THE REGULATION
OF
INTERNATIONAL TRADE

The conclusion of the GATT Uruguay Round negotiations, as well as the emergence of regional trading arrangements and blocs, has underlined the significance of international trade regulation in global politics and economics. As new trade issues emerge and we look into the future of the world trading system it is important that we understand its basic workings.

The Regulation of International Trade introduces the rules and institutions that govern international trade. The authors examine the theory and functioning of international legal regimes, including those of the GATT/ WTO (World Trade Organization), the Canada–US FTA and NAFTA, as well as some aspects of the European Union. Attention is also given to the rise of protectionism through the use of internal trade remedy law, including a detailed comparative analysis of the application of trade remedies to dumping and subsidies in Canada, the USA and the European Union. Settlement of disputes in international trade is given detailed treatment, as well. The book contains individual chapters on trade in agricultural products, trade and development and international labour mobility. In addition, it contains detailed discussion of 'new era' trade issues, such as trade and investment, intellectual property rights, and trade and environment. The book fully reflects the results of the Uruguay Round of trade negotiations.

Throughout the insights of classic and contemporary economics and political economy are related to current issues facing the world trading system. As a comprehensive text *The Regulation of International Trade* will be a valuable guide to students of economics, law and international relations.

Michael J. Trebilcock is a University Professor and **Robert Howse** an Assistant Professor in the Faculty of Law, University of Toronto. They are co-authors, with Marsha Chandler, of *Trade and Transitions*, also published by Routledge.

THE REGULATION OF INTERNATIONAL TRADE

Michael J. Trebilcock and Robert Howse

London and New York

First published 1995
by Routledge
11 New Fetter Lane, London EC4P 4EE

Simultaneously published in the USA and Canada
by Routledge
29 West 35th Street, New York, NY 10001

© 1995 Michael J. Trebilcock and Robert Howse

Typeset in Garamond by
Florencetype Ltd, Stoodleigh, Devon

Printed and bound in Great Britain by
Mackays of Chatham PLC, Chatham, Kent

British Library Cataloguing in Publication Data
A catalogue record for this book is available from the British Library

Library of Congress Cataloging in Publication Data
A catalog record for this book has been requested

ISBN 0-415-08162-9
ISBN 0-415-08163-7 (pbk)

CONTENTS

CONTENTS

CONTENTS

FIGURES AND TABLE

PREFACE

This book is intended to introduce serious students of law, economics, politics, and public policy to the institutions and rules that govern trade between sovereign states. Although we are legal academics, we have not written a traditional legal treatise. Instead, we have sought to bring to bear on our analysis of rules and institutions a wide range of disciplinary perspectives. This includes not only perspectives from the various branches of economics (whether trade theory itself or the theory of finance and economic organization), but also from contemporary political and ethical philosophy and the international relations and political economy literatures.

Although we do discuss extensively the domestic legal regimes of some of the major trading states, most of the law dealt with in this book is international law. There is, of course, an age-old debate as to whether international law is really law in the true sense of the word, as it is not subject to authoritative enforcement by a sovereign. The GATT, the main legal and institutional framework for multilateral free trade, has frequently been judged against a domestic law benchmark and found wanting. Some theorists of international relations question whether rules and institutions matter at all, except as reflections of much more fundamental power relationships.

Our own perspective is that rules, norms and institutions matter a great deal. We see their function as the provision of a framework or structure that permits long-term mutually beneficial co-operation between states. Hence, we take a neo-liberal or new liberal institutionalist view of international relations. This book is not, however, intended as an application or vindication of this particular theory of international relations, which would require a sustained discussion of the theory of international economic co-operation not well suited to an introductory text. Still, in examining the function and evolution of particular rules and norms, we have not hesitated to take stances based on a neo-liberal view nor to be critical of alternative policy stances premised on power-based realist or positivist views of international economic relations.

In general, we see the evolution and maintenance of an open, liberal trading order as to the mutual benefit of states. This view is not premised upon a naive or unquestioning adherence to the economic theory of the gains from trade. On the contrary, throughout our analysis we are highly sensitive to the qualifications to and limits on the case for free trade, as well as the complexities involved in determining the domestic interest in these matters – including concerns about unemployment, worker adjustment, the quality of life and values of human rights and environmental protection. We examine, in a wide range of areas, the multiple challenges that increased economic integration and interdependence pose for domestic and international policymaking. While we frequently see the need to evolve new rules and institutions, or to clarify existing rules and strengthen existing institutions, we also conclude that the basic building blocks of the liberal trading order are not fundamentally defective, and that a protectionist retreat from an open system is likely to reduce both domestic and global welfare.

Compared to the immediacy and directness of the concerns that often result in demands for protectionism – whether job loss within a community or outrage at another state's environmental policies – the basic rules and norms of the global trading order that constrain protectionist responses often appear arcane or obscure. This applies as well to the jurisprudence that has evolved, especially in the GATT, to interpret those rules and norms. We believe that this impression is inaccurate and that in fact there is considerable clarity and coherence to the rules, with interpretation and application to diverse and rapidly changing circumstances being no more difficult and no easier than with respect to other areas of law. But this impression has partly been created because of the often unnecessarily inaccessible and complex presentation of the rules and jurisprudence by trade law experts and officials, and their frequent lack of interest in reaching a broader intellectual and policy community. Ernst-Ulrich Petersmann notes comments by non-experts that 'anyone who reads the GATT is likely to have his sanity impaired' and that there are 'only ten people in the world who understand the GATT and they are not telling'.[1] This book is a modest attempt to show that, to the contrary, international trade law is no more impenetrable or obscure than any other sophisticated body of contemporary law, when it is clearly explained in terms of fundamental concepts, principles and rules.

The topics covered and general organization of this book reflect a number of years' experience in co-teaching an introductory course in international trade regulation at the University of Toronto. The course has typically attracted senior undergraduates both in law and in economics, and we have also been fortunate to have the participation of graduate students in both disciplines, many of whom bring perspectives from undergraduate studies and work experience in a wide variety of countries, both developed and developing. Without this sustained and on-going dialogue with a very diverse and demanding group of students, this book would not have been possible.

We wish to acknowledge excellent research assistance from a number of students or former students at the Faculty of Law, University of Toronto, including Evan Atwood, Ari Blicker, Richard Brando, John Loukidelis, Karen Powys-Lybbe and Presley Warner. Ari Blicker proofread the entire manuscript with care. In addition, on particular chapters, several colleagues and students read earlier drafts or otherwise assisted us with their reflections and advice. In particular, we wish to thank Isis Calder, Kevin Davis, Gary Horlick, Brian Langille, James Odek, Elie Perkins, Craig Scott and Diane Varleau. In the production of the manuscript, we benefited from the superb administrative and secretarial skills of Margot Hall, Merril Randell and Chris Black.

1

THE EVOLUTION OF INTERNATIONAL TRADE THEORY AND POLICY

AN INTELLECTUAL HISTORY OF INTERNATIONAL TRADE THEORY AND POLICY[1]

The central question that must be confronted at the outset of any study of international trade is: why do we need a theory of international trade at all? Why is the analysis of the economic, political or social implications of exchange between traders in two national markets different from the analysis of the implications of exchange between traders within a single national market?

The theory of absolute advantage

In the seventeenth and eighteenth centuries, a school of thought often referred to as 'mercantilism' was concerned that international trade may give rise to an inadequate supply of circulating monetary gold as a result of balance of payment deficits. Silver and gold were mainstays of national wealth and essential to vigorous commerce. Hence the appropriate policy goal was perceived to be the maintenance of a continuing surplus in the balance of payments i.e. sell more to foreigners than one buys from them. Imperial rivalries also led to political concerns about the transfer of *specie* into foreign hands and in part explains colonization efforts in the eighteenth and nineteenth centuries where colonies were seen as a source of raw materials and an outlet for manufactured goods. However, David Hume, in 1752, demonstrated that through the price-specie-flow mechanism, international trade was likely to maintain an equilibrium in the balance of payments. If a country found itself with surplus currency, domestic prices would tend to rise relative to prices of foreign commodities, and money would flow out of the country. If a country found itself with a shortage of currency, domestic prices would become depressed and would attract foreign currency until the shortage had disappeared.[2]

Adam Smith, in the *Wealth of Nations* (1776), mounted a broader assault on mercantilist theories and argued that the case for gains from specialization

1

in domestic economic activities applied equally to specialization in international trade:

> What is prudence in the conduct of every private family can scarcely be folly in that of a great kingdom. If a foreign country can supply us with a commodity cheaper than we can make, better buy it of them with some part of the produce of our own industry.[3]

Thus, to take some simple examples, if countries with tropical climates can produce bananas or pineapples more cheaply than countries with temperate climates, the latter should purchase these products from the former. Conversely, if countries with industrialized economies can produce hydro-electric generators or telephone systems more cheaply and of better quality than those that could be produced by countries that enjoy a cost advantage in producing tropical produce, the latter should buy these products from the former. In domestic economic activities, most of us accept that it makes no sense for an individual to try and produce all his or her own food, clothing, medical services, dental services, home construction services etc., but rather to specialize in producing some goods or services for others and perhaps for some limited subset of his or her own needs, while purchasing requirements to meet remaining needs from others who specialize in their production. It equally follows, on Smith's theory, that similar specialization is likely to generate mutual gains from trade in international exchanges – the division of labour is limited only by the extent of the market. It is important to note that on Smith's theory, *unilateral* trade liberalization would be an advantageous policy for a country to pursue, irrespective of the trade policies pursued by other countries.

The theory of comparative advantage

A central question left open by Smith's Theory of Absolute Advantage (as it came to be called) was: what if a country has no absolute advantage over any of its potential trading partners with respect to any products or services? Is international trade of no relevance or value to it? David Ricardo, in his book *The Principles of Political Economy* published in 1817, answered this question with a shattering insight that continues to form the basis of conventional international trade theory today. His insight has come to be called the Theory of Comparative Advantage. He advanced this theory by means of a simple arithmetic example. In his example, England could produce a given quantity of cloth with the labour of 100 men. It could also produce a given quantity of wine with the labour of 120 men. Portugal, in turn, could produce the same quantity of cloth with the labour of 90 men and the same quantity of wine with the labour of 80 men. Thus, Portugal enjoyed an absolute advantage over England with respect to the production of both cloth and wine i.e. it could produce a given quantity of cloth or wine with fewer labour inputs than England. However, Ricardo argued that trade was still mutually advantageous, assuming full employment in both countries: when England exported to Portugal the cloth produced by the labour of 100 men in exchange for wine produced by 80 Portuguese, she imported wine that would have required the labour of 120 Englishmen to produce. As for Portugal, she gained by her 80 men's labour cloth that it would have taken 90 of her labourers to produce. Both countries would be rendered better off through trade.

Another way of understanding the same intuition is to imagine the following simple domestic example.[4] Suppose a lawyer is not only more efficient in the provision of legal services than her secretary, but is also a more efficient secretary. It takes her secretary twice as long to type a document than the lawyer could type it herself. Suppose, more specifically, that it takes the lawyer's secretary two hours to type a document that the lawyer could type in one hour, and that the secretary's hourly wage is $20, and that the lawyer's hourly rate to clients is $200. It will pay the lawyer to hire the secretary and pay her $40 to type the document in two hours while the lawyer is able to sell for $200 the hour of her time that would otherwise have been committed to typing the document. In other words, both the lawyer and the secretary gain from this exchange. These examples, in an international trade context, generalize to the proposition that a country should specialize in producing and exporting goods in which its comparative advantage is greatest, or comparative disadvantage is smallest, and should import goods in which its comparative disadvantage is greatest.

An unfortunate semantic legacy of Ricardo's demonstration of the gains from international trade that has been perpetuated in the terminology of much subsequent trade literature and debate is that in international trade *countries* are trading with each other. This, of course, is rarely the case. As in purely domestic exchanges, *private economic actors* (albeit located in different countries) are trading with each other. In its most rudimentary form, all that international trade theory seeks to demonstrate is that free international trade dramatically broadens the contract opportunity set available to private economic actors and hence the mutual gains realizable from exchange as parties with different endowments of specialized resources or skills are able to reap the gains from their differential advantages and disadvantages through trade.

It may be argued that in international exchanges, in contrast to domestic exchanges, part of the gains from exchange are realized by foreigners, and that a country would be advantaged by capturing all the gains from exchange for itself. However, this raises the question of whether the domestic gains foregone by foreign trade are greater or less than the additional gains from purely domestic exchange. As a matter of simple economic theory, the gains to domestic consumers from foreign trade will almost always be greater than the additional gains to domestic producers from purely domestic trade.

3

This is so because higher domestic than foreign prices will entail a transfer of resources from domestic consumers to domestic producers (arguably creating matching decreases and increases in welfare), but *in addition* some domestic consumers will be priced out of the market by the higher domestic prices and will be forced to allocate their resources to less preferred consumption choices, entailing a dead-weight social loss. An alternative way in which to conceive of the net domestic loss from foregone foreign exchange opportunities is to ask what compensation domestic producers would need to offer domestic consumers to render them indifferent to these forgone opportunities. Presumably only domestic prices that matched foreign producers' prices would achieve this end.

The factor proportions hypothesis

While Ricardo's theory of comparative advantage still constitutes the under-pinnings of conventional international trade theory, his theory has been refined in various ways by subsequent analysis. Ricardo's theory, for example, assumed constant costs at all levels of production which led to the conclusion that a country would specialize completely in the goods where its compara-tive advantage was greatest (wine in the case of Portugal) or its comparative disadvantage smallest (cloth in the case of England), but this hypothesis rarely seemed to fit the facts. For example, Portugal produced both wine and some cloth. Ricardo's theory was thus modified to take account of increasing opportunity costs. For example, by releasing resources from cloth-making it would not necessarily follow that the addition of these labour inputs to wine-making would continue to increase wine production in constant proportions, especially if the factor proportions in the two activities were different e.g. cloth-making is labour intensive while wine-making is land intensive. In other words, once more than one factor of production was taken into account, it became obvious that combining land and labour at ever increasing levels of output would not necessarily entail similar costs, as the land brought into production at higher levels of output may well (and typically would) be less productive and require more intensive use of labour. On the other hand, the opposite phenomenon may sometimes be true, that is that decreasing costs may be associated with increased scale of operations or levels of output, and may lead to complete international specialization.

Recognition of these considerations led to a reformulation of Ricardo's theory of comparative advantage – often referred to as the Factor Proportions Hypothesis (or the Heckscher-Ohlin Theorem, after two Swedish econo-mists who formulated the theorem in the 1920s). According to the Factor Proportions Hypothesis, countries will tend to enjoy comparative advantages in producing goods that use their more abundant factors more intensively, and each country will end up exporting its abundant factor goods in exchange for imported goods that use its scarce factors more intensively.

4

While the Factor Proportions Hypothesis seems to explain adequately patterns of international specialization in many activities, particularly agriculture and natural resources, it tends to provide a less satisfactory explanation of patterns of specialization in manufacturing activities in modern industrialized economies, where it is common to observe countries specializing in different segments of the same or closely analogous product markets, and simultaneously exporting and importing products in these sectors. Intra-industry trade has accounted for a very high percentage of the total increase in international trade in recent decades.[5] The Factor Proportions Hypothesis assumes that all countries have access to identical technologies of production and that the list of goods which are traded is somehow exogenously given and unaltered by economic activity. However, patterns of specialization and comparative advantage are not exclusively exogenously determined, but are likely to turn in part on a number of endogenous variables, such as savings and capital accumulation rates in different countries; the levels and patterns of investment in specialized human capital, reflecting the country's commitment to investments in education and research and development; and public infrastructure such as transportation and communication systems, which again reflect patterns of collective investments. On this view, comparative advantage is a much more dynamic notion that the static notion implicit in the original formulation of the Factor Proportions Hypothesis, and moreover recognizes the role that governments can play, through a variety of public policies, in shaping comparative advantage over time.

It is also important to note that classical trade theory, as described above, assumed that physical output from production was (subject to transportation costs) mobile across nations but that factors of production, while in most cases mobile within countries, were immobile across nations. While this obviously remains true of land, it has become dramatically less true of financial capital, technology, human capital, and even people, in large part because of advances in communications and transportation technologies. Thus, trade theory has historically focused on *international trade in goods* (a focus reflected in the initial preoccupations of the GATT), and not international mobility of services, capital or people. This focus has been increasingly challenged, as reflected in a rapidly changing trade policy agenda.

The product cycle theory

Largely reflecting the less static, more dynamic and endogenous factors bearing on comparative advantage, noted above, in the 1960s Raymond Vernon of the Harvard Business School formulated a Product Cycle Theory of trade in manufactured goods to explain patterns of international specialization in manufacturing.[6] According to Vernon's Product Cycle Theory, the USA, and perhaps other highly developed and industrialized economies, reflecting their superior access to large amounts of financial capital and highly specialized forms of human capital, would enjoy a comparative advantage in the research and development intensive stage of product innovation. This stage would focus initially on servicing a small, domestic, custom-oriented market. The second stage in the product cycle would see production expanded to cater to a mass domestic market. The third stage would see products exported to other countries and perhaps parent companies setting-up subsidiaries in other countries to undertake manufacture there (the phenomenon of the Multinational Enterprise). A further stage in the product cycle would see the production technology becoming highly standardized and adopted by producers in other countries, particularly countries with lower labour costs, and products perhaps then being exported by these countries back to the USA or other countries where the innovations had originated. According to Vernon, quasi-rents could be earned by domestic firms early in the product cycle, but these rents would be dissipated as the product moved to later stages in the cycle, and comparative advantage shifted to other countries.

The Product Cycle Theory of international trade in manufactured goods seems to explain reasonably well patterns of specialization observable in many countries in the 1950s and 1960s, but has become less compelling over the last two decades, as an increasing number of countries, like Japan and other newly industrializing countries (NICs) have acquired many of the same comparative advantages as the older industrialized economies in early stages of the product cycle, through access to large domestic and international sources of capital that have become increasingly mobile, and through investments of their own in the human capital required to achieve a comparative advantage in the early stages of product innovation and manufacture.

The increasing recognition that comparative advantage is not exclusively ordained by nature but is in significant part, at least in manufacturing, and services, the product of deliberate government policies, has led to an increased focus in many domestic policy settings on issues of so-called industrial policy, and at an international level, concerns and accusations over whether foreign governments' domestic policies are unfairly shaping or distorting comparative advantage.[7] These are issues that we take up in more detail in various contexts later in this book. However, beyond these issues, several long-standing qualifications to the case for free trade, in both economic and non-economic terms, should be briefly noted at this juncture.

Qualifications to the case for free trade

Reciprocity

While classical trade theory emphasized the advantages of unilateral trade liberalization over the protectionist base case, taking the trade policies of trading partners as a given, it is obviously the case that a country is likely to realize additional economic advantages from trade liberalization if it can persuade its trading partners also to liberalize their trade policies, thus generating benefits on both the import and export sides. This raises complex strategic issues for the first country. The modern trade literature distinguishes two kinds of reciprocity – passive and aggressive reciprocity.[8] Pursuing a strategy of passive reciprocity, a country might simply decline to reduce any of its existing trade restrictions until its trading partners agree to reduce some of their trade restrictions. However, if the trading partners appreciate that it is in the first country's interests to liberalize trade whatever the former do, they may choose to withhold any concessions in the hope of gaining the benefits of the first country's trade liberalization for free. This is a classic Prisoner's Dilemma problem, which may inhibit trade liberalization and lead to an inefficient outcome in which everyone is worse off. On the other hand, the trading partners may realize that it could be difficult from a political standpoint for the first country to liberalize on the import side without being able to enlist the support of its export-oriented producers and moderate the effects of contraction in its import-sensitive industries with growth in its export industries. In this case, a strategy of passive reciprocity may produce a mutual agreement on trade liberalization.

A strategy of aggressive reciprocity might take any of several forms.[9] Where two countries have previously negotiated a reciprocal trade agreement, in the absence of a supra-national authority with the ability to enforce the agreement, the threat of retaliation for breach of or defection from the agreement may be the only effective means of ensuring that the agreement is effectively self-enforcing.[10] Retaliation here is likely to entail withdrawal of previous concessions in the hope that this (or the threat thereof) will induce the breaching country to fulfill its prior commitments. Where countries must deal with each other indefinitely, this tit-for-tat strategy may solve repeated Prisoner's Dilemma games by ensuring co-operation rather than defection.[11]

More controversial forms of aggressive reciprocity entail threats by one country to withdraw previous concessions or impose new trade restrictions if trading partners persist in engaging in policies that are perceived by the first country to impact unfairly on its interests – e.g., subsidies in the case of imports, or distribution tie-ups in the case of exports. Adam Smith himself was prepared to contemplate retaliatory reinstatement of previous trade restrictions where foreign countries were maintaining restrictions on imports, although he was concerned that where there was no certainty that retaliation ('revenge') would induce removal of the restrictions, retaliation would simply impose unnecessary costs on domestic consumers.[12] The most prominent contemporary example of such a strategy is the discretionary retaliation provisions of the so-called 'Super 301' regime adopted by the USA in the Omnibus Trade and Competitiveness Act of 1988 which may be invoked where a foreign country's policies are found by the US Trade Representative to be 'unreasonable or discriminatory' and to burden or restrict United States Commerce.[13] Here the threat of retaliatory trade restrictions is primarily designed to induce foreign countries to modify policies or practices that the US government believes are unfairly impeding US exports into foreign markets (the so-called 'crow-bar' theory of trade policy). A major problem with this form of aggressive reciprocity is that it often reflects very divergent understandings of existing obligations – on the one hand that a foreign country is cheating on at least the spirit of previous reciprocal commitments, or on the other hand, that the country threatening retaliation is attempting to coerce new unreciprocated trade or other concessions from foreign countries and is itself cheating on prior commitments by threatening their withdrawal. While in some circumstances the threat of retaliation may involve 'co-operative' solutions to trade disputes, in other cases 'feuds' (counter-retaliation) or 'stalemates' may ensue.[14] Where co-operative solutions do emerge, they are likely to reflect bilateral 'deals' that are antithetical to a non-discriminatory international trading order and may conduce to 'collusive' or managed forms of trade that diverge substantially from the liberal trade ideal. However, some authors argue that once we take into account the transaction costs entailed in monitoring for cheating on, and ensuring compliance with, complex international agreements that lack an effective third-party enforcement mechanism, these arrangements may be the best that can be achieved. While falling short of the (unattainable) first – best liberal trade ideal, they may prevent the world trading system from degenerating into total autarchy or anarchy.[15]

In any event, while reciprocity in any of its various forms played a marginal role in the classical economic theory of trade, it is absolutely crucial to understanding the evolution of the institutional arrangements, both domestic and supra-national, that govern international trade, which are reviewed later in this chapter.

The optimal tariff

A second qualification to the case for free trade, recognized at a relatively early stage in the evolution of trade theory, is the concept of the so-called *Optimal Tariff*. On this theory, countries that account for a very high proportion of international demand for a certain good may, through their governments acting as 'cartel' managers for consumers, possess a significant degree of monopsony power, which they can exercise to their advantage by the imposition of a tariff which forces firms in exporting countries to reduce the price of their products and in effect absorb the tariff. Consumers in the importing countries continue to pay the same price for the goods, but their governments capture additional revenue from foreign exporters through the tariff. While in theory the concept of the optimal tariff may be correct from a national (although not cosmopolitan or global) perspective, the empirical evidence suggests that there are few cases where importing countries possess the degree of monopsony power in international markets necessary to implement effectively such a policy.

Infant industries

A third and equally long-standing qualification to the conventional case for free trade pertains to the case of *infant industries*. As John Stuart Mill argued,[16] along with other nineteenth-century writers like Alexander Hamilton in the USA and Friedrich List in Germany, in the early stages of a country's economic development there may be a case for the imposition of protective tariffs or quotas to allow infant industries, in particular infant manufacturing industries, to develop, by servicing a protected domestic market, to a scale and level of sophistication that will subsequently permit them to compete both with imports and even more desirably to become effective exporters in their own right. This argument has exerted a significant and enduring influence on international trade theory and policy over the past century and a half. It was centrally relied on by the USA in maintaining a high tariff policy throughout most of the nineteenth century and the first quarter of the twentieth century. It has been relied on by less developed countries (LDCs) in the post-Second World War era to justify 'special and differential status' under the GATT in protecting their domestic markets and promoting import substitution policies. It is also, more controversially, claimed to have been a central strategic element in the rise of Japan as a major industrial power. In part, the infant industry argument rests on the proposition that an advanced, mature economy cannot be predominantly dependent upon agriculture or natural resources for its exports, but requires a substantial manufacturing base, partly in order to diversify its economic activities and employment base and reduce the risks associated with excessive reliance on a narrow base of commodity exports, and partly for non-economic reasons associated with national pride in being on the technological frontier along with other advanced countries and providing a concomitant number and range of challenging employment opportunities to its more highly educated or trained citizenry. However, it bears pointing out that some countries have sustained high standards of living without substantial manufacturing sectors, e.g. New Zealand and Denmark through agriculture, Middle Eastern oil-producing states through natural resources.

Strategic trade theory

A contemporary variant on the infant industry argument entails an elaboration on, and application to, the international trade context of the concept

9

of imperfect competition initially developed by Edward Chamberlin and Joan Robinson in the 1930s. Here, it is argued that many modern manufacturing industries fall somewhere between the polarities of the neo-classical economic concepts of monopoly and perfect competition, i.e. essentially oligopolistic industries where prices do not necessarily reflect costs and where quasi-rents can be realized by firms (and hence countries) able to acquire strategically dominant positions in industries in which high minimum efficient levels of scale imply that there is room for only a handful of firms in the global market. In this respect, it is argued that an important role can be played by domestic governments through research and development subsidies, procurement policies, related industrial policies, as well as strategic manipulation of international trade policies, in promoting so-called Schumpeterian industries. This has led to the emergence of Strategic Trade Theory,[17] where it is argued that governments can promote their national interests by assisting firms to establish pre-emptive, first-mover, positions in markets, and to realize learning-curve advantages, in part by maintaining entry barriers to potential competitors. Again, this is a highly controversial aspect of modern international trade theory. As with retaliatory policies designed to secure opening of foreign markets to exports, the theory of the Optimal Tariff, and more general theories pertaining to infant industries, there is a highly speculative but potentially extremely risky and costly aspect to active pursuit by governments of strategic trade theories, because so much depends upon the potential reactions of the governments of foreign countries and competitors or potential competitors based there.[18]

Revenue-raising considerations

Another long-standing qualification to the case for free trade relates to the *revenue-raising* potential of customs duties. In many industrialized countries, it was not until early in this century that income taxes (direct taxes) provided the primary source of government revenues. Until this time, customs duties and to a lesser extent, export taxes were a major source of government revenues. Even today, in developing countries with large informal economies where internal income taxes are difficult or impossible to administer and collect, import and export taxes constitute a major source of government revenue-raising capabilities.

National security considerations

A long-standing non-economic qualification to the case for free trade relates to *National Security* considerations. These may arise on both the import and export sides. With respect to imports, it is argued that there may sometimes be a case for restrictions in order to protect domestic industries which, even though not internationally competitive, may be required in the event of

10

war or other international disruption. Thus, industries such as the steel and ship building industries, have often been protected on this basis, although the concept of national security has proven highly elastic, being invoked to justify restrictions on such unlikely imports as clothes pegs from Poland on the grounds that domestic productive capabilities in clothes pegs would be required in the event of hostilities with the (former) Communist Bloc countries. On the export side, national security considerations have sometimes been invoked to restrict exports of strategically sensitive products or military materiel to 'unfriendly' foreign countries.

Objections to free trade

Apart from the foregoing qualifications to the case for free trade, a number of other more general objections are often raised to free trade: (1) job displacement and wage depression; (2) lowest common denominator effects on domestic social policies; (3) cultural homogenization; and (4) loss of domestic political sovereignty. These will each be briefly considered, drawing primarily, by way of example, on the Canadian experience. Between 1947 and 1986, Canada's merchandise imports grew in value by 552% in real terms and merchandise exports by 564% in real terms. For Canada, post-war multilateral trade liberalization under the GATT has to a large extent entailed bilateral trade expansion with the USA. What have been the effects of this increased trade dependency?

Impact on wages and employment

From 1947 to 1986, per capita GDP in Canada rose in real terms from $7,402 to $19,925 (1986 $) (an increase of 169.2%). Total employment grew from 4,821,000 in 1947 to 12,295,000 in April 1988 (an increase of 155.0%), with manufacturing employment rising 88.7% from 1,131,750 to 2,136,000 during this period. At the same time, of course, Canadian consumers (the silent majority in free trade debates) have enjoyed dramatically wider product choices and lower product prices because of imports. While it would be naive to suggest that these increases in jobs and incomes are wholly or even primarily attributable to trade liberalization and expansion, at least the opposite proposition so often asserted – that continued trade liberalization is likely to reduce real incomes and employment – is revealed as unfounded. While trade liberalization can have negative impacts on jobs and wages in particular domestic sectors which are vulnerable to imports, the net effect on jobs and wages economy-wide has been strongly positive. For workers in sectors adversely impacted by imports, generous and well-conceived domestic adjustment assistance programmes, rather than trade protection, can often deal more cost-effectively with transition costs (as we will argue more fully in a later chapter).[19]

Impact on social policies

Not only has the post-war period of trade liberalization seen these enormous increases in real incomes and employment, it has also simultaneously witnessed the emergence of the modern welfare state. Public expenditures in Canada on education have risen from $147 per capita in 1947 to $1,237 per capita in 1983–4 in real terms (1986 $), or from 1.99% of GDP to 6.79%. Public expenditures on health care have risen from $54 per capita in 1947 to $1,202 per capita in 1985 in real terms (1986 $), or from 0.72% of GDP to 6.18%. Direct financial benefits paid to Canadians under various social welfare programmes amounted to $49,136 million in 1985, compared with 1947 expenditures of $3,838 million on all 'public welfare' programmes (including health) (1986 $). Federal transfer payments to the provinces have risen from the equivalent of 0.12% of GDP in 1947 to 4.04% in 1986. Public expenditures on cultural activities have risen from negligible amounts in 1947 to 0.74% of GDP in 1984–5. Over the same period, greatly increased regulatory attention has also been paid to occupational health and safety, consumer protection and environmental issues. Trade liberalization and trade expansion have not been inconsistent with these redistributional, social, and cultural policies. History again reveals this fear as unfounded. Indeed the simple truism is often overlooked that only relatively prosperous countries can afford generous social policies. Impoverished third world countries do not have such policies, not because they lack commitment to them in principle, but because they do not have the wealth to afford them. Creating wealth is a precondition to redistributing it.

Thus, nothing in the theory or history of trade liberalization and expansion is inconsistent with increasing real incomes and employment or compassionate and civilized social and cultural policies. In fact, there is every reason to believe that only by exploiting our comparative advantage to the fullest can we sustain increasing prosperity and the social policies that prosperity makes possible. Nevertheless, it is important to acknowledge that concerns that international competition will force countries to the lowest common denominator in terms of domestic policies pertaining to, for example, workplace safety laws, employment standards, and environmental laws have recently provoked considerable discussion and debate in the European Union and North America. This is again an issue we return to later in this book, in the context of debates over 'fair trade' [20] and trade and the environment.[21]

Impact on cultural diversity

Another perspective, which figured prominently in the Canada–US free trade debates in the late 1980s, emphasizes the dangers to national cultural identity presented by free trade and international mobility of labour and capital. Distinctive ways of life and cultural values are seen as threatened by the homogenizing effects of economic and technological imperialism. This point of view has its roots in the critique by Rousseau and the nineteenth-century political romantic movement of classical political economy, and also in the Jeffersonian alternative to the commercial republic. Even authors like Fukuyama,[22] who have recently proclaimed the triumph of economic and political liberalism, and 'the end of history', worry about the blandness, homogeneity, and materialism that this may presage.

One cannot help but find somewhat ominous the romanticized 'closed community' conception held by contemporary critics of economic liberalism. Traditional closed societies may have preserved distinctive customs and beliefs against external influences, but only at the cost of racial, religious, and ideological intolerance, and of significant limits on individual self-development. If we were really to avoid the consequences of contemporary cosmopolitanism, trade barriers would hardly be enough – we would need strict censorship, exit visas, limits on ethnic diversity, and other measures aimed at maintaining the 'closedness' of the community.

In any event, during the post-War decades in which Canada has witnessed such enormous increases in international trade, particularly bilateral trade, it has also simultaneously witnessed the flowering of Quebec nationalism and the increasingly confident assertion of a distinct French-Canadian cultural and linguistic identity. In the post-war period, Canada has also witnessed an enormous influx of immigrants from a great diversity of cultural backgrounds that has immeasurably enriched Canada's multi-cultural mosaic, rendering Canada one of the most vibrant and tolerant cosmopolitan societies in the world. This is not the traditional Canada that George Grant so nostalgically recalled in *Lament for a Nation*,[23] but nor have Canadians become part of a homogenized, universalistic American culture as he portended. Canada is and will remain a profoundly different society, as a comparison of daily life in Windsor and Detroit or Toronto and Buffalo should convince the doubtful reader. There are surely deeper measures of a society's cultural evolution than how many minutes are occupied by which country's soap operas on local commercial television networks. While liberal trading policies cannot claim direct credit for our increased cultural diversity and distinctiveness, a close intellectual concomitant of liberal trading policies – more liberal immigration policies – clearly can claim substantial credit. It is not philosophically consistent to urge open and liberal immigration policies but to advocate at the same time closed and illiberal trade policies that deprive potential immigrants of economic opportunities in their home countries, thus leaving them with no option but to sever their roots and emigrate.

Impact on domestic political sovereignty

All international treaties, whether relating to nuclear disarmament, human rights, the environment, the law of the sea, or trade, constrain domestic political sovereignty through the assumption of external obligations. But unless anarchy in international relations is preferred as an alternative, in most cases we accept that the benefits of the reciprocal obligations involved outweigh the costs associated with any loss of political sovereignty. In the trade context, the additional argument is sometimes made that increased economic interdependence constrains political sovereignty in unacceptable ways in that countries – especially smaller countries with major trading relationships with larger countries, such as Canada and the USA – will be concerned that adopting independent foreign policies, for example, may antagonize the larger trading partner and lead to forms of economic 'blackmail' designed to induce policy conformity. This risk cannot be altogether gainsaid. However, trade treaties that structure relations by reference to durable, well-defined substantive norms and objective dispute resolution procedures reduce the risks of larger countries exploiting raw economic power to bully smaller countries, by subjecting power relations to some form of legal ordering. In addition, smaller countries typically stand to gain disproportionately from trade liberalization. This is due to the simple fact that liberalization will provide access to a larger set of potential new trading relationships than in the case of the larger country gaining enhanced access to the smaller country's market.

Public choice theory and the politics of trade liberalization

Over the last two decades or so, economists have developed an increasing interest in the positive analysis of politics. The basic economic model of politics that has been developed – commonly referred to as 'public choice' theory – models the political process as an implicit market with demanders (voters or interest groups) of government policies exchanging political support in terms of votes, information/propaganda, campaign contributions or other material forms of assistance for desired policies. Government (politicians and their agents, bureaucrats and regulators) will supply policies that maximize the governing Party's prospects of re-election (or in the case of opposition Parties, election). This view of the political process contrasts with that conventionally assumed hitherto by economists, which sees governments as attempting to maximize some social welfare function by correcting for various forms of market failure (monopoly, public goods, externalities, etc.). Implicit in the public choice approach is the view that neither the effect nor intent of most government policies is to advance the common good, but rather to construct minimum winning coalitions, often through redistributional policies, even though the impact of such policies will often, perhaps primarily, be to reduce aggregate social welfare.

Applying the public choice model, Downs[24] and subsequently Olson[25] argued that narrow producer interests would tend to dominate over thinly-spread consumer interests in the political process. This is largely a function of the differential mobilization and hence lobbying costs faced by producer and consumer interests. The larger the per capita stakes in an issue, the stronger will be the incentives to overcome information and transaction costs in organizing; and the fewer the affected stake-holders, the easier it will be to overcome the free-rider problem that afflicts large interest groups whose individual members have small per capita stakes in the relevant issues. This framework would tend to suggest that highly concentrated industries with few firms, perhaps also highly geographically concentrated, and possibly with highly unionized work-forces, are likely to be able to organize most effectively and, therefore, are most likely to secure favourable policies from government, including trade protection.

A major theoretical difficulty with this model is that it appears to imply no equilibrium in the political process, at least in the context in which it purports to apply, short of a corner solution entailing infinite protection for the affected industries (a total ban on imports). This is manifestly not what we typically observe, even in concentrated industries, which is sufficient to raise some prima facie doubts about the subtlety of the model. As Destler and Odell point out in a recent, important study,[26] the weakness in the model is its simplistic assumptions that, on the one hand, domestic producers, who are easily mobilized politically, uniformly favour protectionism and that, on the other, the sole or principal cost-bearers are ultimate end-users or lay consumers, who are politically disabled. More specifically, the model first ignores the fact that imports will often be intermediate inputs into another industry, for example, textiles and clothing, steel and automobiles, and that the industry purchasing the inputs will normally find it rational to resist cost-increasing policies. Second, the model ignores the fact that export-oriented industries may have reason to fear retaliation by foreign countries to restrictions on their exports in the form of reciprocal trade restrictions, thus creating an incentive for such industries to resist domestically imposed trade restrictions. Moreover, the potential for growth in export-oriented sectors is likely to moderate the adjustment costs faced by import-impacted sectors, thus reducing the political resistance to trade liberalization. Third, the model overlooks the fact that importers–distributors and large retail chains that import and sell large quantities of lower priced imports constitute a major producer constituency that will be disadvantaged by trade restrictions. Fourth, while it is true that consumers may face information costs, transaction costs, and strategic impediments to effective group mobilization, as individuals they still possess votes which constitute a resource that firms, whatever their other political resources, by definition do not possess. The determinants of the political rate of exchange between various political currencies, for example, votes and financial resources, are not well addressed in the public choice model of the political process. Finally, the model fails to disaggregate what may be complex competing interests *within* firms. As Milner argues, domestic firms with strong international ties often face difficult choices as to whether to support or oppose protection. Protectionist measures which may benefit the firm in a sector where it produces domestically could lead to retaliation by foreign trading partners that could harm the firm's exporting or foreign investment interests.[27] Milner also points out that large, multinational firms have more ability to pursue their own adjustment policies, by moving assembly or other activities offshore to counter any wage-price advantages maintained by foreign competitors. On the other hand, such firms may demand trade restrictions as a kind of 'stick' with which to threaten foreign trading partners to open up their markets, although the evidence that using trade restrictions in this manner can procure significant market opening is quite ambiguous.[28] In sum, the behaviour of firms will often be motivated by complex interests that do not necessarily point to a pro-protectionist rent-seeking outcome.

Various non-public choice models of the trade policy process identified by Baldwin,[29] in contrast to the behavioural assumption of short-run economic self-interest adopted by the public choice models, admit of diverse factors: long-run pursuit of self-interest by economic agents and political actors, autonomous behaviour by public officials who are not simply intermediaries acting on the wishes of the electorate or some part of it, and altruism on the part of public and private actors concerned about the welfare of individuals who may be affected by import competition. Conversely, these public and private actors may arguably be concerned about the welfare of individuals in foreign countries disadvantaged by denial of access to domestic markets for their goods.

The difficulty with these latter models as positive frameworks for predicting trade policy decisions is that their behavioural assumptions are so vague as to be largely untestable, and are likely to provide a positive rationalization for almost any conceivable set of trade policies (and thus predict or explain nothing).

The empirical evidence on most postulated political determinants of trade protection is as ambiguous as the positive theories that underlie the postulates.[30] This ambiguity applies to industry concentration, geographic concentration, industry size (in terms of number of employees), labour intensity, and extent of unionization. Most studies, however, find a positive correlation between protectionism and low-wage, low-skilled industries.

Baldwin concludes that an eclectic approach to understanding this behaviour is the most appropriate one currently. Until the various models are differentiated more sharply analytically and better empirical measures for distinguishing them are obtained, it will be difficult to ascertain the relative importance of different motivations of government officials under various conditions.[31]

An 'eclectic approach' is, of course, no model at all in terms of yielding testable implications or predictions at the level of positive analysis, and in terms of normative implications, provides very little purchase on those features of the policymaking process which, if modified, are likely to yield superior policy outcomes. Perhaps what can be said is that the evidence does not suggest an iron law of politics that inexorably drives governments, in particular sets of circumstances, to the adoption of particular trade restricting policies.

AN INSTITUTIONAL HISTORY OF INTERNATIONAL TRADE POLICY

The advent of free trade

Trading relationships between merchants from different nation-states go back to the dawn of recorded history. Trade was important to many ancient and medieval powers: Athens, Ptolemaic Egypt, the Italian city-states of Venice, Florence, and Genoa, and the German Hanseatic League. Trade regulation through the imposition of tolls (a major source of state revenue) has almost as long a history, as do trade agreements between nation-states – a commercial treaty between the Kings of Egypt and Babylonia existed in 2500 BC.[32]

However, a functional understanding of modern international trade policy on an institutional level necessarily involves some appreciation of the broader forces at work for free trade in the European economies during the late eighteenth and early nineteenth centuries. From this perspective, international trade institutions need to be seen as one aspect of a more general process leading to access to larger, more unified markets, such that by the mid-nineteenth century only national frontiers remained as effective barriers to trade.[33] This process included the repeal of laws banning the export of certain materials previously considered essential to national welfare, the abolition of local regulations regarding manufacturing techniques, the adoption of (national) standards in weights and measures, and the end of restrictions on personal economic freedom (continuing bans against unions being a conspicuous exception to the general trend). Nation-building itself was in part an effort to ensure free trade where such had never existed before: the dismantling of internal tolls and levies was an essential precondition to industrial development in the European economies.[34]

By the mid-nineteenth century, then, most of the advanced European countries had established free trade within their borders. But many nations continued to practice internationally what they had eschewed internally: protection (trade barriers) continued between nations as they vied for wealth and power in international relations. The first major break with these mercantilist-protectionist policies of the past came in Britain with the repeal of the Corn Laws in 1846, spear-headed by Prime Minister Sir Robert Peel, a late convert to the cause of trade liberalization, and Lord Cobden. The repeal of these laws was in part promoted by the increasing intellectual currency of the ideas of Smith and especially Ricardo, and partly by the practical urgency of responding to the desperation of the Irish Famine. Political agitation fed by the wealth and power of commercial and manufacturing interests also played its role, as it would elsewhere in Europe later in the century.[35] The repeal of the Corn Laws was quickly followed by the unilateral removal or reduction of hundreds of tariffs on most imported goods, ushering in, in Britain, a period of resolute commitment to the principle of free trade that extended into the early years of this century.

While British trade policy reflected the insights of classical trade theory that *unilateral* trade liberalization enhanced national welfare over the protectionist base case, Britain also, over the course of the century, negotiated a number of free trade treaties with other countries, beginning with the Cobden–Chevalier Treaty of 1860 with France.[36] France in turn, in 1862, negotiated a comprehensive trade treaty with the *Zollverein*, the German Customs Union, as well as with a host of other European nations in the following decade.[37] These treaties were notable for their espousal of the Most Favoured Nation (MFN) principle, which later became the cornerstone of the GATT. Under this principle, countries negotiating trade concessions with one another agreed that they would extend to each other any more favourable concessions that each might subsequently negotiate with third countries. The MFN principle encouraged multilateralism while discouraging trade discrimination, and because of its presence in most French treaties, free trade swept Europe during the 1860s.[38]

Treaties were not the only institutional results of trade policy in this period. At the same time that countries were negotiating cuts in tariffs, they signed conventions, mainly in the realm of transportation and communication, which helped to facilitate trade in other ways. For example, in 1868 the Rhine was declared a free way for ships of all nations, thus greatly facilitating the transport of goods throughout central Europe.[39] Trading nations also promoted international commerce by setting up organizations to sell domestic products abroad. Commercial attachés date from this period, as do state-run international chambers of commerce. Exhibitions were arranged to show off national wares, and commercial museums were set up to inform manufacturers of the requirements and tastes of foreign markets.[40]

However, the hey-day of free trade was relatively brief and peaked over the period from about 1850 to 1885. In the 1870s Europe suffered a severe and sustained recession, and also found itself facing increasing competition from non-European grain producers. In 1879, Germany retreated from the principle of free trade, when Bismarck raised tariffs substantially on a number of imported items, partly in response to the economic stringencies of the time, and partly in response to the intellectual influence of writers like Friedrich List, who had returned from the United States persuaded of the virtues of a high tariff policy, particularly in manufacturing sectors, in order to promote infant industries. Germany's retreat from free trade was quickly followed by France and a number of European countries, with Britain alone remaining emphatically committed to free trade.[41]

It is perhaps prudent to reflect here on the character of European free trade during the nineteenth century in light of its sudden decline with the advent of hard times. It is important that the history of international trading institutions not be seen as the inevitable result of economic rationality and the triumph of superior economic thought. On the one hand, free trade did not disappear completely after 1879. Germany continued to negotiate trade treaties, although now economic ends tended to be subordinated to those of foreign policy. But perhaps this was no great change of course – free trade was always as much a tool of foreign policy as of economic development. Prussian attempts to establish the *Zollverein* were at least partly motivated by its nation-building aspirations. Similarly, historians have noted that Germany's treaties with France were part of a policy to isolate Austria (Prussia's main competitor for hegemony in the German world), and an attempt to gain French neutrality with respect to Germany's disputes with Denmark.[42] The Cobden–Chevalier treaty may also have been a product of foreign policy desiderata. It was intended, at least in part, to mollify Great Britain over French meddling on the Italian peninsula.[43]

Moreover, if it is a mistake to see treaties as motivated primarily by considerations of economic efficiency, so too would it be wrong to understand the pursuit of markets solely through the instrumentality of trade treaties. Throughout the nineteenth century, the European powers had pursued colonial acquisitions as a means of exploiting the gains from trade.[44] With the onset of depression, and the collapse of the free trade treaties in the late 1870s, this policy was pursued with a vengeance.[45]

The world thus began the present century with the European powers, with the exception of Britain, preferring in large part to reap the gains from trade other than through free trade with other advanced economies. The story had rarely ever been otherwise in the United States. There, with considerable variations over time, a high tariff policy generally prevailed through the nineteenth century, largely promoted by the Republican Party and influenced by the thinking and writings of prominent Americans like Alexander Hamilton, who had vigorously promoted the infant industry rationale for trade protection, in addition to revenue-raising considerations which for much of the nineteenth century were an important function served by tariffs.

The decline of the international trading order

As the world entered the twentieth century, Britain found its economic hegemony rapidly diminishing, and hence it ability to impress the case for free trade on its major trading partners. The advent of the First World War massively disrupted international trading relationships, and the terms of settlement of the war in part contributed to a massive outbreak of beggar-thy-neighbour policies in the 1920s, including competitive exchange rate devaluations and trade restrictions.[46] The Most Favoured Nation system of trade treaties fell into disuse, and trading powers dealt with each other bilaterally instead. In the late 1920s, as the Great Depression set in, many domestic economies, and the world economy at large, largely collapsed. The economic privations of the time prompted many countries to adopt extreme forms of trade protectionism in an attempt to preserve domestic production and employment. The most notorious of such attempts was the enactment by the US Congress of the Smoot-Hawley Tariff in 1930, which raised duties on imports to an average of 60%, and quickly provoked similar retaliatory measures by most of the USA's major trading partners. In the view of most economic commentators, this seriously exacerbated the conditions of the Great Depression, as international trade ground to a virtual stand-still.[47] However, a major shift in policy was signalled by the US Administration in 1934, when President Roosevelt was successful in persuading Congress to pass the Reciprocal Trade Agreements Act, which authorized the Administration to negotiate trade liberalizing agreements on a bilateral basis with its trading partners. In the ensuing years, 31 such agreements were concluded. However, the outbreak of the Second World War decisively shattered visions of a more cooperative international trading environment.[48]

By 1944, it had become reasonably clear to the Allies that the War would shortly be won, and policy-makers, particularly in Britain and the USA, turned their minds to strategies for reconstructing the world economy after the War. Hence, in 1944, in Bretton Woods, New Hampshire, USA, an agreement bearing that name was concluded between Britain and the USA that was designed to lay the groundwork for a co-operative international economic environment following the War. The Bretton Woods Agreement envisaged the creation of three key new international institutions: The International Monetary Fund (IMF), which would be charged with maintaining exchange rate stability, and assisting countries facing balance of payment crises to deal with those crises through access to special drawing rights to be provided by the IMF, rather than by resorting to trade restrictions; the International Bank for Reconstruction and Development (IBRD), commonly referred to as the World Bank, whose mandate initially was to provide reconstruction capital from countries like the USA whose economies had not been devastated by the War to the shattered economies of Europe and Japan; the success of the Marshall Plan that the USA subsequently adopted in promoting this objective meant that the World Bank was able quickly to redefine its focus as providing development capital to less developed countries; and the International Trade Organization (ITO), whose mandate was to oversee the negotiation and administration of a new multilateral, liberal world trading regime.[49]

The formation and evolution of the GATT

Following the end of the War, the IMF and the World Bank were duly created, but the ITO did not come into existence, largely as a result of opposition in the US Congress, which was concerned that both the Organization and many provisions in the Havana Charter that would have created it would excessively constrain domestic sovereignty.[50] Instead, a provisional agreement, negotiated in 1947 among some 23 major trading countries in the world as a prelude to the ITO and the adoption of the Havana Charter, i.e. the General Agreement on Tariffs and Trade (GATT), in fact became the permanent institutional basis for the multilateral world trading regime that has prevailed to this day.[51] Under the GATT, some eight negotiating rounds have now been successfullyconcluded, the latest round (the Uruguay Round) involving about 100 countries, being concluded in December 1993.[52] The first six of these rounds, concluding in 1967 with the Kennedy Round, focused primarily on reciprocal negotiation of tariff concessions. These negotiations were extremely successful and have led to the reduction of average world tariffs on manufactured goods from 40% in 1947 to 5% today. The Tokyo Round that ended in 1979, while also entailing substantial tariff cuts, for the first time directed substantial attention to various non-tariff barriers to trade, such as government procurement policies, subsidy policies, customs valuation policies, and technical standards. In all of these areas, Collateral Codes to the GATT were negotiated on a conditional MFN basis, meaning that only signatories to the Codes are subject to the rights and obligations created by the Codes.[52] The Tokyo Round closed with the world economy and many domestic economies under increasing pressure from a number of sources, including two oil price shocks, a major world recession in the early 1970s and another beginning in the early 1980s, and the rise of Japan, and other newly industrializing countries (NICs), such as Singapore, Hong Kong, Taiwan, South Korea, and Brazil, as major competitive threats in manufactured products. These pressures provoked the rise of the so-called 'New Protectionism' beginning in the early 1970s with countries increasingly resorting to non-tariff barriers to trade, such as quotas, voluntary export restraint agreements, orderly marketing agreements, industrial and agricultural subsidies, and more aggressive unilateral invocation of trade remedy laws, particularly antidumping and countervailing duty laws. In addition, the Short Term Agreement on Cotton Textiles that had been initiated by the USA in 1961 had, by 1973, been generalized to the Multi-Fibre Arrangement (MFA) which permitted countries to negotiate bilateral agreements with exporting countries restricting exports of both natural and synthetic textiles and clothing. This arrangement has been particularly burdensome for many NICs and LDCs which had viewed textile and clothing manufacture, drawing on large pools of unskilled labour and relatively standardized technology, as an attractive entry point into the process of industrialization.

Throughout this period, LDCs in general have played a marginal role in GATT negotiations, which many viewed as a rich man's club. In 1964, LDCs formed the United Nations Commission on Trade and Development (UNCTAD), to address what were perceived to be the special and distinctive economic needs of the LDCs. In 1968, in response to UNCTAD recommendations, Part IV was added to the GATT, providing for so-called 'special and differential status' for LDCs and in particular exempts LDCs from any obligation of reciprocity with respect to trade concessions of developed countries while at the same time urging developed countries to provide unilateral trade concessions to LDCs on trade items of export interest to them. This in turn led to the adoption of the Generalized System of Preferences, where developed member countries of the GATT from the early 1970s onwards granted special trade concessions to LDCs, without seeking reciprocal trade concessions. The special and differential status secured by LDCs under the GATT reflected then widely prevalent thinking in many developing countries that import substitution policies (in effect infant industry promotion policies) were essential to the economic development of these countries, in order to diversify their economic base, provide expanding sources of employment, and reduce dependency on often highly volatile international commodity markets for primary products. With respect to the latter, UNCTAD also promoted the adoption of a variety of international commodity agreements in sectors such as coffee, cocoa, rubber, and tin, in an attempt to stabilize commodity prices and mitigate what were perceived to be deteriorating terms of trade with respect to the exchange of LDC commodities for industrialized countries' manufactured goods.[54]

The Uruguay Round of multilateral trade negotiations under the GATT, which lasted from 1986 to 1993, has proved the most difficult, contentious and complex round of negotiations to have taken place under the auspices of the GATT, in part because of the increasing strains on the world trading system noted above and in part because of the breadth of the negotiating agenda. The Uruguay Round, for the first time, attempted seriously to address the issue of liberalizing international trade in agriculture which had hitherto largely escaped GATT discipline. In addition, the Uruguay Round also sought to reverse the pattern of protectionism with respect to textiles and clothing that had evolved under the Multi-Fibre Arrangement. In addition, several new issues that had previously been viewed as falling outside the ambit of the GATT were for the first time addressed, including in particular international trade in services, trade-related intellectual property issues (TRIPs), and trade-related investment issues (TRIMs).[55]

The formation of regional trading blocs

Running parallel with the evolution of the multilateral trading system under the GATT in the post-War period has been another institutional development of considerable significance – the rise of regional trading blocs. While a significant number of these arrangements have been created, to date by far the most important has been the European Union. The European Union finds its genesis in the Marshall Plan adopted by the USA for the reconstruction of war-torn Europe, motivated not only by economic objectives but also importantly by political concerns to promote a degree of economic integration that would make the devastating military conflicts of the first half of the twentieth century less likely to recur. Efforts at formal economic integration began with the European Coal and Steel Community, which was formed in 1952 and was charged with promoting the rationalization and integration of the European steel industry. In 1957, the Treaty of Rome, which contemplated a much more ambitious agenda of economic integration, was entered into, initially by six member countries: France, Germany, Italy, the Netherlands, Belgium and Luxembourg; and subsequently by the United Kingdom, Denmark, Greece, Ireland, Portugal, and Spain. In the early years, attention was principally focused on the removal of border impediments to trade, especially tariffs and quotas, but over time the European Union has increasingly committed itself to a much more substantial level of economic and political integration, which would provide for the free movement of goods, services, capital, and people within the Community. In 1986, the Community adopted the Single European Act, which set out an ambitious agenda of policy measures with a view to realizing a single European market by 1992.[56] The Maastricht Treaty, ratified in 1993, provides for further forms of economic and political integration. Apart from the European Union, the European Free Trade Association (EFTA) was formed in 1959, with its initial membership comprising Austria, Denmark, Norway, Sweden, Switzerland, and the United Kingdom. The UK and Denmark subsequently joined the European Union, but the remaining members of EFTA have pursued a policy of mutual and substantial tariff reductions. However, EFTA has much more modest ambitions, in terms of degrees of economic integration, than the European Union, and most of the remaining members of EFTA have now applied for full membership in the European Union. In addition, with the recent collapse of the centrally-planned economies in Eastern Europe, a number of these countries now also aspire to eventual membership in the EU.

On the other side of the Atlantic, the conclusion of the Canada–US Free Trade Agreement (FTA) in 1988 marked an important step in the development of an American regional trading bloc. While the FTA is much less integrating than the European Union, it does provide for the removal of all tariffs over a ten year period as well as most other border measures, for largely unrestricted movement of capital and direct investment, and for the liberalization of some trade in services. In 1992 a North American Free Trade Agreement (NAFTA) was concluded by the USA, Mexico, and Canada (subsequently ratified in all three countries), and President Bush spoke of his vision of a trading bloc of the Americas stretching from Anchorage to Tierra del Fuego. The rise of regional trading blocs in the post-war period, alongside the evolution of the multilateral system under the GATT, raises major conceptual and policy issues which will be pursued in greater detail later in this book.[57] While some analysts believe that these trading blocs and the multilateral system can be viewed as complementary and mutually reinforcing, other analysts view regional trading blocs as inherently discriminatory and as a major threat to the future stability and integrity of the multilateral system and to the vision of a co-operative and non-discriminatory world economic order that animated the architects of the Bretton Woods Agreement at the end of the Second World War.

2

THE BASIC ELEMENTS OF THE GATT, THE CANADA–US FREE TRADE AGREEMENT, NAFTA AND THE EUROPEAN UNION

This chapter is intended to provide a brief orientation to, or topography, of the GATT (the heart of the multilateral world trading regime), and the two major regional trading blocs in the world: the Canada–US Free Trade Agreement, now mostly subsumed under the new North American Free Trade Agreement (NAFTA) between the USA, Canada and Mexico; and the European Union. The intention of the chapter is merely to highlight the principal elements of these arrangements, and not to explore them in detail. A number of subsequent chapters in this book will pursue a more detailed analysis of many of these elements. However, given the complexity of these arrangements, there is virtue in having a general road map at hand before embarking on detailed analyses of particular principles or provisions.

THE GENERAL AGREEMENT ON TARIFFS AND TRADE (GATT)[1]

Tariffs

The preamble to the GATT commits member countries ('Contracting Parties') to enter into 'reciprocal and mutually advantageous arrangements directed to the substantial reduction of tariffs and other barriers to trade and to the elimination of discriminatory treatment in international commerce'. Article XXVIII *bis* further provides that the Contracting Parties recognize that

> customs duties often constitute serious obstacles to trade and that negotiations *on a reciprocal and mutually advantageous basis*, directed to the substantial reduction of the general level of tariffs are of great importance to the expansion of international trade.

The Contracting Parties commit themselves under this article to sponsoring such negotiations from time to time either on a selective product-by-product basis or by the application of such multilateral procedures as may be accepted by the Contracting Parties.

Once tariff concessions are agreed to in a particular set of negotiations, these become 'tariff bindings' which are set out in particular Contracting Parties' tariff schedules that constitute an Annex to the GATT. By virtue of Article II of the GATT, all Parties must adhere to these 'tariff bindings' by not imposing customs duties in excess of those set forth in each country's tariff bindings schedule. This is subject to an exception provided for in Article XXVIII, where at scheduled three yearly intervals, any Contracting Party that has made previous tariff concessions can reopen these concessions with other Contracting Parties who have a substantial interest in the concession with a view to modifying or withdrawing the concession, but in that event other concessions must be offered so that a general level of reciprocal and mutually advantageous concessions not less favourable to trade than those existing between the Parties prior to such reopening is maintained.

Obviously, for tariff concessions to be credible, some agreed customs valuation, classification, and administration system is necessary, otherwise a country in agreeing to reduce, for example, a 20% tariff on imports of a particular category to 10%, could negate the concession by arbitrarily revaluing imported goods of this category upwards by 100%, or by reclassifying them into a higher tariff category, or by imposing administrative charges pertaining to the processing of inbound goods that may operate as a *de facto* tariff. Article VII of the GATT requires that the value for customs purposes of imported merchandise should be based on the 'actual value' of the imported merchandise which in turn is defined as the price at which such merchandise is sold or offered for sale in the ordinary course of trade under fully competitive conditions. This definition proved vague and easy to circumvent, and in the Tokyo Round a special Customs Valuation Code was negotiated which stipulates that in the ordinary course of events the 'actual transaction value' as between an exporter and an importer shall be the value for customs purposes, subject to some limited exceptions where the Parties are not dealing with each other at arms length. Similarly, most of the Contracting Parties have agreed to harmonize their systems of customs classification (the HS), based on the Brussels Nomenclature, which reduces room for ambiguity or debate as to the proper tariff classification of a particular good. Finally, Article VIII of the GATT restricts the imposition of fees or charges relating to the administrative processing of inbound goods to the approximate cost of services rendered, which shall not represent an indirect protection to domestic products or a taxation of imports for fiscal purposes.

The principle of non-discrimination

The principle of non-discrimination – often viewed as the cornerstone of the GATT – is referred to in the preamble to the GATT and is amplified in two key provisions: Article I, adopting the Most-Favoured-Nation principle; and Article III, adopting the principle of National Treatment.

The Most-Favoured-Nation (MFN) principle

Under Article I of the GATT, with respect to customs duties imposed by any country on any other member country, any advantage, favour, privilege, or immunity granted by such country to any product originating in any other country shall be accorded immediately and unconditionally to a like product originating in the territories of all other Contracting Parties. Thus, notwithstanding that tariff concessions may be principally negotiated between country A and country B, which may be the chief supplier and purchaser of the products in question respectively, if either country A or country B makes a binding tariff concession to the other, it must extend exactly the same concession to all other member countries of the GATT, without being able to demand *quid pro quos* as a condition for this extension of the concession, at least if these were not part of the initial negotiations. However, the MFN principle is subject to some important exceptions. Article I itself in effect grandfathers preferences that were in force between certain member countries at the time of the inception of the GATT, subject to a rule that freezes the margin of preference, so that it cannot subsequently be increased. This exception has become less important over time as MFN rates have been negotiated down and differences between the preferential rates and the MFN rates progressively reduced. Another exception is the various non-tariff barrier codes negotiated during the Tokyo Round, which operate on a *conditional* MFN basis, meaning that only countries who have chosen to become signatories to the codes are subject to the rights and obligations contained in them.

A third exception is much more important. Article XXIV permits the formation of regional trading blocs, either in the form of custom unions or free trade areas, subject to two basic conditions: namely that the general incidence of duties after the formation of such an arrangement not be higher than the average levels of duties prevailing on the part of member countries to such an arrangement prior to its formation, and that duties and other restrictions on trade must be eliminated with respect to substantially all the trade between the constituent members of the regional trading bloc. It is under this provision that the European Union, the Canada–US Free Trade Agreement, and NAFTA find their legitimacy. By definition, these arrangements would otherwise violate the MFN principle, because they clearly contemplate more favourable duty and related arrangements amongst constituent members than with respect to external trading partners.

Various regional arrangements either in existence or contemplated at the time of the formation of the GATT, including the possible emergence of a European Economic Community, compelled the initial Contracting Parties to recognize this major exception to non-discriminatory multilateralism. As we will see in later chapters, one view of regional trading arrangements is a pragmatic and positive one: that if full multilateral trade liberalization is not immediately possible, partial forms of trade liberalization on a regional basis may be better than nothing, in that they may sustain or nurture over time forward momentum on trade liberalization. This is often referred to as the 'bicycle theory' of trade liberalization. A contrary view argues that partial trade liberalization may be worse than no trade liberalization at all. This view emphasizes a crucial distinction between trade diversion and trade expansion. A simple example will illustrate the distinction. Suppose at one point in time country A maintains a tariff of 20% on textile imports from both countries B and C. Suppose that some of country C's textile producers are 25% more efficient than A's, and that some of country B's textile producers are 15% more efficient than A's. In this scenario C's more efficient textile producers will successfully surmount A's 20% tariff barrier and sell textiles into A's market 5% cheaper than A's producers. B's producers, on the other hand, will find that the 20% tariff more than neutralizes their 15% efficiency advantage over A's producers and renders their product 10% dearer in A's market than textiles produced in C. If countries A and B at a subsequent point in time agree to form a free trade area and to abolish all tariffs between them but to maintain tariffs against external Parties, including the 20% tariff on textiles that A formerly had in place against C, C finds itself in a position where it can still sell textiles 5% more cheaply than A's producers, but they are now 10% dearer than those produced by B. Conversely, B's producers can now sell textiles into A's market 15% cheaper than A's producers, and 10% cheaper than C's (in effect the tariff retained by A against C neutralizes the efficiency advantage that C's producers enjoy over B's of 10% and imposes a further 10% penalty on C relative to B). The result of the formation of a free trade area in this example is that production of textiles will shift from C, the most efficient producer amongst the three countries, to a less efficient producer, B. In other words, trade has been diverted from C to B, despite C's comparative advantage over both B and A. In this example, partial trade liberalization has actually further distorted the efficient allocation of resources.

In considering institutional arrangements to promote regional economic integration, it is useful to think of an integration continuum. First, there are Free Trade Areas (like the Canada–US Free Trade Agreement), where two or more countries agree to remove border restrictions on goods amongst themselves but each reserves the right to maintain whatever external trade policy it wishes with respect to non-member countries. A particular problem raised by this kind of arrangement is importation of goods through low tariff member countries and trans-shipment to higher tariff member countries, which can only be resolved with complex rules of origin. Second, there are Customs Unions where in addition to removing border restrictions on trade in goods amongst member countries, member countries also agree to harmonize their external trade policies *vis à vis* non-member countries. Third, there are Common Markets or Economic Unions (like the European

Union), where in addition to removing border restrictions on trade in goods amongst member countries and harmonizing external trade policy, free trade in or free movement of services, capital, and people, as well as perhaps a common monetary policy, might be contemplated. Fourth, there are Federalist structures, like the USA, Canada, Australia, and Germany, where economic units form a single state, with the central government being vested with the dominant jurisdiction over economic functions, but with some agreed division of economic powers between the central and sub-national levels of government, with constitutional or other arrangements designed to guarantee internal free movement of goods, services, capital, and people, and minimization of internal barriers to trade. Finally, there are Unitary States, where over a given geographic region, one government, to all intents and purposes, possesses exclusive jurisdiction over all significant economic functions, so that problems of inter-governmental coordination of economic policies within the geographic area are eliminated.

The National Treatment principle

The MFN principle set out in Article I of the GATT is designed to constrain discrimination by Contracting Parties amongst different foreign exporters i.e. playing favourites among foreigners. The principle of National Treatment set out in Article III of the GATT addresses another form of discrimination, namely where a Contracting Party adopts internal or domestic policies designed to favour its domestic producers *vis à vis* foreign producers of a given product, even though the latter may all be treated in a uniform way. Article III:4 provides that the products of the territory of any Contracting Party imported into the territory of any other Contracting Party shall be accorded treatment no less favourable than that accorded to like products of national origin in respect of all laws, regulations and requirements affecting their internal sale. In effect, what the principle of National Treatment dictates is that once border duties have been paid by foreign exporters, as provided for in a country's tariff schedules, no additional burdens may be imposed through internal sales taxes, differential forms of regulation etc. on foreign exporters where domestic producers of the same product do not bear the same burden. The particular application of the National Treatment principle to given situations has been the source of a number of important GATT Panel decisions, where difficult decisions arise as to whether a domestic law, regulation or administrative policy, which may be neutral on the face, nevertheless has either the intent or effect of imposing differential burdens on foreign exporters. A specific example of this problem has been addressed in the GATT Code on Technical Standards, initially negotiated during the Tokyo Round, which attempts to promote harmonization of domestic product standards that might otherwise discourage international trade.

An explicit exception to the National Treatment principle is contained in Article III:8 of the GATT, which permits government agencies to favour local producers in purchasing goods for governmental purposes and not with a view to commercial resale. However, this provision is now subject to a detailed government procurement code initially negotiated during the Tokyo Round that requires many departments and agencies of government (although in federal systems, not sub-national levels of government) with regard to government procurement contracts over a certain size to respect the National Treatment principle, and avoid preferences in favour of local producers or unreasonable tendering processes that unfairly disadvantage foreign producers from tendering on government contracts.[2]

Quantitative restrictions

The original framers of the GATT contemplated that the GATT would heavily constrain most border restrictions on trade other than tariffs, so that border restrictions would principally take the form of tariffs which could then be negotiated down over time. In particular, Article XI of the GATT prohibits the use of quotas or import or export licences (i.e. quantitative restrictions) on the importation or exportation of goods into or out of any Contracting Party. Quantitative restrictions on imports clearly protect domestic producers. Less obviously, restrictions on exports may provide local producers for the domestic market with privileged access to 'captive' inputs, or protect local processing plants if exportation of raw materials is constrained. The theory behind Article XI was that if quantitative border restrictions could be avoided, the greater transparency and commensurability of tariffs relative to quantitative restrictions would make their reduction through successive rounds of negotiation more tractable. However, Article XI has been markedly unsuccessful in this ambition, and increasingly so over time.

Exceptions to Article XI

First of all, Article XI itself, until recently, contained a major exception for quantitative restrictions on agricultural imports where these are maintained in order to protect domestic supply management or agricultural marketing board schemes. In addition, Article XII permits the imposition of quantitative restrictions (albeit, by virtue of Article XIII, on a non-discriminatory basis) if a country is facing serious balance of payments problems. Article XVIII of the GATT also permits less developed countries (LDCs) to impose quantitative restrictions either for balance of payments reasons or infant industry reasons against a very relaxed set of criteria. Finally, a major defining characteristic of the rise of the so-called New Protectionism has been the dramatic escalation in the use of quantitative restrictions, typically negotiated on a bilateral basis under threat of unilateral action, and in clear violation of either the letter or spirit of Article XI and Article XIX (relating to safeguard actions, discussed below). These proliferating forms of quantitative restrictions have occurred under the Multi-Fibre Arrangement, and on a more *ad hoc* basis through voluntary export restraint agreements (VEAs) or orderly marketing agreements (OMAs) in sectors such as steel and automobiles.

The safeguard provision

Under Article XIX (often referred to as the safeguards or escape clause), if as a result of unforseen developments and of the effect of obligations incurred by a Contracting Party under the GATT, including tariff concessions, any product is being imported into the territory of that Contracting Party in such increased quantities or under such conditions as to cause or threaten serious injury to domestic producers of like products in that territory, the Contracting Party is entitled to suspend or modify obligations or concessions on a temporary basis in order to alleviate the injury. However, where safeguard action is taken, either in the form of reinstatement of a tariff or the imposition of quantitative restrictions, it must be taken on a non-discriminatory (i.e. non-selective) basis, and the Party taking such action must offer compensation acceptable to other Parties whose trade is prejudiced by such action in the form of substantially equivalent concessions, failing which the latter may retaliate by imposing trade restrictions of equivalent value on exports from the country invoking the safeguard clause. Article XIX was initially envisaged as a kind of safety valve permitting Contracting Parties to buy temporary breathing-space and moderate adjustment costs when confronted with unexpected surges of imports that were causing serious injury to domestic producers. However, the requirements that action be taken on a non-discriminatory basis and be accompanied by compensating concessions has rendered it an unattractive option for Contracting Parties with import-impacted sectors relative to bilateral arrangements like the MFA, VERs, and OMAs, extracted under threat of a unilateral action, principally through the imposition of antidumping or countervailing duties or in the case of the USA unilateral action under section 301 of the Omnibus Trade and Competitiveness Act of 1988.

Trade remedy laws

Article VI of the GATT recognizes the right of Contracting Parties to take unilateral action under domestic trade laws where domestic industries are being materially injured because of unfair foreign trading practices, specifically either dumping or subsidization.

Dumping occurs in its most typical form where foreign producers are selling goods into another country's market at prices below those which they would normally charge in their home market (perhaps because they have a protected market at home). Where this pricing practice is causing material injury to domestic producers of like products, antidumping duties in the amount of the difference between the export market price and the home market price may be imposed on the imported goods. Many member countries of the GATT have enacted anti-dumping laws, and over the late 1970s and 1980s, such laws were invoked with increasing frequency, especially by such countries as the USA, Canada and Australia, and the EC. Article VI has now been amplified by an anti-dumping code initially negotiated during the Kennedy Round and revised in the course of the Tokyo and Uruguay Rounds.

In the case of countervailing duties, the complaint is not the private pricing practices of foreign producers, but rather that foreign governments are unfairly subsidizing the production of foreign exports, artificially advantaging them in importing countries' markets. Where foreign government subsidization of foreign exports is causing material injury to a domestic industry producing like products, domestic trade laws enacted in many countries permit the unilateral imposition of countervailing duties on the subsidized imports so as to offset or neutralize these foreign subsidies. Again, over the late 1970s and 1980s, as a characteristic of the New Protectionism, countervailing duties, along with antidumping duties, began to be more frequently invoked, although in the case of countervailing duties almost exclusively by the USA. A special code on subsidies was initially negotiated during the Tokyo Round and revised during the Uruguay Round, partly with a view to disciplining the invocation of countervailing duty laws and partly with a view to providing an alternative multilateral dispute resolution track for adjudicating disputes over all forms of subsidies that may have trade effects.

The issue of subsidies is one of the most sensitive and complex subjects in international trade law. At one level, the objectionability of subsidies is obvious, in that a subsidy can be devised to replicate the effects of almost any tariff. For example, if country A agrees to reduce tariffs on country B's widget exports from 20% to 10%, and binds itself to this concession, this concession can effectively be undermined by country A then providing subsidies to its own domestic producers of widgets in the amount of 10% of production costs. Conversely, if country A declines to negotiate a reduction of its 20% tariff on country B's widget exports, but country B seeks to undermine the reciprocal bargaining process contemplated for tariff reductions under Article XVIII *bis* by unilaterally subsidizing its exports of widgets into country A's market in the amount of 10% of production costs, country A's right to elect which tariffs to bind itself to would be undermined. On the other hand, given that almost all significant domestic policies of governments, e.g. investments in physical infrastructure, education, health, research and development, telecommunications, law and order, directly or indirectly affect the pattern of economic activities that evolve in each country, and by extension the pattern of international trade activities to which each country contributes, the charge of unfair subsidization has no natural limits. A burgeoning political discourse has emerged over the last few years surrounding the notion of 'fair' (or 'unfair') trade, or 'level playing fields'. Professor Jagdish Bhagwati has described the rise of fair trade discourse as 'the truly greatest threat since the 1930s' to the world trading system.[3]

Article XVI of the GATT requires a Contracting Party that grants or maintains any subsidy which has the effect of increasing exports or reducing imports to notify the Contracting Parties of the nature and extent of the subsidization and its likely effects on trade, and where serious prejudice is caused or threatened to the interests of any other Contracting Party to discuss with that Party the possibility of terminating the subsidization. With respect to export subsidies, Article XVI provides that where export subsidies are granted on a primary product, these should not result in the exporting country gaining 'more than an equitable share of world export trade in that product', relative to pre-existing shares. With respect to export subsidies on non-primary products, a number of signatories have agreed to forsake these where such a subsidy would result in export sales at lower prices than domestic sales. The new Uruguay Round Subsidies Agreement attempts to provide more precise definitions of prohibited, actionable, and non-actionable subsidies.

For clarity of understanding, it is helpful to keep in mind a basic taxonomy of subsidy scenarios. The first scenario is one where country A subsidizes its exports into country B's market. This is the scenario which has classically attracted the potential for countervailing duties under Article VI and complementary domestic trade remedy laws. These subsidies could relate exclusively to exports or to all domestic production, wherever consumed. The second scenario is where country A subsidizes its exports into country C's market, and in so doing displaces country B's exports from country C's market. In this scenario, the subsidized goods are not moving from country A to country B and thus cannot be countervailed by country B, so that country B is remitted to a complaint under the GATT Subsidies Code for resolution under the Panel dispute resolution process. The third subsidy scenario is the case where country A is subsidizing its domestic producers to service principally country A's own domestic market, and in so doing displaces country B's exports from country A's market. Again, as in scenario two, the subsidized goods are not moving from country A to country B so as to attract possible countervailing duties in country B, so that country B is again remitted to the multilateral dispute resolution process.

The considerable, and apparently growing, attraction of antidumping and countervailing duties for import-impacted sectors, relative to the safeguard regime contemplated by Article XIX, reflects the fact that selective (i.e. discriminatory) action is permitted, no compensation is required in the form of counterbalancing trade concessions, and the duties are imposed automatically by administrative rather than political decision (unlike safeguard actions which ultimately require executive political action, typically following discussions and negotiations with affected foreign country governments).

State trading enterprises

Under Article XVII of the GATT each Contracting Party undertakes that its state trading enterprises shall, with respect to its purchases or sales involving either imports or exports, act in a non-discriminatory manner and make such purchases or sales solely in accordance with commercial considerations. This provision does not apply to imports of products for immediate or ultimate consumption in governmental use and not otherwise for resale.

This provision recognizes that state trading enterprises have the potential for distorting international trade through explicit or implicit subsidy policies or artificial pricing strategies. For example, a state enterprise selling into export markets may artificially subsidize its exports. Conversely, a state enterprise in its purchasing policies may explicitly or implicitly favour domestic producers over foreign producers of the same products. Article XVII, in its initial conception, was principally addressed to a significant number of state-owned enterprises that existed in the jurisdictions of Contracting Parties at the time of the formation of the GATT, even though these countries were largely committed to market economies. Article XVII is not nearly as well equipped to address the systemic problems of countries which are members of the GATT, or aspire to be, that are predominantly centrally planned or command economies, or which are in the process (as with Eastern European countries and China) of transition from command to some form of market economy. In these countries, because prices, input costs, and wages have traditionally been set by command or administrative fiat, determining, as is required by Article XVII, whether a state enterprise is operating according to 'commercial considerations' involves the intractable counterfactual exercise of determining what the country in question would import or export *if* there was a functioning market.

In consequence, where in the past command economies have participated in the GATT, they have done so on special terms that have involved either specific commitments to increase imports from non-Communist countries, or have entailed expectations of partial liberalization of the trade and payments system. Special arrangements of this nature have applied in the case of Poland, Hungary and Romania, and to a much more limited extent to the former Yugoslavia.[4] As well, in many instances, Contracting

Parties have not granted full MFN status to these countries despite their membership in the GATT, and the terms of accession in the case of some of these command economies have permitted imposition of discriminatory safeguards or quantitative restrictions, which were frequently invoked by European Community countries in particular.

With the fall of the Communist bloc, the issue of normalizing the GATT membership of the former command economies has come to the fore. As well, the question of the admission of Russia and other former Soviet republics looms large, as does the application for re-admission of Communist China, which continues to remain in many important respects a command economy. We address these issues in greater depth in the concluding chapter.

Less developed countries

'Special and differential status' is accorded to LDCs under the GATT both with respect to actions which they are permitted to take and with respect to actions that developed countries are expected to take towards them. Under Article XVIII, LDCs have been given broad latitude to impose restrictions on imports, typically through quantitative restrictions such as quotas and licenses, for balance of payments reasons or in order to foster infant industries. Under Part IV of the GATT, added in 1964, Article XXXVI:8 provides that developed Contracting Parties do not expect reciprocity for commitments made by them in trade negotiations to reduce or remove tariffs and other barriers to the trade of less developed Contracting Parties. Article XXXVII in turn provides that developed countries commit themselves to according high priority to the reduction and elimination of barriers to products currently or potentially of particular export interest to less developed Contracting Parties. These latter provisions led to the introduction of the Generalized System of Preferences in the early 1970s and the unilateral adoption of special preferences by industrial countries with respect to some exports of less developed countries. The degree of success of either of these two elements of the special and differential status accorded to LDCs under the GATT will be the subject of a more detailed discussion in a later chapter.[5] For the moment, it is sufficient to note that with respect to the first element in this status i.e. authorization of import substitution – infant industry promotion policies by LDCs – this reflects a debate going back to John Stuart Mill about the case for protectionism in this context (discussed in the previous chapter). The second element in the special and differential status, i.e. non-reciprocal trade concessions by developed countries, raises the strategic question of whether countries will find themselves willing to engage in unilateral trade liberalization, and reflects the long standing intellectual debate about the virtues of unilateral trade liberalization relative to reciprocal trade liberalization.

General exceptions to GATT obligations

Under Article XX of the GATT, a number of dispensations from GATT obligations are provided with respect to the adoption or enforcement by Contracting Parties of measures, for example, necessary to protect public morals; necessary to protect human or animal health or life; necessary to secure compliance with laws or regulations which are not inconsistent with the GATT; imposed for the protection of national treasures; necessary for the conservation of exhaustible natural resources.[6] Under Article XXI of the GATT, various national security exceptions are provided for that permit a Contracting Party to take any action which it considers necessary for the protection of its essential security interests relating to fissionable materials, traffic in arms and munitions or which reflect the exigencies of war or other emergency in international relations.[7] Article XXV (5) provides that in exceptional circumstances not otherwise provided for in the Agreement, the Contracting Parties may waive an obligation imposed on a Contracting Party by the GATT, provided that any such decision is approved by a two-thirds majority of the votes cast and such majority comprises more than half of the Contracting Parties. This waiver provision has been invoked on a number of important occasions, including the 1955 US agricultural waiver application and the Canada–USA Auto Pact in 1965.

The governance of the GATT

With the failure of the initial Contracting Parties to endorse the creation of the International Trade Organization and the Havana Charter of which it was part, the GATT, at least on its surface, was born with an anaemic institutional structure relative to many other international organizations, such as the International Monetary Fund and the World Bank. These other organizations were seen as largely addressing and coordinating matters of external economic and political relations, while the ITO and Havana Charter were perceived as possessing the potential for constraining many domestic policies and hence trenching, to a greater extent, upon domestic political sovereignty. However, over the course of time, various institutional structures have evolved that appear to have proven reasonably serviceable in the management of the GATT. A committee of ministers of trade from member countries meets periodically, although most of the effective collective decision making is channelled through the Council of Representatives, which meets on a monthly basis in Geneva, and is drawn from permanent GATT delegations of member countries, with each country entitled to one vote. The Council of Representatives is supplemented by various specialized committees and working parties as well as dispute resolution panels appointed on an *ad hoc*, case-by-case basis. The full-time staff of the GATT is headed by a Director-General, appointed on a fixed term basis by consensus of the Contracting Parties. Article XXV (4) of the GATT provides that decisions of the Contracting Parties shall be taken by a majority of the votes cast, except as otherwise provided for in the Agreement. Article XXXIII provides for the accession of new members, if supported by a vote of a two-thirds majority of all Contracting Parties. Article XXX provides for amendments to the GATT provisions. Part I of the agreement containing the Most Favoured Nation principle and the principle of tariff bindings may only be amended by consent of all the Contracting Parties. Other provisions may be amended by a two-thirds majority of all the Contracting Parties, but amendments become binding only with respect to those Contracting Parties which accept the amendment.

With respect to specific disputes between Contracting Parties (which it must be emphasized are governments, not private parties), Article XXII imposes an obligation on Contracting Parties to accord sympathetic consideration to complaints of other Parties and adequate opportunity for consultation with such Parties. If the Contracting Parties cannot resolve a dispute through mutual discussions, perhaps assisted by mediation of a third Party, including the Director-General of the GATT or his staff, the dispute must then be addressed within the framework of Article XXIII. Under this Article, if a Contracting Party considers that any benefit accruing to it directly or indirectly under the GATT is being 'nullified or impaired' by a policy or practice of another Contracting Party, the complaining Party can refer its complaint to the Contracting Parties as a group – effectively the Council of Representatives, which in turn will decide whether to appoint a Panel to investigate the complaint and make recommendations to the Council of Representatives for resolution of the dispute. Panels typically comprise three individuals, drawn from countries other than the disputing Parties, who meet privately with the disputing Parties to ascertain the facts and the precise nature of the allegations, and if possible to resolve the dispute informally. If this is not possible, the Panel will make recommendations to the Council of Representatives as to the resolution of the matter. The Council of Representatives makes decisions on Panel recommendations on a consensus basis, which effectively requires unanimity, including the support of both Parties to a dispute. If the Council adopts the recommendations of a Panel then a Contracting Party is required to modify or withdraw its policy or practice to bring itself into conformity with the Council's decision. If it fails to do so, the Council can authorize retaliatory action by the aggrieved Party in the form of a suspension of trade concessions or other obligations. Despite a number of seemingly odd features of this dispute resolution process, when compared with domestic adjudication processes, in many respects it has worked reasonably well over the years. Several hundred complaints have been investigated since the inception of the GATT, as we will see in a later chapter. There has been a very high compliance rate with Panel recommendations and Council decisions, despite the hypothetical ability of losing Parties to veto adoption of adverse Panel recommendations. Moreover, aggrieved Parties have almost never found it expedient to pursue retaliatory action against Parties adversely affected by Panel or Council decisions.

The Uruguay Round Agreement

On 19 December 1993, member countries of the GATT reached a wide-ranging and ambitious agreement on many trade and related issues, after seven years of negotiations which were characterized by much higher levels of rancour and controversy than any of the previous MTN rounds. While the Round seemed often at the point of collapse, the agreement eventually reached signifies substantial progress on a number of important issues.

With respect to goods, substantial across-the-board cuts in tariffs (of the order of one-third) on many products were agreed to. In the case of agricultural products – a key area of controversy – the EU agreed to significant cuts over time in export subsidies, and member countries agreed to abandon quantitative restrictions, which are to be replaced by tariffs. In the case of textiles and clothing, the MFA will be dismantled by degrees, with quantitative restrictions again being replaced by tariffs, which are to be reduced over time. The general safeguard regime has been significantly strengthened by adoption of firm time limits for safeguard measures and for limiting their re-adoption; by improving multilateral notification and surveillance; and by requiring existing grey-area measures to be brought into compliance with the new regime or terminated. A modestly revised Antidumping Code was also negotiated, as well as a more fully elaborated Subsidies Code. A revised Government Procurement Code provides for somewhat greater coverage of government contracting than the Tokyo Round Code. With respect to intellectual property, substantial harmonization of domestic intellectual property regimes around norms prevailing in the USA and a number of other industrialized countries was agreed to.

With respect to international trade in services, a process for liberalization on a sector-by-sector basis, governed by a conditional MFN principle and an effects-based National Treatment principle, has been set in motion. With respect to trade-related investment measures, local sourcing and minimum export requirements as conditions for approval of foreign investments have been prohibited.

With respect to the governance of the GATT, a World Trade Organization (WTO) has been created to oversee an integrated dispute settlement regime and to undertake a pro-active trade policy surveillance role. In addition, membership of the WTO now entails commitment to most of the GATT codes, which are fully integrated into the GATT/WTO, and no longer operate on a conditional MFN basis.

We pursue many of these issues in much greater detail later in this book.

Recent estimates suggest that by the year 2002, net world welfare may be around $US270 billion higher, in current prices, than it would be if current levels of protection remained unchanged.[8]

THE CANADA–US FREE TRADE AGREEMENT[9]

History

Canada and the USA have a long and tangled history of bilateral arrangements pertaining to trade. In 1854, both countries agreed to the Reciprocity Treaty which provided for a measure of free trade with respect to Canadian exports of certain agricultural products and natural resources and US access to Canadian inshore fisheries. However, the USA cancelled this treaty in 1865, in part reflecting US unhappiness with what was perceived to be Canadian complicity with Britain in supporting the Confederacy side in the US Civil War, and in part due to opposition by US agricultural interests.[10] In 1879, Prime Minister John A. MacDonald announced the National Policy, which entailed high levels of tariff protection for manufacturers in central Canada, complemented by policies to support western settlement and provide markets for these goods, which would be encouraged through the development of a national transportation system. In 1911, the Liberal government led by Sir Wilfred Laurier negotiated a tentative free trade agreement with the USA, partly in response to dissatisfaction by farmers in western Canada with the cost of domestically produced farm implements. However, debate in Parliament forced Laurier to call an election, during which the Conservatives strongly opposed a free trade agreement with the USA on the grounds that this would mean increased competition for Canadian farmers because of the earlier US growing season, would jeopardize relations with Britain, and would risk importing US economic difficulties such as unemployment. The Liberals lost the election, and the agreement was never ratified. In 1934, the US Congress, on the initiative of President Roosevelt, enacted the Reciprocal Trade Agreements Act and in 1935 pursuant to this Act a Canada–US bilateral agreement was negotiated which provided for some modest tariff reductions. In 1948, Canadian and American negotiators negotiated a comprehensive bilateral free trade agreement, but Prime Minister William Lyon Mackenzie King refused to present the agreement to Parliament for adoption on the grounds that it would lead ultimately to union with the States and separation from Britain. In 1965, Canada and the USA negotiated the Auto Pact which provided for conditional duty-free trade between Canada and the USA in original equipment, auto parts, accessories, and most types of motor vehicles. In a 1975 report entitled *Looking Outward*, the Economic Council of Canada proposed that Canada contemplate substantial trade liberalization with the USA. In 1978, the Senate Committee on Foreign Affairs took a similar position. In

1983, the Department of External Affairs issued a Review of Foreign Trade Policy that recommended that the government consider the advisability of sectoral free trade with the USA in urban transport equipment, textiles, agricultural equipment, and petro-chemicals. In 1986, the Macdonald Royal Commission on the Economic Union and Development Prospects for Canada, after undertaking an extensive review of all of Canada's trade policy options, strongly recommended that Canada initiate negotiations with the USA to secure a comprehensive bilateral trade agreement. The Mulroney Conservative government, which was elected in 1984, initiated formal negotiations with the USA in 1986. Negotiations culminated in the Canada–US Free Trade Agreement, which was signed by the two countries on 2 January 1988 and subsequently ratified by the legislative bodies in both countries. As of 1988, two-thirds of Canada's imports came from the USA and three-quarters of its exports went to the USA. About one-fifth of US imports came from Canada and one-quarter of US exports went to Canada. The trading relationship between Canada and the USA is the largest bilateral trading relationship in the world. The basic elements in the Agreement are briefly reviewed below.

Trade in goods

Under the FTA, all tariffs between Canada and the USA will be phased out in varying stages by 1 January 1998. The FTA also eliminates a number of quotas and embargoes on the import and export of goods between Canada and the USA. Minimum price requirements for exports cannot replace prohibited quotas and minimum price requirements on imports are similarly eliminated. Canada has also agreed to phase out prohibitions on importation of used automobiles and used aircraft. Some existing quotas have been maintained. Canadian vessels will continue to be prohibited from coastal activities in US waters, and Canadian export controls on logs and east coast prohibitions on the export of unprocessed fish will remain in force (Chapter 4).

Only goods originating in either country are entitled to the benefit of the reduced tariffs provided for by the FTA. Goods which are wholly obtained in either or both countries are deemed to originate in the country from which they are exported and are entitled to FTA treatment. Goods incorporating third country materials generally qualify for FTA treatment provided sufficient processing has occurred to cause them to have a tariff classification different from that of the component materials. In other cases, special content rules must be satisfied as well (Chapter 3).

With respect to government procurement, the FTA lowers the GATT Code threshold from $US171,000 to $US25,000 for purchases by Code-covered federal agencies of covered goods. Each Party must use criteria for decisions on qualifying suppliers, valuing bids, and awarding contracts that are objective, free of preference and clearly specified in advance. The

FTA establishes a bid challenge procedure that may result in re-evaluating offers, recompeting, or terminating contracts (Chapter 13).

With respect to energy, the FTA introduces free trade between Canada and the USA in crude oil, natural gas, electricity, uranium, petroleum products, petrochemicals, and oil field equipment. Export restrictions, whether quantitative or price based, are in general prohibited. Exceptions relate to conservation, price stabilization and national security, but permitted restrictions must be applied on a proportional sharing basis so as to ensure that the burden of restrictions applies equally to domestic and export markets (Chapter 9).

With respect to agriculture, the FTA removes all tariffs on agricultural goods over a ten year period. All export subsidies on agricultural goods exported by one country to the other are eliminated. Some quotas are also prohibited, in particular quotas on meat goods, and import permit requirements imposed by Canada on wheat, oats or barley and their products will be eliminated if the level of US subsidies for these goods is less than or equal to the level of Canadian subsidies. Minimum quota levels, which are in excess of the current levels, are established for poultry and eggs imported into Canada. Supply management programmes for Canadian dairy farmers appear to be unaffected by the provisions in the FTA. Processes are also stipulated for developing harmonized standards and inspection procedures to facilitate an open border policy for bilateral trade in agricultural food, beverages, and related products (Chapter 7).

With respect to bilateral trade in automotive goods, the Auto Pact is preserved, but export-based duty remission schemes have been prohibited, and assembly plants established in Canada or the USA subsequent to the 1989 model year do not qualify for Auto Pact treatment. However, duties on automotive trade outside the Auto Pact will end ten years from the date of the Agreement, subject only to the goods meeting rules of origin requirements. The Auto Pact will continue to permit duty-free importation into Canada of automotive goods from third countries and to require domestic manufacturers to produce one vehicle in Canada for every vehicle sold in Canada. These residual benefits, which accrue only to Canada, will likely cause the USA to serve the one year notice that terminates the Auto Pact when duties end in ten years on bilateral trade (Chapter 10).

The FTA also attempts to end discriminatory pricing and distribution practices that have been adopted by federal, state, and provincial governments with respect to the retail sale of distilled spirits and wine. The FTA does not apply to beer distribution or beer retailing regulations and practices, although both Parties have expressly reserved their rights under GATT Article III (the National Treatment principle) with respect to existing measures affecting pricing and distribution of beer, and GATT dispute resolution panels have recently held that both countries are in violation of this provision (Chapter 8).

The FTA provides a two-track system for invoking safeguard relief against rapid increases in imports where such increases are causing or threaten to cause serious injury to domestic industries. The first track safeguard system provides for emergency tariff rate freezes or increases for USA–Canada trade affected by the FTA's removal of tariff and non-tariff barriers. Such safeguards cannot be maintained for more than three years, or be invoked more than once by either Party for any good. The regime expires ten years after the date of the agreement. The second track safeguard system attempts to deal with imports of one Party in the event of multilateral safeguard action taken by the other under Article XIX of the GATT. In the past, such global actions have adversely affected Canadian exporters who have been 'side-swiped' by US safeguard actions taken under the GATT and directed principally at European and Pacific rim imports. Imports from either Party are exempt from global safeguard action where they are not substantial and are not contributing significantly to the injury caused by imports. Imports in the range of 5% to 10% or less of total imports are normally not to be considered substantial. The FTA establishes a system of binding arbitration to resolve disputes relating to either bilateral or multilateral safeguard actions (Chapter 11).

Investment

Under the FTA, Investment Canada's screening threshold with respect to US acquisitions of domestic enterprises is increased from $5 million Canadian to $150 million in terms of gross assets of the acquired enterprise. Screening requirements are removed entirely for indirect acquisitions involving transfers of control from one foreign-controlled firm in Canada to another. Existing restrictions on foreign ownership in Canadian cultural industries and the Canadian oil, gas and uranium sectors are exempt from the Agreement. The Agreement also exempts restrictions in both Canada and the USA on foreign ownership in the communication and transportation industries. The two countries have agreed to prohibit investment-related performance requirements e.g. local content or import substitution require-ments, if these significantly distort bilateral trade. Nationalization of industries for public policy purposes may occur, but due process and fair compensation requirements must be satisfied (Chapter 16).

With respect to foreign investment in the financial sector, US banks are exempted by Canada from the 16% foreign ownership ceiling on total banking assets in Canada. Canada has also agreed to exempt US firms and investors from the 25% ceiling on non-residents holding shares in a federally-regulated, Canadian-controlled financial institution, although they will still be subject to any 10% maximum rule applicable to any individual investor in the shares of any such institution. Under the FTA, Canadian banks operating in the USA will be able to underwrite and deal in securities of Canadian governments and agencies. Canadian banks are also granted 'grandfather' status that permits them to operate in more than one State, unlike many of their US competitors. Canadian financial institutions have been guaranteed that they will receive the same treatment accorded US financial institutions under any amendments to the Glass–Steagall Act, which prohibits US commercial banks from engaging in investment banking or securities underwriting (Chapter 17).

Trade in services

The FTA adopts a National Treatment principle in a range of service sectors, including advertising, collection agencies, telephone-answering, commercial cleaning, security and investigation, management consulting, insurance, engineering, computer, architectural, and accounting services. However, the requirement of National Treatment has had little immediate impact on these service industries because the FTA grandfathers existing measures which do not conform to this principle, and applies only prospectively to new measures introduced after the FTA. With respect to such measures, differential treatment of persons of the other Party is permitted provided that the difference in treatment is no greater than necessary for prudential, fiduciary, health and safety, or consumer protection reasons. The Agreement commits the two Parties to pursuing efforts at harmonization of licensing and certification standards in covered sectors so as to ensure that these relate principally to competence and do not have the effect of discriminatorily impairing the access of nationals of the other Party to such sectors (Chapter 14).

The FTA also provides for a regime of temporary entry visas for business persons who require entry into the other Party incidentally to trade in goods or services or investment activities (Chapter 15).

With respect to cultural industries, the FTA provides that nothing in the Agreement affects the ability of either Party to pursue cultural policies that favour national cultural enterprises, with four exceptions: (1) the elimination over a ten-year period of tariffs on goods used and produced by cultural industries; (2) mandatory purchase by Canada at fair open market value of any foreign-owned cultural industry enterprise where divestiture has been ordered by Investment Canada; (3) non-discriminatory copyright protection and remuneration for owners of programmes broadcast by distant stations and retransmitted by cable companies; and (4) the termination of Canada's Income Tax Act requirement that a magazine or newspaper be typeset and printed in Canada in order for advertisers to have the right to deduct expenses for advertising space (Chapter 20).

Institutional provisions

The FTA creates the Canada–United States Trade Commission on which both Parties are represented equally by their trade ministers. Where disputes arise as to the interpretation or application of FTA provisions to actual or proposed measures of either Party, the Party complaining that such a measure will cause nullification or impairment of any reasonably expected benefit under the FTA can refer the matter to the Commission. The complaining Party must first notify and consult with the other Party, but in the absence of agreement can then request a meeting of the Commission. The Commission may appoint a mediator. If this fails to result in agreement, the Commission must refer disputes over safeguards and may refer other disputes to a binding arbitration panel if the two Parties agree on such a reference. If a Party fails to implement the finding of an arbitration panel, or the Parties cannot agree on compensation or remedial action, the other Party can retaliate. If the Commission does not send the dispute to arbitration, then upon the request of either Party, it must name a panel of experts, drawn primarily from permanent lists maintained by each Party, to find facts and recommend a resolution. The Commission must then attempt to reach agreement on the resolution of the dispute as recommended by the panel. In the absence of agreement, the aggrieved Party may retaliate. Only the Canadian and US governments can participate in this process; private Parties and provincial or state governments are excluded (Chapter 18).

Beyond these general dispute resolution mechanisms, the FTA has set up a new bilateral panel review process for final domestic antidumping and countervailing duty determinations, which mechanism replaces domestic judicial review processes. The FTA provided that this mechanism would be temporary, pending negotiation of new legal regimes on dumping, subsidies and countervailing duties in the five to seven years from the commencement date of the Agreement. Under the mechanism, if aggrieved Parties so demand, binational panels must be struck as an alternative to pursuing domestic judicial review processes. These binational panels, which comprise five experts drawn from permanent lists provided by each Party (two from each Party with agreement normally on a fifth person as chairperson) may only review final antidumping and countervailing duty determinations for consistency with applicable domestic laws using domestic standards of judicial review. The decision of a panel is binding on the Parties. Each Party reserves the right to change or modify its antidumping or countervailing laws, provided that any such amendment expressly stipulates that it shall apply to goods from the other Party. Where a Party complains that such an amendment is inconsistent with the other Party's obligations under the GATT or with the object and purpose of the FTA, that Party may request that the amendment be referred to a panel for a declaratory opinion. Where the declaratory opinion reports an inconsistency, the Parties must consult and seek a mutually satisfactory solution to the dispute, including remedial legislation with respect to the statute of the amending Party. If remedial legislation is not enacted within nine months from the end of the ninety day consultation period provided for and no other agreement has been reached, the complaining Party may take comparable executive or equivalent legislative action, or terminate the entire FTA upon sixty days written notice to the other Party (Chapter 19).

THE NORTH AMERICAN FREE TRADE AGREEMENT (NAFTA)[11]

Negotiations formally commenced on 12 June 1991 between the USA, Mexico, and Canada to attempt to secure a North American Free Trade Agreement. Negotiations concluded on 12 August 1992 with a draft agreement which has now been ratified in the three countries involved. In many respects NAFTA is an extension to Mexico of the Canada–US Free Trade Agreement. Major features of the Agreement are described in the following seven sections.

Trade in goods

Most tariffs between the three countries will be eliminated over a ten-year period, in accordance with stipulated phase-out schedules. Most import and export restrictions, in particular quotas and import licences, will be eliminated. The principle of National Treatment is reaffirmed. Rules of origin similar to those contained in the Canada–US Free Trade Agreement are adopted, although there are special rules applicable to particular classes of products. With respect to automobiles, 62.5% of NAFTA content is required to qualify for preferential treatment. In the case of textiles, a 'fibre forward' rule is adopted that in effect requires NAFTA fibres to be used to qualify for preferential treatment, and in the case of clothing a 'yarn forward' rule is adopted which requires clothing to be made from NAFTA produced yarn in order to qualify for preferential treatment. There are some limited exceptions to these latter rules, through a system of Tariff Rate Quotas (TRQs), which allows preferential treatment of exports up to agreed ceilings even though the rules of origin are not met. The textile and clothing provisions of the Agreement also contain a safeguard mechanism that enables a country to impose trade restrictions to provide temporary relief during a transition period.

With respect to energy and basic petrochemicals, similar provisions apply as under the Canada–US Free Trade Agreement, except that Mexico has reserved to the Mexican State activities in oil, gas, refining, basic petrochemicals, and the nuclear and electricity sectors.

With respect to agriculture, the USA and Mexico have agreed to eliminate all non-tariff barriers to trade and to convert these to tariffs or TRQs. The operation of these provisions is deferred in the case of sensitive products, such as corn and dry bean exports to Mexico, and orange juice and sugar exports to the USA. Canada and Mexico have agreed to remove all tariff and non-tariff barriers to agricultural trade except with respect to dairy products, poultry, eggs and sugar. The agricultural provisions also contain a special safeguard provision that can be invoked during the first ten years of the Agreement if imports exceed specified trigger levels. The use of export subsidies for agricultural products is generally discouraged and permitted only in response to non-NAFTA country subsidies, but subject even in this event to consultation procedures. The Agreement provides for efforts at harmonization of grade and quality standards with respect to agricultural products.

Sanitary and phytosanitary (SPS) measures maintained or introduced by any NAFTA country are permitted provided they are not a disguised form of trade restriction and are based on scientific principles and a risk assessment. Where possible, NAFTA countries commit themselves to using relevant international standards and to working towards equivalent SPS measures without reducing any country's chosen level of protection of human, animal or plant life or health.

Along the lines of the provisions in the Canada–US Free Trade Agreement, both bilateral and multilateral general safeguard provisions are included in the Agreement. Similar but permanent provisions have also been adopted with respect to binational panel review of domestic antidumping and countervailing duty determinations.

With respect to government procurement, National Treatment obligations are adopted with respect to purchases by government departments or agencies over $US50,000 of goods and services and over $US6.5 million for construction services. With respect to federal government enterprises, these thresholds are raised to $US250,000 and $US8 million respectively. Transparency and bid-challenge provisions similar to those found in the Canada–USA Free Trade Agreement are adopted.

Trade in services

With respect to trade in services, both the National Treatment and Most Favoured Nation Principles are adopted. The Agreement provides that no local presence is required to provide covered services. A number of reservations have been entered with respect to which services are covered and which are not. With respect to licensing and certification of professionals, the Agreement provides that entry requirements should be related solely to competence and endorses a qualified mutual recognition principle. In the case of land transportation services, the Agreement provides for cross-border provision of bus and trucking services to be phased in over a transitional period.

The Agreement recognizes the right of establishment with respect to banking, insurance, securities, and other financial services, and adopts the National Treatment and Most Favoured Nation Principles with respect to financial services generally. Canada commits itself to extending the exemption from the 25% non-resident rule to Mexico and the exemption from the aggregate asset ceiling on foreign banks operating in Canada. Mexico has reserved the right to impose market share limits on foreign firms in the financial services sector during a transitional period expiring in the year 2000.

The Agreement also provides for temporary entry for business persons into any NAFTA country along the lines of the provisions in the Canada–US Free Trade Agreement.

Investment

Both the National Treatment and Most Favoured Nation Principles are adopted. Performance requirements of foreign investors are generally prohibited. Some reservations are registered with respect to particular sectors and Canada has reserved the right to continue reviewing foreign investments as provided under the Canada–US Free Trade Agreement. Mexico is committed to raising its foreign investment review threshold to $150 million within ten years of the implementation of the Agreement. The Agreement also provides that no NAFTA country is to lower its environmental standards in order to attract investment.

Competition policy, monopolies, and state enterprises

Each country commits itself to maintaining laws regulating anti-competitive practices. In the case of state enterprises and domestic monopolies, these enterprises are not to discriminate against other NAFTA firms or citizens in buying or selling goods and services and are to follow normal commercial considerations in their contractual activities. A tri-lateral committee is to be created to review the relationship between competition laws and trade matters, including presumably trade remedy laws. A side-accord initiated by Canada commits the member countries to atempting to negotiate new legal regimes on dumping, subsidies and countervailing duties within two years of the implementation of the Agreement.

Intellectual property

The Agreement has an extensive set of provisions protecting patent, copyright and trademark rights, and providing for their effective enforcement. These provisions largely build on the intellectual property chapter in the Uruguay Round Draft Agreement of the GATT.

Institutional arrangements

The Agreement provides for the creation of a NAFTA Trade Commission, to be supported by a full-time Secretariat, and complemented by various working groups and committees. Dispute resolution mechanisms similar to those provided for in Chapter 18 of the Canada–US Free Trade Agreement are included, where binational panels will adjudicate on disputes between two member countries of the NAFTA, with the third member reserving the option of either participating in the proceedings or pursuing its own process of consultation and dispute resolution. Where complaint procedures are open to a NAFTA country either under the GATT or NAFTA, a complainant country is entitled to choose which regime it pursues its complaint under, except where the complaint pertains to health, safety, or environmental standards, where the respondent country can insist on dispute resolution under NAFTA. In this event, the Agreement provides for the creation of scientific boards to provide expert evidence to panels adjudicating on questions pertaining to health, safety and environmental standards.

Side-accords on environmental and labour standards

Subsequent to the negotiation of NAFTA, the current US Administration initiated a further set of negotiations on environmental and labour standards that resulted in trilateral side-accords that set up an elaborate institutional machinery to ensure that existing environmental and labour laws in each of the three countries are effectively enforced with the possibility of fines and trade sanctions as penalties for non-compliance. The Accords also provide for consultative mechanisms designed to promote a higher degree of harmonization of standards in these areas in the future.

THE FRAMEWORK OF ECONOMIC INTEGRATION IN THE EUROPEAN UNION[12]

The 'constitution' of the European Union is the Treaty Establishing the European Community, usually known as the Treaty of Rome.[13] It states the basic principles of economic union – the free movement of goods, persons, services and capital – and contains a variety of legal norms aimed at the realization of these freedoms. In addition to provisions that prohibit customs duties on imports from Member States, quantitative restrictions and 'equivalent measures' are prohibited (Article 30), as are certain State aids to industry.

The Treaty imposes constraints on Member States' governments as well as positive obligations. However, even where the Treaty of Rome requires further positive action in the form of cooperation between governments, this is much more than a 'best efforts' exhortation. In fact, it has the status of a juridical norm. To those accustomed to Anglo-American understandings about the rule of law, this may at first appear strange, since court action is not apparently available to force governments to bring into being the positive measures in question. It is, however, quite consistent with continental notions of constitutional law as embodying the most general legal norms. In turn, these norms are realized by the enactment of secondary or derivative norms by governments.

The Treaty of Rome establishes several institutional mechanisms for the realization of the Treaty norms: the European Court of Justice, the European Commission, The Council of Ministers, and the European Parliament. Some of the most important 'economic union' provisions in the Treaty of Rome are directly enforceable by the European Court. These provisions allow a citizen (or in some instances a corporation) in a Member State to apply to the judiciary for relief against measures of her own or another State that violate provisions of the Treaty. While direct enforceability or application only exists for some aspects of the Treaty, it has been of major importance in making the Union something more than a common market or customs union. In most free-trade agreements, dispute settlement is an intergovernmental process. As a result, dispute settlement has strong political and diplomatic dimensions. By contrast, the Treaty of Rome is in significant respects a *supranational constitution*, conferring enforceable legal rights on Union citizens.[14]

In addition, a number of provisions of the Treaty are explicitly enforceable by the European Commission, but are subject to judicial review. This is, in particular, the case with competition policy and the prohibition of State aids (subsidies) that distort competition within the Union. The Commission is an executive body consisting of representatives appointed from the Member States, but obliged by law to act independently of their governments. Appointments must be acceptable to all Member States.[15] The Commission must always have a member from each Member State. Decisions of the Commission must be approved by a simple majority of the members (i.e., at least seven commissioners) with a quorum of at least eight commissioners. In practice, where the Commission makes decisions in individual cases with respect to subsidization, it depends to a large degree on the advice of an extensive technical staff of European civil servants. Decisions of the Commission (e.g. with respect to State aids) are directly binding on Member States, and do not require any kind of political approval or agreement by the governments of the Member States of the Union. The Member States may, however, by unanimous vote, override Commission decisions on some matters (a highly unlikely occurrence).

With respect to harmonization of regulatory regimes through European law, the Commission plays a crucial role, as does the Council of Ministers. The Council consists of political representatives from all major States. It makes regulations and directives, upon the initiative of the Commission.

Regulations are directly binding in the legal systems of the Member States, whereas implementation of directives requires domestic legislation. Directives allow some flexibility as to the manner of implementation by the Member States, although there is some protection against the possibility that Member States will mis-implement or fail to implement them. In those circumstances, the directive may become directly enforceable in court, even by an individual or firm, if it is adequately specific to give rise to a determinate legal meaning.[16] In addition, the Commission or another Member State can take a recalcitrant Member State to the European Court to force it to properly implement a directive. In some instances, the key issue will be whether the domestic implementing legislation adequately achieves the result intended by the directive. The important point is that directives are not just exhortations to national political authorities to make 'best efforts', but are legally binding with respect to *result*. Whether a given domestic statute *achieves* a result is a question of *law* to be determined by independent supranational authorities.

As discussed below in connection with harmonization, directives generally no longer require unanimous approval of the Council. Instead, they must be endorsed by a weighted majority of votes.[17] Harmonization through unanimous agreement between member states proved to be difficult because of hold-out problems.[18]

We now turn to the substantive law and policy of economic integration developed in the European Union.

Non-discrimination norms vs legitimate public purposes

The major legal limits to non-tariff barriers with respect to goods are contained in Articles 30 and 34 of the Treaty of Rome. They prohibit quantitative restrictions and 'all measures having equivalent effect' on imports and exports. Article 36, in turn, provides specific derogations from these strictures, based on public objectives related to health and safety, public security, and morality, and protection of national cultural treasures, among others.[19]

Early in the jurisprudence of the Union, the scope of Articles 30 and 34 was extended beyond measures that discriminated on their face against non-domestic products to those that merely had a disparate impact. Thus, in the *Cassis de Dijon* case,[20] the Court held that a German law that prohibited the sale of the liqueur cassis with less than 25% alcohol content violated Article 30. It prevented the import of French cassis which had an alcohol content below 20%. However, the Court suggested that where measures are not facially discriminatory but have a disparate impact, they may be saved if they are 'necessary in order to satisfy mandatory requirements relating in particular to the effectiveness of fiscal supervision, the protection of public health, the fairness of commercial transactions, and the defence of the consumer'.

The test of necessity involves consideration of whether alternative measures less restrictive of intra-Union trade might adequately satisfy the 'mandatory requirements' at issue.[21] Hence, if the goal was to ensure that consumers were not misled by an assumption about the domestic product into thinking that the foreign product contained an equivalent amount of alcohol, labelling requirements would suffice. Similarly, in the *German Beer Standards*[22] case, the Court impugned a German law which required any product sold with the label 'Beer' in Germany to meet German purity standards. The Court reasoned that consumers could be informed of the difference between beers through the use of appropriate labelling requirements. Where health risks are claimed as a basis for content requirements that affect trade, and where less stringent requirements are in place elsewhere in the Union, the Court places some burden on the defendant Member State to produce empirical evidence of the risks in question.

State aids

State aids (e.g., subsidies) are dealt with under a separate regime from that in Articles 30, 34, and 36 of the Treaty of Rome. The major relevant provision is Article 92 (1) which prohibits 'any aid granted by a Member State or through State resources in any form whatsoever which distorts or threatens to distort competition by favouring certain undertakings, in so far as it affects trade between Member States'. Certain derogations are permitted, including aid to underdeveloped areas or 'to remedy a serious disturbance in the economy of a Member State'.[23] Article 93 makes the Commission responsible for monitoring and enforcement of the State aid prohibitions. A process is mandated whereby the Commission must be informed of any new State aid with sufficient advance notice to determine its consistency with the Treaty. Moreover, it can require the subsidizing State to amend an aid programme to make it consistent with the Treaty. Decisions of the Commission are reviewable by the Court.

Placing review of State aid measures in the hands of the Commission reflects the fact that an approach which emphasizes legal rules and orders is unsuited to dealing with the complex subsidy and tax incentive programmes of advanced, mixed economies. Furthermore, the procedure of *ex ante* review takes into account the possible consequences for workers and other relatively vulnerable constituencies if an existing aid programme were suddenly to be declared invalid by the court. Finally, the possibility of adjustment to an aid programme through negotiation between the Commission and the granting State allows for positive-sum solutions. These solutions might involve, for instance, aid earmarked to sustain existing production in a surplus capacity sector being modified in the direction of a managed exit approach.

Harmonization

The 'Europe 1992' initiative, launched by the coming into force of the Single European Act in 1987, reflects the fundamental recognition that negative constraints on government actions that impede economic mobility are far from sufficient to achieve economic union. An essential thrust of the move towards completion of the internal market by 1992 is the harmonization of regulatory regimes with respect to financial services, securities, insurance, company law, and telecommunications, as well as community-wide standards with respect to product safety, technical specifications, etc. The importance of this aspect of 1992 is well-illustrated by Hufbauer:

> Differing national technical and licensing regimes create major obstacles to a unified market. These are by far the most important barriers, for they restrict market entry on a grand scale. The Cecchini Report puts the gains from opening market entry, and the consequent intensification of competition and realization of scale economies, at about $240 billion. Differing product standards and certification procedures hamper the Europe-wide acceptance of numerous items ranging from autos to pharmaceuticals to packaged cereals.[24]

Various initiatives of the harmonization enterprise being undertaken appear to fall short of truly centralized regulation, in that they involve a process of mutual or reciprocal recognition. In this process, if a firm, product or service complies with domestic regulatory requirements in the Member State which is its 'home', it is allowed into the market of other Member States without being subject to further or different regulatory requirements by the other States. While this approach allows regulatory control to be retained at the level of Member States, a *sine qua non* is the setting of minimum, community-wide standards for regulation. Depending on the area, this can entail quite detailed Community-level regulatory requirements. Moreover, as disputes or concerns emerge whereby the receiving State is dissatisfied with the degree of regulatory protection afforded by the 'home country' regime, an on-going institutional mechanism exists to promulgate new or better defined Community-level standards or rules. The endpoint of the process of mutual recognition may indeed be detailed, unified regulation. This is consistent with the fact that mutual recognition was regarded as a means of speeding up harmonization by generating, from the bottom up, the requirements of harmonization rather than engaging in predicting all the requirements of a uniform regulatory regime.

The Maastricht Treaty

The Treaty on European Union,[25] better known as the Maastricht Treaty, was signed by the heads of government of the European Union in February

1992 and has now been ratified by all Member States. It is intended as a blueprint for a fundamental deepening of European integration. Undoubtedly the most radical and ambitious aspect of Maastricht is the framework for creation of a single European currency by the end of this century, to replace national currencies of the Member States, including the establishment of a European Central Bank (ECB). The plan for European Monetary Union envisages as a prerequisite for a single currency the alignment of macro-economic policies of Member States, including the achievement of price stability (low inflation) and the elimination of excessive budget deficits (Article 109j).

As well, the Maastricht Treaty calls for the creation of a common European foreign and security policy (Title V). Where the Council takes a common position on foreign policy, individual Member States are to be bound by it in their own conduct (Title V, Article J.2). However, this requirement is of limited significance, since unanimity is required for Council decisions on foreign policy (Article J.8.2).

Another important feature of Maastricht is a strengthening of the social agenda of the Union, with the Council being given the explicit mandate to adopt directives binding on Member States with respect to working conditions, occupational health and safety, and equality in employment. Importantly, qualified majority voting is to apply with respect to adoption of these directives by the Council (Protocol on Social Policy, Article 2.2). However, with respect to social security, protection of workers in the case of termination of employment, and the work conditions of *Gastarbeiter* the unanimity rule will apply (Article 2.3).

As well, the Treaty would establish immigration policy (i.e. with respect to immigration into Community countries from outside the EC) as a matter of common interest, with measures implementing joint action on these matters to be adopted by the Council according to the qualified majority voting rule (Title VI, Articles K.1, K.3).

Finally, the Maastricht Treaty envisages a number of institutional changes that address (albeit in a rather modest way) concerns about the Union's 'democratic deficit'. An Office of Ombudsman is to be established under the aegis of the European Parliament to address citizen complaints about 'maladministration' by non-judicial Union institutions and officials (Article 138(e)). Also, the Parliament is given a specific mandate to be pro-active – it can request the Commission to submit a proposal to it on any matter where Union action is required to implement the Treaty. In addition, the number of matters on which co-decision (i.e. approval by the European Parliament) is required, as opposed to mere consultation between the Commission and the Council, has been somewhat expanded.[26]

A number of obstacles have emerged to implementing the Maastricht Treaty. First of all, the United Kingdom only agreed to Maastricht on condition that it was able to opt out of the social policy and monetary union provisions of the Treaty. Particularly on the single currency and monetary union, this opt out represented a calculated wager that a more pro-European stance would emerge in Britain, and the opt out would thus be temporary.

Perhaps more importantly, the virtual collapse of the existing arrangements for coordination of exchange rates within the European Union (the EMS, European Monetary System)[27] in the Autumn of 1992 and the Summer of 1993, in the presence of over-heated speculative market activity anticipating currency realignments, has cast a long shadow on the capacity to move forward with much more radical plans for monetary integration. While some supporters of European Monetary Union see these crises in the EMS as reinforcing the logic of moving to a single currency in order to eliminate exchange rate instability, many observers have viewed the crises as suggesting that the political pressures on individual countries to adopt different monetary policies remain too great to allow the degree of common macroeconomic policy discipline needed to sustain fixed exchange rates, let alone a single currency.[28]

Furthermore, the initial rejection of the Maastricht Treaty in a referendum in Denmark in the Spring of 1992, and its near rejection in a French referendum in September 1992,[29] have slowed the pace of ratification, although the Union authorities seem determined to find a way around these setbacks. For instance, a set of modifications and qualifications with respect to Denmark's obligations under Maastricht eventually succeeded in securing Denmark's ratification of the Treaty. But the populist backlash against deepening of European integration has led to more sober second thought in European political circles more generally about the appropriate pace of deepening. One range of concerns that deserves noting is that the provisions respecting immigration policy in the Maastricht Treaty have served as a flashpoint for rejection by the right and far-right in a number of European countries, most notably France and Germany, where immigration is already an extremely sensitive political issue. Some commentators worry that the possibility of loss of national control over immigration policies raised by Maastricht might serve to fuel growing anti-immigrant and racist sentiment in some EC member states.[30]

It should be emphasized that while Maastricht has become the main focus for public anti-Union sentiment, less public attention has been paid to the increasing activism of the European Commission and Council in implementing the Europe 1992 agenda of harmonization of regulations and standards in many important areas of economic activity (e.g. financial services). An increasing number of harmonization measures, in matters such as product standards and environmental control, are being justified as necessary for the completion of the internal market. The principle of subsidiarity, as explicitly recognized in the Maastricht Treaty, is that the Union should only act where 'the objectives of the proposed action cannot be sufficiently achieved by the member states' (Article 3b). However, this principle is only to apply to matters that do not fall within the 'exclusive competence' of the Union, and therefore does not limit the scope of Union action with respect to completion of the internal market.

3

TRADE, EXCHANGE RATES, AND THE BALANCE OF PAYMENTS

INTRODUCTION

The theory of comparative advantage that we outlined in Chapter 1 suggests that it will benefit a country to produce domestically those products in which it has a comparative advantage and import those in which other countries have a comparative advantage. While the theory shows how a country that does not have an absolute advantage in anything will still be able to export and benefit from trade, it by no means demonstrates that the value of a country's exports of products in which it has a comparative advantage will equal the value of imports in which it has a comparative disadvantage.

To return to the Ricardian example of the exchange of wine and cloth between England and Portugal, what if England's wine imports yield Portugal £100 a year, yet the English cloth it requires costs £200? In this example, to maximize the gains from trade, Portugal must draw down its national reserves of wealth (e.g. gold) in order to obtain the additional £100 it needs to purchase English cloth. It thus seems that the mercantilist objection that liberal trade could reduce accumulated national wealth has not really been met by the theory of comparative advantage.

The philosopher David Hume is thought to be the first to have developed a theory of the balance of payments that could meet this objection.[1] In essence, the theory suggests that since the demand for a country's currency depends on demand for its exports, where the latter rises, so will the former. Where a country has a trade surplus, the extra demand for its exports will increase the value of its currency and therefore make its exports more expensive and its imports cheaper. This, in turn, will reduce the surplus, as demand for exports goes down in response to their relatively higher cost, whereas demand for imports goes up due to their relatively lower cost. In theory, an equilibrium will eventually be reached where trade and payments are balanced at a given exchange rate.

This 'market equilibrium'[2] view of exchange rates and the balance of payments is fundamental to understanding the interface between the legal order of international trade and the international monetary system. The post-war Bretton Woods arrangements contemplated a system of fixed exchange rates tied to the gold standard. Under this system, a country would in theory be required to hold sufficient reserves of gold to back the quantity of its currency in circulation. Where a temporary imbalance of payments occurred (i.e. where a country could not meet payments for imports with its receipts of foreign currency from export sales without selling gold for foreign currency), this would be financed by a country borrowing from the International Monetary Fund.[3] In the case of a structural or persistent imbalance, a country would devalue its currency under the supervision of the IMF, which might recommend domestic policy adjustments to ensure that further devaluations were not required in order to maintain the balance of payments.[4] In the case of a country running a persistent trade surplus, foreign demand for its currency, i.e. by purchasers of its exports, would eventually exceed the amount of its currency that could be backed by gold reserves, therefore calling for a revaluation of the exchange rate and/or domestic policy changes to dampen exports and/or boost imports.

Paul Volcker has said of the Bretton Woods system of IMF-managed fixed exchange rates: 'The irony is that no sooner did it become mechanically operative than worries about its sustainability began. Nor was it purely a coincidence that the first sign of stress appeared about the same time the system began to blossom'.[5] When the European currencies became convertible in the 1950s, the United States was running an enormous trade surplus with its trading partners. However, this was balanced by large outflows of dollars in the form of development assistance to Europe and Japan. As the European and Japanese economies began to recover, the US trade surplus started to decline, while outflows of US currency due to foreign aid and investment continued to increase. By 1960, the United States no longer had sufficient gold reserves to cover all of the dollar holdings abroad, and for the first time there was a crisis of confidence in the US dollar.

During the 1960s, and particularly in the early 1970s, the Johnson and Nixon administrations, respectively, largely refused – contrary to what was contemplated by the founders of Bretton Woods – either to devalue the dollar or to alter US domestic policies so as to reduce the payments deficit. Devaluation would have increased the costs of foreign borrowing to finance the Vietnam War, and the appropriate domestic policy changes (tighter macroeconomic policies to dampen US consumer demand for imports) were considered politically infeasible. At the same time, Germany and Japan did not wish to revalue *their* currencies, since this would dampen trade expansion by making exports from these countries to the United States more expensive. Finally, in 1971 the United States unilaterally refused to back the dollar with gold any longer, and proposed that a new system of floating exchange rates be negotiated to replace the Bretton Woods system. The dominant position of the United States in the world economy, as well as the extent of foreign dollar holdings, permitted this unilateralism. In effect, if other countries did not agree to the new system, the crisis in confidence in the dollar would be disastrous for them as well as the United States, since their dollar holdings were enormous and their exports to the United States were a very important source of economic growth.

Although between 1971 and 1973 an attempt was made to manage floating rates within a fixed margin or band, by the mid-1970s any attempt at multilateral management of exchange rates was abandoned, although since then there have been occasional negotiated realignments of exchange rates through central bank intervention on the currency markets and through some co-ordinated adjustment of domestic policies among the major monetary powers, the so-called G-7 (e.g. the Plaza Agreement of 1985 and the Louvre Accord of 1987).[6]

What are the implications for the international trading order of the key relationships between trade, exchange rates, and the balance of payments as they have played themselves out in the post-war period under both fixed and floating rate systems?

First of all, while a decline in the exchange rate seems a logical way to correct a trade deficit (i.e. by making imports more costly and exports less costly), this may be not without significant cost to other pressing domestic policy objectives. In many instances, higher costs for imports may have socially unacceptable effects – for instance, in the case of developing countries, a falling exchange rate could make imported medicines, foodstuffs and other essential requirements prohibitively expensive. More generally, as Fisher notes, 'a depreciation directly affects domestic inflation by raising the prices of imports. Further by increasing the profitability of exports and increasing aggregate demand, depreciation affects wage claims and thereby indirectly increases the inflation rate.'[7] On the other hand, in the case of a country that is running a trade surplus, an appreciation in the value of its currency will lead to unemployment at least in the short run, as sales of exports decline and imports increase – a consequence that may be politically unacceptable.

These are just two illustrations of why countries may be unprepared to accept adjustments to exchange rates in order to move towards a balance of payments equilibrium. A further concern, however, is *liquidity*. Even if countries were prepared to accept the domestic consequences of the indicated adjustments, there is, of course, an assumption that until the adjustment takes place the country running the deficit in trade will have sufficient reserves of wealth, such as gold or the currency of its trading partners, to meet demands for currency to purchase imports that exceed its foreign currency receipts from exports.

Where liquidity is thin, an imbalance of payments inevitably leads either to import restrictions or to limits on the convertibility of currency (exchange controls). Both such measures represent a fundamental threat to liberal trade, and yet may be seen as an unavoidable outcome of free trade between countries that lack reserves of foreign currency or gold.

An equally fundamental challenge to liberal trade is the presence of a variety of factors quite apart from the trade balance that affect exchange rates, such as the movement of capital across national boundaries for investment reasons, remittances of expatriate workers, and speculation on the future value of currencies by currency traders. As Kenen notes: 'The rapid growth of international transactions have [sic] been reflected in an even faster growth of foreign-exchange trading. In 1980, daily trading in American currency markets averaged less than $18 billion; in 1986, it averaged almost $60 billion; and in 1992 it averaged more than $190 billion. Daily trading in London, the world's largest currency market, averaged $300 billion in 1992'.[8] By contrast, the *annual* value of world trade in goods was $US2,035 billion in 1980 and $US3,506 billion in 1991.[9]

Taken together, the implication of these figures is clear; today the bulk of foreign exchange transactions is not accounted for by payment for traded goods. Indeed, it has been suggested that comparative advantage in trade can easily be wiped out, at least in the short run, by changes in exchange rates due to these non-trade factors.[10] There are several dimensions to the problem. The first is that the *volatility* of floating exchange rates threatens to upset the cost and price calculations of exporters and importers, making trade more risky than purely domestic economic activity that does not involve exchange of currencies. The second, mentioned above, is that non-trade domestic macroeconomic objectives, such as the control of inflation, may deter a country from adjusting its currency so as to permit the achievement of an equilibrium in trade. Lack of macroeconomic policy co-ordination between major currency countries can thus place considerable strain on the commitment to liberal trade (this is often referred to as the problem of misalignment).

Third, the actual experience of the United States in the mid-1980s, when it allowed the dollar to fall in order to redress its trade deficit, puts in question whether Hume's equilibrium theory still applies in contemporary circumstances. Briefly, an apparently substantial decline in the value of the dollar did not result, even after the required time period for adjustment in consumers' expectations, in a significant reduction in the US trade deficit.[11] Among the reasons often given is that upward pressure on the dollar from high US interest rates (a reflection of the financing requirements of the US budget deficit) made it virtually impossible for the dollar to fall to the point where adjustment in the prices of US imports and exports respectively would lead to an elimination, or significant reduction, of the trade deficit.[12]

It is sometimes argued that a return to fixed exchange rates (where governments determine exchange rates in accordance with economic fundamentals) would help to resolve the instability and imbalance in trade attributable to floating rates. However, in the past, fixed exchange rates co-existed with a financial system where private actors did not trade currency except, largely, to pay for imports and exports. A return to fixed or managed rates would probably entail a reimposition of exchange controls, at least on the capital account (thereby entailing a retreat from the globalization of capital markets). As was demonstrated in the crisis in the European Monetary System in 1992–3 (discussed later in this chapter) even an open-ended commitment by governments to intervene in the markets to sustain fixed rates in the presence of market forces that threaten to destabilize them may not be enough under conditions of free capital flows, where speculators are free to make their own assessment of the credibility and sustainability of these interventions.

A final challenge to liberal trade is much more straightforward – the *substitutability* of currency restrictions for protectionism. Imposing a quota or tax on the sale of foreign currency to purchase an import is likely to have a similar protectionist impact as imposing a quota or tariff on the import of the product itself. Effectively maintaining bargains about the elimination or reduction of tariffs and quotas, therefore, also implies some rules to constrain parallel currency measures. A different but related issue is that of *transaction costs* on trade payments that occur due to government policies that are not motivated by protectionism (for instance, requirements that foreign exchange transactions be reported to the authorities).

Having sketched in brief some of the key relationships between trade and money, and the challenges they present to maintenance of liberal trade, we turn to the legal rules that have been devised to deal with these various challenges.

LIQUIDITY, ADJUSTMENT AND SUBSTITUTABILITY

Liquidity was viewed from the outset of the Bretton Woods system as a fundamental challenge. Few countries had the reserves necessary to be able to wait until a devaluation brought imports and exports back into balance. Therefore, the system had to be designed to permit temporary imposition of both trade restrictions and currency controls in order to manage a balance of payments crisis. At the same time, it was important to ensure that these measures were temporary and did not lead to permanent protectionism. This would involve supervision of a process of domestic policy adjustment with a view to balancing of exports and imports, encompassing domestic policy reforms and/or including exchange rate adjustment.

The legal rules of both the GATT and the IMF, and the institutions of the latter, were designed to reflect this approach to liquidity.

The GATT

Articles XII to XIV of the GATT elaborate a complex code designed to govern and discipline the use of trade restrictions for balance of payments purposes. Article XII:1 states the basic right of any Contracting Party to impose quantitative restrictions in derogation from Article XI 'in order to safeguard its external financial position and its balance of payments ... '. Article XII:2 establishes that such restrictions shall be limited to what is 'necessary: (i) to forestall the imminent threat of, or to stop, a serious decline in monetary reserves, or (ii) in the case of a Contracting Party with very low monetary reserves to achieve a reasonable rate of increase in its reserves'. As well, such restrictions must be progressively relaxed as the balance of payments improves.

Furthermore, Contracting Parties 'undertake, in carrying out their domestic policies, to pay due regard to the need for maintaining or restoring equilibrium in their balance of payments on a sound and lasting basis, ... ' (XII:3). At the same time, no Contracting Party is obligated to take domestic balance of payments measures that would threaten the objective of full employment (i.e. Contracting the domestic money supply to dampen demand for imports (XII:3 (d)). A process of consultations is envisaged with the GATT Council concerning any new restrictions or increase in restrictions, with periodic review of the necessity of the trade measures and their consistency with Articles XII–XIV. In addition, Article XII contains provisions on dispute settlement, including the authorization of retaliation where a Party persists in trade restrictions that have been found by the Contracting Parties to violate the GATT. Articles XIII and XIV contain respectively the requirement that measures taken pursuant to Article XII:1 be implemented on a non-discriminatory basis and certain narrow exceptions to this non-discrimination requirement, e.g. where discriminatory exchange controls have been authorized by the IMF (see the discussion of substitutability below).

In the case of developing countries, there is a much broader exemption for balance of payments-based trade restrictions. Hence, Article XVII:2 (b) states the principle that developing countries should have additional flexibility 'to apply quantitative restrictions for balance of payments purposes in a manner which takes full account of the continued high level of demand for imports likely to be generated by their programmes of economic development'. What this suggests is that even though a developing country could address its balance of payments difficulties through exchange rate adjustments or tighter macroeconomic policies, it should not be expected to do so given the harm to development that may come from the resultant decline in needed imports. It is recognized that quantitative restrictions will allow a developing country to conserve its limited foreign currency resources for purchases of imports necessary for development

– whereas an exchange rate devaluation would result in *all* imports becoming more expensive. In this connection, it bears emphasis that balance of payments restrictions in general may be discriminatory with respect to products although not with respect to countries. Indeed, it is explicitly stated that 'the contracting party may determine (the) incidence (of restrictions) on imports of different products or classes of products in such a way as to give priority to the importation of those products which are more essential in the light of its policy of economic development; . . .' (XVIII B (10)). Finally, Article XV:2 provides for deference to the IMF in the determination of what constitutes a balance of payments crisis as well as other financial issues involved in the application of Articles XII and XVIII.

There have been few invocations of Article XII by developed countries since the 1960s.[13] One of the most anomalous features of Article XII is its application to quantitative restrictions exclusively, rather than to re-imposition of tariffs (as contemplated by Article XIX Safeguards against import surges, for example). Perhaps this exclusive emphasis on quantitative restrictions may be in part explained by the assumption that re-imposition of tariffs would not operate rapidly enough to stem a drain on foreign exchange reserves. In the event, Contracting Parties turned out to be *more* inclined to use import surcharges (i.e. tariff-like measures) than to invoke Article XII explicitly in response to balance of payments difficulties. In some cases, the surcharges were made consistent with the GATT through an explicit waiver. In others, they were simply tolerated as a kind of *de facto* expansion of Article XII.[14]

Finally, in 1979 the Contracting Parties, without formally amending the General Agreement, made the 'Declaration on Trade Measures taken for Balance-of-Payments Purposes'[15] which expanded the ambit of Articles XII–XIV and XVIII beyond quantitative restrictions to include 'all import measures taken for balance of payments purposes'. The Declaration also imposes an obligation on Contracting Parties taking such measures to 'give preference to the measure least restrictive of trade', which, as Petersmann suggests, would usually involve a preference for tariffs and surcharges over the quantitative restrictions explicitly mentioned in Article XII.[16]

Through much of the history of the GATT, balance of payments-based trade restrictions were not subject to much direct scrutiny. Developing countries, in particular, made liberal use of such restrictions. However the increasing invocation of these restrictions in the wake of the LDC debt crisis, combined with a new emphasis on the importance of trade liberalization to development in more recent thinking on the subject, had led to increasing concern by the mid-1980s, particularly on the part of the United States and some other developed countries.[17] Another, in some sense, almost opposite source of concern was the continued maintenance of restrictions by countries that were growing rapidly, e.g. the Asian NICs. Thus, in a 1989 case, the United States complained that South Korea continued to impose

Article XVIII B restrictions on imports of beef despite improvements in its balance of payments position.[18] The approach of the GATT Panel was quite straightforward – it deferred to the conclusion of the GATT Balance of Payments Committee, in its 1987 consultation with Korea, that the country's current and prospective balance of payments was such that continued restrictions could not be justified. The Committee in turn had acted on the advice of the International Monetary Fund, in accordance with Article XV:2.

The Understanding on the Balance of Payments Provisions of the General Agreement on Tariffs and Trade 1994, incorporated in the Uruguay Round Final Act, is aimed at improving GATT/WTO discipline of trade measures taken for balance of payments purposes. Members commit themselves to publish, as soon as possible, time-schedules for the removal of such trade measures. Such schedules may, however, be modified 'to take into account changes in the balance-of-payments situation' (Article 1). Further (and perhaps the most important modification of the existing GATT regime) Members commit themselves to give preference to trade measures of a price-based nature, such as tariff surcharges, and only to resort to new quantitative restrictions where 'because of a critical balance-of-payments situation, price-based measures cannot arrest a sharp deterioration in the external payments position' (Articles 2, 3). The Understanding further sets out an elaborate set of procedures for review by the Committee for Balance-of-Payments Restrictions of both the time-schedules for elimination of existing restrictions and notifications of any new restrictions. The overall intent appears to be that of placing balance-of-payments trade restrictions under on-going scrutiny, with a view to their elimination as soon as possible. This is consistent with the original GATT regime, where such restrictions are envisaged as temporary, and not an appropriate longer-term solution to payments imbalances. It is also, however, something of a retreat from the more permissive approach to such restrictions reflected in the Tokyo Round declaration.

While Articles XII–XIV and XVIII of the General Agreement deal with trade restrictions taken to address a balance of payments crisis, Article XV concerns the trade effects of currency and other monetary restrictions. Here a fundamental concern is the substitutability of exchange measures for trade restrictions. Thus, Article XV:4 states that Contracting Parties shall not 'by exchange action frustrate the intent of the provisions of this Agreement, nor, by trade action, the intent of the provisions of the International Monetary Fund'. Contracting Parties are required to obtain membership in the IMF, or alternatively, to negotiate a 'special exchange arrangement' with the GATT. Article XV:4 is subject to the proviso that any exchange measures explicitly authorized by the IMF are to be considered consistent with the General Agreement (XV:9).

The IMF

The provisions of Article XV of the GATT, taken together, suggest considerable reliance on the IMF to ensure an open payments system that sustains liberal trade. At the time the General Agreement was negotiated and came into effect, however, currency controls were pervasive not only in developing but also in most developed countries. As mentioned earlier in this chapter, the Bretton Woods system was designed in such a way as to permit countries eventually to stabilize their balance of payments without resort to such measures, through lending from the IMF's own resources to sustain liquidity, and through Fund-approved adjustments of exchange rates in connection with appropriate domestic policy reforms. However, it was considered that this state of affairs would not occur, for most countries, until after a considerable transition period.

Countries were therefore provided with an option of accepting the full convertibility obligations of Article VIII of the Fund Articles of Agreement, or joining the Fund through the transitional provisions of Article XIV of the Articles of Agreement. Even the convertibility obligations of Article VIII still permitted a member of the Fund to impose exchange controls with Fund approval.

Thus, Article VIII:2(a) prohibits 'restrictions on the making of payments and transfers for current international transactions' without Fund approval. The expression 'current international transactions' certainly encompasses all import or export sales, but does not include, for example, many forms of foreign investment, securities transactions, etc. In this respect, it is important to note that most developed countries maintained, consistent with Article VIII, restrictions and controls on the *capital* account until the 1980s.[19] Article VIII does not provide any explicit criteria for the authorization of current account restrictions by the Fund, nor does any other provision of the IMF Articles.[20]

Article XIV allows a member of the Fund to impose exchange restrictions in 'the post-war transitional period' provided the member declares to the Fund its intent to do so. The Fund may decide that any such measure is no longer necessary, i.e. that the transition period has elapsed, but must in the first instance give the member country 'the benefit of the doubt' (Article XIV:5).

Particularly during the LDC debt crisis, the Fund played an important role in sustaining liquidity in LDC debtor countries and preventing the economic collapse of the debtor states. However, the Fund insisted on macro-economic and trade policy reforms as a condition for liquidity assistance, thereby forcing painful domestic adjustment as the appropriate response to the crisis in the balance of payments. Similarly, today the Fund encourages the Newly Liberalizing Countries (NLCs) of Central and Eastern Europe to move rapidly towards liberalization of trade and payments. Much of Western assistance is premised on the need for liquidity support to underpin these rapid policy shifts. However liquidity is only part of the problem – the domestic adjustment costs are the other part and these can be enormous.

Interaction between the GATT and IMF rules

A number of legal issues have arisen concerning interaction between GATT rules on trade restrictions for balance of payments purposes and IMF rules concerning exchange controls and monetary restrictions. One such issue is the characterization of measures that can be plausibly viewed as one or the other. This issue was raised but not resolved by a GATT Panel in a 1952 case that involved a Greek tax on foreign exchange for imports, which varied depending on 'the usefulness and necessity of the products imported'.[21] Eventually, largely through a decision of the IMF Directors, it was clarified that a measure will be considered an exchange restriction if the *technique* used involves restricting access to foreign exchange, even though the principal intent and effect is to restrict *imports*.[22] Under this approach, the Greek tax would have been deemed an exchange restriction and therefore subject to IMF as opposed to GATT discipline, despite the fact that it was quite directly targeted at imports.

There is some evidence that Contracting Parties have sought to minimize IMF scrutiny of *trade* measures, by advocating a narrow interpretation of Article XV:4, which would limit the IMF's role to that of providing statistical findings concerning a balance of payments crisis.[23] However, in the *Korean Beef Import* case discussed above, a GATT Panel took a more expansive view of the IMF's role, deferring to a finding based not just on facts provided by the IMF, but also upon but the Fund's 'advice'. In addition, as noted above, the IMF itself, as a condition of assistance, may well impose a requirement that trade restrictions, not just exchange restrictions, be lifted. The overall effect of these developments is that today, whether a Contracting Party chooses to enact trade restrictions or currency measures to address a balance of payments crisis, it will find its actions subject to a similar level and kind of scrutiny by the IMF.

The OECD Invisibles Code

The OECD Code on Liberalisation of Current Invisible Transactions is intended to go beyond the obligations of Article VIII of the IMF Articles in seeking to eliminate all restrictions on 'current invisible transactions and transfers' between OECD member countries. Indeed, members are encouraged to extend the benefit of the Code to all IMF members (Article I (d)). Whereas Article VIII of the Fund Articles applies only to restrictions on payments and transfers themselves, such as rationing of access to foreign currency, the Code applies also to taxes and charges, as well as administrative requirements imposed on the actual *transactions* required to make payments and transfers abroad. These measures fall between the cracks of the GATT and IMF rules, in that they apply neither to imports and exports of products nor do they directly restrict payments on the current account. Obligations under the OECD Code on Invisibles are subject to various reservations filed by individual member states. However, in recent years reservations have been reduced and the Code strengthened.[24]

VOLATILITY

As mentioned earlier in this chapter, the original Bretton Woods arrangements were intended to function with fixed exchange rates. A country would be permitted to adjust these fixed rates in order to correct 'a fundamental disequilibrium'.[25] The intent of these arrangements was that exchange rate changes would occur only occasionally, and would be supervised by the IMF to ensure that they did not cause undue harm to the trading or other economic interests of other countries, i.e. that they reflected changes in the terms of trade rather than constituting an attempt to unilaterally alter those terms in favour of the devaluing country. Thus a country would be permitted to devalue where its exports had been declining relative to imports, but not in order to create a trade surplus where its existing trade was not in disequilibrium (i.e., competitive, beggar-thy-neighbour exchange rate devaluations that characterized the inter-war period).

Under the system of floating rates that emerged in the 1970s after the collapse of the Bretton Woods fixed rate system, what determines exchange rates is supply and demand with respect to the various currencies. Central banks can and do intervene in the market to alter the value of their countries' currency, in accordance with domestic policy objectives. However, because currencies are no longer fixed in value as against a common, objective standard (such as the price of gold), or subject to adjustment only in accordance with internationally agreed criteria ('fundamental equilibrium'), volatility is much greater.

Blame is often placed on the US for undermining the fixed rate system and thereby introducing fundamental volatility into exchange rates.[26] However, greater volatility was arguably inevitable. With the terms of trade changing rapidly, and moreover with globalization of capital markets, enormous and rapid shifts in capital flows would have probably required very frequent adjustments to exchange rates even under a fixed rate system – or, alternately, curbs on globalization itself. As Spero notes, during the 1980s, 'most developed countries . . . abolished or relaxed exchange controls, opened domestic markets to foreign financial institutions, and removed domestic regulatory barriers. A revolution in telecommunications, information processing, and computer technologies made possible a vastly increased volume, speed, and global reach of financial transactions.'[27]

Those who advocate a return to fixed rates with a view to addressing volatility and sustaining the gains from trade thus also tend to argue for deglobalization, and reimposition of controls on the import and export of capital.[28] However, this perspective fails to consider the extent to which liberalized capital flows themselves contribute to the expansion of trade through globalization of production (Foreign Direct Investment), and the exploitation of comparative advantage in the financial services sector.

There is a serious empirical issue as to the extent to which exchange rate volatility has negatively affected trade.[29] Sophisticated actors on world markets can hedge the foreign exchange risk from their trade transactions by buying and selling in a variety of currencies, or by actively trading in currencies themselves. Nevertheless these possibilities are significantly less open to smaller traders, and there are always transaction costs entailed in the hedging of currency risks. In order to reduce volatility, it has been proposed that a tax be placed on foreign exchange transactions. The tax would be set low enough that it would not affect trade in goods and services but would impose a high cost on 'short term in-and-out transactions' of a speculative nature.[30] However, this kind of proposal presumes that speculation is the driving force behind exchange rate volatility – if, however, such volatility is endemic to globalized capital markets, then short-term transactions may be critical to hedging endemic foreign exchange risk, and therefore the tax may be fundamentally self-defeating.[31]

MACROECONOMIC POLICY COORDINATION AND PROPOSALS FOR MANAGED EXCHANGE RATES

Under the system of fixed exchange rates that prevailed until 1971, changes in macroeconomic policies did not automatically result in changes to exchange rates and thereby did not directly affect the trade interests of other countries or the demand for protection in the country making the policy change. Under the system of flexible rates, however, no rules or institutions have been created for the international management and supervision of macroeconomic policies.

These policies continue to put considerable pressure on the liberal trading order. Occasionally the G-7 countries, i.e. those nations with the major international currencies including the United States, Germany and Japan, have agreed on certain targets and goals. But Germany and Japan, for instance, have often been very reluctant to stimulate spending and expand their money supply so as to increase imports from the United States. At the same time they have been disinclined to revalue their currencies, because this would make their exports more expensive and threaten jobs. The United States, by contrast, has refused to act unilaterally to raise taxes to finance its deficit rather than resort to further foreign borrowing. This has meant continued upward pressure on the US dollar, further exacerbated by interest rates that have reflected a tight monetary policy. The consequence is that US exports remain expensive in terms of other currencies and imports into the USA relatively cheap, creating unremitting pressures for selective trade protection. One recent positive sign, however, is the commitment of the Clinton Administration to reduce significantly the US budget deficit.

Some economists – most notably John Williamson[32] – have developed proposals for targeting zones for exchange rates. This does not represent a return to fixed rates and strict domestic controls on the movement of capital. Rates are still set by supply and demand in the currency markets. Should, however, rates move outside the target zone, countries commit themselves,[33] through central bank intervention and/or policy adjustments, to a return within the zone. This kind of solution seems to offer a number of advantages. First of all, unlike a return to fixed rates, it appears to avoid the kind of limits on financial market liberalization that would be entailed by the (re)imposition of controls on capital movements or restrictions on the markets. In theory, at least, governments sustain the target zones not by constraining the markets but by playing them. Second, since the zones are established by some kind of objective standard, such as a current account target, i.e. what a country's account should look like given a number of external (e.g. trade) and internal (e.g. inflation) factors, the indeterminacy that characterizes open-ended discussions on policy coordination would appear to be avoided.

The problem is, as Cooper notes, that 'the setting of current account targets would be an intrinsically arbitrary exercise in a world of high capital mobility and open markets in goods and services'.[34] Given the multiplicity of reasons why money flows in and out of countries – investment, repatriation of earnings, capital markets transactions such as the purchase and sale of bonds and other securities – how does one begin to determine the balance between in-flows and out-flows that a given country should maintain at a given point in time? A further difficulty, in the absence of exchange controls, is that governmental commitments to maintain the zones must be credible to speculators – otherwise governments will find themselves in the almost impossible position of fighting the expectations of the market. When speculators believe that governments' commitments to their domestic interests are sufficiently pressing that they will not be able to sustain in future their internationally-agreed exchange rate targets, the collapse of the targets can easily become a self-fulfilling prophecy. In sum, without either a return to controls or a move forward to macroeconomic policy harmonization and the kind of supra-national control of domestic policies envisaged in the Maastricht blueprint for monetary union, 'coordination' is likely to remain at the level of a very occasional adjustment in rates which reflects a saw-off between conflicting interests of the major financial powers, or perhaps even more likely, the unilateral threat of protection from the USA if exchange rates are not adjusted appropriately.

More generally, despite the fact that economists still speak of over or under-valuation, it may even be difficult for a country to determine its optimal exchange rate from the perspective of *domestic interests*. For example, the Canadian government has maintained a tight monetary policy to fight inflation, and thereby sustained high interest rates and consequently a high Canadian dollar. As a result, freer trade with the United States has yielded relatively fewer gains for Canadian producers and has resulted in considerable unemployment in Canada. Should the Canadian government have let the Canadian dollar fall against the US dollar, at the cost of lower interest rates and some inflation? (It is important to note that popular discontent with high unemployment was directed at free trade much more than at the government of the day's tight monetary policy.)

THE EUROPEAN MONETARY
SYSTEM (EMS)

The European Monetary System (EMS) provides an interesting case study of the difficulties of maintaining a system of managed or fixed exchange rates under conditions of increased liberalization and globalization of financial markets and in the absence of an agreed common macroeconomic policy approach.[35] Established in 1978, the EMS applied to many but not all of the members of the European Union (for instance, the UK chose to stay out of the System until quite recently). The core of the EMS was an agreement to maintain currencies within a ±2.5% band of a fixed rate against the ecu, the common EU currency. This agreement was made possible, it is generally thought, by the presence of Germany in the system as a hegemonic financial power. If other members of the system engaged in substantially looser monetary and fiscal policies than the traditionally conservative Bundesbank, confidence in their currencies would weaken, with investors switching their holdings into Deutschemarks. Eventually, to sustain the exchange rate within the 2.5% band, these other countries would have to alter their monetary policies so as to conform with those dictated by the Bundesbank.

In fact, however, this happened only to a limited degree. Until the full liberalization of financial markets in the EU in 1992, a number of the countries with weaker currencies continued to maintain exchange controls. Through these controls, the countries concerned (e.g. Italy) were able to maintain looser macroeconomic policies than those of Germany, since they could limit outflow of capital in response to higher interest rates and a stronger currency in Germany. As well, the system had permitted the fluctuation of some currencies outside the ±2.25% band. In addition, some devaluations and revaluations of currencies actually did occur, despite the commitment in principle to fixed rates. These (albeit infrequent) realignments would eventually create further pressure on the system, by inducing in currency traders and speculators the expectation that at a certain point, where particularly currencies in the system were under sustained pressure, the EMS members would act to realign the fixed rates. The expectation of a devaluation would intensify sale of the currencies already under pressure, and therefore increase that pressure enormously (especially after the lifting of capital controls).

The breakdown of the EMS in September 1992 can be attributed to the interaction of the above factors.[36] In the 1990s, Germany's macroeconomic policies could no longer be considered an adequate benchmark for economically sound price stability goals. Instead, they reflected Germany's special needs to finance German reunification. Because of the politically-motivated refusal of the Chancellor to raise taxes to finance unification, the Bundesbank was required to raise German interest rates beyond a level required by macroeconomic fundamentals, in order to finance unification by borrowing. Under these circumstances, with capital controls removed, other EMS members faced extreme pressure on their currencies. They did not want to raise interest rates to match those set by Germany's extraordinary borrowing requirements for reunification, because this would worsen the recession in their countries. At the same time, the French did not want to devalue the Franc, because a strong Franc was viewed as necessary to maintain investor confidence in the French economy.

One logical solution would have been revaluation of the Deutschemark. Revaluation would, of course, have reduced Germany's exports and increased its imports, therefore countering at least to some extent the effects on other currencies of *capital* in-flows to Germany.[37] And, indeed, such a solution was favoured by the Bundesbank – thereby creating speculation on the markets that currency realignments were imminent. However, the German Chancellor rejected revaluation, probably for political reasons (it will be recalled that, in the short term, revaluation costs domestic jobs, as exports decline and imports rise). Finally, one important factor that continued to hold the system together, and dampen somewhat investor speculation that it was under fundamental threat, was the expectation that the Maastricht plan for a single European currency, once it shifted into full gear, would result in greater co-ordination of macroeconomic policies in the transitional phase of moving to a single currency, thereby restabilizing the system, or perhaps more accurately putting it on a new, surer footing.

In September 1992, with expectations that Maastricht might be rejected in the French referendum running high, with capital controls now completely removed, and with no resolution in sight to the problem of German interest rates, there was a speculative run on a number of the other currencies in the EMS. Perhaps even more ominous than the speculative run itself, was the discovery by governments and central banks that – with the end of exchange controls – the possibilities of restabilizing their currencies through intervention were dramatically reduced. Even overnight increases in interest rates in the hundreds of percentage points did not succeed, and several countries, including Britain, had to withdraw from the Exchange Rate Mechanism (ERM) of the EMS.

The breakdown of the EMS initially created considerable doubt as to whether plans to proceed with a single currency, as envisaged in Maastricht, are at all feasible. As well, numerous proposals exist for putting the EMS back together again, at least in the short run. However, with the French referendum result narrowly supporting the Maastricht Treaty, and Denmark's eventual acceptance of the Treaty, the project for monetary union received renewed momentum. As for the EMS, it was rehabilitated in a much weakened form by an August 1993 decision to allow currencies to float within a 15% band (Germany and the Netherlands nevertheless undertook to keep their currrencies within a 2.5% band).[38]

Finally, it is arguable that the crisis of the EMS reinforces rather than undermines the Maastricht approach of monetary *union*, which requires as a prerequisite to the movement to a single European currency a substantial degree of harmonization of macroeconomic policies. For example, in order for a country to enter the monetary union it must, *inter alia*, have a relatively low rate of inflation, it must not be running an 'excessive' budget deficit, and its interest rates must not exceed a norm based upon the interest rate performance of the three EU countries with the lowest inflation rates.[39] As Kenen remarks, on the basis of these prerequisites, 'nobody really believes that every EC country will be ready for monetary union, even in 1999'.[40]

CONCLUSION

An examination of the rules and institutions that govern the inter-relationship between trade and finance suggests that despite the 'casino' of currency speculators and globalized capital markets, the Bretton Woods rules and institutions did in many respects prove well-adapted, or at least adaptable, to sustaining a relationship between trade and money conducive to liberal trade. The liquidity and balance of payments adjustment problems are increasingly being addressed through IMF assistance, conditioned upon acceptance of an open trade and payments system. While the LDC debt crisis represented a serious setback, its end result is more rather than less liberalization of trade by the LDCs affected. Moreover, the GATT and IMF rules and the institutional arrangements of the IMF have proven effective in addressing the substitutability problem, whereby countries attempt to undercut trade concessions by resorting to currency measures. With respect to volatility under floating rates, and the corresponding increase in the riskiness of trade transactions, the system has proven less effective in explicitly addressing the challenge. However, in the end it may turn out that hedging techniques are a relatively effective means of private actors themselves reducing foreign exchange risk in trade, although smaller and less sophisticated actors have less access to these strategies. Where the system has been least effective is in addressing the trade pressures that result from and/or intensify conflicts over domestic macroeconomic policies. Yet the major powers have nevertheless avoided a spiral of beggar-thy-neighbour devaluations, even if they find it impossible to agree on a positive strategy for targeting exchange rates.

4

TARIFFS, THE MFN PRINCIPLE, AND REGIONAL TRADING BLOCS

THE ECONOMIC EFFECTS OF A TARIFF

The economic effects of a tariff on both importing and exporting countries are best understood by first examining the case of a prohibitive tariff – that is a tariff that is so high that it prevents all imports. Here we draw on an example provided by Ruffin and Gregory.[1]

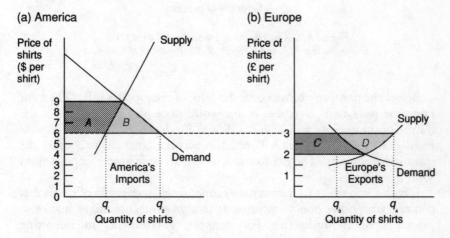

Figure 4.1 The costs of a prohibitive tariff
Source: Ruffin R. J. and Gregory, P. R., *Principles of Economics*

With a prohibitive tariff, the prices paid in each country are determined by the supply and demand curves in each country. To compare prices, we assume that \$US2 = £1. If there were no tariff, prices would be the same in the two countries. The prohibitive tariff in America raises the price in America from \$US6 to \$US9. Consumers lose area A + B, but producers gain area A. The net loss to America is area B. In Europe, prices fall from £3 to £2, and producers lose area C + D, while consumers gain C. The gain to consumers is less than the loss of producers. The net loss to Europe is area D.

73

One can next consider a non-prohibitive tariff, which does not preclude all imports of the product. Ruffin and Gregory graph this example as in Figure 4.2.

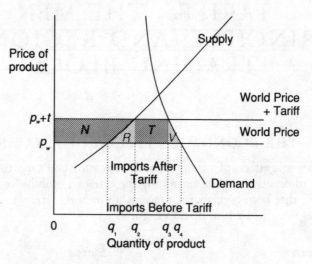

Figure 4.2 The effects of a non-prohibitive tariff
Source: Ruffin R. J. and Gregory, P. R., *Principles of Economics*

Before the non-prohibitive tariff, the price of the product is P_w. The tariff raises the price to P_w + t; that is, the world price plus the amount of the duty. Consumers lose area N + R + T + V. Producers gain N. The government gains the tariff revenue T, which equals the tariff per unit times the quantity of imports. The net loss is R + V. The tariff lowers imports from $(q_4 - q_1)$ to $(q_3 - q_2)$.

It is also important to note certain economic characteristics of tariffs that contrast with other policy instruments that governments might invoke to protect domestic industries. For example, governments in importing countries may seek to protect domestic industries by quantitative restrictions (or quotas). As protectionist devices, these have the virtues of definitively limiting the volume of imports that will be permitted, and thus provide stronger assurances to domestic producers of protected market shares. On the other hand, they exhibit the corresponding vice, depending on their design, of insulating domestic producers from most forms of foreign competition and thus encouraging inefficiency. In contrast, with a non-prohibitive tariff, highly efficient foreign producers may be able to surmount the tariff and still compete effectively with domestic producers, thus creating some incentives for the latter to enhance their productive efficiency. Another difference between tariffs and quotas relates to who collects the scarcity

74

rents that they engender. With tariffs, governments in importing countries collect revenues from non-prohibitive tariffs. With quotas, depending on how they are allocated, domestic holders of import quotas or licenses may collect scarcity rents (rather than the government collect tariff revenues). If the quotas are allocated to foreign exporters, these firms will collect scarcity rents by charging more for their goods in the protected market, without being under any obligation to pay customs duties on the imports.

Tariffs should also be distinguished from production subsidies designed to make domestic industries artificially competitive with imports. Such subsidies will distort domestic production decisions by attracting resources into the subsidized activity, but will not necessarily (depending on how they are financed) distort domestic consumption decisions, in that the goods in question will still trade at world prices. Tariffs, in contrast, distort both domestic production and consumption decisions, first by attracting resources into the protected sector and second by raising prices to consumers above world prices, which in general reflect least cost means of production, thus inducing consumers to allocate their resources to less preferred forms of consumption.

As noted in Chapter 2, these characteristics of alternative instruments of protection find rough analogues in the provisions of the GATT. The GATT in Article XI purports to take a strong prohibitory approach towards quantitative restrictions. On subsidies, Article XVI reflects a much more ambivalent position, and while the Tokyo and Uruguay Round Subsidies Codes (especially the latter) take a somewhat less equivocal stance, only a narrow range of subsidies are subject to outright prohibition. Tariffs are not presumptively good or bad and there is no obligation under the GATT to reduce them, although Article XXVIII *bis* contemplates periodic negotiations on a reciprocal and mutually advantageous basis directed to the substantial reduction over time of the general level of tariffs.

THE MOST FAVOURED NATION PRINCIPLE

The Most Favoured Nation principle, found in Article I of the GATT, has its clearest application to tariff concessions. Under Article I, any concession made by one country to another must be immediately and unconditionally extended to like products originating from other Contracting Parties. While, as indicated in Chapter 1, the Most Favoured Nation principle has a long history, controversy still surrounds the purposes served by the principle.[2] At one level, it seems to encourage rampant free-riding by countries on concessions negotiated between other countries, and at the limit might encourage every country in turn to withhold concessions in the hope of being able to free-ride on concessions made by others, thus paralysing the process of trade liberalization. On the other hand, it might be argued that trade, or specifically tariff, concessions might be more readily negotiated between country A and country B, if each country is assured that the other country will not subsequently negotiate more generous concessions with third countries and thus undermine the benefits associated with the initial exchange of concessions. Whatever the strength of these offsetting arguments, the bargaining structures that member countries of the GATT have employed in negotiating tariff concessions clearly reflect sensitivity to the free-rider problem and the importance, at least politically if not economically, of extracting reciprocal concessions from other countries who stand to benefit from importing countries' concessions.

The political centrality of the concept of reciprocity is illustrated by the ritual which has followed each previous Round of tariff negotiations, where major participants have announced, presumably principally for domestic political consumption, the balance-sheet on the value of tariff concessions given and received, typically representing that a net gain has been realized. The method commonly employed for calculating the value of concessions has no economic foundation. For example, if Country A obtains a 10% tariff cut on widget exports to Country B that in previous years have averaged $US10 million, this concession will be valued at $US1 million. But this assumes a demand elasticity in Country B of unity, i.e. for every one percentage decline in price, quantity demanded will increase by one percent. This may or may not bear any resemblance to reality. Moreover, to value the concession accurately from Country A's perspective requires some knowledge of how other suppliers of widgets are likely to react to these new opportunities. That is to say, without a firm knowledge of these underlying demand and supply elasticities, simply calculating the value of a tariff concession by reference to trade coverage is next to meaningless.

While these political dimensions of the concept of reciprocity are clearly important to the optics of trade policy, we have also acknowledged in Chapter 1 that reciprocity may be an economically rational strategy – while unilateral trade liberalization may be welfare enhancing, reciprocal trade liberalization may generate even greater welfare gains. In any event, for both political and economic reasons, reciprocity has been central to most tariff reductions under the GATT.

A number of important exceptions or qualifications to the MFN principle should be noted at this point.

1 Historical preferences in force at the time of coming into effect of the GATT are grandfathered under Article I of the GATT, although subject to the requirement that the margin of preference cannot subsequently be altered in such a way as to exceed the difference between the MFN rate and preferential rates existing as of 10 April 1947. The provision contemplates that the absolute, not proportional difference between MFN and preferential rates must be maintained when MFN rates are reduced or raised. For example, if the MFN rate is 20% and the preferential rate

10% on imported widgets, and the MFN rate is subsequently reduced to 15% (a 25% reduction), the preferential rate can be reduced to 5% and not merely 7½% (which would be a 25% reduction).

2 The Generalised System of Preferences (GSP) provided for in Part IV of the GATT in favour of developing countries obviously entails preferences that would otherwise violate the MFN principle.

3 Antidumping and countervailing duties imposed by importing countries pursuant to Article VI of the GATT clearly involve duties that are selective and discriminatory.

4 Quantitative restrictions imposed pursuant to Article XII or Article XVIII of the GATT for balance of payment reasons may, by virtue of Article XIV, temporarily deviate from the principle of discrimination in respect of 'a small part of a country's external trade' where the benefits to that country substantially outweigh any injury which may result to the trade of other countries.

5 National security exceptions, recognized in Article XXI of the GATT, may justify the imposition of trade restrictions on a discriminatory basis.

6 Where retaliation is authorized under the nullification and impairment provision of the GATT (Article XXIII) or the safeguard provision (Article XIX), such measures will typically be selective and hence discriminatory.

7 The various non-tariff codes negotiated during the Tokyo Round were typically negotiated on a Conditional MFN basis, meaning that only Contracting Parties who were prepared to become signatories to the codes and thus accept the obligations so entailed are entitled to the correlative benefits. Under the Uruguay Round Agreement, these codes will be fully integrated into the GATT, and membership in the WTO will entail adherence to them.

8 By far the most important exception to the MFN principle is the authorization of customs unions and free trade areas under Article XXIV of the GATT, provided that two basic conditions are met, i.e. trade restrictions are eliminated with respect to 'substantially all the trade' between the constituent territories, and customs duties shall not be higher thereafter than the duties prevailing on average throughout the constituent territories prior to the formation of a customs union or free trade area. Subject to these two conditions, constituent territories are permitted to establish more favourable duty and other arrangements amongst themselves than pertain to trade with non-member countries. This exception is so important that the third part of this chapter is devoted to a discussion of the relationship between regional trading blocs and the multilateral system.

A final comment on the principle of non-discrimination requires a mention of how the National Treatment principle, enshrined in Article III of the GATT, bears on tariff concessions. In the absence of this principle, negotiated tariff concessions could be easily sabotaged. For example, if country

A agreed to reduce its tariffs on imported widgets from 20% to 10%, and then imposed differential domestic sales taxes on domestic and imported goods of 5% and 15% respectively, the tariff concession would effectively have been negated. More subtle forms of discriminatory treatment of imports relative to domestically produced goods may equally nullify or impair the benefit of previous tariff concessions to exporting countries and provoke a complaint under Article XXIII.

ALTERNATIVE BARGAINING STRUCTURES

Product-by-product negotiations

In the five negotiating rounds under the GATT prior to the Kennedy Round (1964–7), tariff concessions were negotiated on a product-by-product basis. Under the Principal Supplier rule that was adopted by the participants, countries who were principal suppliers of goods into international markets would prepare 'request' lists of goods where they were seeking tariff concessions from importing countries. Countries preparing request lists would at the same time prepare offer lists indicating products on which they were prepared to make concessions. Because of the MFN principle, requests and offers were typically directed by principal suppliers to principal importers, thus essentially bilateralizing tariff negotiations. A principal supplier would have no interest in directing a request to a minor importer because trade concessions negotiated with such a country, while entailing MFN obligations on the latter's part, would entail no such obligations on the part of major importers. Similarly, the principal supplier of product X would have no interest in making concessions on imports of product Y from a minor exporter, where this concession would have to be generalized to major exporters without being able to extract from these exporters major concessions on products of which the importing country was the principal supplier. According to Finger,[3] product-by-product negotiations achieved very high internalization rates, in the sense that benefits of trade concessions were confined, to a very large extent, to Parties offering countervailing trade concessions, with very little free-riding (pursuant to the MFN principle) on the part of exporters who offered no reciprocal concessions. To the extent that there were likely to be significant spill-overs benefiting non-reciprocating Parties from tariff concessions, typically product-by-product negotiating rounds concluded with a settling-up session where concessions previously tentatively negotiated were subject to threats of withdrawal or revision unless non-reciprocating countries agreed to offer concessions as well.

While this process may have led to deeper tariff cuts on items that were subject to negotiations, it arguably substantially restricted the range of products with respect to which active negotiations occurred, thus restricting the coverage of the resulting tariff reductions. Product-by-product negotiations had other limitations: first, small exporting and importing countries were largely frozen out of the negotiating process; second, by focusing negotiations on particular products, domestic producer constituencies were encouraged to become active in resisting tariff concessions on products in which they were interested; third, the negotiating process was highly transaction cost intensive because of its focus on line-item negotiations.

Linear-cuts with exceptions

In the Kennedy and Tokyo Rounds, the Contracting Parties chose to substitute for product-by-product negotiations a linear cutting formula, with a provision for exceptions lists where countries could take products out from the linear cuts and negotiate, as before, on a product-by-product basis. Obviously, with this approach, the coverage of products embraced by tariff reductions was likely to be much larger, although the degree of internalization of concessions exchanged was likely to have been lower, and according to Finger would have created incentives for shallower cuts. Finger refers to this as the internalization – coverage trade-off. In fact, both the Kennedy and Tokyo Rounds produced average tariff cuts of about 35% – well in excess of tariff reductions negotiated in the four rounds that had intervened between the initial GATT negotiations and the Kennedy Round. However, linear-cutting formulae present problems of their own. Now, negotiations must focus on the appropriate formula, and in both Rounds these negotiations proved problematic in various respects. For example, countries that already had low tariffs on average argued that it was unreasonable to expect them to cut these tariffs by the same percentage as high tariff countries, the reasoning being that, for example, a 50% cut of a 60% tariff would still leave a 30% tariff in place, which if one assumes that the initial tariff contained a lot of 'water', might still be largely prohibitive of imports, while a country cutting a 10% tariff to 5% might well find that this would have a significant impact on the volume of imports.

In both Rounds, formulae were finally agreed to which required, in one respect or another, larger cuts of higher tariffs than of lower tariffs. Another problem with the linear-cutting approach was the risk that countries would abuse the right to take items out from the linear-cutting formula and place them on an extravagant exceptions list where they would be subject only to product-by-product negotiations. Indeed, a number of countries with import sensitive sectors like textiles, clothing and footwear adopted this expedient. Also, countries primarily engaged in the exportation of agricultural products or natural resources, where tariffs were in many cases quite low but whose manufacturing sectors were highly protected (like Canada) viewed product-by-product negotiations as more advantageous than linear-cuts and in the Kennedy Round were entirely exempted from the linear-cutting process, but not in the Tokyo Round although subject to extensive exceptions lists.

Notwithstanding these problems, as noted above, between linear-cuts and product-by-product negotiated tariff reductions, the average level of tariffs was substantially reduced in the course of both Rounds.

Sector-by-sector negotiations

In both the Kennedy and Tokyo Rounds, efforts were made to negotiate reductions in trade barriers in selected sectors, such as steel, chemicals, and forest products. Canada was a prominent proponent of this approach. It was largely a failure. The reasons are not hard to identify. To focus negotiations on a particular sector (e.g. steel), is likely to engage the interest principally of producer interests in this field and rather than reducing or eliminating trade restrictions instead runs the risk of a managed trade arrangement effectively entailing cartelization of the global industry. Alternatively, because negotiations amongst producer interests in the same field in different countries tend to have a zero-sum quality to them, no agreement at all will be possible. While a code on trade in civil aircraft and components was successfully negotiated during the Tokyo Round and did reduce some trade barriers, the Multi-Fibre Arrangement that emerged in the 1970s is a stark example of the cartelization scenario. More generally, by attempting to negotiate trade liberalization within sectors, the political room for manoeuvre in cross-product or cross-sector exchanges of concessions, as entailed in product-by-product or linear-cutting negotiations, is dramatically reduced.

Non-reciprocal concessions

As recognized in Part IV of the GATT, developing countries are not expected to offer reciprocal commitments in trade negotiations, and developed countries are expected, to the fullest extent possible, to accord high priority to the reduction of barriers to products of particular export interest to developing countries. Pursuant to these provisions, in the early 1970s many industrialized countries adopted the Generalized System of Preferences (GSP), and unilaterally extended preferential tariff rates on certain items of export interest to developing countries. However, these preferential tariffs typically are not bound, usually entail escape clause provisions that permit the termination or reduction of the preferences in the event of import surges, and contain graduation provisions whereby developing countries lose their preferences when in the view of the country extending them they have reached a state of development where they no longer require them. As well, GSP preferences have typically not been extended on items produced by politically sensitive domestic sectors such as textiles, clothing, and footwear, even though these are of major export interest to many developing countries early in the process of industrialization. Moreover, as MFN rates have declined as a result of subsequent multilateral negotiations, the margin of preference between GSP and MFN rates has contracted.[4]

OUTSTANDING TARIFF ISSUES

While the first seven Rounds of tariff negotiations under the GATT since the Second World War dramatically reduced world tariffs on average (from about 40% on manufactured goods in 1947 to about 5% today), Laird and Yeats[5] identify a number of tariff issues that remained outstanding at the outset of the Uruguay Round Multilateral negotiations. First, despite low average tariffs, most countries still maintain very substantial tariffs on particular items, as the appended table from Laird and Yeats sets out. Moreover, there is still a good deal of unevenness in tariff levels from one industrialized country to the other with respect to particular items, suggesting that the low tariff–high tariff debate in negotiating modalities for reducing these disparities has not yet been fully resolved.

Second, many national tariffs are still not legally bound; this applies particularly to GSP tariffs. Third, there are different and adverse effects of specific tariffs on developing countries' exports (i.e. a fixed charge per unit), as opposed to *ad valorem* tariffs (a percentage of value). Specific tariffs are still quite common. Fourth, the cost-insurance-freight (CIF) as opposed to free-on-board (FOB) procedures for customs valuation continue to discriminate against geographically disadvantaged developing countries, particularly those that are least developed and land locked. Fifth, a serious problem still exists as to how to liberalize tariffs for products that are also simultaneously covered by non-tariff barriers (such as quotas). Sixth, developed countries still commonly apply escalating tariffs to imports depending on their stage of processing, in order to protect domestic processing industries, often at the expense of developing countries who would derive substantial advantages from being able to engage in value-added processing of what otherwise are purely commodity or raw materials exports.

Caves and Jones[6] provide a simple example (adapted slightly here) to illustrate how nominal tariff rates in fact may be substantially less than effective rates of protection as a result of escalating tariffs on different stages of processing: Initially, yarn is sold on the world market at 40¢ a yard and a particular unit of clothing made from this yarn is sold at a world price of $US1. A country importing the yarn and manufacturing the clothing produces value-added of 60¢. Subsequently the importing country imposes a 40% tariff on imported clothing, raising its price to a $US1.40 per unit. Now, when the importing country manufactures clothing from the imported yarn and sells it domestically, it has produced value-added of $US1 (US$1.40 – 40¢). The 40¢ increase in value-added ($US1 – 60¢) as a result of the 40% tariff on imported clothing amounts to a 66.7% effective rate of protection of domestically produced clothing (40¢/60¢ × 100/1). As a result of sharply escalating tariffs, effective rates of protection in a number of countries on processed goods are several orders of magnitude higher than nominal tariff rates. For example, according to Caves and Jones in Chile in 1961 the nominal rate of duty on processed food was 82%, while the effective rate of protection was 2,884%.[7]

Table 4.1 Post-Tokyo, applied and GSP tariffs in selected developed countries

Product group	Australia	Austria	Canada	EU	Finland	Japan	Norway	New Zealand	Sweden	Switzerland	USA	All developed
						Average MFN tariff rates						
All Food Items	4.9	8.0	6.2	3.7	8.9	9.7	2.8	9.7	1.6	10.0	4.1	6.4
Food and live animals	2.8	5.9	6.8	3.2	9.3	10.0	3.0	5.7	1.4	9.0	3.8	6.5
Oilseeds and nuts	4.1	1.9	6.0	10.3	7.9	5.6	4.5	0.9	3.3	7.5	1.4	5.3
Animal and vegetable oils	2.0	0.8	0.0	0.1	0.8	0.3	0.0	0.0	0.0	0.2	0.9	0.1
Agricultural Raw Materials	5.1	2.3	0.0	3.4	1.1	0.7	0.6	1.0	1.7	1.9	0.3	0.8
Ores and Metals	10.2	5.6	2.1	2.8	1.9	2.5	1.5	6.0	2.5	1.4	1.9	2.3
Iron and steel	17.2	8.4	5.4	5.5	3.9	5.0	1.8	8.0	4.8	2.0	4.3	5.1
Nonferrous metals	3.9	6.1	2.2	3.2	1.2	5.5	1.9	4.0	1.0	1.2	0.7	2.3
Fuels	0.0	2.1	1.4	0.1	0.1	1.5	0.0	0.2	0.0	0.0	0.4	1.1
Chemicals	5.4	6.3	6.4	8.4	2.4	5.5	5.9	6.7	5.0	0.9	3.7	5.8
Manufactures excl. chemicals	17.7	14.1	7.0	8.1	8.2	5.7	6.1	22.6	5.4	3.3	5.6	7.0
Leather	17.8	3.3	3.8	10.2	11.8	11.9	4.7	20.9	4.1	1.8	4.2	5.1
Textile yarn and fabrics	15.3	18.2	9.4	17.3	22.7	8.6	12.8	16.2	10.6	6.0	10.6	11.7
Clothing	49.3	30.2	12.6	19.9	32.0	15.0	20.3	93.0	13.6	8.6	20.3	17.5
Footwear	43.9	25.9	11.9	22.5	16.0	14.2	11.2	40.3	14.3	9.6	11.7	13.4
Other Items	0.2	3.3	0.1	4.8	1.3	2.3	2.0	1.2	1.8	0.4	n.a.	n.a.
All Products	n.a.	n.a.	n.a.	n.a.	n.a.	n.a.	n.a.	n.a.	n.a.	n.a.	n.a.	n.a.

Product group	Australia	Austria	Canada	EU	Finland	Japan	Norway	New Zealand	Sweden	Switzerland	USA	All developed
					Average applied tariff rates							
All Food Items	3.1	6.8	3.0	4.4	5.2	9.4	1.4	7.8	0.8	9.1	3.5	5.3
Food and live animals	1.7	4.9	2.9	4.8	5.7	9.7	1.5	3.9	0.8	8.4	3.2	5.3
Oilseeds and nuts	2.0	1.5	4.6	4.9	5.5	4.8	4.3	0.7	2.2	7.4	1.0	4.0
Animal and vegetable oils	2.4	0.8	0.1	0.0	0.8	0.3	0.0	0.0	0.0	0.2	1.0	0.2
Agricultural Raw Materials	0.7	1.6	3.7	0.4	1.0	0.3	0.4	0.7	1.4	0.7	0.3	0.5
Ores and Metals	4.3	0.3	2.7	0.7	0.1	1.8	0.4	4.2	0.2	0.1	2.2	1.5
Iron and steel	7.3	0.5	5.6	2.3	0.1	2.9	0.7	6.4	0.4	0.1	5.0	3.4
Nonferrous metals	2.4	0.2	2.8	0.5	0.0	4.3	0.1	2.1	0.1	0.1	0.7	1.3
Fuels	0.0	1.5	0.2	0.3	0.0	1.2	0.0	0.0	0.0	0.0	0.4	0.6
Chemicals	4.0	0.5	3.0	3.4	0.1	4.8	0.4	4.9	0.4	0.1	3.9	3.1
Manufactures excl. chemicals	11.5	2.0	6.2	4.6	1.3	4.6	1.3	18.3	1.4	0.4	4.9	4.7
Leather	10.9	0.9	11.0	2.1	2.3	10.7	0.8	21.4	0.3	0.1	2.7	3.1
Textile yarn and fabrics	11.3	2.0	18.3	5.3	1.0	7.1	1.6	10.9	1.7	0.6	12.1	7.9
Clothing	35.6	5.1	17.2	7.3	7.7	10.0	3.0	75.6	4.8	1.7	18.1	11.9
Footwear	27.9	1.2	23.4	6.5	3.8	12.5	2.4	28.4	2.8	0.6	9.5	9.0
Other Items	0.1	1.1	4.7	0.1	0.1	0.7	0.4	0.9	0.1	0.2	3.6	3.3
All Products	8.3	2.0	4.4	2.5	1.0	3.1	1.0	11.0	0.8	1.0	3.4	3.0

Source: Calculations on the basis of the GATT Tariff Study and UNCTAD Series D Trade Tapes

Product group	Australia	Austria	Canada	EU	Finland	Japan	Norway	New Zealand	Sweden	Switzerland	USA	All developed
	Average tariff for GSP beneficiaries											
All Food Items	1.3	9.0	1.5	5.0	7.0	11.1	0.3	6.2	0.4	6.3	3.6	5.5
Food and live animals	1.0	8.9	1.3	5.1	7.2	11.7	0.3	0.8	0.4	6.5	3.4	5.6
Oilseeds and nuts	0.7	0.1	5.6	6.2	8.8	5.0	3.2	0.0	1.7	9.0	0.3	4.5
Animal and vegetable oils	0.3	0.3	0.0	0.0	10.7	1.2	0.0	0.0	0.0	0.1	0.1	0.4
Agricultural Raw Materials	0.1	1.4	3.1	0.5	5.5	0.5	0.5	0.0	2.1	0.3	0.1	0.5
Ores and Metals	1.6	0.9	0.5	0.5	0.1	1.3	0.3	0.2	0.1	0.4	1.1	0.9
Iron and steel	4.9	2.9	4.0	3.3	0.4	2.0	0.4	2.3	1.0	0.4	3.5	3.0
Nonferrous metals	0.3	1.1	0.9	0.5	0.0	3.1	1.7	0.5	0.1	0.9	0.3	1.1
Fuels	0.0	1.5	0.0	0.2	0.0	1.3	0.0	0.0	0.0	0.0	0.3	0.6
Chemicals	4.2	4.0	6.1	4.1	0.1	5.1	0.2	1.1	0.6	0.4	1.0	3.7
Manufactures excl. chemicals	11.4	18.9	13.8	6.4	9.3	4.2	5.9	14.3	6.9	2.7	6.6	6.7
Leather	9.6	6.6	9.6	2.8	6.1	8.4	5.5	18.0	1.2	1.1	1.4	3.2
Textile yarn and fabrics	6.3	17.5	19.8	7.6	6.0	6.1	11.0	8.5	6.8	2.7	9.0	8.4
Clothing	35.1	27.2	16.2	9.3	23.6	8.6	18.9	82.8	13.2	7.6	17.8	14.6
Footwear	25.6	24.4	23.3	9.1	14.8	7.9	11.6	22.1	13.4	4.4	9.4	10.1
Other Items	0.0	5.2	5.6	0.1	0.1	1.0	0.1	1.7	0.0	0.4	0.4	3.8
All Products	4.3	4.9	4.4	2.1	4.6	2.3	2.8	3.3	2.3	2.3	3.6	2.7

The Uruguay Round Agreement contemplates average cuts in developed countries' tariffs of 38%. Some tariffs fall to zero either immediately or over a phase-out period. Many peak tariffs will be reduced by 50%; escalating tariffs on processed goods will be substantially reduced; and the number of bound tariff rates are substantially increased. Unlike the previous two Rounds, negotiations proceeded on a sectoral or product-by-product basis.

DOMESTIC ADMINISTRATION OF TARIFFS

Each country's customs authorities are responsible for administering the country's customs laws. Primarily their task involves calculating the duties owed by the importer, completing the required paperwork, and collecting the payments. However, calculating import duties involves a number of tasks: valuing the imported goods; locating the goods in the appropriate product classification; and identifying the goods' country of origin. Each stage of the process, from the valuation system to the paperwork and administrative fees, is a potential barrier to trade; domestic administration can increase the level of protection afforded by tariffs or even make the importing process prohibitively complicated. As someone once said: 'Let me write the Administrative Act and I care not who writes the rates of duty.'[8] In the areas of customs valuation and classification there has been general acceptance of harmonized rules, but little progress has been made on rules of origin, and administrative fees still remain at each country's discretion. Under Article X of the GATT, every Contracting Party is obligated to publish in accessible form all laws, regulations, rulings, etc., pertaining to classification, valuation, and customs administration and to institute a system of judicial or quasi-judicial review to enable prompt review and correction of administrative actions relating to customs matters. In Canada, tariff schedules are set out in great detail in the *Customs Tariff*, running into several thousand items. Five major tariff rates often exist for a given item: (1) the MFN tariff rate; (2) the FTA or NAFTA rate; (3) the General rate (for non-GATT members); (4) the British Preferential rate (for some Commonwealth countries); and (5) the GSP rate for some developing countries. In turn the Customs Act creates the domestic administrative machinery for the collection of duties through the Department of National Revenue. Internal appeal mechanisms within the Department on classification, valuation and related issues are provided for. Appeals from final Departmental determinations may be made to the Canadian International Trade Tribunal and thence, on matters of law, to the Federal Court of Appeal.

Valuation[9]

Most tariffs today are *ad valorem*, requiring the importer to pay a certain percentage of the good's value in duty.[10] Hence, the value of the imported goods is an important determinant of the ultimate import duty: 'any advance in value is accompanied by a commensurate increase in both duties collected and in the level of protection'.[11] It is in the interest of all countries that valuation techniques be uniform and predictable. A system that is unpredictable, or unfair to exporters serves as a non-tariff barrier to trade and undermines the effects of tariff reductions. Further, differences in valuation methods make tariff negotiations more complex.[12] In negotiations, a country must take into account the different effects of tariffs due to the different valuation techniques employed to ensure that it is receiving reciprocal trade concessions.

The current international rules on the valuation of goods for customs purposes are found in the Agreement on Implementation of Article VII of the GATT (the Customs Valuation Code).[13] The Customs Valuation Code was initially negotiated during the Tokyo Round in order to 'provide a uniform, neutral valuation system that conforms to commercial realities and prohibits arbitrary values for duty'.[14] A slightly revised Code was negotiated during the Uruguay Round.[15] Prior to this, the rules were found in Article VII of the GATT. Article VII was intended to ensure that signatories used fair systems of valuation that conformed with certain principles. It requires that Parties to the agreement base 'value for customs purposes of imported merchandise . . . on the actual value of the imported merchandise . . . not . . . on the value of merchandise of national origin or on arbitrary or fictitious values'.[16] Actual value is defined as the 'price at which . . . such or like merchandise is sold or offered for sale in the ordinary course of trade under fully competitive conditions'. The article does not specify the valuation method to be used and it gives the importing country discretion over the time and place for determining price.

Prior to the Tokyo Round negotiations over one hundred countries (including Japan and the countries of the EU) had adopted the valuation system called the Brussels Definition of Value (BDV).[17] However, two major GATT trading nations retained separate systems of valuation: Canada and the United States. Because of the Protocol of Provisional Application (the Grandfather Clause),[18] many of the signatories to the GATT were only bound to apply its Articles to 'the fullest extent not inconsistent with existing legislation'. Along with the general nature of Article VII, this provision allowed the perpetuation of very different, sometimes unfair, systems of valuation. For example, the United States used, in part, the American Selling Price (ASP) method of valuation which was viewed as 'a device to keep the American public from seeing in all its nakedness the exorbitant level of duties contemplated by rampant protectionism'.[19] The American system was made up of nine different methods of valuation and was 'stupefying in its complexity'.[20] In addition, Canada's valuation system was long considered to be inconsistent with Article VII of the GATT.[21] Countries which traded with the USA and Canada raised the issue of customs valuation in the Tokyo

Round negotiations in an attempt to have them abandon their systems.[22] The original intention of countries using the BDV was that it would become the worldwide system but a compromise was reached with the USA.[23] The Customs Valuation Code that was concluded in 1977 was based in part on the US system and was accepted by the major trading nations.[24] Signatories were obliged to render their legislation consistent with the Code by 1 January 1981 but many countries, including Canada, reserved the right to postpone implementation in order to ensure the maintenance of tariff protection at pre-code levels.[25]

A major objective of the Code was to constrain the exercise of administrative discretion. Both the Tokyo and Uruguay Round Codes establish 'transaction value' as the primary standard of valuation.[26] Transaction value is the price paid or payable for the goods when sold for export to the country of importation, plus certain additions such as the cost of packaging and the value of various items provided to the buyer free of charge in connection with the sale of the goods (assists). There are also some items that can be deducted from the price such as the cost of transportation, handling and insurance from the place of direct shipment. The transaction value can only be used for the purposes of valuation in certain circumstances. It can be used if there are no restrictions on the disposition or use of the goods other than those that are imposed by law or that restrict the resale area or that do not substantially affect the value of the goods.[27] In addition, to use transaction value the price of the goods cannot be subject to any conditions or consideration, such as an undertaking by the buyer to buy more goods at a later date. Sales between related persons (generally officers of each other's companies, partners, direct or indirect controlling interests) are eligible for use of transaction value provided it is demonstrated that the relationship did not affect the price.[28] There are a number of valuation methods outlined in the current Code to be used in the event that the transaction value cannot be used. Authorities must make resort to these methods in a particular order; for example, only if the first and second cannot be used can resort be made to the third. In the prescribed order, they are:

- transaction value of identical goods exported to the same country of importation at approximately the same time;
- transaction value of similar goods exported to the same country at approximately the same time;
- deductive value based on resale price in the country of importation; and
- computed value based on the cost of production of the imported goods.[29]

In many cases, the use of one of the alternate methods of valuation will be inappropriate because of information limitations or difficulties in calculation. Generally, resort will be made to the third or fourth methods when the price is affected by the relationship between the Parties to the transaction or when there is no selling price at the time of importation.

Certain methods of valuation are expressly prohibited in the Code, such as the use of arbitrary or fictitious values, and the use of the selling price in the country of importation.[30] In the Canadian and American legislation, customs officials are authorized to apply one of the above methods flexibly if goods cannot be valued under any of the above methods; this is the residual or alternative method. Part II of the Code also provides for the establishment of a Customs Valuation Committee that is responsible for furthering the objectives of the Code and facilitating consultation and dispute resolution with respect to the valuation system.

Classification

Because there is wide variation in the level of tariffs from product to product, goods must be located in the correct product category to receive proper tariff treatment. As with valuation, the problem with classification for customs purposes is that it can be used as a protectionist device. A country that has agreed to reduce its tariffs in exchange for reciprocal concessions can use the classification system to ensure the benefit is only received by the reciprocating country. This selectivity can be achieved if the product's classification can be subdivided so that the goods from the reciprocating country are in a distinct category. Then the tariff on the distinct category of goods can be reduced and other countries that would normally receive the benefit of the reduction through Most Favoured Nation treatment receive no benefit.[31] This same technique of product classification is also used to reduce the tariffs on inputs for domestic manufacturers and processors while maintaining the overall level of protection.[32]

The Customs Cooperation Council was established in 1950 and given a mandate to develop and harmonize customs systems of the world. The result of the committee's work is the Harmonized Commodity Description and Coding System. The Harmonized System (HS) was open for signing in 1984 and was implemented in some countries by 1987.[33] The basis of the Harmonized System is that goods should only be classified by their essential or intrinsic nature (i.e. by what they are and not how they are used) and should only fall into one category.[34] In Canada's previous classification system it was not uncommon to find the same good in several different categories carrying different rates of duty.[35] The nomenclature consists of a mandatory six digit classification system that is used by all signatories. Countries who find the classification too imprecise for their needs may use up to four more digits, as Canada has done.[36] Along with the numbers and descriptions, the System includes legal notes that are binding on the signatories. The notes provide definitions of terms and phrases essential to the classifications and set boundaries on the goods to be included in each. In addition, the notes list specific goods to be included or excluded in each category and give directions for locating the appropriate classification for excluded goods. Finally, there are extensive explanatory and interpretive notes; the latter are legally binding.

Rules of origin

The final task in calculating the appropriate duty on imported goods is establishing the country of origin of imports. Tariff treatment is often dependent on the country of origin of the imports. As noted earlier, in Canada there are five major tariff treatments. In order to qualify for a particular tariff treatment an importer must establish the product's origin. Establishing origin is often difficult: goods may be processed, assembled, packaged or finished in a variety of different countries, or shipped to the importing country via another country where they may or may not enter the commerce of that country.

There are presently no comprehensive multilateral rules that govern determinations of rules of origin. Moreover, in many countries, rules of origin are not internally harmonized. That is, there are different rules for establishing origin within the country depending on the context, for example, for tariff purposes or during a dumping investigation. This can pose a difficulty for exporters: a good that originated in country A may pay the tariff rate for country B, where it was processed, but face antidumping duties levied against goods from country A. Even within one context, rules are often imprecise as exemplified by the rules of origin laid out in the FTA. For the purposes of the FTA goods are deemed to originate in the territory of a Party if they are wholly produced or obtained in the USA or Canada. Also, they may contain offshore materials or components if they are transformed in Canada or the USA so as to be 'subject to a change in tariff classification'.[37] The difficulty with this system for origin determination is that the kind of change in tariff classification required to satisfy the FTA varies between goods.[38] In some cases a change at the statistical level is sufficient but in others the good must be under a different heading (first four digits). According to Palmeter,

> Change in tariff heading, as employed in the FTA, is not a rule of origin, but an agglomeration of ad hoc decisions devoid of any discernible principle . . . it is difficult to imagine how a similar system might be negotiated multilaterally.[39]

The Uruguay Round Agreement on Rules of Origin contains a similar approach to the FTA, with some important differences. First, the Agreement sets out plans for transition to a harmonized system of origin determination to be developed by a Committee on Rules of Origin and a Technical Committee assisting it within three years of the acceptance of the Agreement. The first step requires all countries to harmonize their own rules of origin.[40] During this period the rules applied by each country must be based on a positive standard (i.e. what confers origin not what does not confer origin). Once this harmonization is achieved countries will be required to base determinations of origin either on the country where the good was wholly obtained or the country where the good underwent its last substantial transformation. The rule of last substantial transformation is not fully defined in the Agreement[41] but it combines the change in tariff classification method with supplementary criteria based on percentage of value added or specific manufacturing or processing operations. The NAFTA also contains a number of new and complex rules of origin designed to clarify and harmonize determinations of content.[42]

Customs fees

Aside from the calculation of duties on imported goods, customs authorities are also responsible for processing documentation and collecting duties and administrative fees from importers. Both fees and documents may be barriers to trade. Documentation requirements can make the importation process more costly or prohibitively burdensome. In 1952 a Code of Standard Practices for Documentary Requirements was accepted by the GATT. The Code's main purpose is to restrict the kind and number of documents required. The result of the Code was the abolition in many countries of consular invoices which were previously a heavy burden on international trade.[43]

With respect to fees, there is no international agreement beyond the basic provisions of the GATT. Article VIII provides that:

All fees and charges of whatever character imposed by contracting parties on or in connection with importation or exportation shall be limited in amount to the approximate cost of services rendered.

The terms of Article VIII are vague and do not significantly constrain domestic practices. For example, importing countries often charge fees equal to a set percentage of the value of imports, leading to total charges far in excess of the cost of services rendered; the protective effect of such fees can be significant.[44] At present, domestic authorities retain a great deal of discretion in this area of customs administration.

MULTILATERALISM VERSUS REGIONALISM

The emergence of regional trading blocs, most prominently the European Union and the Canada–US FTA, and now NAFTA in the post-war period, collateral to the evolution of the GATT and sanctified by Article XXIV of the GATT, constitutes easily the most important exception to the MFN principle of non-discrimination embodied in the GATT and on that account requires an extended discussion.

While the record of the GATT in reducing tariffs on manufactured products has been impressive, it is also true that it has proven less effective in disciplining tariffs on primary products and non-tariff border measures, especially quantitative restrictions, let alone most other forms of trade-distorting policies of its members. If the reference point against which the GATT is to be judged is the deep integration being realized in the EU, with integration being pursued with respect to not only goods, but also services, capital, and people, co-ordination of exchange rate and monetary policies, and harmonization of a plethora of domestic fiscal and regulatory policies, it is impossible not to adopt a relatively gloomy prognosis for the future of the GATT.[45] However, it is important to be explicit about the premise on which this prognosis rests. Only with a hegemonic pro-free trade presence in the case of the multilateral system, or heavily centralized policy-making institutions in the case of the EU, is it likely that deeper economic integration can be achieved.

Thus, in the case of the GATT, now with a declining US hegemonic influence and with about 100 members (compared to 23 at the outset) in very different stages of economic development and with widely differing political, economic and cultural orientations – a heterogeneity that is likely to be increased in the future with the admission of countries in transition from command to free market economies – it is difficult to imagine the emergence of centralized integrating institutions to whom member states are prepared to surrender major aspects of their political sovereignty. Thus, if one insists on viewing the GATT, as traditional liberal institutionalists do, as a system of international legal rules designed to constrain domestic self-interest, which system can only be reinvigorated by stressing the importance of a global vision, of farsighted statesmanship that places global welfare and common interest over immediate domestic self-interest and of the importance of the global rule of law,[46] the GATT is now and will always be a disappointment.

However, a somewhat more optimistic (and realistic) view of the GATT is possible. Sometimes referred to as the new liberal institutionalist approach,[47] this view stresses that multilateralism should rather be seen as a decentralized framework for the negotiation and maintenance of mutually advantageous bargains among states. Liberal internationalists seek ways for designing or re-designing processes that, by reducing information, transaction, surveillance and verification costs, will facilitate Pareto-superior deals between or among states that are largely self-enforcing contracts. Performance of these contracts is promoted by reputation effects and tit-for-tat retaliation strategies that tend to solve the Prisoner's Dilemma problem in multi-period games.[48] This is precisely what describes the greatest achievement of the GATT – the dramatic reduction in tariffs, but it bears recalling, over a 40-year period and over eight successive bargaining rounds.

While it has become fashionable to talk of a 'borderless' world economy, the growth of global federalism, the decline in the significance of the nation state, and the rise of consumer sovereignty,[49] it is as plausible to view the rapidly integrating world economy as overlain with 'a splintering world polity'.[50] The rise of regional trading blocs arguably reflects this latter trend. Over 80 regional arrangements have been notified to the GATT under Article XXIV between 1947 and 1990. Many arose during the 1960s, and a second generation during the 1980s.[51]

Regional trading blocs have generally enjoyed a bad press from trade economists.[52] The reasons are straightforward enough. At a political or foreign policy level, they necessarily entail playing favourites and risk reducing international relations to mutually self-destructive factionalism of the kind that was so dramatically evidenced in the 1930s. From an economic perspective, regional trading blocs, whatever their trade expansion properties with respect to intra-regional trade, almost necessarily also entail some measure of trade diversion (in the sense that lower-cost producers outside the regional trading blocs are discriminated against), thus distorting the efficient global allocation of resources and hence reducing global welfare.[53] But this said, the question must be asked, 'compared to what?'. Compared to complete, undistorted global free trade, regional trading blocs are clearly second-best. But compared to the world trading system that actually prevails, or is likely to prevail in the foreseeable future, the case against regional trading blocs is not so clear.[54]

In this second-best world, Lawrence and Litan[55] provide a balanced assessment of their strengths and weaknesses. In the end, their assessment is cautiously positive. Central to this assessment is, on the one hand, their view that regional trading blocs may be able to achieve a deeper degree of economic integration than the multilateral system – negotiations typically involve a much smaller number of 'like-minded' nations, and (less explicitly claimed) the necessary centralized or federalizing policy-making and enforcement institutions (as with the EU) are more likely to emerge – and on the other hand, their view that the trade diversion potential of regional trading blocs is often over-stated, given both the size of inherent intra-regional trade flows already involved, at least in the EU and NAFTA,[56] and the empirical evidence on the importance of extra-regional trade to all of the major regions that might conceivably become involved in regional trading blocs. That is, it is reasonable to assume (or hope) that regional trading blocs will remain 'open', rather than become 'closed'.

We are less confident about both sides of this coin. With respect to the trade diversion argument, it is easy to be persuaded of the opposing view. For example, Stoeckel et al.[57] point out that the EU has been remarkably unforthcoming about how it plans to standardize external NTBs, especially quantitative restrictions, in 1992 or thereafter. Some member countries have relatively liberal import policies towards, for example, textiles and automobiles; others much more restrictive policies. On the assumption that the EU adopts a compromise between the Union-wide average protection level for each group of manufactures and the 'lowest common denominator' (the most restrictive), Stoeckel *et al.* project that this would lead to a contraction of imports of $US34 billion per year. In addition, because the EU would lose competitiveness due to higher cost imports, exports would fall by $US58 billion per year (9%). Overall, GNP of the EU would fall by over 1% or $US52 billion.[58]

Now, one might argue, as Lawrence and Litan implicitly do, that it would be economically irrational for the EU to constrain extra-regional trade when this has such self-destructive properties. But this can equally be said of most of the plethora of protectionist policies that have ever been adopted by any country anywhere. In the case of the EU, history suggests that economic rationality has not been the only force at play in the evolution of the Common Market. The Common Agricultural Policy (CAP) has transformed the EU at high cost over the post-war period from the world's largest importer of temperate zone agricultural products to the world's second largest exporter, with massive trade diversionary effects.[59] The rise of the New Protectionism (especially quantitative restrictions) in recent years has been particularly pronounced in both the EU and the USA, both of which figure most prominently in discussions of present or prospective regional trading blocs, as the following graph from Stoeckel *et al.*,[60] showing the growth in proportion of imports covered by trade restrictions, amply demonstrates (Figure 4.3).

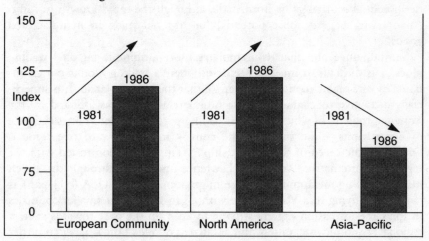

Figure 4.3 Trends in non-tariff barriers in the three regions
Source: Stoeckel *et al.*, *Western Trade Blocks: Game, Set or Match for Asia Pacific and the World Economy?*

Even if the existence of a hegemonic power is a necessary condition to the maintenance of a liberal trading regime, it clearly is not a sufficient condition – as exemplified by the historical role of the Soviet Union in Eastern Europe and the non-leadership role of the USA in the first third of this century.[61] Similarly, while it may also be the case that the existence of strong centralized institutions in a regional trading bloc is a necessary condition for deep economic integration, it would seem equally hazardous to assume that it is also a sufficient condition.

But this leads us to the first of the two reasons offered by Lawrence and Litan for their relatively positive view of regional trading blocs as conducive to deeper economic integration – negotiations occur among fewer and more like-minded countries than in the multilateral system. Under these circumstances, countries will be more willing to cede the kind of political sovereignty to federalizing central institutions that is required for deeper economic integration. Then presumably once these regional trading blocs have achieved a high degree of economic integration, it is assumed that negotiations between a handful of major trading blocs, all oriented towards progressive trade liberalization, will be conducive to inter-regional economic integration. We are less sanguine than the authors about this scenario.

First, as they would acknowledge, many actual or potential regional trading blocs offer very small prospects for intra-regional trade expansion, even setting aside their effects on external trade. This is true for actual or potential trading blocs in Africa, Latin America, the South Pacific and the Caribbean, where similarity of natural endowments often sharply limits the potential mutual gains from trade, although the rapid growth in intra-Asian trade suggests more potential for regional trade in manufactured goods.

Second, once one then contemplates more ambitious regional trading blocs, it is difficult to imagine scenarios where a trading bloc is not dominated by one major economic power – either the USA or Japan. It is superficially attractive to characterize the multilateral system as afflicted by the 'convoy problem' in which 'the least willing participant determines the pace of negotiations – the speed of the convoy moving toward free trade is limited by the speed of the slowest ship'.[62] This can be contrasted with the regionalist alternative evoked by Lawrence and Litan through the much more appealing metaphor of a geese migration, with the USA (or Japan) as head goose flying in a V-formation with a gaggle of other smaller countries in the same formation eagerly striving to keep up the pace towards at least regional economic integration. But as citizens of one of the smaller countries in such a formation, our judgement, after observing the ferocity of political debates in Canada over adoption of the Canada–US Free Trade Agreement, is that this entirely ignores political sensitivities to loss of sovereignty. If the virtue of regional trading blocs is their capacity for achieving a deeper degree of economic integration than the multilateral system, this view, as noted earlier, is premised either on a hegemonic theory of trade liberalization or strong federalizing central policy-making and enforcement institutions.

To take the Canada–US or Canada–US–Mexico case, we cannot imagine Canadians (or for that matter Mexicans) tolerating an arrangement whereby the USA is free to impose a common set of policies on all three countries across the spectrum of issues being addressed by the EU in its drive to integration (e.g. possibly a common currency, centrally coordinated monetary policy, regulation and directive powers over many domestic fiscal and regulatory policies). On the other hand, it is equally difficult to imagine the USA accepting a set of federalizing central institutions in which member countries are accorded equal or nearly equal standing (recall the demise of the Havana Charter and the ITO). Thus, we conclude, as the Canada–US FTA and NAFTA largely corroborate, that most regional trading blocs will not be conducive to deep economic integration. We believe the EU is a *sui generis* case. Partly because of the much greater symmetry in size and resources of the participating countries (perhaps about to be tested by the role of a reunified Germany), and partly because of special historical and political considerations largely related to the ravages of recurrent wars, member countries have been prepared to cede significant political sovereignty to federalizing central institutions. Even in the case of the EU, intense internal debates and divisions over the implications for domestic political sovereignty of the Maastricht Treaty suggest growing reservations about this trend.

Third, even if we are wrong, we believe that it is highly speculative to assume that following deep regional integration, regional trading blocs will then readily move to inter-regional economic integration through negotiations with other trading blocs. It is easy to assume that if political forces within each of these blocs have been amenable to regional trade liberalization and perceive the economic gains associated therewith, they would as readily perceive the virtue of just keeping on going, so to speak, and integrating inter-regionally. But the problem here is that regional patterns of integration and specialization that develop may (depending on how much trade diversion is created) significantly exacerbate the adjustment costs of subsequent inter-regional integration, where different patterns of integration and specialization may be entailed.[63] Moreover, regional trading blocs unquestionably place a premium on foreign investment relative to foreign trade (partly because of its domestic employment-enhancement effects), and as foreign firms, principally MNEs, establish substantial presences in each of the major trading blocs, a major political force for broader trade liberalization is attenuated (so-called 'co-operative protectionism').[64]

Fourth, one should not underestimate the sequencing problems in maintaining an 'open' regional trading bloc,[65] in the sense of it remaining open to membership by subsequent Parties. First-movers in such an arrangement face considerable uncertainty in determining the value of the preferences they are receiving in return for putatively deep concessions of their own, when these preferences may be eroded by subsequent admissions to the bloc. This will lead countries to be more reluctant to enter into a bloc in the first place, or to make deep concessions if they do, at least without a right of veto on new memberships (creating hold-out problems). Alternatively, negotiations with all prospective members will need to occur simultaneously, but in this event the large numbers problem said to afflict negotiations in the multilateral system will tend to re-emerge.

Canada has had to confront these issues in deciding on its role in the US–Mexico free trade negotiations. The strategy adopted in this case may set the mould for future free trade negotiations between the USA and other Latin American countries (e.g. Chile, Brazil, Argentina). The risk to Canada in staying out of such negotiations was that its preferences in the US market under the FTA would be eroded by similar preferences extended by the USA to Mexico while gaining nothing in return (in contrast to the USA) in terms of enhanced access to Mexico's market for exports and foreign investment. These effects would be exacerbated with each new bilateral agreement that the USA negotiates with another country – in the limiting case, a free trade area from Anchorage to Tierra Del Fuego, in President Bush's words. In turn, there will be strong incentives for export-oriented firms to invest in operations in the USA, relative to other Parties to these bilateral (hub-and-spoke) agreements, because this will assure them of unrestricted access to all affected markets.[66] In recognition of these considerations, Canada joined the negotiations that led to the recently concluded North American Free Trade Agreement (NAFTA).

The reservations noted above about the economic implications of regional trading blocs constitute strong reasons for being slow to abandon or attenuate the commitment to the non-discriminatory multilateral world trading regime envisaged by the founders of the GATT. Rather, we need a reconceived role (and a more patient set of expectations) for the GATT in promoting Pareto-superior and largely self-enforcing deals between countries on NTB's and other trade distortions in successive bargaining rounds modelled as closely as possible on the tariff-reduction bargaining process that GATT has so successfully facilitated in the past. Reducing most trade distortions to a common metric – a tariff equivalent or effective rate of protection – would be an important first step in pursuing this strategy.

5

ANTIDUMPING LAWS*

INTRODUCTION

Goods may be considered dumped when the price that exporters charge to their foreign customers is less than the price they charge to their home-market customers. Among countervailing duty, safeguard, and antidumping actions, antidumping actions were the most popular of the trade remedies in the 1980s. By the end of 1989, twenty-eight countries had adopted antidumping laws.[1] Nearly 1,200 actions were initiated between July 1980 and June 1988.[2] Four countries' actions accounted for 97.5% of all actions brought: 30% were brought by producers in the United States; 27% were brought in Australia; 22% in Canada; and 19% in the European Union.

The targets of these actions are more diverse. The EU was the largest single target, defending 27% of the actions, while Canada, the USA and Australia in total were targeted in fewer than 14% of the actions. The second most targeted group of countries were the Newly Industrialized Countries (NICs), representing 18% of the defenders. The actions against the NICs were most often initiated by the USA and Australia, who, along with the EU, also initiated 106 actions against Japan. The EU's main targets were the socialist countries of Eastern Europe, who defended 15% of the world's actions. Overall, western industrialized countries accounted for 58% of the targets and developing countries (other than NICs) only 9%. Finally, of the actions initiated by the major users, the success rate ranged from 44% for Australia to 71% for the EU. Recent GATT data for 1989 to 1993 suggest some interesting new trends, with the USA, China, Japan, Korea, Taiwan, and Brazil (in that order) emerging as the leading targets of antidumping cases.

In this chapter, we review the GATT provisions on dumping and the domestic application of dumping laws in Canada, the USA, and the EU. We then develop a fundamental critique of dumping laws and argue for their replacement with harmonized domestic competition laws focusing on cross-border predation.

THE GATT PROVISIONS ON ANTIDUMPING

Article VI of the GATT contains general rules governing the application of antidumping and countervailing duties. The first paragraph of the Article condemns export sales below normal value when they

> cause or threaten material injury to an established industry in the territory of the contracting party or materially retard the establishment of a domestic industry.

In addition, the article describes the basis for determining when sales are below normal value: when the export price is less than 'the comparable price, in the ordinary course of trade, for the product when destined for consumption in the exporting country'.[3] When these criteria are satisfied the importing country is entitled to levy an antidumping duty equal to the difference between the normal value and the export price.

However, the wording of the article is vague in important respects, leading to inconsistent interpretations and applications of the provision. Moreover, two of the biggest users of antidumping duties – Canada and the USA – did not consider themselves bound by its terms.[4]

The Kennedy Round Antidumping Code

In the Kennedy Round negotiations, beginning in 1963, many concerns about Article VI were addressed. The result was the 1967 Agreement on the Implementation of Article VI (the Antidumping Code) which laid out detailed criteria and procedures for the invocation of antidumping actions.[5]

Among the procedural rules contained in the Code is the requirement in Article 10(a) that provisional duties only be imposed following a preliminary finding of both dumping and injury. The imposition of retroactive duties is restricted by Article 11 of the Code, and Article 6 establishes rules of confidentiality and evidence. Finally, a notable feature of the Code is that it states a preference for the imposition of a duty that is less than the dumping margin when the lesser duty will alleviate the injury.[6]

With respect to substantive issues, the first problem with Article VI is that it does not define the 'industry' whose injury justifies imposing antidumping duties. Article 4(a) of the 1967 Code clarifies this issue, defining industry as 'the domestic producers as a whole of the like products or . . . those of them whose collective output of the products constitutes a major proportion of the total of those products'. A like product is defined in Article 2(b) as

> identical, i.e., alike in all respects to the product under consideration, or in the absence of such a product, another product which, although not alike in all respects, has characteristics closely resembling [the dumped product].

These two definitions in combination identify a relatively narrow group of producers which must be injured in order for an action to be successful.

The second ambiguity in Article VI is in the requisite causal link between the dumping and the injury. The 1967 Code specifies that the dumping has to be 'demonstrably the principal cause'[7] of the injury.

The Tokyo Round Antidumping Code

Signatories to the Antidumping Code in 1967 committed themselves to ensuring that their domestic trade legislation was rendered consistent with the Code. For the USA this task posed a substantial problem. The Code's test for causality was quite stringent and inconsistent with the US Antidumping Act.[8] The inconsistency between the Code and the Act led to unwillingness on the part of Congress to amend its laws or restrict the discretion of the administering authorities.[9] While the USA claimed that its applications were not inconsistent with the Code, the wording of the domestic law remained unchanged.[10] Having adopted the Code's definitions, the EU sought to ensure compliance by the USA and insisted on reopening the Code during the Tokyo Round.

The main revisions to the 1967 Code related to causality and injury determination. Rather than requiring that the dumping be 'demonstrably the principal cause', the 1979 Code only specifies that any 'injuries caused by other factors must not be attributed to the dumped imports',[11] making it more consistent with the US position. The EU also now supported a relaxation of the causation requirements. With respect to injury, the factors to be used in evaluating the impact of the dumping are explicitly laid out, i.e.:

> actual and potential decline in output, sales, market share, profits, productivity, return on investments, or utilization of capacity; . . . effects on cash flow, . . . wages, . . . growth.[12]

Also, the rules on the acceptance and administration of price and quantity undertakings are expanded in the 1979 Code (although their thrust remains the same). Finally, the Code requires that except under special circumstances a proceeding should be completed within one year and that the rules permitting retroactive duties be more restricted.

The Uruguay Round Antidumping Agreement

The 1979 Code left unresolved a number of problems and ambiguities.[13] The incompleteness of the Code results in inconsistent antidumping practices and procedures throughout the world. The Antidumping Code received further attention in the recent Uruguay Round negotiations. The main changes reflect a growing tension between developed countries, especially the USA and the EU, which bring a substantial percentage of all antidumping actions, and NICs and developing nations who are typically defenders rather than complainants.

In an attempt to make injury determinations more objective, Article 3.5 of the Uruguay Round Antidumping Agreement makes explicit those factors whose effects must be separated from those of the dumped goods in evaluating causality, for example, the volume and prices of imports not sold at dumped prices. Article 5 expands the procedural rules that govern the initiation and investigation of a dumping charge. Article 5.8 requires that an investigation should be terminated when a dumping margin is *de minimis* (less than 2% of the normal value) or when the volume of dumped products is negligible (i.e. if the volume of dumped imports from a particular country accounts for less than 3% of imports of the like product in the importing country unless countries that individually account for less than 3% of imports collectively account for more than 7% of imports). The rules on evidence (Article 6) are also expanded providing for assurances of disclosure and improved opportunities to make a full defence or argument, while still preserving essential confidentiality. Evidence provided by foreign Parties shall not be disregarded even if it is not clear in all respects (Annex II). Article 11 includes a 'sunset review' clause which limits, subject to review, the duration of duties to five years from their imposition. Article 9.5 requires the individual assessment of exporters who did not export during the period of investigation. This treatment replaces the typical application to uninvestigated exporters of the highest duty levied in a case.

While all these provisions can be viewed as enhancing the discipline imposed on the invocation of antidumping duties, other provisions cannot be viewed in quite such a benign light. A new provision bearing on the constructed cost measure of normal value permits the administering authorities, in the absence of firm-specific data, to use the weighted average of administrative, selling and other costs, and profits of other exporters under investigation, thus penalizing more efficient foreign producers (Article 2.2.2 (ii)). Member countries were unable to agree on provisions to prevent circumvention of antidumping duties by exporters subject to duties setting up local assembly plants using imported inputs ('screwdriver plants'); this issue has been remitted to the Committee on Antidumping Practices, set up under the Agreement, for resolution. Complaints over non-compliance with the Agreement may be referred to the integrated Dispute Settlement Body established by the broader Uruguay Round Agreement. Under Article 17.6, dispute resolution panels shall determine whether domestic agencies' establishment of the facts were proper and whether their evaluation was unbiased and objective. However, deferring to US concerns, Article 17.6 then provides that if the establishment of the facts was proper and the evaluation was unbiased and objective, the evaluation shall not be overturned even though the panel might have reached a different conclusion. Also, where a panel finds that a provision of the Agreement admits of more than one permissible interpretation, the panel shall find the agency's determination to be in conformity with the Agreement, if it rests upon one of these permissible interpretations.

ANTIDUMPING LAWS: CANADA, THE UNITED STATES AND THE EU[14]

History and background

Canada amended its *Customs Tariff* in 1904 to provide for antidumping duties and in so doing became the first country in the world to establish an antidumping regime.[15] The current legislation is set out in the Special Import Measures Act 1985 (the SIMA).[16] The first specific American antidumping statute, which is still in force, is known as the Antidumping Act of 1916.[17] Because of the onerous predatory intent requirement, there has never been either a successful prosecution or a civil judgment under this Act. This parallels experience under predatory pricing provisions in domestic antitrust laws where convictions or successful civil suits are rare. The US Congress enacted the Antidumping Act of 1921[18] to provide complainants with a greater scope for relief than the 1916 Act. The current American legislation is embodied in Title VII of the Tariff Act of 1930. Institutions of the European Union have had the authority to take action against dumped imports since 1968.[19]

Institutional arrangements

In Canada and the USA, the institutional responsibilities for determining 'dumping' and 'material injury' are separated. 'Dumping' determinations are made by the Deputy Minister of National Revenue (DMNR) in Canada[20] and by the International Trade Administration of the Department of Commerce (DC) in the United States. 'Material injury' determinations are made by the Canadian International Trade Tribunal (CITT) and by the US International Trade Commission (the ITC).

The institutional arrangements in the EU are very different from those in the USA and Canada. The principal institution involved in the administration of the EU antidumping system is the Commission, specifically Directorate C in the Directorate-General in Charge of External Relations of the Union, which has the primary responsibility for the enforcement of the antidumping regime. It is responsible for all stages of the investigation, including the decision to initiate a proceeding. Following an investigation, the Commission can impose provisional duties or submit proposals for definitive action to the Council. It also has the authority to accept undertakings by the exporter and terminate the proceeding. Finally, the Commission makes recommendations to the Council with respect to antidumping legislation.

The Council's main role is to approve the provisional determinations of the Commission and to order the collection of the imposed duties. It also has legislative responsibility for the antidumping regulation. The role has usually been a *pro forma* one.

An advisory committee made up of a Commission representative and an official from each member state is consulted by the Commission at various stages in the investigation. The committee's primary involvement is in determining the appropriate relief to be granted for an injury. An undertaking from the exporter cannot be accepted if there is not complete agreement from the Member States. Through their customs authorities, the Member States also help to ensure that duties are collected. Again, in practice the Committee's role is largely *pro forma*.

In certain circumstances the Court of Justice has the authority to review antidumping decisions. It can review the legality of Commission or Council determinations and redress 'manifest errors' in the assessment of facts or violations of procedural rules, although in practice the Court exercises its review function with restraint.

Finally, the European Parliament has an advisory role and issues non-binding opinions on EU legislation. In addition, its Committee on External Economic Relations serves as a forum for discussion of the administration of the antidumping system.

Substantive law

Dumping

The GATT Antidumping Agreement[21] requires that both dumping and injury be shown before action against the exporter will be taken. In Canada, the DMNR will make a finding of 'dumping' when the computed margin of dumping is positive and non-negligible. Section 2(1) of the SIMA defines 'margin of dumping' as 'the amount by which the normal value of the goods exceeds the export price thereof'. The American definition is similar,[22] although the American provision refers to 'fair value' instead of 'normal value'.[23] Once the normal value is determined, the DC constructs a weighted average of the home market price over a six-month period and compares it to each individual sale in the USA over this period. In the EU, the dumping margin is calculated as the weighted average of the difference, as determined on a transaction-by-transaction basis, between the normal value (a weighted average) and the export price.[24]

Normal/Fair value

The objective of the normal value inquiry is to establish a benchmark against which to measure the prices charged by the exporter in the export market. There are three ways to calculate normal value: the home-market method, the constructed-cost method and the third-country method. The GATT Agreement evinces a preference for the home market method, but contemplates the use of other methods when home market sales are an inappropriate benchmark.

Home-market method

The GATT Agreement defines 'normal value' as 'the comparable price, in the ordinary course of trade, for the like product when destined for consumption in the exporting country'.[25] The Canadian DMNR uses this home-market method if it can identify buyers in the exporting country who are at the same or a similar[26] trade level to buyers in Canada. The home-market price is deemed to be the preponderant[27] price charged for the goods in the home market within a 60-day period selected by the DMNR.[28] When there is no preponderant price, the DMNR uses a weighted average of the prices throughout the 60-day period.[29]

In the United States, the DC uses the exporter's weighted average home-market price provided home-market sales exceed 5% of the total export sales of the exporter.[30] Canada, the United States, and the EU exclude from normal-value calculations home-market sales which occur at less than their 'fully allocated cost'; these sales are deemed to be 'not in the ordinary course of business'.[31]

The EU regulations contemplate that the home-market method should be used in the typical case. However, the Commission will only use this method of calculation if the domestic sales (above cost) represent at least 5% of exports by volume to the Union.[32] The EU bases the normal value on the prices charged in domestic sales during an investigation period of six to twelve months prior to the initiation of proceedings. Beginning in 1985,[33] sales by companies related to the alleged dumper are also included in this home-market calculation.

Once the home market price is calculated, it is adjusted to reflect quantity discounts and differences in the terms of sale and the tax treatment of the imports.[34] The American regulations allow for adjustments to reflect advertising and promotion costs. The EU and Canadian legislation make no allowance for such expenditures.[35]

Constructed-cost method

Antidumping authorities depart from the home-market method when the sales in the domestic market are an inappropriate basis of comparison for one of the following reasons: (1) domestic sales of the like product are of insufficient quantity; (2) a substantial amount of home-market sales occur at a price below the 'fully allocated cost' of the goods; (3) the home market is not a market economy; or (4) domestic sales are primarily to 'associated' companies or to companies with 'compensatory arrangements' with the exporter.[36] Canada uses the constructed-cost method for both cases (1) and (2). The US uses the constructed-cost method for case (2) and the EU tends to use this method in all cases but (3).

When they use the constructed-cost method, both Canada and the USA examine all costs incurred by the exporter, including production and overhead. They then add a profit margin to those costs based on the profit the exporter makes in the home market. In Canada, the DMNR presumes an 8% profit when it is unable to calculate the actual profit margin.[37] In the USA, the DC attaches a minimum profit margin of 8% to the exporter's sales, regardless of the exporter's actual profit. The DC also adds a flat 10% to the exporter's computed costs to reflect overhead.[38] Canada computes the exporter's actual overhead, and does not add minimum overhead percentages to the exporter's computed costs.

For the EU, the constructed cost is the same as the cost measure used in the domestic-market calculation to determine if sale prices are 'in the ordinary course of trade'. As in the USA and Canada, it is the sum of the average cost of production (including average fixed costs) and other general expenses[39] plus a reasonable margin of profit. In calculating the margin of profit, the Commission tries to find an average based on all profitable sales in the market where the producer has sufficient profitable sales of the product. Producers whose dumping margin is being calculated under this method are unlikely to have sufficient profitable sales to have their profit margin determined by this method. A number of alternative methods are laid out in the Agreement. For example, the lowest weighted average profit of producers with sufficient domestic sales can be used.[40] The profit margin used in determining the constructed value ranges from 5% to as much as 60%.[41]

There are two main problems with the constructed-cost calculation. The first is the inclusion of minimum profits and overhead costs. There is little basis for the choice of profit or cost level and their inclusion needlessly penalizes efficient exporters who have low overhead costs or low expected profits as a percentage of costs (but high turn-over). The imposed profit levels make a finding of dumping more likely under the constructed-cost method than under the home-market or third-country method.

The second problem with the constructed-cost provision is the treatment of home-market sales which occur at a price below the goods' fully allocated cost: they are deemed 'not in the ordinary course of business'. This treatment ignores generally accepted antitrust jurisprudence which recognizes that sellers may price below their full costs for legitimate business reasons.[42] By including all fixed costs, average unit costs will increase as demand declines, e.g. in a recession, thus compelling an increase in prices in a depressed market.

Third-country method

Where the home country is not a market economy, the EU and Canada use analogue country exporters as a benchmark. Under this method, in Canada the DMNR approaches a third-party exporter in a 'surrogate' country and asks that exporter to volunteer its cost and pricing information. This information is then used to calculate a normal value for the exported goods. The choice of a comparable surrogate is crucial to the dumping calculation and difficult to make. Under this method, the DMNR's dumping determinations are largely arbitrary because there is no mechanism for adjusting cost differences between the surrogate country and the home country.[43] In contrast, the USA calculates a hypothetical constructed value for exports from non-market economies. For market economy exporters with insufficient home market sales from which to infer a home-market value, the USA will often use as a benchmark sales by those exporters to a third country.

In the EU, the procedure used for calculating the normal value in the case of non-market economies was first introduced in 1979 and is laid out in Article 2(5) of the regulations.[44] The Commission chooses an analogue country, preferably a third-country, in which the normal value of the like product will be assessed.[45] The Commission tries to find a country which manufactures a similar product with the same processes and technical standards as the exporting country. As in Canada there are no adjustments for cost or competitive differences between countries.[46] Once the analogue country has been chosen, one of the previous methods is used to establish the normal value. The choice of an analogue country introduces an additional element of uncertainty into the evaluation, so that the exporter has little idea what price will constitute dumping.[47]

The third-country approach in general has been heavily criticized. The costs incurred by surrogate country producers do not reflect those of non-market economy exporters, yet they form the standard against which the latters' prices are measured. Indeed, as Bhagwati notes, 'there is no way in which "true" or "fair" costs and prices can be meaningfully determined for centrally planned economies in the first place'.[48]

Export price calculation

Relative to the normal value calculation, the export price calculation is straightforward. The Canadian SIMA declares the export price to be the lower of the exporter's sale price and the importer's purchase price.[49] The American provision is similar.[50] In the EU, the export price is 'the price actually paid or payable for the product sold for export to the community'.[51] In many cases the Community will construct the export price because of the existence of particular compensatory relationships between the exporter and importer.[52]

Injury

According to the GATT Agreement, only dumping that 'causes or threatens material injury to an established industry or materially retards the establishment of an industry' can attract relief. There are three components to the injury inquiry: (1) the definition of the domestic industry; (2) whether that industry is being injured;[53] and (3) whether dumping is causing the injury.[54]

Domestic industry and like goods

The GATT Agreement defines 'domestic industry' as domestic producers as a whole of 'like products'.[55] Both Canada and the United States have adopted this definition of 'domestic industry'. In deciding which domestic goods are 'like' those being dumped both Canada and the United States focus on the functional uses of goods.[56] The Canadian 'like goods' test asks whether dumped goods 'closely resemble' domestic goods.[57] The American test is stricter, and asks whether dumped goods are 'most similar in characteristics' to domestic goods.[58] A narrow construction may make an injury finding more likely by restricting the inquiry to whether the producers of the *most* similar goods are being injured without regard to impacts on the broader industry.

For the EU, the domestic industry being injured need only be a Union producer(s) whose output constitutes a major proportion of the total Union production of the like product.[59] The definition of a like product is identical to that in the 1993 GATT Antidumping Agreement[60] and is construed by the Union quite narrowly. According to Bellis

> There has to be a close physical relationship between the exported product and the domestic product; domestic producers of merely similar or substitute merchandise are not protected by the antidumping law.[61]

Material injury

Article 3.4 of the GATT Agreement provides a non-exhaustive list of indicators of material injury. These include: negative effects on the output of domestic industry; negative effects on employment, market share, profits and growth; high inventories; capacity underutilization; and price erosion. The Canadian definition of 'material injury' follows these criteria.[62]

In the United States, 'material injury' is defined as 'harm which is not inconsequential, immaterial, or unimportant'.[63] The ITC is required to examine the volume of dumped goods, the effect of dumped goods on the domestic market price and the effect on domestic producers.[64]

The typical ground for imposing duties in the EU is actual material injury or actual material injury combined with threat of injury, but there is no definition of these concepts. Article 4(2) of the regulations lists a number of factors to be considered, such as changes in capacity utilization in the community industry, relative market shares, profits and employment. The investigated period for the determination of 'injury' is often several years, unlike the six to twelve month reference period for dumping.[65]

Causation

Once antidumping authorities find injury, the crucial question is whether that injury is caused by dumped goods or by other competitive pressures. The Canadian SIMA does not articulate the required causal link between dumping and injury to domestic producers.[66] The CITT requires dumped imports to constitute an 'important', 'significant'[67] or 'direct'[68] cause of injury to domestic industry, and considers actual or likely decreases in output, sales, productivity, return on investment, and utilization of capacity.[69] The CITT has dismissed some antidumping complaints by attributing domestic injury to declining markets, limited production ranges and production problems.[70] During the material injury inquiry, the Director of Investigation and Research of the Canadian Competition Policy Bureau can make submissions on the extent to which domestic injury is caused by general competitive forces.[71]

The US legislation requires only that injury be 'by reason of' dumping. The US Court of International Trade recently declared that the ITC must make a positive finding of injury if dumped imports contribute 'even minimally' to depressed conditions of domestic industry.[72] The ITC's position is that '[t]he injury caused by [dumping] need not be the "principal" or a "major" or "substantial" cause of overall injury to an industry'.[73]

The EU regulations[74] parallel the GATT Agreement and require that all factors influencing the domestic industry be analysed and that the role of dumping be separated from other factors. The dumping must cause the injury contemplated by the Agreement.

Procedure

Standing of complainants

The GATT Agreement requires antidumping complaints to be initiated on behalf of the industry affected, which is defined as 'domestic producers whose collective output of the products constitutes more than 50 percent of the total domestic production of like products produced by that portion of the industry expressing either support for or opposition to the application'. No investigation shall be initiated where domestic producers supporting the application account for less than 25% of total domestic production of the like product.[75] Both Canadian[76] and US[77] laws incorporate provisions similar to the GATT requirement. In the EU, the Commission has the authority to investigate an exporter's price of its own accord or at the request of a member state but in practice only initiates proceedings when a complaint is launched on behalf of a Union industry. European trade associations usually file complaints on behalf of aggrieved industries.

Preliminary investigation

Once a complainant is found to have standing, the GATT Agreement[78] requires antidumping authorities to undertake a preliminary investigation to determine whether the dumping complaint discloses sufficient evidence of dumping, material injury, and a causal link. The preliminary investigation must yield simultaneous *prima facie* findings of dumping and material injury for a formal investigation to be initiated.[79]

In Canada, after receiving a properly documented[80] complaint, the DMNR has thirty days to determine whether the complaint is supported by evidence of both dumping and of past, present or future material injury. If there is such evidence, the DMNR commences a formal investigation to determine whether dumping is in fact occurring.[81]

In the United States, the preliminary process involves more steps. An investigation generally begins when the complainant simultaneously files a petition with the DC and the ITC, although the DC may initiate an investigation of its own accord. The DC and ITC then undertake preliminary investigations to determine whether there is *prima facie* evidence of dumping and *prima facie* evidence that the dumping is causing material injury. If both preliminary investigations produce positive findings, the DC begins an investigation to determine whether dumping is in fact occurring. In practice, the ITC tends to find a reasonable indication of injury unless there is clearly no threat of material injury, nor any possibility that contrary evidence would arise if an investigation were launched.[82]

In the EU, the complaint must contain 'sufficient evidence' of dumping and injury in order to lead to a formal investigation, but in practice the threshold tends to be low.[83]

Formal investigation

The DMNR in Canada solicits information on home-market sales and production costs from exporters and importers of the impugned goods. Importers must provide extensive information on the prices at which the goods are sold into the Canadian market.[84] On the basis of this information, the DMNR decides whether the impugned goods are being dumped. If there is evidence of dumping, the DMNR makes a provisional determination of the dumping margin and imposes provisional antidumping duties equal to the margin of dumping on the imports. The CITT then undertakes a more thorough material injury inquiry. Over the next ninety days, while the

CITT inquires into material injury, the DMNR may revise its provisional determination of the dumping margin before making a final determination. This process is open to affected Parties.[85]

In the course of its material injury inquiry, the CITT gathers extensive economic data and constructs a model of the domestic market for the dumped product. This culminates in an adversarial hearing which is generally held immediately following the DMNR's final determination of the dumping margin. The CITT must complete its inquiry and reach its decision within 120 days of the DMNR's provisional dumping determination. If the CITT makes a finding of material injury, antidumping duties are imposed which reflect the DMNR's 'final margin of dumping' determination. If the CITT does not find material injury, the investigation is terminated and any provisional duties paid by exporters are refunded.[86]

Following the initiation of the formal investigation, the US procedure is similar to that in Canada. If the DC finds dumping to be occurring, it makes a provisional determination of the dumping margin and refers the matter back to the ITC for its final determination of material injury. At the same time, importers are required to post a bond sufficient to cover the calculated margin of dumping. The ITC then undertakes a second, dispositive, inquiry into whether the dumping is causing material injury. Like the CITT, the ITC gathers data from both petitioners and respondents.

In the EU, after the complaint is received questionnaires are sent to the exporter, importers, and community producers for their submissions. The submissions may relate to the existence of a dumping margin or injury, or the appropriate remedy. The questionnaires must be returned within thirty-seven days of being issued and must contain all of a Party's arguments on any point. In the past few years, the Commission has held Parties strictly to the time and procedural constraints laid out in the regulation.[87]

The case handlers then conduct on-site verifications in order to corroborate the questionnaire responses and test the reliability of the data provided by exporters and importers as well as Union producers. Any Party to the complaint may make oral representations at a hearing after submitting written comments. The significance of hearings in the antidumping process has varied over the past decades. Given the current strict enforcement of deadlines, Parties are now using the hearings more often to amplify arguments presented in the questionnaires or to comment further on the injury sustained by the Union industry. In general, the investigation is not public; hearings are held in private in meetings of the officials of the Commission.[88] No Party can be compelled to attend and the evidence that is available is limited. Finally, hearings are only held at the request of a Party to the case who has a representation to make.

Once the Commission has made a decision, it issues a public notice of the termination of the case or the imposition of provisional duties but does not produce a reasoned judgment. Usually following the provisional determination of the Commission, the Parties to the complaint can obtain the information upon which the Commission's decision was made.

Assessment of antidumping duties

In Canada, antidumping duties are imposed following the DMNR's final determination and the CITT's positive finding of material injury.[89] Antidumping duties are imposed on an entry-by-entry basis, so Canadian importers know the extent of their antidumping duty liability as it accrues. Canada sets a normal value and if exporters sell above it, there is no duty, deposit, or bond. The CITT's positive finding of injury automatically expires after five years.[90] Thereafter, complainants must file new petitions which form the basis for new investigations.

In the USA, once the ITC makes a positive finding of injury, importers pay duties equal to the 'final' dumping margin computed by the DC during its formal investigation. These antidumping duties represent an estimate of the importers' actual liability. At the end of each year, the DC revises its 'final' dumping margin to reflect actual sales of dumped goods during the year. The DC uses the revised margin to compute retroactively importers' actual antidumping duty liability for the year. The importers' periodic payments of antidumping duties throughout the year are deducted from the final antidumping duty liability, and importers are liable for the remainder. As Palmeter notes, by accepting dumped goods importers expose themselves to an open-ended contingent liability.[91] While the US system has the advantage that antidumping duties are based on actual data, an importer cannot be certain in advance of the antidumping duty liability.

Antidumping orders in the USA expire after five years unless an interested Party requests an administrative review during that period.[92] Antidumping orders can also be lifted if the dumper shows that it has not sold the goods at less than fair value for at least three consecutive years.

In the EU, once dumping and material injury are found, the Commission will impose provisional duties which apply for four months. When these are approved by the Council they become definitive and under the new 'sunset review' procedure lapse after five years unless an interested Party can show that there is still a threat of injury.[93] Duties are generally prospective, although there is provision for their application to goods imported up to ninety days prior to the imposition of provisional duties.[94]

Consulent with the GATT Agreement, Article 13(3) of the regulations specify that the duty shall be less than the dumping margin if this is sufficient to remove the injury. A new provision in Article 13(11) also ensures that the duties are not absorbed by the exporter; the price must increase by the amount of the duties or further duties will be applied to the importer. The importer can claim a refund of duties paid if it can be shown that they exceed the dumping margin, although Bellis suggests that this is more of a theoretical than practical possibility.[95]

In the regulation imposing the duties, the specific duties owed by each exporter are specified. Exporters not specified – typically those who begin exporting after the case is decided – in the past have been subject to residual duties which are the highest duties imposed in the case. In addition, because they were not exporting during the investigation period, prospective importers cannot offer undertakings in order to avoid antidumping duties.[96]

The 'parts' or 'screwdriver' provision in Article 13(10) allows the extension of duties to products assembled or produced in the Union. This extension is allowed when specific circumstances are present suggesting that the production in the Union is for the purpose of circumventing antidumping duties. The imposition of duties also depends on the percentage of EU-originating parts in the final product, the amount of research and development carried out and technology applied in the Union. This practice of imposing duties on parts is controversial because it imposes duties on goods without first finding that they have been dumped or are causing injury. There is also a very obvious 'buy European' bias to this provision.

A case can be settled without the imposition of duties in a number of ways. First, the exporter can give an undertaking to eliminate the dumping or the injury by revising the export price, or to stop exporting. If the undertaking is accepted the proceeding is terminated. This kind of settlement was popular but is being used less frequently as the Commission has begun treating settlement as a favour to the exporter. Second, the foreign and domestic industries can negotiate a settlement. Such a private settlement will not terminate a proceeding but can prevent its initiation. Finally, a voluntary restraint arrangement can be concluded to end the action.

Public interest considerations

In Canada, once the CITT has determined material injury it may consider the potential effect of antidumping duties on 'the public interest'.[97] If the CITT is of the view that imposing antidumping duties would be contrary to the public interest, it must both publish a report in the *Canada Gazette* and report to the Minister of Finance, who has the discretion to lower or remove the duty.[98] The provision reflects the concern that 'concentration on producer interests alone is too narrow a focus and the consumer interest must be considered'.[99] In practice, however, only three public interest hearings[100] have been convened since the provision was enacted in 1985, and consumer groups did not initiate or participate in any of the hearings. The United States does not have a public interest provision. The EU regulations provide that duties should only be imposed when doing so serves the Union's interest,[101] but the typical reason for invoking the clause is to avoid domestic producers paying more for dumped inputs.[102]

Rights of appeal

While the CITT's decision is 'final and conclusive',[103] the CITT may review its own findings if it is satisfied that such a review is warranted.[104] There are also appeals to the Federal Court of Appeal[105] and the Supreme Court of Canada, principally on issues of law.[106] In the United States, an appeal lies to the Court of International Trade from both DC and ITC decisions.[107] Under the FTA and NAFTA, appeals may be referred to binational dispute settlement panels.[108] The EU system has a limited right of appeal. As previously noted, the Court of Justice is reluctant to review a Commission decision. The EU antidumping system is characterized by discretion and secrecy; the reluctance of the Court to review the Commission's decisions increases the appearance (at least) of unfairness in the system's administration.[109]

THEORETICAL RATIONALES FOR ANTIDUMPING LAWS

Economic rationales for antidumping laws

There are three ways in which dumping can be characterized: as international price discrimination, as predatory pricing, or as intermittent dumping. These characterizations, if well-founded, each give rise to possible economic justifications for the existence of antidumping laws.

International price discrimination

Canada was the first country in the world to enact antidumping legislation and there is some evidence that this was prompted by fears of international price discrimination. According to Jacob Viner, Canada's first antidumping legislation was a response to the US Steel Corporation's practice of selling its exports at prices substantially below its domestic prices.[110] US antidumping laws are also often characterized as a means of responding to international price discrimination.[111]

Both Canadian[112] and US[113] antitrust laws prohibit various forms of domestic price discrimination. These laws have intricate and detailed requirements which make the legal definition of price discrimination complex. However, a standard economic definition of price discrimination is as follows:

> It is discriminatory to charge significantly different product prices to two or more customers when there are no significant differences between the costs to the seller of supplying those customers.[114]

A seller thus price discriminates when selling an identical product in different markets for different prices. The seller must have some degree of control over the market price (or 'market power') to be able to price discriminate, and the seller will only have market power under conditions of imperfect competition.[115]

There are essentially two arguments for prohibiting domestic price discrimination.[116] First, a monopolist's[117] total output may decrease when it shifts from a single-price policy to a discriminatory pricing policy. Because a monopolist sells less output than is optimal, a further decrease in its output might exacerbate the scarcity and impose greater welfare losses on society. Once the monopolist price discriminates between the two markets, some existing customers will be forced out of the higher priced market, and new customers will be attracted to the lower priced market. The total output produced and sold will decrease if the higher priced market forces out more customers than the lower priced market attracts.

The second argument against allowing price discrimination reflects two forms of social cost imposed on society. The first costs are those that the monopolist incurs in segregating its markets and computing its customers' elasticities of demand. If price discrimination were prohibited, resources invested in administering the price discrimination scheme could be put to socially beneficial uses such as product innovation, plant expansion or research and development. Second, according to Posner,[118] the lure of monopoly profits induces competing sellers to seek monopolies. Sellers compete with each other to obtain, for example, licences and protectionist legislation in the hope of achieving a monopoly. In the monopoly contest, sellers may invest resources up to their expected monopoly profits. The monopoly rents gained by the ultimate victor may be wholly offset by the socially wasteful expenditures of the competing sellers. If price discrimination is allowed, expected monopoly profits will be higher, sellers will invest more resources in achieving monopolies, and resulting social costs would be higher than under a nondiscriminatory pricing policy.

These traditional arguments for prohibiting price discrimination are inconclusive. Among antitrust scholars there is no consensus on whether domestic price discrimination should be prohibited.[119] First, whether output will increase or decrease under price discrimination is an empirical question.[120] In a wide range of circumstances, it is likely to increase. Second, while the costs that the monopolist incurs in acquiring and segregating its market may be wasteful, if the monopolist produces more output under price discrimination those costs may be outweighed by the benefits of the increased output. Third, since some monopolies are efficient, expenditures to secure such monopolies are not wasteful.

Even if one assumes the validity of the arguments for prohibiting domestic price discrimination (although they are often contested), the case for prohibiting dumping is not analogous. Domestic price discriminators and dumpers have different effects on the export country. A seller only 'dumps' if it charges a lower price to its export market customers than it charges to its home

113

market customers.[121] Therefore, while domestic price discriminators create both a higher priced market and a lower priced market in the same country, dumpers create only a lower priced market in the country to which they are exporting.

The export country benefits from low import prices. The consumers in the export country enjoy more consumer surplus since they receive more output at a lower price per unit. When the export country imposes anti-dumping duties on low-priced imports, its consumers lose these benefits. By increasing the price of dumped goods to the exporter's monopolistic home market price, antidumping duties impose supra-competitive prices on consumers in the export market and force them to settle for an inefficiently low level of output. Those consumers who remain in the market pay higher prices and enjoy less consumer surplus, and some consumers are priced out of the market, generating a dead-weight social cost.

In addition, when dumping occurs, the higher priced market is by definition located in the dumper's home country. The dumper's home country thus bears the dumper's costs of identifying and segregating its markets, and any social costs associated with the dumper's monopoly profits. The efficiency losses associated with domestic price discrimination, which drive the arguments for prohibiting price discrimination, are borne entirely by the dumper's home market. Hence, the arguments for prohibiting domestic price discrimination do not justify a corresponding prohibition against dumping; dumping gives the export country the benefit of the price discriminator's low priced market without the social costs of its high priced market. Even if the export country were concerned about the dumper's home market problems through some altruistic motive, forcing domestic consumers to pay the dumper's home market monopoly price is a wholly ineffective response. On this point, Trebilcock and Quinn note

> Although equality of exploitation has a certain egalitarian ring to it, it seems a little difficult to see any other virtue in replicating other people's miseries, particularly when in so doing we are in no way ameliorating the lot of our fellow sufferers.[122]

Finally, while the potential reduction in output is an argument against price discrimination, and whether total world output will rise or fall under international price discrimination is an empirical question, in the case of dumping prices are by definition lower in the export market, so the output available to the export country is unambiguously higher with dumping, rendering highly problematic the appropriateness of providing any remedy to producers in the latter country on this account. The losses to consumers will almost always outweigh any gain to producers who are thereby protected.

It should be added that international price discrimination is only viable if foreign exporters can segregate their markets and prevent arbitrage between the low- and high-priced markets. Where a country like Hong Kong, with few trade barriers or other restrictions, is found guilty of dumping, almost by definition the rationale cannot be price discrimination.

Predatory pricing

The traditional arguments for prohibiting domestic price discrimination do not support the case that dumping as a form of international price discrimination should be prohibited. Clearly, antidumping laws cannot be supported on efficiency grounds unless dumping involves something more than price discrimination. Predatory pricing is the second characterization of dumping that gives rise to an economic rationale for antidumping laws. It consists of 'systematically pricing below cost with a view to intimidating and/or eliminating rivals in an effort to bring about a market price higher than would otherwise prevail'.[123]

US antidumping laws were initially enacted out of a concern for predatory pricing by foreign competitors.[124] Canadian, US and EU antidumping laws penalize predatory pricing in addition to international price discrimination by authorizing the constructed-cost method of calculating the normal value. This penalization of below-cost pricing suggests that predatory pricing may be an additional rationale for current antidumping laws.

Canadian,[125] US,[126] and EU[127] domestic antitrust laws prohibit predatory pricing. A seller who engages in predatory pricing (the predator) ultimately harms competition by driving other sellers from the market and acquiring market power. Once the predator gains market power it restricts its output and captures monopoly profits. Predatory pricing is unlikely to occur frequently.[128] An extensive antitrust literature argues that predatory pricing is not often an effective means of achieving market power,[129] and economic theory suggests that systematic below-cost pricing is infeasible and irrational unless certain structural conditions are present. In order to compensate for the extensive losses suffered while selling at artificially low prices, the predator must achieve a monopoly position by driving its competitors from the market and preventing new competitors from entering. This will be difficult: competitors will only leave the market if there are low barriers to exit, and low exit barriers imply correspondingly low barriers to entry. Thus, even if the predator is successful in driving out its current competitors, it may face competition from a new wave of competitors. As well, as Hovenkamp[130] and McGee[131] argue, if the initial competitors are driven into bankruptcy, other sellers may acquire their facilities at fire-sale prices and compete with the predator while incurring lower fixed costs. Since it is unclear whether the predator will succeed in creating a monopoly, the potential gains from predatory pricing are uncertain.

Predatory pricing allegations are also difficult to assess. As Areeda and Turner note:

[U]nhappy rivals may automatically assume predation when a competitor's price is below their costs, disregarding the possibility that the alleged predator's cost is well below theirs and more than covered by his price.[132]

In both Canada and the USA, prices below the seller's marginal cost[133] or average variable cost[134] tend to be deemed predatory, although courts have experienced some difficulty in measuring those costs.[135] The rejection of average total cost as a reference point is important because there are many instances in which a seller may be forced to sell below cost. For example, in times of slack or declining demand, the seller may not be able to sell enough output to cover all of its costs. As long as the seller prices its output above its variable costs, the revenue in excess of its variable costs will defray a portion of its fixed costs. Thus, the seller suffers lower losses than it would by halting production (in which case it would suffer losses equal to its full fixed costs).

The gains from predatory pricing are even more uncertain in the international arena. For a predator to achieve a monopoly in its export market it must not only drive out domestic competitors from the export market, but other foreign competitors as well. Foreign producers compete with each other just as vigorously as they compete with domestic competitors in their export markets.[136] Thus, the likelihood of one seller achieving a worldwide monopoly is slim, and vigorous competition among foreign competitors implies a small likelihood, in most markets, of successful oligopoly formation.[137]

Although true international predatory pricing (predatory dumping) may be expected to occur infrequently, where it does occur it harms competition in the export market. Indeed, predatory dumping is more harmful than wholly domestic predatory pricing because resulting monopoly profits are captured by the foreign exporter. On efficiency grounds, antidumping laws are justifiable insofar as they prevent predatory dumping. However the current antidumping regimes of Canada, the USA and the EU penalize behaviour which may be neither predatory nor prohibited by antitrust legislation. Indeed, Hutton and Trebilcock conclude that of the thirty cases between 1984 and 1989 in which Canada imposed antidumping duties, none could be supported on predatory pricing grounds.[138] Currently, antidumping duties are imposed when 'fully-allocated costs' exceed export market prices. As argued above, below-total-cost pricing need not be predatory. In fact, by attaching arbitrary minimum profits of 8% to cost calculations, antidumping laws penalize pricing which may be slightly above cost. Hence, antidumping laws penalize non-predatory behaviour.

Moreover, even below-marginal-cost pricing by the exporter need not reflect an underlying predatory intention. When the exporter makes its production decisions, it estimates the price its output will eventually realize in the export market. As long as the estimated export market price exceeds its marginal cost, it will produce output for sale in the export market. If, owing for example to fluctuating exchange rates or changed market conditions, the actual export market price turns out to be lower than estimated the exporter will have no choice but to sell its output at the best available price. This price may be lower than the *ex ante* marginal costs the exporter faced when it made its production decision. However, the exporter will continue to sell in the export market because the output has already been produced and it can recoup a portion of its sunk costs by selling its output.[139] Although the exporter is engaging in below-marginal-cost pricing, there is no predatory intention. The exporter is doing what it can to minimize its losses in the face of its inaccurate *ex ante* estimate of the market price. Hutton and Trebilcock find that frustrated *ex ante* market price estimates accounted for below-marginal-cost pricing in four antidumping actions initiated in Canada against US exporters.[140]

Finally, in some cases below-marginal-cost pricing may actually promote competition. Depending on the product, sellers may engage in below-marginal-cost pricing to compete for market share. Deardorff[141] identifies two product characteristics, 'experience' and 'learning by doing', that make below-marginal-cost pricing likely for some goods. Consumers may pay more for 'experience' goods after their first and subsequent purchases than before their first purchase. This is because the quality of 'experience' goods is only discernible after their first use. To induce consumers to sample their goods for the first time, as a marketing strategy sellers may initially price their goods below their marginal cost. Sellers will recoup their initial losses once consumers pay more for the goods on their subsequent purchases.[142] Sellers produce 'learning by doing' goods when they experiment with new technology or new products. When they first enter the market with new goods, sellers may be inefficient and suffer losses. At this point, marginal costs may exceed the sale price. Sellers gradually reduce their costs as they 'learn' more about efficient production methods. In the meantime, they gain a valuable toehold in the market.[143]

Below-marginal-cost pricing for 'experience' or 'learning by doing' goods is typical for sellers expanding into new markets and cannot be viewed as predatory. In fact, it increases consumer demand, competition, and productive efficiency, and sellers can recoup their costs without acquiring market power. Many sellers, regardless of their degree of market power, may increase their market share by selective below-marginal-cost pricing. These legitimate roles for below-marginal-cost pricing suggest that antidumping laws should not categorically penalize below-marginal cost pricing. Significantly, domestic antitrust laws permit these kinds of activities.[144]

Intermittent dumping

The final characterization of dumping that gives rise to an economic rationale for antidumping laws is intermittent dumping. Jacob Viner defined intermittent dumping as systematic dumping which lasts for several months or years at a time.[145] Viner viewed this form of dumping as objectionable because it lasts long enough to injure domestic producers without providing consumers with a constant long-run supply of goods.[146] A situation in which intermittent dumping might occur is in the context of oversupply of perishables. Agricultural producers often make planting decisions long before selling their produce. Because of the cyclical nature of supply in agricultural markets, producers often find they have excess produce and rather than allowing it to rot they sell at low prices. For these agricultural producers, the relevant cost at the time of selling is the cost of packaging and marketing. Hutton and Trebilcock[147] find that the only Canadian antidumping cases that exhibited any indication of intermittent dumping were agricultural cases. They argue that the case of perishables is not a dumping problem and that agricultural price instability should be addressed, if at all, through income stabilization programmes rather than antidumping laws.[148]

Non-predatory intermittent dumping cannot occur unless certain structural conditions are present.[149] First, exporters must be unable to compete with domestic producers under normal market conditions. Otherwise, exporters would provide a permanent source of supply instead of an intermittent one. Second, intermittent dumping must be so extensive that it substantially disrupts domestic production. The heavy losses incurred by selling below-cost products into export markets makes it unlikely that the dumping will last long enough to disrupt domestic production. As well, disruption will only occur if domestic purchasers substitute foreign goods for domestic goods. By substituting foreign goods for domestic goods during the intermittent dumping period, domestic purchasers will disrupt domestic production. As a result, when the intermittent dumping period is over domestic producers will charge higher prices than before to recoup their post-intermittent-dumping readjustment costs. Domestic purchasers can avoid the higher price by not substituting away from domestic goods in the first place.

The conditions necessary for non-predatory intermittent dumping to occur are unlikely to arise. Moreover, the effect of non-predatory intermittent dumping on welfare is ambiguous. When foreign exporters dump, domestic producers in the export market must adjust to meet lower import prices. Some domestic producers may be forced out of the market and if the dumping is only temporary, domestic producers will then have to readjust to fill the vacuum left by the departing dumper. The adjustment and readjustment costs incurred by domestic producers unquestionably harm *producer* welfare, as Trebilcock and Quinn note.[150] Corporate resources which would go to skills training, expansion, or research and development are diverted to maintaining the producer's market share in the more competitive market. Losses incurred during the dumping period may force some producers into bankruptcy. Since domestic capital markets may be imperfect, the producers forced into bankruptcy may not be the least efficient.[151]

Adjustment and readjustment costs associated with intermittent dumping may also be passed on to consumers. Intermittent dumping harms consumers if they end up paying a higher long-run average price for goods than they would pay if there were no dumping. If intermittent dumping occurs with sufficient frequency that the domestic producer's cost of capital is higher over the long run (reflecting higher risk) than it would be in the absence of intermittent dumping, this cost will be passed on to consumers. However, the dumping margin may so depress prices during the period of dumping that, notwithstanding the producers' increased cost of capital, the consumer ends up paying lower long-run average prices. The net effect of intermittent dumping on consumer welfare is thus uncertain.

Given both the uncertain effect of intermittent dumping on consumer welfare and the low probability of the structural conditions for intermittent dumping being satisfied, it is questionable whether antidumping laws should seek to prevent intermittent dumping. In any event, the present anti-dumping laws of Canada and the United States are ill-adapted to addressing problems of intermittent dumping. Antidumping investigations assess dumping margins and material injury without regard to whether the dumping is temporary or permanent. This conclusion is borne out by Hutton and Trebilcock's finding that the *possibility* of intermittent dumping concerns was present in only four of the thirty Canadian cases they examined in which antidumping duties were imposed.[152]

Non-efficiency rationales for prohibiting dumping

The standard literature on dumping generally considers only economic or efficiency-based rationales for prohibiting dumping.[153] However, efficiency-based rationales may not tell the whole dumping story. Typically, antidumping laws can be justified politically because they address the perceived 'unfairness' of low-priced foreign imports. A US Senate Committee has called dumping 'pernicious',[154] and American courts have characterized dumping as an 'unfair trade practice'.[155] The global increase in antidumping actions may therefore reflect growing domestic political objections to the unfairness of low-priced foreign imports. The previous section showed that the only economic justification for antidumping laws is the prohibition of international predatory pricing, but notions of fairness may offer different justifications.

Fairness is a difficult concept.[156] Bhagwati characterizes the fairness

119

terminology in antidumping laws as 'inherently vague',[157] and remarks that it is 'reflective of the psychological mood of a nation losing hegemony in the world economy'.[158] The perceived unfairness of non-predatory dumping may result from the disruptive impacts of low-priced imports on domestic industry and work-forces. By increasing the net price of imports, antidumping duties make domestic goods relatively more attractive to consumers and allow domestic producers to avoid direct competition with foreign exporters. Direct competition with low-cost suppliers may eventually force domestic producers to leave the market. This exit is likely to result in domestic workers losing jobs and shareholders of affected producers losing capital. Thus, while consumers would benefit from lower prices if antidumping duties were abolished, domestic producers might suffer severe losses from low-priced imports.[159]

Hutton and Trebilcock examine distributive justice and communitarian rationales for antidumping laws.[160] Antidumping laws would be justified on a distributive justice rationale if they were to enhance the welfare of the least-advantaged members of society.[161] The least-advantaged group would include immobile, unskilled, and low-income workers.[162] Antidumping laws would be justified on a communitarian rationale where they minimized the disruptive effect of imports on established communities and their corresponding network of family and social relationships.[163]

However, both theoretically and empirically, antidumping laws cannot be sustained on these non-economic rationales. First, there is no principled reason to distinguish between the harm caused by non-predatory dumping and the harm caused by non-dumped low-priced imports. Undeniably, low-priced imports inflict losses on domestic interests; however, the severity of these losses does not depend on the home-market price of those imports, which is what distinguishes dumped imports from other imports.

Empirically, most Canadian cases in which antidumping duties are imposed do not reflect distributive justice or communitarian rationales. Hutton and Trebilcock show that of the thirty Canadian antidumping cases in which antidumping duties were imposed between 30 October 1984 and 3 February 1989, two cases could be justified by a distributive justice rationale alone, five cases could be justified by a communitarian rationale alone, and four cases could be justified by a combined distributive justice/ communitarian rationale. Nineteen of the thirty cases examined could not be justified on any normative rationale, either economic or non-economic.[164] Thus, not only do non-economic rationales fail to justify a prohibition against dumping, but antidumping authorities appear to ignore these rationales when they impose antidumping duties. Indeed, Hutton and Trebilcock find that most Canadian antidumping cases benefit those workers and communities who are already better off than the majority of workers and communities in Canada,[165] suggesting that the current Canadian regime actually violates distributive justice concerns.

REFORMING ANTIDUMPING LAWS

Current antidumping regimes might seek to prevent international price discrimination, international predatory pricing and intermittent dumping. However, only predatory pricing gives rise to a legitimate economic rationale for prohibiting dumping: when dumping is merely international price discrimination, the export market benefits. Intermittent dumping can be expected to occur only rarely and its net welfare effects are ambiguous.[166] Yet antidumping laws are ill-designed to identify and penalize true international predatory pricing. Instead, they result in duties being levied upon goods priced at non-predatory levels, thereby imposing severe costs on consumers in export markets through supracompetitive prices.

Non-economic rationales for antidumping laws, such as concerns over distributive justice or communitarian impacts of low priced imports, are more appropriately dealt with under safeguard regimes or, better still, under domestic adjustment assistance programmes. This conclusion leads us to propose that antidumping laws should be replaced by either supra-national or harmonized domestic antitrust regimes which penalize international predatory pricing without at the same time penalizing non-predatory international price discrimination. Price discrimination laws should play no role in regulating cross-border trade. Amongst Member States of the European Union, this solution has largely been adopted, with the abolition of antidumping duties with respect to inter-member trade and replacement with Union competition laws which bind Member States and their citizens. However, EU competition laws constrain not only predatory pricing but also price discrimination, including cross-border price discrimination.[167] Therefore, the European model is more expansive than our analysis suggests is warranted. Moreover, with respect to trade with non-member countries, the prospect of a binding supra-national body of competition law at this time seems remote.[168]

Instead, the more modest goal of harmonizing domestic antitrust laws, ideally under the aegis of the GATT, with respect to international predatory pricing seems a more appropriate goal. In this respect, the 1988 Protocol between Australia and New Zealand, pursuant to the Australian–New Zealand Closer Economic Relations Trade Agreement (ANZCERTA) between the two countries is much more apposite. Both countries have agreed that as of July 1990, all antidumping actions between the two countries should cease and that any antidumping duties then in place should be terminated. In their place have been substituted harmonized provisions in both countries' competition law pertaining to abuse of dominant position. These provisions permit a complainant located in one country to complain of abusive behaviour by a firm or firms located in the other country. The courts in the first country are then authorized to hold hearings in the second country and to use the second country's courts to enforce subpoenas and other orders. The provisions on abuse of dominant position clearly focus on cross-border predatory pricing, and not cross-border price discrimination. Warner has recently proposed a similar harmonized antitrust regime for bilateral Canada–US trade.[169] Here the political trade-offs seem promising. Between 1980 and 1988, US producers brought 22 antidumping actions against Canadian exporters, while Canadian producers brought 50 actions against US exporters. Canada imposed duties in 23 of the 50 actions, while the US imposed duties in 14 of the 22 actions. In principle, such a regime could also be implemented multilaterally, through a GATT cross-border predatory pricing Code, which would require signatories to harmonize their domestic antitrust laws in line with the Code, in very much the same way that at present domestic antidumping laws must conform with the GATT Antidumping Agreement. In moving in this direction, one of the major forms of the 'New Protectionism' would be radically constrained, while legitimate concerns about domestic impacts of surges in low-priced imports would be dealt with through a well-conceived multilateral safeguards regime[170] and domestic adjustment assistance programmes.[171]

THE INTERFACE BETWEEN TRADE AND COMPETITION POLICIES

We should note in concluding this chapter that the relationship between competition policy and trade policy extends well beyond the issue of replacing domestic antidumping laws with harmonized predatory pricing laws.[172] While dumping practices engage unfair trade concerns, excessively lax or excessively stringent domestic competition laws which impact adversely on foreign interests may similarly raise unfair trade concerns. The harmonization of domestic competition laws more generally is emerging as a major area of debate on the trade policy agenda. With accelerating trends towards globalization of domestic economies, firms are often multinational in their structure and operations, and transactions and arrangements between or among firms often span many jurisdictions. Moreover, as international investment flows have come to dominate international trade flows, and trade flows increasingly involve intra-enterprise trade, issues of effective market access, with the decline in the significance of tariffs, increasingly entail domestic policy divergences with respect to competition and investment policies.[173] For example, mergers now often involve acquiring and acquired firms located in different jurisdictions. Even when the merging firms are located within the same jurisdiction, the principal impact of the merger may be felt in either input or output markets located in other jurisdictions. In these cases, antitrust or competition authorities in the various jurisdictions may all regard themselves as legitimately responsible for reviewing the competitive implications of the merger. However, multiple reviews increase the costs and delays for the Parties involved, and generate a significant risk that these reviews will reach conflicting determinations. This is due to the wide diversity in both procedural and substantive aspects of merger law in the competition laws of many countries.[174] Horizontal arrangements amongst domestic producers may also prejudice foreign competitors or consumers, most obviously in the case of export cartels or import cartels (group boycotts). There is a proliferation of new forms of horizontal arrangements, which do not neatly fit into conventional competition law categories like mergers or collusion. These arrangements are often referred to as 'strategic alliances', and encompass joint research or production ventures; minority shareholdings, long-term reciprocal contractual supply arrangements, research consortia, etc.[175] These new forms of corporate arrangements raise a number of difficult issues. On the one hand, to the extent that domestic antitrust or competition law regimes permit cooperative or collusive arrangements amongst domestic rivals, this might be argued to prejudice unfairly foreign competitors both in the domestic market and in export markets. For example, it is sometimes claimed that lax competition laws that facilitate anti-competitive behaviour in domestic markets enable firms to use the supra-competitive profits so generated to engage in 'strategic dumping' in foreign markets.[176] On the other hand, given that these arrangements often involve both foreign and domestic firms and may impact on input or output markets in yet other jurisdictions, the same potential for multijurisdictional conflict arises as with mergers. In the case of vertical restraints (such as exclusive territories or exclusive dealing arrangements) domestic competition laws in the USA, Canada, the European Union, Japan and other jurisdictions differ sharply in the stringency of the legal constraints imposed on such arrangements. For example, it is argued that vertical relationships between domestic input suppliers and manufacturers, and between manufacturers and distribution networks in Japan (often referred to as *keiretsu*) unfairly inhibit access by foreign exporters and investors to the Japanese market, and that the quiescent state of Japanese competition law, in effect, constitutes an unfair non-tariff barrier to trade (and investment). On the other hand, excessively aggressive competition laws may also improperly prejudice foreign competition. For example, private actions against alleged predatory pricing by foreign competitors or mergers involving foreign acquirers may constitute forms of anti-competitive (and protectionist) strategic harassment.

How these interfaces between trade policy and competition policy are best resolved is far from clear. Within most industrialized member countries of the GATT, trade policy and competition policy tend to be administered by different agencies of government. At the same time, international institutional arrangements for harmonizing competition laws, whether under the aegis of the GATT (as the original Havana Charter contemplated), or the OECD, or through bilateral arrangements such as the recent agreement between the USA and the European Union on international merger review, are at this juncture, for the most part, weakly developed and poorly coordinated.[177] We feel confident, however, in predicting that the relationship between international trade policies and domestic competition policies is likely to emerge as one of the major new issues on the trade policy agenda in the years ahead.

6

SUBSIDIES, COUNTERVAILING DUTIES, AND GOVERNMENT PROCUREMENT

INTRODUCTION

Under Article VI of the GATT, countervailing duties can be levied by member countries on imports that are causing harm to domestic industries due to subsidization by a foreign government.[1] After antidumping actions, counter-vailing duty actions are the most frequently initiated trade-remedy actions, accounting for 18% of all import relief measures initiated between 1979 and 1988.[2] However, unlike antidumping actions, one country is the main user: between 1979 and 1988 the United States initiated 371 actions while all other countries initiated only 58.[3] According to Messerlin: 'To the United States, the [GATT Subsidies] Code is an instrument to control subsidies. To the rest of the world, it is an instrument to control US countervailing duties.'[4] The predominance of the USA as a user of countervailing duties illustrates the distinctive view of subsidies held by the USA, and the lack of international agreement on the status of subsidies as policy instruments. In the USA, subsidies are often viewed as illegitimate distortions of international trade, while in other countries industrial subsidies are considered a legitimate instrument of domestic policy.

Despite US protests at the use of subsidies by other countries,[5] there is a significant incidence of subsidies in the United States itself, particularly at the state level where subsidies (including tax incentives) are pervasive. Fry estimates that 'at the end of the 1980s, the total annual tab for targeted assistance at the subnational level was over $20 billion for non-agricultural businesses; expenditures and lost revenues for the states approached $200 billion'.[6] Moreover, many of these state aids are highly visible, rather than being hidden in procurement policies, utility rate rebates, etc.[7]

With respect to subsidies at the federal level, recent empirical work by Bence and Smith, based upon data from the mid-to-late-1980s, concluded that, excluding the defence sector, the average subsidy rate (subsidies as a percentage of the value of industry outputs) was about 0.5% for the United States.[8] However, once defence procurement in the United States is taken into account, the US average rate of subsidies jumps to 2%. Bence and Smith, however, do not explain the methodology used to discern the subsidy component in defence procurement, and hence the 2% estimate should be regarded as speculative. At the same time, it should be noted that neither estimate fully reflects off-budget items such as loan guarantees and tax expenditures which are generally regarded as among the most pervasive instruments of subsidization in the United States.[9]

Parties to the GATT are authorized to levy countervailing duties in response to injury caused or threatened by subsidized imports.[10] However, there are three situations in which subsidies can distort trade, and in only one can countervailing duties be used directly to address any resulting distortions. First, if country A subsidizes its exports to country B, causing domestic producers in country B to be disadvantaged, country B can respond by countervailing those imports. Second, if country A subsidizes its domestic production, disadvantaging the exports of country B to country A, the only actions country B can take are to respond with equivalent subsidies, retaliate by imposing duties on other imports from A, or complain of nullification or impairment of prior tariff concessions to a GATT dispute resolution panel.[11] Finally, if country A subsidizes exports to C, disadvantaging exports of country B into C's market, again there is little that country B can do other than respond with equivalent subsidies or retaliate with duties on other imports from A.[12] It is necessary to consider both the rules on subsidies and those on countervailing duties in order to address the problems raised in these three scenarios.

GATT PROVISIONS ON SUBSIDIES

Article VI

Article VI of the GATT contains general rules governing the application of antidumping and countervailing duties. In section 3, countervailing duties are defined as 'a special duty levied for the purpose of offsetting any bounty or subsidy bestowed directly or indirectly upon the manufacture, production or export of any merchandise'. The fact that countervailing duties are linked with antidumping duties in this Article suggests that subsidies are actionable for the same reason that dumping is: because they result in below-normal value pricing;[13] however, early commentators distinguish subsidization from dumping on the grounds that the former is a distorting practice of *government* whereas the latter is a pricing policy of a private firm.[14]

Few rules are laid out in this Article. In order for a countervailing duty action to be authorized, the effect of the subsidization must be to cause or threaten material injury to an established domestic industry or to retard materially the establishment of a domestic industry. Section 5 specifies that no product may be subject to both antidumping and countervailing duties and that any countervailing duties should be no more than the estimated bounty or subsidy determined to have been granted. Finally, two specific practices are exempted from countervailing duty actions. First, the exemption of a product from duties or taxes borne by that product (or a product like or competitive with that product) when not destined for export (i.e. when destined for consumption in the country of origin) is not a countervailable subsidy.[15] Second, the maintenance of price stabilization systems for producers of primary commodities is not countervailable if such systems lead to both high and low export prices and are not intended to stimulate exports or cause distortions.[16]

Article XVI

Article XVI of the GATT contains general provisions on subsidies. At the time of the formation of the GATT, Article XVI contained only one provision whose main purpose was to encourage notification and consultation on the use of subsidies. Section A requires Parties to notify the GATT of any subsidies that affect imports or exports, directly or indirectly, and to consult with any Parties whose interests are threatened by or are suffering serious prejudice from such subsidies. This provision of the GATT was: 'something less than an effective brake on the use of subsidies ... [and] there is no record of any country ever having limited a subsidizing practice as a result of consultations under Article XVI, paragraph 1'.[17]

In 1955, Article XVI was expanded to include a more specific provision on export subsidies.[18] The provision is relatively weak and in any event not all countries accepted it.[19] Under section B, Parties were obliged to seek to avoid the use of subsidies on the export of primary products. Any such subsidy should not be applied in such a way as to result in that Contracting Party having a 'more than equitable' share of world export trade in the subsidized product. With respect to non-primary products, Parties were to seek to avoid the use of subsidies that would result in export sales of a product at prices below the comparable price for the sale of the like good in the domestic market. The different treatment of primary and non-primary products was interpreted by developing countries as discrimination against their trade and they did not endorse this section of the Article.[20] The final amendment to Article XVI was made in 1960 when an illustrative list of export subsidies was developed to aid Parties in interpreting the provisions.[21]

The Tokyo Round Subsidies Code

As was the case with antidumping, the presence of an injury requirement in Article VI of the GATT did not affect the administration of countervailing duty laws in the USA. By virtue of the Protocol of Provisional Acceptance, domestic laws that were in existence at the time of the signing of the GATT took precedence over GATT obligations, leaving the US government 'free to countervail without demonstrable economic justification'.[22] For most nations, subsidies other than export subsidies were considered matters of national or internal policy. Therefore, the aim of the Tokyo Round negotiations on subsidies was to secure a binding requirement that countervailing duties only be imposed on subsidized products that are causing material injury to domestic producers. However, the USA, which felt strongly about the unfairness of subsidies, insisted that rules on countervail should only be addressed if an agreement to discipline subsidies more generally was reached.[23] In essence, there was a fundamental difference in approach to the issue of subsidies/countervailing measures.[24] The result of the conflict between the USA and other countries was the two-track approach laid out in the Tokyo Round Code on Subsidies and Countervailing Duties.

Track I

Track I of the Tokyo Round Subsidies Code deals entirely with unilateral responses to subsidies – i.e. the imposition of countervailing duties on subsidized imports causing injury to a domestic industry. Signatories have the authority to impose countervailing duties sufficient to counteract the foreign subsidy, or a lesser duty if this would be sufficient to alleviate the injury.[25] The procedural and substantive provisions are very similar to those on antidumping. Article 2(1) requires that sufficient evidence of subsidization, injury and a causal link between the imports and the injury be furnished before an investigation can be launched. The main weakness in the Code is that there is no clear definition of a countervailable subsidy. Because of the Code's silence on this issue, countries are given a great deal of latitude in defining 'subsidy' for countervailing duty purposes.[26]

Early in the negotiations, US negotiators conceded that an injury test was needed but they were concerned that '"material injury" meant something in US law – a degree of injury difficult to demonstrate – that went well beyond the understanding given the term under the GATT or under foreign country countervailing duty practice'.[27] The injury provision in the Subsidies Code is consonant with that in the Antidumping Code, also negotiated during the Tokyo Round. Rather than specifying the kind of injury that qualifies as sufficient for retaliation, it includes a list of criteria that should be used in making a determination of injury. The primary factors to be considered are the volume of subsidized imports, any increase in imports, either absolutely or relatively, and the existence of any price undercutting.[28] Moreover, the investigation shall also include an evaluation of 'all relevant economic factors and indices having a bearing on the state of the industry'. As in the Antidumping Code, causation is not defined. Article 6 of the Subsidies Code specifies that injury caused by other factors should not be attributed to the subsidized imports.[29] It is far from clear, however, that these guidelines are adequate to distinguish the effect of subsidization *per se* from that of import competition more generally.

There are extensive rules on the procedures to be followed in counter-vailing duty cases, including the right of Parties to have access to materials not 'by nature confidential' and the power of signatories to conduct investigations. For example, Article 8 authorizes signatories to conduct investigations in the territory of other signatories and on the premises of firms. According to Article 9, if any interested Party refuses to cooperate with the investigating authorities then the final determination can be made on the basis of the best available information. Upon determination of subsidization and injury, duties cannot be levied retroactively except for a period for which provisional measures have been applied (i.e. for the period following the initiation of the investigation). Except in special circumstances, investigations shall be concluded within one year of their initiation. Finally, countervailing duties can be maintained only as long as and to the extent necessary to counteract the subsidization which is causing the injury.

Track II

Track II has been the multilateral route for addressing subsidies. According to Barceló, it is 'a promising way of dealing with the genuine issues raised by subsidies'.[30] It is primarily concerned with obligations undertaken by signatories to reduce the incidence of trade-distorting subsidies and for the most part is an elaboration of Article XVI of the GATT. Countries agree to notify the Contracting Parties of any subsidies that may impact on exports or imports and undertake to avoid granting export subsidies[31] on other than primary products. Moreover, signatories are expected to avoid export subsidies on certain primary products if they serve to increase the signatory's share of world trade beyond what is equitable, account being taking of the share of the signatory in trade during a previous representative period. If an export subsidy is being maintained in a manner inconsistent with the Code, a signatory may request consultation with the offending country under Article 12(1). The matter may be referred to conciliation and panel review under Part VI of the Code if a mutually acceptable solution is not reached in thirty days.

Expanding on Article XVI of the GATT, the Code addresses domestic subsidies in Article 11. Signatories recognize that domestic subsidies are important instruments for the promotion of social and economic policy. The policy objectives that are recognized in the Code[32] are:

(a) the elimination of industrial, economic and social disadvantages of specific regions;
(b) to facilitate the restructuring, under socially acceptable conditions, of certain sectors, especially where this has become necessary by reason of changes in trade and economic policies, including international agreements resulting in lower barriers to trade;

(c) generally to sustain employment and to encourage re-training and change in employment;

(d) to encourage research and development programmes, especially in the field of high-technology industries;

(e) the implementation of economic programmes and policies to promote the economic and social development of developing countries;

(f) redeployment of industry in order to avoid congestion and environmental problems.

Furthermore, signatories 'do not intend to restrict the right of signatories to use such subsidies to achieve these and other important policy objectives which they consider desirable'.[33] When adopting policies that involve the granting of subsidies, Parties shall 'weigh, as far as is practicable, taking account of the nature of the particular case, possible adverse effects on trade'.[34] While they are recognized as legitimate, domestic subsidies can be challenged if they cause one of three effects:[35]

- injury to the domestic industry of another signatory;
- nullification or impairment of the benefits accruing to another signatory under the General Agreement;
- serious prejudice to the interests of another signatory.[36]

Unlike the Track I procedure, Track II does not permit the complainant to impose duties unilaterally to counteract an offensive subsidy. Articles 12 and 13 and Part VI lay out the dispute settlement procedure. First, the complainant signatory must consult with the country providing the subsidy. If no mutually acceptable solution to the matter can be reached then a panel will be formed by the Committee on Subsidies and Countervailing Measures.[37] This panel will be made up of three or five individuals, selected with a view to ensuring the independence of the members, a sufficiently diverse background and a wide spectrum of experience, from countries who are not Parties to the dispute.[38] The panel will review the facts and within sixty days after its establishment it will present to the Committee a report on its findings with respect to the rights and obligations of the signatories who are Parties to the dispute.[39] After consideration of the report, the Committee shall make recommendations to the Parties to the dispute. If these recommendations are not followed within a reasonable amount of time, the Committee can authorize countermeasures – including the withdrawal of GATT concessions or obligations. It is to be noted, however, that the obligations of the Parties are extremely weak beyond the prohibition of export subsidies on non-primary products.

Treatment of developing countries

It was clear during the negotiations that developing countries felt disadvantaged by the distinction between subsidies on primary and non-primary products. Most developed countries were interested in retaining the right to subsidize agriculture and other primary industries. Developing countries had different interests; specifically, many countries wanted to retain the right to use subsidies to encourage economic development. Article 14, in Part III of the Code, includes a recognition of the role of subsidies in the economic development policies of developing countries and lays out somewhat stricter rules governing actions against them under Track I. For example, there shall be no presumption that export subsidies granted by developing countries result in adverse affects to other signatories and therefore developing countries are not subject to the blanket prohibition of export subsidies. There are also restrictions on the rights of other signatories to take action against them under Track II. For example, with respect to domestic subsidies, action can only be taken against a developing country if the subsidies result in nullification or impairment of tariff concessions or other obligations in such a way as to displace or impede imports of like products into the subsidizing country, or unless Track I type injury occurs. Finally, if a developing country enters into a commitment to reduce or eliminate export subsidies, for the period of that commitment its subsidy practices shall not be subject to review by the Subsidies Committee.

The Uruguay Round Subsidies Agreement

Under the new Uruguay Round Subsidies Agreement, subsidies will be deemed to exist if there is a financial contribution by government or any public body where the government practice involves a direct transfer of funds (e.g. grants, loans, and equity infusion); potential direct transfers or liabilities (e.g. loan guarantees); government revenue that is otherwise due but is foregone; government provision of goods or services other than general infrastructure; government payments to a funding mechanism or direction to a private body to carry out any of the foregoing functions (Article 1.1). A definition of specificity is also adopted, which closely follows existing US countervailing duty law. This definition includes subsidies that are on their face limited to an enterprise or industry (or group of enterprises or industries), as well as subsidies that are *de facto* specific.

Subsidies are classified as actionable, non-actionable, and prohibited. Non-actionable subsidies include general non-specific subsidies such as spending on education or infrastructure, as well as some specific subsidies (Article 8). First, specific assistance for research activities conducted by firms or by higher education or research establishments on a contract basis with firms is not actionable if the assistance covers not more than 50% of the costs of basic industrial research or 25% of the costs of applied research.[40] Second, assistance to disadvantaged regions given pursuant to a general framework of regional development, and non-specific within eligible regions, is not actionable subject to certain conditions. Each disadvantaged region must be a clearly designated, continuous geographical area with a definable economic and administrative identity. The region must be considered as disadvantaged based on neutral and objective criteria, indicating that the region's difficulties arise out of more than temporary circumstances. The criteria include some measure of economic development which shall be based on at least one of the following factors (as measured over a three-year period): one of either income per capita or household income per capita, or GDP per capita, which must not be above 85% of the average for the country concerned; the unemployment rate which must be at least 110% of the average for the country concerned. Even these two forms of specific subsidies may be objectionable if a signatory can demonstrate that they have resulted in serious adverse effects to its domestic industry. Third, assistance to promote adaptation of existing facilities to new environmental requirements is non-actionable provided it is a one-off measure, is limited to 20% of the adaptation costs, does not cover the cost of replacing and operating the assisted investment, is directly limited to planned reduction in a firm's pollution and does not cover any manufacturing cost savings, and is available to all firms that can adopt the new equipment or processes.

Two kinds of subsidies are prohibited *per se*: subsidies contingent in law or in fact upon export performance (illustrated in an Annex to the Agreement), and subsidies contingent upon use of domestic rather than imported inputs (Article 3). Subsidies that are neither prohibited nor non-actionable are placed in the actionable category. Actionable subsidies are defined as specific forms of government assistance to firms or industries (Article 5). The list of legitimate grounds for domestic subsidies found in Article 11 of the Tokyo Round Subsidies Code has been dropped. Actionable subsidies may be objectionable if they cause injury to the domestic industry of another country, if they entail nullification or impairment of benefits accruing to another country under the GATT, including the benefits of concessions bound under Article II, or if they cause serious prejudice to the interests of another country. Serious prejudice may arise where the effect of the subsidy is to displace or impede the imports of like products into the market of the subsidizing signatory; where the effect of the subsidy is to displace or impede the export of a like product of another signatory from or to a third country market; where the effect of the subsidy is a significant price-undercutting by the subsidized products as compared with the price of a like product of another signatory in the same market; or where the effect of the subsidy is an increase in the world market share of the subsidizing signatory in a particular subsidized primary product or commodity as compared to the average share it had during the previous period of three years (Article 6.3). Prohibited (export) and actionable subsidies are subject to challenge under either the multilateral dispute resolution track or the domestic countervailing duty track. Non-actionable subsidies are immune from challenge under both tracks (Article 10, note 33). The imposition of countervailing duties in the case of a non-actionable subsidy could presumably lead to a request for review under the dispute resolution provisions of the Agreement, thus, for example, rendering US applications of the specificity criteria subject to multilateral review.

Part V of the Agreement sets out detailed rules governing countervailing duty actions. In most respects they follow the Tokyo Round Code. However, countervailing duties may only be imposed in respect of actionable or prohibited subsidies as defined in the Agreement. Article 11.9 also contains a *de minimis* provision which requires an investigation to be terminated if the amount of a subsidy is less than one percent *ad valorem* or where the volume of subsidized imports or the injury is negligible. Under Article 15.5, in determining material injury from subsidized imports, injuries caused by factors unrelated to the subsidized imports cannot be attributed to the imports; a number of these extraneous factors are enumerated in the Article. Under Article 21.3, duties must be terminated within five years of their imposition unless renewed following a review by the relevant domestic agency prior to that date.

With respect to institutional arrangements, the Subsidies Committee constituted under the Agreement shall establish a permanent Group of five Experts to prepare opinions on the existence of prohibited subsidies and to provide advisory opinions to the Committee on the existence and nature of any subsidy. The Group of Experts may be consulted by any signatory and give advisory opinions on the nature of any subsidy proposed to be introduced or currently maintained by that signatory, although such advisory opinions may not be invoked in proceedings before the Committee itself (Article 24). The consolidated dispute resolution mechanisms provided elsewhere in the Uruguay Round Agreement empower the Committee to constitute panels to review subsidy complaints.

Under Part VII of the Agreement, substantially enhanced notification and surveillance procedures with respect to subsidies are instituted, requiring signatories to report annually to the committee the existence of subsidies (as defined by the Agreement), and to provide substantial detail on the nature and effects of the subsidies. The Committee itself is required to engage in regular surveillance of these notifications.

With respect to developing countries, Part VIII provides some partial exemptions from the strictures in the Agreement. The provisions on prohibited subsidies do not apply to least developed countries, and other developing country signatories are provided with an eight year grace period to bring themselves into compliance with the prohibited subsidy provisions. The presumptive rules providing when actionable subsidies shall be deemed to result in serious prejudice (Article 6(1)) do not apply to developing countries with respect to whom such prejudice must be demonstrated by positive evidence. With respect to actionable subsidies, the dispute resolution process may not be invoked unless the subsidy entails nullification or impairment of tariff concessions or other obligations under the GATT in such a way as

to displace or impede imports of like products into the market of the subsidizing country or unless injury to the domestic industry in the importing
market of a signatory occurs as defined in the Agreement. Moreover,
countervailing duty actions shall not proceed if a domestic agency determines that the overall level of subsidy granted by a developing country upon
the product in question is 2% or less of its value calculated on a per unit
basis, and that the volume of the subsidized imports represents less than 4%
of the total imports for the like product in the importing signatory. This
exemption from countervailing duties only applies where developing countries collectively account for no more than 9% of the total imports for the
like product in the importing country. The comparable *de minimis* rule in
the case of subsides originating in developed signatories is one percent *ad
valorem* (Article 11.9). In the case of signatories in the process of transformation from a centrally planned to a market economy, prohibited subsidies
must be phased out within a period of seven years from the date of entry into
force of the Agreement. Subsidy programmes involving forgiveness of government debt and grants to cover debt repayment are not actionable for the
same period under the dispute resolution processes of the Agreement. With
respect to other actionable subsidies, the provisions applicable to developing
countries, which require nullification or impairment of tariff concessions or
other obligations under the GATT, are adopted (Article 29).

Protectionism in Government Procurement[41]

Government procurement policies pose a problem closely related to that of
potentially trade-distorting subsidies. In most countries, the government is
the largest single purchaser in the economy. In common law jurisdictions
(like Canada), the government's procurement contracts are usually
governed, in principle, by the same contract law that applies to private
transactions.[42] The process of government procurement is, however, unlike
private contracting in that governments tend to use their large purchasing
power as a tool to promote various domestic political, social, and economic
policies. These purposes of government procurement contracting lead to
the adoption of a wide range of measures that qualify the objective of
obtaining the best product or service for the lowest price.[43] The three most
common areas for domestic preference in government procurement are: (a)
to protect employment in declining industries; (b) to protect the supply of
'strategic' defence goods; and (c) to support emerging domestic high-tech
industries.

Domestic preference in government procurement contracting is usually
expressed in the form of either official domestic preference policies (overt
discrimination against foreign suppliers) or exclusionary tactics 'hidden' as
something else (less visible forms of discrimination).[44] Overtly discriminatory
tactics include:

1 Price differentials applied against foreign bids (whereby foreign bids may be accepted only if the lowest domestic bid is more than a certain percentage higher than the foreign one).[45]
2 'Discounts' for the domestic content of the bid.
3 Selective sourcing policies (whereby only domestic firms are invited to bid).[46]
4 Set-asides of certain procurements to specific domestic sectors.
5 Assignments of certain procurements for domestic industries only (for example, defence spending).
6 Requiring foreign contractors to procure from the local market as a condition of the award of the contract.

Less visible forms of discrimination include:

1 Selective tendering procedures, employed to (unofficially) exclude foreign competition.
2 Manipulating the time and method of giving notice of tender solicitations to favour domestic suppliers.
3 Short deadlines for submitting bids, which foreign suppliers are unable to meet.
4 Product or service standards which are only readily met by domestic producers.

The GATT Tokyo Round Code on Government Procurement

The GATT initially refrained almost completely from regulating government procurement policies: paragraph 8(a) of Article III makes government procurement an exception to the National Treatment obligation. However, this issue was re-examined during the Tokyo Round, and it was decided that the eventual elimination of discriminatory procurement practices was desirable.[47] The result of the ensuing negotiations was the Agreement on Government Procurement (the Code).[48]

The Tokyo Round Code on Government Procurement seeks to achieve greater liberalization of government procurement through the establishment of an agreed framework with respect to regulations, procedures and practices regarding government procurement. The Code not only establishes the obligation of National Treatment, but also sets out detailed rules for transparent procurement procedures that are to be followed in order to ensure that foreign suppliers indeed receive fair treatment.

The Code is, however, quite limited in scope and coverage. It only applies to contracts of a value of SDR 130,000 or more,[49] although there are procedures to prevent the evasion of this threshold.[50] Service contracts are not covered at all by the Code,[51] and Article VIII provides for other exceptions, notably in the area of defence spending. As well, the Code only applies to government agencies that 'contributed' to the Code, as listed in Annex I:13;

signatories normally exclude numerous departments from this list. State or municipal governments are also not covered by the Code.

The Code's provisions for National Treatment also raise several difficulties. First, these provisions are only available to suppliers from other signatories to the agreement, thus requiring rules of origin.[52] Second, these principles do not exempt foreign suppliers from customs duties. Third, Article V:15(b) allows governments to continue to demand offset industrial benefits (such as local content, licensing of technology, investment requirements, counter-trade or similar requirements) from potential foreign suppliers as a condition for awarding a contract.

The key mechanism of the Code is a set of detailed and transparent tendering procedures. The preferred procedure under the Code is the 'open' tender, in which a notice of each proposed purchase (NPP) is published in the designated publications, containing all of the information necessary for the timely submission of both foreign and domestic bids.[53] 'Selective' tendering procedures are also allowed, either by the use of previously established lists of suppliers, or by a qualification requirement as a precondition for the submission of bids; however, such lists and qualifications must be published, and they must not be used as a means of excluding foreign suppliers.[54] More problematic is the use of 'single' tendering procedures, where the government only considers tenders from a single source. In order to control the protectionist abuse of single tendering, the Code requires a report of justification to be published in an appropriate publication (as defined by the Code) in the event of a single tendering.[55]

The Code requires that a contract shall be awarded to the lowest tender, or to the tender which in terms of the specific evaluation criteria set forth in the NPP is determined to be the most advantageous.[56] The use of technical specifications to refuse the award to a foreign firm, a common device used by governments to exclude foreign suppliers from tender competition, is regulated under Article IV:2(a). Technical specifications prescribed by procurement entities shall be in terms of performance rather than design, and should also be based on international standards if possible.

The Code provides for a system of enforcement and dispute resolution. The emphasis has been on the settlement of disputes between the states involved, rather than the granting of a private right of action to an aggrieved supplier: mechanisms for the hearing of private complaints have been left to the discretion of the procuring agency.[57] Between governments, Article VII of the Code envisages a three-stage complaints proceeding: first, bilateral consultations will be held; second, if these produce no result, the Committee on Government Procurement will mediate; and third, if mediation fails, the Committee will constitute an *ad hoc* panel to make recommendations. Panel decisions are non-binding, but the Committee may recommend the authorization of the suspension of the application of the Code *vis-à-vis* the suppliers of the non-complying Party.[58]

Changes in government procurement under the Uruguay Round Agreement

The GATT Code has been substantially revised during the Uruguay Round negotiations in an attempt to address the difficulties in the Code's operation noted by the Parties.[59] These revisions have the effect of harmonizing the GATT Code with the NAFTA agreement on government procurement (see below). There are three key areas of change in the revised GATT Agreement: first, the scope and coverage of the agreement has been expanded to include service and construction contracts;[60] second, contracting entities are no longer able to demand offsets as a condition for the awarding of contracts;[61] and third, the Parties are now required to establish effective bid challenge procedures.[62]

The establishment of mandatory bid challenge procedures, by which aggrieved foreign suppliers may challenge alleged breaches of the Agreement directly, is potentially the most important change in the Uruguay Round Code. Under this requirement, each Party to the Agreement will have to establish impartial review bodies to adjudicate procurement disputes in a timely fashion. However, as is noted in Article XX:7(c), the compensation provided to the aggrieved supplier may be limited to the costs for tender preparation or protest, a sum which may be insufficient to deter governments from effectively breaching their obligations under the Agreement.

An important new aspect of the Uruguay Round Agreement is the expansion of the scope and coverage of the Agreement to include certain 'sub-central government' (or state, provincial and municipal) entities. Each Party is responsible for listing in Appendix I all entities within its jurisdiction to be covered by the Agreement, and each Party may withdraw one of the listed entities at will (subject to objections from other Parties, which are to be resolved in accordance with the procedures on consultations and dispute settlement contained in Article XXII). If major changes to the existing structure are requested by one of the Parties, such as transfers of entities between categories within Appendix I, the Committee on Government Procurement (established by Article XXI) will consider the proposed change and determine if compensatory adjustments are necessary.

The Uruguay Round Procurement Agreement will enter into force on 1 January 1996, with the exception of the procedures on consultations and dispute settlement (Article XXII), which are contingent on the entry into force of the WTO Agreement.

Government procurement under the Canada-US FTA

As a result of the limited coverage of the pre-Uruguay GATT Code, many Canadian and US firms were still subject to the protectionist procurement policies of each other's governments. In the USA, these measures included the Buy American Act, which required that only domestic supplies be purchased for public use, subject to an exception for 'unreasonably' priced domestic alternative products. The American government also protects domestic concerns through various 'set-aside' provisions, notably to benefit businesses owned by 'socially or economically disadvantaged individuals', a category which automatically excludes foreign suppliers.

The Canadian procurement policies are not regulated by statute, but rather by administrative directives. The most important of these is the Canadian Content Premium Policy, under which the Department of Supply and Services will apply a premium of 10% of the difference in foreign content on competing bids in favour of sources with greater Canadian content. As well, when the value of a procurement exceeds $2 million, the 'procurement review mechanism' is triggered, with the purpose of ensuring that the awarding of the contract will achieve the 'maximum benefit to Canada'.[63] These administrative directives are only in effect for government contracts not covered by international agreements, but before the implementation of the FTA they were an important method of ensuring domestic preferment for contracts not covered by the GATT Code.

The FTA represents an attempt to liberalize government procurement that was not covered under the GATT Code from the effects of these domestic preference policies. However, Chapter 13 of the FTA actually changed little from the Code.[64] The most important changes it made were: first, to lower the threshold of eligibility from SDR 130,000 to $US25,000; second, to enable eligible Canadian goods to be treated like US goods (including 'Buy American' differentials);[65] and, third, the establishment of a requirement for domestic procurement review, available to aggrieved suppliers.

In Canada, the Procurement Review Board was established to fulfil this obligation. Governed by both the procedures of the GATT Code and the 'expanded' obligations under Article 1305 of the FTA, the board has the authority to order the government to postpone the awarding of a contract pending the termination of the board's investigation. However, the board is subject to a bizarre limitation: in order to reserve the benefit of the board to Canadian and American suppliers, it may only review procurements of a value more than the FTA threshold, and yet less than the GATT threshold. Large procurement awards are thus immune from scrutiny by the board. Of course, with the establishment of an international obligation for bid challenge procedures under the Uruguay Round GATT Agreement, this limitation will no longer be necessary.

Changes in government procurement under NAFTA

NAFTA's Chapter 10 provides for considerably wider coverage than either the pre-Uruguay Round GATT Code or the FTA, both in terms of entities and types of contracts covered. Not only does NAFTA extend the improvements available under the FTA to Mexico, it also extends coverage to many federal government agencies not covered by either the FTA or the Code.[66] NAFTA also closed some previously-existing exclusions in the earlier agreements, such as construction and service contracts (which are now covered) and the imposition by procurement entities of offset requirements (which are now prohibited).[67]

Threshold values were, however, raised under NAFTA to $US50,000 (this provision, however, applies only to Mexico: for Canada and the USA, the FTA threshold of $US25,000 still applies). For the newly-covered area of construction services, the threshold has been set at $US6.5 million. For 'government enterprises', as opposed to federal government entities, the thresholds are higher still: $US250,000 for goods and services, and $US8 million for construction services.

One major problem with the NAFTA procurement rules lies in the area of tendering procedures. Article 1009 of NAFTA allows more restrictive 'qualification procedures' than the FTA, which may be used to exclude foreign tenders.

The process of liberalizing North American government procurement markets under NAFTA is still far from complete. Under Article 1024, the Parties have agreed to commence further negotiations no later than 1998, with a view to further liberalization of their respective government procurement markets. Prior to that date, the Parties have agreed to attempt to obtain the voluntary acceptance, by state and provincial government entities, of the principles contained in this chapter. As well, the Parties have also agreed to increase their obligations and coverage under this chapter to a level at least commensurate with the final version of the GATT Agreement.

Procurement markets in the European Union

The European Union has attempted to regulate the domestic preferment policies of its Member States with regard to government procurement through a series of co-ordination directives. The legal effect of these directives are that aggrieved suppliers can, at least in principle, invoke the provisions of the procurement directives directly in the national courts of the Member States.

The original directives issued by the commission were the Public Works directive and the Public Supplies directive.[68] These directives were based on three main principles: first, community-wide advertising of contracts, in order to give equal opportunity to firms from all Member States; second, the banning of 'discriminatory' technical specifications; and third, the use of objective and non-discriminatory criteria in tendering and award procedures.

The major problems with these directives were their limited coverage (the so-called 'excluded sectors' included energy, water, transportation and telecommunication), and their high value thresholds (after amendment, ECU 5,000,000 for the Works directive, and ECU 130,000 for the Supplies directive). Another major problem lay in the excessive discretion given to awarding entities to choose their tendering procedures.

Under the co-ordination directives, three different tendering procedures are allowed: 'open' and 'restrictive' competitive tendering, and non-competitive 'negotiated' tendering. In 'restrictive' tendering, the awarding authority advertises its intention to receive requests to participate in the tender for a specific contract; the authority may then choose the applicants to whom invitations to submit tenders will be sent. This system can obviously be abused, although amendments to the directives now curtail the awarding authorities' discretion somewhat (requiring, for example, justification for the use of 'restrictive' tendering procedures under the supplies directive, and the publication of the reasons for both winning and losing bids under the works directive). An additional opportunity for abuse was created by the fact that non-competitive tendering was originally allowed in exceptional circumstances, although the Member State's use of these exceptions was required to be reported.[69]

Experience with the operation of the co-ordination directives soon demonstrated that redress for aggrieved suppliers in the offending nation's national courts was uneven. To remedy this situation, the Review directive was implemented.[70] This directive requires members to provide effective domestic review procedures with the power to suspend the awarding of contracts, to set aside awarding entities decisions, and to award damages to aggrieved suppliers.

The Commission also made an attempt to apply the Union procurement rules to the traditionally excluded utilities sectors by implementing the Utilities directive.[71] This directive applies both to public authorities and to private firms operating on the basis of 'special or exclusive rights' granted by a member state (to avoid the public/private distinction in the legal status of the entities involved). Due to the 'special nature' of the concerned undertakings, awarding entities were allowed considerable discretion in their choice of tendering procedures, and were in addition allowed to use an unspecified 'qualification system' to screen potential tenders.

The Commission, recognizing the special status of the 'excluded sectors', also adopted a Utilities Review directive applicable only to the Utilities directive.[72] Like the regular review directive, it requires Member States to provide effective review procedures in relation to all decisions taken by their contracting entities. As an alternative to this mandatory remedy, the Utilities Review directive adopted two voluntary procedures: the attestation system, in which the awarding entity submits to systematic review by attestors (independent and objective witnesses to the entity's conformity with the requirements); and the conciliation procedure, in which aggrieved bidders and contracting entities settle their disputes through a non-litigious process of negotiation mediated by a Commission-appointed conciliator. In general, these review procedures allow the Member States wide discretion in determining what procedures they will follow.

DOMESTIC ADMINISTRATION OF
COUNTERVAILING DUTY LAWS[73]

Institutional context

Because the USA is almost the exclusive user of countervailing duty laws, it is important to understand the institutions and methodologies it employs to administer those laws. Four institutions are involved in the administration of US countervailing duty laws: the International Trade Administration of the Department of Commerce (DC), the International Trade Commission (ITC), the Court of International Trade (CIT) and the review panels established under Chapter 19 of the Canada-USA Free Trade Agreement (FTA) and NAFTA.

The International Trade Administration is the branch of the DC responsible for the enforcement of antidumping and countervailing duty laws. It is responsible for conducting antidumping and countervailing duty investigations and has the authority to initiate investigations.[74] In countervailing duty cases the DC determines whether the products under investigation are being unlawfully subsidized, and if so, calculates the margin of subsidization and the appropriate duties. Further responsibilities include conducting administrative reviews of outstanding countervailing duty orders and ensuring that these orders are properly administered by customs officials.

The ITC is the body responsible for establishing the existence of actual or threatened material injury due to subsidized imports. The CIT is the American court with competence to review determinations of the DC and ITC. Under Chapter 19 of the FTA and NAFTA, binational panels are appointed to hear disputes arising out of countervailing duty actions between the Parties to the Agreement.

Substantive law

In the USA, laws dealing with unfair foreign subsidization date back to the Tariff Act of 1897. Current US legislation is found in the Trade Agreements Act of 1979 which amended the Tariff Act of 1930. In a countervailing duty action, there are two central questions that must be answered: Is the foreign producer who is selling into the domestic market receiving an actionable subsidy from its home government? Are domestic producers of products like or competitive with those being subsidized suffering or being threatened with material injury as a result of the subsidized imports?

Subsidies

According to the Tariff Act, a countervailing duty will be imposed on imported goods when it is found that the country is directly or indirectly subsidizing the manufacture, production, or exportation of goods imported into the USA.[75] The application of this provision depends on the meaning given to the word 'subsidy'. Defined broadly, the term could include everything from the provision of basic infrastructure to government financed education and regional development programmes. Such a definition would effectively undermine liberal trade 'since virtually every product would benefit from these kinds of government assistance'[76] and hence could be subject to a countervailing duty. The US legislation begins its definition in §1677(5) by making clear that the term 'subsidy' has the same meaning as the phrase 'bounty or grant' and includes but is not limited to export subsidies and domestic subsidies.

Export subsidies

As reflected in Track I of the Tokyo Round Code and the definition of prohibited subsidies in the Uruguay Round Agreement, export subsidies are probably considered the most objectionable form of government assistance. An export subsidy can be defined as government programmes or practices that increase the profitability of export sales without similarly increasing the profitability of domestic sales.[77] The US legislation has no explicit definition of this concept, and instead refers in §1677(5)(A) to the illustrative list of export subsidies found in the Tokyo Round Subsidies Code (largely reproduced in Annex I to the Uruguay Round Agreement). Some examples of the enumerated practices are:

- the provision by governments of direct subsidies to a firm or an industry contingent upon export performance;
- currency retention schemes or any similar practices that involve a bonus on exports; and
- internal transport and freight charges on export shipments provided or mandated by governments, on terms more favourable than for domestic shipments.

The DC has the authority to find that practices not on the list are export subsidies.[78] Even with the benefit of the list, it is often difficult to identify export subsidies.[79] Because export subsidies will generally result in assessment of larger duties than would be applicable to domestic subsidies, the determination of whether a subsidy is an export or domestic subsidy is important.[80]

Domestic subsidies: the Specificity Test

International rules are more lenient with respect to subsidies not targeted specifically at exporters. The hostility to pure export subsidies probably reflects the view that most legitimate domestic policy rationales for subsidies would not differentiate between production intended for domestic consumption and production intended for export. In addition, export subsidies raise concerns over the prospect of mutually destructive international export subsidy wars. However, in the countervailing duty provisions of the Tokyo and Uruguay Subsidies Codes there is no differentiation between domestic or export subsidies. In the USA, practices that cannot be characterized as export subsidies are countervailable if they fall within the definition of domestic subsidies in §1677(5) of the Tariff Act. Countervailable domestic subsidies are defined as subsidies targeted to a *specific* enterprise or industry, or group of enterprises or industries. In addition, the subsidies must provide some opportunity or advantage to the targeted producers that would not otherwise be available to them in the marketplace.[81] The wording of this definition has given rise to the Specificity Test for the assessment of the countervailability of domestic subsidies. This test has developed over time into one that investigates not only *de jure* but also *de facto* specificity. Under this test, where either the purpose or the effect of a government programme is to benefit a specific enterprise or industry, or group of enterprises or industries, the DC will find that a countervailable benefit has been conferred. Included in this definition are forms of assistance such as capital, loans or loan guarantees on terms inconsistent with commercial considerations, goods or services at preferential rates, funds or forgiven debts to cover operating losses, and the assumption of costs or expenses of manufacture, production or distribution.

In the early 1980s, there was a significant degree of controversy in the USA over whether the specificity test should be retained in its current form.[82] The CIT, on review of DC decisions also created some confusion on this issue. In *Carlisle Tire and Rubber Co.* v. *United States*,[83] the Court upheld the DC's decision in favour of Korean exporters benefiting from a generally available accelerated depreciation programme. The court found that in order for a countervailable domestic subsidy to exist, there must be evidence of a regional or industry preference. However, subsequent cases suggest that this interpretation of the specificity test no longer obtains. For example, in *Cabot Corp.* v. *United States*,[84] the CIT held that the specificity test upheld in *Carlisle* is not the correct legal standard to apply; it would erroneously allow the recipients of subsidies purportedly of general availability to avoid countervailing duties even though the subsidies in fact only benefit specific industries or enterprises.

The *Cabot* decision resulted in a change in DC methodology. It led to the articulation of the DC's current approach: the three pronged specificity test.[85] The DC now proceeds through a series of steps in its investigation before being satisfied that the subsidy in question is not countervailable. First, a *de jure* limitation on the availability of a subsidy is sufficient to find specificity. Second, if the subsidy is generally available but few enterprises actually use the programme, or if there are disproportionate or dominant users, the DC will find *de facto* specificity. Third, if a foreign government is exercising its discretion in such a manner that a *de jure* generally available programme is *de facto* specifically targeted, the DC will again find *de facto* specificity. This formulation of the specificity test has increased the DC's discretion and thus reduced predictability for exporters in countervailing duty cases.[86] This definition of specificity is largely adopted in the Uruguay Round Agreement definition of actionable subsidies.

There are a number of noteworthy aspects of US countervailing duty laws.[87] First, countervailing duty actions cannot be taken against non-market economies,[88] although given the recent transformation of many of the former command economies, there is considerable room for ambiguity as to which countries presently are non-market economies. Second, subsidies indirectly received by an exporter, such as through a subsidized input source, can be countervailable. However, if it is alleged that an indirect subsidy was received by a company via a subsidy given to another company upstream,[89] the DC will not assume that benefits conferred by the subsidy are passed on to the second company.[90] In cases entailing allegations of these 'upstream subsidies', it must be shown that there is an indirect subsidy before countervailing duties will be assessed. In addition, the upstream subsidy must confer a competitive benefit on the goods under investigation and have a significant effect on their cost of production.[91] It is also not sufficient to show that a subsidy programme exists; the specific product being investigated must have been subsidized.[92] Benefits conferred by private individuals may be countervailable if the evidence indicates that the benefit was conferred at the request of the government.[93] Finally, countervailing duty petitions or orders cannot be suspended or overturned by the executive for political reasons.[94]

Calculation of countervailing duties

According to Article 19.4 of the Uruguay Round Subsidies Agreement: 'No countervailing duty shall be levied on any imported product in excess of the amount of subsidy found to exist, calculated in terms of subsidization per unit of the subsidized product and exported product.' Article 19.4 provides that it is desirable that the duty should be less than the total amount of the subsidy if such lesser duty would be adequate to remove the injury to the domestic industry and that procedures should be established which would allow domestic authorities to take account of representations by domestic interests, including consumers, who may be adversely affected by the imposition of duties.

The task of the DC at this stage of proceedings is to determine the amount of the countervailing duty required to protect US producers from the injury created by the subsidy.[95] In order to achieve this, the value of the subsidy is measured with reference to the benefit conferred upon the targeted industry rather than the cost of the subsidy to the government.[96] However, the DC does not evaluate the effect of the subsidy on the cost of production, quantities produced, or prices charged by the foreign exporting firm. Nor does it evaluate its effect on similar aspects of the sales of US firms. As a result it is not clear that the methodology accurately captures competitively salient benefits to the firm. The subsidy may not result in lower costs or higher production; it may, for example, result in greater inefficiency on the part of the producer. Alternatively, the subsidy may have no effect on the costs of production because of the nature of the subsidy. For example, if the grant is to pay for the decommissioning of an old plant, there would no be effect on the marginal costs of production of the firm.[97]

The net subsidy is found by making certain adjustments to the subsidy amount conferred.[98] The countervailing duty is found by dividing the net subsidy by the total sales of the company receiving the subsidy. If the government practice is found to be an export subsidy then the counter-vailing duty is calculated by dividing the net subsidy by the total exports of the company receiving the subsidy; since total sales will generally be larger than exports, export subsidies will generally result in higher duties.[99] The DC will not impose duties against subsidies that are *de minimis*, comprising less than 0.5 % of the *ad valorem* value of the merchandise (increased to one percent under Article 11.9 of the Uruguay Round Agreement).

Injury[100]

Prior to the Tokyo Round, US law on countervailing (and antidumping) duties did not contain an injury requirement; both forms of duties could be applied without any showing of harm to domestic firms from the foreign action. The purpose of an injury test is to ensure that duties are only imposed in cases in which a causal nexus is found between the unfair foreign practice and harm suffered by the domestic industry. This requirement is intended to reduce protectionist use of the laws by uncompetitive domestic industries. The injury requirement adopted in the GATT Codes is the same as that in the Antidumping Code and antidumping and countervailing duty cases are treated in the same way by the ITC.[101] The subsidized imports must cause material injury or a threat of material injury to a domestic indus-try, or material retardation to the establishment of a domestic industry. There are three components to the injury test: (1) the definition of domes-tic industry; (2) evidence of material injury; and (3) a causal nexus between that injury and the subsidized imports.

Domestic industry

The injury proceeding before the ITC requires that the ITC first define the relevant US industry. The Uruguay Round Subsidies Agreements defines 'domestic industry' as 'domestic producers as a whole of the like product or those of them whose collective output of the products constitute a major proportion of the total domestic production of those products'.[102] The US legislation adopts a similar definition.[103] Under the Uruguay Round Subsidies Agreement, no investigation may be initiated if the domestic producers expressly supporting the application account for less than 25% of total production of the product by the domestic industry (Article 11.4). In special circumstances the ITC can divide the industry into separate geographical markets if two conditions are met: (1) the companies in that region must sell all or almost all of their output of the like product in the geographical region; and (2) demand in that region must not be substantially supplied by US producers outside of the region.[104] As is the case with antidumping investigations, a narrow construction of the relevant domestic industry can make a finding of injury more likely.

The 'like product' is defined as 'a product which is like, or in the absence of like, most similar in characteristics and uses with' the product under investigation.[105] The 'characteristics and uses' test has led to determinations such as that in *Lamb Meat from New Zealand*[106] that fresh and frozen lamb meat are one like product. In analysing the complaint, the ITC must focus on the narrowest range of products that includes the like product, but in many cases must investigate a broader industry due to the unavailability of data. In addition, there may be more than one like product.[107]

Material injury

There is no definition in the Uruguay Round Agreement of 'material injury' but the Agreement directs authorities to examine a number of specific factors such as changes in output, prices, employment or profitability in the domestic industry.[108] In the USA, most cases focus on actual or threatened material injury, which is defined as harm that is not 'inconsequential, immaterial or unimportant'.[109] The injury test requires an analysis of domestic industry conditions. The factors that are to be considered in this analysis are laid out in 19 U.S.C. §1677(7)(B). The factors typically considered by the ITC in this determination are the volume of subsidized imports, their effect on domestic prices of like products, and their impact on domestic producers of like products. In its evaluation of the volume of imports, the ITC considers both the absolute level of imports at the time of the proceeding and whether the level is increasing either relatively or absolutely.[110] With respect to the effect on prices, the ITC considers any evidence of undercutting and determines whether there is any indication that the effect of the subsidization has been to depress domestic prices.[111] The presence of certain negative factors such as plant closures or unprofitability will often be sufficient to convince the ITC that the injury test has been satisfied. In other cases the ITC will compare certain economic variables to their levels in previous years, inferring from a decline in such variables the presence of injury.[112] Such variables might include capacity utilization, employment, or return on equity. If these factors do not provide the ITC with evidence of material injury, the investigation will be terminated and no duties will be assessed against the exporters. The ITC's investigations are divided into a preliminary and a final phase. In the preliminary phase the ITC must determine if there is a reasonable indication of injury. Inconclusive or incomplete evidence related to the key elements may support an affirmative preliminary finding of injury but not be adequate to support a final determination of injury. In both cases, the ITC must make its determination on the basis of all the evidence before it.

Causation[113]

There is no precise definition in the Uruguay Round Agreement of 'cause', beyond a list of factors that may be examined,[114] leaving the appropriate standard to the discretion of the investigating authorities. The ITC looks for a causal nexus between the subsidization and the effects on the domestic industry. Factors that are typically considered in this context are the presence of underselling, evidence of lost sales, and import trends in the industry.[115] There are a number of weaknesses with this approach to causation. First, these three factors do not define a test capable of resolution: 'the test mixes analysis of trend information unrelated to dumping or subsidization with analysis of the effects of dumped or subsidized imports'[116] and the US legislation does not 'identify a method of integrating these factors into a cogent analytical structure'.[117] Moreover, the assumption that declining performance alone is evidence of harm caused by imports does not account for other factors that affect performance, or the possibility that the harm is due to import competition and not subsidization. Thus, because the ITC methodology focuses on the imports rather than the subsidization, an affirmative finding might result when the harm is caused by reason of comparative advantages that the imported goods might possess. Finally, the three criteria usually considered – evidence of underselling or lost sales, and import trends – do not serve to identify clearly the relationship between the subsidization and the harm. For example, evidence of lost sales suffered by the domestic industry only provides relevant causal information if it can be shown that those sales were gained by the subsidized importers by reason of the subsidization. At present the ITC does not evaluate the kind of evidence or perform the kind of counterfactual that would justify a determination of causation.

Rights of appeal

The Court of International Trade (CIT) is the US Court vested with jurisdiction to review ITC and DC rulings. In practice, the CIT has been highly deferential to these administrative bodies. Underlying this disposition is the view that administrative bodies have extensive expertise and therefore have comparative competence in those matters that fall within their jurisdiction.

One limitation that the CIT has regularly imposed is that the ITC and DC provide the reasons supporting their determination. However, if those reasons allow the CIT 'reasonably to discern the agency's path,' a decision of 'less than ideal clarity' will be upheld.[118] In some cases, the CIT requires that the agency determination be supported by substantial evidence on the record,[119] but this approach is infrequently adopted.

Chapter 19 of the FTA provides for the establishment of binational review panels to hear disputes arising between the Parties to the Agreement.[120] Either Party may request review by the binational panel and its determinations are final except in extraordinary circumstances.[121] These panels have authority to determine that there has been either an error of law by the administrative agency or that the evidence on the record was insufficient to support the decision at that level. While the panel cannot overturn the administrative decision, its remanding of the decision to the appropriate agency generally forces compliance due to political repercussions that would result if no action were taken. Evidence to date suggests that the binational panel review process has led to significant improvements in the level of rigour required of the ITA and ITC in countervailing and antidumping duty determinations.[122] Similar procedures are provided for in Chapter 19 of NAFTA.

RATIONALES FOR EXISTING LAWS

Traditionally, the legitimacy of countervailing duty laws has depended on the characterization of subsidies as harmful in some way and on evidence that offsetting countervailing duties repair that harm. Advocates of countervailing duty laws offer two main characterizations of subsidies that give rise to an argument in favour of countervailing duties. First, subsidies are often characterized as inefficient and introducing distortions into world trade. Second, subsidies are characterized as being unfair and disturbing the 'level playing field' of international trade.

Efficiency rationales

The traditional argument for countervailing duties is that subsidies distort comparative advantage and hence lead to the inefficient allocation of global economic resources. However, plausible characterization of many subsidies is that they correct or compensate for market imperfections or externalities that would otherwise exist, and thus enhance efficient-resource allocation.[123] In many cases subsidies serve to produce 'a more efficient resource allocation, that is, resource allocation more consonant with the actual production possibilities and consumer preferences than that yielded by wholly private transactions'.[124] The task of evaluating whether subsidies contribute to or derogate from efficient resource allocation is daunting. According to Schwartz and Harper, the exercise is at best highly indeterminate because of three factors: (a) the pervasiveness of externalities which subsidies may help internalize; (b) what the authors rather opaquely call potential private–public intersectorial economies, which embrace the collective validation of all kinds of preferences that may not be adequately captured in private market transactions (e.g. protection of national security, preserving the family farm and rural lifestyles, promoting regional development, etc.); and (c) the possibility that a positive government benefit to a firm may be designed to offset some other burden that has been imposed by government (e.g., high minimum wage laws, stringent occupational health and safety requirements, plant closing or environmental obligations).

Even if subsidies are truly distortive of international trade, the question that remains is whether countervailing duty laws improve resource allocation. It is clear from the previous section that the methodology currently used in the calculation of subsidy margins does not serve to determine accurately the duties needed to offset the effects of trade distortions. Moreover, it has now been convincingly demonstrated[125] that in almost every conceivable set of circumstances, countervailing duties reduce domestic social welfare in the *importing* country, where social welfare is defined as the maximization of producer, consumer and government surplus. Gains to domestic producers from the higher prices induced by the duties are offset by losses to consumers who remain in the market and pay the higher prices, while some consumers who would have purchased the product are priced out of the market and suffer welfare losses. Even accounting for the increase in government surplus in terms of increased revenue from duties, consumer losses outweigh all gains, leaving total welfare lower. Thus, however, ambiguous the welfare effects of a subsidy either in the country providing it or globally, there is nothing ambiguous about the welfare effects of the subsidy in the importing country. This analysis suggests that rather than condemning foreign subsidies, importing countries should send expressions of their gratitude to the subsidizing country, noting only their regret that the subsidies are not larger and timeless.

A further efficiency argument that is sometimes directed against subsidies is that government support in the form of export subsidies is intended or at least serves to assist firms in practising predatory pricing. It is argued that subsidies enable a firm to sell at a lower price in the foreign market in order to eliminate competition and thereafter reap monopoly profits.[126] Predation nationally or internationally is a practice that unambiguously lowers economic welfare. However, in the previous chapter on antidumping laws, we argued that there is little theoretical or empirical basis for allegations of predation in international trade. Moreover, current countervailing duty laws do not consider factors that would support a claim of predation, such as industry concentration and barriers to entry. As in the case of antidumping, concerns over predation (potentially a valid reason for the prevention of some forms of subsidization) do not justify existing countervailing duty laws.

Fairness rationales

The level playing field rationale

Some advocates of countervailing duties argue that subsidies constitute unfair trade and disturb the 'level-playing field' in international trade. Professor Robert Hudec, a distinguished international trade law scholar, in a recent paper[127] provides a useful taxonomy of many of the unfair trade claims that presently enjoy wide currency. He draws a basic distinction between what he calls offensive 'unfairness' and defensive 'unfairness'. With respect to offensive unfairness, the claim is often made that domestic policies adopted by governments in exporters' countries of origin provide them with unfair advantages in competing in importing country markets or in third country markets. With respect to defensive unfairness, the claim is often made that a country is adopting domestic policies that unfairly favour its own products and unfairly penalize foreign producers who wish to sell into this country's market.

In the case of countervailing duty laws, the complaint of offensive unfairness focuses on the fact that foreign firms are able to out-compete domestic firms in the latter's market as a result of some artificial advantage that the foreign firms enjoy by virtue of government subsidies or other benefits conferred on them in their country of origin. This unfairness claim is difficult both to unravel and to contain.[128] At one level, even in the case of an explicit export subsidy, one can reasonably argue that, as suggested above, consumers in the export market are better off as a result of the foreign subsidy and that it should be viewed as a form of foreign aid that on balance increases the welfare of citizens in the importing country. At another level, the claim of unfairness relating to foreign governments' actions has no natural limits to it. Unless one is prepared to adopt a *laissez-faire* baseline as one's normative reference point, and to view every government deviation from this baseline as a form of unfairness where it has some impact on the pattern of international trade, one is quickly forced to accept that almost everything that modern governments do is likely, either directly or indirectly, to affect the pattern of economic activities within a country and therefore, by extension, the pattern of international trade flows to which that country contributes. For example, such basic activities of governments as investments in physical infrastructure e.g. roads and communication systems, investments in public education and basic research, investments in law and order, investments in health care systems etc. all shape in one way or another a country's comparative advantages or disadvantages in international trade.

According to liberal trade theory, only if differing productive conditions exist across countries can gains be derived from international trade; countries will specialize in the production of the goods that they can produce relatively cheaply, and purchase from abroad, at lower cost, goods in which they have a comparative disadvantage. If all countries were to have identical productive conditions, then no country would have a comparative advantage in the production of any good and there would be no gains from trade. Thus, if subsidies disturb the 'level playing field' they serve to increase potential gains from trade.[129] At least, it could be argued that differing subsidization policies across countries, like different education levels or different tax structures, are simply one of the factors that contribute to different productive conditions across countries. Moreover, it is to point out the obvious that, given an assumption of scarce resources, a country that chooses to subsidize one set of activities cannot subsidize another set of activities, which some of its trading partners may, as a matter of domestic policy priorities, choose to subsidize instead.

In recent debates where these kinds of claims of offensive unfairness are made, three new areas have emerged.[130] First, it is sometimes argued that the quiescent state of Japanese competition/anti-trust law permits Japanese firms, through acquisition of dominant market positions or through collusive arrangements in Japan, to garner supra-normal profits in the Japanese market and to use these to fund subsequent aggressive export initiatives. Second, it is widely claimed that lax environmental laws in many countries constitute a form of implicit subsidy that confer on firms originating in these countries an artificial advantage in export markets. Third, it is often argued that weak labour laws pertaining to such matters as minimum wages, hours of work, child labour, workplace safety conditions, again operate as implicit subsidies to firms located in countries with such policies and confer on them an artificial advantage in export markets. In all three cases, the policy choices for governments in importing countries are either to attempt to persuade or induce the country of origin to harmonize its laws up to the standards prevailing in the importing country; or for the importing country to harmonize its laws down to the level of those prevailing in the exporting country; or to harmonize to some agreed intermediate solution; or to impose unilaterally some border measure, like a countervailing duty, designed to neutralize whatever artificial advantages are claimed to be associated with these domestic policy differences.

As Bhagwati points out,[131] fairness arguments can be pushed to almost any lengths:

If Bangladesh has a current comparative advantage in textiles, due to lower wages, we no longer need to worry about being scolded as protectionists when we reject imports of Bangladeshi textiles as unfair trade caused by her 'pauper labour'. After all, the low Bangladeshi wages are a result of inadequate population control *policies* and of inefficient economic policies that inhibit investment and growth and hence a rise in real wages. In like manner, if the United States continues to produce textiles, which rely heavily on immigrant labor, often illegal, this is unfair trade, since American immigration *policy* encourages this outcome, and therefore a Structural Impediments Initiative demand for changed immigration policy needs to be made against the United States simply to ensure level playing fields.

This is not to argue that claims of unfairness have no role at all in international trade law. The impact of the EU Common Agricultural Policy, and offsetting US subsidy policies, on the Prairie wheat economy in Canada is a particularly pressing and immediate example of what is at stake. Current debates within the European Union, the negotiation of side accords to the North American Free Trade Agreement (NAFTA) on labour and environmental standards, and indeed constitutional debates within Canada, over the case for a social charter or social base-lines as a necessary corollary to proposals for greater economic integration, all serve to further highlight the importance that these issues have assumed. Issues pertaining to recognition or harmonization of environmental and labour standards are pursued in later chapters.[132] With firms and corporate business arrangements increasingly assuming a multi-national character, the harmonization of competition laws has also taken on increasing importance, if only to avoid interjurisdictional conflicts, as noted in the conclusions to the previous chapter.[133] Rather, it must be emphasized that economists, lawyers and other trade policy analysts now face an urgent task in introducing a substantial measure of coherence and discipline into these fairness claims, both at the theoretical and operational level, so that they can be contained within defensible bounds. We return to this question in the concluding chapter of this book.

Unfair impact rationales

Even if there are no efficiency or fair trade rationales that justify counter-vailing duty laws, there are possible arguments for countervailing duty laws that take account of the disruptive impact of imports on vulnerable members of society. In particular, it may be that distributive justice or communitarian values can be vindicated through the use of this form of protectionism. On distributive justice grounds, countervailing duty laws might be justifiable to the extent that they improve the lot of the least-advantaged members of society.[134] However, countervailing duty laws are not designed to address these concerns. As was suggested in the previous section, the application of countervailing duties focuses on factors ill-suited to uncovering any injury suffered by an industry as a result of foreign subsidies and factors even less well-suited to discovering the impact on the least advantaged stake-holders in these industries. In addition, as noted in the previous chapter on antidumping, it is clear that in practice distributive justice concerns have not been addressed through antidumping cases; it is unlikely that the evidence is any different for countervailing duty cases. Moreover, there is no principled reason to treat some of the least advantaged as more deserving of protection because the threat to their welfare derives from subsidized imports rather than unsubsidized imports, domestic competition, or other internal factors.

Similarly, the vindication of communitarian values would require that policies be adopted that prevent the disruption of long-standing communities. However, countervailing duty laws are also poorly suited to the achievement of this end. Current formulations of the injury test inquire into the adverse impacts on the domestic industry without investigating whether these impacts are being sustained by dependent communities. Finally it must be emphasized that, in general, protectionist trade remedies such as countervailing duties are not the most appropriate policy instruments for vindicating these values. Instead, as we argue in the next chapter, labour adjustment assistance programmes, or short term safeguard relief where appropriate, more directly and effectively address transition costs suffered by workers. Such an approach would be a non-discriminatory means of dealing with disruptive impacts of competition from any source on the most vulnerable members of our society without excessively burdening consumers with the costs of trade protectionism.

REFORMING SUBSIDY LAWS[135]

There are two basic problems with countervailing duty laws: their unilateral nature serves to increase international trade frictions and perhaps protectionist tendencies; and they fail to distinguish between subsidies that are distortionary and those that are benign. Reform of the laws on subsidies must address both these concerns. There has been some debate in the current literature about whether reform proposals should focus on the theoretically defensible or the politically feasible;[136] the approaches that follow are grouped into regimes that represent varying degrees of trade liberalization and, correspondingly, varying degrees of political realism.

The US cash-flow approach: the status quo

There are substantial problems with the current administration of countervailing duty laws by the USA. In a recent paper, Diamond undertakes a full-scale critique of current and proposed DC practices in the administration of US countervailing duty law. His analysis leaves them in shambles and his conclusion seems fully warranted:

> The rules promulgated and proposed cannot be squared with any known purpose which countervailing duty law may serve. Surrogates are chosen which have no conceivable relationship to the effect which the foreign subsidy has on the ability of the foreign firm to compete.

Internal inconsistencies arise when [DC's] intuitive grasp of competitive effects causes it to over-ride the cash-flow principle which it has adopted. Conceptual lacunae arise where [DC] can find no answer to questions regarding implementation and can only declare that the necessary economic and financial principles do not exist.[137]

The thrust of Professor Diamond's critique of current and proposed DC practices is as follows: in determining the existence of a countervailable subsidy, and in determining the appropriate level of the countervailing duty, the cash-flow or benefit-oriented approach adopted by the DC fails to make consistent distinctions between benefits accruing to a foreign firm from a subsidy and *competitive* benefits accruing from a subsidy. Under the cash-flow or benefit-oriented approach, government action confers a countervailable subsidy on a foreign firm whenever such action allows the foreign firm to receive something of value which it would not have received in a free market. The difference which occurs in the firm's cash flow as a result of the subsidy is *prima facie* the benefit which a countervailing duty will be set to neutralize by pro-rating the value gained by the company (and hence the countervailing duty) over the amount of merchandise produced. As Diamond points out, this approach generates all sorts of largely intractable difficulties. It does not distinguish between subsidies that alter a firm's production costs and those that do not – a subsidy to decommission a plant and under-write adjustment costs for displaced workers or to clean up environmental damage is treated in the same way as a wage subsidy or output-related subsidy. In the case of foreign firms with multiple product lines, pro-rating capital subsidies over product lines is arbitrary. Determining the amount of the subsidy in the case of equity infusions or loans is also arbitrary, as is the allocation of the benefit over time (when the subsidy may in fact be received upfront). The issue of causation is also problematic: is it the impact of foreign imports, which happen to be subsidized, on domestic producers that is central, irrespective of the competitive significance of the subsidy, or is it the latter? But if the latter, this requires a prior determination of the competitive significance of the subsidy, which the cash-flow or benefit-oriented approach explicitly eschews. Diamond's description of the contortions of the DC over time in adopting, rejecting, revising, and re-adopting various rules of thumb to address these issues reflects the inherent arbitrariness and, in a conceptual sense, futility of the exercise.

The entitlement approach

As a more coherent alternative to the cash-flow or benefit-oriented approach, Diamond develops an entitlement theory of countervailing duties,[138] building on an approach initially proposed by Goetz, Granet and Schwartz.[139] The entitlement theory is premised on the notion that US producers should be entitled to an outcome which limits the direct impact of the subsidized firm in the US market to what it would have been had the government subsidy not been available. This entails an analysis of the impact of subsidies on foreign exporters' marginal costs of production. If the subsidy reduces marginal costs, leading a firm to equate marginal revenues and marginal costs at higher levels of output and to increase its sales in the USA at the expense of US producers, the latter's entitlement to 'fair competition' has been violated and countervailing duties are *prima facie* in order.

This entitlement theory differs from the cash-flow or benefit-oriented approach currently taken by the DC because of its focus not simply on benefits conferred by governments on foreign firms that export into the USA, but on *competitively salient* benefits. Thus, causation and injury requirements would emphasize the extent to which subsidies that reduce the marginal costs of imports cause injury to domestic firms by reducing their market share. The entitlement theory also differs from the economic distortion approach, which would target countervailing duties on foreign subsidies that distort the globally efficient allocation of resources.

Diamond proposes the entitlement theory as some form of potentially coherent and tractable middle ground between the cash-flow or benefit-oriented approach on the one hand, which he views as incoherent, and the economic distortion theory on the other, which he rejects as indeterminate. However, his approach is problematic at the operational level. The entitlement approach, given the central role it assigns to the impact of a subsidy on foreign firms' marginal costs of production and the causal linkage between this and alleged injury to domestic producers, is highly data intensive, which is likely to exacerbate problems of data manipulation and lack of transparency in decision-making. Measuring marginal costs is a notoriously difficult exercise, exacting in its data demands and inherently error-prone. Firms do not record their costs in this fashion, and so one would likely quickly be driven to the concept of average variable costs as a compromise. Even then, in multi-product firms, problems of joint cost allocation are likely to be pervasive. Moreover, the counterfactual with which the subsidy-impacted marginal cost function of a foreign firm must be compared is likely to be highly speculative. Is it the *status quo ante* of the firm before the conferral of the subsidy, or alternative courses of action that the firm might have taken to reduce its production costs in the absence of a subsidy?

Problems well known in antitrust law and public utility regulation[140] suggest that in the countervailing duty context these difficulties would be even more pronounced. Here one is dealing with *foreign* firms, typically more than one, each with its own cost functions. Nor do the problems stop with estimating marginal cost functions for foreign firms. Even where subsidies are found to reduce the marginal costs of production of foreign firms with respect to exports into the USA, it will still be necessary to address causation and injury issues, and then to determine the correct level of duty. Diamond suggests that injury will largely be a function of the elasticity of domestic demand for the product: the more elastic the demand the less the injury. But again we know from antitrust experience in defining relevant product and geographic markets that these elasticities are often highly speculative. Even in cases where domestic demand is relatively inelastic so that increased sales by subsidized foreign exporters *prima facie* will erode the market shares of domestic producers, it is easy to envisage cases where loss of market share would occur absent the subsidy.[141] Thus, again, a counterfactual which is necessarily highly conjectural is required not only at the foreign firms' end of the process, but also at the domestic end of the process. Moreover, these comparisons presumably cannot be excessively static, but once a duty is imposed would require constant review in the light of changing circumstances over time at either end of the process. Finally, should foreign firms be able to argue that the subsidies they have received are wholly or partially offset by subsidies received by domestic producers, and that only the net subsidy advantage should qualify as a countervailable subsidy? Goetz, Granet and Schwartz are frank enough to acknowledge these complexities:

> Admittedly, the neutralization approach would often be difficult to implement because of the empirical issues that it implicates ... Experience with this approach might well yield useful generalizations so that 'rules of thumb' could, in some situations, effectively replace detailed case-by-case enquiry. This is not to suggest that coherent implementation of the protectionist rationale will ever be anything but a very costly and error-prone process ... Facing the implications of mandating this approach may also lead some legislators to become less certain of the desirability of implementing the protectionist [entitlement] rationale. It is no doubt clear by now that this is a result which would not be uncongenial to us.[142]

Taxonomizing subsidies

In the Tokyo Round, no agreement was reached regarding the classification of domestic (non-export) subsidies as acceptable or unacceptable (countervailable). Thus, an approach that has been pursued in the Uruguay Round Agreement is to spell out more definitively the different categories of subsidies. Under a first-best regime, our preference would be to abandon this approach. The development of a three-way taxonomy of subsidies as benign ('white'), prohibited ('black'), and ambiguous ('grey') is, in many respects, problematic. First, conventional understanding has it that pure export subsidies are the most objectionable and trade-distorting forms of subsidies and provide the strongest case for both international and domestic countervailing sanctions.[143] This understanding is reflected in the Tokyo and Uruguay Rounds Subsidies Codes. It may be that such subsidies represent a foolish misallocation of resources by the subsidizing state – in effect giving away its goods to foreigners below cost – and may distort the efficient global allocation of resources by squeezing out more efficient third country producers from the importing country's market, who should perhaps be entitled to make a claim for nullification or impairment under Article XXIII of the GATT. However, in terms of its own economic welfare, the importing country has no grounds for objection. The general economic case for countervailing duties in the case of pure export subsidies is as tenuous as the general economic case against dumping.[144] While we recognize the broader international risk of 'Prisoners' Dilemma' type export subsidy wars, negotiated reductions of, or restrictions on, such subsidies in given contexts, as reflected in the Uruguay Round Agreement on agricultural subsidies or the Tokyo Round Code on Trade in Civil Aircraft, seem an appropriate response to this problem. We also recognize that pure export subsidies will be typically harder to justify in terms of non-trade related domestic policy objectives, most of which can be better served by subsidies or other policy instruments that are not targeted exclusively on exports, but again it is not clear why this should be of concern to the importing country.

Similarly, generally available subsidies under the Uruguay Round Agreement are not seen as trade distorting with respect to either imports or exports, presumably because they do not disproportionately influence the price of particular categories of goods. However, this view reflects a rather static conception of comparative advantage; most modern international trade theorists believe comparative advantage is a dynamic concept and is not entirely exogenously determined.[145] Clearly, many developed countries owe a significant part of their international comparative advantage to social investments in health, education, law and order, basic research and physical infrastructure. It may be the case that generally available subsidies are more benign than selective subsidies because they are less likely to be the product of rent seeking by special interest groups. It may also be the case that generally available subsidies are reflected more fully in exchange-rate adjustments than selective or targeted subsidies. But in an international environment where exchange rates are determined increasingly by international capital flows rather than goods flows, it is not clear how robust this assumption is, or when one can be confident that generally available subsidies have induced appropriate exchange-rate adjustments while more selective subsidies have not.

Finally, in the context of countervailing duty law, there remain selective domestic subsidies with export spillovers. In this case, the economic analysis is the same as that for the case of pure export subsidies: the importing country receives lower priced goods and increases its welfare. To the extent that such subsidies squeeze out a third country's exports, then the third country should, as in the case of pure export subsidies, have a right to bring a nullification and impairment claim before a GATT dispute resolution panel.

A first-best alternative to countervailing duty law: negotiated reciprocity

The preceding analysis illustrates the normative incoherence as well as the technical difficulties associated with current and proposed countervailing duty laws. Our first-best reform proposal would be to abandon the attempt to develop a taxonomy of subsidies and to admit that 'unfair' subsidies are a largely incoherent idea. The protectionist tendencies that drive countervailing duty actions should be disciplined by being subjected to the strictures of a revamped Article XIX on Safeguards. To advocate the replacement of 'unfair' trade remedy laws with a comprehensive safeguards regime is not to deny that global economic welfare might be enhanced by the reduction of government subsidies to industry. Rather it is the case for countervailing duties that makes no sense, not the case for reducing some subsidies. Although it has been suggested that the appropriate use of countervail may actually lead to a reduction in the use of subsidies, there is little empirical evidence to suggest that the imposition or threat of contingent protection actually alters states' domestic policies.[146]

However, the GATT may have an appropriate role to play in facilitating agreement among states to reduce subsidies. The GATT is more likely to achieve success, not through a ban of some supposedly pernicious subclass of subsidies enforceable through unilateral retaliation, but through facilitating negotiation of mutually advantageous concessions among the Contracting Parties. It is through negotiated reciprocity that the GATT has achieved its clearest success – the dramatic reduction in tariff barriers. The enhanced notification and surveillance procedures in the Uruguay Round Subsidies Agreement may indeed facilitate such an approach to disciplining subsidies.

When subsidy wars threaten a tragedy of the commons, mutual agreement to halt or constrain subsidization in a particular sector may be possible. In comparison, tariff reductions did not occur because trading states suddenly recognized the cogency of the economic arguments that tariffs distort global allocative efficiency. Similarly, the focus regarding subsidies should be on facilitating, through the GATT, Pareto-superior bargains, where subsidies are reduced reciprocally, or 'traded' against reductions of other trade restrictions.

A particularly forceful case for mutual reduction of subsidies exists where several states are sustaining excess capacity in declining industries through constantly increasing subsidization. At some point, the cost of matching the increases of every other state's subsidy becomes prohibitive, thereby making negotiated restraints attractive. Such restraints might involve an agreement to focus subsidy policies on orderly reduction of capacity through severance pay settlements to older workers, other public assistance for worker retraining and relocation, or regional subsidies to create jobs in other sectors in the region concerned.

Although there are quite broad prohibitions on subsidies in the Treaty of Rome, from the beginning the European Commission has not viewed the prohibitions on State Aid as reflecting a *laissez faire* paradigm of non-intervention in markets.[147] The Commission only began to intervene actively in the aid policies of Member States during the sectoral crises of the 1970s and early 1980s when Union producers were faced with excess capacity in a variety of sensitive sectors such as steel, autos, and textiles. In this context, subsidization appeared as a beggar-thy-neighbour attempt by each subsidizing country to maximize its share of a declining world market for Community production as a whole. The subsidizing countries then externalized onto other member countries the adjustment costs of sectoral decline. Political norms of interstate cooperation, and the 'race to the bottom' effects of intra-Union subsidies wars, justified intervention. The intervention occurred without the Commission having to decide on an appropriate normative base-line for government intervention in mixed economies, i.e. how much intervention is compatible with free competition, or the *laissez-faire* ideal. Moreover, in many cases, the Commission's response was to accept readjustment of the aid in question with a view to restructuring and reducing capacity. The latter was aimed at alleviating the crisis of surplus capacity within the Union as a whole.[148] Finally, the Commission has taken a positive view of subsidies aimed at development of new environmentally safer production processes, as well as development of disadvantaged regions (as the Uruguay Round Subsidies Agreement now does). Nevertheless, the Commission has insisted on justification of the specific measures in question, and has not sustained measures to prop up failing firms just because they happened to be located in underdeveloped regions. Instead, the Commission has sought evidence that the aid in question will contribute to long-term development of the local economy. Backed by technical expertise and capacity for on-going monitoring and scrutiny of government policies, the Commission has been able to engage in a fruitful (although occasionally tense) dialogue with aid-granting Member States about the relationship between means and ends, in which the broader social goals behind government intervention have been accepted at the outset as legitimate, as well as the principle that one Member State should not impose on another the costs of attaining those goals within its own borders. The Union jurisprudence on subsidies has, therefore, a much less Lochnerist tone than that of US domestic trade tribunals applying American countervailing-duty law, which presume the illegitimacy of any foreign subsidy that is not generally available.

Following the EU experience, the GATT requires better institutional machinery for negotiation and supervision of these kinds of subsidy regimes. However, creating an institutional framework to facilitate such specific regimes is a more appropriate task for the GATT than the elusive search for a universal taxonomy of good and bad subsidies. A transparency agency operating under the aegis of the GATT, now to an important extent contemplated in the detailed notification and surveillance mechanisms of the Uruguay Round Subsidies Agreement (Articles 25 and 26), could also play a positive role by monitoring subsidy policies and calculating subsidies in tariff equivalents, thus providing a kind of common bargaining currency. For instance, in the steel sector, the USA might agree to remove some existing voluntary export restraints or contingent protection actions in return for EU commitments to use subsidies to reduce, rather than sustain, excess capacity. Clearly, in order to make such commitments plausible, some kind of independent surveillance mechanism is essential that can conduct verifications and ensure against flagrant cheating. Current GATT machinery is not designed to handle this verification function but were such machinery developed (perhaps through the new World Trade Organization) we might see more agreements that address domestic subsidies. Thus, the reduction of subsidies should be treated as has tariff-cutting in previous GATT rounds: the aim should be periodic global welfare enhancing bargains based on a broad balance of concessions (negotiated reciprocity).

Second-best reforms

It must be acknowledged that at least in the short run it is unlikely that the first-best solution of removing all *a priori* general constraints on subsidies and leaving their reduction to negotiated reciprocity in particular contexts would be acceptable to the USA. The second-best solution accepts the general taxonomic approach embodied in the Uruguay Round Subsidies Code. However, on our preferred approach,[149] the regime would consist primarily of Track II, and unilateral application of countervailing duties (Track I) would be restricted to a narrow class of prohibited pure export subsidies perhaps defined as subsidies where at least 80% of the output of subsidized foreign firms is exported, provided that the subsidies are competitively salient subsidies (as discussed above with respect to the entitlement approach). Track II would be the exclusive avenue of recourse for addressing actionable subsidies and no remedy of any kind would be available in the case of non-actionable subsidies. If a subsidy has some trade effects but is also serving legitimate non-trade related domestic policy goals, remedial action should only be taken following investigation by a multilateral panel. The panel would determine whether the subsidy is objectionable and the Committee of Signatories to the Subsidies Code would mandate appropriate remedial or retaliatory action. In formulating the standards to be applied by subsidies panels, the experience of review panels established under Chapter 18 of the FTA may be helpful.[150] In recent cases involving disagreements about the legitimacy of government policies that influence trade, the panels have adopted a least restrictive means test. For example, in the case, *In the Matter of Canada's Landing Requirement for Pacific Coast Salmon and Herring* (1989), it was argued that a Canadian requirement that all catches of these fish be landed in Canada before processing was an essential component of resource conservation which is exempted by Article XX(g) from the GATT prohibition on export restrictions under Article IX.[151] However, because the objectives of the policy could have been achieved through sampling and other monitoring requirements less restrictive of trade, the policy was not sustained by the panel.

The paradigmatic formulation of the least restrictive means test is found in the case law under section 1 of the Canadian Charter of Rights and Freedoms.[152] In order for a limit on a Charter right to be sustained, the limit must have a valid objective, and the means chosen to reach that objective must be rationally connected to the objective and must be the least restrictive means, or the means that impairs minimally the right in question. This approach should be adopted to deal with the indeterminate class of reviewable (actionable) subsidies; if a subsidy is rationally connected to a legitimate non-trade related policy objective (such as those previously set out in Article 11 of the Tokyo Round Subsidies Code), and is the least trade-restrictive policy instrument available to achieve that objective it should be sustained, but not otherwise. This test should encourage governments to seek out domestic policy instruments that will minimize trade distortions.

In summary, we envision that an international subsidies regime could feasibly aspire to define a category of subsidies that are immune from challenge either multilaterally or unilaterally, along the lines of 'non-actionable subsidies' in the Uruguay Round Subsidies Code, and another category of subsidies (principally subsidies that are *de jure* or *de facto* pure export subsidies) that are *per se* objectionable both multilaterally and unilaterally. For the wide array of intermediate subsidies that do not fall into either of these two categories, we envisage only a multilateral complaints route, with panels applying a least trade-restrictive means test, and an adverse determination by the Subsidies Committee being required before retaliation can be undertaken. Invocation of domestic countervailing duty regimes would not be possible unless and until such a determination had been made. We believe that this approach recognizes the complex welfare judgements entailed in evaluating the economic effects of subsidies and is respectful, within reasonable limits, of the domestic sovereignty of member states to pursue a wide range of non-trade related domestic policy objectives of their choosing without risking unilateral punitive measures from other countries with divergent perspectives on the wisdom of those policies.

7

TRANSITION COSTS
Safeguard regimes, domestic adjustment, and labour policies

THE GATT SAFEGUARD REGIME

Introduction

Article XIX of the GATT is widely known as the Escape Clause or Safeguard Provision. It allows a GATT signatory in certain circumstances to avoid GATT obligations that cause serious injury to domestic industries of a product like, or competitive with, one whose importation is increasing.[1] When the increase in imports is caused by unforeseen developments and prior GATT obligations, a Contracting Party can modify or withdraw the relevant trade concessions. Measures taken under Article XIX are intended to be temporary, lasting only long enough to prevent or remedy the injury, and applied in a non-discriminatory way to all Parties exporting the product. Finally, they can only be undertaken when Parties with substantial interests have been consulted and agree to the import restraint or receive proper compensation.[2] A new Agreement on Safeguards was negotiated during the Uruguay Round and is discussed later in this chapter.

Between 1950 and 1986, 132 actions under Article XIX were notified to the GATT.[3] As with antidumping, over 80% of the actions were taken by four main users: 29% by Australia, 21% by the USA, 17% by Canada, and 14% by the EC. Compared with other trade remedies, safeguard actions are infrequently initiated: from 1979 to 1988, 1,833 antidumping actions and 429 countervailing actions were initiated,[4] while in 1988, 261 export restraint arrangements (ERAs) were known to be in existence.[5] The predominance of antidumping and countervailing actions may seem surprising since they respond to 'unfair' forms of trade and would seem to carry a heavier burden of proof. Moreover, the number of ERAs is striking and disconcerting; these actions are not legal under the GATT,[6] but are increasingly the preferred form of safeguard action. Because they are often unofficial, secret and discriminatory, ERAs are a serious threat to the integrity of the GATT multilateral trade regime, specifically undermining the integrity of the safeguard regime.

History and background

Article XIX is a direct derivative of the escape clause found in the 1943 Reciprocal Trade Agreement between the USA and Mexico.[7] Prior to 1943, escape clauses to protect against specific risks had been contemplated by trade agreements, but never a general escape clause.[8] Then in 1947, responding to concerns in Congress over impending GATT trade liberalization, a US executive order required that all trade agreements entered into by the USA include a general escape clause similar to the one found in the Reciprocal Trade Agreement.

Among the Contracting Parties, there was general agreement during the initial GATT negotiations that an escape clause was desirable, but there was some controversy about its scope.[9] The rationale for the inclusion of a safeguard provision was twofold:[10] to encourage greater trade liberalization, and to increase the trade regime's flexibility. The goal of the GATT was to remove all trade barriers except customs duties (tariffs), and then to reduce these duties through successive, binding multilateral negotiations. Safeguards were believed to be necessary to protect against unforeseen economic difficulties that would result from liberalization. It was thought that with the existence of a form of relief from obligations in extreme circumstances, countries would be more likely to agree to broad reductions in trade barriers in the first place. Second, it was believed that the flexibility provided by safeguards would increase the long-term stability of the system. If nations were able to protect their import-sensitive industries temporarily within the GATT regime then they would be less likely to abandon the multilateral system in favour of protectionism or some other trading system.

Substantive requirements

The escape clause agreed upon in 1947 is 'extraordinarily oblique, even for GATT language',[11] resulting in difficulty in interpretation and uncertainty in application.[12] Very few rules define the required procedure for invocation of the safeguard. The safeguard user must notify the Contracting Parties and afford those with a substantial interest an opportunity for consultation with respect to the proposed action. A striking feature of the regime is that the importing country is responsible for the substantive determinations, and while notification to the GATT is mandatory there is no requirement of surveillance or external confirmation. The lack of international involvement encourages informal, secret negotiation since exporters feel their interests are inadequately protected by the formal mechanism. In addition, actions that are taken under Article XIX must be taken by the executive branch of the government of the Contracting Party and are thus political, not administrative actions like antidumping and countervailing duty actions. The need for executive approval forces an invoking government to justify the action to its constituents and to foreign governments. In addition, it may be difficult if the action is prompted by a genuine emergency to explain why it is necessary to pay compensation. By creating greater political costs, the safeguard regime creates incentives to substitute relief through less accountable mechanisms like ERAs.

Increased imports

According to Article XIX, the importing country must show that the imports in question are increasing, either relatively[13] or absolutely, due to unforeseen developments and GATT obligations. While integral to the invocation of the safeguard provision, neither of the two causative factors is defined in the article. The increased importation of the product must be affected by GATT obligations, but the kind of obligation is uncertain. The article includes more than simply tariff concessions – a large proportion of the actions involve quantitative restrictions – but there is a debate over whether the Most Favoured Nation (MFN) clause is applicable. Some argue that the MFN requirement of the GATT may be the obligation causing the injury,[14] and so Parties should be able to restrain imports on a selective basis – by suspending MFN treatment. However, others insist that it is unlikely that the MFN obligation is responsible for the increased imports.[15] Leaving aside the MFN issue, this requirement is easily satisfied if all the safeguard user has to show is that *but for* the GATT obligation, protective measures would have been taken to prevent the increase in imports; there is little evidence that this clause is more strictly construed.[16]

The second causality requirement is that the increased imports be caused by 'unforeseen developments'. This criterion is the least onerous aspect of the safeguard clause. Indeed, according to some, interpretation has rendered both of the causative requirements 'virtual nullities'.[17] In the *Hatter's Fur Case* in 1951, the USA alleged that imports of Czechoslovakian hatter's fur were causing injury to domestic producers. The change in the preferred style of women's hats was declared sufficiently 'unforeseen' to justify an Article XIX action; this conclusion was supported by a GATT report on the case.[18] Such interpretations suggest that almost anything can be considered an unforeseen development:

> Any increase in imports, even if through normal changes in international competitiveness, could therefore be considered actionable under Article XIX.[19]

Serious injury

The increased imports must cause or threaten serious injury to domestic producers of like or directly competitive products. There are three ambiguities in this requirement: (1) what is needed to establish causation?; (2) what constitutes serious injury?; and (3) what qualifies as a like or competitive product? First, serious injury is different from material injury (the requirement for antidumping and countervailing actions) but whether it requires proof of more or less harm than material injury has not been established. Second, the range of producers that can be protected by a safeguard action are more diverse than those contemplated by an antidumping action, extending to producers of competitive as well as like products. But what kinds of competitive products are eligible for protection remains unsettled. What has been established, in the *Hatter's Fur Case*, is that the Party invoking safeguard protection is entitled to the benefit of the doubt that serious injury has been sustained or is threatened.

Remedy and compensation

The GATT obligation that is causing or threatening the injury can be suspended or modified 'to the extent and for such a time as may be necessary to prevent or remedy such injury'. Some Contracting Parties, particularly the EU, argue that GATT obligations can be suspended selectively so that the concession is only withdrawn with respect to the particular trading nations who are causing the injury. This argument is inconsistent with the Article XIX interpretation developed during the Havana Charter negotiations,[20] and with the GATT's apparent historical insistence on nondiscriminatory application of safeguard actions.[21] However, the right to restrain imports selectively has been at the centre of the debate on the reform of the safeguard clause and contributes to the greater attractiveness of ERAs and other trade remedies like antidumping and countervailing duties, all of which are selective.

The safeguard remedy seems designed for temporary relief but no precise requirements are specified under Article XIX in this respect. Before taking action the Contracting Party must consult with the Parties substantially affected to try to obtain agreement on the need for such action. Ultimately, the safeguard provision can be invoked without agreement from trading partners but, according to Article XIX(3), if the restrained Parties are dissatisfied with the action they have the right to suspend concessions of substantially equivalent value or other obligations. This aspect of the safeguard regime has been interpreted as establishing a right to compensation. Compensation usually takes the form of other trade concessions by the Party invoking the safeguard relief and requires negotiations between the injured country and all exporting countries. Owing to the generally low level of tariffs, it is becoming increasingly difficult for countries to compensate with equivalent concessions; few tariffs are high enough for meaningful reductions except for products which are already sensitive to imports.[22] Thus, the requirement is often politically difficult to meet and it increases pressure to find alternative escape routes. Sykes argues that the compensation requirement reduces the likelihood that the safeguard provision will be used inappropriately.[23]

However, it also reduces the chance that it will be used at all, as countries instead negotiate ERAs or invoke other trade remedies.

Other escape clauses

Article XIX is not the only provision of the GATT that allows signatories to suspend their obligations. Articles XII and XVIII(b) permit the imposition of import controls to relieve temporary balance-of-payments pressures and economic development problems of less-developed countries. In addition, Article XXVIII provides for the renegotiation of concessions during specified renewal periods.

Outside of the GATT there is a further safeguard regime worthy of note: Chapter 11 of the Canada–US Free Trade Agreement (FTA).[24] It differs from the GATT clause in a number of important ways. First, bilateral emergency actions are only permissible within the ten year transition period.[25] Second, these actions have several features distinguishing them from those allowed under the GATT: they must be limited to three years; there is no right to renew; the increase in imports causing the serious injury has to be absolute, so if the import's share of the market increases due, for example, to a decline in purchases of domestic goods no action can be taken; the only actions permitted under the clause are tariffs, which (along with auctioned quotas) provide revenue to the country imposing them which can help finance adjustment programmes;[26] and binding arbitration must be used to resolve disputes over actions taken. In addition, in order to address the problem of 'side-swiping', the Chapter provides for the exemption of Canada or the USA from the impact of actions taken by the other under the GATT multilateral safeguard regime if their imports are not 'substantial' or 'contributing importantly to the serious injury'. Article 1102(1) of the FTA specifies that 'imports in the range of five percent to ten percent or less of total imports would normally not be considered substantial'. This exemption does not apply if it would undermine the effectiveness of the relief and the domestic industry would continue to suffer injury. Before restraining the other Party to the FTA there must be notification and consultation. Finally, the restraint must not have the effect of reducing the other Party's imports below the trend of imports over a reasonable base period with allowance for growth. Similar safeguard provisions are included in the North American Free Trade Agreement.[27]

Theoretical rationales for the safeguard regime

Trade liberalization

In 1970 Kenneth Dam observed that 'the GATT escape clause is a useful safety valve for protectionist pressures'.[28] In his view, the clause, in addition to being a prerequisite for essential US participation, encouraged trade liberalization more generally. According to Dam, the GATT escape clause 'encourages cautious countries to enter into a greater number of tariff bindings than would otherwise be the case'.[29] Sykes develops this observation into the primary rationale for a safeguard regime.[30] His thesis is not unlike the traditional argument for the inclusion in the GATT of a safeguard regime: that broader liberalization will be undertaken when there is an opportunity to suspend those obligations. His approach is novel in its use of public choice theory to explain the role of this trade remedy.

Public choice theory predicts that policy-makers will be more concerned about trade impacts on producers than on consumers because the former are both better organized and more influential than the latter. According to Sykes, the consequence of the self-interested behaviour of policy-makers is that they may not liberalize trade even if the current environment is favourable to such an action. Their reluctance will result from knowledge

that unanticipated changes in economic conditions may create circumstances in which political rewards to an increase in protection (or the political costs of an irrevocable commitment to reduce protection) are great.[31]

The safeguard is therefore essential to any liberalizing scheme. This conclusion depends on two important and challengeable assumptions: that adequate substitutes do not exist for the formal safeguard regime, and that signatories feel bound by their obligations and will generally not wish to abrogate them.[32] In Sykes' view, the *ex ante* nature of the safeguard regime implies that it is different from bilateral negotiations over ERAs which occur *ex post*. The increasing use of grey-area and other contingent measures to avoid obligations, combined with the infrequent use of Article XIX, challenges both these assumptions. By modelling Article XIX, Sykes shows how the criteria for invoking the safeguard serve to maximize political gains from protection. In addition, he argues that requirements such as compensation reduce illicit use of the escape clause. The optimal safeguard regime would constrain protection to cases in which the gains to the importing country are greater than any losses to other countries.

Economic adjustment

Jackson advances an economic adjustment rationale for safeguards:

Imports, particularly recently increasing imports, often cause harm to select groups within an importing society, even though they may in the long term and in the broader aggregate increase the welfare of that society. Competing firms will be forced to 'adjust' to the imports ...

a temporary period of time of some relief from imports will allow the domestic competing industry to take the necessary adjustment measures.[33]

This rationale can be reformulated in different terms: the safeguard remedy provides an opportunity for domestic industries to improve their competitiveness with imports. Hufbauer and Rosen have studied the effectiveness of various programmes for facilitating adjustment of US industries being impacted by import competition. Their study focuses on three trade policies: special trade protection, such as exceptional restraints on imports that go well beyond normal border or tariff restrictions; trade-related adjustment assistance to labour in affected industries; and escape clause relief.[34] Hufbauer and Rosen find that among the various policies, the escape clause is the most effective at inducing adjustment. Of the sixteen industries studied ten received tariff increases, two obtained orderly marketing arrangements, and the other four received quota protection. The adjustment of these firms was relatively successful since twelve no longer required protection:[35] one of these adjusted by expanding; the rest contracted either to a competitive core or out of the industry. The relative success of escape clause relief results from three factors: the relief is temporary, which gives firms a strong incentive to adjust quickly; labour adjustment programmes in the USA are inadequate and incapable of effectively inducing or easing adjustment; and the escape clause in the USA is administered by the International Trade Commission and while the President authorizes the granting of relief, the primary mechanism is not political lobbying as it is for special trade protection.

The adjustment rationale does not, standing alone, support a role for safeguards. Its inadequacy stems from the distinction that it draws between competitive impacts from imports and from domestic sources. If there are social gains to be realized from facilitating adjustment to economic changes why should not all firms experiencing competitive pressures receive such assistance? The answer is clearly that in competition within domestic industries there are at least two sets of domestic producer interests, differently affected, whereas foreign firms causing harm to domestic industries do not have any political 'allies'. There are few real political losses to be suffered from harming a foreign industry so that there are incentives to provide adjustment assistance to domestic firms suffering from import competition through safeguard relief.

Non-economic rationales

There may be important non-economic rationales for the protection offered by the safeguard regime. Despite the efficiency gains to be achieved through trade liberalization, substantial losses resulting from unconstrained imports may justify protection of domestic interests. Vulnerable domestic interests may include less-well endowed and immobile workers and long-established communities whose viability substantially depends on domestic industries that are facing contraction or collapse due to import competition. Distributive justice and communitarian values would require sensitivity to these vulnerable interests and justify policy initiatives to alleviate adverse impacts.

However, trade protection is a very costly way to vindicate these values. The cost to consumers for each job saved by trade protection typically far outweighs the average compensation per worker in the industry affected.[36] To cite some recent examples, the cost to US consumers of protection of the specialty steel industry was $1 million per year for each job preserved when the annual compensation was less than $60,000 for those jobs. United States consumers of automobiles paid $160,000 per year for each job saved through protection when annual compensation in this industry was less than one quarter of this figure.[37] In Canada, the statistics are similar: consumers of footwear were 'taxed' through trade protection between $53,668 and $69,460 per job saved, while compensation per year for a worker in the industry was $7,145; consumers of textile and clothing were 'taxed' between $40,600 and $50,982 per year for each job saved when average earnings were $10,000; and consumers of automobiles paid between $179,000 and $226,394 per year for each job saved when average compensation in the industry was between $29,000 and $35,000.[38] Given the substantial cost to domestic consumers of trade restrictions, it is likely that other policy instruments can vindicate distributive justice and communitarian values at lower cost.

Reforming safeguard laws

As noted earlier, the frequency of the use of safeguard protection has been low, as has been the incidence of retaliation.[39] To some, this evidence suggests that the safeguard regime is an effective part of a liberal regime: it encourages broad liberalization without leading to substantial avoidance of obligations.[40] On this view, the principal challenge may be to make the regime stricter so that it contributes more positively toward greater trade liberalization. However, this optimistic conclusion requires the drawing of an artificial distinction between Article XIX actions and grey-area measures such as ERAs. The distinction is drawn by Sykes on the grounds that if *ex post* negotiations of import restraints were a perfect substitute for the safeguard regime then there would be no need to have a formal regime at all; the very existence of Article XIX shows that *ex post* negotiation is not a substitute for the safeguard regime. However, his view is inconsistent with the growing tendency of countries to negotiate ERAs in response to injurious import competition rather than resort to Article XIX.[41]

Thus, the challenge for reform of the safeguard regime is a substantial one. On the one hand it is necessary to restore the relevance of the safeguard regime by making it more attractive than alternative escape actions such as ERAs.[42] This can be accomplished by relaxing the criteria for invocation of the safeguard regime and bringing grey-area measures within the ambit of the GATT. On the other hand, if the regime is excessively relaxed then it will no longer serve to lower the overall levels of trade protection. Thus, the challenge is to balance these two objectives: to encourage the use of the safeguard regime rather than illicit substitutes, but to maintain its positive, liberalizing influence.

Selectivity

The issue of selectivity in the application of safeguard remedies has been central to ongoing debates over reform of the GATT safeguard regime. In 1947, there seemed to be consensus on the importance of the application of safeguard remedies to all exporters on a non-discriminatory basis. This position seems to have been confirmed in subsequent GATT practice.[43] According to Bronckers,[44] the principle of non-discrimination in the context of Article XIX of the GATT serves two principal purposes. First, it promotes economic efficiency by minimizing the trade distortions associated with safeguard remedies. It achieves this purpose by imposing a common burden on all exporters of the product found to be causing serious injury to domestic producers. By not unduly burdening the most efficient exporter with trade restrictions, distortions in the global allocation of resources are minimized. Moreover, second-order distortionary effects such as trade diversion to unconstrained third countries are avoided. Second, it is argued that the principle of non-discrimination increases the number of adversely affected exporting countries, and their combined pressures against the initial invocation of safeguard relief or for the removal of existing safeguard measures or for the granting of compensation operates as a deterrent against unwarranted or abusive exercise of the safeguard remedy. These pressures coincidentally protect weaker or smaller exporting countries who might otherwise be singled out for trade restrictions, whether their exports were or were not the principal cause of injury to domestic producers in an importing country, and for whom demands for compensation or the threat of retaliation may not be viewed as credible.

Despite these arguments for non-discrimination in the application of Article XIX, there have been recurrent demands, particularly from some developed countries, for selective application of import restraints under the safeguard regime. The case for selectivity was first advanced when Japan acceded to the GATT in 1955. Some Contracting Parties took the view that applying restraints against all exporters when Japanese exports were principally causing the harm in question would lead to a destructive, overall increase in trade protectionism. No change was made in the regime at that time, leaving the issue unresolved. The case for selectivity can be shortly stated.[45] First, if it is appropriate to provide an exceptional form of relief to countries suffering serious injury from imports, obviously the most effective form of relief will target the principal source of the imports, rather than adopting a shotgun approach that restrains imports from all sources, whether or not they are contributing importantly to the injury in question. Second, the increasing invocation of 'unfair' trade remedy regimes, particularly antidumping and countervailing duty regimes, which impose duties selectively on particular sources of imports, and the proliferation of various forms of 'voluntary' export restraints, which also impose restrictions on imports by country of origin, implies a high degree of substitutability amongst these various trade remedies. This suggests the futility of insisting on a principle of non-discrimination under Article XIX, rendering it increasingly a dead letter.

It was clear prior to the Tokyo Round negotiations that countries were reluctant to use the safeguard regime because it disrupted the trade of nations that was not causing any harm, and required complex negotiations and compensation schemes. Instead, nations were concluding 'voluntary' ERAs with the main sources of disruptive imports. This practice mainly disadvantages NICs and developing countries who are vulnerable to pressure from the larger economies; they agree to these arrangements in order to avoid more adverse impacts that might result from resort to unilateral formal remedies. There are also benefits to exporters from ERAs, especially the opportunity to reap monopoly rents from the artificial scarcities induced by quotas, but this does not imply that they are necessarily supported by exporting countries. There was a strong desire on the part of developing countries to strengthen the GATT Safeguard regime, making grounds for invocation clearer and stricter. Knowing what alternatives they faced in formal mechanisms, they would then have greater bargaining power in bilateral negotiations. Essential to their view of the regime was the incorporation of safeguards, and alternative escape actions, into a system of nondiscriminatory application. To relax the discipline of Article XIX was thought likely to encourage, rather than constrain the incidence of bilateral, managed trade arrangements, which are antithetical to the founding premises of the multilateral system. An opposing view was taken by the EU which advocated the right to apply Article XIX selectively. Selectivity was believed necessary to enhance stability in international trade. As Winham observes:

> [D]eveloping countries are less well served by stability than by rapid changes in traditional trading patterns ... the effort to negotiate selective safeguards was motivated by a desire to force developing-country exporters to adjust to a pace of change that would not create dislocation in competing industries in the developed countries.[46]

When safeguard negotiations began in 1978, near the end of the Tokyo Round, selectivity was the focus of discussions but the developing countries and the EU could not reach agreement.[47] Developing countries were prepared to compromise on the issue of selectivity in exchange for multilateral surveillance. This compromise was reflected in the Secretariat Draft of April 1979, which specified that in cases where serious injury would result from unusual (not just unforeseen) circumstances, restraints could be taken selectively, either with the agreement of the exporting country or with the approval of a proposed international safeguard committee. This compromise was acceptable to Canada, the USA, Japan, and developing countries,[48] but the EU was unable to accept such a system of review: the administration of international trade laws in the EU is not very transparent, and because of the competing interests in the Union public scrutiny may have caused political difficulties. The right to make determinations of injury without being monitored by an international agency became an issue of economic sovereignty and put an end to any chances of agreement. Ultimately, the only decision made at the Tokyo Round was that a committee should meet to try to elaborate supplementary rules and procedures to provide 'greater uniformity and certainty'[49] in implementing the Safeguard Clause. Following the negotiations, the committee collected data on safeguard use and met to discuss problems of reform but 'no further progress ha[d] been made toward a common approach to the matter'.[50]

Developing countries, while committed to the issue of nondiscrimination, were willing to compromise if selectivity was combined with other reforms advantageous to them. The two major adjuncts to selectivity are surveillance and clearer criteria for invocation. One such package that Wolff recommends would entrench very specific criteria for selective restrictions, aimed at ensuring that the exporter being targeted is really the principal cause of the injury and does not suffer excessive prejudice from the selective treatment.[51] In addition to the requirement that the supplying countries involved have increased their market share, the products of these countries must 'differ in terms of quantities, prices, or kind from other imports not being restricted so that these products can reasonably be determined to be the cause of the serious injury or threat thereof'.[52] Further, other countries' imports must not be injurious and if a substantial advantage in terms of acquisition of market share is being conferred on unrestricted suppliers there should be a mechanism for the targeted suppliers to seek redress. Wolff's reforms would also include a provision for multilateral surveillance. This approach to selectivity is consistent with the multilateral emergency provisions in the Canada–US Free Trade Agreement, in which exports that are 'not contributing importantly to the serious injury' are exempt from restraints.

The Uruguay Round Agreement on Safeguards resolves the issue of selectivity as follows: Under Article 5, safeguard measures shall be applied to a product being imported irrespective of its source. Under Article 9, where a quota is employed, if agreement amongst all affected Parties on the allocation of the shares of the quota is not feasible, shares shall be allocated amongst exporters based on proportions of imports supplied during a previous representative period. This rule may be departed from where: (a) imports from certain Parties have increased disproportionately to the total increase in imports; (b) the reasons for the departure are justified; and (c) the conditions of the departure are equitable to all suppliers. Such a departure may not exceed four years in duration. In the case of developing countries, safeguard measures may not be applied against their exports if in the case of a given country exports do not exceed 3% of all imports of the product in question, provided that developing countries with less than a 3% import share collectively do not account for more than 9% of total imports (Article 19).

Injury

While the ultimate stumbling block to agreement on a new safeguards regime in the Tokyo Round negotiations was the issue of selectivity, the determination of injury was also controversial. The definition of injury in Article XIX is very imprecise and there was disagreement on the appropriate test to adopt. Because of the conflict over selectivity, the issue was not resolved. Approaches to the question vary dramatically. Some advocate a substantial loosening of the criteria for invocation combined with a reduction in the number and scope of measures available.[53] One improvement in this area would be to make safeguard protection on proof of injury available to industries as of right, like protection from dumping, rather than a matter of political discretion. Others advocate a tightening of the requirements.[54] Ways of achieving such a tightening vary. One possible system would have two tiers: governments could negotiate agreements with other states undertaking to satisfy stricter criteria for invoking safeguard relief and in return be relieved of the obligation to pay compensation; those without such agreements would follow the less restrictive criteria and pay normal compensation.[55]

Another proposal contemplates that an industry should only be protected if injury is being suffered by 'less-endowed and immobile workers or long-established and dependent communities'.[56] This injury test is more attractive than the status quo because the cost of protection borne by consumers would be balanced against the gains by another vulnerable group 'able to make normatively defensible claims not vulnerable to a utilitarian social welfare calculus'.[57] In addition, the concept of worker and community interests as the only legitimate interests justifying protection suggests a link between revenues from protectionist measures and adjustment programmes which these revenues can help finance. Along with the altered injury requirement could also be a condition that the country invoking safeguard relief show that there are no less drastic (less trade distortive) policy instruments available to vindicate these values.

The injury test adopted in the Uruguay Round Safeguards Agreement is a modest improvement over the ambiguities of Article XIX. Serious injury is defined in Article 6 as 'a significant overall impairment in the position of the domestic industry'. The factors to be considered in this determination are specified: rate and amount of the increase in imports in absolute and relative terms, the share of the domestic market taken by increased imports, changes in the level of sales, production, productivity, capacity utilization, profits and losses, and employment. However, the need for GATT obligations and unforeseen developments to cause the increase in imports appears to have been removed or at least rendered marginal; as long as there is an increase in imports that is causing injury, relief is available.

Surveillance

While the developing countries were prepared to compromise on selectivity, the Tokyo Round negotiations ultimately foundered on the issue of multilateral surveillance. The Uruguay Round Safeguards Agreement now provides for a Safeguards Committee which will monitor the implementation of the Agreement and compliance with its procedural and substantive requirements by Contracting Parties. All decisions to initiate or implement safeguard actions must be notified to the Committee, along with evidence justifying the measures. The Committee will also oversee the phasing out of grey-area measures and report as appropriate to the Contracting Parties through the Council for Trade in Goods on the operation of the Agreements. The general dispute resolution mechanisms of the GATT will apply to the new Agreement (Article 38).

Compensation

One of the problems with the Article XIX regime is the obligation of Parties to pay compensation for invoking safeguard protection. As Tumlir states:

> [I]t is destructive of the spirit of reciprocity for a country in an emergency to be obliged to pay for taking *bona fide* temporary action, to negotiate such a payment and to be threatened with retaliation if it does not offer enough.[58]

In addition to the fact that compensation requirement forces payment for *bona fide* emergency actions, the requirement increases the burden of the safeguard regime and the attractiveness of alternative escape routes. Rather than negotiate with a number of exporters over the appropriate compensation for all or face retaliation, a country will find it more attractive to conclude a bilateral arrangement. However, supporters of the compensation requirement, like Sykes, insist that it discourages use of the regime in non-emergencies or in circumstances in which the gains are insufficient to justify the real costs. The Uruguay Round Safeguards Agreement retains the obligation to compensate, but if the escape measure lasts less than three years the right of exporters to suspend concessions of equivalent value is withheld (Article 18), thus reducing their leverage in demanding compensation.

Duration

One of the most significant aspects of the Uruguay Round Safeguards Agreement is the introduction of provisions for limited duration and digressivity of relief. The Agreement specifies that no action shall be maintained for longer than four years (Article 19). It may be extended for up to an additional four years if there is evidence that the industry is adjusting and the protection is shown still to be necessary to remedy serious injury (Articles 11 and 12). Any measure of more than a year in duration must be progressively liberalized so that the amount of protection decreases over the duration of the measure (Article 13). In addition, there are limits on the application of new restrictions to a product that has already been subject to restraint: effectively, no new measure can be introduced for a period of time equal to that during which the previous measure was in effect (Article 14). There is some risk that being aware of the need to progressively remove the restraint, Parties will impose initially tighter restraints than are necessary. The surveillance of the GATT Safeguards Committee is designed to discourage any such overprotection.

Grey-area measures

As noted at the outset of this chapter, the integrity of the safeguard regime has been undermined by measures taken outside the framework of the GATT. The obvious solution would be to bring these other measures into the system and then restrict their use or ban them. Some fear that to legalize other trade measures would be to encourage their use.[59] Some proposals for reform have suggested that the other contingent trade remedies be subject to some of the same criteria for invocation. This harmonization would imply, for example, that the kind of injury required to sustain antidumping measures would be similar, in order to prevent domestic producer interests from attempting to substitute one form of contingent protection for another.[60]

The Uruguay Round Safeguards Agreement attempts to constrain grey-area measures as follows: Article 22 provides that a Contracting Party shall not seek, take or maintain such arrangements nor encourage or support the adoption or maintenance by public and private enterprises of equivalent non-governmental measures. In addition, those currently in existence shall be brought into conformity with the Safeguards Agreement or be phased out within four years of the coming into force of the Agreement, with an exception permitted for one specific measure per Contracting Party subject to review and acceptance by the Safeguards Committee and subject to termination not later than 31 December 1999.

Conclusion

In many respects, the Uruguay Round Safeguards Agreement is a substantial improvement over Article XIX of the GATT: in bringing existing grey-area measures within its purview and prohibiting further such measures; in establishing firm time limits; in achieving a compromise on the issue of selectivity; and in improving multilateral notification and surveillance. There are a number of other reforms that should be considered in future. First, some relaxation of the principle of non-discrimination seems justified in order to avoid pointless 'side-swiping' of exporters who are not contributing importantly to the serious injury in question. Here, a *de minimis* provision along the lines of that to be found in the Canada–US Free Trade Agreement and NAFTA, would seem appropriate. Second, a radical reconceptualization of the injury test also seems appropriate, so that while firms or industries may be able to petition for safeguard relief, the success of such petitions should depend on a showing that imports are causing serious injury to less well endowed and immobile workers or long-established communities, and that alternate remedies less distortive of trade are not available, in the form of various domestic adjustment assistance policies, to redress such injury. Third, the only forms that safeguard relief should be permitted to take should be either tariffs or auctioned quotas, in part because these two forms of relief render the cost to domestic consumers more transparent, and more importantly, because they generate a source of revenue out of which generous domestic assistance policies can be financed. Fourth, safeguard relief should be available as a matter of administrative rather than political decision (like antidumping and countervailing duties), so that incentives to substitute away from the safeguard regime are reduced.

DOMESTIC ADJUSTMENT ASSISTANCE POLICIES

Each of the major industrialized nations has adopted its own policy approaches to the challenge of economic adjustment, including adjustment to trade liberalization and shifts in comparative advantage. We have reviewed these policies extensively elsewhere.[61] We confine ourselves to some brief comments on one class of such policies – industrial subsidies – and offer a somewhat more extended set of comments on labour market adjustment policies.

Industrial subsidies

In many industrialized countries, beginning in the early 1970s, sectors like ship-building, coal, steel, textiles, clothing and footwear, and in some cases, automobiles, experienced substantial competitive pressures from imports. Apart from trade restrictions, countries under import pressure often had resort to various kinds of industrial subsidies. In general, these subsidy policies have not been effective in avoiding the ultimate need for adjustment or moderating its severity. Pure output related subsidies have been the least effective in this respect in that they flatly deny the need for adjustment, and while they maintain output and employment in an industry this typically can only be sustained if the subsidies are endless and often increasing. Other forms of industrial subsidies have been designed to facilitate the modernization of obsolete capital. Here it is argued that state assistance to facilitate capital modernization may be necessary to make a distressed industry internationally competitive again. However, obsolete plants are often the result, and not the cause, of the loss of international competitiveness. Firms which are only able to cover variable costs are constrained to allow their fixed assets to run down and with them their long-term capacity. If an adequate return could be made on new fixed assets, presumably private capital markets would provide the funds required to make the investment. A governmental judgement that such an investment will yield long-run competitiveness and profitability will typically be at variance with these private capital market judgements and should, for this reason, be viewed with extreme wariness.

Much less frequently, industrial subsidies have been provided to ease exit costs. Japan has most prominently invoked industrial subsidies for this purpose in industries like coal mining and steel. It is argued in this context that if there is some degree of indivisibility in plant or firm size so that efficient industry adjustment to a decline in demand requires that firms exit in some orderly temporal sequence, market forces may not produce this sequence. A case may thus arise, so it is argued, for a governmental role in managing adjustment to the contraction in demand, perhaps through recession cartels, active promotion of mergers, or compensation for scrapping physical capacity. While Japanese policies seem to have registered some successes in this context, there are reasons for caution in assigning a pro-active role to government in facilitating firm exit. First, this view assumes that governments can economize on transaction costs in this context in ways not open to private firms, through mergers, specialization agreements, and other means. Also, there are clear dangers of bureaucratic involvement

177

in detailed industrial restructuring in terms of relative institutional competence, and also dangers of fostering anti-competitive forms of collusion in seeking agreement on future industry structure.

Labour market adjustment policies

The case for active labour market adjustment policies is substantially more compelling. Under conditions of close to full employment, there would be little reason to be concerned about the dislocation effects of trade liberalization. The market, in effect, would soon reabsorb the dislocated workers, although even here, from a number of ethical perspectives, it might be appropriate for governments to bear some of the transition costs faced by these workers.

If, more realistically, we assume that re-employment is likely to be far from automatic, then the question arises as to what measures are required to facilitate it. The concept of adjustment is complex. At one level, the adjustment problem may be understood as the time lag between a worker being displaced from one job and finding another that is an adequate replacement. From this perspective, provision of temporary income support and search, counselling, and relocation assistance would seem obvious and appropriate to address the problem.

However, the fact that employment is being created primarily in sectors other than those where jobs are being lost raises serious questions about the adequacy of the unemployment insurance model. It may be necessary to go far beyond this model, and provide training and retraining of workers for new types of employment within the economy. This is well-expressed in the Canadian de Grandpré Report, which contrasts the trampoline approach (which emphasizes training and retraining), with the unemployment insurance model (the 'safety net' approach).[62] The report suggests:

> The 'trampoline' approach seeks to prepare Canadian workers to prosper in a world of increasing technological change and international competition, in which Canada must use its access to the larger North American market to achieve greater economies of scale and higher productivity.[63]

In terms of economic efficiency (i.e. allocative efficiency), it may seem unclear why either income support or a trampoline ought to be provided by the state to trade-dislocated workers. Kaplow, for example, has argued strongly that from an efficiency perspective compensation for regulatory change (of which trade liberalization is one example) makes no sense absent convincing proof that markets are incapable of allocating the risks of such changes.[64]

In fact, however, there are certain inherent limits to the efficient private *ex ante* allocation of the risk of job loss from trade liberalization. It is very difficult to make sound *ex ante* predictions as to the nature and extent of these risks.[65] As a consequence, although worker self-insurance through personal savings undoubtedly exists, such savings are very likely to be too high or too low, given lack of good information about risk. With respect to private insurance, one simply does not observe such markets. Their absence cannot be explained by the presence of basic public unemployment insurance in most industrial democracies, since it is unclear why a market for supplemental benefits would not exist. After all, public insurance benefits cover only a portion of income loss and in some countries only for relatively short periods of time. An additional explanation for the absence of such private insurance would be the arguably quite severe moral hazard problems involved. Full insurance of the risk of dislocation due to trade liberalization would very likely lead some workers and firms to take greater risks, or to underinvest in precautions against the risks in question (e.g. skill diversification). It should be emphasized that these possible market failures do not suggest that government will be any better at *ex ante* allocation of risks of job loss from trade. However, the absence of viable private insurance markets may argue for government intervention based upon the desirability of the existence of insurance that would otherwise not be provided, a desirability to be established on independent normative grounds.

A further possibility would be contractual allocation of risk between employer and employee through bargaining of notice periods in the event of dislocation. While such notice periods are the subject of contractual bargaining in some subset of cases, there is empirical evidence that the existence and nature of such provisions are very poorly correlated to the actual risk of dislocation in the industry and region in question.[66] This suggests that serious information failures may plague *ex ante* allocation of these risks through contractual bargaining between employer and employee.[67] In addition, it is often very difficult for workers to address the risk of dislocation through *ex ante* diversification of their skills. Indeed, powerful incentives exist for workers to increasingly specialize in firm-specific knowledge and skills, as it is these investments that usually have larger pay-offs in promotions and bonuses.

Naturally, firms themselves are likely to invest most heavily in those training programmes that involve highly firm-specific skills. They have little incentive to train workers to be able to move to other sectors or firms, and indeed, arguably, a disincentive since the longer a worker stays with a particular firm, the greater will be that firm's return on the investment in that worker. Of course, if the firm is a conglomerate encompassing a wide range of economic activities (i.e. highly diversified in its operations) it may have an incentive to provide training that is not narrowly job specific, with a view to workers moving between diverse activities within the firm. Yet, even in this case, it is far from clear that in the absence of a long-term employment contract or implicit contract (such as company loyalty in Japan) workers would not take the newly acquired skills and apply them elsewhere.

A somewhat different economic efficiency rationale for adjustment policies stems from the very real danger that, absent appropriate government intervention, trade-induced worker dislocation may result in an erosion of human capital. Workers who lose their jobs due to freer trade, or other structural changes, may out of desperation and in the absence of retraining assistance, seek employment at lower wage levels, and in occupations of lower skill and labour productivity. Empirical evidence suggests that a significant percentage of dislocated workers end up in lower-wage, lower-skill occupations, and, in fact, never regain the earnings levels of their previous employment.[68] Worse still, a protracted period of unemployment – especially when uncushioned by adequate income-support – may also entail physical and mental illness, family break-up, alcoholism, and drug use, which in addition to creating added costs for various social safety nets, is almost certain to reduce the productive capacity of workers and reduce the chances that they will return to the workplace, leading instead to dependence on the social welfare system. All of these factors are likely to be aggravated by the problem of 'sour grapes'[69] or adaptive preferences: the longer workers are unemployed or underemployed in an occupation, the less likely they will be to *believe* in their own inherent capabilities, and hence to actively seek better opportunities.[70] In sum, the *human* effects of dislocation on workers and their families may well lead to long-term sub-optimal deployment of workers' capacities, absent positive adjustment measures.

Many of the most important, and most controversial, arguments about the justification for trade-linked adjustment assistance measures centre around the notion that it is desirable to compensate the losers from freer trade. In economic theory, the notion of Kaldor-Hicks efficiency, applied to the analysis of policy change, suggests the desirability of a given policy change where the benefits to the winners from this change outweigh the losses to the losers. However, unless one adopts a very crude or extreme utilitarian position, the complete sacrifice of particular groups in society for the sake of the common good is ethically problematic.

There are important political and social reasons for attempting to spread across society the costs of adopting particular measures to improve the general welfare. The attitudes of particular groups towards the political process, and their sense of citizen solidarity with the community as a whole, may be adversely affected by having to pay the largest part of the price for a given improvement. The common good itself may be lost sight of as acrimonious debates about who wins and loses increasingly dominate the political process. This range of concerns has been evoked by Michelman in his discussion of demoralization and disaffection costs,[71] and is well-expressed by Calabresi:

> A decision which recognizes the values on the losing side as real and significant tends to keep us from becoming callous with respect to the

moralisms and beliefs that lose out . . . it tells the loser that, though they lost, they and their values do carry weight and are recognized in our society, even when they don't win out.[72]

Comparative experience with labour market policies in various industrialized countries yields a very mixed record. Countries like the UK, France, Canada, the USA, and Australia have tended to favour a safety net approach, rather than proactive labour market policies. In contrast, Sweden, Japan, and to a lesser extent Germany, tend to favour much more proactive labour market policies that provide generous assistance to workers for training, retraining, and relocation. The empirical evidence strongly suggests the superiority of the latter class of policies in terms of facilitating adjustment.

Another controversial issue relates to whether special labour market policies should be adopted in trade-impacted sectors. For example, the US Trade Expansion Act of 1962 and the 1974 Trade Act both sought to provide adjustment assistance to workers dislocated by import competition. The 1962 Act, with its very strict eligibility criteria (to be eligible for assistance it was necessary to demonstrate that imports were a more important factor than all others combined in causing injury and that tariff concessions and injury must have occurred simultaneously), was largely unsuccessful as an instrument of assistance. From 1962 to 1974, only 54,000 workers were certified for assistance involving total expenditures of $US85 million.[73] Adjustment assistance grew substantially under the 1974 Trade Act, under which the level of benefits was increased and the eligibility criteria were greatly relaxed. Between 1977 and 1981, 1.2 million workers received benefits. Spending on TAA in 1981 reached $US1.5 billion, although subsequently the programme budget was severely cut.[74] However, for the most part assistance under the Trade Act turned out to be an instrument of compensation for temporarily laid off workers rather than an instrument to promote adjustment out of declining industries.[75]

These are not arguments against trade-related adjustment assistance programmes *as such* – rather they suggest that policies should be designed to ensure that priority is placed on job losses that are likely to be permanent, and that eligibility criteria are not tilted in favour of sectors that are represented by powerful lobby groups.

A second, but related argument against linking adjustment assistance with trade liberalization is that singling out trade-displaced workers from other displaced workers is morally arbitrary and unfair. This kind of argument assumes that *only* trade-displaced workers are being offered assistance beyond that provided by the general social safety net (including UI benefits). However, when a variety of programmes exist that are targeted at specific groups of workers, and with a range of eligibility requirements, it is much less clear that providing a programme for trade-displaced workers is giving them an unfair advantage.

The logic of targeting or disaggregating adjustment assistance is that workers displaced for different reasons have different needs. Workers displaced by trade liberalization, for example, may be more likely to require retraining than those who lose their jobs due to cyclical downturns or the bankruptcy of a particular firm, since trade-induced dislocation may reflect a need to restructure an entire industry or sector in response to enhanced import competition. As Peter Morici suggests, in the wake of NAFTA:

> In the United States and Canada, jobs in low- and medium-technology activities must make way for jobs in high-technology activities. Generally this will entail the loss of low-skill/wage jobs in industries such as consumer electronics and the gain of high-skill/wage jobs in industries such as advanced telecommunications equipment.[76]

It might reasonably be argued that a *worker's* right to adjustment assistance in the case of trade induced displacement would, on both efficiency and ethical grounds, be a superior alternative to the right to safeguard relief presently accorded to *firms* under import pressure.[77] One of us has suggested that such a right to worker adjustment should be entrenched in a parallel accord to NAFTA.[78] The right could be satisfied by governments providing domestic adjustment assistance programmes that are generally available to all displaced workers (unemployment insurance, retraining and reskilling benefits, job counselling etc.) or alternatively, by programmes more directly targeted at workers displaced by trade. Where workers believed that domestic policies of their own countries did not satisfy the right to adjustment they would, on this scheme, be able to petition a Trinational Committee of Experts, which would examine and rule on the adequacy of the adjustment programmes in the country concerned. Ideally, once a right to adjustment was in place, a country would be permitted to invoke traditional safeguards only if it could show that domestic adjustment policies that satisfied the right to adjustment were nevertheless insufficient to cope with the nature or scale of the social and economic disruption caused by import surges.

Unfortunately, from a political perspective, incentives on the part of both demanders and suppliers of public policies tend in the direction of a complete inversion of the policy prescriptions implied by the analysis in this chapter. That is to say, in the face of trade-related adjustment pressures, politicians will face strong pressures to maintain or increase trade restrictions, in part because these entail off-budget expenditures and in part because they buy off investor, worker, and other dependent interests. As a second-best policy, industrial subsidies will be favoured because while they, to a greater or lesser extent, involve on-budget expenditures, they are responsive to demands not only by workers but also by investors and other affected interests. As a distinctly third-best policy option, labour market adjustment policies may be favoured, but even then with a bias toward stay-oriented labour policies rather than exit-oriented labour policies. Most labour market policies involve on-budget expenditures and are responsive only to the demands of workers and not of investors and other affected interests; and stay (safety-net) oriented labour policies avoid an acknowledgement by government that the sector cannot or will not be preserved in its present form or on its current scale. The new Safeguards Agreement discussed earlier in this chapter may help tilt domestic political forces more strongly in the direction of proactive labour market adjustment policies, enhancing simultaneously domestic and global economic welfare.

Labour standards, free and 'fair' trade

The interrelationship between labour and trade policies extends, however, far beyond the context of domestic adjustment assistance. Many critics of free trade have argued that it is unfair that producers in the developed industrial world should have to compete with imports from countries with very low wage rates and poor labour standards. Already, US trade law provides for withdrawal of trade concessions with respect to countries that engage in 'unfair labor practices'. For example, s. 301 of the U.S. Trade and Tariff Act of 1974 provides the United States Trade Representative (USTR) with discretionary authority to recommend a wide variety of trade sanctions against countries which, *inter alia*, engage in acts, policies, and practices that 'constitute a persistent pattern of conduct denying internationally recognized worker rights'.[79] In addition, with respect to developing countries in particular, trade preferences granted under the GSP[80] are denied to a country that is determined not to be 'taking steps' to implement 'basic worker rights'.[81] These are defined as: the right of association; the right to organize and bargain collectively; freedom from any kind of forced or compulsory labour; a minimum age for the employment of children; and acceptable conditions of employment with respect to minimum wages, hours of work, and occupational safety and health.[82] Although application of trade sanctions against unfair labour practices involves a unilateral judgment by the US authorities about the domestic policies of other countries, the language of the US statute does suggest as a reference point certain widely accepted international norms, as reflected in the *Conventions* of the International Labour Organization.[83] In other words, although the process is unilateral, it refers to substantive standards that are of a multilateral nature.

In the context of NAFTA, US concerns in particular about Mexican labour practices led to the negotiation of a parallel accord on labour standards. Mexican labour laws do provide for most of the workers rights contained in the ILO Conventions, but are widely believed to be un- or underenforced.[84] Some proponents of NAFTA attribute this un- or under-enforcement to a shortage of labour inspectors.[85] However, the problem is likely much more deeply rooted – reflecting widespread corruption of politicians or public officials (especially at the regional or local level), and the use of intimidation and violence to keep workers from organizing in some parts of Mexico, such as the economically important *Maquiladora* zone. Furthermore, as Morici suggests, there may be collusion between the Mexican government and the official Mexican trade union movement to keep workers unorganized in the *Maquiladoras* so as to attract more foreign investment into Mexico.[86]

Adjustment and the North American Agreement on Labor Cooperation

The North American Agreement on Labor Cooperation, usually referred to as the NAFTA Labor Side-Agreement or side-deal, has two major components. The first is a hard legal obligation on the part of NAFTA Parties to enforce adequately their own domestic labour laws, particularly with respect to occupational safety and health, child labour and minimum wage standards (Articles 3, 27). This obligation may be described as hard, in that a binding dispute settlement process may, where there is 'persistent failure' to enforce these labour laws, lead to a monetary judgment against the offending party. In the case of a successful action against Canada, the monetary judgment can be enforced through an order of a Canadian domestic court; in the case of the US and Mexico, it may be enforced through withdrawal of concessions under NAFTA. Another substantive obligation of the Side-Agreement is that 'each Party shall ensure that its labor laws and regulations provide for high labor standards consistent with high quality and productivity workforces, and shall continue to strive to improve those standards in that light' (Article 2). However, this obligation is hedged by the qualifying language that it is subject to 'the right of each Party to establish its own domestic labor standards, . . .', and – unlike the Article 3 obligation – no means of legal enforcement is contemplated for this obligation.

These obligations, and particularly the partly enforceable Article 3 obligation, may appear to have a bearing on labour adjustment, especially if one believes that un- or underenforcement of Mexican labour laws is likely to be a major cause of adjustment pressures. While there may be strong moral reasons for requiring some enforcement of basic labour standards as a condition of liberal trade, there is little convincing evidence that non-enforcement of these standards is likely to be a major source of Mexican competitive strength. Instead, legally low-paying adult jobs are likely to be the major source of competitive pressure, assuming – given a large pool of available labour and increased investment in physical and human capital – that productivity of Mexican labour can increase faster than wage rates themselves.[87]

This is not to deny that some North American firms may exploit labour law abuses in Mexico, as has already been the case with the

Maquiladoras. However, it is far from clear that under NAFTA this kind of exploitation is likely to *increase* to the point where it affects comparative advantage such as to create significant adjustment issues in other NAFTA countries.

Potentially of greater significance to the evolution of adjustment policies is the institutional framework for ongoing discussion and cooperation on labour matters that the Labor Side-Agreement provides. A Commission for Labor Co-operation is to be established, comprised of a Council and a Secretariat (Article 8), charged with, *inter alia*, promoting the collection and dissemination of data on labour issues, the production and publication of reports and studies, and the facilitation of consulation between the Parties on labour matters (Article 10). Article 11 provides a list of specific matters regarding which the Council 'shall promote cooperative activities between the Parties, as appropriate, . .'. Adjustment policies or programmes are not mentioned as such on this list. However, a number of the specific heads bear on adjustment issues, including: (d) 'human resource development'; (g) 'social programs for workers and their families'; (h) 'programs, methodologies and experiences regarding productivity improvement'; and (n) 'forms of cooperation among workers, management and government'. Moreover, the Commission is to have a mandate to facilitate cooperation not just on those matters set out in the list, but 'on such other matters as the Parties may agree'.

Perhaps more importantly, the Secretariat of the Commission – which is to have a permanent expert staff – does have an explicit mandate to engage in *reporting* on adjustment issues. Thus Article 14 stipulates that 'the Secretariat shall periodically prepare background reports setting out publicly available information supplied by each Party on . . . (d) human resource development issues such as training and adjustment programmes'.

There are several specific reasons why the Commission, and in particular, the Secretariat should make adjustment policies and programmes an important part of its mandate. At the most general level, signing a trade agreement such as NAFTA far from guarantees the disappearance or even reduction of protectionist pressures. Moreover, the Agreement leaves broad scope for the continued utilization of unilateral protectionist instruments such as antidumping and countervailing duties. Responsible monitoring of the adjustment costs of North American free trade has the potential to reinforce a balanced view of the costs and benefits of the Agreement; monitoring of countries' adjustment policy responses can focus the spotlight on whether they have been taking appropriate measures to develop adjustment-oriented alternative responses to the inevitable protectionist backlash as domestic interests feel the effects of intensified competition.

At a more specific level, there would be value to the Secretariat intervening in sectoral disputes (for instance, steel in the case of Canada and the USA) where clearly problems of excess capacity, restructuring, and intensified global competition form the background to the escalating use of unilateral protectionist instruments. The Secretariat might suggest ways in which adjustment programmes and policies could effectively address some of the background difficulties that plague the sector with a view to reducing protectionist pressures. The Commission as a whole could go further, and facilitate consultations between the Parties with a view to funding an agreed set of adjustment policies from the revenues from countervailing and anti-dumping duties. Finally, in the case of a sectoral accord or understanding to settle this kind of dispute, the Secretariat could be active in proposing an adjustment component to such an accord, where for example each Party agrees to a given set of measures to facilitate orderly exit of workers from the sector, as part of restructuring and the reduction of excess capacity.[88]

Finally, the NAFTA contains a 'safeguard' or 'escape clause' provision modelled on that in Article XIX of the GATT. Under this provision, where (during the transitional period for phase-out of tariffs) imports of goods from another NAFTA Party increase to the extent that the increases alone 'constitute a substantial cause of serious injury, or threat thereof, to a domestic industry', tariffs may be re-imposed up to the pre-NAFTA level of duty (Article 801). Reimposition of duties must be, however, to 'the minimum extent necessary to remedy or prevent the injury'(Article 801). It is arguable that, in interpreting the 'minimum extent' requirement, account should be taken of the degree to which the country whose industry is facing injury has taken non- or less trade-restrictive measures to address the problems posed by increased imports and ensure longer-term adjustment to higher levels of imports. Here also, it is arguable that the Secretariat could appropriately give itself a mandate to examine adjustment issues surrounding invocation of escape clause relief. While the Labor Commission clearly has no formal involvement in settlement of disputes concerning emergency action under Article 801,[89] nevertheless Secretariat staff could be charged with preparation of a report – in consultation with the affected Parties – on the nature of any adjustment-related problems in the industry on whose behalf emergency action has been taken.

Whether the institutional framework established under the NAFTA Labor Side-Agreement is effective in addressing the links between adjustment and trade policies will depend decisively upon the quality and priorities of the Secretariat's Executive Director and the staff, to be comprised initially of fifteen members. Clearly, this is a small group to cover the entire horizon of trade-related labour policies and laws. However, with the appropriate degree of will and determination, much can be done within these constraints. Furthermore, the Side-Agreement explicitly contemplates that the number of staff may be changed in future by the Council (made up of Ministerial representatives of the NAFTA Parties). In any event, a useful beginning would be to encourage governments to report their own expectations with respect to adjustment costs entailed by trade liberalization under

NAFTA, and the policies and programmes they expect will be in place to address those costs. At the same time, the Secretariat should encourage stakeholder (e.g. industry, trade union, etc.) responses to these reports from the various NAFTA governments. A defect of the Labor Side-Agreement is that it provides virtually no formal channels for stakeholder participation in the activities of the Labor Commission. It is clear, however, that the Secretariat may receive information from a 'person or organization' since the Labor Side-Agreement contains specific provisions concerning protection of the confidentiality of the source or content of such information (Article 6).

Race to the bottom concerns

Even beyond the issue of compliance with internationally recognized norms of workers rights, some critics of free trade argue that the mere existence of large differentials in labour costs between trading partners puts in question the gains from trade. A major concern is that of a 'race to the bottom' – the need to compete with imports from countries with lower labour costs and/or standards can be expected, it is argued, to exert downward pressure on wages and standards in developed industrial countries. 'Race to the bottom' concerns influenced the European Union's decision to link a Community Social Charter and Social Programme, that covers a wide range of labour laws and standards, to increased economic integration.[90]

In our view, the 'race to the bottom' is much more likely to occur under conditions of very deep economic integration between countries that already have similar levels of economic development, worker productivity etc., so that few barriers or factors other than relative labour costs remain in place to influence where products are manufactured. This, however, is not the case with respect to existing levels of economic integration between, say, the United States and Bangladesh, or even Mexico – although it may be the case for the various members of the European Union. With respect to many products, the higher levels of skill and productivity of developed country workers will continue to give these countries a comparative advantage in many sectors. In addition, where relatively low labour costs do constitute a decisive part of the comparative advantage of one's trade competitors, lowering one's own wages or labour standards is by no means the logical domestic policy response: it may make much more sense, along the lines of the discussion on adjustment earlier in this chapter, to retrain or reskill one's own workers for higher-value-added jobs in other sectors of the economy.[91]

Critics of trade with low-wage countries may respond, however, that low wages and other poor conditions of work do not reflect underlying economic realities as much as oppressive social and political arrangements. In theory, in a world with no barriers to exit and entry for workers (i.e. a world where immigration was completely liberalized) workers who were underpaid for a given level of productivity (due to social and political arrangements in their country of origin) would simply move to other countries where that level of productivity is rewarded with higher wages. A labour shortage would develop in countries with relatively low wages and a surplus would be created in countries that happened to have wages that were particularly high relative to productivity. The result would be that wages would be pushed up in low wage countries and/or pushed down in high wage countries. The truth is that barriers to labour mobility constitute a major reason why some countries can sustain wage rates that are low relative to productivity – *and* why others may be able to sustain wage rates that are high relative to productivity. Thus, by virtue of their restrictive immigration laws, the major industrial nations with high wage costs are in fact complicit with whatever social or political oppression may be keeping wages low in some developing countries. But rarely do critics of the role that trade plays in reinforcing supposed exploitation of cheap labour also argue against restrictive immigration policies.

In fact, as has been noted by the United Nations Development Program (UNDP) in its 1991 *Development Report*, higher exports in a number of LDCs have indeed led to higher wages, including a higher social wage and increased public investment in education, health care and other social services.[92] Employment of workers even at initially very low wages has in some countries reduced the ranks of the starving and totally destitute, and resulted in a significantly larger percentage of the population at least being capable of mobilization by progressive political movements.[93] Of course, in other countries the record has not been so positive. However, we are persuaded that on balance trade is likely to improve the lot of the least advantaged in most developing countries. This is not to say that it is inappropriate to link closer trade ties with such countries, as well as trade preferences, to compliance with internationally agreed human rights norms, including worker's rights under the *ILO Conventions*. But low wages in and of themselves should not be viewed as an objection to trade. Moreover, even the unilateralist American approach to unfair labour practices of trading partners entails the recognition that compliance with international standards must be considered relative to a country's level of development.

With respect to existing trade concessions that are legally bound in the GATT, withdrawal of these concessions as a response to labour practices in violation of international rights norms would nevertheless constitute a violation of the GATT – unless the practices in question could be characterized as 'negative subsidies' that confer an advantage or benefit on producers in the country concerned by reducing the costs of production. Imposition of countervailing duties, however, would prove to be a largely arbitrary means of aiding the process of compliance with human rights norms in developing countries, since which practices are targeted will be a function of the demand for protection in the importing country, not the seriousness of the rights violations or the concerns of human rights activists.

In our view, rather than encouraging the use of countervailing duties in these situations, it would be preferable to amend the GATT to permit Contracting Parties to restrict trade in goods produced in a manner that reflects systematic violation by the producing country of widely accepted international workers' rights or other human rights norms. This would most appropriately be done by making an addition to Article XX(d), which already permits restrictions or prohibitions on imports of products manufactured with prison labour. The general limitations of Article XX would apply to such otherwise GATT-inconsistent trade measures – namely that they not be applied in a discriminatory fashion and that they not constitute 'disguised restrictions on trade'. Non-discrimination is important, since it places a limit on the ability of Contracting Parties to target countries not on the basis of their workers' rights records as such, but rather in response to protectionist pressures. If a Contracting Party, for instance, believed that it was subject to such trade measures for purely protectionist reasons while many other countries with worse worker's rights records were left unaffected it could invoke the GATT dispute settlement process and argue that the measures did not conform to the general criteria of Article XX. In addition, it could be provided in Article XX that before taking trade measures against a Contracting Party for violation of internationally recognized worker's rights, the importing state must consult with the International Labour Organization, the international body responsible for the oversight of the *ILO Conventions*. Alternately, or in addition, where a dispute arises under this proposed new provision in the General Agreement, the Panel or Working Party should be required to consult with the ILO, or perhaps even to defer to the ILO's judgement of whether the country(ies) in question are indeed systematically violating worker's rights.

CONCLUSION

With the new Uruguay Round Safeguards Agreement, with future reforms to the regime along the lines discussed earlier in this chapter, and with adequate domestic labour market adjustment policies implemented along with carefully defined constraints on oppressive labour practices of trade rivals, we believe that the adjustment costs associated with trade liberalization or shifting patterns of comparative advantage will have been adequately addressed. In particular, the case for retaining broadly-cast domestic antidumping and countervailing duty regimes, either to address the impact of growth of imports on domestic industries or to address claims of 'unfair trade', will have been substantially refuted. While trade-related transition costs are an important policy concern, the existing panoply of trade remedy laws lack any normatively coherent structure for dealing with these costs. Radical reform of existing trade remedy laws, operationalizing an effective right on the part of workers to adjustment assistance, and multilateral agreement on baseline labour market standards, are issues that are likely to continue to occupy a central place on the future international trade policy agenda.

8

TRADE IN AGRICULTURE

INTRODUCTION

Over the last two decades, trade in agriculture has become one of the most prominent and acrimonious issues on the world trade agenda. A solution to some of these controversies, particularly those surrounding agricultural export subsidies and related domestic measures (such as price supports and production quotas) was crucial to the successful conclusion of the Uruguay Round of GATT negotiations. Protectionism has been pervasive in the agricultural sector in Canada, the United States, the EU and Japan. Prior to the Uruguay Round Final Act, the GATT itself placed fewer strictures on agricultural protection than was the case with most other sectors. Moreover, a number of the major exporting states had come close to ignoring GATT requirements altogether, even to the point of refusing to implement GATT panel decisions. The International Monetary Fund recently estimated that the costs of agricultural protection to taxpayers and consumers in the OECD countries alone amounts to about $US300 billion each year. The IMF has also found that liberalization of this sector, involving both trade and domestic policy reforms in these countries, would result in gains to consumers and taxpayers far outweighing losses to agricultural producers.[1]

Despite the economic welfare case for liberalizing trade in agriculture, a number of rationales are still often invoked for treating the agricultural sector as a special case. These rationales include: supposedly exceptional price and income instability; the importance to national security of agricultural self-sufficiency; and the cultural and social value of preserving rural lifestyles. At the same time, liberalization – while leading to eventual substantial net gains in welfare, both global and domestic – poses significant adjustment and transitional equity issues.

In this chapter, we will consider the existing treatment of agriculture in trade law and practice; the extent to which it is justifiable to treat agriculture as a special case; and the liberalization achievements of the Uruguay Round Final Act, with particular attention to managing the challenge of adjustment.

191

TRADE IN AGRICULTURE AND THE
PRE-URUGUAY ROUND GATT

Historical origins of special treatment for agriculture

The special treatment of agriculture in the General Agreement was largely, if not exclusively, a reflection of the power and influence of the United States at the end of the Second World War. The negotiators of the GATT did not, generally speaking, see any need for a special regime for agriculture. Import quotas and export subsidies were, however, an integral feature of the American supply management system for agricultural products that existed at the time, and as Dam suggests, 'no treaty that impinged upon the U.S. Farm program could receive the constitutionally required senatorial approval'.[2] As will be discussed in detail below, the special treatment of agriculture contained in the General Agreement has led to a large number of disputes over the interpretation of the GATT. Moreover, in this area – more so than in any other – Contracting Parties found it impossible to live with GATT panel decisions limiting their capacity to engage in agricultural protection. Thus, for the United States, the special treatment it won under the General Agreement for import restrictions linked to domestic supply management proved insufficient, leading the US Administration to seek a waiver of Article XI GATT obligations as early as 1955, with respect to a variety of agricultural products, including sugar, peanuts and dairy products.[3] Similarly, the European Union has either blocked the adoption of, or refused to implement, Panel decisions that threaten elements of its Common Agricultural Policy.

Quantitative restrictions

Article XI of the GATT prohibits quantitative restrictions on trade, subject to certain exceptions. Several of the exceptions are of particular relevance to trade in agriculture. First of all, Article XI (2) (a) permits export 'prohibitions or restrictions' of a temporary nature in order to address critical food shortages in the exporting country. Second, XI(2)(b) permits 'import and export restrictions'[4] necessary to the application of standards or regulations for the classification, grading or marketing of commodities in international trade'. Third, and most importantly, XI (2) (c) permits import restrictions on 'any agricultural or fisheries product' where necessary to enforce domestic restrictions on the marketing or production of a similar product or product substitute. Import restrictions are also permitted where necessary to remove a temporary surplus of a domestic like product or product substitute. Article XIII sets out detailed rules on the use of quantitative restrictions in cases where one or more of these exceptions apply.

In theory, at least, an important constraint on the protectionist impact of these exceptions to the ban on quantitative restrictions is that the import restrictions in question must be accompanied by like domestic measures. Foreigners cannot be singled out or targeted – hence, import restrictions must not reduce the total value of imports proportionate to domestic production below that 'which might reasonably be expected to rule between the two in the absence of restrictions' (Article XI:2). If this condition were applied rigorously, it would mean that domestic price supports could be operated in a manner consistent with comparative advantage. If, for example, a Contracting Party placed a quota of 10 million chickens a year on domestic marketing of poultry, and chickens from another Contracting Party would have had a 60% market share under *unrestricted* market conditions, then the other Contracting Party would be entitled to a share of 6 million chickens.

This, of course, involves a difficult counterfactual exercise – i.e. determining comparative advantage in agriculture absent the price distortions created by domestic price support policies in the import-restricting country. Nevertheless, in theory, it should make quantitative restrictions a rather unattractive instrument of agricultural protection, since foreigners end up with a market share equal to that which would exist in the absence of protection.

Perhaps for this very reason this condition on the use of quantitative restrictions has never been effectively enforced. An attempt in the 1950s to enforce the even more general condition that import restrictions be 'necessary' to enforce domestic marketing and production limits resulted in a threat from the United States that it would leave the GATT. A GATT Working Party found that US import restrictions on dairy products were not accompanied by domestic restrictions on the production of the raw material for the products (milk), and retaliation was authorized under Article XXIII when the United States failed to remove the restrictions in question.[5] In the face of the threat of US withdrawal from GATT, the United States was granted a non-time-limited waiver from the strictures of Article XI with respect to agricultural products. This exemption for the United States may well have had the effect of dampening efforts to enforce strictly Article XI against other Contracting Parties – given that the United States was granted a waiver, it might have been difficult, on principled grounds, to have refused one to others.

Nevertheless, in several recent panel decisions, a stricter view of the provisions of Article XI has been taken. For instance, in ruling on an American complaint concerning Japanese quantitative restrictions on a wide variety of agricultural product groups, a GATT panel held that Article XI:2(c)(i) should be construed narrowly, and, in particular, that there was a burden of proof on the import-restricting state to show that it had granted to foreign producers the market share that would exist if there were no restrictions.[6] The Panel decision did not, however, establish a methodology or detailed guidelines for making such a determination – the Panel merely held that Japan had not attempted to discharge the burden of proof. In another case, which concerned import restrictions imposed by the

European Union in the face of a surplus of apples, a Panel held that the exemption in Article XI:2(c)(ii) did not apply, because the surplus was not temporary, but rather a chronic side-effect of the Union's own agricultural price support policies.[7] In a case that concerned Canadian quantitative restrictions on imports of yoghurt and ice cream from the United States, Canada argued before the Panel that these restrictions were 'necessary' to render effective domestic production restrictions on milk, in the sense that the higher cost of milk generated by these restrictions made secondary products manufactured with the higher cost Canadian milk vulnerable to imports. Therefore, Canada claimed, the requirements of Article XI:2(c)(i) had been met. The Panel took a narrow view of the word 'necessary', finding that it did not include import restrictions aimed at neutralizing the competitive disadvantage to other domestic industries of higher domestic prices for agricultural inputs. In effect, without the restrictions, Canada would still be able to enforce domestic restrictions on milk production and hence keep the price of milk high – albeit at some cost to Canadian yoghurt and ice cream makers. This ruling is arguably quite important, since it prevents Article XI:2(c)(i) from being used by Contracting Parties to shift the costs of their agricultural protectionism from their own agrifood industries on to foreign competitors in these industries.

Export subsidies

Article XVI of the General Agreement prohibits export subsidies, subject to an exception for 'primary products'. These are permitted, with the proviso that 'they shall not be applied in a manner which results in that contracting party having more than an equitable share of world export trade in that product, . . .'. In defining what constitutes an equitable share, 'shares of the contracting parties in such trade in the product in a previous representative period' are to be taken into account. This suggests that the essential issue is whether the export subsidy has caused an increase in market share over that which prevailed in the period before the subsidy was introduced. A 'primary product' is defined in an Interpretive Note to Article XVI as 'any product of farm, forest, or fishery at an early stage of processing'.

These provisions were incorporated into the Tokyo Round Subsidies Code (Article 10), with minor variations. In particular, the expression 'more than an equitable share of world trade' was defined to apply to those cases where 'the effect of an export subsidy granted by a signatory is to displace the exports of another signatory bearing in mind the developments on world markets' (Article 10(2)(a)). As well, the 'previous representative period' would normally be 'the three most recent calendar years in which normal market conditions existed' (Article 10(2)(c)).

Even with these criteria, it proved very difficult to interpret the concept of 'an equitable share of world trade'. In a 1958 case that concerned French subsidies on the export of wheat flour, the Panel ruled that the subsidies did not comply with the GATT because France had attained more than an equitable share of the world market. Three considerations formed the basis of this finding: (1) France's exports of flour to the market in question (Southeast Asia) had increased over a previous period; (2) the complainant's (Australia's) exports to the same market declined; and (3) the subsidy was found to be a 'substantial cause' of the displacement.[8] In a more recent case,[9] however, a Panel found that European Union subsidies on wheat flour were permissible under Article XVI, even though the Union's share of the world market had increased from 29% to 75% between 1962 and 1981, while the complainant (the United States) had seen its share over the comparable period decline from 25% to 9%. The Panel noted the difficulty in determining whether, in fact, changes in market share could be attributable to a particular export subsidy, as opposed to other factors. It seemed to be suggesting that specific evidence of price undercutting in the market in question would be required to establish that export subsidies were unambiguously resulting in displacement – shifts in market share alone were insufficient, however dramatic.

The United States objected strongly to this approach, and vetoed adoption of the Panel report. However, the Report is defensible on at least two grounds: (1) As Jackson notes, the United States itself was marketing its own wheat in the same market on non-commercial terms, through a food aid programme,[10] and therefore neither country's market share could be considered over the period in question to have been based on undistorted market conditions; and (2) although dramatic increases in market share had occurred, this had taken place over a period of twenty years, whereas the text of the Subsidies Code itself suggested that market share changes should be considered in terms of changes occurring within a three year representative period. More generally, by the time of this dispute world trade in agriculture had become so distorted by the domestic and export policies of the main producers that the Panel's difficulty in finding a clear benchmark against which the distorting effect of one particular subsidy could be measured was entirely understandable.

In the *Pasta* case, the United States argued that subsidies paid by the European Community to exporters of pasta violated Article 9 of the GATT Subsidies Code, which prohibits export subsidies on 'non-primary' products.[11] The EU responded that the subsidy should be viewed as a subsidy on primary product inputs into pasta production, in particular European durum wheat. The effect of the subsidy, according to the EU, was simply to compensate EU pasta exporters for the higher than world prices of EU flour, thereby allowing them to be competitive on world markets despite purchasing wheat at higher prices than foreign competitors. This argument was rejected by a majority of the Panel, which read Article 9 literally to include all subsidies *paid* to exporters of non-primary products, without regard to whether the intended or actual effect was to subsidize indirectly a primary product. One of the four panellists, however, wrote a dissenting opinion, taking the view that in negotiating the Tokyo Round Subsidies Code, governments had generally understood or assumed that subsidies on primary components of non-primary products would not be prohibited by Article 9.

The EU blocked adoption of the majority ruling by the Subsidies Committee and eventually reached a negotiated settlement with the United States of the dispute in question. But the ultimate consequence was continued uncertainty about the legality under GATT of one of the most pervasive and controversial features of the European Union's Common Agricultural Policy – export subsidies on products that use EU agricultural inputs.

Domestic subsidies and related domestic support measures

A more recent GATT ruling narrowed the scope for granting *domestic* subsidies to users of a product rather than its producers. As discussed in a previous chapter, domestic subsidies are not prohibited by the GATT, although, in accordance with the rules set out in the Subsidies Code, they may be countervailable. However, in the *Oilseeds*[12] case, a GATT panel found that a subsidy paid to European Union users of oilseeds violated Article III, the National Treatment principle of the GATT. Here, the Panel took a quite literal approach to the wording of Article III, which only exempts subsidies from the National Treatment obligation if they are paid 'exclusively' to domestic producers of the subsidized product (Article III:8 (b)). The EU revised the form of assistance so that it appeared to comply with the requirements of Article III. However, a subsequent panel found this new form of assistance still constituted non-violation nullification or impairment of a benefit that the United States could reasonably have expected from previous GATT concessions. Here, the United States was able to point to an early GATT tariff binding on oilseeds by the EU, which gave it reason to expect at least some level of access to the EU market.[13] Bilateral negotiations between the EU and the USA concerning implementation of the panel's ruling were initially unsuccessful; the dispute was finally resolved within the framework of a broader US/EU agreement on negotiating positions in the Uruguay Round (the Blair House Agreement, discussed in a later section of this chapter).

Health and other technical standards

Article XX (b) of the GATT permits the adoption of measures that would otherwise constitute violations of the General Agreement where 'necessary to protect human, animal or plant life or health'. This is subject to the general proviso that the measures in question be applied on a non-discriminatory basis (i.e. in a manner consistent with the MFN principle), and that they not constitute a 'disguised restriction on trade'. It has been a long-standing concern of the United States in particular that sanitary and phyto-sanitary regulations with respect to the importation of meat are often used as disguised restrictions on trade. However, there are few Panel rulings that relate to this issue, in part because since the adoption of the GATT Standards Code in 1980, a separate, more scientific or expertise-based dispute resolution process is available where technical barriers to trade are at issue. The Standards Code obliges Contracting Parties to attempt to harmonize technical standards, and, as Hillman notes, there are a number of international standard-setting entities in the agricultural area.[14]

However, science-based approaches are not necessarily able to settle disagreements about technical barriers. This is well-illustrated by the so called *Beef Hormone*[15] case. In this case, the United States filed a complaint against the EU under the GATT Standards Code, alleging that an EU ban on US hormone-fed beef had no basis in scientific evidence of a health danger from human consumption of the hormones. The EU viewed the ban as a legitimate response to public concerns about use of hormones as growth stimulants, while admitting that there was little scientific support for these concerns. The more technical legal disagreement surrounded whether the Code applied to standards which were not product standards in the strict sense but rather which applied to the 'process or production method' (PPM) by which a product was produced (clearly, the ban on hormone-fed beef went to the method of production of the beef). The EU replied that the Code did not apply to PPMs. The United States, however, invoked a provision of the Code that suggested PPMs would be covered in circumstances where their effect was to circumvent the primary obligations of the Code not to create 'unnecessary obstacles to trade'.

In the event, a technical panel under the Code was never established to decide the matter, since the EU refused to accept its jurisdiction, arguing that the Code did not apply at all to the kind of measure at issue. The EU was prepared to have a special panel of legal experts address the threshold issue of the Code's jurisdiction over the dispute, but this was unacceptable to the United States. The USA undertook trade retaliation and eventually a negotiated settlement of the dispute was reached.

THE CANADA–US FREE TRADE AGREEMENT (FTA) AND THE NORTH AMERICAN FREE TRADE AGREEMENT (NAFTA)

Chapter Seven of the FTA deals with trade in agriculture. The main impact on agricultural trade is the phased-in reduction and eventual elimination of tariffs on many agricultural commodities. However, because the FTA contains few strictures with respect to domestic support measures, its overall liberalizing effect is quite modest. Article 701 does, however, prohibit export subsidies on agricultural goods moving from one FTA partner to the other. It should be noted that this does not prohibit the use of export subsidies when Canada and the USA are competing against each other in third-country markets. Instead, there is a weak obligation to take into account the harmful effects of such subsidies of exports to third countries on the other FTA partner (Article 701.4).

As well, although the FTA does not contain a general prohibition on non-tariff border measures, such as quotas imposed to implement supply management schemes, the United States was able to obtain from Canada minimum market access commitments under some of these schemes. For instance, with respect to chicken and chicken products, the United States is entitled to an import quota no less than 7.5% of the previous year's domestic production of chickens in Canada (Article 706). In addition, the Parties agree to work towards harmonizing technical standards, and a number of technical working groups are established for this purpose (Article 708).

In the case of NAFTA, there is, generally speaking, little substantial progress over the FTA with respect to trilateral trade liberalization, due largely to Canadian intransigence with respect to supply management schemes (which, of course, will now have to be modified in light of the Agreement on Agriculture in the Uruguay Round Final Act).[16] However, the NAFTA contains much more promising provisions with respect to US–Mexico agricultural trade, including a waiver of GATT rights with respect to imposition of quantitative restrictions connected to domestic supply management (Article XI:2(c) of GATT). There is a complicated scheme for tariff reductions, with tariffs on some commodities to be eliminated between all three countries immediately, whereas tariffs on other commodities are to be phased out in either a five, ten, or fifteen-year period, again depending upon the commitments each country has made with respect to that particular commodity. Canada insisted on excluding poultry, milk and eggs from these commitments. However, in some other areas, Canada has agreed to lift quantitative restrictions on imports from Mexico, including cereals, meats, and margarine (with respect to the United States, US rights of market access where Canada maintains quantitative restrictions remain governed by the provisions of the FTA which have been substantially incorporated into the NAFTA). NAFTA also contains provisions on technical barriers that resemble very closely those in the Uruguay Round Final Act (to be discussed later in this chapter).

An economic model of the effects of liberalization commitments in NAFTA with respect to agricultural products predicts that, when NAFTA is fully implemented, agricultural trade between the USA and Mexico will be 15% greater than it was in the 1988 base year.[17] US exports to Mexico are predicted to increase more rapidly that Mexican exports to the USA, in part because Mexico's pre-NAFTA level of border protection on these commodities was substantially higher than that of the USA.[18] A major shortcoming of this kind of model, is of course, the difficulty of predicting other factors such as exchange rate movements, changes in agricultural demand and supply in other countries, etc. that may affect the impact of the NAFTA. Significantly, Canada was not treated in the model as a NAFTA partner, because the impact of NAFTA on its agricultural trade was assumed to be minimal.

RATIONALES FOR DIFFERENTIAL TREATMENT OF THE AGRICULTURAL SECTOR: A CRITICAL OVERVIEW

Although much agricultural protectionism can be attributed to the influence of powerful farm lobbies in North America, Europe, and Japan, there are a number of long-standing rationales for the justification of protection that are specific to this sector.

Self-sufficiency/National security

In the most literal sense, a nation's survival can be said to depend upon access to food. Famines have appeared periodically throughout history, and continue to do so in much of the developing world, whether caused by war, pestilence, or drought. In times of shortage, access to food from foreign imports may well dry up, as countries impose export restrictions to ensure their own populace gets fed first. As we noted above, this kind of export control is in fact explicitly authorized by the GATT. Under these circumstances, it is not surprising that self-sufficiency is often cited as a rationale for agricultural protection, or more precisely, as a rationale for measures that maintain agricultural production in a country where it would be more efficient for most or all of its needs to be met from imports. A variant on the self-sufficiency argument is the purported advantage of not having to rely on foreigners who may be one's enemies in war (or potential enemies) for the supply of food.

Exceptional price instability

Agricultural commodities are subject to price fluctuations often considerably greater than many other goods that are traded, in significant part because supply is so susceptible to unpredictable factors such as weather. As a consequence, farmers' incomes are highly volatile. On the other hand, their costs (debt service on land, equipment etc.) are likely to be fixed to a significant extent. In the end, it is argued, unless supply is restricted, or prices stabilized by other means, a single bad year may well result in many farmers being put out of business altogether, although in some sense they nevertheless have an on-going comparative advantage in producing food. Although much of the agricultural industry in developed countries is now constituted by large commercial producers, the image of the family losing its farm, and therewith a lifetime of work together, remains a powerful and poignant image in popular culture.

Preservation of the rural way of life/environment

Over the last few decades, efficiency of agricultural production has increased enormously in most developed countries. Therefore, even if a certain level of domestic food production could be seen as necessary for self-sufficiency reasons, or even if price stabilization could be justified as a means of making farm incomes less volatile, nevertheless there would still be a long-run shift of both land and people away from agricultural production – one can simply meet existing demand with less land and fewer people. Hence, in recent years an often heard argument for agricultural protection has been that keeping land and people in farming is a social good in itself. With respect to land, the implicit assumption is that, but for agricultural usages, the countryside would be much more heavily burdened with ugly, polluting industries, or simply replaced by industrial or commercial towns. A closely related argument is that agriculture sustains rural *communities*, which would either disappear or lose their distinctive character if economic activity in the countryside were shifted away from agricultural production.

Wilson and Finkle suggest, writing primarily of the Canadian context:

Farmers enjoy an undercurrent of sympathy among urban voters which confers political power on them quite out of proportion to their numbers . . . most urbanites are attracted to the idealized image of the countryside: the hard working farm family, the noble virtues and traditional values which they imagine motivate their rustic compatriots. It is not a lifestyle most urbanites would care to live themselves but they are glad someone is doing it and they are willing to pay a bit to see it maintained.[19]

As well, Europeans in particular are fond of arguing that their countryside is a natural and cultural treasure that would be fundamentally threatened if land were taken out of agricultural production.

None of these three main kinds of rationales is entirely bogus, although assumptions that the agricultural industry is largely composed of needy farm families or that modern farming operations are more aesthetically or environmentally friendly than other kinds of contemporary economic activity deserve critical scrutiny. The more fundamental issue is whether any of these goals really necessitates measures that radically distort world trade and cost non-farm households more than a $1000 per year in both higher food prices and in taxes that pay for farm subsidies. For example, with respect to the price instability of agricultural products, the real issue is the stability of farmer's incomes. Farmer's incomes could be stabilized directly, through income averaging techniques or income insurance, rather than distorting domestic prices and limiting foreign competition in order to maintain artificially high domestic prices. With respect to rural life-style values, careful regional development plans seem a more finely-tuned instrument than agricultural protection to ensure balanced economic activity in the countryside. As we shall argue below, much of the potential for reforming agricultural trade comes from this potential for 'decoupling' of policy goals such as income stabilization from trade distortive policies.

INSTRUMENTS OF AGRICULTURAL PROTECTION

Domestic price control and supply management systems and related trade measures

The European Union Common Agricultural Policy (CAP)

In theory, the Common Agricultural Policy (CAP) is based on the objectives in Article 39 of the Treaty of Rome, including market stabilization, increased agricultural productivity, and reasonable agricultural prices for consumers. During the 1960s and 1970s, the CAP developed into a complex web of price and sales guarantees, subsidies, and other support measures that largely insulated farmer's incomes from market forces. For most agricultural products, a minimum price was set to apply to all sales within the EU. In order not to undermine this price, it was essential that lower-priced imports be prohibited. This was achieved by a Variable Import Levy – a charge on imported goods equivalent to whatever difference exists at the time of entry between world price and the Union price. In effect, through the levy, the Union is able to neutralize whatever price advantage a foreign competitor might enjoy.

As Martin has remarked, 'European farmers have demonstrated beyond a shadow of a doubt that they are economically rational.'[20] Hence, in the face of guaranteed prices considerably above world prices and no production controls, they expanded production. It should be remembered that since the price was set so that the least efficient producers in Europe could make a profit, it offered significant rents or *supra*-normal profits to the more efficient producers. In addition, given that technological developments were increasing the efficiency of *all* farmers, it is not surprising that enormous surpluses soon developed. Since prices could not be lowered, there was no obvious way to dispose of the surplus in an orderly fashion. In consequence, the Union came to make undertakings to farmers to purchase their surplus at the high Union price. Enormous stockpiles of many commodities soon developed, and by the 1980s close to 80% of the Union budget was spent on agricultural programmes. Once again, farmers behaved entirely rationally, and now that they had not only prices but also sales guaranteed, further invested to expand production.

It is in the context of these pressures that the Union established a rebate on export sales, where in order to encourage disposal of the surpluses on world markets, the Union pays exporters the difference between the high Union price and the world price. Although these rebates have often been characterized, and condemned as export subsidies, in theory it should be noted that they do not actually undercut the world price. However, critics of the CAP have often charged that, in practice, rebates are given which exceed the difference between the Union and the world price, because the EU authorities tend systematically to underestimate world price in their calculation of the rebates. What is certainly true is that the CAP went from a programme that affected trade by keeping foreign producers out of the EU market to one that, at the same time, because of the massive surpluses being disposed of through the rebate scheme, made it increasingly difficult for foreign producers to sell their agricultural products in *third country* markets.

North America

Although Americans have tended to single out the CAP as the main villain in the agricultural trade wars, it must be remembered that it was US agricultural protection that led to weak GATT rules in agriculture in the first place. These have included price support measures, coupled however with production restrictions. There is a legitimate argument that these measures were less harmful than the CAP price support mechanism – since production restrictions were in place, keeping prices high did not result in the generation of massive surpluses. Also, since the mid-1980s, the United States has attempted to permanently reduce production by paying farmers to take land out of service. As well, instead of keeping the market price artificially high, for some commodities the United States now pays to farmers the difference between the price they can get on the market and a target price based on a formula that reflects the revenue farmers need to break even.

Although Americans often claim that US export subsidies are a competitive response to EU and other foreign programmes, in fact such subsidies long predate the CAP. However, it is true that during the 1960s and 1970s the United States' use of export subsidies declined considerably, until in 1985 a new set of aggressive subsidies was introduced in response to the CAP.[21]

Canada maintains marketing and production restrictions on poultry and eggs, enforced through domestic and import quotas. These import quotas have been justified under Article XI: 2(c) of the GATT, discussed earlier in this chapter. In addition, Canada actively subsidizes the sale of wheat and other grains, often through concessional financing by the Canadian Wheat Board, which actively tries to undercut competitors' in many export markets. However, Canada tends to view these subsidies as a response to similar behaviour on the part of its competitors, particularly the European Union, where a grain industry would be largely non-existent but for the CAP.

In addition, both Canada and the United States both provide a variety of forms of assistance to farmers that, arguably, do not directly distort world or domestic prices, such as crop insurance and low-interest loans and loan guarantees for purchase of land and equipment and generous tax write-offs (the latter, in the case of Canada, have created a new class of 'gentlemen-farmers'). The arguments concerning whether such subsidies are objectionable as leading to inefficient or unfair trade are much the same as for any other domestic subsidy.

Japan

Japan's domestic market for agricultural products is one of the most protected in the world, at least with respect to some commodities. A wide range of instruments is employed that includes price stabilization, control of supply by state or quasi-state monopolies, coupled with import quotas and extremely high tariffs. According to Gilson,[22] in 1988, the Japanese domestic price for wheat was eight times the world price. Rice is often estimated to cost 10 or 11 times as much in Japan as on world markets and beef is heavily protected as well. Japan, however, is not a major exporter of agricultural products, and therefore does not participate in the export subsidy war between North America and the European Union.

Costs and benefits of agricultural protection

There have been many estimates in recent years of the costs and benefits of agricultural protection, using different methodologies and different definitions of what constitutes protection.[23] With respect to costs, these include the expense to the taxpayers of on-budget measures such as export and domestic subsidies, and commitments to purchase surpluses, costs to consumers of more expensive food, and allocative efficiency losses as resources are misdirected to agricultural production where no comparative advantage exists in the farm sector.

Figure 8.1, taken from a recent Survey by the *Economist*[24] magazine, contains estimates of the per household per year costs of agricultural protection in the United States, Western Europe and Japan (including both higher taxes and higher food prices):

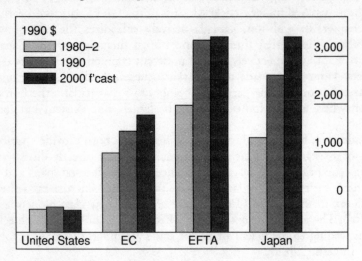

Figure 8.1 *Cost of agricultural support per non-farm household*
Source: 'Disarray in world food markets', by Tyers and Anderson

These costs, which globally average around $1400 per household per year for the countries concerned, represent a considerable welfare loss. To these costs must be added the environmental costs of over-farming due to incentives to increase production in the European Union, and the dead-weight loss of resources devoted to lobbying for protection. As well, the effect of protection in the developed countries is to shut out to a large extent the developing countries and the Newly Liberalizing Countries of Central and Eastern Europe from many agricultural markets, thereby further retarding growth and adjustment (although some developing countries may benefit, at least in the short run, from lower food prices due to subsidized food exports of developed countries).[25] As well, developed countries such as Australia and New Zealand, which have undertaken unilateral liberalization of their own agricultural support policies see themselves as having much to gain from more open policies elsewhere, and have been leading forces behind the Cairns Group, which has pressed for comprehensive agreement on agriculture as part of the Uruguay Round.[26]

The effects of protection on farmers' incomes in various countries, including industrialized and developing countries, are displayed in Figure 8.2.

The gains to farmers in the EU and Japan are clearly very large. As the *Economist* notes,[27] since the gains from protection are proportional to the amount produced, small or poor farmers receive a small percentage of these gains, and highly efficient, large 'industrial' farms capture the lion's share.

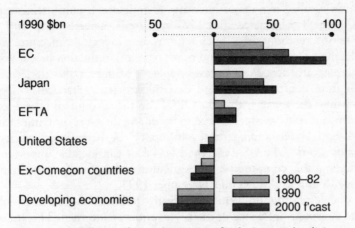

Figure 8.2 Effect on farmers' incomes of rich countries' policies
Source: The Economist

These gains, however, do not easily translate into the purported rationales for or social benefits from agricultural protection discussed above. First of all, while prices have been supported domestically, protection has led to increased instability in world prices, as surpluses have rapidly developed in various commodities. This in turn has made domestic price support increasingly costly. Second, even very high levels of protection have not saved the family farm – the exodus to the cities continues, because increased efficiency means that more can be produced with fewer farmers, and because small family farms often do not have access to the capital needed to invest in the expansion of production and particularly the technology that would allow them to capture major gains from protection. Finally, agricultural protection does not appear to have prevented environmental and aesthetic degradation in rural areas – indeed, as mentioned earlier, over-farming with intensive use of fertilizers and other chemicals has begun to contribute significantly to environmental degradation.

THE URUGUAY ROUND AGREEMENT ON AGRICULTURE

Given the extremely high costs and dubious benefits of agricultural protection – and particularly the increasing cost of beggar-thy-neighbour subsidy wars – the case for removing agricultural protection is a particularly strong one, and was accepted at the level of principle by both the United States[28] and the European Union as a basic goal of the Uruguay Round negotiations. Indeed, as early as 1982, the OECD Ministerial Council had adopted a declaration that 'agricultural trade should be more fully integrated into and within the open and multilateral trading system', also agreeing that multilateral negotiations should address 'adjustments in domestic policies'.[29] This ultimately resulted in a major initiative on agricultural policy reform in the OECD, which culminated in a 1987 ministerial agreement to undertake major reforms without delay. Such reforms were to include 'measures which, by reducing guaranteed prices and other types of production incentives, . . . will prevent an increase in excess supply'.[30] Ministers also undertook to 'refrain from confrontational and destabilising trade practices'.[31] Despite this apparent consensus within the OECD on the need for and the direction of reform, agricultural issues proved to be among the most contentious in the Round, and understanding the evolution of the bargaining positions of the major actors – the USA and the EU – is of considerable importance in appreciating the compromise on agriculture that finally permitted the Uruguay Round to close in mid-December 1993.

At one level, the problem was clearly political. Agricultural lobbies exercise enormous influence in the key countries concerned. This influence is usually quite disproportionate to the percentage of the population at large engaged in agricultural production. In some countries (Canada is an example) the boundaries of legislative districts have not changed in such a way as to fully reflect the shift in population from rural to urban areas, thereby resulting in the former being over-represented in legislatures. In some European countries, the electoral politics are such that forming a governing coalition may be difficult, if not impossible, if some rural-based Parties are not included. As well, in some countries, of which Germany is a prime example, the shift away from agricultural production to other economic activities as the major source of employment has not necessarily been accompanied by a population shift of comparable magnitude from the rural areas to the cities, and electoral boundaries are based on where people live not where they work. Philip notes: '[in the Western part of Germany] a majority of the population is still living in rural areas, even though they don't necessarily work there'.[32]

Just as the American agricultural lobby was adamant that US negotiators accept nothing less than radical reductions in EU export subsidies, the European (and especially the French) farm lobbies were equally adamant that the basic level of protection in the CAP be preserved. However, even where they had the political will to resist the most extreme demands of the farm lobbies, EU policymakers had a series of legitimate concerns about adjustment and the management of transitional costs during the shift to a more liberal regime for agriculture.

Rapid removal of protection would lead to massive bankruptcies and significant job losses, as farm revenues plummeted in those countries with the highest costs of production. In addition, and perhaps most difficult of all, land values that now reflected rents from protection would decline dramatically[33] – as would the market value of quotas in supply management systems such as that of Canada. Here there would be a transitional gains trap[34] problem, because while older farmers who saw the value of their land go up as rents from protection increased arguably have done very well from protection over the years and may not be deserving of further compensation, there is a much greater difficulty in the case of those who acquired quotas or land more recently, paying a price that reflected an expected income stream based on the assumption of continued protection. The removal of protection in these instances might be viewed as a 'regulatory taking' and therefore require extremely costly compensation for the reduction in the value of land or quotas. Containment of transitional costs generally implies an incremental approach to the removal or at least restructuring of agricultural protection – a process that already had begun on a small scale in the mid- to late -1980s in the United States but has been overshadowed by subsidies wars that are a result of the excess capacity produced by past protectionist practices. An incremental approach, however, has its own drawbacks. First of all, a basic principle of equity suggests that each country should pull its own weight in the overall reduction in protection, but the setting of targets is made more difficult by the diversity of policy instruments employed by different countries. It is necessary to achieve consensus on a methodology for reducing the protectionist impact of these instruments to a common measure.[35] There are a variety of alternative techniques for doing this, each of which has its strengths and weaknesses.[36] A related requirement is effective monitoring of a complex variety of domestic policy changes to ensure that these changes are indeed being made in such a way as to reduce each country's common measure of protection by the targeted amount.

These are some of the transitional issues that set the scene for a dispute between the United States and the European Union over the approach to liberalization which lasted from the intensification of the Uruguay Round negotiations towards the end of the 1980s until the very last days of the Round in December 1993.

Although it showed rather early in the negotiations some flexibility with respect to its opening position that all protection (including domestic support) be eliminated within a ten-year period, the United States insisted that a major thrust of liberalization must be very substantial reductions in one particular instrument of protection, export subsidies, over a ten-year period. This intransigence was probably the result of a variety of factors, including scepticism concerning the ability to monitor more complex domestic policy shifts[37] and an increasing sense of frustration at European unwillingness to comply with existing GATT strictures (which reached a peak, as mentioned above, with the European refusal to implement the 1991 Oilseeds ruling). In addition some of the negotiating positions of the EU seemed almost calculated in their manner of presentation to raise the ire of the United States – for instance, at one point the EU, while offering to reduce domestic support by 30% over ten years (an apparently substantial concession) insisted that the offer be backdated to 1986, so the 30% target would be significantly met by reductions that had already occurred.[38]

The European Union, although prepared to make some concessions with respect to domestic support measures, insisted on the continuing capacity to subsidize exports, if only because as long as the other measures were to be phased out gradually, incentives to over-production would continue to exist, and there would be a continued need to use export subsidies to reduce surpluses. The European Union also insisted on the ability to pay income support to farmers as a substitute for protection.[39] From the European perspective any move away from price- and trade-distorting policies would necessarily require adjustment policies that would include a significant element of domestic support, even in the medium or long term.[40] The Union argued that adjustment-oriented measures such as income support were not trade-distorting and therefore ought not to be disciplined under GATT. The USA was sceptical; income support might nevertheless preserve incentives to farmers to continue overproduction, thereby perpetuating the pressure to resort to directly distortive measures, such as export subsidies, to reduce the resulting surpluses.

The 1991 'Dunkel Draft' of a possible Uruguay Round Agreement attempted to set forth a compromise aimed at breaking the impasse in negotiations between the USA and the EU. The Draft proposed: reduction of domestic support measured in terms of a common standard (the Aggregate Measure of Support or AMS) by 20% from 1993 to 1999 with credit to be given for reductions that occurred since 1986; tariffication of border measures other than tariffs (e.g. the import quotas used by Canada to sustain its supply-management system); and reduction in export subsidies by 36% between 1993 and 1999 in terms of outlays (aggregate expenditures) and by 24% in terms of quantities of output subsidized (Part B, para. 11). The Dunkel Draft was ambiguous as to whether income support payments to farmers, as conceived by the EU in the MacSharry Report on CAP Reform[41], would be viewed as exempt from domestic support reduction commitments.

Negotiations based on the Dunkel Draft made limited headway until, after intense internal discussions, in May 1992, the European Council adopted a revised version of the plan for agricultural reform contained in the MacSharry Report. This entailed a substantial reduction in price support for cereals, accompanied by compensation in the form of income support to farmers, in most instances conditional upon their willingness to 'set aside', or take out of cereals production, a part of their land. In other areas, however (livestock and particularly dairy) the agreed reforms were much less significant – reflecting a difficult intra-European bargain (and above all, the compromises required to gain acceptance by France). In November 1992, the USA and the EU reached a bilateral agreement concerning the liberalization of agricultural trade, the so-called Blair House Agreement. Under the Blair House Agreement, the USA and EU agreed to support the following reductions as a basis for a Uruguay Round Agreement: a 20% reduction in domestic support in terms of the AMS, with 1986–1988 as a base period;

a 21% reduction in the volume of export subsidies and a 36% reduction in the cash amount of export subsidies, with the base period as defined in the Dunkel Draft; exemption of income support to farmers from domestic support reduction commitments provided that these payments are made on only a limited part of the total production of each farm (so as not to encourage future over-production).[42] These agreed terms for a Uruguay Round settlement on agriculture certainly represented very substantial concessions by the United States to the European Union, at least in terms of previous US negotiating positions. For instance, the USA ended up accepting a 1986 baseline for domestic support commitments – an element that it had rejected when it appeared in earlier EU negotiating positions. In return, however, the USA received satisfaction on a number of specific bilateral concerns, foremost among them the oilseeds controversy. Here, the EU agreed to reduce subsidies on oilseeds once oilseed acreage reached a certain trigger level. The EU also agreed to facilitate market access for US corn to Spain and Portugal. A mutually satisfactory resolution of bilateral disputes between the Parties with respect to corn gluten feed and malted barley sprouts was also achieved.

The Blair House Agreement represented an important breakthrough, but the future of the Uruguay Round was still clouded due to the unwillingness of the French to accept Blair House as a definitive basis for CAP reform. Finally, an adjustment of the Blair House Agreement was achieved through discussions between US Trade Representative Mickey Kantor and EU External Affairs Commissioner Leon Brittan at a meeting in Brussels on 7 December 1993 – just a week before the final deadline for the Uruguay Round negotiations. The major new US concession was to allow back-loading of commitments for reduction in export subsidies, so that smaller reductions would be possible in the first few years of the six-year transition period.[43] A new feature was, however, added to what had been agreed on at Blair House with respect to the basis for a Uruguay Round settlement on agriculture – a commitment to a minimum level of market access for foreign producers equivalent to 3% of domestic production, rising to 5% at the end of a six-year period.

Overview

In terms of general structure and basic principles, the key elements of the Agreement reflect, in the first instance, the Dunkel Draft. With respect to specific commitments, the Agreement is largely based upon the bilateral understandings between the United States and the EU in the Blair House Agreement, as modified by the 7 December Kantor/Brittan meeting (not surprisingly, some smaller countries, including developing countries, found it a source of irritation at the end of the Round that the final Agreement should be closely modelled on a bilateral deal between the USA and the EU).

The key elements may be summarized as follows:

1 *Domestic support* (including price support policies such as the EU Variable Levy) is to be quantified in terms of a common metric, the Aggregate Measure of Support (AMS) (Article 1 (a); Article 6; Annex 3) with mandatory minimum reductions amounting to 20% over a six-year period, with 1986–8 as the base period (i.e. at the end of six years from the entry into force of the Agreement on Agriculture domestic support must be 20% lower than it was in the 1986–8 base period). 'Direct' payments to farmers, when made under 'production-limiting programmes' are not subject to reduction commitments, provided the payments are based on fixed area and yields, or are made on 85% or less of the base level of production, or (in the case of livestock) on a fixed number of head (Article 6.5 (a) (i)–(iii)). Where these payments also conform to the more specific exemption criteria contained in Annex 2, they are also *non-countervailable.*[44]

2 *Export subsidies* are to be reduced over a six-year period by 21% in terms of the volume of agricultural products that receive such subsidies and 36% in terms of total cash value. Except for certain permitted minor adjustments (Article 9.2), members undertake not to expand export subsidies beyond the levels reached after the achievement of their six-year reduction commitments. This in effect alters, with respect to agricultural products, the operation of Article XVI of the General Agreement, which permits export subsidies on primary products.

3 *Existing non-tariff border measures,* such as import quotas, VERs, and the EC Variable Import Levy are to be converted into tariffs (Article 4.2, footnote 1), and *new* measures of this kind are to be prohibited (Article 4.2). This modifies Article XI:2(c) of the General Agreement, which permits quantitative restrictions on agricultural and fisheries products where necessary to the enforcement of the domestic marketing scheme. In addition, existing non-tariff border measures *must* be reduced to the extent required to allow foreign producers a minimum of 3% market access in terms of total domestic production of each product category, rising to 5% at the end of the six-year phase-in period.

4 *Tariffs* (including existing non-tariff border measures that have been converted to tariffs) are to be reduced by at least 36% overall by each Member over the six-year phase-in period, with a minimum 15% reduction on *each* product category.

Operationalizing the commitment to liberalization; other selected features of the Agreement on Agriculture

It is impossible in this chapter to do full justice to the complex definitional and methodological framework which the Agreement on Agriculture establishes for the operationalization of the reduction commitments sketched

210

above. The Agreement contains finely-crafted provisions that set out basic rules for the calculation of Aggregate Measure of Support in the case of domestic support measures (Annex 3) and for the calculation of tariff equivalents in the case of non-tariff border measures (Attachment to Annex 5). For instance, with respect to domestic price support measures (characteristic of the CAP), these are included in the AMS by calculating the difference between a 'fixed external reference price' (i.e. a world price) and the higher administratively-set domestic price, and multiplying this difference by the volume of production to which the administered price applies (Annex 3, Article 8).

Annex 2 of the Agreement provides a very detailed set of criteria for determining which domestic support measures are exempt from reduction commitments, including income support measures for farmers. To be exempt, domestic support measures must meet the 'fundamental' requirement that 'they have no, or at most minimal, trade distortion effects or effects on production' (Annex 2, Article 1). Measures are considered to have met this requirement where they conform to the following two criteria: (1) they are provided through a publicly-funded government programme that does not involve transfers from consumers; and (2) the measures in question do not have the effect of price support (Annex 2, Article 1). Several pages of much more specific criteria and examples of exempt measures follow, and these are based on the general concepts of Article 1 of the Annex. Some of the exempt measures include: research and training programmes; inspection services for health, safety, grading or standardization purposes; and various forms of adjustment assistance to farmers, including income support, where the measures meet very specific conditions aimed at ensuring that the effect is not to reward and thereby perpetuate current levels of production. Article 13 of the Agreement stipulates that domestic support measures that are exempt from reduction commitments by virtue of Annex 2, are to be *non-countervailable* (Article 13.1 (a)). 'Due restraint' is also to be exercised in the initiation of countervail investigations of measures exempt from reduction commitments under Article 6.5 ('direct' payments to farmers in connection with a production-limiting programme).

There is a special safeguard provision in the Agreement on Agriculture, which permits imposition of an additional level of duty (but not reimposition of non-tariff measures) in the case where imports of a particular product exceed a trigger level in a given year or where the price of imports falls below a trigger price.

The trigger level for *volume* of imports varies between 125% and 105% as against the quantity imported over the last three years, depending on the level of existing market access opportunities for imports of the product in question. Thus, for example, where existing market access opportunities for imports amounted to 10% or less of domestic production, an additional 'safeguard' level of duty could only be imposed where imports of the product increased by 25% in the year in question over the average annual quantity imported for the previous three years. However, if existing market opportunities for imports were above 30% of domestic production, a safeguard could be imposed if the volume of imports of the product surged by only 5% over the average annual quantity imported over the previous three years. Where the volume of domestic consumption has changed, the volume of imports must exceed the sum of the trigger level *and* domestic changes in consumption. This reflects the fact that increases in domestic consumption are likely to mitigate the extent to which domestic producers are injured by import surges – there is a larger domestic market to absorb the additional imports. On the other hand, where imports surge at the same time as domestic consumption is decreasing, the injury to domestic producers is likely to be aggravated.

The trigger *price* level is set at an average 1986 to 1988 reference price. Varying levels of 'safeguard' duties may be imposed depending upon the extent to which the price in a given year falls below this trigger price level. For instance, where the price in a given year is 40% less than the trigger price level, a 10% duty would be permitted. If, on the other hand the price were 60% less than the trigger price level, a duty of 20% would be permitted. The formulae for calculating these various rates of safeguard duty are contained in Article 5.5 (a)–(c) of the Agreement.

THE URUGUAY ROUND AGREEMENT ON THE APPLICATION OF SANITARY AND PHYTOSANITARY MEASURES

The Uruguay Round Final Act, contains – separate from the Agreement on Agriculture discussed above – an Agreement on the Application of Sanitary and Phytosanitary Measures, which constitutes a comprehensive code on the most disputed technical barriers to trade in agriculture.

The basic rights and obligations of the Agreement are contained in Articles 5:5–8. Article 6 provides that 'members shall ensure that any sanitary or phytosanitary measure is applied only to the extent necessary to protect human, animal or plant life or health, is based on scientific principles and is not maintained without sufficient scientific evidence, . . .'. This is subject to Article 22, which allows Members to take provisional measures 'on the basis of available pertinent information' where 'scientific evidence is insufficient'. Where a Member acts on the basis of Article 22, it is required to seek a more objective evaluation based on fuller evidence within a reasonable period of time. Article 7 requires that 'members shall ensure that their sanitary and phytosanitary measures do not arbitrarily or unjustifiably discriminate' between Members where identical or similar conditions prevail, including between their own territory and that of other Members. Further, 'sanitary and phytosanitary measures shall not be applied in a manner which would constitute a disguised restriction on international trade'.

Other provisions of the Agreement on Sanitary and Phytosanitary Measures amplify the obligations in Articles 6 and 7. Articles 9–13 require that, to facilitate harmonization, Members base their sanitary and phyto-sanitary standards on 'international standards, guidelines or recommen-dations' wherever possible. Significantly, Article 11 makes it clear that a higher level of protection requires scientific justification to be GATT-consistent, whereas any other kind of difference from international standards (i.e. inferior protection) shall be deemed to be GATT-consistent. Articles 16–18 require that all sanitary and phytosanitary measures be based upon risk assessments that take into account 'risk assessment techniques developed by the relevant international organizations' (Article 16). There appears to be some potential tension between Articles 10–11 and the thrust of Articles 16–18. If a Member adopts sanitary or phytosanitary measures that are based on international harmonized standards, should it really be required to go to the expense of making its own domestic risk assessment, as appears to be required by Articles 16–18?

Finally, the Agreement provides for the establishment of a Committee on Sanitary and Phytosanitary Measures to act as a forum for consultations on the implementation of the Agreement, and also to monitor progress with respect to the evolution of harmonized international standards with respect to sanitary and phytosanitary measures (Articles 38–44). The general GATT dispute settlement process is not explicitly made available to enforce the Agreement on Sanitary and Phytosanitary Measures. However, as is clear from explicit language in several provisions of the Agreement, compliance with its strictures would generally result in the application of the Article XX (b) exemption by a panel in any dispute under the General Agreement (e.g. Article XI) with respect to the trade-restricting impact of sanitary and phytosanitary measures. By contrast, non-compliance might well give rise to a presumption that, where a Member's sanitary or phytosanitary measures result in a *prima facie* violation of a provision of the General Agreement, the measures in question cannot be saved by Article XX (b) as 'necessary' for reasons of health and safety.

CONCLUSION

The Uruguay Round Agreement on Agriculture marks a vital turning point with respect to the regulation of trade in agricultural commodities. Implementing the Agreement, and particularly its complex disciplines on domestic policies, will be a major challenge for the WTO. It will be equally important, however, for political leaders to maintain the courageous stance that ultimately allowed them to sign the Final Act, and to win domestic legitimacy for freer trade in agriculture. This will entail carefully crafted adjustment policies for affected farmers and their communities, as permitted by the Agreement on Agriculture. It should also involve, however, a vigorous public defence of the justification for liberalizing agricultural trade, including a clear explanation of the gains to domestic and global economic welfare. Disappointingly, some governments have instead responded to the farm lobbies' predictable criticisms by pretending that little has changed.[45] The extent to which the Agreement realizes its promise, however, will be significantly affected by the capacity of governments to obtain public support for liberalization, thereby permitting specific commitments to liberalization that eventually exceed the rather modest minimum reductions required by the Agreement itself. Some trade diplomats and policy analysts place great hopes in the new institutional framework of the WTO as a means of sustaining and intensifying the liberalization commitments of the Uruguay Round.[46] Ultimately, however, the full potential of the Agreement will only be realized if citizens view the Uruguay Round liberalization of trade in agriculture, not as a damage control exercise or a concession to the unreasonable demands of others, but rather as a promising new beginning.

9

TRADE IN SERVICES

INTRODUCTION

In the developed industrial countries, services now account for 50% to 60% of GNP[1] and in North America in particular are at present the largest source of new jobs in the economy.[2] At the same time, trade in services is thought to account for only about 20% to 25% of world trade.[3] As comparative advantage in the production of many manufactured goods has shifted to the Newly Industrializing Countries (NICs), the developed industrial countries have become increasingly concerned with enhancement of trading opportunities in services, particularly in areas such as financial services, insurance, telecommunications, transportation, computer and professional services (e.g. architecture, consulting engineering, law).

The pre-Uruguay Round GATT framework applies only to trade in goods, reflecting traditional assumptions that services are not easily tradeable. These assumptions have come into question for a variety of reasons. First of all, because of technological developments, it is possible to effect many services transactions without physical proximity between the provider and consumer of the service.[4] For example, many international banking or insurance transactions can be accomplished through electronic data transfers. Second, in almost all countries through most of the post-war period, many important service industries had been highly regulated, or maintained as state monopolies (telecommunications, transportation). The regulatory reform trend during the 1970s and 1980s resulted in a removal or loosening of prior substantial limits on domestic competition in these industries,[5] thereby focusing new attention on the possibilities of international competition. It is of significance that regulatory reform in a wide range of countries has led to (at least partial) liberalization of markets in service industries such as telecommunications and transportation that themselves provide the means to bring together providers and users of many *other* services; for example, in many countries on-line computer services have become both more feasible and less expensive as a result of regulatory reform in telecommunications.[6]

Third, many services have traditionally been viewed as functions integral to the production of goods, e.g. storage of customer or other data or engineering designs. The 'splintering'[7] of services from goods, and the increasing use of external contracting to obtain service inputs into the production of goods (or, indeed, inputs into other services) has created new explicit markets. The logic of external contracting for services within a domestic economy (i.e. that better contract terms can be had outside the firm) seems equally applicable to external contracting with foreigners. Conversely, the globalization of production functions within the multinational corporation (discussed in Chapter 11, Trade and Investment), can be extended to include international *intra*-firm trade in service inputs into production *either* of goods *or* of other services. Sauvant notes the example of an American insurance company that processes claims in Ireland: 'Insurance claims collected in the United States are shipped daily by air to Ireland, where they are processed. The claim information is then sent through transnational computer communication systems back to the United States, where checks are printed and explanations of benefits are mailed out.'[8]

In light of these various developments, all of which create increased potential for international trade in services, the reduction or elimination of barriers to services trade became a major priority of a number of developed countries in the Uruguay Round of GATT negotiations.

In this chapter we will consider the characteristics of traded services and the nature of the barriers to such trade. We will then examine provisions related to trade in services in a range of international agreements, including the Canada–US Free Trade Agreement, the North American Free Trade Agreement, the OECD Code on Invisibles and, most importantly, the Uruguay Round General Agreement on Trade in Services (GATS). The chapter will conclude with a consideration of the issues in trade in services in two sectors of particular importance to the global economy – financial services and telecommunications. Here, a major focus will be on the sector-specific provisions of the FTA, NAFTA, and GATS, as well as the future prospects for negotiation of further commitments to liberalization within the GATS/WTO framework.

THE NATURE OF SERVICES

There is a wide range of economic literature that attempts to define the nature of services, the intrinsic differences between goods and services, and how these differences affect (if at all) the application of the neo-classical theory of comparative advantage to trade in services.[9] At the level of general principle, there is no reason why the logic of gains from specialization and trade should not apply to services. Nevertheless, the factors that determine comparative advantage in services may often be rather different from those that determine comparative advantage with respect to goods. For instance, 'natural' factor endowments such as land and minerals will be of less importance than in the case of many goods, while 'man-made' factors such as knowledge and skill will be of paramount importance.[10] Nevertheless, one should be wary of exaggerating these differences – for example, countries with beautiful scenery may have an advantage in the export of tourist services.

Traditionally, economists have attempted to define services largely by contrast with goods. Therefore, definitions have emphasized the intangibility or invisibility of services, their supposedly non-durable or transitory character, or the notion that, unlike with goods, consumption and production occurs simultaneously.[11] It is, however, possible to find exceptions to each of these definitions. For example, is there anything intangible or invisible about an architect's drawing or a design for an integrated circuit? With respect to transitoriness, as Nicolaides notes, 'a lecture, or occasionally a bank transaction, is longer than the lifetime of an ice-cream'.[12] Also, with respect to some services (e.g. most television programmes) consumption and production are *not* simultaneous. Understandably, given these kinds of anomalies, none of these definitions has attracted any kind of consensus within the economic literature.

It has sometimes been argued that services that are inputs in the production of *traded goods* should not be viewed as traded at all. The *real* trade transaction, it is claimed, occurs when the good itself, in which various service inputs are embodied, crosses national boundaries. This view was taken by the United States when it first sought to place the issue of services on the Uruguay Round agenda. The United States argued that the negotiations should be limited to trade in nonfactor services, i.e. services that could themselves be viewed as finished products, such as financial services, thereby excluding services that could be viewed solely as inputs into production (e.g. construction crews).[13] This distinction rather transparently served US self-interest: liberalization would occur with respect to knowledge- and technology-intensive services in which the USA had a comparative advantage, but would not occur with respect to labour-intensive services in which developing countries might have an advantage over the United States.[14]

It is not difficult to appreciate the artificiality of the distinction between services as final products and services as inputs. Most of the services often described as final products are also important inputs into the production, marketing and distribution of goods, including financial services that provide the capital required for production. At the same time, since *goods* that are primarily inputs into the production of other goods are governed by trade rules on goods, it seems illogical that services that are inputs into the production of goods (or indeed other services) would not also be governed by trade rules that apply to services.

A particular conceptual difficulty exists with respect to services that are embodied in goods as a *medium* for the delivery of the service. Literature and recorded music, for instance, could plausibly be considered as services that are embodied in or transmitted to the user through goods. However, trade in these services has been traditionally conceptualized as trade in the goods which embody them. Would it be more appropriate to subject the trade in question to rules on services?

These various definitional quagmires are largely avoidable, however, if instead of attempting an abstract definition, one looks to the purpose of creating trade rules on services in the first place. The purpose is to reduce or eliminate barriers to trade that are not caught by existing rules, since those rules have been designed largely with a view to liberalizing trade in goods. From the perspective of trade law and policy, what is most important is to be able to identify a set of barriers that should be reduced or removed to facilitate trade in services. Of course, the nature of these barriers arises from certain identifiable characteristics shared by a significant number of service industries (such as a high degree of domestic regulatory control or the importance of free movement of capital and labour to trading opportunities) but some non-service industries may also possess some of these characteristics. For this very reason, the knowledge of which traits of service industries are important from the point of view of trade liberalization may not generate a satisfactory abstract or conceptual definition of services, i.e. a definition that rigorously delineates goods from services in an essentialist manner. With these considerations and caveats in mind, we now proceed to develop a taxonomy of barriers to trade in services.

BARRIERS TO TRADE IN SERVICES

The following taxonomy of barriers is intended to illustrate the discrete issues involved in the liberalization of trade in services.

Direct and facially discriminatory barriers to trade in services

These are explicit barriers to trade specifically directed at service industries. Examples would include domestic content regulations for television and radio broadcasting, prohibitions on the practice of law by foreign nationals, or restrictions on the ownership and establishment of financial institutions by foreigners. These kinds of barriers can in principle be addressed by extending the principles of National Treatment or non-discrimination to services either on a conditional or unconditional MFN basis. However, some of these barriers may often be seen by countries as vital to legitimate domestic social, cultural, and political interests. These concerns may be addressed either through a general exemption to National Treatment where discriminatory measures can be justified as necessary to achieve legitimate domestic objectives; and/or through reservations on National Treatment

218

with respect to particular industries or even particular regulatory measures that apply to an industry in one or more countries.

Indirect but facially discriminatory barriers to trade in services

These are forms of discrimination against foreigners, or barriers to international movement of factors in service production (such as people, information and capital) that are not targeted at, or limited to, specific service sectors. Examples would be general limitations on immigration or temporary entry into a country for work purposes, limitations on foreign investment not specific to service industries, and controls on remittances and payments abroad (e.g. for liquidity reasons). The issues raised by these kinds of measures go beyond domestic or international regulation of service industries as such, yet their impact on services trade is generally agreed to be of great significance. One way of addressing this dilemma is to deal with these kinds of barriers in international agreements that approach the barriers in a general manner, i.e. on their own terms and not only on the basis of their effects on services trade (examples would be the OECD Code on Invisibles or the general principle of personal mobility within the European Union that is entrenched in the Treaty of Rome). Another approach is to negotiate removal or relaxation of these barriers with respect to specific service sectors or service industries. This is the approach to mobility of people taken in the Canada–US FTA. Unlike the Treaty of Rome, the FTA does not establish free movement of people as a basic principle or norm, but instead contains some specific (and very limited) mobility guarantees that apply to provision of particular (mainly professional or technical) services.

Direct but facially neutral barriers to trade in services

Much domestic regulation of service industries falls into this category. For example, maintaining a railway or telecommunications network as a national monopoly directly impedes market access by foreign providers, but is non-discriminatory with respect to foreigners because would-be *domestic* competitors are excluded as well. These barriers would not be in violation of a general National Treatment obligation with respect to services. Another example is setting of rates for services such as telecommunications (regardless of whether provided by nationals or foreigners): these can be set at levels that eliminate any cost/price advantage a foreign competitor may possess, while not being facially discriminatory against foreigners.

Removal of these kinds of barriers would in many cases involve a fundamental change in domestic regulatory approach in some countries. This is one reason why, in particular, US demands for removal of these kinds of barriers through GATT in order to achieve 'free market access' has met with considerable resistance from a number of countries.

Indirect and facially neutral barriers to trade in services

These barriers arise as well out of domestic regulation. They include the additional costs to foreign providers of adapting to distinctive national regulatory standards or requirements. Barriers of this nature can be described as indirect because they do not limit or prohibit competition as such, but impose some disadvantage on foreigners who must adapt their activities and practices to the idiosyncratic regulatory structure of the country concerned. Such barriers may occur as well with respect to professional services, where a country has distinctive requirements for training and certification of professionals and does not recognize licences, diplomas or other credentials acquired abroad.

Ultimately, removal of these barriers would require harmonization of domestic regulatory regimes or (as in the European Union blueprint for liberalization of financial services) home country regulation, whereby a service provider is given the right to enter a foreign market provided it complies with its home country's regulatory requirements. In the case of professional services, the equivalent to home country regulation is mutual recognition of qualifications or licences, whether in accounting, engineering, law or architecture (law is perhaps the most problematic of all these cases, since a country-specific knowledge base may often be seen as a legitimate pre-condition for professional competence).

Many advocates of liberalization of trade in services see the argument for free trade internationally as linked to the purported benefits of deregulation domestically.[15] Yet whether strict or liberal regulation (and these terms arguably conceal a much more subtle set of instrument choices[16]) maximizes *domestic* welfare depends on complex judgements about market failures, and the costs and benefits of a particular regulatory approach in light of the risk preferences of one's own citizens. Three important and related observations follow from this insight. First of all, the global gains from liberalization of trade in services should be conceptually separated from gains or losses to domestic welfare that may be entailed by the regulatory changes required to produce a level playing field to sustain liberalization. If we assume a beginning point where the regulatory choices of each member state represent a social optimum that maximizes domestic welfare within that state, then any changes in regulation needed to sustain liberalization in trade are likely to reduce domestic welfare – the global gains from trade that are yielded by liberalization must be then traded off against domestic welfare losses. Of course, if some countries' domestic regulatory regimes are suboptimal from the perspective of domestic welfare, then liberalization may yield gains in excess of those from liberal trade itself.

On the other hand, in the absence of a high but level playing field, free trade in services may lead to spillovers that distort the global allocation of resources. For example, where lax regulation of a bank in one country results in failure of financial institutions or prejudice to depositors in another that have placed large deposits in that bank, significant costs will be incurred by the public authorities in that other country. The possibility of free trade in services allows countries to shift beyond their own borders some of the negative welfare effects of their regulatory approaches, thus driving a wedge between domestic and global welfare. Thus in the absence of agreed minimum regulatory standards, free trade in services may actually result in a net reduction in aggregate global economic welfare – i.e. the gains from free trade are more than outweighed by the reduction in global welfare due to the opportunities for externalizing the costs of domestic regulatory approaches abroad that are created by liberalization.

However, the existence of such spillovers has already led to considerable regulatory co-operation in a number of highly significant service sectors. The world's leading financial powers have accepted guidelines for capital adequacy of banks under their regulatory control (the Cooke Committee guidelines, negotiated under the auspices of the Bank for International Settlements in Basel (BIS))[17]; cooperation between domestic securities regulators has become increasingly effective in containing contagion effects where instability or regulatory failure in one market undermines market confidence elsewhere;[18] and in telecommunications and aviation, coordination of a wide variety of domestic regulatory policies that have transboundary impacts occurs through a variety of bodies, including the International Telecommunications Union (ITU) and the International Civil Aviation Organization (ICAO).

It would be wrong to suggest that any of these fora or processes is leading or can lead in the foreseeable future to a genuinely level playing field, or to a resolution of all important conflicts over differences in domestic regulatory philosophy or regulatory interests. At the same time, the evidence does indicate that, as markets in service sectors have become increasingly globalized, cooperative mechanisms have emerged to manage regulatory spillovers and constrain 'beggar-thy-neighbour' regulatory competition.

INTERNATIONAL AGREEMENTS FOR THE LIBERALIZATION OF TRADE IN SERVICES

The Canada–US Free Trade Agreement (FTA)

Article 1402.1 of the Canada–US FTA states a basic National Treatment obligation with respect to services: 'Each Party shall accord to persons of the other party treatment no less favourable than that accorded in like circumstances to its persons'. This general obligation applies to a wide range of measures, including the right of establishment, access to domestic distribution systems, and generally any measure related to 'the production, distribution, sale, marketing and delivery of a covered service'. The National

Treatment obligation applies to a limited number of sectors listed in an Annex to these provisions. The sectors range from construction to insurance to public relations.

The general National Treatment obligation is followed by a limitations clause, which permits deviation from national treatment, where 'the difference in treatment' is 'no greater than that necessary for prudential, fiduciary, health and safety, or consumer protection reasons'. (Article 1402 (3) a). Such deviations must be 'equivalent in effect to the treatment accorded by the Party to its persons for such reasons'. Suppose, for instance, a Canadian province was to require American construction service providers to post a bond to assure that funds were available to pay occupational health and safety or workers' compensation claims, but did not demand the same of local firms. The argument would first of all be made that the differential treatment of Americans is due to the fact that they are unlikely to have valuable assets in the jurisdiction that can readily be seized or attached in case of non-payment of these claims. Equivalence in effect would be established by showing that this required bond has much the same *regulatory impact* on American operators as provisions permitting seizure and attachment in the case of local providers. On the other hand, if it turned out that local laws did not provide means of securing judgment against local firms for such payments, the American firm could argue that the regulatory impact was not, indeed, equivalent in effect. Finally, prior notification of differential treatment must be provided to the other Party, and the Party imposing the differential treatment must bear the burden of justifying it.

The National Treatment obligation in the FTA is subject to grandfathering, i.e. it does not apply to existing measures, or to continuation, 'prompt renewal', or amendment of existing measures. In the case of amendment, however, the effect must not be to *decrease* conformity with National Treatment. Obviously, the distinction between an amendment and a new measure is one that has no self-evident legal meaning. New comprehensive legislation would almost certainly be considered in the nature of a new measure, but the case of alterations that are more than caretaking amendments but less than a basic policy overhaul would be more difficult to classify.

The grandfathering provision may reflect in part expectations arising from the tendency toward deregulation and regulatory reform that was among the most prominent policy trends in both the United States and Canada – as well as in many other countries – during the late 1980s.[19] As these dynamics led to liberalizing reforms in both countries, the new measures, presumably more conducive to free trade in themselves, would then be caught by the FTA, which would prohibit a future retreat to more restrictive approaches.

It should be noted that the National Treatment obligation in the FTA is not accompanied by an MFN obligation. Therefore, a Party to the FTA is free to treat services provided by a third country more favourably or less favourably than those provided by the other FTA partner, where this treatment is also superior to that provided to its own nationals. Also, there is a provision that serves the same function as do rules of origin in the case of trade in goods. Hence, Article 1406.1 permits the other Party to deny the benefits of the National Treatment obligation with respect to services where it can be established that 'the covered service is indirectly provided by a person of a third country'. Clearly, this is a very rough rule of thumb – for instance, would a Japanese insurance company or architectural firm that provides services to the US market through a Toronto office where both Japanese and Canadian nationals are employed, be viewed as 'a person of a third country'? Or what of a Canadian engineering company that supplied advice on a particular project to an American client, but on the basis of groundwork done by a multinational team of mining engineers?

In addition to the general National Treatment obligation, sectorally specific treatment is given to telecommunications and financial services (to be discussed in detail in the final part of this chapter). As well, there are provisions that mandate in some instances, and encourage in others, the development of common standards in various professional disciplines, e.g. architecture – enabling mutual recognition of some professional qualifications and facilitating movement of some service providers (but not labour in general) across the Canada–US border.

The North American Free Trade Agreement (NAFTA)

The NAFTA takes an approach to liberalization of trade in services that is similar to that of the Canada–US FTA. However, one significant difference is that, unlike the FTA, the NAFTA contains an MFN obligation that applies with respect to both Parties and Non-Parties (Article 1203). A second significant difference is that both the National Treatment (Article 1202) and MFN obligations in NAFTA are not limited to specific service sectors but are applicable to services[20] generally. Instead, a 'negative list' approach is adopted, whereby reservations are noted with respect to particular service sectors or particular measures within certain sectors to which a Party does not want these obligations to apply. The only service industries excluded altogether from coverage by the Services Chapter of NAFTA are those 'associated with energy and basic petrochemical goods and air services'. However, the reservations noted by Canada, the United States and particularly by Mexico in Annexes to the NAFTA apply to a wide range of measures in various service industries. Very extensive reservations apply for one or more of the NAFTA Parties with respect to transportation (especially maritime shipping) and some professional services (especially law). In addition, further Annexes are to contain reservations with respect to measures of sub-national governments. These lists may well be quite lengthy, as in both Canada and the United States provincial and state governments (respectively) are deeply involved in the regulation of many services, and particularly professional services.

In contrast to the FTA, existing services measures are not grandfathered in the NAFTA, although there is to be a two-year delay with respect to state and provincial measures to allow these governments adequate time to elaborate satisfactory lists of reservations (Article 1206). As in the FTA, the communications and financial services sectors are dealt with in separate, sectorally-specific chapters (Chapters 13 and 14), to be discussed in the final part of this chapter.

In addition to the National Treatment and MFN obligations, which address direct and facially discriminatory barriers to trade in services, the NAFTA provides a framework for removal of other classes of barriers. For instance with respect to direct but facially neutral barriers – defined in the NAFTA text as 'non-discriminatory measures relating to the cross-boundary provision of a service' (Article 1208) – Parties are invited to list specific commitments in Annex VI of the NAFTA (to date, very few such commitments have been made). As well, the NAFTA Parties are to engage in further negotiations with respect to temporary licensing of engineers on the basis of mutual recognition of professional credentials. These negotiations are to take place within a year of the entry into force of the NAFTA itself (Annex 1210 (Professional Services) Section C).

The OECD Invisibles Code

The Invisibles Code[21] requires OECD Members to eliminate between each other 'restrictions on current invisible operations' (Article 1). The expression 'current invisible operations' refers to a wide variety of trans-boundary service transactions, listed in Annex A of the Code. These include, *inter alia*, many forms of technical assistance to businesses, including training, market research, and provision of plans and blueprints, construction and maintenance services. As well, 'current invisibles operations' includes transactions that *facilitate* transboundary services provision. Thus, transboundary movement of the salaries and wages of non-resident workers is included in the list in Annex A.

Members are permitted to lodge reservations and (in some circumstances, such as a domestic economic or financial crisis) derogations from the basic obligation to remove restrictions on current invisible operations, but must indicate their reasons for doing so. These reasons are periodically scrutinized by the Committee on Capital Movements and Invisibles Transactions. The Committee may recommend to a member that it remove a reservation, but these recommendations do not have binding legal force. Reservations appear to be lodged most frequently with respect to audio-visual, maritime transport and insurance services.[22]

The Invisibles Code contains a general limitation clause that allows

Members to take measures that they consider necessary for reasons of public order, protection of public health morals and safety, or for reasons of domestic or international peace and security (Article 3).

The General Agreement on Trade in Services
(Uruguay Round Final Act)

Overview

It was largely due to the insistence of the United States that trade in services was placed on the Uruguay Round agenda.[23] This initiative generated much controversy and disagreement among other Contracting Parties, especially (but not exclusively) developing countries.[24] The reasons for this controversy can be traced to two interconnected factors. First of all, a major motivation for the United States' initiative was the belief that unlike many basic manufacturing sectors where it was losing global markets as well as part of its domestic market to NIC competitors, service sectors remained a strength of the United States, especially sectors like financial services and telecommunications, considered to be highly knowledge- and technology-intensive. Some developing countries responded to this logic, and drew the conclusion that liberalized trade in services would result in their domestic providers being out-competed by American firms. Moreover, most developing countries could see little benefit accruing to them through access to the services markets of other countries. It was argued that the comparative advantage that developed countries possessed with respect to services was due to their overall higher level of economic and technological development, and if liberalization of trade in services occurred under these conditions, developing country providers would lose their domestic services markets before even having had a chance to acquire comparative advantage in service sectors. This was, in essence, a variant of the infant industry argument for protection that had often been invoked by developing countries in previous GATT negotiations with respect to trade in goods.

Some economists, the most prominent among them Jagdish Bhagwati, challenged the notion that developing countries possessed no comparative advantage in service sectors.[25] They noted that a range of developing countries (e.g. India) possessed significant numbers of highly-trained professionals such as engineers and accountants who were typically paid far less than equivalent professionals in the developed industrial countries. Moreover, some services (such as construction) were labour intensive, thereby potentially conferring a comparative advantage on developing countries with abundant supplies of skilled or semi-skilled labour. Finally, the NICs, which had already acquired the capacity to manufacture medium- and some high-technology goods, could be expected to have some export potential with respect to related services, such as computer software.

In fact, these claims seem to be borne out by recent statistics. Between 1980 and 1987, a significant number of developing countries increased substantially the share of their total exports accounted for by services (including Egypt, Chile, and the Philippines).[26] Moreover, in at least a dozen developing countries, in 1987 the percentage of total exports accounted for by services approached, equalled or even exceeded that of many developed countries.[27]

Although at the level of general principle the United States espoused the idea that negotiations on services should have a comprehensive scope, the US position on the definition of services themselves had the effect of focusing the negotiations on those sectors of most export interest to the United States and other developed countries (e.g. cross-border transactions in sectors such as telecommunications and financial services), while excluding liberalization of factor movements, especially labour,[28] where developing countries might often have a comparative advantage (e.g. ship's crews, construction gangs, etc.).

A second, important concern shared by many countries as well was the aggressive 'market access' approach to an accord on services that appeared to be taken by the United States. The United States appeared interested not only in the extension of the National Treatment obligation to services, but also in negotiating whatever changes in countries' domestic regulatory structures might be necessary to allow market access by foreigners. Since, as we discussed in 'Barriers to Trade in Services' (this chapter) many of the barriers to trade in services do indeed result from fundamental choices of regulatory instrument by individual countries (e.g. state monopolies, licensing, or rate-setting), or from regulatory diversity itself, there was some substantive justification for a market access approach. However, the ultimate implications for domestic policy sovereignty would be profound. While all international trade obligations involve some surrender of domestic sovereignty, it was understandably far from clear to many Contracting Parties that the benefits of liberalization would outweigh the costs of substantially constraining or altering their domestic regulatory approaches. Since the Reagan Administration was firmly persuaded that the domestic changes required to meet its market access demands (e.g. privatization and deregulation) would also be of considerable benefit to the countries adopting these changes, it did not see any profound conflict of domestic and global interests in trade in services. Indeed, a range of countries (including some developing nations) had embarked unilaterally on ambitious programmes of deregulation and privatization and it could be argued that a GATT services agreement would be one means of attaining some reciprocal trade benefit from these policy shifts. Nevertheless, contrary to crude 'free market' rhetoric, deregulation and privatization entail complex transitional issues and formidable challenges of regulatory redesign.[29] It is not surprising, therefore, that even countries with short- or long-term intentions of liberalizing domestic competition in key service sectors did not want their room to manoeuvre fundamentally constrained or pre-empted by a multi-lateral market access agreement.[30] As well, negotiated reciprocal market access could easily turn into a market-sharing or managed trade arrangement, in tension with the general principles and philosophy of the GATT. This would be especially true if the position of some American experts were adopted[31] and these market access commitments were negotiated on a discriminatory non-MFN basis.

As the negotiations evolved, insistence on a non-MFN approach became an important means of the US backtracking from its original 'open borders' rhetoric, as many US providers became increasingly worried about having to compete with foreigners in their own market. Where domestic US service providers were opposed to more competition at home, it would always be possible to insist that commitments in the area in question should be negotiated on a reciprocal basis, on the grounds that other countries were not prepared to open up their markets sufficiently to justify free access for foreign producers to the US market. The large degree of indeterminacy in assessing how much other countries' specific commitments to liberalization were worth in terms of reciprocal access to one's own markets actually permitted a wide scope to the United States for justifying on reciprocity grounds its increasing refusal to make broad multilateral commitments to liberalize access to its own markets.

The negotiations, despite numerous impasses, were brought to at least a partial resolution (i.e. agreement on a framework with negotiations in some sectors to continue) on the basis of a number of carefully-negotiated compromises. First of all, it was agreed that liberalization of trade in services would be negotiated under the 'umbrella' of the Uruguay Round, but with a view to the conclusion of an accord that would be legally separate from the GATT itself, i.e. a General Agreement on Trade in Services (GATS). Since agreement was reached on the institutional framework for a World Trade Organization (WTO), it was possible to maintain GATS (as well as the Agreement on TRIPs) as separate from GATT, but to place GATS nevertheless within the overarching framework of the WTO. With respect to the debate over MFN, however, the United States insisted to the very end on being able to exclude almost entirely certain sectors (e.g. maritime services) from the general framework of the GATS, and also on being able to negotiate on a reciprocal basis market access commitments with specific countries, which would be excluded from MFN treatment. With respect to financial services (to be discussed in the final section of this chapter), it was necessary to provide a special accommodation for the United States with respect to MFN exemptions in order to allow the Round to close at the mid-December deadline.

The GATS is a highly complex accord. It is also incomplete, in as much as agreement was not reached on a comprehensive set of initial specific sectoral market access commitments. Parts I and II of the GATS provide a set of general rules and principles with respect to liberalization of trade in services. Here, the GATS may be said to apply or adapt some of the key concepts and principles of the GATT to trade in services. Parts III and IV provide a framework for the negotiation of specific market access commitments to be bound in the schedules of individual Members. Part V contains provisions concerning dispute settlement and enforcement of obligations. Part VI deals with a variety of definitional issues in the application of the GATS. There follow a series of Annexes on exemption from MFN treatment, movement of persons, financial services, telecommunications, and air transport services. In addition, there is a series of eight Decisions concerning various aspects of implementation and interpretation of the GATS (ranging from financial services to dispute settlement).

The following discussion covers all of these various provisions and instruments, except those specifically addressed to the financial services and telecommunications sectors, which will be dealt with in the final part of this chapter.

Part I

The definitions in Part I evoke a very broad view of the meaning of trade in services, without thereby attempting to define services themselves. Along these lines, the GATS is to apply not only to 'supply of a service . . . from the territory of one Member into the territory of any other party' (I.2 (a)), but also to such 'supply' 'in the territory of one Member to the service consumer of any other Member' (I.2 (b)) and through 'the presence of service providing entities of one Party in the territory of any other Party' (I.2 (c)), as well as 'by natural persons of one Party in the territory of any other party' (I.2 (d)). Clearly, I.2 (c) directly bears upon the treatment of foreign investment, including the right of establishment, and I.2 (d) on the right to enter a state of which one is not a national. What kind of measure would involve a restriction on the supply of a service on the territory of one Party to the consumer of another may at first glance seem obscure. An example might be a requirement that nationals of Country A engage in certain banking or securities transactions only within Country A and not in other Contracting Parties. Here, what is being restricted is not the flow of other Contracting Parties' services into A but access of A's customers to services offered by providers of other Contracting Parties.

Article I.2 (d), which refers to supply of services 'through presence of natural persons of a Member in the territory of any other Member', would seem to imply that the scope of the GATS extends to include liberalization of movement of persons. However, this is not an area where, pursuant to Parts III and IV of GATS, Members are under any *obligation* to negotiate specific commitments. This is reinforced by the Annex on Movement of

Natural Persons Supplying Services Under the Agreement, which states that 'In accordance with Parts III and IV of the Agreement, Members *may* negotiate specific commitments with respect to movement of natural persons' (emphasis added). The Annex also states that the GATS does not apply in respect of 'measures affecting natural persons seeking access to the employment market of a Member, nor shall it apply to measures regarding citizenship, residence or employment on a permanent basis' (Article 2). However, a limited concession to the concern of developing countries that the GATS extend to movement of people is to be found in the Decision on Movement of Natural Persons, which provides that negotiations on movement of persons are to continue beyond the Uruguay Round through the establishment of a 'negotiating group on movement of natural persons'. The negotiating group is to conclude negotiations within six months of the entry into force of the Agreement establishing the WTO and to present a final report to the Council on Trade in Services at that time, when any commitments that result from the negotiations will be inscribed in Members' individual schedules.[32]

Article I.3 sets out the entities to which GATS strictures on services will apply. This includes not only three levels of government (described as 'central', 'regional', and 'local') but also 'non-governmental bodies in the exercise of powers delegated' by these three levels of government. This last inclusion represents an important departure from typical GATT practice of only seeking to bind governmental entities, whether directly in the case of Members' central governments or indirectly in the case of sub-national governments. The departure reflects the fact that in some countries, various professional services are often self-regulating in whole or in part (legal services, accounting, architecture and some health services are typical examples). A rather different kind of example would be the Canadian Radio and Television Commission – a public body created pursuant to statute but explicitly intended to exercise public authority independent from the Government of the day. An important question will become whether a formal or functional definition of delegated powers is to be employed in the interpretation of this sub-section. Some self-regulating bodies (e.g. the Committee that promulgates the City rules that apply to London securities houses) do not exercise directly delegated powers, but could be argued to perform a function that in many other Contracting Parties would be given to a government agency (in this case a Securities Commission like the US SEC). The formal perspective would be more in keeping with the GATT tradition of relating disciplines only to direct government action, but could result in an arbitrary asymmetry of obligations, with Members that choose a self-regulating approach to certain sectors being subject to less discipline than those that adopt more direct regulatory instruments, or at least structure self-regulation as explicitly delegated regulatory power.

In any case *Members* (i.e. states) remain responsible for the compliance of these non-governmental entities with GATT provisions. One view of such an obligation, that would go hand in hand with the functional view of delegated powers, is that a positive obligation is imposed on governments to curb the practices of these entities that violate the GATS. The notion that the GATS – as a liberalizing agreement – could involve an obligation to regulate may seem, at first, odd. However, it should be noted that numerous provisions of the Agreement on TRIPs (Trade-Related Intellectual Property Measures) impose requirements of this kind with respect to protection of intellectual property rights.

Part II

MFN treatment

Article II:1 requires that MFN treatment be accorded 'immediately and unconditionally to services and service providers of any other country'. Article II:2 however, allows a Member to maintain exemptions to MFN treatment, provided that the Member lists the exempted measure in the Annex on Article II Exemptions, and provided that the conditions listed in that Annex are complied with. The conditions include: that exemptions granted for more than five years shall be reviewed by the Council for Trade in Services to determine 'whether the conditions which created the need for the exemptions still prevail' (Annex: Articles 3, 4 (a)); that exemptions should not last for more than ten years and must be subject to negotiation in subsequent rounds of multilateral negotiations.

These provisions reflect a compromise between American insistence that, at least in many key sectors, the USA should not be required to open up its markets to countries not prepared to provide an adequate equivalent degree of market access, and the concerns of many other Members that the GATS do not evolve into a tangled web of bilateral sectoral deals, i.e. into a regime of sectoral managed trade at odds with basic GATT principles of rules-based multilateral liberalization. In essence, the USA and other countries that so wish are permitted to continue to pursue liberalization arrangements based on reciprocity, but the justification for refusing to extend these arrangements to other Members on an unconditional MFN basis is subject to ongoing scrutiny within the framework of the WTO.

Article II:3 exempts from the MFN requirement 'advantages' conferred on 'adjacent countries in order to facilitate exchanges limited to contiguous frontier zones of services that are both locally produced and consumed'. Part II contains a range of substantive obligations that are binding on all Members. Some of these obligations apply to trade in services generally, while others apply only where a Member has made specific commitments to market access in its schedule. Article III:1 requires prompt publication of 'all regulations of general application, which pertain to or affect the operation' of GATS, and Article III:3 requires, at a minimum, annual reporting to the Council for Trade in Services of any new measures 'which significantly affect trade in services' covered by specific commitments in a Member's schedule. Article VI:1 provides that in sectors where specific commitments are undertaken, each Member shall ensure that all measures of general application affecting trade in services are administered in a 'reasonable, objective and impartial manner' and Article VI:2 requires that administrative and/or judicial review of decisions that affect trade in services be available, subject to any constraints that may arise due to a Member's constitution or the nature of its legal system.

Among the most important substantive provisions of Part II is the framework for scrutiny of technical barriers to trade in services set out in Articles VI:4–5. The Council for Trade in Services is to develop a set of disciplines on these barriers (including 'qualification requirements and procedures, technical standards and licensing requirements') so as to ensure that these measures do not 'constitute unnecessary barriers to trade in services'. This work is to occur under 'appropriate bodies' established by the Council. The resultant disciplines will ensure that measures such as qualification requirements and technical standards are, *inter alia*: ' (a) based on objective and transparent criteria, such as competence and the ability to supply the service; (b) not more burdensome than necessary to ensure the quality of the service; (c) in the case of licensing procedures, not in themselves a restriction on the supply of the service' (Article VI:4). The Decision Concerning Professional Services, which is part of the Uruguay Round Final Act provides that 'the work programme foreseen in Article V, paragraph 4 . . . should be put into effect immediately'. For these purposes a Working Party is to be established, which is to give priority to the elaboration of multilateral disciplines with respect to regulation of the accounting profession (Article VI:5 (a) of GATS makes the criteria in Article VI:4 immediately and directly[33] applicable to domestic measures in a sector where a Member has already made specific commitments in its schedule, at least where there is a possibility that the measures in question may nullify or impair specific market access commitments in a Member's schedule).

Article VII is aimed at the multilateralization of existing arrangements for recognition of educational and other credentials in the licensing or certification of service providers. Whether such recognition is afforded to particular countries unilaterally or on the basis of negotiated reciprocity (i.e. mutual recognition), other Members must be given the opportunity of demonstrating that credentials, licensing or certification in their country are also worthy of recognition. Moreover, 'a member shall not accord recognition in a manner which would constitute a means of discrimination between countries in the application of its standards or criteria for the authorization, licensing or certification of service suppliers, or a disguised restriction on trade in services' (Article VII:3).

231

Articles VIII and IX concern monopolies and restrictive business practices. Article VIII requires that Members ensure that monopoly service suppliers act in a manner that is not 'inconsistent' with the Article II MFN obligation, or with specific commitments in the Member's schedule. Moreover, Members are required to prevent 'abuse' of monopoly position, where a domestic monopolist is competing in the supply of a service over which it does not have monopoly rights (Article VIII:2). An obvious example would be that of a telecommunications concern that has a monopoly over local service but competes with respect to long distance and other services. Article IX provides for mandatory consultations where a service provider is believed to be restricting competition through business practices other than those described in Article VIII.

Part II of the GATS contains safeguards provisions and a set of general exemptions to GATS obligations. Article X of GATS provides that a permanent safeguards provision shall be negotiated within a three-year period. In the interim, Members are free to modify or withdraw specific commitments under the GATS provided that the Member justifies before the GATT Council that its measures are urgently needed and must be taken before the end of the three-year period contemplated for negotiation of a permanent safeguard instrument. There is an additional provision that permits the reimposition of restrictions on trade in services that would otherwise be inconsistent with a Member's specific commitments, where necessary to address serious balance-of-payments difficulties or other 'external financial difficulties' (Article XII). Such restrictions must, *inter alia*, be applied on a non-discriminatory basis and be consistent with the IMF Articles of Agreement.

Article XIII exempts government procurement from the MFN and National Treatment[34] obligation of the GATS, subject to a requirement that negotiations on government procurement of services take place within two years of the establishment of the WTO. Articles XIV and XIV bis contain general exceptions to GATS obligations, modelled respectively, on Articles XX and XXI of the GATT. Article XIV, exempts from GATS discipline measures 'necessary to protect public morals or to maintain public order' as well as 'human, animal or plant life or health', provided these are not 'a means of arbitrary or unjustifiable discrimination between countries where like conditions prevail, or a disguised restriction on trade and services'. In addition to these exceptions, virtually identical to some of those in Article XX of the GATT, exceptions are also provided that reflect particular concerns with respect to service sectors, for example privacy concerns with respect to trans-border data flow (Article XIV (c) (iii)). As well, Article XIV (d) exempts from the National Treatment obligation differential tax measures for foreign service providers, where these special measures are necessary, for example, to counter tax avoidance or evasion. Article XIV bis provides an exception for measures taken for the 'protection of essential security interests', and is for all relevant purposes, virtually identical to Article XXI of the GATT. Finally, Article XV requires Members to enter into negotiations with a view to multilateral disciplines on subsidies that affect trade in services, as well as on the issue of countervailablility of subsidies to service providers. Currently only subsidies on goods are countervailable under domestic trade remedy laws of the major trading states, and the GATT provisions on subsidies can be taken to authorize countervailing duty actions only with respect to trade in goods. Subject to the future negotiations contemplated by Article XV, GATS may be said to prohibit the imposition of countervailing duties in as much as these would violate the general MFN obligation in Article II of GATS. Article XV also provides that a Member that deems itself adversely affected by the subsidy of another Member may request consultations with the other Member. Such requests for consultations must be given sympathetic consideration.

Parts III and IV

Parts III and IV of the GATS apply with respect to specific market access commitments provided by Members in their schedules.

Article XVI:1 reaffirms the application of the MFN principle to specific commitments. A footnote to this article also specifies that where a Member makes a particular market access commitment, and where 'cross-border movement of capital is an essential part of the service itself' the Member is thereby committed to liberalizing the movement of capital. Article XVI:2 prohibits the imposition of quantitative restrictions on trade in services with respect to those sectors where a Member has made specific commitments. The prohibited quantitative restrictions include limitations on the number of service providers, on the total value of service transactions, and limitations on the participation of foreign capital, either in terms of a percentage limit on foreign shareholding or on the total value of foreign investment, either in the aggregate or by a single entity.

Article XVII contains a National Treatment obligation with respect to sectors listed in a Member's schedule. 'Formally different treatment' of foreign suppliers may be consistent with the National Treatment obligation – provided of course that such formally different treatment nevertheless is 'no less favourable' in effect. However, this is very much a two-edged sword – for 'formally identical treatment' may be deemed to *violate* the National Treatment obligation where the measure in question nevertheless 'modifies the conditions of competition in favour of domestic service suppliers'. This approach to National Treatment, which goes beyond a ban on intentionally discriminatory measures, reflects the view that equal treatment implies adjustment of domestic regulatory regimes so that foreign suppliers have *substantively* equal competitive opportunities.

Article XVIII states explicitly that Members may negotiate and bind within their schedules additional commitments beyond those that Articles XVI and XVII require with respect to any sector listed in a Member's schedule of specific commitments. Thus, a ban on quantitative restrictions (Article XVI) and National Treatment (Article XVII) may be said to constitute (subject to any reservations that are lodged; see below) the *minimum required content* of liberalization commitments with respect to any specific sector contained in a Member's schedule. However, it is anticipated that additional commitments to particular regulatory changes (e.g. 'qualifications, standards or licensing matters') will also occur with respect to those sectors on a Member's schedule.

Article XIX commits Members to enter into 'successive rounds of negotiations ... with a view to achieving a progressively higher level of liberalization'. Liberalization is to occur 'on a mutually advantageous basis' and should secure 'an overall balance of rights and obligations'. It is made explicit that what is involved is not merely the discipline of measures that discriminate against foreign suppliers directly or intentionally, but more generally 'the reduction or elimination' of measures which have '*adverse effects* on trade in services'. This legitimizes the notion that Members should be prepared to put on the bargaining table *any* domestic regulatory measure that has the effect of limiting market access. The far-reaching implications of this provision for domestic policy sovereignty are somewhat balanced by the statement in Article XIX:2 that 'the process of liberalization shall take place with due respect for national policy objectives and the level of development of individual Members, both overall and in individual sectors'.

Article XIX:2 further specifies that 'there shall be appropriate flexibility for individual developing countries for opening fewer sectors, liberalizing fewer types of transactions, progressively extending market access in line with their development situation and, when making access to their markets available to foreign service suppliers, attaching to it conditions aimed at achieving the objectives referred to in Article IV', which include *inter alia* the strengthening of developing countries' capacity in service sectors as well as liberalization in service sectors of export interest to these countries.

Article XIX must be read in conjunction with the delicate compromise concerning the MFN obligation in Article II and in the Annex on Article II Exemptions. As discussed above, in light of US refusal to proceed with certain sectoral negotiations on an MFN basis it was necessary to allow for certain exemptions from MFN treatment for specific sectoral commitments. However, as also noted above, these exemptions will be subject to ongoing scrutiny by the Council for Trade in Services, which will 'examine whether the conditions which created the need for the exemptions still prevail' (Annex on Article II Exemptions). Arguably, Article XIX provides some significant guidelines to the Council in its examination of whether an exemption from MFN treatment is needed. Article XIX:2 may be said to set reasonable expectations with respect to the pace and extent of liberalization, particularly for developing countries. If, on the whole, the specific commitments of such countries are consistent with these reasonable expectations, an exemption from MFN treatment in the schedule of a developed country should not be justifiable on the basis that developing countries have not sufficiently opened up their own markets to allow for, in the words of Article XIX:1, 'an overall balance of rights and obligations'. Article XX sets out a number of items that must be specified in Members' schedules of specific commitments. These include any 'terms, limitations and conditions on market access' (i.e. with respect to the elimination of quantitative restrictions contemplated in Article XVI) and 'conditions and qualifications on National Treatment'. Article XXI provides that a Member may permanently withdraw or alter a specific commitment in its schedule at any time after three years following the entry into force of the Agreement. This is subject to a requirement of three years' advance notice, and to prior negotiation of a 'compensatory adjustment' where necessary. Such compensatory adjustments are to be made on an MFN basis, and are aimed at maintaining 'a general level of mutually advantageous commitments not less favourable to trade than that provided for in schedules of specific commitments prior to such negotiations' (Article XXI:2 (a)). This provision makes it clear that modification or withdrawal of specific commitments by a particular country or countries is not to be used as a pretext for a broader move by other countries to narrow the scope of MFN-based liberalization. Where negotiations on compensation fail, binding arbitration under WTO auspices shall decide what compensatory adjustment, if any, is required.

The provisions of Article XXI clearly go beyond the traditional GATT 'safeguards' concept of temporary reneging on commitments. However, it should be emphasized that much of what Members will be binding in their schedules will consist of specific domestic regulations or regulatory changes. As technology, as well as social and economic conditions, evolve it is essential that Members have some scope for adjusting their domestic regulatory frameworks.

Parts V and VI

Part V contains provisions that relate to the institutional framework of the Services Agreement, and more specifically, to dispute settlement. The Council for Trade in Services is to have a very broad mandate for implementing the Agreement. It 'shall carry out such functions as may be assigned to it to facilitate the operation of [the] Agreement and further its objective'. The Council, and normally any subordinate body of the Council, is to be open to participation by all Members. This makes it clear that failure to provide a given level of specific liberalization commitments will not exclude any Member from participation in the decision-making of the Council (including decision-making about where exceptions to MFN treatment are justifiable). With respect to dispute settlement, the normal WTO procedures apply to GATS (these are outlined in the Understanding on Rules and Procedures Governing the Settlement of Disputes, which builds on Articles XXII and XXIII of the GATT). One difference, however, is that with respect to GATS, the Dispute Settlement Body (DSB) may only authorize suspension of concessions where 'it considers the circumstances are serious enough to justify such action, . . .' (Article XXIII:2). Moreover, it is only concessions under GATS that may be suspended – retaliation may not be authorized in the form of suspension of concessions under any other Agreement in the WTO. By virtue of Article XXIII:3 the concept of non-violation nullification or impairment is extended to GATS. The Decision on Certain Dispute Settlement Procedures for the General Agreement on Trade in Services provides that a special roster of panellists is to be established for purposes of settlement of disputes under GATS. These panellists are to have 'experience in issues related to the General Agreement on Trade in Services and/or trade in services, including associated regulatory matters'(Article 3). Moreover, 'panels for disputes regarding sectoral matters shall have the necessary expertise relevant to the specific service sectors which the dispute concerns' (Article 4).

Part VI represents a very basic attempt to state rules of origin for services. Article XXVII specifies that a Member may deny the benefit of the Agreement, where it establishes that the 'service is supplied from the territory of a non-Member' or to a corporation that is not a 'service supplier' of another Member. Neither of these rules permits of straightforward application. With respect to the first, the concept of 'territory' is very difficult to apply in the case of multinational service provision. Take, for instance, the case of a multinational law firm that provides legal services to nationals of a GATS member with respect to a business deal that involves a non-Member (e.g. Russia). Some of the work may be done in the firm's Moscow office, but many of the client contacts and even the negotiations may take place on the territory of GATS Members. How, then, can one decide whether the service in question is being provided from the territory of a non-Member? In the case of rules of origin for trade in goods, this is dealt with by specifying a threshold percentage of the value of the good that must be accounted for by economic activity within a Member country. With respect to the second rule, it depends upon the determination of corporate nationality, a very difficult issue in many service sectors where trade in services is dominated by multinational enterprises that have no unambiguous national identity (unless one invokes purely formal criteria such as the place of incorporation of the parent company, the head office location, etc.).

FINANCIAL SERVICES

The OECD Code on Liberalisation of Capital Movements

The Capital Movements Code[35] requires OECD Members to 'progressively abolish between one another, . . . restrictions on movements of capital to the extent necessary for effective economic cooperation'(Article 1 (a)). Annex D establishes a list of capital movements to which the Code applies. This includes a very wide range of transactions required for the trans-boundary supply of financial services, including banking, insurance, and securities. Members may lodge reservations and (in some circumstances) derogations with respect to the general obligation of progressive removal of restrictions. There is an MFN obligation with respect to domestic regulation that affects providers of financial services from other member countries as well as an MFN obligation with respect to other OECD members. However, the Code also encourages, without requiring, members to extend the advantages of liberalizing provisions of the Codes to non-members.

The European Union

Liberalization of trade in services within the European Union is stated as an objective in the Treaty of Rome, and is a major aspect of the Europe 1992 programme, reflected in the Single European Act (1986).[36] In the financial services sector,[37] the approach of the Union to liberalization of trade is based on the closely related principles of mutual recognition, home country rule, and minimum regulatory harmonization.[38] Mutual recognition entails the granting of market access to an institution from another EU Member state, based on the institution's compliance with regulatory requirements in its home country. The related principle of home country rule stipulates that the regulatory authorities in the home country retain responsibility for prudential supervision of the institution even where what is involved is activities in other EU states. Hence, market access is not granted on terms of compliance with the (non-discriminatory) regulation of the 'importing' country (as with National Treatment) but on condition that the entity meet relevant regulatory requirements in its own country.[39] Unlike National Treatment-based approaches, mutual recognition and home country rule, taken together, imply not only the elimination of direct and facially discriminatory barriers to service provision by foreigners but also the removal of those indirect and facially neutral barriers that exist where the foreign providers face costs in adapting products or operations so as to meet the distinctive regulatory requirements of the importing or host state.

However, since mutual recognition and home country rule necessarily entail reliance on another state's regulators and regulations to protect one's own citizens, an essential *quid pro quo* is a set of minimum standards sufficient to provide even the country with the strictest regulatory requirements the needed confidence in the regulatory regimes of the others. This is reflected in the third principle, minimum regulatory harmonization.

The minimum standards to which EU Member states' regulatory regimes must conform are set out in the 1989 Second Banking Directive.[40] As Kim notes, these standards cover a very wide range of regulatory requirements, including 'initial capital requirements, disclosure of a credit institution's major shareholders, limitations on the size of participation in nonfinancial undertakings, standard solvency ratios, and permissible activities'.[41] 'Minimum' regulatory harmonization thus entails, in fact, a very significant degree of harmonization.

It is important to note that the European Union has a strong, permanent institutional structure that allows for ongoing consultation and cooperation among the regulators of the various Member states, and for further harmonization. This allows for ongoing adjustment of common minimum standards in response to experience with liberalized trade in financial services, and allows adaptation of harmonized requirements to changes in the industry, such as the introduction of new products and the changing interrelationship between banking and other financial services. It may be difficult to extend the EU approach to bilateral or regional contexts where this kind of common institutional framework does not exist. As well, unless the minimum common standards are in fact set quite high, the EU approach may lead to 'unfair trade' complaints from domestic institutions who must now compete with foreign providers who have lower regulatory costs because their home country's regulatory standards are laxer. In such a situation, an EU-style approach could create downward pressures on the regulatory standards of the stricter countries. Where, however, it is the stricter countries that have the bargaining power to ensure that the common minimum standards remain high, or are moved upward, the end result may in fact be a higher standard. It should be noted that, within the European Union, the two major powers, France and Germany, have what are generally considered relatively strict, rather conservative approaches to regulation of financial services (in comparison, say to Italy or the UK). This may give an important clue as to why liberalization of trade in financial services has not led to downwards harmonization.

The Canada–US Free Trade Agreement (FTA)

The Canada–US FTA takes a National Treatment approach to liberalization of trade in financial services between the Parties. The failure to move to an approach based on regulatory harmonization or mutual recognition reflects significant assymmetries in domestic regulatory approaches in Canada and the United States prior to the FTA, especially with respect to banking.[42] In Canada, there are strict entry requirements for the banking sector, but once a bank is chartered or licensed, it can engage in banking business, as well as in securities business, throughout the country. The United States regime is characterized by ease of entry into the banking business, but by continued prohibition, under the Glass–Steagall Act, of bank participation in the securities business, as well as strict limits on inter-state banking. Prior to the FTA, Canadian banks had already obtained important exemptions from the limits on inter-state banking in domestic US regulation. Canadian banking laws prohibit concentrated ownership of banks – no one share-holder may own more than 10% of a Canadian chartered bank. In addition, strict limits are also imposed on foreign ownership – the aggregate of foreign-held shares in a chartered bank may not exceed 25%. Given these limitations, a foreign-owned bank that wishes access to the Canadian market must establish itself as a 'Schedule B' bank, with limited powers to engage in branch banking, and also limitations on assets. The aggregate assets of foreign 'Schedule B' banks may not constitute more than 16% of the total assets of the Canadian banking system.

Under Article 1703 of the FTA, the United States is exempt from the main limitations imposed on foreign 'Schedule B' banks in Canadian banking regulation, and from discriminatory treatment under federal laws that apply with respect to non-bank financial institutions such as trust companies (except the 10% limit on a single shareholder's stake). However, since most regulation in the non-bank financial sector in Canada is provin-cial, the commitments are of less significance than with respect to banking. Canada also makes a general commitment to go beyond National Treatment and to 'liberalize further the rules governing its markets' (Article 1703.4).

While US institutions thus gain considerably enhanced access to the Canadian market, Canadian institutions do not gain a comparable increase in access to the US market. Canadian banks do preserve some of their *existing* rights and privileges under US law, such as exemptions from restrictions on inter-state branching (1702.2) and the right to deal in government securities (1702.1). As well, Canadian institutions are promised National Treatment with respect to future changes to domestic US regulation, including the Glass–Steagall Act (1702.3). However, unlike Canada, which commits itself to liberalize further its domestic regulatory regime for financial institutions, the United States itself makes no such commitment. Instead, the preser-vation of Canada's *existing* access to the US market is premised on further Canadian *unilateral* liberalization of regulations (1702.4). In the FTA, the USA may thus be said to have succeeded in achieving a one-sided agreement on financial services – obtaining considerably greater market access in Canada, while yielding no immediate effective increase in access to its own markets. This success in the bilateral context may be one underlying reason why the United States, as will be discussed below, was so resistant to accept-ing a genuine multilateral approach to liberalization of trade in financial services within the GATS.

The North American Free Trade Agreement (NAFTA)

Unlike the FTA, the NAFTA contains general MFN (Article 1406) and National Treatment (1405) obligations with respect to financial services, as well as a Right of Establishment. The Right of Establishment is, however, recognized only as a 'principle' and this principle is subject to requirements that separate financial institutions deliver separate services (1403.2 (a)), thereby protecting the provisions of the US Glass–Steagall Act from scrutiny under NAFTA. As well, although the Right of Establishment includes the right to 'expand geographically' within the territory of another Party (1403.2 (b)), compliance with the principle of a Right of Establishment is only to be subject to review by the NAFTA Parties once the United States has chosen of its own accord to lift domestic restrictions on interstate banking activity by foreign institutions (1403.3).

The National Treatment obligation in Article 1405 is based not upon the notion of facially non-discriminatory treatment, but rather of 'equal competitive opportunities'(Article 1405.5–7). This provides considerable scope for claims that neutral domestic regulation nevertheless does not create a level playing field for competition.

Article 1407.1 provides that 'each Party shall permit a financial institution of another Party to provide any new financial service of a type similar to those services that the Party permits its own financial institutions, in like circumstances, to provide under domestic law', subject to any non-discriminatory domestic regulatory control over the 'the institutional and juridical form through which the service shall be provided'. Article 1407.2 provides for free transboundary flow of data between NAFTA Parties in connection with the provision of financial services. Significantly, this is not subject to any obligations with respect to the protection of personal privacy or commercial confidentiality.

Pursuant to Article 1408, Parties may make reservations with respect to their adhesion to the Right of Establishment, National Treatment, MFN and other obligations set out in Articles 1403–1407. Mexico, in particular, has filed a complex schedule for phasing in these obligations over a six-year period (1994–2000), as well as a safeguard provision to apply between 2000 and 2007 (Annex VII (B)–Mexico). The schedule entails an expanding set of limits on the aggregate market share of foreign institutions (whether from NAFTA Parties or Non-Parties), as well as the individual market share of any one foreign institution. Separate limits apply with respect to each individual part of the financial services sector (banking, securities, insurance, etc.). For example, aggregate limits on banks will increase from 8–15% from 1994 to 2000, and may be frozen at 25% between 2000–2007 under the safeguard provision. It should be noted that the safeguard provision applies only with respect to aggregate limits on market share; individual firm limits are to be phased out completely by the year 2000.[43]

Article 1410 exempts from the obligations contained in the NAFTA Chapter on Financial Services, 'reasonable measures [taken] for prudential reasons'. These will include measures taken to protect investors and other market participants, as well as for purposes of maintaining the 'safety, soundness, integrity or financial responsibility' of financial institutions, or to ensure 'the integrity and stability of a Party's financial system'. There are special provisions with respect to dispute settlement concerning the NAFTA financial services chapter. Members of dispute panels are to be chosen from a special roster of individuals with expertise in 'financial services law or practice, which may include the regulation of financial institutions'(Article 1414.3 (a).

The Uruguay Round Services Agreement (GATS)

The GATS contains two Annexes on Financial Services as well as an Understanding on Commitments in Financial Services and a Decision on Financial Services. These various instruments reflect the incompleteness of the negotiations on financial services at the closure of the Uruguay Round in December of 1993, as well as a compromise between different views as to how the negotiations should be completed. The United States took the view, during the final period of negotiations leading up to the December deadline, that other countries had not offered sufficient sectoral liberalization commitments in financial services to justify US adherence to a multilateral, MFN-based framework. The United States therefore stated its intent to take an MFN exemption with respect to its own commitments under a GATS agreement on financial services, and to proceed with bilateral and regional negotiations on liberalization of trade in financial services.[44] This would, in effect, amount to an opting out of the multilateral track towards liberalization. Through a mechanism described in more detail below, a compromise was reached whereby the United States would suspend its MFN exemption for a six-month period after the coming into force of the Final Act in 1995, during which period a further attempt would be made at multilateral negotiation of liberalization commitments within the GATS/WTO framework. If this attempt succeeded, the USA would permanently withdraw its MFN exception. If these further negotiations resulted in an impasse, the USA would be free to reinstate the exception and proceed along bilateral and regional lines.

The Annex on Financial Services does not contain any specific liberalization commitments with respect to trade in financial services, but rather concerns the application of the GATS to the financial services sector. Article 2.1, for example, provides an exemption from GATS strictures of measures taken 'for prudential reasons, including for the protection of investors, depositors, policy holders or persons to whom a fiduciary duty is owed by a financial service supplier, or to ensure the integrity and stability of the financial system'. This is, however, subject to the requirement that any such non-conforming measures not be used to circumvent GATS obligations. Article 3 permits either unilateral or mutual recognition of other countries' 'prudential measures'. This limited exception to the MFN principle is subject to the requirement that, where recognition is accorded through a negotiated agreement or arrangement, a Member must provide an opportunity for other Members to accede to the agreement, or to negotiate a comparable deal (Article 3.2).

In Article 5.1 of the Annex, the financial services sector is defined very broadly as including 'any service of a financial nature offered by a financial service supplier of a member'. This is followed by a lengthy list of services that fall within this general definition. The list includes a comprehensive range of insurance services, 'traditional' banking activities such as deposit-taking and lending, as well as underwriting of securities and trading in virtually every existing form of security or negotiable instrument. In addition, consulting and brokering services connected with these transactions are included within the ambit of financial services. As is suggested by the wide-ranging character of this summary of the list, the clear intent of Article 5.1 is to include as many activities as possible under the rubric of financial services.

The Second Annex on Financial Services allows Members a period of six months following the entry into force of the Agreement Establishing the WTO within which to 'improve, modify or withdraw' any specific commitments in their schedules with respect to financial services, and also to finalize any MFN exemptions in their schedules. The Decision on Financial Services stipulates that, until the expiration of this six-month period, Members shall suspend the *application* of any MFN exemption already filed in their schedules. These provisions were required in order to implement the crucial compromise discussed above, whereby the United States agreed to extend provisionally its participation in multilateral negotiations on financial services, without prejudice to its right to proceed on a bilateral or regional basis if the negotiations were not to succeed within the agreed time period.

The Understanding on Commitments in Financial Services outlines a framework for liberalization of trade in financial services which provides an alternative to that set out for services generally in Part III of the GATS. Members are free to choose to schedule specific commitments in the financial sector either in accordance with Part III or in accordance with the Understanding. The Understanding sets out a series of specific commitments that some, but not all Members, have inscribed in their individual schedules, *and which gain legal force not from their inclusion in the Understanding but from their presence in the schedules*. This contrasts with the approach in Part III of the GATS, where Members are *legally bound* to inscribe certain basic commitments within their schedules.

The commitments contained in the Understanding, taken together, represent a very extensive degree of liberalization. Members are obligated to list in their schedules monopoly rights with respect to financial services provision and to 'endeavour to eliminate them or reduce their scope' (Article 1). Both National Treatment and MFN obligations are to apply to government procurement of financial services (Article 2). Market access is to be conferred on non-resident suppliers on a National Treatment basis in the areas of marine, commercial aviation and space travel insurance (e.g. of satellites), as well as with respect to financial data processing and transmission. A Right of Establishment is provided in Articles 5 and 6, including a right to establish a commercial presence in the territory of another Member through acquisition of an existing enterprise. There is also a right of temporary entry for certain classes of personnel from the financial services providers of other Members, including senior management, specialists in financial services operations, and certain other technical specialists (e.g. computer services personnel) (Article 9). Article 10 of the Understanding entails a commitment to 'endeavour to remove' a wide range of *non-discriminatory* regulatory measures which are deemed to have an adverse effect on the market access of financial services suppliers from another Member. A notable instance is that of 'non-discriminatory measures that limit the expansion of the activities of financial services suppliers into the entire territory of the Member', which would apply to limits on inter-state branching in US domestic banking law. It is to be noted that the language 'endeavour to remove' stops short of formal legal commitment to actually eliminate the measures in question. Furthermore, a Member may, as an alternative to endeavouring to remove a measure, instead endeavour to limit its adverse effects on other Members (for example, by not applying the measure to service providers of other Members or applying it in a different manner). Finally, the Understanding requires that providers of other Members be given access, on a National Treatment basis, to 'payment and clearing systems operated by public entities, and to official funding and refinancing facilities available in the normal course of ordinary business', with the exception of 'lender of last resort' facilities. As well, the providers of other Members must be able to join any 'self-regulatory body, securities or futures exchange or market, clearing agency' in a Member's territory, on the same terms as the Member's own financial service providers. This applies whenever joining any such body or institution is a requirement for providing financial services in the Member's territory on a National Treatment basis (Article 11.2).

TELECOMMUNICATIONS

The Canada–US FTA

The FTA provides for the liberalization of trade only with respect to what are termed in the Agreement as enhanced telecommunications services. The relevant provisions are contained in an annex to the Services Chapter of the FTA (Chapter 14), entitled 'Computer Services and Telecommunications-Network-Based Enhanced Services'. Each Party is required to maintain the existing access to the basic telecommunications network that it currently provides to the other Party (Article 4). Moreover, where a Party maintains a monopoly over basic services, it must insure that the monopoly does not abuse its power to compete unfairly in the area of enhanced services. This means, *inter alia*, that a Party's monopoly must provide access to its basic network on terms that do not discriminate against enhanced service suppliers of the other Party (Article 5).

As Globerman, *et al.* observe, the significance of these provisions for liberalization of trade in telecommunications services depends on how 'basic' services are defined in contrast to 'enhanced' services.[45] The definitions in the Annex itself are of limited assistance. Basic telecommunications transport service 'means any service as defined and classified by measure of the regulator having jurisdiction that is limited to the offering of transmission capacity for the movement of information'. Enhanced service is defined as 'any service offering over the basic telecommunications transport network that is more than a basic telecommunications transport service as defined and classified by the regulator having jurisdiction'. It seems clear enough that local and long distance telephone services fall within the 'basic' category, and indeed at the time the FTA was negotiated these were largely subject to monopoly provision in Canada. With respect to many other services, however, it is unclear whether they should be viewed as offering 'transmission capacity for the movement of information' or as providing something more. For example, there are services that store or transform information, and thus from one perspective can be viewed as 'enhanced', but which do so primarily to *facilitate* its movement or transmission, rather than – as with computer services – to provide new or additional information (Store and Forward Telex and Pager Services are two examples).

NAFTA

Chapter 13 of NAFTA is devoted to telecommunications, and embodies a rather more extensive set of obligations than the FTA. Article 1302 requires that a Party provide 'persons of another Party' access to its basic telecommunications network 'for the conduct of their business, on reasonable and non-discriminatory terms'. This refers to private communications and data networks maintained by firms for their internal use, and to the kind of enhanced services covered by the FTA. It does not imply a right to sell or resell telecommunications capacity itself. Thus Article 1301. 3 (c) states that nothing in Chapter 13 prevents a Party 'from prohibiting persons operating private networks from using their networks to provide public telecommunications transport networks or services to third persons'.

Article 1302 contains a series of rather technical provisions that define many of the elements of the right of access to the basic network (for example, the right to attach one's own equipment to the basic network). The right of access may be limited where necessary, *inter alia*, to protect the privacy of basic network subscribers or to protect the technical integrity of the public telecommunications network (Articles 5–6).

Unlike the FTA, which refers to enhanced services, the NAFTA uses the expression 'enhanced and value-added services'. This expression is defined with some precision in Article 1310 as including services that 'act on' aspects of a customer's information, provide 'additional, different, or restructured information'; or 'involve customer interaction with stored information'. This is a very explicit and broad definition, which clearly encompasses most services beyond the basic local and long distance telephone service. There is a correspondingly narrow definition of public telecommunications transport service as a service 'required by a Party, explicitly or in effect, to be offered to the public generally, . . . that typically involves the real-time transmission of customer-supplied information between two or more points without *any* end-to-end change in the form or content of the customer's information'.

It should be noted that, unlike the FTA, the NAFTA confers on enhanced service providers something more than a right to non-discriminatory access to the public telecommunications network. Enhanced and value-added service suppliers are also to be exempt from requirements that they cost-justify their rates or that they provide enhanced services to the public generally (Article 1303.2 (a), (b)). Finally, the NAFTA requires that the Parties 'consult with a view to determining the feasibility of further liberalizing trade in all telecommunications services, including public telecommunications transport networks and services'(Article 1309.2).

The Uruguay Round Services Agreement (GATS)

The GATS contains an Annex on Telecommunications, which is very similar in its substantive provisions and terminology to Chapter 13 of NAFTA. Thus, the Annex establishes a right of access for persons of another Party to a Party's public telecommunications transport networks and services on 'non-discriminatory and reasonable terms' (Article 5.1). However, the extent to which this right may be used by persons of a non-Party to supply telecommunications services to others (including, presumably, what are referred to in NAFTA as enhanced and value-added services) will depend on the specific commitments inscribed in the schedules of individual Members (Article 2.3.1).

In addition to the GATS Annex on Telecommunications, the Uruguay Round Final Act also contains the Decision on Negotiations on Basic Telecommunications. This Decision entails the conduct of future negotiations 'on a voluntary basis with a view to the progressive liberalization of trade in telecommunications transport networks and services ... within the framework of the General Agreement on Trade in Services' (Article 1). These negotiations are to be 'comprehensive in scope, with no basic telecommunications excluded *a priori*'. Although the negotiations are to be open to all members, so far only twelve countries have announced their intention to participate. Significantly all of these are developed countries, except Mexico (which is obligated by NAFTA to undertake 'consultations' of a similar nature in the NAFTA framework). The Decision provides for the establishment of a Negotiating Group on Basic Telecommunications, which must conclude its negotiations and make a final report by 30 April 1996.

For those who adhere to a truly multilateral vision of the GATT/WTO there is something troubling about the establishment within the GATT/WTO umbrella of a negotiating agenda of interest, with but one exception, to a sub-set of developed countries. Of course, there have been occasions where agreements negotiated within the GATT only attracted the signatures of a minority of Contracting Parties (for instance, the Tokyo Round Subsidies Code). However, the Decision on Negotiations on Basic Telecommunications establishes a negotiating process on matters on which, *at the outset*, there is far from a consensus as to the appropriateness of trade strictures.

CONCLUSION

Given the highly diverse nature of the barriers to trade in services, and the interconnection of many of these barriers with a wide range of complex domestic regulations and policies, liberalization of trade in services is not achievable through the general multilateral rules and negotiated removal of border measures that have characterized the GATT's approach to liberalization of trade in goods. While some barriers are caught by a National Treatment obligation, many others can only be addressed either through commitments to remove or alter non-discriminatory domestic regulations or to international regulatory harmonization (at least with respect to minimum standards or qualifications).

The attempt to insert a process for negotiation of specific commitments to regulatory change within a multilateral rule-based institutional and legal framework has been less than entirely successful – as witnessed by the severe tensions between different Members concerning the place of the MFN principle in this process. This has led to an incomplete result, and one that has already been declared unsatisfactory by many of those who had sought deeper liberalization in many of the most important service sectors, such as telecommunications, financial services, and transportation.[46] There is a significant possibility that liberalization will in future be pursued further either through the elaboration of bilateral or regional accords that already deal with services (NAFTA and the OECD Codes, for instance), or through negotiations within the WTO framework on a basis which is, in fact, not genuinely universal or multilateral. The danger is that a set of liberalization commitments may emerge that closes off major markets for services from countries unwilling or unable to make particular kinds of commitments to deregulation of their own service industries. Of course, a convergence of approaches to regulation and deregulation among an increasingly wide range of countries would significantly attenuate this problem, and make a multilateral approach more feasible and attractive.

Such a convergence is arguably occurring, at least among a significant number of both developed and developing countries,[47] although not at a pace always satisfying those seeking the fullest possible liberalization. It is important nonetheless to recognize that, in theory and perhaps also in practice in at least some areas, important trade-offs may still exist between the gains from liberalized trade in services on the one hand and, on the other, the resultant sacrifice in regulatory diversity and innovation. Finally, if the initial, quite limited bargains within the GATT/WTO on services are to be sustained over the long term, it will be quite important that the WTO deliver on the promise of becoming a genuine supranational organization, capable of facilitating ongoing negotiation and adjustment of commitments with respect to trade in services, in light of technological and other changes that affect the covered sectors and that present new or renewed regulatory challenges.

10

TRADE-RELATED INTELLECTUAL PROPERTY (TRIPs)

INTRODUCTION

Over the last two decades, a number of the most economically advanced industrialized nations, including the United States and some members of the European Union, have faced increasing competition in manufactured exports from Newly Industrializing Countries (NICs) in Asia and Latin America. This increasing competition has focused attention on domestic policies of these nations that may adversely or (as is often claimed) even unfairly disadvantage American or European trading interests. It is in this manner that the issue of intellectual property rights has become a prominent item on the trade agenda, as reflected in the extensive provisions on intellectual property in both the Uruguay Round Final Act and the North American Free Trade Agreement.

Two main concerns have dominated the debate. The first is that many developing countries, including some NICs, have often afforded a shorter period of patent protection (and in some cases more narrowly defined protection) to products such as pharmaceuticals than do the United States and most European Countries. The result is that domestic imitations of these products often dominate developing country markets, with a resultant loss of potential foreign sales to the original North American or European producer who financed the innovation in the first place. In addition, the patent-granting process and the enforcement of patent protection in many developing countries has been viewed as lacking in transparency and legal security and certainty. The second concern is the tolerance of some developing country governments (and lack of vigilance in some other states as well) with respect to the production and sale of pirate sound recordings and videos, as well as the 'theft' or appropriation of trade marks and symbols (like 'Rolex' or 'Pierre Cardin') and their attachment to cheap imitations that have no relationship to the original producer's own manufactures.

American business interests have estimated losses in the billions of dollars annually from these kinds of supposed inadequacies in intellectual property protection, primarily in developing countries. From a trade theory perspective, however, it is far from clear that all countries should be required to maintain the same level of intellectual property protection. Patent protection constitutes a form of monopoly rent to the innovator. This provides incentives for innovation, but also may entail at least short-term consumer welfare losses and may discourage imitation and adaptation by competitors, which themselves constitute valuable economic activities. The level of intellectual property protection each country decides to afford will thus be rationally related to whether its comparative advantage resides more in innovation or imitation and adaptation of innovations made elsewhere, and the relative weight it gives to the interests of consumers (including its own producers who are consumers of inputs), imitators, and innovators.

Two kinds of justification for the protection of intellectual property dominate the debate on TRIPs. The first centres on fairness or compensatory justice concerns, the second on arguments about the relationship between protection of intellectual property and domestic and global economic welfare.

The use of inventions or creative works of others without their permission is often labelled as piracy or theft. Of course, unless the act in question is defined in those terms in the positive law of the country concerned, or in international law, such a characterization merely states a normative conclusion that inventors and creators *should* have a proprietary entitlement to the fruits of their labour. One (Lockean) line of argument to support this view is that persons are naturally owners of the fruits of their own labour, and that the taking of these fruits represents an attack on the autonomy – or even the integrity – of the person.[1] Pushed to its limits, this view would point to a perspective that suggests that taxation – or any non-voluntary appropriation by society of some of the value of an individual's labour – is expropriation. While we cannot here explore all the theoretical difficulties with such an understanding of property,[2] it is worth mentioning one problem that presents particular complications with respect to intellectual property. Society provides the context in which creative activity takes place – few inventions or works of art or literature spring fully grown from the inventor's head. They usually depend on education within society, and build on the work of many others. There is thus a limit to the extent that creators can declare the work totally their own, and exclude any claim by society on some of that value.

In fact, despite the rhetoric of natural rights or proprietary entitlements that is often invoked to argue for strengthened protection of intellectual property, the debate centres around whether protection should be limited, say, to 15 years for patents or extended to 20 or 25 years. It is hard to imagine a natural right that miraculously disappears after 20 or 25 years! Once we have established that the issue is actually the *level* of compensation to which a creator is entitled, then it is clear that at least implicitly the creator's claims are being balanced against other social interests.

A complete absence of compensation, or a social expropriation of all the benefit of an individual's creativity would, essentially, amount to slavery (with the one significant difference being that the inventor or creator could presumably choose not to invent or create, whereas the slave must work for another's benefit). Proprietary entitlements over one's creative product are, however, not the only form in which such compensation may be provided. For instance, in many countries, a large percentage of inventors or creators work in government laboratories and universities, and even literary and artistic activity is subsidized by the state. Invention and creation may be regarded as a salaried occupation like any other.

Once we view the relevant normative concern as that of compensation, a wide variety of factors may well enter into the determination of what a fair level of intellectual property protection would be. Just as inadequate compensation for valuable inventions may constitute exploitation, so could profiteering on the monopoly control over, for instance, the formula for some life-saving drug.[3]

The economic argument for the protection of intellectual property rights is relatively straightforward – unless invention or creation is compensated at its full social value there will be sub-optimal incentives to undertake it. Central to this insight is the 'free-rider' problem – an individual or firm will be much less likely to make an investment if someone else (the free rider) can capture or appropriate at little or no cost a significant part of the economic returns from the investment in question. However, as is widely recognized in the economic literature,[4] this must be weighed against the economic effects of creating a monopoly on knowledge, namely higher cost products and the exclusion from the market of competitors who may be able to imitate or adapt the invention in such a way that its social value is increased.

To take a simple example, let us suppose that currently in a given country, 15 years of patent protection is extended to the development of new widget technologies. If protection is extended to 20 years, incentives for innovation are increased, and some new valuable widget technologies that otherwise might go undeveloped and unexploited would come into being. However, lower cost products based on competitors' imitations or adaptations of existing widget technologies will take longer to get to market. Extending protection from 15 to 20 years will *only* make sense if the welfare gain from the added incentive to innovation outweighs the welfare loss from deterring competition with respect to imitations of the technology. In the abstract, we cannot tell which is more important to a given country – cheaper widgets from existing technologies or more new widget technologies.

Before we introduce the implications of this basic insight for trade, it is important to note that rarely will a single level of protection for all technologies or sectors maximize domestic welfare. After all, the trade-off between the economic benefits of innovation and imitation will vary quite considerably depending, say, upon whether we are dealing with computer technologies or pharmaceuticals. Recent work in economics on patent protection suggests the possibility that very strict protection could result in wasteful outlays on research and development – due to the 'winner takes all' nature of such protection firms may compete to be the first past the post with a patent in hand. This 'patent racing' argument points to the social efficiency, in some contexts, of treating R and D as a public good.[5] Third, it should be noted that the gains from imitation and the corresponding losses from increased patent protection may be of two kinds – first, higher costs to consumers from the monopoly position that the patent confers on the holder and second, the loss with respect to imitation industries, where revenues and employment will decline.

Similarly, the overall trade-offs between innovation and imitation may well differ from country-to-country. A country where innovation is not a major source of economic activity and growth is likely to choose, on balance, a less stringent intellectual property regime than would a country whose economy is highly dependent on innovation. From this perspective, there is nothing suspect or unreasonable with the preference of many developing countries for a relatively lax system of intellectual property rights. These countries have much to gain, in terms of consumer welfare, from countenancing cheap domestic imitations of innovations made elsewhere, and perhaps little to lose if they are not at a stage of development that makes domestic research and development an important ingredient in domestic welfare. From the point of view of at least some developing countries, then, an agreement on TRIPs that raised intellectual property protection to developed-country levels could rightly be seen as a welfare-reducing or Pareto-inferior bargain.

Several arguments have nevertheless been advanced to show that such a bargain could be in the long-term self-interest of developing countries. The first is that these countries, like all others, benefit from innovation which occurs outside their own borders, and that the increased incentives to inventors due to increased global revenues from their innovations, will yield greater amounts of innovation, and therefore new benefits in which developing countries will share. Often, industry estimates of 'foregone' revenues from sub-standard intellectual property protection in developing countries assume that if proper protection were afforded, a quantity of original products would be consumed equal to that of the imitations now being purchased. This, as is widely noted in more recent economic literature,[6] may be quite misleading – since original products (i.e. patent as opposed to generic drugs) would likely be much more expensive, one could expect a considerable decline in demand. Deardorff questions whether the marginal benefit of extra protection, in terms of products that would not have been invented but for the additional incentive from higher monopoly rents in developing countries, is likely to outweigh the reduction in consumer welfare due to higher prices.[7] It is also possible that the optimal level of innovation has already been achieved or exceeded – in which case further protection of intellectual property might actually result in, or even intensify, a misallocation of productive resources to research and development. At the margin, would welfare be increased more by an extra dollar being spent on innovation or on applications of existing inventions and technologies?

Another line of argument is that developing countries will attract greater amounts of foreign investment and technology transfers if foreigners believe that products, processes and trade secrets will be adequately protected. Empirical evidence that this is the case is, however, sketchy and anecdotal.[8] In addition, the appropriate response might be to negotiate specific guarantees with investors, rather than increasing intellectual property protection across the board.[9]

TRADE THEORY AND INTELLECTUAL PROPERTY RIGHTS

In terms of neo-classical trade theory, whether a particular country will want stronger or weaker intellectual property protection will depend on whether its comparative advantage lies more in innovation or in the imitation and adaptation of others' innovations. This is simply an extension of the argument concerning the allocation of resources domestically between imitation and innovation. More precisely still, a rational country would have different levels of protection for different industries, representing different trade-offs between innovation and imitation in each industry, depending upon where its comparative advantage lies.

The United States traditionally has been a country with a significant comparative advantage in innovation, reflected in the fact that a higher percentage of its exports contain domestically-generated technologies than those of any other country, far exceeding even Japan.[10] Under these circumstances, a high level of protection for intellectual property rights within the United States would seem to be well-justified. From the perspective of the *national* interest of countries that have a comparative advantage that lies more in imitative than innovative activity, however, a lower level of protection would likely be optimal. This argument, it should be stressed, does not apply only to developing countries. Much of Japan's dramatic economic growth in the 1960s and 1970s can be accounted for by its success at imitation and adaptation of innovations developed elsewhere, aided by a strategic use of intellectual property protection to stimulate imitation in some sectors and industries and innovation in others.[11] The strength of Canadian multinational enterprises has been linked to their capacity to find and adapt technology from elsewhere.[12] In sum, it is far from clear that increased intellectual property protection would benefit even developed countries with a strong advantage in imitation.

The conclusion that stronger intellectual property protection may benefit some countries but not others suggests a fundamental difference between the theoretical case for trade liberalization, as we developed it in Chapter I, and the case for mandating high levels of intellectual property protection throughout the world. In the former instance, the neo-classical theory of trade suggests that further liberalization will, with certain defined exceptions, be *always* beneficial *both* to the domestic economic welfare of the liberalizing state, and to *global* economic welfare (defined in terms of global allocative efficiency and/or the aggregate of the domestic welfare of all member states).

With respect to intellectual property protection, however, the case cannot be stated in these terms – for a requirement of strengthened protection, in the case of at least some sectors, could increase economic welfare in some countries, while reducing it in others. Mandated stronger protection for intellectual property rights is not necessarily, therefore, Pareto-superior – and must be justified instead as a fair bargain or trade-off between the competing or conflicting economic interests of different states.

In addition, it is highly questionable whether increased protection is even Kaldor–Hicks efficient – i.e. whether the gains to economic welfare to countries who benefit from stricter protection outweigh the losses to those countries who lose by it. In a seminal and provocative article, Allan Deardorff has argued that global aggregate welfare may well be maximized if certain countries *are exempted completely* from requirements for intellectual property protection. The reason is that, with respect to these poorer countries, the marginal increased rents to the patent holder are unlikely to be substantial enough to constitute significant incentives to further innovation. However, the losses to developing countries from being forced out of imitation or buying imitations from elsewhere would probably be more substantial.[13] Additionally, if the effect of increased protection is to shift productive resources from an activity in which a country has a comparative advantage (imitation) to that in which it has less comparative advantage (innovation), then global allocative efficiency would be reduced by increased protection.

Deardorff's basic insight has been developed independently by Maskus as a formal model of the global welfare effects of IP protection. His empirical studies using this model, which are based upon United States International Trade Commission data with respect to impacts of lower IP protection in other countries, yielded the result that 'static global welfare would suffer from the extension of IP protection by information-importing countries' under most assumptions about elasticities of supply and demand.[14] Only under highly speculative dynamic assumptions (i.e. that increased protection would create enough incentives for technology transfer to, and new R and D within, developing countries to *create* a comparative advantage in innovation), could global welfare be predicted to rise. Work by Grossman and Helpman also suggests that global welfare may be reduced by higher levels of intellectual property protection in developing countries, since the effect may be to slow the process whereby products invented in the North come to be imitated and manufactured in the South at lower cost (i.e. more efficiently).[15]

THE PRE-URUGUAY ROUND INTERNATIONAL LEGAL FRAMEWORK

Having considered the case for strengthening of intellectual property rights from a number of perspectives, we now canvass the existing international rules on this subject. The international legal and institutional framework for co-operation in the protection of intellectual property rights that has emerged over the last hundred years, as we shall see, falls short of elaborating a set of universal, harmonized standards for intellectual property rights. Yet from the fairness, domestic and global welfare perspectives discussed above, the case for such harmonization is, as we have seen, far from compelling. At the same time, the existing framework reflects long-standing recognition by a wide range of states that intellectual property rights are a legitimate subject of international legal discipline.

The GATT

By virtue of Article XX of the General Agreement, intellectual property has been largely excluded from the ambit of GATT. Article XX states a number of exceptions to the basic obligations of the GATT with respect to trade, and these include 'measures . . . necessary to secure compliance with laws or regulations which are not inconsistent with the provisions of this Agreement, including those related to . . . the protection of patents, trademarks and copyrights, and the prevention of deceptive practices' (Article XX(d)). However this exception, like all the others in Article XX, is subject to the following qualification: such measures must not be 'applied in a manner which would constitute a means of arbitrary or unjustifiable discrimination between countries where the same conditions prevail, or a disguised restriction on international trade, ...'.

Students of the GATT have long been divided as to whether the meaning of this qualification is that the principle of National Treatment as defined in Article III nevertheless applies to Article XX exemptions, or whether the intent is to define an alternative, weaker, national treatment standard applicable only to the matters listed in Article XX (the standard would be weaker because of the qualifying words, 'between countries where the same conditions prevail', which imply a 'similarly situated' test).[16] To some extent, this issue has been resolved in favour of the latter view in a GATT panel decision on the GATT-consistency of s. 337 of the US Tariff Act.[17] In that case, the Panel held that, in some circumstances, an Article XX (d) exception might be claimed for measures that, but for the exception, would be in violation of the Article III National Treatment obligation. This, of course, would be impossible if Article XX (d) itself were to imply the same National Treatment standard as Article III.

The Paris Convention

The Paris Convention[18] is the principal instrument of international law with respect to protection of patents and trademarks, described within the Convention by the general label 'industrial property'. The Convention was established in 1883 and has 98 signatories whose countries represented (in 1985) 88% of world trade in goods.[19]

The cornerstone of the Convention is the National Treatment principle, expressed in Article II (1), which provides that 'Nationals of any country of the Union shall, as regards the protection of industrial property, enjoy in all the other countries of the Union the advantages that their respective laws now grant, or may hereafter grant to nationals . . .'. In addition to the same substantive protections, Article II (1) also provides that nationals of other members of the Union shall have 'the same legal remedy against any infringement of their rights, provided that the conditions and formalities imposed upon nationals are complied with'. One important aspect of these obligations is that they apply to legal instruments defined as 'industrial property' in Article 1 (2) – including patents, trade marks, industrial designs and trade names. Thus, for instance, it is unclear whether the National Treatment obligation would apply to new *sui generis* forms of intellectual property rights. In the light of efforts by the United States to negotiate bi-laterally with some countries special agreements for protection of the intellectual property of its nationals, it is also important to note that, on its face, the National Treatment obligation of the Paris Convention does not include a Most Favoured Nation requirement.[20]

In addition to the National Treatment obligation, the Convention sets some minimum standards with respect to both patent and trademark protection. A priority registration system is created whereby if a patent is filed in one member country nothing which occurs within a twelve-month period that runs from the first filing will affect the right to a patent in other member countries (e.g. exploitation or use of the invention within that twelve-month period in a country where a patent has not yet been filed). The provision for trademarks is identical, except that the period is six months. (Articles 4A–4B).

With respect to trademarks and trade names, there is a further set of much more rigorous obligations. Other countries are *required* to accept a trademark for registration and to protect it fully, once the mark has been properly registered according to the laws of the country of origin, subject to certain exceptions e.g. where third-party rights are violated or where the marks are 'contrary to morality or public order' (Article 6). In addition, member states are obliged to seize, upon importation, all goods 'unlawfully bearing' a trademark or trade name entitled to legal protection in the importing country (Article 9).

National Treatment clearly prohibits one kind of national strategy for intellectual property that, as suggested above, may in fact be domestic welfare-maximizing for certain kinds of countries – e.g. extending generous intellectual property protection to domestic innovators (to provide an incentive for domestic innovation) while providing minimal protection to foreigners (so as to maximize consumer welfare and provide incentives for imitation and adaptation of foreign innovations). However, indirect pursuit of such a strategy is possible within a literal reading of the Convention.

For instance, as Lesser suggests, 'a member state may offer no patent protection for certain product groups, provided that the absence of protection applies equally to nationals and non-nationals'.[21] This permits very significant *de facto* discrimination against foreigners to occur through selection of product groups. Countries can (and do) exempt from protection products in whose innovation they themselves have no comparative advantage (e.g. pharmaceuticals in the case of many developing countries). *A fortiori*, a country would have little or no interest in protecting intellectual property rights in products of which it is solely an imitator and intends to remain so – here the national interest is above all consumer welfare, i.e. sourcing the product as cheaply as possible.

At what point differential protection for particular products, industries, or technologies becomes a *de facto* violation of National Treatment is of course very difficult to determine. Such differential treatment need not have a discriminatory intent – even assuming a country did not trade at all, it might well provide varying levels of protection depending upon the trade-offs between the benefits of encouraging innovation and those of encouraging imitation that existed in a particular sector. Here, the National Treatment principle itself, if it is to be effectively implemented, may point to some international minimum standards, i.e. to some kind of determination in international rules as to which balances between innovation and imitation are legitimate domestic policies and which constitute unfair trade practices.

An additional difficulty that arises with respect to National Treatment concerns rules or procedures that pertain to the granting and enforcement of intellectual property rights. Some legal systems place a premium on the exercise of administrative discretion in the determination of what intellectual property rights, if any, to grant to a particular innovation. Borrus notes with respect to Japan, for example,

The exercise of discretion is enabled mightily by a lack of transparency in decision-making. The JPO (Japanese Patent Office) rarely documents its reasoning . . . when using the system to disadvantage foreign filings JPO examiners have been known to fail to communicate in a penetrable way. The resulting speculative interpretation of the examiner's intent leads to misinterpretation and instant justification for hindering or rejecting foreign filings.[22]

With respect to these kinds of complaints it is very difficult to know whether, in fact, discrimination against foreigners is actually occurring, or whether they simply find it burdensome working within a different legal and political environment. Despite the fact that foreigners may incur special costs in seeking intellectual property protection in another member state (such as translation, hiring of local lawyers or patent experts able to guide them through the system), the Paris Convention clearly states that to avail themselves of National Treatment foreigners must 'observe the formalities and conditions imposed upon nationals' (Article 2(1)).

Related complaints concern the enforcement of intellectual property rights. Particularly with respect to developing countries, Primo Braga notes: 'Problems often mentioned include: the slowness of the enforcement process; discrimination against foreigners; biased court decisions; inadequate civil and or criminal remedies; and corruption'.[23] Not surprisingly, much of the evidence of these difficulties is anecdotal. It is probably true that foreigners are in some sense discriminated against in legal systems characterized by corruption and bias, inasmuch as locals are likely to have access to 'back channels' that foreigners lack. Yet these are symptoms of broader social and political issues that may be difficult to address in the rather specific context of international rules on intellectual property rights. As well, in some cases, foreigners may incorrectly assume that outcomes that appear unfamiliar, anomalous or unfavourable are the product of discrimination or improper dealing. Even if they are based on ignorance of law and institutions in other countries, such assumptions contribute powerfully to the notion that the National Treatment principle, as elaborated in the Paris Convention, is inadequate to discipline discriminatory practices.

The Berne Convention

The Berne Convention,[24] established in 1885, sets certain minimum standards with respect to authors' rights, and also contains a National Treatment and a Most Favoured Nation obligation.[25] In general, the required minimum length of protection is the author's life plus fifty years (Article 7(1)). During this period, authors (or their estate) 'enjoy the exclusive right of authorizing' any reproduction or communication of the works they have created (Articles 9–14). These minimum standards are subject to certain limitations or exceptions, such as for quotation and utilization of works in other publications or works (e.g. TV broadcasts). These are exceptions not only to the minimum standard itself, but also to National Treatment and MFN obligations; hence the Convention contemplates 'special agreements' on these matters between particular member states of the Berne Union (Article 9 (2)).

The Convention also contains special provisions applicable to developing countries, permitting them to substitute compulsory licensing for the minimum standards of the Convention. The (perhaps somewhat 'imperialistic') reasoning is that the dissemination of literary and artistic works from abroad is crucial to the development needs of these countries, and would often not be possible if the works had to be purchased as imports from the developed world, or reproduced on the basis of the kinds of royalties or fees that might be demanded in return for authorization by an author holding a copyright. The compulsory licensing provisions only apply where, after five years (or in certain cases three or seven years), the work has not been disseminated by the owner of the right of reproduction 'at a price reasonably related to that normally charged in the country for comparable works' (Appendix, Article III (2)). Thus the authors/owners retain the option of asserting their rights, if they are prepared to authorize reproduction at a price that is comparable to normal prices in the developing country in question. Moreover, for compulsory licensing to apply, the intent must be to disseminate the work 'for use in connection with systematic instructional activities' (Article III (2)(a)).

The language of the Convention clearly suggests an intent to cover virtually every kind of creative work.[26] However, with respect to certain kinds of scientific work or industrial and architectural design, the question arises of whether patent rather than copyright protection is more appropriate. This question has become of considerable importance as countries grapple with the appropriate means of protecting creative rights in computer software.[27]

The Berne Convention currently has more than 75 signatories. It is noteworthy that the United States only joined the Convention in 1988, having previously chosen to rely upon unilateral measures and bilateral reciprocity-based treaties to protect copyright.[28]

The World Intellectual Property Organization (WIPO)

WIPO was established in 1967[29] to administer multilateral agreements on intellectual property rights, including the Paris and Berne Conventions, and since 1974 has had the status of a specialized agency of the United Nations. WIPO does not embody a formal court-like mechanism for the resolution of disputes under these agreements, but regularly produces studies and reports on issues that arise in their implementation. As well, WIPO has been active in assisting developing countries in establishing their own systems of intellectual property protection, and has provided financial aid and technical advice for this purpose. At the outset of the Uruguay Round, it was the position of most developing countries that WIPO, not GATT, was the appropriate forum for evolving stronger international rules on the protection of intellectual property rights. This position was undoubtedly influenced by the perception that developing countries have traditionally had more influence in the UN system than in the GATT. It could also be defended on the basis that WIPO's accumulated expertise and experience in the intellectual property field make it a more appropriate forum for negotiations on TRIPs.[30]

Other international agreements

Besides the Paris and Berne Conventions, a number of other international agreements exist with respect to other forms of intellectual property rights, including the Rome Convention[31] (Performers' Rights), and the International Convention for the Protection of New Varieties of Plants (UPOV) (Plant Breeder's Rights),[32] and most recently (1989) the Washington Treaty (Integrated Circuits).[33] Although this last agreement addresses an increasingly important form of intellectual property, its significance is greatly circumscribed by the fact that the United States, Japan and the EU (i.e. the world's leading producers of these devices) have refused to sign the Treaty, apparently preferring to negotiate reciprocal accords among themselves rather than accept the general National Treatment approach embodied in the Treaty.[34]

In addition, agreements exist to facilitate co-operation between countries in the administration of patent laws (e.g. The Patent Co-operation Treaty). These agreements vary considerably in importance and in the number of countries that are signatories; reasons of space do not permit a detailed discussion in this chapter.[35]

AGGRESSIVE UNILATERALISM: US TRADE REMEDY LAW AND THE EU NEW TRADE POLICY INSTRUMENT

United States trade remedy law has long provided for unilateral retaliatory trade action against foreign products, based upon violations of intellectual property norms by the producing countries. Section 337 of the US Tariff Act of 1930 as amended applies to products imported into the United States, where the products in question have been produced in such a way as to violate intellectual property rights that American individuals or firms hold under domestic US law. There is no requirement of injury to the American producer, and a positive finding results in the complete exclusion of the product from the United States, unless the American holder of intellectual property rights and the foreign producer enter into a voluntary settlement (usually a licensing agreement). Conceptually, Section 337 can be considered either as a means of extra-territorial enforcement of domestic American intellectual property or – more consistent with the overall framework of American trade law – as a counter to an unfair advantage acquired by a foreign producer in competition with domestic American producers for the American market. However, the remedy provided by s. 337 – a ban on the imports in question rather than a duty aimed at neutralizing the supposed unfair advantage – comports more with the former interpretation than the latter. Nevertheless, the scope of s. 337 is limited to products imported in the United States, and does nothing to discourage use of American innovations in violation of domestic US law with respect to home market sales or exports to third countries.

Where a developing country is determined to have 'weak' intellectual property protection, tariff concessions extended to it under the Generalized System of Preferences can be withdrawn, which has apparently occurred in the case of Korea, Mexico, Brazil and Thailand. There is no requirement to prove injury to a particular American industry. Nor need it be shown that the intellectual property laws of the country concerned discriminate against American or other foreign holders of intellectual property rights or otherwise do not meet international norms as set out, for example, in the Berne or Paris Conventions. It should be noted that these provisions apply *only* to countries within the GSP; clearly, a discriminatory withdrawal of other tariff concessions provided to a GATT member would violate the MFN obligation of GATT and/or specific tariff bindings under the Agreement.

Broader in sweep still is the so-called Special 301 provision of the Omnibus Trade and Competitiveness Act of 1988, which provides that trade sanctions may be taken against countries named as engaging in 'unfair' trade practices.[36] Such sanctions would likely be contrary to the GATT MFN principle. To date, however, Special 301 has been used as a weapon to extract from named countries specific policy changes desired by US interests, or (it is also sometimes claimed) more sympathy for American positions in the Round negotiations – including on intellectual property.[37] The countries named to date under Special 301 have included Japan, Brazil and India. The aggressively extra-territorial dimension of Special 301 is highlighted by the fact that it does not refer to any set of norms or principles in order to define adequate intellectual property protection among US trade partners – the implicit assumption being that any level of protection inferior to that provided by US law is an unfair trade practice.

S. 337 of the Tariff Act has come under challenge in the GATT. A GATT panel held in 1989 that the Section violated the GATT National Treatment obligation, since it entailed a method of enforcement – through the office of the United States International Trade Commission (USITC) – that provided weaker procedural protection to foreigners than that accorded to American firms and individuals accused of violating American intellectual property laws.[38] While (as mentioned earlier in this chapter) Article XX (d) provides, under certain circumstances, exception from GATT strictures for measures 'necessary' to the enforcement of domestic intellectual property laws, the Panel found that measures provided in s. 337 were not 'necessary' in this sense, since other countries had found it possible to enforce adequately their intellectual property laws against foreign nationals by subjecting the foreigner to the same legal processes as applied to domestic actors.

A further provision of US law, contained in the Process Patents Amendment Act of 1988, may also be vulnerable to challenge under GATT rules: the provision makes importers or retailers who bring products made in violation of US intellectual property laws into domestic US commerce liable to civil suit by the US holders of the violated intellectual property rights.[39] Since importers and retailers will often not have the knowledge to determine whether a particular product has been made in contravention of intellectual property rights, the result is arguably a 'chilling' effect where buyers simply avoid products from countries with reputations for poor intellectual property protection, in order to obviate the risk of civil liability. In the result, arguably, the National Treatment principle of the GATT is violated – since it is only to imported products that the risk of such liability is attached.

An instructive contrast with the American law is to be found in the approach of the EU. In 1984, the Union created what is called 'the new trade policy instrument'. The instrument allows the Union to engage in trade retaliation[40] against 'illicit commercial practices' of non-Union countries that affect EU economic interests. 'Illicit commercial practices' are defined as violations of 'international law or generally accepted rules'.[41] According to the European Commission *Green Paper* on copyright, 'in the field of intellectual property, and copyright in particular, the instrument could conceivably play a significant role in the future, particularly as regards countries which practise a policy of more or less active connivance in the pirating of goods and services developed elsewhere'.[42] In the intellectual property area, the instrument would be used primarily against countries in violation of existing treaty obligations, under both the Paris and the Berne Conventions. However, Brueckmann notes that pursuant to Article 113 of the Treaty of Rome, which gives the Union jurisdiction over a common commercial policy, bilateral action has also been taken (in particular against Korea) along the lines of the US Tariff Act – i.e. suspension of GSP concessions.[43] The background of this action was however rather unusual. Korea had agreed, as part of a negotiated settlement of action under s. 301 of the Tariff Act, to provide intellectual property protection for US innovations but did not extend such protection to other countries. The EU claimed at least as favourable treatment, hence – although from one perspective unilateralist

– the Union's action countered a discriminatory arrangement arguably in violation of provisions of the Berne Convention requiring equally favourable treatment for all foreigners.

INTELLECTUAL PROPERTY PROVISIONS IN TRADE AGREEMENTS

The Canada–USA FTA

Apart from a general commitment of the Parties to 'co-operate in the Uruguay Round of multilateral trade negotiations and in other international forums to improve the protection of intellectual property' (Article 2004), the only provisions on intellectual property rights in the FTA concern retransmission of broadcasts. This reflects a long-standing complaint of American broadcasters that Canadian cable companies rebroadcast their programming without any compensation, and moreover often remove the original advertising and replace it with advertising purchased from the Canadian cable company. Article 2006 of the FTA provides for a scheme whereby the holder of the programme copyright must be compensated for any retransmission. Furthermore, in the case of retransmission of pay TV programmes – i.e. those 'signals not intended in the original transmission for free, over-the-air receptions by the general public' – such retransmission must be with the permission of the original copyright holder. Finally, retransmission in altered form or non-simultaneous retransmission shall only be allowed where permitted by the original copyright holder. This last provision reflects the complaint that, where Canadian viewers are capable of receiving the American signal directly (the case for a large part of the population), Canadian cable companies are in direct competition with the American broadcasters for audience and hence for advertising. There is thus a danger that Canadian cable companies will rebroadcast at a time or in a format more congenial to Canadian viewers, and therefore take away audiences from the original transmission.

The Uruguay Round and Intellectual Property Rights

Background

Not surprisingly, it was the United States that spearheaded the movement to have intellectual property rights included as an integral part of the Uruguay Round negotiations. The overall American goal was clear from the outset: to obtain a set of international rules that ensure that American innovators' intellectual property rights are as extensive and as effectively enforced abroad as in the United States itself. In general, Japan and the European Union were generally supportive of the American approach, although at first they required some prodding from high-technology industries and other domestic interests that stood to benefit from high international standards for IP protection.

Developing countries, however, generally opposed the negotiation of intellectual property rights within the GATT, arguing that WIPO was the more appropriate forum for these discussions. Underlying this concern about the institutional appropriateness of the GATT was, however, a more fundamental substantive concern that the American objectives, particularly with respect to patent protection and the curbing of compulsory licensing, were contrary to the economic interest of developing countries. As suggested by our analysis earlier in this chapter, this concern has a sound basis in economic theory.

The globalization of the American standard of patent protection was far from the only objective of the United States in the Uruguay Round negotiations. The United States, like some other developed countries, was also concerned that *existing* international obligations, under the Berne and Paris Conventions, were not enforced adequately by many developing countries, and that WIPO did not provide a credible institutional framework for settlement of disputes under these agreements.[44] These were particularly acute concerns with respect to the Berne Convention, whose provisions the United States saw routinely ignored in a number of developing countries where piracy of American creative works was rampant. In the case of the Paris Convention, the United States had a related concern – the supposed difficulty that American patent-holders encountered in attempting to enforce their rights in foreign legal systems. Unlike the case with copyright, where the focus was on the lack of effective criminal or regulatory sanctions for piracy, in the patent context the emphasis was on the supposed lack of expeditious due process in the civil courts of other countries. This last concern, it should be noted, extended beyond the case of developing countries and encompassed complaints about several aspects of the patent registration and enforcement process in Japan. Developing countries, in particular, bristled at the notion that their domestic legal systems, and the level of scarce administrative and enforcement resources allocated to those systems, should have to pass muster according to American standards. There was considerable merit in the developing country position. Operating a truly effective patent system is a costly enterprise, given the high demand for patent registration, and the substantial component of technical expertise required to make such a system work properly.[45] As well, the problems of administration of justice complained of by the United States were often arguably of a general nature (slow courts, lack of written reasons[46] for decisions, and corruption) and not attributable either to an intention to disregard the intellectual property rights of foreigners or a reckless disregard for these rights. Perhaps, however, a 'win-win' or Pareto-optimal solution to this difference of perspectives would be to link expectations for improvements in patent registration, administration and enforcement in developing countries to the provision of technical assistance and funding to those countries so as to enable these improvements to be made.

A further dimension of the American position in the Uruguay Round negotiations was to ensure that developed country approaches to the provision of intellectual property protection to new, technology-based forms of innovation would set the international standard. In the biotechnology field, for instance, US industrial and scientific interests were concerned that, as these technologies took on increasing economic importance, they be fully protected by intellectual property rights.[47] For many countries, however, the patenting of life itself raises not only economic, but also important ethical issues.[48] The Biodiversity Convention, concluded at the Rio Environmental Summit, acknowledges the legitimacy of a country extending intellectual property protection at least to the genetic material of plants, but also states that individual countries have the sovereign right to determine on what terms and conditions private interests should have access to biological resources.[49]

The Uruguay Round Final Act

Despite these basic differences of perspective between the United States and some other developed countries, and most of the developing world, the Uruguay Round was successful in producing a comprehensive agreement on TRIPs. The TRIPs Agreement in the Uruguay Round Final Act represents a complex balance between conflicting national perspectives and interests with respect to the protection of intellectual property rights.

The Agreement consists of seven Parts: (1) a statement of general principles and of the interaction of the Agreement with the Paris and Berne Conventions; (2) substantive norms with respect to the protection of the various forms of intellectual property; (3) obligations with respect to the domestic enforcement of intellectual property rights; (4) obligations with respect to the facilitation in domestic legal systems of the acquisition and maintenance of intellectual property rights; (5) dispute settlement; (6) transitional arrangements; and (7) a WTO-based institutional framework for TRIPs.

General principles of intellectual property protection

Part I of the TRIPs Agreement sets out both National Treatment (Article 3) and MFN obligations (Article 4) with respect to Intellectual Property Rights. The National Treatment obligation is subject to the exceptions that already exist in the Paris, Berne and Rome Conventions and the Washington Treaty. The MFN obligation does not apply with respect to rights and privileges conferred on a reciprocal basis to certain GATT Members through bilateral or multilateral agreements in force prior to the Uruguay Round TRIPs Agreement. An example would be the bilateral accords for microchip (semi-conductor) protection in force between the USA, the EU and Japan. However, to be exempted from the MFN requirement these agreements must not operate so as to 'constitute an arbitrary or unjustifiable discrimination against other Members' (Article 4 (d)). Similarly, where the WIPO strikes new multilateral agreements with respect to 'the acquisition or maintenance of intellectual property rights', the National Treatment and MFN obligations in the GATT Agreement will not apply (Article 5). This allows for the evolution of 'mutual recognition' type regimes for the filing and registration of claims for intellectual property protection.

Part I also contains a statement of principles, which acknowledges that a balance of legitimate (potentially competing interests) must be struck in determining the appropriate level and kind of intellectual property protection guaranteed by the GATT. According to Article 7,

> the protection and enforcement of intellectual property rights should contribute to the promotion of technological innovation and to the transfer and dissemination of technology, to the mutual advantage of producers and users of technological knowledge and in a manner conducive to social and economic welfare, and to a balance of rights and obligations.

Moreover, Article 8 states that 'appropriate measures, provided that they are consistent with the provisions of this Agreement, may be needed to prevent the abuse of intellectual property rights by right holders through the resort to practices which unreasonably restrain trade or adversely affect the international transfer of technology'.

A broad, purposive interpretation of Article 7 and Article 8 taken together would permit GATT Members considerable scope to impose competition policy or investment policy-related measures on foreign patent-holders, provided the level of intellectual property protection itself conforms to that provided in the TRIPs Agreement. It remains an open question whether, for instance, a foreign patent holder who refused to comply with policy measures aimed at facilitating technology transfer or preventinganti-competitive abuse of patent protection could be legally denied the level of protection specified in the TRIPs Agreement. In other words, are domestic policy measures that *condition* the granting of rights under the TRIPs Agreement on compliance with the kinds of measures contemplated in Articles 7 and 8 'consistent' with the TRIPs Agreement? A further interpretative issue is whether Articles 7 and 8 could be used as a 'shield' by developing or other countries against unilateral US action in response to policies in conformity with the Uruguay Round TRIPs Agreement but nonetheless considered 'unfair' by US trade authorities. Thus, arguably, in the presence of such unilateral action a GATT member could make a complaint in the GATT TRIPs dispute settlement forum that the United States was in violation of Article 7 and/or Article 8 in prejudicing its ability to implement the kinds of intellectual property-related domestic policies contemplated in these provisions. This would reinforce a more general complaint that unilateral action violated other GATT provisions, such as Articles II, III, or XI of the General Agreement itself (which would likely be the case if the action in question consisted in trade sanctions or discriminatory treatment of the Member's products under domestic US law; see the discussion of the s. 337 GATT Panel above).

Standards concerning the availability, scope and use of Intellectual Property Rights

Copyright The basic obligations and rights contained in the Berne Convention[50] are incorporated into the TRIPs Agreement (Article 9). With respect to computer software, the Agreement clearly specifies that 'computer programs, whether in source or object code' shall be protected as 'literary works' under the Berne Convention (Article 10). This entrenches an approach to software protection long-favoured by the United States, and increasingly deployed in the developed world (despite initial interest by the EC and Japan in the development of a *sui generis* form of protection).[51] However, the extent of required copyright protection for software may be significantly affected by the general proviso in Article 9 (2) that 'copyright protection shall extend to expressions and not to ideas, procedures, methods of operation or mathematical concepts as such'. Arguably, given this proviso, copyright will protect the originality of a computer programme as a whole, but will not extend to preventing use of ideas, functions, etc. in the development of new programmes. Clearly, interpreting such a distinction on a case-by-case basis may involve quite difficult technical judgments.

With respect to databases, if these merit the status of 'intellectual creations' by virtue of the 'selection or arrangement' of their contents, they are to be afforded copyright protection. However, this does not create any entitlement to the protection of the underlying data or material out of which the database was generated. Moreover, where a pre-existing copyright exists with respect to the data or material itself, any protection of the database as an intellectual protection 'shall be without prejudice' to the subsisting copyright on the material (Article 10 (2)).

With respect to rental of films and computer programmes, authors are to be provided with 'the right to authorize or to prohibit the commercial rental to the public of originals or copies of their copyright works' (Article 11). In the case of films, however, a Member may exempt itself from this requirement, provided that rentals have not resulted in widespread violation of authors' rights through copying.

Article 12 establishes that the minimum term for copyright protection is 50 years from the initial date of authorized publication, or alternately, 50 years from the making of the work.

Trademarks The Agreement states that

> the owner of a registered trademark shall have the exclusive right to prevent all third parties not having his consent from using in the course of trade identical or similar signs for goods or services which are identical or similar to those in respect of which the trademark is registered where such use would result in a likelihood of confusion (Article 16.1).

There is a requirement that all 'signs' with sufficient distinctiveness be accepted for registration by the Parties. This is, however, subject to the right of Parties to deny registration on other grounds (i.e. than lack of distinctiveness), provided that those grounds are consistent with the provisions of the Paris Convention. It should be recalled that the Paris Convention explicitly permits refusal to register, where the trademark is 'contrary to morality or public order (Article VI),[52] where it is 'of such a nature as to deceive the public' or where the mark's use would constitute unfair competition.[53] A further exemption – specific to the GATT agreement – applies to 'fair use of descriptive terms'. Thus, where a trademark becomes a common expression applied generically to a particular process of product (e.g. nylon), Parties may allow for its use by others without permission of the owner of the mark, 'provided that such exceptions take account of the legitimate interests of the owner of the trademark and of third parties'. Parties are permitted to provide for revocation of a registered trademark after an uninterrupted period of three years of non-use, unless non-use can be shown to be due to certain kinds of obstacles presented to the holder, e.g. import restrictions on the goods in question or other 'government requirements' that may impede their use in the country concerned (Article 19).

An extensive set of provisions with respect to sound performances and recordings places positive obligations on states to provide to performers the right to prevent unauthorized recording of their performances, unauthorized reproduction of authorized recordings, unauthorized broadcasting of any performance or recording, whether itself authorized or not. However, only 'broadcasts by wireless means' are included, which may indicate an intention to exclude cable re-broadcasts.[54] With respect to sound performances and recordings, the exemptions and limitations[55] contained in the Rome Convention are incorporated into the Agreement.

Patents The provisions with respect to patents reflect the largest modification of the existing international regime, in that a substantive standard of protection is required of all Members. That standard is 20 years from the filing date. Protection applies to both product and process patents. With respect to process patents, however, the obligation to protect from unauthorized use extends only to products 'obtained directly' from the patented process. This means that Members are not required to protect the rights of patent holders where a process they own is merely the basis for production, i.e. where significant alteration or innovation in a patented process is at issue as opposed to direct use (Article 28.1).

Furthermore, patent rights must be 'enjoyable without discrimination as to the place of invention, the field of technology and whether products are imported or locally produced'(Article 27(1)). At the same time, the Agreement acknowledges the concern of developing countries, and some developed countries, to protect the scope for legitimate domestic trade-offs of social and economic interests in the determination of patent rights. For instance, Members are permitted to exclude from patentability 'plants and animals other than microorganisms, and essentially biological processes for the production of plants or animals other than non-biological and microbiological processes' subject to providing some protection for plant varieties, either through patenting or a *sui generis* system (Article 27 (3) (b)). However, this provision is to be reviewed every four years after the establishment of the WTO, and during this time the USA can be expected to exercise pressure (perhaps through unilateral trade instruments) for the inclusion of a requirement of patentability of life within the Agreement on TRIPs.

Most importantly, from the perspective of those countries with concerns about negative social and economic consequences from high levels of patent protection, the Agreement permits *compulsory licensing* during the period of required patent protection, provided certain conditions are fulfilled (Article 31). The proposed user must first have attempted to obtain explicit authorization for use from the patent holder on 'reasonable commercial terms' and have been refused. Once this condition is met, compulsory licensing is permitted. However, such licensing must be non-exclusive (i.e. anyone who applies must be granted a licence on similar terms and conditions); production under licensing must be intended primarily for the internal market of the licensing Party; and 'adequate remuneration' must be paid to the patent holder, taking into account the 'economic value' of the patent (Article 31 (j)).

In interpreting the expressions 'reasonable commercial terms' and 'adequate remuneration', account should be taken not only of the claim of the patent holder to just compensation, but also of the various social and economic interests stated in Part I of the Agreement on TRIPs, including the 'transfer and dissemination of technology to the mutual advantage of producers and users of technological knowledge and in a manner conducive to social and economic welfare' (Article 7). In addition, the need 'to prevent abuse of intellectual property rights' (Article 8) should also be considered in interpreting the conditions of compulsory licensing in Article 31.

Other forms of intellectual property In addition to these three main types of intellectual property rights, the Agreement also contains provisions on

Industrial Designs, Geographical Indications for Wines and Spirits, integrated circuits and protection of trade secrets. In the case of Industrial Designs, Members are required to provide a minimum of 10 years protection to 'independently created industrial designs that are new or original', subject to the right of Members, if they so choose, to protect other designs (Articles 25; 26 (3)). Furthermore, 'members may provide that such protection shall not extend to designs dictated essentially by technical or functional considerations' (Article 25). This last provision reflects a significant lobbying effort by US insurance companies, consumer groups and replacement parts manufacturers, all of whom sought language on industrial designs that would not allow automobile manufacturers to protect the design of car parts, thereby threatening the 'generic' replacement parts and potentially raising the costs of replacement parts.[56]

The provisions on Geographical Indications, and particularly those that apply to Wines and Spirits, address long-standing European concerns about the use of labels to describe imitation products with no direct connection to the geographical area denoted by the label. The main operative provision, Article 23 (1), requires each Member to 'provide the legal means for interested parties to prevent use of a geographical indication identifying wines for wines not originating in the place indicated by the geographical indication in question, ... even where the true origin of the goods is indicated or the geographical indication is used in translation or accompanied by expressions such as 'kind', 'type', 'style', 'imitations' or the like. This obligation applies identically to spirits. However, exceptions are provided with respect to geographical appellations in use for at least ten years preceding the conclusion of the Uruguay Round negotiations (Article 24 (4)). In the case of geographical indications for products other than wines and spirits, protection need only be provided by Members against use of geographical indication 'which misleads the public as to the geographical origin of the good' (Article 22 (2) (a)).

With respect to Lay-out Designs (Topographies) of Integrated Circuits, the required protection is more extensive than that provided in the Washington Treaty, to which, it will be recalled, most developed countries had refused to adhere. Hence, the term of protection is 10 years as opposed to 8 in the Washington Treaty, and compulsory licensing or governmental use can only occur under the same conditions as those set out for compulsory licensing in the TRIPs Agreement provisions on patents (Articles 38; 37(2)). It is significant that among the main reasons that the United States and Japan refused to sign the Washington Treaty was their opposition to the Treaty's provisions on compulsory licensing.[57] However, the applicable provisions on compulsory licensing in the TRIPs Agreement are, in the end, very similar to those contained in the Washington Treaty. This reflects at least some compromise with the concerns of developing countries.[58]

Enforcement, Dispute Settlement, and Institutional Design

Enforcement There is a wide range of obligations to provide other Members with access to appropriate mechanisms to enforce intellectual property rights. These provisions constitute a largely unprecedented degree of control by an international regime over domestic civil and administrative procedures. It is required that enforcement procedures 'not be unnecessarily complicated or costly, or entail unreasonable time-limits or unwarranted delays' (Article 41.2); decisions are 'preferably' to be in writing and to contain reasons; and a right of judicial review is to be provided in the case of administrative decisions, at least with respect to matters of law. These quite far-reaching obligations are balanced by the qualification that they create no 'obligation with respect to the distribution of resources as between enforcement of intellectual property rights and the enforcement of laws in general' (Article 41.5).

With respect to remedies, the TRIPs Agreement requires that 'judicial authorities' be empowered to issue injunctions (Article 44 (1)); award damages and legal costs to successful right holders (Article 45); and to dispose of goods tainted by infringements of intellectual property rights 'outside the ordinary channels of commerce' (Article 46). In addition, the judicial authorities are to be authorized to grant interim or provisional injunctions, including in *ex parte* proceedings, 'where any delay is likely to cause irreparable harm to the right holder' (Article 50 (3)).

These requirements would seem, at first glance, to be a massive intrusion into domestic legal systems, and especially the balance that those systems strike between the rights of defendants and those of plaintiffs. In some systems, for instance, there may be constitutional limitations on the capacity of courts to grant relief without hearing the other Party – even for certain kinds of interim relief. However, it is to be noted that where any of the remedies is 'inconsistent with domestic law', the domestic law is to prevail, subject to a requirement that 'declaratory judgments and adequate compensation' be available (Article 44 (2)). It should also be noted that while the Agreement provides that judicial authorities be authorized to grant certain classes of remedies, the use of these remedies is not *mandated* by the GATT Agreement. Judicial authorities are, therefore, free to use their discretion to grant or deny a particular remedy, and to weigh plaintiffs' and defendants' rights in the exercise of that discretion.

A final important obligation with respect to enforcement relates to counterfeit or pirated goods. Rights holders are to have access to a procedure whereby customs authorities suspend 'the release into free circulation' of such goods, for example by seizure or by turning them back (Article 51). This is subject to the right of the importer that such suspension be promptly removed except where a judicial or administrative determination is made that, in fact, the goods are counterfeit. Moreover, members who have eliminated border customs inspection as between themselves are not obligated to provide such a procedure (e.g. the case of the European Union).

Monitoring and dispute settlement A two-fold approach to monitoring and dispute settlement is set out in the TRIPs Agreement. First of all, a new institution is to be created, the Council on Trade Related Aspects of Intellectual Property Rights (TRIPs Council), charged with the monitoring of domestic compliance with the Agreement. Members are obliged to notify the Council of their domestic laws and regulations with respect to intellectual property protection (Article 63 (2)). The Council may also provide a forum for consultations on intellectual property issues, and is 'to provide any assistance requested by them in the context of dispute settlement procedures' (Article 68). This might include, for example, a kind of mediation or the provision of advisory opinions concerning Members' interpretations of the Agreement. Nevertheless, no special dispute settlement process is established in connection with the Council – instead the general GATT procedures are to apply (Article 64).

With respect to settlement of disputes under the TRIPs Agreement the provisions in Articles XXII and XXIII of the GATT are to apply, subject to suspension of the operation of dispute settlement under Articles XIII:1 (b) and XXIII:1 (c) of the GATT for the period of five years. This refers to complaints of non-violation nullification or impairment, which are to be referred to the TRIPs Council and the Ministerial Conference during the five-year period.

Developing countries

As discussed in an earlier section of this chapter, one of the main aims of the United States in placing TRIPs on the Uruguay Round agenda was to address what it considered ineffective protection of intellectual property rights in developing countries. It is not surprising, therefore, that developing countries do not enjoy many special exemptions from these obligations. They are entitled to a one-year delay with respect to implementing most of the obligations of the Agreement and a further four-year delay upon application to the Council. The further four-year delay does not apply, however, to the general requirements of National Treatment and MFN treatment in Part I. A further five-year delay applies, where a particular area of technology is currently unprotectable under the domestic law of a developing country. This reflects the fact that extension of protection may result in loss of entire industries in some developing countries (e.g. pharmaceuticals), with attendant adjustment costs.[59] Finally, *least*-developed countries are exempted entirely from the Agreement.

The North American Free Trade Agreement (NAFTA)

The provisions on intellectual property rights in the NAFTA are, in most important respects, largely identical to those in the draft Uruguay Round Agreement, discussed in detail in the previous section. Unlike the Uruguay Round Agreement, the NAFTA does not contain substantive provisions on performers' rights. Performers' rights would seem to be covered by the National Treatment obligation with respect to intellectual property rights. An exception to National Treatment is, however, that '... a Party may limit rights of performers of another Party in respect of secondary uses of sound recordings to those rights its nationals are accorded in the territory of such other Party' (Article 1703.1).

The NAFTA also contains a provision on the decoding of encrypted satellite signals that is not present in the Uruguay Round TRIPs Agreement. Under this provision each Party would be required to make it a criminal offence to manufacture or sell any device used for the purpose of decoding encrypted satellite signals, and a civil offence to decode or improperly receive these signals. These provisions would appear to be primarily aimed at protecting the rights of Pay-TV broadcasters. Finally, unlike the Uruguay Round TRIPs Agreement, the NAFTA does not contain any special provisions on dispute resolution with respect to intellectual property rights, suggesting that the general dispute resolution mechanism in the NAFTA will apply to disputes under the intellectual property provisions of the NAFTA.

The NAFTA represents a major victory for mostly US based multinational pharmaceutical companies. Canada had a significantly shorter period of patent protection for pharmaceuticals (10 years) after which compulsory licensing was provided under Canadian law.[60] The consequence was a wealth of low-cost generic drugs, with major cost savings to consumers, as well as to government programmes that provide free or subsidized medications to the elderly and the poor. In order to comply with NAFTA and a possible Uruguay Round Agreement on TRIPs the previous Government in Canada changed the law to provide 20 years of patent protection to patent pharmaceutical producers. However, under the letter of both NAFTA and the Uruguay Round Agreement on TRIPs, compulsory licensing is still permissible, provided reasonable compensation is offered to the patent-holder and some other conditions are met. This suggests that there was some kind of informal understanding between Canadian and American authorities that Canada's approach to pharmaceuticals must be dismantled if the spirit of NAFTA is to be respected. Perhaps also influential with the Canadian authorities was a massive, high-profile lobbying effort on the part of patent drug manufacturers stressing the amount of new R and D activity that would engage in Canada with the adoption of these changes. In any case, despite these major changes in the Canadian domestic regulatory regime to the advantage of American proprietary drug interests, Canada failed completely to win any insulation from US aggressive unilateralism, including actions under s. 337 of the Tariff Act.[61] The current Government in Canada is apparently considering the reintroduction of measures to provide for the compulsory licensing of pharmaceuticals, on terms consistent with NAFTA and the Uruguay Round TRIPs Agreement.

CONCLUSION

While trade theory provides little basis for mandating uniform standards of intellectual property protection across all countries, intellectual property rights is an issue that is here to stay on the international trade agenda. The Uruguay Round TRIPs Agreement, while at the level of general principle promoting a uniform approach, in fact allows for a balance to be struck between countries' legitimate interests in limiting intellectual property rights for consumer welfare and economic and social development reasons, and the interests of their trading partners in sustaining adequate incentives for innovation. Maintaining this balance through monitoring and dispute settlement will be a major challenge for the World Trade Organization.

11

TRADE AND INVESTMENT

INTRODUCTION

The last decade has seen a dramatic increase in foreign direct investment, defined as ownership and (normally) control of a business or part of a business in another country. Foreign direct investment is usually distinguished from portfolio investment, where a foreign actor purchases securities in a domestic company solely to earn a financial return, without any intent to own, control or manage the domestic firm.[1] Foreign direct investment generally takes one of 'three forms: an infusion of new equity capital such as a new plant or joint venture; reinvested corporate earnings; and net borrowing through the parent company or affiliates'.[2] It is estimated that between 1983 and 1989, foreign investment increased at an annual rate of more than 30%, three times the comparable percentage of increase in merchandise trade over the same period.[3] Perhaps the most remarkable trend has been towards developed countries themselves becoming significant hosts for foreign investment. Thus, with respect to the United States alone, inward foreign investment totalled $56 billion between 1971 and 1981, whereas between 1981 and 1989 the figure was close to $307 billion.[4] While many developing countries have come in recent years to take a more positive view of foreign investment and have moved to dismantle many explicit barriers and disincentives (such as limits on the percentage of an enterprise that can be foreign-owned and on repatriation of profits), ownership by foreigners has become of increasing concern in certain industrialized countries, particularly the United States, that traditionally complained about illiberal attitudes elsewhere towards foreign investment.[5] As well, increased interest in foreign investment in Japan by nationals of other major industrialized countries, especially the United States, has focused attention on a range of domestic policies and practices in Japan that (including competition policies that provide few constraints on domestic cross-ownership of enterprises) supposedly create obstacles to foreigners wishing to acquire business assets there.[6]

The issue of foreign investment is closely linked to the role of multinational corporations in the global political economy. Some see such corporations as powers unto themselves, capable of buying or intimidating governments, or at least with the capacity to spread production and other functions around the globe so as to exploit regulatory differences between states – taking advantage of one country's cheap labour, another's tax haven, and yet another's favourable rules on intellectual property, and perhaps creating a race to the bottom.[7] Others view the multinational corporation as a logical and desirable extension of the inherent logic of comparative advantage – combining the benefits of organizing production within a single firm with the gains from free trade.[8]

Much of the contemporary controversy over foreign investment has surrounded measures that aim not to exclude investment but to direct it in a manner that benefits the economic development of the host country. In fact, measures aimed at channelling foreign investment to benefit the economies of host countries actually challenge two of the major assumptions that have traditionally underpinned hostility to foreign investment and the multinational firm: first and most obviously that foreign ownership is necessarily harmful to development; and second, that developing countries are powerless to determine the way in which foreign firms exploit their productive resources.[9] Also of significance are incentives to attract foreign investment, such as tax holidays or subsidies.[10] Indeed, incentives are often used in conjunction with export performance or local sourcing requirements, and may have the effect of offsetting some or all of the disincentive effects of such restrictions or conditions on foreign investment.[11]

As will be described in the next section, in a world completely free of restrictions on the movement of goods, services, and capital, any measure that distorts the global allocation of productive resources would be world-welfare reducing from the perspective of neo-classical economic theory.[12] However, within the GATT, the focus of attention has been on investment measures that have direct effects on trade in goods, such as measures that require or encourage foreign owned firms to discriminate between domestically produced and imported inputs in production in the host country (local content requirements), as well as measures that require that a certain percentage of the foreign firm's output be exported.[13] The investment provisions of the Uruguay Round Final Act would subject some investment measures with direct effects on trade to more explicit scrutiny against existing GATT norms. These are relatively modest disciplines on investment disincentives and incentives in comparison with those found in the Canada–US FTA and the NAFTA, both of which include a National Treatment obligation with respect to foreign investors, as well as a general right to invest (right of establishment) subject to certain limitations and exceptions. Finally, the equivalent of a right to establishment is also entrenched in the OECD Code of Liberalisation of Capital Movements (1991) and a National Treatment obligation with respect to foreign investors is contained in the OECD 1976 Declaration on International Investment and Multinational Enterprises.

FOREIGN INVESTMENT AND TRADE THEORY

The theory of comparative advantage outlined in Chapter 1 shows the gains to both domestic *and* global economic welfare from specialization of each country in the production of those goods in which it has a comparative advantage. However, most goods – including Ricardo's classic examples of wine and cloth – can be understood as composites of other goods and services. It is unlikely that a country that has an overall comparative advantage in the production of a particular good also has a comparative advantage with respect to all the inputs required to produce the good in question. To return to Ricardo's example, England's comparative advantage in cloth may arise from the skill of its weavers, and in fact Portugal may have a comparative advantage in the production of wool or cotton; similarly, Portugal's comparative advantage in wine may arise from the quality of its grapes, and would not exclude English comparative advantage in the production of wine-making technology. In such a case, it may still make sense for Portugal to make wine and trade it for English-produced cloth – but it will also make sense for Portugal to export its cotton or wool to England and for England to export wine-making technology to Portugal.

Such an outcome need not, of course, lead to any foreign investment. Wholly Portuguese companies may make wine with technology produced by wholly British companies. However, just as it may make sense to produce domestically a good through internalizing different activities required for production within a given firm, rather than through contracts between discrete individuals or firms, so too it could make sense for Portuguese vineyard-owners to purchase British producers of wine technology – or for the British producers to buy Portuguese vineyards. According to the modern theory of the firm, production will be organized within a given firm where the agency costs of internal contracting between the firm's owners, agents, and employees are lower than the costs of external contracting between independent producers or providers of each component or element required to make the final product.[14] The rapid growth in intra-firm trade over the last few decades testifies to the economic logic of trans-boundary internal contracting.[15]

Increasingly, the production of complex goods may entail both cross-boundary internal and external contracting. For instance, many of the activities required to produce an automobile may be subsumed within a given auto-maker, which in turn will locate production facilities globally in order to maximize comparative advantage, but other important components will be obtained through external contracting with both domestic and foreign firms.[16]

Nicolaides suggests that there may be some archetypal cases where cross-boundary internal contracting will occur, rather than or in addition to external cross-boundary contracting (trade):

> The multinational company (MNC) exists precisely because it is not easy to trade intangible assets in open markets. It is difficult, for example, to write contracts for experience and newly-developed technology which is in the process of being adapted for commercial applications. The reasons that encourage corporate integration are that production costs are reduced, information flows faster and actions of individual units are more effectively coordinated.[17]

Some of the reasons for engaging in foreign investment as opposed to or in addition to external contracting may be endemic to, or particularly salient to, the international context. For instance, the greater difficulty in enforcing external contracts across borders may lead to increased agency costs of contracting.[18] As well, intellectual property and related laws in other countries may provide inadequate protection of firm-specific innovations or knowledge, leading to a reluctance to transfer these to domestic firms through arms-length external contracts (e.g. licensing arrangements or direct sale of technology or processes).[19]

Dunning has analysed a vast literature on the theory of the multinational firm and the globalization of production, and has developed what he calls an 'eclectic' theory, which emphasizes a wide range of factors, including transportation and wage costs, greater suitability of internal contracting to the development and dissemination of firm-specific technology and processes, and hedging of the political risk of locating in a single country in a volatile world environment.[20] In many respects, this pluralistic approach is quite consistent with contemporary views on the nature of comparative advantage in trade, which take into account a wide variety of factors that may determine the comparative advantage or disadvantage of a particular country, including dynamic factors that change with changes in governments' domestic policies, technologies, consumer preferences and other rapidly evolving domestic and international realities.

ECONOMIC RATIONALES FOR GOVERNMENT INCENTIVES AND DISINCENTIVES TO FOREIGN INVESTMENT

Do the combined insights of the neo-classical theory of free trade and the modern theory of the firm suggest that economic welfare could actually be increased by government incentives or disincentives with respect to foreign investment? In a world where (apart from background rules of contracting) government action does not influence the allocation of productive resources, markets themselves should generate optimal levels of foreign investment.

In such a world, government intervention would, almost by definition, distort the allocation of productive resources, inasmuch as disincentives reduced the level of investment below the market optimum, or incentives increased the level above that optimum.

A number of important qualifications to this view have been proposed by trade scholars and merit serious examination.

For example, according to one prominent theory of industrial competitiveness – that of Michael Porter and his associates – much economic development is attributable to the creation of 'clusters' of industries in a given country or region. Clusters are groups of industries that are interdependent or complementary.[21] According to Porter, many industries develop in response to the needs of other industries within a particular region or country. Most firms form part of an industry cluster in their home-base – they have developed over time a complex web of relationships with suppliers and customers, including suppliers who have incurred sunk costs in developing or adapting products and services to the needs of the particular firm. When a firm establishes operations abroad, it or its foreign subsidiary, is likely to continue to source many inputs from the firm's 'home base', thus failing to help build a cluster in the host country. On this view, local content or sourcing requirements may have desirable domestic welfare effects, if they can effectively counter the 'home-base' bias identified by Porter, and lead to the development of functioning clusters in the host country.

In addition, host-country local content requirements, or local hiring and manufacturing requirements, may offset the cumulative effects of subsidies or other governmental measures in the 'home base' of the investing firm. The pressures to source in the 'home base' may come less from the market than from government. These pressures may be informal, as well as formal. Formal pressures would include subsidies linked to job creation in the domestic economy and local content requirements in 'home base' government procurement contracts. More informally, the perception that a firm is a good local 'corporate citizen' may be viewed as important in effectively lobbying 'home base' governments on a wide variety of regulatory matters of concern to the firm, whether environmental standards, labour policies, or taxation issues. Often, the treatment a firm receives from its 'home base' government may be linked to the perception and reality that the firm really 'belongs' to that country.

Finally, it may make sense to impose special burdens or requirements on foreign firms where these firms are able to elude more general or neutral forms of redistributive regulation. For instance, multinational corporations, especially those characterized by high levels of intra-firm trade, may find it easy to manipulate transfer pricing[22] so as to avoid taxation on actual earnings in a foreign country. Many developing countries, in particular, do not have the sophistication in the design and enforcement of corporate tax regimes required to counter effectively this kind of conduct. As well, manipulation of transfer pricing may allow a multinational corporation to 'cheat' on tariff restrictions by significantly underpricing imports of inputs. Seen as a response to this kind of behaviour, local content or sourcing requirements may be viewed as a substitute for ineffective tariff protection.

These various considerations do not, admittedly, add up to a decisive argument in favour of local content and related requirements, which may have negative consumer welfare and allocative efficiency effects within the host country. This does, however, weigh against any kind of general assumption that trade would be undistorted, or less distorted, in the absence of such requirements.

Investment and trade protection

There is a complex interaction between foreign investment and trade protection. First of all, foreign investment may occur as a means of jumping tariff walls or avoiding harassment of imports under the trade remedy laws of the host country (so-called 'co-operative protectionism'). If much of its comparative advantage is portable, consisting of know-how, processes and technology, a company may avoid border restrictions simply by manufacturing within the domestic market. Enhanced access to host country markets generally ranks high among the factors that industries cite as reasons for foreign investment.[23]

Protection-avoiding foreign investment has both opportunities and risks attached to it. One such opportunity is the strategic use of tariffs or, more likely, administered protection, to encourage foreign investment. Where a tariff (or other trade protection) induces a foreign producer to relocate production facilities to the protecting state, new jobs in that state are created, and in fact there is a possibility of shifting some of the foreign firm's comparative advantage itself to the host-country. For instance, when Honda or Toyota sets up production in Canada or the United States, it brings with it the processes, know-how, and so forth, that arguably constitute much of its comparative advantage.

It is important, however, to note that in one important sense consumers in the protecting state will still be worse off than under conditions of liberal trade, because the foreign firm that does relocate will be able to price up to tariff or other trade barriers (e.g. VERs), thereby still charging consumers prices higher than would be the case without trade restrictions.

A simple example will illustrate this point. A and B are both foreign car manufacturers who have been exporting cars into C. A and B both produce a mid-sized car that would sell, in the absence of protection, for £6000 and C's consumers are indifferent as between the car produced by A and that produced by B. Assume that a tariff of 30% is imposed on imports and an elasticity of demand for this kind of car that results in two-thirds of the tariff being passed on to the consumer in higher prices. If A and B both export their cars to C, C's consumers will pay £7200 per car. If A starts to produce the car in C, and comes inside the tariff wall it *may* be able to underprice B while still earning more than the non-tariff price per car. As long as consumers are indifferent between A's car and B's, A will be able to outcompete B at any price below £7200. The end result will be somewhat less of a consumer welfare loss than if both A and B's cars are imported and subject to tariffs, but consumers will still be somewhat worse off than they would be if there were no protection.

At the same time, because *some* of the rents of protection have been shifted from domestic firms to the foreign firm producing domestically, this may compensate in whole or in part for additional costs incurred in shifting some production to the importing country – including compliance with export performance, technology transfer or other requirements imposed by the host-country government. A disturbing implication, especially for consumer welfare, is that the higher the amount of protection, the more attractive the shift of production is, because the rents from protection that accrue to the domestically-producing foreign firm are correspondingly higher.[24]

The dynamic effects of foreign investment in protected markets

In reality, when foreign firms have come within a tariff wall, they have often found it to be something less than a safe haven. Domestic firms are apt to petition government for relief from the increased competition, frequently arguing that the foreign plants are little more than screwdriver operations aimed at circumventing tariffs or other border restrictions, and that they create less employment per car sold, for instance, than domestic firms, which source domestically to a greater degree and thus create jobs in a wider range of sectors that produce inputs. As a consequence, once inside the tariff wall, foreign firms may well find themselves confronted with new obstacles to exploitation of the domestic market. A prominent example of this has been the effort of the European Union to limit the market share of cars manufactured by Japanese producers within Europe, claiming that these are not really European automobiles.[25] Quite commonly, local content requirements are imposed upon the foreign firm.

At one level, such *ex post* adjustments of the 'bargain' between the protecting country and the foreign firm could be viewed as opportunism – once it has sunk substantial costs in the creation of factories or other production facilities, the foreign firm may have little choice but to stay. On the other hand, it is arguable that domestic welfare is improved by such measures – some of the rents from protection against competing foreign firms that accrue to the investing firm are clawed back in the form of boosted sales for domestic providers of inputs.

In theory, there are losses in allocative efficiency since otherwise uncompetitive manufacturers of inputs are being kept in business. However, in the case of inputs for some complex products, arguably the effect is to transfer comparative advantage to input providers as well. Where a firm is unhappy with the quality of domestic inputs but must use them to circumvent the tariff wall through foreign investment, it may still be in the firm's interest to produce locally but also to work with domestic input providers on quality control, making their products genuinely competitive with imported inputs.

Alternatively (or additionally), the host country may find a way of increasing the rents from protection to compensate the investing firm for the costs of complying with new local content or local sourcing requirements. Quotas and VERs, because of their discriminatory potential, are a simple way of increasing such rents. In return for local content requirements, for instance, a foreign car manufacturer producing domestically could be offered larger quotas on models that it continues to produce offshore. Consumers will benefit from the increased quota (a larger supply will result in somewhat lower costs), but will of course not benefit as much as when quotas on all imported cars in a similar category or competing for the same market are increased or at the limit eliminated. Conversely, the foreign firm with the increased quota benefits from greater sales, but at the same time loses fewer of the scarcity rents than it would if the supply of its foreign competitors' comparable products were also increased.

The dynamics of the relationship between trade protection and foreign investment described above have broader implications that should dampen the enthusiasm of advocates of strategic protection. First of all, a clear consequence is to reinforce the dominant position of the strongest firms in a given industry, thereby reducing global competition. In order to play the game, a firm must be large enough and have sufficient resources to expand production globally, investing large amounts of capital in new production facilities. Second, in the host country, a whole new set of jobs is created that, in effect, depends upon continued protection. If comparative advantage has genuinely been transferred to the host country, of course it may still make sense to continue production even after the removal, or reduction, of protection. But the closing of American branch plants in Canada, and their relocation to the United States, that has occurred in the wake of the Canada–US Free Trade Agreement, is a powerful reminder that jumping the tariff wall may remain a decisive consideration in a plant's continuing operation in the host country. Arguably, as well, this suggests that if protection is to be used to induce foreign investment, then it is important to attach conditions that actually assure a real transfer of comparative advantage (such as requirements for reinvestment and renewal of the plant, training of workers, and technology transfer).[26]

NON-ECONOMIC RATIONALES AND EFFECTS OF INVESTMENT POLICIES: SOVEREIGNTY AND THE FOREIGN FIRM

The discussion so far has focused exclusively on economic and trade policy dimensions of foreign investment measures. Traditionally, however many of the reasons for which states have imposed restrictions on foreign investment have been connected with political arguments about sovereignty. These arguments concern a wide range of specific harms that are believed to flow from ownership of a country's productive resources by foreigners. They include national security and defence considerations; the supposed difficulty of subjecting foreign or multinational firms to domestic jurisdiction; concerns that foreign investors or foreign firms will become a vehicle for inappropriate influence by their home governments on politics and society within the host country; and concerns about the protection of cultural autonomy or distinctiveness.[27] We will briefly consider several of these pre-occupations with the potential drawbacks of foreign investment.

Defence and National Security

A traditional dictum of security policy, at least since Machiavelli,[28] is that no state should rely on others to furnish the weapons needed for its own defence. Nevertheless, the global arms trade flourishes, and only a handful of relatively industrially advanced nations are capable of manufacturing sophisticated weapons systems in any quantity.

The concern about having one's own arms often extends to autarchy with respect to the inputs necessary to produce those arms, whether steel or computer chips. For instance, as Japan and some European countries have become world leaders in the development and manufacture of products and technologies considered to have critical defence applications, the United States has become increasingly concerned that it may be placing its vital security interests in the hands of foreigners. This concern has been deployed as a rationale for trade protection to sustain uncompetitive national industries considered vital to the security of the United States. It has also resulted in measures intended to control foreign ownership of productive assets in the United States. The United States has justified prohibitions or restrictions on foreign investment in many sectors on national security or related grounds (i.e. vital national interest). These sectors include: air transportation, coastal shipping, commercial fisheries, communications, energy resources, and real property.[29]

In 1988, an amendment was added to the Omnibus Trade and Competitiveness Act (the Exon–Florio Amendment, named after the US legislators who proposed the bill) providing the President of the United States with the authority to block mergers or acquisitions involving foreign firms on grounds that US national security interests would be impaired by the resulting foreign ownership.[30] The Committee on Foreign Investment in the United States (made up of representatives of various agencies in the US Government, including the State Department, the Defense Department, the Commerce Department and the office of the United States Trade Representative) is given the authority to conduct investigations of mergers, acquisitions and takeovers that may threaten US national security. On the basis of these investigations, the Committee makes recommendations to the President as to whether national security interests justify blocking a transaction or altering its terms. Until recently, at least, there have been few investigations, and even fewer instances where the result has been Presidential intervention in a transaction.[31] Nevertheless, the need to avert the threat of such intervention may, in a wider range of cases, lead to various 'voluntary' undertakings by the potential investor, making the terms of the investment more favourable to American interests.[32] However, as Graham and Ebert note,[33] there is strong pressure in Congress to make investigation of proposed investments mandatory, at least with respect to some sectors.

Does foreign ownership of strategically-sensitive enterprises really jeopardize security? First of all, if in fact foreign producers do have a monopoly over products or processes that are vital to a country's security interests, the country in question is certainly better off having those products or processes developed within its borders. Dependency on imports is much riskier since a foreign government can, in effect, control the export of the needed materials. In a national emergency, by contrast, domestic production facilities (even though foreign-owned) could be commandeered by the government, or made directly subject to its orders.

What, however, of the case where there currently exist two suppliers of a given technology or product, one domestic and one foreign, and where the foreign supplier chooses to buy out the domestic supplier? Here, the acquisition may be motivated by the desire to obtain a monopoly, and in fact could result in *all* production, or much of it, being moved offshore. In such an instance, it may be quite justifiable to weigh carefully national security implications within any overall review of the impact of such an acquisition.

In addition, foreign firms in the defence sector are likely to have particularly close relationships with their home country government – often reflected in the presence of former politicians and senior bureaucrats on their board of directors, government subsidies, procurement and R and D contracts, or partial government ownership. Where this is the case, some concern that foreign powers will be able to exercise influence or control over the firm's strategy, and have privileged access to its products or research, may be warranted. Again, however, this concern would be justified mainly where a merger or acquisition results in a monopoly in a particular product or process.

In the instances just discussed, national security concerns may in fact be warranted with respect to foreign investment. However, in the United States in particular, the national security argument has been extended far beyond the case of very sensitive defence industries to sectors that produce a wide variety of inputs into military products, or whose production facilities might, in war time, need to be converted to military uses (steel, cars, civil aircraft). In most of these instances, a variety of producers, domestic and foreign, currently exist. Taken to its logical conclusion the argument would end up justifying something close to complete autarchy – since there are few sectors of civilian production that do not contribute something of importance to the materiel needed, in the broadest sense, to sustain an all-out war effort.

Furthermore, blocking a foreign takeover or merger will itself far from guarantee either the continuation of a domestic source of supply for the products in question or protection against foreign influence. For example, where the merger or acquisition is required to rescue the domestic firm, or to ensure its continuing viability, the alternative may well be bankruptcy – with the result that the foreign firm becomes the monopolist anyway but produces abroad, and hence the source of supply becomes even more insecure. Hence, in a number of instances, one suspects that national security arguments against *foreign* acquisitions are disguised attempts to attract a government supported bail-out at home, or more protection. Once the firm is considered a domestic producer vital to national security, the logical consequence is not just that foreigners should be prevented from acquiring it, but that its survival as a domestic firm should be guaranteed by the state.

Inadequate regulatory or political control over the foreign investor

The multinational firm is often described as a kind of power unto itself, able to slip through the normal control of national jurisdictions through the global diffusion of its activities. There are few inherent legal constraints on the application of domestic jurisdiction to the activities that multinational corporations engage in within a particular country; however, there may be significant practical constraints, where the bulk of the firm's assets and much of the information about its activities and decisionmaking are located abroad. Of course, while it is true that offshore activities and decisions of a foreign multinational may affect the regulatory interests of its host country, so may the foreign activities and interests of the host country's *own* firms. Thus, the problem concerns both inward and outward foreign investment.

In some sectors the regulatory issues may be particularly acute. In the case of financial services, for instance, regulators may be concerned with the overall stability of an institution, the quality of its investments etc. Ultimately, domestic deposit holders are dependent upon the stability of the overall institution, including the soundness of its lending practices and other activities abroad. As is illustrated by the Bhopal disaster, regulatory issues may also arise where multinationals are engaged in high-risk activities in a host country, but where they retain elsewhere the assets necessary to satisfy potential liabilities for these risks, or information about the risks.

These kinds of regulatory issues may justify some kinds of differential treatment of foreign investors – the requirement to carry liability insurance, to maintain a minimum level of assets within the host country, or to post a bond or a deposit to guarantee regulatory compliance.

Extraterritoriality

Another set of concerns about foreign investment may be considered the 'mirror image' of the concern about lack of domestic control of the foreign-owned company or subsidiary – that is, the possibility that foreign ownership will result in the extraterritorial application of the laws and regulatory authority of the firm's home country to its activities in the host country.[34] Extraterritoriality has been particularly a concern raised by the explicit extraterritorial sweep of a number of US regulatory regimes. One important example is export controls – the United States has sought to prevent foreign subsidiaries of American firms from exporting products to countries that are embargoed by United States law, such as Cuba.[35] From the perspective of the law of the GATT, this can rightly be seen as an interference with the trade relations of another Contracting Party. However, export controls based upon national security considerations are explicitly exempted from normal GATT rules by Article XXI,[36] although, it is highly questionable whether even Article XXI provides scope for a Contracting Party to interfere with exports and imports flowing between another Contracting Party and a third state.

It bears emphasis that extraterritoriality is not a problem that is limited to the context of foreign investment. Ownership by nationals is but one basis among many that the United States, for instance, uses as a grounds for exercising jurisdiction beyond its borders. For instance, US anti-trust law is applied extraterritorially not just to American-owned companies, but to any activity that materially affects United States commerce, including for example participation of foreign-owned firms in cartels with US firms that restrict competition in the US market.[37]

The most promising avenue for resolving problems of extraterritoriality is not restrictions on investment, but the evolution of multilateral processes to deal with particular cases of conflicting exercise of jurisdiction, and eventually to evolve a set of detailed principles or guidelines broadly consistent with international law norms on state sovereignty. In this regard, it should be noted that a 1991 Decision of the OECD Council allows any member

State of the OECD to refer to the Committee on International Investment 'any problem arising from the fact that multinational enterprises are made subject to conflicting requirements'.[38] With respect to extraterritorial application of anti-trust laws, the OECD has developed a separate process intended to address directly issues of restrictive business practices and the multinational enterprise.[39] A number of constructive approaches to inter-jurisdictional conflict have been suggested, including harmonization of domestic competition laws and designation of a lead jurisdiction for review of international mergers.[40]

In addition to the matters discussed above, developing countries have traditionally had an additional (although often overlapping) range of concerns about foreign investment, which have been used to justify severe restrictions on the activity of foreign firms. These have included concerns that foreign investors often will deploy technologies that are inappropriate for exploitation of and development of local skills for best advantage, that may aggravate or create balance of payments problems by heavy reliance on imported inputs in the production process; and that foreign investors will perpetuate existing patterns of Southern dependency in exploiting cheap, unskilled labour in developing countries without transferring the skills and technologies required for economic development.[41]

On balance, the recent empirical evidence seems to suggest that foreign direct investment has had a positive impact on growth and development in LDCs.[42] In addition, it appears that on a comparative basis developing countries with relatively restrictive policies towards foreign investment have experienced much lower rates of economic growth over the last 30 years than those (e.g. Malaysia) with relatively open policies.[43] However, it may be that what distinguishes, at least in part, the countries with more open policies, is that instead of placing general (and severe) restrictions on, for example, repatriation of earnings or the right of establishment as such, these countries negotiated specific agreements on issues like technology transfer and local employment with individual firms. Thus, instead of adopting either a generally negative stance towards FDI, or a completely open attitude, they proceeded in a more selective fashion to impose requirements or conditions on some foreign investors, where it was believed this would serve the interests of domestic economic development. This case-by-case approach, however, is more transaction-cost intensive and heightens the risk of corruption in the administration of foreign investment policies.

This being said, in the aftermath of the LDC debt crisis (which has resulted in substantial reduction of new debt financing available to many developing countries) and given what many observers consider to be a world shortage of capital (considering, for instance, the substantial needs of the Newly Liberalizing Countries in Central and Eastern Europe), many developing countries have adopted a much more liberal attitude towards foreign investment, and see the issue for governmental policy much more as that of attracting foreign investment rather than restricting or limiting it. This led the *Economist* magazine to remark, in a recent survey of multinationals, that

> too many governments see foreign investment as a shortcut to prosperity, bringing in skills, capital and technology to push their countries rapidly from the 1950s to the 1990s. . . . Those governments that rely too heavily on multinationals are likely to look for a foreign scapegoat when inflation heads for triple figures, unemployment fails to drop and demonstrators surround the ministry.[44]

ALTERNATIVE APPROACHES TO INTERNATIONAL DISCIPLINE OF FOREIGN INVESTMENT MEASURES

The pre-Uruguay GATT

Investment measures and the General Agreement: An overview

Our discussion in 'Foreign Investment and Trade Theory' and 'Economic Rationales' (this chapter) has emphasized the complexity of the relationship between foreign investment measures, liberal trade and protectionism. The dramatic expansion in foreign investment in recent years has depended heavily on liberal rules governing trade in goods, yet this expansion has also provided new opportunities and incentives to exploit the rents from protection, thus leading to new kinds of protectionist pressures. At the same time, the interdependencies created by the globalization of production have brought into being new interests that would lose enormously from a fundamental unravelling of the liberal trading order.

As a matter of law, only a few of the investment measures that can be deployed strategically along with trade protection arguably fall within the ambit of the GATT. The most clear-cut example is that of local content or sourcing requirements, which explicitly discriminate against imports and in favour of like domestic products – hence violating the National Treatment obligation of the GATT (Article III:4). Export requirements are a somewhat more complicated case. As will be discussed below, a GATT panel decision with respect to Canadian foreign investment measures held that export requirements did not *per se* violate any provision of the General Agreement. However, as we will argue, export requirements linked with a subsidy to the foreign investor may in some circumstances constitute an export subsidy, the only kind of subsidy explicitly banned in the General Agreement (Article XVI). Export requirements may also lead to dumping, inasmuch as they lead to the product being exported below cost or at a price lower than that which applies in the domestic market.

In addition to local content and export requirements, the law of the

GATT may be violated by trade balancing requirements, which typically limit the value of what a foreign investor is allowed to import into the host country to the value of exports. Here, two sets of provisions in the GATT are relevant. First of all, the limitation on imports might be considered, like a domestic sourcing requirement, as a form of discrimination against imported goods. However, it might be argued that this need not be the result, since with a trade balancing requirement (unlike a direct local sourcing requirement) a foreign firm wishing to import more inputs will be permitted to do so if this is balanced by an increase in exports of finished products (and, as we have just mentioned, *export* requirements are not as such illegal under GATT). A stronger case can be made that trade balancing restrictions violate the Article XI ban on quantitative restrictions, as they place (albeit variable) quantitative limits on imports. Because Article XI bans restrictions on exports as well as imports, a *prima facie* violation of Article XI might also occur where the host country places limits on the percentage or amount of production that it can export, i.e. requiring that a portion of the production be set aside for the domestic market. Such a requirement might be imposed where, perhaps for technology transfer reasons, a country wishes domestic users to have access to what is being produced by the foreign firm. The requirement might go hand in hand with an additional provision that the percentage of production in question be made available to domestic users for local currency or at a lower than world market price.

Additional investment measures that implicate GATT law are requirements that foreign investors re-invest a percentage of earnings within the host country and, conversely, limitations on the repatriation of profits in convertible currency. In the former communist countries (of which several were long-standing GATT members) such requirements were commonplace, and they still exist today in many developing countries. Arguably, both re-investment requirements and limitations on the repatriation of profits could constitute violations of Article XV of the GATT, which requires Contracting Parties to adhere to IMF rules with respect to balance of payments and exchange arrangements. However, as has been discussed in detail in Chapter 3, these rules allow considerable scope for developing countries to restrict foreign exchange, including exchange of local earnings into foreign currency. In addition, it should be noted that trade-balancing requirements or other investment measures that would otherwise be in violation of Article XI of the GATT may nevertheless be saved by Article XII, which permits some, mainly non-discriminatory, quantitative restrictions where necessary to address a balance of payments crisis. Although the drafters clearly had temporary measures in mind, Article XII has been used to sustain much longer-term restrictions. In addition, Article XVIIIB: 9 explicitly authorizes a broader range of quantitative restrictions – including discriminatory quantitative restrictions – where these are measures undertaken by developing countries to protect or enhance their balance of payments.

The FIRA Panel Decision

The FIRA Panel Decision[45] represents the only case where foreign investment measures were the central focus of a GATT panel, and therefore deserves detailed analysis. At issue were various undertakings obtained from foreign investors pursuant to Canada's Foreign Investment Review Act. The Act established a governmental agency, the Foreign Investment Review Agency, to screen investment proposals by foreign interests. The Agency was to review the proposals and either accept, reject, or modify them. The essential criterion was whether the investment would be of significant benefit to Canada, significant benefit being defined to include increases in employment and exports, technology transfer, and advancement of 'national industrial and economic policies'. Under the Act, foreign investor applicants were able to make undertakings with respect to any aspect of the operation of their business in Canada, with a view to more favourable treatment of their application. Such undertakings were not, however, mandatory or a formal prerequisite for the success of an application. Once an investment application was approved, however, the undertakings were legally enforceable.

The United States argued that three kinds of undertakings violated provisions in the GATT: local content, local manufacturing, and minimum export.

Local Content and Local Manufacturing Requirements

With respect to local content requirements, the main argument was that these undertakings violated Article III:4 of the General Agreement (National Treatment). Given that the undertakings were not formally *required* by the Canadian law, a threshold issue was whether they could be considered, for purposes of Article III, as 'laws, regulations, or requirements'. The United States argued that such undertakings could not be viewed as simply voluntary, since no firm would make them unless it would gain some advantage or avoid some penalty by doing so. The Panel, however, sidestepped the issue of voluntariness, simply stating that 'private contractual obligations entered into by investors should not affect the rights which contracting parties, including contracting parties not involved in the dispute, possess under Art. III:4, . . .'.

A second issue was raised by the Canadian argument that these undertakings merely constituted predictions of what foreign investors intended to do based upon commercial considerations. The panel rejected this argument, pointing out that the specific content of some of the undertakings showed that firms were expected to act in a manner not consistent with commercial considerations or in explicitly discriminatory terms, for instance binding themselves always to purchase a Canadian product when available on similar terms to an import.

The Panel's approach seems justified in light of the economic analysis developed earlier in this chapter. Because the foreign firm producing domestically can capture rents from protection by pricing up to the tariff, there are good reasons to believe that commitments investors make about how much local sourcing they will undertake are not simply in the order of a prediction about how they will behave in future in accordance with market forces, but also reflect a 'price' investors are willing to pay to capture some of the rents of protection.

A further important issue raised by the economic effects of local content or local manufacturing undertakings is that of injury. The Panel chose to sidestep this issue, noting that 'under standing GATT practice, a breach of a rule is presumed to have an adverse impact on other contracting parties' (para. 6.4). It is not obvious that foreign investors who make undertakings are worse off under a scheme for screening foreign investment than under circumstances where investment is unimpeded. As discussed earlier, the rents from protection that a foreign investor gains from coming within the tariff wall (i.e. from being able to price up to the tariff) may be substantial, and may more than compensate for the costs of compliance with domestic content or other performance requirements. Also, such requirements may in some situations be balanced with explicit subsidies or other incentives to investment (such as tax holidays). There is clearly, however, a trade-related injury from local content and local manufacturing requirements that is borne by producers and suppliers of imported goods that would otherwise compete favourably with locally produced imports. These producers *may*, of course, include the foreign investor itself, or other firms from its 'home-base' country – but they may be entirely from other countries.

Thus, it is incorrect to conceive of the debate over the trade effects of these measures as simply a conflict between host country and home country interests. Even though developed countries are more likely to be home than host countries, developing countries or other countries that are not major sources of foreign investment still can lose significantly from investment restrictions in the nature of local content requirements, if the result is discrimination against their exports.

Export performance requirements

The FIRA Panel also considered the legality of export performance requirements under the GATT. The United States had argued that these requirements violated the obligation in Article XVII:1 of the GATT for certain enterprises to act 'in accordance with commercial considerations'. The Panel found that this obligation only applied to state-trading enterprises as defined in the general provisions of Article XVII, and therefore was not relevant to foreign investors. However, the panel also found that 'there is no provision in the General Agreement which forbids requirements to sell goods in foreign markets in preference to domestic markets. In particular, the General Agreement does not impose on contracting parties the obligation to prevent enterprises from dumping' (para 5.18).

Here, the Panel seems to have overlooked the spirit (although perhaps not the strict letter) of the prohibition of export subsidies in Article XVI:2 B of the General Agreement. The Panel's general position – that undertakings are not made gratuitously but in exchange for a benefit that flows from the host country government to investor – would argue in favour of the view that in fact export undertakings are likely to be subsidized, at the very least by the rents from protection that the host government 'grants' to the investor in authorizing the investment. Article XVI:4 B, furthermore, prohibits Contracting Parties from granting 'directly or indirectly any form of subsidy' on exports, at least where the result is a lower price for exports than the domestic price of the product.

The case for deeming export performance requirements as equivalent to an export subsidy is, of course, particularly strong where an investor is attracted to the host country by explicit financial incentives to establish operations there. However, at the same time, the GATT rules on subsidies do not refer explicitly to investment incentives as such. Some such incentives may constitute countervailable subsidies under the GATT Subsidies Code, but only because domestic *products* are being subsidized, not because of the impact of such subsidies on the location decisions of foreign firms.

The evolution of the GATT rules: TRIMs and the Uruguay Round

Clearly, the GATT rules extend only to a relatively narrow range of investment measures with direct and immediately identifiable impacts on trade. In the Uruguay Round of GATT negotiations, the United States in particular sought a much more comprehensive GATT code on investment based upon the principle of free access to foreign markets. On this free access approach, the investment measures disciplined by the GATT would no longer be limited to measures such as local content requirements that discriminate against imported products, but would extend to a potentially vast range of domestic policies of Contracting Parties that create barriers to in-bound foreign investment regardless of whether specific trade impacts are present. The free access approach, it should be noted, gains some normative weight from the allocative efficiency arguments for liberal investment policies explored in 'Foreign Investment and Trade Theory' (earlier in this chapter). These imply that, in principle, almost any incentive or disincentive to investment can be regarded as a distortion of the optimal global allocation of productive resources. However, under real world conditions of imperfect competition and tariff and other trade restrictions, important qualifications exist on these allocative efficiency arguments – qualifications explored earlier in this chapter. In addition, the free access approach provides no obvious means of weighing against allocative efficiency considerations the non-economic rationales for investment restrictions discussed above in 'Non-Economic Rationales' (this chapter).

Unlike the United States, most other Contracting Parties have been sceptical of the free access approach, and have seen the task of the Uruguay Round negotiations on TRIMs as that of developing more detailed and explicit rules with respect to measures that appear inconsistent with well-established GATT principles, such as National Treatment with respect to products. This suggests a cautious extension of the kind of analysis undertaken by the FIRA Panel to a somewhat broader set of measures (such as trade balancing requirements or export performance requirements) that directly affect trade flows. A concrete example will elucidate how the much more comprehensive US view of what is trade-distorting conflicts with the more text-bound view of other Contracting Parties. The US views technology transfer requirements as distorting trade, in that a possible result is to transfer to the host country the capacity to develop products and processes that it would otherwise have to import from the home country.[46] Other countries question whether this impact is very well established: it might be the case, for instance, that absent such a transfer, some developing countries would not be able to afford such products and processes at all, and therefore that imports would be negligible.[47]

The Uruguay Round Final Act reflects a rather subtle compromise between these differing perspectives.[48] On the one hand, there is a binding obligation not to apply any investment measures 'inconsistent with the provisions of Article III or Article XI of the General Agreement' (Article 2(1)). There is thus a clear re-affirmation of the principle that existing GATT provisions do apply to some investment policies. Moreover, an 'illustrative list' of such measures is provided, which includes local content, sourcing, and some trade balancing requirements (which violate National Treatment) and import and export restrictions (which violate the ban on Quantitative Restrictions, in Article XI of the General Agreement).

On the other hand, the illustrative list does not contain any of the measures with more indirect or questionable effects on trade for which United States negotiators had been seeking explicit disciplines, such as technology transfer requirements. In addition, the existing exceptions with respect to Article XI that apply to developing countries are re-affirmed (Article 4). As well, developing countries are provided with substantial transition periods (5 years and 7 years in the case of the least-developed countries) for elimination of TRIMs that offend Article III and/or Article XI (Article 5).

However, it should also be noted that the illustrative list is just that – the text leaves it open for GATT panels to find that measures not on the list violate the GATT, and in addition, the fact that no list of 'green light' or explicitly non-GATTable measures is provided, means that no further protection is extended to Contracting Parties against unilateral retaliatory action by the United States on the basis of its market access approach. Indeed, additional legitimacy could well be conferred on the US approach in that the Final Act provides for a five-year review of the provisions on TRIMs, possibly with a view to including new provisions on 'investment policy and competition policy' (Article 9). The Final Act Agreement on Trade Related Investment Measures also calls for the creation of a Committee on TRIMs whose functions are, *inter alia*, to 'monitor the operation and implementation of' the Agreement.

The FTA and NAFTA

Overview

The provisions on foreign investment in the FTA and the NAFTA are much more reflective of the US free access approach than is the Uruguay Round 'Agreement on TRIMs'. The two pillars of the investment provisions in these regional trade pacts are the right of establishment and National Treatment. The right of establishment provides a direct legal guarantee that investors from any one of the Parties to these agreements will be permitted to own business assets and engage in productive activities within the jurisdiction of the other Parties. The National Treatment obligation requires that the foreign firm, once established, will be treated under the host country's laws in the same way as domestic firms. In addition to being incorporated into the FTA and NAFTA, this free market access approach is also embodied in a variety of bilateral investment treaties initiated by the United States with a number of its trading partners.[49]

The FTA

In the Canada–US FTA, the right of establishment and National Treatment obligation are both subject to the grandfathering of existing investment restrictions, including some of those provided for in the Canadian foreign investment regime (Article 1602). An exception to grandfathering is that minimum thresholds for review of foreign investment by Canadian federal authorities are increased substantially upon the entry into effect of the FTA. In addition, one particular sub-set of performance requirements, i.e. local content and local manufacturing requirements, are banned forthwith. Here, in terms of disciplining the kinds of undertakings given under the *existing* Canadian foreign investment regime, it should be noted that the United States won more in the FTA negotiations than it received from the FIRA Panel decision, in that not only local content and local manufacturing requirements are banned by Article 1603 of the FTA, but so are export performance requirements which the GATT panel found not to be in violation of the General Agreement. Unlike the rules on investment that the USA has negotiated bilaterally with some other countries, the FTA investment provisions do not, however, contain an MFN provision. This means that Canada and the United States remain free to treat investors from third countries *more favourably* than investors from the other FTA partner, as long as investors from the other FTA partner are treated as well as *domestic* investors. In consequence, discriminatory *incentives* are permitted – for instance, each government is free to provide subsidies or tax breaks or regulatory advantages to investors from non-FTA countries on a discriminatory basis.

From an allocative efficiency perspective, an approach based on a right of establishment and National Treatment is in itself insufficient to prevent distortions in the global allocation of productive resources, because such distortions can come equally from incentives as from disincentives. For example, tax concessions or subsidies aimed at attracting investment and production from one jurisdiction to another could arguably induce a misallocation of productive resources. From an allocative efficiency perspective, it is just as undesirable to encourage a higher level of investment than would occur on the basis of market forces alone, as to discourage investment that would occur on the basis of such forces alone.[50] Perhaps the failure to consider incentives in the investment provisions of the FTA can in part be attributed to the fact that the FTA envisages a subsequent negotiation on subsidies, leading to the conclusion of a Subsidies Code within five to seven years of the entry into force of the FTA itself (Articles 1906 and 1907). However, it might be open to a Party to argue that it has met the National Treatment standard even though differential treatment is accorded to an investor from the other FTA partner, since incentives compensate (or more than compensate) for any additional burden placed on the investor from the other FTA partner. National Treatment, as defined in the FTA, entails 'treatment no less favourable' (Article 1602(1)), as distinct from identical treatment or a ban on every single, discrete measure that discriminates against investors from the other FTA partner.[51]

The FTA addresses in one respect investment policies of Parties towards non-Parties. Article 1602 (3) of the FTA prevents either Party from imposing on investors from third Parties' local content or export performance requirements 'as a term or condition of permitting an investment in its territory, or in connection with the regulation of the conduct or operation of a business enterprise located in its territory' where such requirements 'could have a significant impact on trade between the two Parties'. This would occur where, for instance, local content requirements imposed on a Japanese investor by Canada result in that investor discriminating against American exports in favour of Canadian products. However, it is important to note that even with this extension to third country investors, the FTA does nothing to prevent investment measures that have harmful effects on the trade of those third countries themselves. And, strictly speaking, the FTA ban on performance requirements does not extend to requirements that an investor, either from one of the FTA partners, or from a third country, source within the FTA area. Thus, Canada (for example) would be within its rights under the FTA in insisting that an American investor buy a certain percentage of inputs from either Canadian or American sources – this would still be disadvantageous both to the investor and to world trade, where the most efficient producer of the import was neither a Canadian nor an American firm. Of course, such requirements might still be illegal under the GATT, pursuant to the FIRA panel decision, but because (as discussed above) the panel did not analyse the nature of the injury at issue, it is less than clear whether the panel's approach would really imply a GATT-based remedy where *only* the trade of a third country was harmed, and not the interests of the home country of the investor.

In the FTA, investment restrictions based on non-economic concerns such as national security or political sovereignty can be addressed through deviations from the requirement of National Treatment. Thus, the FTA contains a national security exemption that applies so as to exempt from all FTA strictures any action which either Party '*considers* necessary for the protection of its essential security interests . . .' (Article 2003 (b)). These interests are defined to include 'traffic' in weapons but also other items 'directly or indirectly for the purpose of supplying a military establishment' (2003 (b)(1)). The language 'considers necessary' parallels that in Article XXI of the GATT, which has been used by the USA to argue that it is the sovereign right of each state to determine what is required by its security interests, and therefore that whether a measure is actually necessary for security reasons should not be subject to scrutiny by supranational dispute mechanisms.[52] As we have already noted, a vast number of sectors can be deemed essential for direct or *indirect* military supply.

The end result is an asymmetrical constraint on Canada. In both countries, many investment restrictions may be driven by protectionism, but these policies have in Canada been much more transparently conceived as economic development measures while the US justification has mostly focused on national security.

The North American Free Trade Agreement (NAFTA)

Once one moves beyond the context of an agreement between two countries such as the United States and Canada that share many of the same political and social values, a normative consensus among states as to what range of political and social concerns constitute justified limits on freedom to invest is likely to be much harder to strike. The North American Free Trade

Agreement (NAFTA), however, represents an attempt to build on the FTA approach but so as to include a developing country which, although now strongly committed to attracting new foreign investment, has traditionally insisted on limiting access to its economy by foreigners for a variety of economic, social and political reasons.

Mexico's distinctive concerns about domestic economic sovereignty are addressed in the Investment Chapter of the NAFTA (Chapter 11), primarily through reservations and exceptions to the general obligation of National Treatment, including the right of establishment, and certain other disciplines, which in themselves are very similar to those found in the FTA. These reservations and exceptions are listed in various Annexes to the NAFTA (especially Annexes I–III) and in the case of Mexico include measures related to the following sectors: transportation, telecommunications, petrochemicals, the postal service, professional services, and social services. Canada and the United States, however, have also included reservations with respect to some of these sectors in Annex II, in some cases out of specific policy concerns and in others simply to preserve reciprocity or symmetry between the obligations of Mexico and its NAFTA Partners.[53] Where not reserved, existing non-conforming measures must be eliminated within ten years.

In addition, a general provision has been added in the introductory section ('Scope') of Chapter 11 stating that 'Nothing in this Chapter shall be construed to prevent a Party from providing a service or performing a function such as law enforcement, correctional services, income security or insurance, social welfare, public education, public training, health and child care in a manner that is not inconsistent with this Chapter' (Article 1101.4). This reflects Canadian as well as Mexican concerns that some provisions of the Investment Chapter, particularly the right of establishment, could be interpreted as providing to private investors of other NAFTA partners a right to compete in areas that are characterized by complete or substantial public sector provision in Mexico and Canada, but where some or all of delivery is provided by the private sector in the United States. One may question, however, the legal significance of this clause, since it protects only those measures that are *in any case* 'not inconsistent' with the provisions of Chapter 11, and thus does not override the application of Chapter 11 to public provision of essential services. In addition, on its terms, the clause only seems to apply to direct governmental provision: thus, once a government begins contracting out some of these functions, even to the non-profit sector, it might be required to permit a direct business presence in that sector by private interests in other NAFTA countries, on a National Treatment basis. The effect may be to deter governments from innovative experiments with delivery through non-governmental actors such as non-profit community groups, for fear of losing adequate scope for regulatory control or being required to allow competition on essentially commercial criteria.[54]

Unlike the FTA, the NAFTA provides some protection for investors from non-NAFTA countries who already have 'substantial business activities in the territory' of one of the NAFTA Parties. These investors from non-NAFTA Parties are to enjoy the full rights of NAFTA country investors if they choose to expand their activities into the territory of another NAFTA Party (Article 1113.2). Thus, for example, a German-owned company operating in Canada that wishes to engage in business activities in the United States would be entitled to the same benefits of the NAFTA as would be a Canadian-owned company operating in the United States.

Arguably the most innovative feature of the NAFTA investment provisions, however, is the establishment of dispute settlement processes based on arbitration according to international arbitral rules, in particular those of ICSID, the International Convention on the Settlement of Investment Disputes. The NAFTA Parties consent to submission to arbitration of investment disputes under Chapter 11, at the request of the private investor itself. This makes NAFTA the first comprehensive international trade treaty[55] to provide to private Parties direct access to dispute settlement as of right.

The Codes of Conduct approach: Negotiating the rights and responsibilities of multinationals and sharing the costs and benefits of foreign investment

A third approach to international discipline of foreign investment measures is embodied in the various multilateral and bilateral Codes of Conduct that have been negotiated between states as well as between states and multinational firms themselves. The Codes of Conduct generally aim at striking an explicit balance between concerns of investors (compensation for expropriation, repatriation of earnings) and concerns of host countries about the conduct of foreign firms (whether corruption and bribery, avoidance of domestic regulatory and tax regimes, or unfair labour practices). In return for commitments of 'fair treatment' from the host country the firm commits itself to behave there as a good corporate citizen. Reflective of this approach are the 1976 OECD Guidelines for Multinational Enterprises[56] and the United Nations Draft Code on Transnational Corporations, as well as Guidelines for Investment developed by international business groups such as the International Chamber of Commerce for inclusion in negotiated agreements between multinational enterprises and individual countries.[57]

One attractive feature of the Codes and guidelines is their inherently pluralistic character – involving an explicit balance of economic and a variety of political, ethical, and social concerns in the regulation of foreign investment. Another, often cited advantage with respect to some Codes and guidelines is that they result from a multilateral process where there is a relative equality of bargaining power between large and small countries, and between the developed and developing world. This is particularly true of instruments developed within the UN system, including the UN Draft Code on Transnational Corporations.

Often, however, the language of these instruments reflects a high level of generality and diplomatic vagueness. They therefore often provide very limited guidance for the resolution of specific disputes or conflicts. For instance, an obligation to abstain from bribery is specific enough, but what of the obligation on multinationals by the OECD Guidelines 'To take fully into account established general policy objectives of the Member states in which they operate'? How would one go about determining whether this vague obligation had been sufficiently complied with by a particular foreign investor? Despite their voluntary character, and the vagueness of many of their prescriptions, the Guidelines have been credited with improving channels of communication between multinational corporations and host country governments (as well as local trade unions) in OECD countries. Implementation of the guidelines is monitored by the OECD Committee on Investment and Multinational Enterprises (CIME), which however does not serve the function of settling specific disputes between multinationals and host governments. The CIME does issue 'clarifications' of the Guidelines, and these 'clarifications' are usually triggered by specific disputes which involve disagreement about the meaning of the Guidelines.[58]

In contrast to the Guidelines, two other OECD instruments contain strict substantive commitments by OECD member states with respect to liberalization of investment measures. The OECD Code of Liberalisation of Capital Movements and the Code of Liberalisation of Current Invisibles contain specific disciplines on measures that impede the flow of capital between OECD member states.[59] Cumulatively, these disciplines are viewed by the OECD as the equivalent of a right of establishment.[60] The Codes of Conduct are legally binding on OECD members. A commitment to National Treatment of foreign investors is contained in Article II of the OECD Declaration on International Investment and Multinational Enterprises (1976). Unlike the Codes, the Declaration is not binding in international law. Subsequent Decisions of the OECD Council (which *are* binding) have, however, required that member states lodge with the OECD any exceptions to National Treatment in their national policies. Such exceptions are to be examined by the CIME at regular intervals (at least once every three years) with a view to 'making suitable proposals designed to assist Members to withdraw their exceptions'.[61] In addition, any member country 'which considers that its interests may be adversely affected by significant official incentives and disincentives to international direct investment' by another member country may demand consultations in the CIME 'to examine the possibility of reducing such effects to a minimum'.[62] The National Treatment commitment in the Declaration is subject to '. . . needs [of member states] to maintain public order, to protect their essential security interests and to fulfil commitments relating to international peace and security . . .'[63] Member states are, nevertheless, required, for transparency purposes, to notify to the OECD measures that may be justified on these terms.

In contrast to these OECD instruments, most multilateral investment codes, especially those concerned with investment relations between developed and developing countries, only become effective through explicit or implicit understandings between host countries and individual multinational corporations. This is the case for example, with the UN Draft Code on Transnational Corporations. Here, all the inherent difficulties of inequality of bargaining power between developing and developed countries – supposedly redressed in part through multilaterally-developed Codes – return as countries and firms bargain as to what sub-set of rights and obligations will be adopted and complied with in these explicit or implicit bilateral understandings.[64] At the same time, some observers have noted that the Codes of Conduct have succeeded in influencing the settlement of some investment disputes through private litigation, due to the willingness of judges and arbitrators to invoke them as interpretative aids or sources of guidance on matters of international economic policy.[65]

An attempt to remedy the problem of inequality of bargaining power, at least in part, is reflected in the Convention on the Settlement of Investment Disputes Between States and Nationals of Other States (ICSID).[66] ICSID provides a vehicle by which host countries, home countries and multinationals can agree to submit investment disputes to third-Party arbitration. ICSID responds both to the concerns of developed country foreign investors that they may not be fairly treated in the domestic legal processes of host countries and to the parallel concerns of the developing countries about investment disputes being adjudicated in, for example, American or British courts (as would often be provided in the choice of forum clause of an investment agreement, at the insistence of the developed country investor). While a variety of bilateral investment treaties and agreements between host countries and multinationals provide for arbitration through the ICSID process, it has rarely been resorted to in order to resolve investment disputes, for reasons that are not entirely clear.[67] ICSID's future may now, however, be somewhat brighter by virtue of the incorporation of the ICSID arbitration process into the dispute resolution provisions of the NAFTA Chapter on investment. Finally, inasmuch as principles in the codes end up being part of bilateral, reciprocal bargains that strike a balance of interests between investors and host countries, they present the same kind of danger as any managed trade, bilateral reciprocity-based approach to liberalization. The balance of interests struck may ignore effects of investment measures on third countries (e.g. import substitution effects) with a global welfare perspective being lost sight of entirely.

At the same time, these dangers may be somewhat attenuated through the development of general norms of international law with respect to compensation for the expropriation of the property of foreign nationals and extra-territoriality, as well as more specific regimes that deal with inter-jurisdictional dimensions of corporate taxation or anti-trust policies. As discussed earlier in the chapter, these are matters that loom large in invest-ment relations between states, but overlap with other international and domestic regimes not specific to the foreign investment context.

CONCLUSION

Subject to a number of important qualifications, the allocative efficiency case for free trade also implies the desirability of liberal rules on foreign direct investment. Nevertheless, there is considerable uncertainty as to whether and how GATT rules apply to many investment measures. Some regional trade treaties, most notably the FTA and NAFTA, contain much more comprehensive coverage of investment measures than does the GATT at present. This is also the case with certain instruments of the OECD, such as the Code on the Liberalisation of Capital Movements and the Declaration on International Investment and Multinational Enterprises.

However strong the allocative efficiency case for liberal rules on invest-ment, a variety of non-economic policy concerns are also implicated in the determination of the rights and responsibilities of foreign investors and host-country governments. For this reason, many of the issues that predominate in this area are likely to continue to be addressed through bilateral or regional agreements and multilateral codes of conduct and guidelines specific to the investment context, rather than a comprehensive GATT-based set of general rules. The 'Agreement on TRIMs' in the Uruguay Round Final Act should, by contrast, be seen as advancing the more modest goal of clarifying the application of existing GATT rules, while at the same time creating an institutional avenue for negotiation of broader-ranging disciplines on trade-restricting investment measures.

12

TRADE AND DEVELOPING COUNTRIES

INTRODUCTION

Developing countries[1] currently account for about a quarter of world exports, and about the same percentage of world imports.[2] Although some developing countries were included within GATT from the outset,[3] they had a marginal influence on the original Bretton Woods negotiations.[4] By the 1960s, developing countries had come to predominate numerically in the GATT, and during the 1960s and 1970s their share of world trade, and particularly of exports grew rapidly, although in this respect the performance of some developing countries was vastly superior to that of others.[5] Throughout this period, developing countries complained that their influence on the design and functioning of the GATT rules remained marginal, and increasingly pressed demands for more preferential treatment within GATT, as well as attempting to evolve other fora for the creation of rules on trade (particularly, UNCTAD, the United Nations Conference on Trade and Development) where they could wield greater influence.

While some developing countries continued through the 1970s to experience considerable growth, particularly those with more open or outward-oriented trade policies, the strategy that was adopted by most LDCs and that predominated in the development literature at the time – import substitution and protection of infant industries – yielded disappointing results.[6] The conclusion most often drawn was that the rules of the game of international trade and finance were so heavily skewed to the disadvantage of the LDCs that a radically new strategy was necessary, based upon a fundamental redistribution of wealth and opportunities between North and South. Developed in UN fora such as UNCTAD, the strategy was termed the New International Economic Order.[7] While the NIEO remained at the level of ideology or at most the 'soft law' of UN resolutions, the developed countries did, at a practical level, respond to these pressures by granting further tariff preferences to developing countries on a non-reciprocal but also a non-binding basis (the Generalized System of Preferences). At the same time the availability of recycled petrodollars promised to give the strategy of protected, state-assisted rapid industrialization a new lease on life.

The further failure of this strategy, combined with the second oil shock and recession in the developed world (which produced high interest rates and low demand for developing country exports), led to the debt crisis of the early 1980s. The rescheduling of loans to developing countries was premised upon the undertaking of domestic reforms, including price liberalization, movement towards convertible currency, and unilateral trade liberalization. Thus, many developing countries moved towards an outward-oriented, export-driven approach to development and growth.[8] While these policy shifts can be in part understood as imposed from the outside through institutions like the IMF as a price for cooperation by the North in solving the debt crisis, they also reflect increasing recognition of the extraordinary success enjoyed by the Asian NICs (newly industrializing countries) through an export-oriented, as opposed to import-substitution-based strategy, for growth. They also may reflect, or at least be reinforced by, the intellectual and political decline of Marxism, which in its Leninist/centralist and neo-Marxist variants was an important ideological source of resistance to economic liberalism.[9]

The treatment of developing countries in the GATT that emerged during the first few decades after the General Agreement came into force reflects what Bela Balassa has aptly termed a 'Faustian bargain' between the North and the South.[10] On the one hand, developing countries were granted significant exemptions from GATT disciplines, so as to allow them considerable scope to adopt import-substitution, infant-industry-protecting strategies of development. Eventually, as well, developing countries were granted preferential tariff concessions or complete removal of tariffs on a non-binding basis, with respect particularly to raw materials. On the other hand, with respect to exports that could immediately figure in an export-led growth strategy, such as textiles, light manufactures, and processed agricultural products, developed countries maintained extremely high trade barriers, including high tariff rates, and also in the case of textiles, quantitative restrictions under a special GATT-exempt arrangement that has come to be known as the Multi-Fibre Arrangement. Thus, although it is fashionable to blame leftist theories of development economics and the influence of Soviet bloc central planning approaches for the protectionist follies of the developing world in this epoch, the treatment of developing countries in the Western-dominated global trading order made inward-oriented policies easy, while it set up obstacles to export-led growth.

We now proceed to examine in some detail the nature of this treatment.

THE LEGAL AND INSTITUTIONAL FRAMEWORK FOR DEVELOPING COUNTRY TRADE

The pre-Uruguay Round GATT

Article I

Article I, which establishes the MFN (Most Favoured Nation) principle, nevertheless allows for the *continuation* of preferential tariff rates – i.e. tariffs below the bound, MFN rate negotiated within the framework of the GATT – between countries that shared a common sovereignty before the Second World War, and also between countries that formed part of the Ottoman Empire until the settlement at Versailles that ended the First World War. Under the first category, preferences given by (ex-colonial) powers such as Britain, France, and Spain to their former colonies are permitted, and this would have included a substantial part of trade between developed and developing countries at the time the GATT was created. The margin of preference, however, cannot exceed that which existed between the MFN rates and the preferential rates in question at the time of entry into force of the GATT (1947). Thus, further preferential treatment has required an explicit GATT waiver from the MFN obligations of Article I.

Quantitative restrictions
(Articles XI, XII, XIII, XVIII)

As discussed in earlier chapters, Article XI of the General Agreement contains a general prohibition on quantitative restrictions on imports and exports, subject to a narrow range of exceptions. The balance of payments exceptions defined in Articles XII and XIII were not especially aimed at the needs of developing countries – at the beginning of the post-war era, very few of the *developed* countries possessed stable, or even convertible currencies.[11] Nevertheless, Article XII does contemplate that a Contracting Party may assert an exception to Article XI on balance of payments grounds, where its balance of payments difficulties are due to 'domestic policies directed towards the achievement and maintenance of full and productive employment or towards the development of economic resources' (XII:3 (d)). This has the effect of immunizing a developing country from the claim that, since its balance of payments crisis is induced or prolonged by its own illiberal or distortive domestic policies, the appropriate solution is to change those policies rather than to increase trade protection.

Article XVIII, in the form that emerged after the 1954–5 review of the General Agreement, contains much more explicit recognition for development-based exceptions from GATT strictures. Article XVIII begins with a lengthy preamble that states the agreement of the Contracting Parties that developing countries[12] 'should enjoy additional facilities to enable them (a) to maintain sufficient flexibility in their tariff structure to be able to grant the tariff protection required for the establishment of a particular industry and (b) to apply quantitative restrictions for balance of payments purposes which take full account of the continued high level of demand for imports likely to be generated by their programmes of economic development' (XVIII:2). This statement is notable for its incorporation within the terms of the GATT itself of the infant-industry-protecting view of economic development – the notion that the goal of 'establishment of a particular industry' is an appropriate rationale for protection where pursued by a developing country.

The preamble to Article XVIII is followed by Sections A, B and C, which set out the specifics of the 'additional facilities' to be granted to developing countries. Section A provides that a developing country may, where it wishes 'to promote the establishment of a particular industry', reopen negotiations on bound tariffs with any Contracting Party 'with which such concession was initially negotiated' (A 7(a)). It is foreseen that the developing country would offer compensation for the withdrawal or modification of a concession, perhaps in the form of a reduction of tariffs on other products. If, despite an offer of adequate compensation, the developed Contracting Party or Parties in question refuse(s) to allow the concession to be withdrawn or modified, the developing country can apply to the GATT Council for the right to proceed unilaterally. Section B reiterates but also expands the balance of payments exceptions to Article XI strictures already contained in Article XII. For instance, developing countries may impose quantitative restrictions for balance of payments purposes on a discriminatory basis, i.e. 'in such a way as to give priority to the importation of those products which are more essential in the light of its policy of economic development' (XVIII(B):10).

Section C applies where a developing country 'finds that governmental assistance is required to promote the establishment of a particular industry with a view to raising the standard of living of its people ...' (XVIII (C):13). If the developing country is experiencing difficulties in the achievement of this goal, it may notify the GATT Council of the difficulties and any GATT-inconsistent measure with respect to imports that may be indicated. Upon notification, the GATT Council may, within 30 days, either request consultations with the developing country in question, or allow it to proceed with measures that would otherwise be in contravention of provisions of the General Agreement. There are two limits on this relief from GATT strictures: first, where the measures in question affect products for which there are already tariff bindings, the developing country must first consult with, and seek the consent of, the Contracting Party with whom the initial concession was negotiated; second, no deviation from Articles I, II and XIII of the General Agreement is permitted under Section C. Hence, whatever import-restricting measures are adopted pursuant to Section C must be implemented on a non-discriminatory basis.

In practice, as is described in detail by Hudec,[13] Article XVIII provided a basis for the granting of sweeping exemptions from GATT strictures to many developing countries, usually with a view to import substitution and protection of infant industries, as contemplated in the very terms of the General Agreement. The GATT Council routinely accepted such deviations from the general provisions of the GATT, and without insisting on the consultation requirements and other formal criteria embodied in Article XVIII. The explanation for this laxity is to be found less in development theory than in the fact that developed countries simply did not feel threatened by infant industries in developing countries. These industries posed little threat to developed country dominance in the sectors concerned, both in home markets and third country markets. In more recent years, there has been increased pressure for scrutiny of developing country trade practices, in part because a number of the larger and relatively more prosperous developing countries have come to be seen as significant potential markets for developing country exports, whether goods, services, or technology. This has been reflected to a large extent in US pressure to include disciplines on services and intellectual property in the Uruguay Round (the implications for developing countries are discussed below) but also in demands that developing countries' Article XVIII exemptions be re-examined and eliminated wherever not justified, or no longer justified, by the wording of the GATT.[14]

Part IV

Part IV of the General Agreement, entitled 'Trade and Development', was added in 1965, in response to the increasingly insistent demands of developing countries as they emerged through UNCTAD, which had been formally established in 1964.[15] Unlike Article XVIII, which had as its focus the relaxation of GATT strictures to enable developing countries to pursue inward-looking growth policies based on protection and promotion of infant industries, Part IV concerns the access of developing countries to developed country markets, and therefore appears to at least implicitly endorse the theory of export-led growth. Hence, the preambular section of Part IV states (in part): 'the export earnings of the less-developed contracting parties can play a vital part in their economic development . . .' (Part IV: Article XXXVI:1(b)).

Nevertheless, the persistence of the inward-looking approach is reflected in the statement that 'the developed contracting parties do not expect reciprocity for commitments made by them in trade negotiations to reduce or remove tariffs and other barriers to the trade of less-developed countries' (Part IV: Article XXXVI:8). This principle of non-reciprocity is often referred to as 'special and differential status' for developing countries. The clear implication is that export-led growth is consistent with, and indeed should go hand in hand with, protection of developing countries' domestic markets – a mercantilist view in profound tension with the neo-classical perspective that protectionism which distorts domestic price mechanisms and insulates industries from international competition is likely to frustrate the development of viable export industries.[16]

A pervasive characteristic of the substantive provisions of Part IV is that they lack the clearly binding or obligatory character of most provisions of the General Agreement. Thus the developed countries 'shall to the fullest extent possible – that is, except when compelling reasons, which may include legal reasons, make it impossible – give effect' to commitments to reduce and eliminate trade barriers with respect to 'products currently or potentially of particular export interest to less-developed countries' (Part IV: Article XXXVII:1(a)). In other instances, developed countries are 'to make every effort' to, *inter alia*, 'give active consideration to the adoption of other measures designed to provide greater scope for the development of imports from less-developed countries . . .' (Part IV: Article XXXVII:3(b)). The only remedy specified in Part IV where developed countries are not living up to these loosely-worded commitments is the possibility of a developing country Contracting Party requesting consultations either with individual developed countries or in the GATT Council (Part IV: Article XXXVII:2).

Other GATT provisions

The Tokyo Round Codes

Serious tensions arose between developed and developing countries in the GATT due to the refusal of the United States to grant the benefit of the Tokyo Round GATT Subsidies and Antidumping Codes to countries that have not signed the Codes, which includes most developing countries. In the 1960s, India had obtained a legal ruling from the GATT Secretariat that MFN obligations applied to the Kennedy Round Antidumping Code, thereby obliging the United States to provide the benefits of the Code to non-signatories.[17] In the Tokyo Round, the United States pressed for an explicit conditional MFN approach to the revised Antidumping Code and the new Subsidies Code. The resultant Codes, on their face, required that benefits only be extended to signatories. However, the Codes did provide some special treatment for developing countries. In the case of the Antidumping Code this only amounts to a general provision (Article 13) requiring Parties to explore 'possibilities of constructive remedies provided for by this Code [i.e. price undertakings]' before 'applying anti-dumping duties where they would affect the essential interests of developing countries'. This supposed special consideration for developing countries has not been translated into concrete provisions in the domestic trade remedy law of major developed nations. In the case of the Subsidies Code, developing countries are exempted from the general ban on export subsidies, provided these subsidies are not 'used in a manner which causes serious prejudice to the trade or production of another signatory' (Part III, Article 14, (2), (3)). It is, however, an open legal question whether this exemption only applies to the export subsidies provisions of the Code (Article 9) itself, or whether it extends by implication to the restrictions on export subsidies in Article XVI of the General Agreement. The latter view seems to be more plausible, since the entire Subsidies Code can be seen as an elaboration and detailed application of the subsidies provisions of the General Agreement.

In addition, the Code states that with respect to *any* subsidy granted by a developing country signatory (i.e. either export or domestic) no action may be taken under the dispute resolution provisions of the Code, unless the subsidy has nullified or impaired a tariff concession 'or other obligations under the General Agreement' (Article 14 (7)). Nullification and impairment is defined narrowly as displacement of imports into the subsidizing country or 'injury to domestic industry in the importing market of a signatory, . . .'. However, this provision is of little practical significance, since it only applies to subsidies actions under the multilateral dispute resolution process provided for in the Code, and does not constrain the unilateral application of countervailing duties.

Dispute settlement

The dispute settlement procedures of the GATT are rarely invoked either by or against developing countries. From 1947 to 1986 only 12.5% of GATT complaints were initiated by LDCs and LDCs were respondents in only 15% of the cases.[18] One reason for this state of affairs may be the consequences (perceived or real) of power imbalances between developed and developing countries. The GATT enforcement mechanism is ultimately based on retaliation as the sanction of last resort – a sanction that most developing countries would be hard-put to apply to developed countries. Since few developing countries represent, individually, major export markets for developed countries, withdrawal of concessions would not normally be a very powerful sanction. On the other hand, where developed countries wish to get developing countries to comply with trade rules, they possess very effective leverage, including development aid and GSP preferences. In addition, because of the power imbalance, unilateral measures can often be applied to developing countries with relative impunity. Significantly, as developing countries acquire greater political and economic power and influence they do tend increasingly to be taken to the GATT; hence, in the last few years NICs such as Korea and Chile have been the subject of GATT complaints.[19]

The Generalized System of Preferences and the Lomé Convention

Despite the absence of self-contained and self-activating 'hard' legal obligations in Part IV, it set the scene for the granting of non-reciprocal trade preferences to developing countries through mechanisms outside the GATT. The two main mechanisms are the Generalized System of Preferences and the Lomé Convention. The GSP was initiated under the auspices of UNCTAD in 1968. The intent was to build on existing colonial preferences which (as discussed above) had been grandfathered in the GATT MFN requirement – no longer would only the ex-colonial powers grant such preferences and the ex-colonies be their only recipients (hence the expression 'generalized'). Each developed country would be free to grant or not grant such preferences as it chose. And the preferences are not 'bound' in the GATT – therefore they may be removed or modified at any time. A 'waiver' – pursuant to Article XXV of the GATT – was granted in 1971 to permit the derogation from Article 1 MFN obligations that would be needed to introduce new preferences. However, the GATT waiver did require that each Contracting Party's GSP programme benefit developing countries generally – a potential constraint on open-ended discrimination between developing countries and the use of the GSP to strike bilateral side-deals with particular developing countries.[20]

In the case of the European Union, preferences have been embodied in the Lomé Convention which first came into force in 1975, and has been renewed and revised several times since.[21] While containing non-reciprocal tariff preferences, these agreements also deal with a wide-ranging agenda for commercial cooperation between the EU and some 65 developing countries (almost all of them ex-colonies of Britain or France).[22] Since the preferences contained therein do not benefit all developing countries, it might be argued that in principle they do not conform with the terms of the GATT waiver. However, it has been suggested that the Lomé system could be viewed as a free trade area or customs union, therefore consistent with the GATT even absent a waiver, provided that it conforms to the provisions of Article XXIV:5.

In contrast to the European Union, the United States and other developed countries such as Canada and Australia have embodied trade preferences for developing countries in domestic customs legislation rather than in agreements with the developing countries themselves. Given the importance of the United States as a market for developing country exports, the American GSP system has loomed large in debates about the desirability of the GSP approach to promoting export-led growth in developing countries. The United States initially opposed the granting of preferences to developing countries, but finally established its own GSP system in the mid-1970s.[23]

The present version of this system is found in the Trade Act of 1974, as amended in 1984. The Act contains a number of provisions that open the door to discrimination between different developing countries, and to use of the threat of withdrawing GSP status as a political and economic weapon. For instance, the Act gives the American President authority to waive GSP status if the country in question fails to provide 'reasonable access to its markets and to its commodities' and if it does not afford 'adequate and effective protection of intellectual property rights'.[24] In addition, the Act provides for 'graduation' of developing countries from GSP status once they reach a certain level of per capita GDP ($US8,500 in 1984, indexed to a formula based on half the annual US growth rate).[25] This threshold is relatively high, but some of the most prosperous NICs are now beginning to pass it.[26] As well, detailed rules exist for removal of preferences on particular products, even where a country does not meet the threshold for complete graduation. A preference will be removed when a developing country has become a major world exporter of a product – arguably a highly perverse approach that punishes the most successful LDC exporters (i.e. those who are most competitive in developed country markets).[27] This partial graduation has occurred with respect to particular exports of more than a dozen LDCs.

Aside from the issue of graduation, and the obvious drawbacks of trade preferences that are non-binding and that can be used as political and commercial leverage by developed countries, there is a more general question to be raised about whether, in fact, the kinds of preferences actually granted have done much to assist export growth in the developing world. As Balassa suggests, the GSP itself excludes 'product groups of principal interest to developing countries such as steel, textiles,[28] clothing, and shoes'.[29] In addition, trade remedy laws (countervail and antidumping) have frequently been used against developing countries, thereby clawing back much (and in some cases, all) of the benefit provided by tariff preferences – in recent years, for instance, the number of anti-dumping cases initiated by the United States and the European Union against developing countries has often equalled or even exceeded the number of cases against developed country exporters.[30]

Furthermore, preferences do not appear to have responded adequately to developing countries' concerns about 'tariff escalation'. Tariff escalation denotes the tendency for developed countries to impose very low tariffs on imports of raw materials and much higher tariff rates on processed or finished products that are made from those raw materials. This practice makes it very easy for developing countries to export raw materials in an unprocessed state and much more difficult to export products that have a significant value-added component. The escalation effect occurs because while developed country producers of the processed or finished products have access to raw materials at almost the same price as developing country producers (due to the low tariffs on the raw materials), they also have a protected market against the developing country producers by virtue of the significant tariff imposed on the processed or finished products in question. The end result is to discourage export-driven strategies of moving up the value chain from the extraction of raw materials to increasingly sophisticated processing industries. Balassa found that, even on the basis of GSP and Lomé preferences, effective protection afforded against higher value-added products from developing countries due to tariff escalation ranged from three to almost nine times the applicable nominal tariffs.[31]

More generally, as MFN tariff rates have fallen in successive rounds of GATT negotiations the value of the GSP to developing countries has inevitably eroded. As well, GSP arrangements have often contained 'safeguard' provisions, allowing re-imposition of higher tariffs or other import restrictions where a surge of developing country imports threatens developed-country domestic producers.

The Multi-Fibre Arrangement(MFA)

The MFA is an agreement between nine importing developed country signatories (including the EU) and 31 exporting developing countries. It provides a framework for Voluntary Export Restraints (VERs), primarily quotas, limiting developing country exports of textiles and clothing to the nine developed country signatories. The MFA was formally established in 1974. It superseded two earlier agreements, the Short and Long Term Arrangements, that applied to a far narrower range of developing country exports.[32]

The Short-term Arrangement on cotton textiles was in force from 1961 to 1962, and had been negotiated at the initiative of the Kennedy Administration. It was replaced in 1962 with the Long-term Arrangement Regarding International Trade in Cotton Textiles. It is important to note that these Arrangements did not initiate restrictive trade practices with respect to these sectors, which had existed since the end of the Second World War, particularly in the Western European countries.[33] Indeed, at the beginning these Arrangements held the promise of an orderly codification of restrictions with a view to their eventual phase-out, as developed country producers adjusted to new competitive realities through technological innovation and gradual labour shedding.[34]

In the 1970s, however, competitive pressure from the NICs in particular became much more intense than had previously been experienced, and the MFA became a convenient vehicle to respond to these pressures through further restricting trade in these sectors with the use of special safeguards, VERs and quotas.[35] In addition, the incorporation of protectionism in a formal interstate agreement disguised to some extent the GATT-inconsistency of most of the measures in question, which were discriminatory quantitative restrictions, in violation of both Articles I and XI of the General Agreement. Jackson goes so far as to suggest that 'the countries who have accepted the textile or multifibre arrangements have arguably partially 'waived' their GATT rights'.[36] In our view, this claim is highly suspect, because (as Jackson himself acknowledges) developing countries have accepted these arrangements only under the threat of even more restrictive GATT-inconsistent measures.

It is sometimes argued that developing countries are nevertheless protected by the MFA because the right to impose import restrictions is limited to cases where 'real risks of market disruption' exist in the import-restricting country (Article 4), and also because the MFA provides for gradual expansion of quotas, as well as exemptions for new entrants in the market and small suppliers. However, as Dao remarks, despite the existence of a monitoring mechanism (the Textiles Surveillance Body or TSB), 'importing countries are reluctant to adhere to the Arrangement and often take additional restrictive measures beyond the Arrangement, . . . '.[37]

The fundamental reality is that developing countries suffer very large losses from import restrictions imposed by developed countries in these sectors. It has been estimated that if *all* trade restrictions on LDC textile and clothing imports were lifted by the EU, Japan and the United States, the gains to LDCs 'would be no less than 50.8 per cent of total possible gains related to all trade'.[38] It has been further estimated that if all import restrictions were removed, developing country textile exports would increase by about 50% and clothing exports by 128.9%.[39]

The last extension of the MFA, which occurred in 1986, further sanctified the increasing restrictiveness of developing country measures. Thus, coverage was extended to include new types of fibres and developed countries gained new rights to take unilateral measures against developing country imports. Developing countries gained very little, save a statement that the final objective of the Parties was eventual submission of trade in textiles to GATT strictures and some strengthening of the (in any case little used and little heeded) TSB.[40]

The Uruguay Round Final Act contains an ambitious plan for sweeping reform and the eventual phasing out of the MFA, which is described in detail in a later section of this chapter.

UNCTAD (The United Nations Conference on Trade and Development)

UNCTAD was founded in 1964 as a periodic conference of all UN members, with an ongoing institutional framework (the Secretariat). The intent was to establish a forum on trade where developing countries would find themselves less marginalized in the decision-making process than was thought to be the case with the GATT.[41] Under the stewardship of Raoul

Prebisch, UNCTAD became a leading forum for the elaboration of the 'import-substitution', protectionist view of economic development in the Third World. Prebisch was an Argentinian economist who had written extensively on economic development in Latin America. His perspective on trade and development had three main elements: (1) the view that balance of payments problems were endemic to underdevelopment, thereby making liberal trade between developed and developing countries infeasible; (2) the hypothesis that the terms of trade were likely to deteriorate further, because of a supposed long-term trend to declining prices in primary commodities, the major source of export earnings of developing countries, at least relative to the prices of manufactured goods; and (3) the proposal that to reverse these further impoverishing trends ('immiserizing growth'), developing countries must engage in rapid industrialization aimed at import-substitution, to be assisted both by subsidies for industrial development as well as 'infant industry' trade protection.[42] At times, the developing countries appeared to be prepared to withdraw from GATT and to utilize UNCTAD as a forum for evolving an alternative legal order for world trade.[43] However, this threat never materialized, and instead UNCTAD became an instrument for applying pressure on developed countries to liberalize trade unilaterally with developing countries (i.e. while permitting developing countries themselves wide exemptions from GATT strictures in order to sustain import-substitution-based growth policies, such as protection of infant industries). The main product of UNCTAD has been the non-law or at most 'soft law' of UN Resolutions. In the 1970s and early 1980s, UNCTAD sought to develop a New International Economic Order, a grandiose project aimed at a fundamental restructuring of North–South relations. In fact, the NIEO was largely a recasting of the old demands for unilateral developed country trade liberalization in a new ideological language – that of the moral imperative of redistribution of wealth from developed to developing countries.[44]

The Generalized System of Trade Preferences

A much more concrete initiative of UNCTAD is the Global System of Trade Preferences (GSTP). Unlike the GSP, this is a system of preferences negotiated between, and applicable to, trade among developing countries themselves. It reflects UNCTAD's enthusiasm for the promotion of South–South trade as a response to supposed developed country domination of the rules and terms of North–South trade. In fact, however, South–South trade continues to account for a very small percentage of world trade (about 7%, holding constant through much of the 1980s).[45]

The GSTP developed from the 1971 GATT 'Protocol Relating to Trade Negotiations Among Developing Countries', which obtained an explicit Article XXV waiver to allow preferences in contravention of the Article I

MFN requirement.[46] Despite official UNCTAD ideology that South–South preferences should reflect the relative economic development needs of the various developing countries, it appears that GATT-type reciprocity or trading of concessions on the basis of mutual self-interest dominated the most recent (1988) negotiations on GSTP preferences. The resulting agreement embodies 1300 tariff concessions, and has been signed by 46 developing countries.[47]

With some exceptions, the GSTP provides for an MFN principle to apply with respect to concessions negotiated between the signatories. It appears, however, that the legal text of the GSTP permits the signatories, if they so desire, to confer the same preferences, or even more preferential treatment on *non-signatories*, even where this may erode the value of concessions to signatories. This latitude was made necessary by the overlapping of the GSTP with various South–South regional trade agreements and customs unions.[48]

The GSTP contains a provision that obligates signatories not to undermine concessions negotiated in the GSTP through the application of any charge or measure restricting commerce other than those existing prior thereto, with exceptions for countervailing and antidumping duties, border tax adjustments, and balance of payments measures (Article 10).

International Commodity Agreements and Export Earnings Stabilization

Given the prominence of concerns about deteriorating terms of trade (particularly as related to primary commodities) in the UNCTAD view of trade and development, it is not surprising that a major thrust of UNCTAD's work has been in the area of commodity price stabilization. Under the auspices of UNCTAD's Integrated Programme for Commodities, established in 1976, numerous International Commodity Agreements (ICAs) were struck, including cocoa, coffee, copper, cotton, and tin, among other commodities. These Agreements are in essence producers' cartels. Each producer country that is a member of the Agreement is assigned an export quota, with the global total of such quotas determined in such a way as to sustain world prices at a level acceptable to the membership. Some of the ICAs also provide for Stabilization Funds that purchase surplus production at times of oversupply with a view to selling when there are shortages.

The ICAs have not been particularly successful at sustaining commodity prices at the desired levels. The core difficulty is that which is endemic to most cartelization arrangements – the tendency of individual members to 'cheat' on the supply constraints.[49] As well, a cartel can only function effectively if all or almost all the producers of the commodity in question are members, and this has not been the case with a number of the ICAs.[50]

In addition to ICAs, UNCTAD has also sought to establish a system of export earnings compensation, which would involve loans or grants to developing countries when their export earnings decline below a certain level due to supply and price fluctuations with respect to primary commodities. A limited facility for export earnings compensation, called the STABEX, exists under the Lomé Convention but applies only to exports of a limited number of agricultural commodities to the EU.

The UNCTAD scheme involved the creation of a Common Fund that would apparently finance both the Stabilization Funds of individual ICAs (i.e. funds for purchase of buffer stocks or surpluses) as well as export earnings compensation. However, although first proposed in 1976, the Common Fund has yet to become a reality. The United States has consistently refused to participate, and a number of other developed countries (while agreed in principle on the idea) have failed to ratify the Agreement to create the Fund.[51]

TRADE AND DEVELOPMENT: THEORY AND POLICY

Having reviewed the legal rules and institutions that apply to developing country trade we now proceed to examine the evolving theoretical and policy stances with respect to the relationship between trade and development that have influenced the evolution of these rules and institutions over the last forty years.

The theory of comparative advantage and economic development: The limits of neo-classical theory

Despite the intense interest of their eighteenth and nineteenth century predecessors – particularly Smith, Hume, and Mill – in the causes of wealth and poverty among nations, modern neo-classical trade economists have until recently not devoted a great deal of attention to articulating a rigorous theory of the linkage between trade and economic development.[52] As discussed in an earlier chapter, neo-classical theory can explain why a country will experience welfare gains when it specializes in those products in which, given existing factor endowments, it possesses a comparative advantage. Comparative advantage is generally taken to be *revealed* comparative advantage, leading to a static perspective that largely ignores the issue of how nations actually come to acquire comparative advantage in particular products in the first place. Today, of course, it is widely recognized that much more goes into the determination of comparative advantage than fixed, 'natural' factors like endowments of natural resources, and there is an important and expanding economic literature on the causes of and constraints on economic growth and development.[53]

314

Quite early in the post-war period, however, the creation of comparative advantage became a persistent concern of development theory and for a quite straightforward reason – the existing specialization of economic activity in developing countries seemed to provide no guarantee of generating sustained economic growth. On the basis of the example of the developed world (and the early experience of Soviet Bloc industrialization), specialization in large-scale manufacturing industries was viewed as the key to growth. In addition, the existing specialization patterns of many developing countries could with justification be viewed as the historically contingent product of colonialism – developing countries served as ready sources of raw materials on the one hand, and as markets for the finished products of the colonial powers, on the other. This suggested not only the artificiality of existing comparative advantage in developing countries, but also its foundation in fundamentally unjust power relationships.[54]

Trade and development in the Import-substitution theories of the 1950s and 1960s

The most influential early attempts to provide a rigorous explanation of these phenomena are to be found in the work of Raoul Prebisch[55] and Ragnar Nurkse.[56] In the previous section of this chapter we briefly alluded to Prebisch's 'export pessimism', or concern with the supposedly deteriorating terms of trade between developing and developed countries. This concern is admirably summarized by Gilpin: 'the nature of technical advance, cyclical price movements, and differences in demand for industrial goods and primary products cause a secular deterioration in the terms of trade for commodity exporters, that is deterioration of the prices the LDCs receive for their commodity exports relative to the prices of the manufactured goods they import from developed countries'.[57] Nurkse's analysis emphasized the view that developed country markets would not be able to absorb significantly increased imports from the developing world.[58]

The policy implications drawn from these analyses suggested an inward-oriented growth strategy for LDCs. Industrialization would have to be achieved through government support for infant industries, including protection against competing developed country imports. Since it was assumed that the terms of trade in industrial products would continue to favour the developed countries, the aim was not to create 'global winners' in the developing world but rather to create viable industries to serve the domestic market.[59]

Although sometimes its intellectual success is blamed on the popularity of Marxist or neo-Marxist views of political economy, import-substitution-based development theory rapidly gained acceptance as an orthodox policy prescription for developing countries even among the developed, 'capitalist' countries and among liberal policy analysts. The simple fact is that neo-classical liberal economists did not possess an alternative theory of growth and development, based on liberal trade, with which to launch an effective response.

Perhaps the one significant exception was Raymond Vernon's 'product cycle' theory.[60] Vernon's key argument is well-summarized by Grossman and Helpman: 'Most new goods ... are developed in the industrialized North and manufactured there until their designs have been perfected and production techniques standardized. Then the innovating firms move the locus of production to the less developed South where wage rates and perhaps materials prices are lower. In a final stage of the product's life, new and superior goods may impinge upon this market share and ultimately render it obsolete.'[61] Vernon's approach did provide a plausible strategy for developing countries to acquire comparative advantage in increasingly sophisticated manufactured products through foreign investment-based technology transfer. However, from the developing country perspective, the theory had a number of unattractive features. First of all, it supposed, and accepted, that developing countries would never actually 'catch up' with the North, but would always remain a stage or two behind in the product cycle. Second, it was premised upon the acceptability of foreign ownership and investment, and was therefore susceptible to the critique that developing countries themselves (as opposed to foreign investors and multinational corporations) would realize few of the gains from their place in the product cycle, and would become subject to a new kind of economic colonialism.

In any event, the predominance of the import-substitution view is reflected in the wide range of exemptions from GATT strictures afforded to developing countries, which we have outlined above, as well as the approaches and initiatives of UNCTAD. The many developing countries that adopted import-substitution policies typically erected extremely high tariff and non-tariff barriers to imports, maintained artificially high exchange rates and stringent exchange controls, and in many cases domestic price controls (for instance, the prices of agricultural products were often controlled in order to contain the cost of living of industrial workers in the cities).[62]

Dependency theory and the beginnings of a neo-classical response to import-substitution approaches

It quickly became apparent that import-substitution policies were producing disappointing, or even disastrous, results in the many developing countries that had attempted them.[63] This produced two diametrically opposed responses in development theory. Many of those who advocated import-substitution approaches turned to dependency theory to explain the continued failure to generate adequate economic growth in developing countries. According to dependency theory, these countries remained economically and socially backward due to complicity between the local power élites and the forces of developed-country capitalism. Early efforts at industrialization could easily be exploited by multinational corporations, who – with the support of corrupt and avaricious local élites – would build branch plant facilities in developing countries, but without contributing to development through significant technology transfer or training of local workforces.[64] The policy implications were a general continuation of import-substitution policies but with a new emphasis on control of the multinational corporation, support for democratization movements, and guarantees that developed countries would not interfere with the sovereignty of developing nations.[65]

While many of those who had from the beginning supported import-substitution approaches resorted to dependency theory to explain the early failure of these approaches, neo-classical trade economists began to reflect on the interesting fact that those few developing countries, mainly in East Asia, that had eschewed import-substitution for outward-oriented strategies were experiencing relatively high levels of economic growth.[66] As Anne Kruger suggests,

> the results were far more spectacular than even the most ardent proponents of free trade would have forecast. Growth rates rose to heights that had previously been regarded as unattainable. South Korea achieved a rate of growth of real GNP in excess of 10 per cent a year over the entire decade from 1960 to 1970 and weathered the oil price increase of 1973–74 better than almost any other oil-importing country. Taiwan, Hong Kong, Singapore, and Brazil also thrived on outer-oriented trade policies to an extent not previously deemed feasible.[67]

According to Balassa, the share of Korea, Singapore and Taiwan in total LDC manufactured exports increased from 6% in 1963 to 42% in 1984. Over the same period, per capita incomes quadrupled in these three countries, while they increased at a much slower pace in inward-oriented LDCs such as India, Argentina, and Mexico.[68]

In reflecting on the empirical evidence of export-led growth, some neo-classical economists began to sketch a liberal alternative to import-substitution-oriented development theory. The flavour of this alternative is captured by the following passage from an essay by Bela Belassa, one of the leading exponents of liberal development theory:

> At the early stages of development, countries will generally benefit from specializing in natural resource products. In the process of industrialization, it will be advantageous to concentrate first on products utilizing mainly unskilled labour, with subsequent upgrading in the product composition of exports as the country accumulates physical and human capital.[69]

317

The theory thus emphasizes how developing countries can move up the 'value chain' beginning from a pre-existing comparative advantage in the least value-added exports (unprocessed raw materials). It thereby directly counters the claims of the import-substitution-oriented theorists that absent the creation of protected industries by the state, developing countries will be fated to remain 'hewers of wood and drawers of water' under constantly deteriorating terms of trade.

A further focus of the liberal theory is the negative consequence for economic growth of 'the chaotic nature of differential incentives among diverse activities in IS (import substitution) regimes'.[70] The effect of this chaos is largely to destroy the market signals that would normally lead to efficient resource allocation. In addition, the pervasive government 'rigging' of economic activity diverts considerable resources to 'directly unproductive profit-seeking activities', i.e. rent seeking, bribery of government officials, etc.[71] Finally, a liberal import policy can provide a substitute for domestic rivals which may be few or non-existent in many developing countries, thereby inducing competitive pressures to increase productivity.[72]

The direct policy implications of the liberal theory of trade and development are the liberalization of *both* developed *and* developing country trade policies. Liberalization of the former gives developing countries new opportunities to achieve growth through export expansion, allowing these countries to move their exports up the 'value chain'. And liberalization of developing country trade policies bring the gains from more efficient resource allocation that we have just described, with a corresponding increase in the competitiveness of developing country products on world markets.

However attractive to proponents of liberal trade (such as ourselves), the theory and evidence of export-led growth still leave much to be explained and debated concerning the relationship between trade liberalization and development. First, it has been pointed out that those developing countries characterized by significant export-led growth did not simply replace import-restrictive policies with a *laissez-faire* approach. While, on the one hand, reducing tariffs and other barriers to trade and reforming exchange rate regimes, on the other hand these countries initiated or activated a wide range of alternative government policies aimed at encouraging exports, including significant subsidies and loans to export-oriented industries.[73] A recent study by the World Bank of growth in East Asian economies concluded that while targeted industrial policies (e.g. subsidies to specific firms) made little positive contribution to the Asian economic miracle, more generally available export subsidies and other export incentives had a modest but significant impact on the extraordinary economic success of these countries.[74] Second, the results of applying the export-led growth formula in other developing countries have, in general, been disappointing (this is particularly the case for Africa).[75] This has led to speculation with respect to whether the dynamic Asian and Latin American economies display certain 'exceptionalist' political, social, or cultural characteristics that explain in large part the success of the export-led model of development. Factors that have been suggested include: a relatively pragmatic, 'this-worldly' orientation in the mainstream culture; superior human resources (higher literacy rates, etc. among the general population);[76] and a state that is relatively 'autonomous', i.e. to some extent insulated from tribal, ethnic sub-group, or concentrated interest group domination.[77]

The LDC Debt Crisis

The Debt Crisis arguably marks a crucial watershed in the evolution of approaches to LDC economic development. Owing to the Petrodollar surplus of the 1970s, major American, European and Japanese commercial banks found themselves with unprecedented amounts of money to lend on world markets. The banks became increasingly interested in lending to developing country governments. They often presumed that since a sovereign could not go bankrupt, the very fact that the debtor was a government would provide adequate security for the loans. For developing country governments, these loans represented an opportunity for another attempt at import-substitution based industrial development. The loans were particularly attractive since they offered the capital needed for indus-trialization, but without the strings attached to foreign direct investment or multinational corporate activities. Developing country governments would have direct control of the money, and full rights to distribute or reinvest domestically the profits from successful investments. In the event, commercial banks lent to developing country sovereigns an average of over $US40 billion per year between 1977 and 1982.[78]

By the early 1980s, a number of developing country debtors were having increasing difficulty in paying off these loans. First of all, once again import-substitution based industrialization failed to yield high rates of growth. Second, the recession in the developed world had considerably dampened demand for developing country exports, while at the same time leading to increased protection against those exports even where demand continued to be strong. At the same time, interest rates increased as the United States and other Western countries adopted an anti-inflationary monetary policy. Since the developing country loans were based on floating rates, this meant that just at a time when their foreign currency earnings from exports were declining, developing country debtors were faced with very substantial increases in the cost of servicing their loans.[79] Finally, in 1982 Mexico announced that it could not continue to pay its creditors according to schedule, and a number of other LDC debtors soon followed suit.[80]

The initial response of the creditor nations was that of debt rescheduling. Repayment of loans would be stretched out over a much longer period, without any debt reduction. The debtors would be required to have the rescheduling backed by an IMF stand-by credit, which in turn would be conditional on domestic policy reforms to provide some assurance that the countries in question would attain the balance of payments stability required to repay on the rescheduled terms. The reforms in question included anti-inflationary policies, currency devaluation, and also liberalization of prices and (to some extent) foreign trade. Not only did some of the policy conditions of rescheduling cause severe human hardship in LDCs (for instance rapid increases in food costs due to removal of price controls) but frequently, at the outset, the policy prescriptions were internally contradictory (for instance, tight money policies to fight inflation alongside inflation-inducing currency devaluations and price liberalization), although eventually IMF officials paid greater attention to the interaction and sequencing of the various policy reforms.

During the 1970s, even despite the disappointing results from import-substitution policies, many of these LDCs nevertheless continued to experience strong, albeit far from adequate, export growth, and increases in GDP. The effect of the debt crisis was to halt this growth almost entirely, as the debtor countries' foreign exchange earnings were eaten up by debt service requirements and they were unable to make investments in industrial production. In consequence, developing country imports from the developed world declined significantly, further worsening the recession. This led to the fundamental recognition by the Reagan Administration of the dependency of world economic recovery on the renewal of growth in developing countries, and a sense of urgency to find a solution to the LDC debt crisis that would permit such a renewal of growth.

The Baker Plan (named after the then US Treasury Secretary, James Baker) was the first such effort. Launched in 1985, it involved a proposal that commercial banks loan fresh money for investment in economic renewal to a select group of LDC debtors who were prepared to make major structural economic reforms, to be backed by structural adjustment lending by the World Bank and the IMF.[81] While it appears that some new loans were made pursuant to this Plan, the overall level of lending by commercial banks to LDC debtors actually declined from 1985 to 1987, and per capita income in debtor countries continued to fall.[82]

While the Baker Plan did not provide for debt reduction, some LDC debtors were, towards the end of the 1980s, beginning to have some success with debt reduction, through repurchase of debt on the secondary market at discounted rates and also through debt/equity swaps. The swaps were most successful in the case of the countries such as Chile and Mexico, who eventually were able to make credible commitments to provide an attractive climate for the foreign investment to be purchased with debt. At the same time, in part due to pressure from domestic regulatory authorities, many developed country creditor banks were increasing reserves on LDC loans, and their ability to do so lessened the sense of fear or panic that eventual debtor default could bring down the international financial system.

It was in this context that the United States proposed the Brady Plan in 1989. It would involve the commercial banks for the first time accepting debt reduction, but in return for a degree of backing for repayment of the remaining debt through various kinds of securities, with active participation in this backing by the US Treasury. After an (albeit somewhat shaky) beginning in Mexico the Brady approach came to play an important role in debt restructuring in the Philippines, Venezuela, Uruguay, Costa Rica and Nigeria.[83] Mexico, Chile and the Philippines in particular have recognized the potential for credible domestic policy reforms to induce significant influxes of capital, both foreign investment and (often more importantly) funds taken out of the country by its own nationals in order to avoid onerous taxation.

Trade policy reform at the end of the 1980s

The lessons that have emerged from the debt crisis, along with the collapse of central planning in the Soviet Bloc, and the general decline of Marxist-inspired ideology, as well as the brilliant success of more liberal trade policies in the Asian NICs, have led a variety of developing countries to move towards liberalization of their trade and related domestic policies even without the pressure of strict IMF conditionality. It has been estimated that, since the mid-1980s some 36 LDCs have undertaken significant trade policy reforms, and 17 of these have undertaken comprehensive reforms of distortionary policies, including exchange rate, price and wage policies.[84] Frequently, these reforms have been supported by lending facilities from the World Bank and the IMF.

Two issues that loom large with respect to these reforms are *adjustment* and *sequencing*. Lifting of trade restrictions can lead to rapid decline of protected industries that would never have existed but for government intervention and isolation from global competitive forces. The result is often widespread labour dislocation, because of a lag before the positive growth effects of more liberal policies are felt. Moreover, because liberalization is unilateral, increased competition from abroad is not immediately offset by greater access for developing country products in global markets. While they have undertaken very substantial lending to assist in the stabilization of the balance of payments during macroeconomic and related reforms, the International Financial Institutions have been very reluctant to engage in lending to facilitate labour adjustment. Worker adjustment is narrowly conceptualized as a distributional issue, and there is often suspicion that displaced workers may not be the most deserving beneficiaries of assistance. A recent World Bank paper suggests, for instance, that 'workers displaced from protected industries are not among the poorest groups in society'.[85]

This is arguably a short-sighted view, as unemployment among relatively advantaged segments of the population gluts the labour market in general and reduces consumer demand, therefore indirectly inflicting hardship on other, possibly less-advantaged segments of the population.[86] A further difficulty is that, in some developing countries, particularly those with poor tax collection systems, tariff revenues may constitute an important revenue source, and removal of tariffs therefore actually reduces the income stream which the government has at its disposal to fund labour adjustment programmes.

A second issue is that of sequencing: should import controls be removed before macroeconomic and other domestic reforms are already in place? There is a strong argument that until distortions in domestic prices and wages (inputs into production) are removed, and exchange rates become more realistic, it is unlikely that import competition will send the appropriate signals to domestic producers. It has been found that trade policy reforms can be effective when introduced either simultaneously with other reforms or shortly thereafter.[87]

POLICY OPTIONS AND PROSPECTS FOR THE FUTURE

Unilateral trade liberalization

This option, which has just been described from the perspective of structural policy reform, has the obvious limitation that the adjustment process is not facilitated through any additional access to developed country markets. However, in many developing countries the costs of distortive policies to productivity and growth may have become so high as to justify not delaying liberalization until reciprocal trade liberalization can take place. Balassa suggests that in these instances developing countries should proceed with liberalization, and that in eventual negotiations on the basis of reciprocity they can credibly demand concessions for making liberalization that has already taken place binding and irreversible.[88] This depends on the credibility of the implicit threat that such liberalization would be reversed in the future – the fact that many of the original protectionist policies are now seen as fundamentally pernicious to the developing countries themselves reduces the credibility of the threat considerably.

South–South trade liberalization

Despite the increasing activity with respect to South–South trading arrangements, and the implementation of the GSTP, South–South trade remains, as we have noted, a very small percentage of global trade. However, in the wake of structural domestic reforms, particularly those directed towards currency convertibility, this may change somewhat. (In the past, trade between developing countries rarely took place in convertible currency and therefore was less attractive than trade with developed countries.) Moreover a pattern is already discernible whereby the more developed LDCs, particularly the Asian NICs, relocate some of the production processes for their exports to lesser-developed LDCs with lower wages and less skilled workforces.

Regional trading arrangements between developed and developing countries

This option is most clearly reflected in the possibility of a North American Free Trade Agreement encompassing Canada, the United States and Mexico, with future extension to other Latin American LDCs. Unlike multilateral liberalization, liberalization through a regional arrangement may bring with it adjustment and technical assistance from the more developed members of the grouping. On the other hand, there is the possibility that the developed country or countries in the grouping will exercise overwhelming power and influence over the way in which the arrangement is implemented.

Multilateral liberalization: Developing countries and the Uruguay Round Result

The Uruguay Round provides a number of attractive trade-offs for (at least some) developing countries. On the one hand, many developing countries have been (particularly at the outset of the negotiations) resistant to American demands that their domestic policies with respect to regulation of service industries, foreign investment, and intellectual property become subjects of negotiation in the GATT. On the other hand, the prospect of substantial reduction in agricultural protection and the phasing out of a significant part of textiles and clothing protection offers the prospect of real gains for many developing countries. In previous chapters on trade in services, intellectual property and investment, we have discussed in greater detail the issues that these Uruguay Round agenda items raised for many LDCs. However, as we note in these chapters, the Uruguay Round Final Act reflects a number of compromises between developed country demands and the concerns of developing countries. For instance, in the case of TRIPs, compulsory licensing of patented inventions is permitted subject to certain conditions being met, including compensation to the patent holder. This reflects a significant compromise of the American view, shared to a large extent by the EU and Japan, that no compulsory licensing should be permitted within the 20-year period of required patent protection. In the case of TRIMs, the Final Act stops short of characterizing, for instance, technology transfer requirements as violations of trade rules, and leaves considerable scope for investment measures aimed at ensuring that foreign enterprises further the developing goals of host countries – again, the United States in particular, had pushed hard for a much more restrictive approach to investment measures.

While the general provisions of the Final Act thus reflect developing country concerns in a number of areas, the tendency has not been to grant developing countries broad exceptions to compliance with GATT rules. In some instances, developing countries may be given a somewhat longer period of time to phase in domestic compliance with the new rules, but the Uruguay Round result reflects, in large measure, a rejection of the view that developing countries should not be required to make reciprocal commitments to trade liberalization. The following brief survey of the Final Act canvasses many of the specific references to developing countries as well as issues such as the MFA of direct, specific relevance to developing country trade. It is intended to be illustrative, not exhaustive.

Understanding on the Balance of Payments Provisions of the GATT This Understanding, discussed in detail in Chapter 3, reflects concern by the United States and some other developed countries about insufficiently rigorous application of the conditions or criteria established in Articles XII and XVIII:B of the GATT to justify trade measures taken for balance-of-payments reasons. This mostly concerns, in contemporary circumstances, measures taken by developing countries.

Agreement on Agriculture The Agreement allows developing countries the flexibility to implement their commitments to reduction of protection and domestic support over a 10-year period (Article 15; the normal implementation period for developed countries is 6 years). The least-developed country Members are not required to make reduction commitments.

The existing system of agricultural support in developed countries is widely viewed as having depressed world prices for temperate zone agricultural commodities.[89] The effects on developing countries of the liberalization process set out in the Agreement on Agriculture are, therefore, mixed. As Winters suggests: 'Exporters of the temperate products whose prices are most affected by industrial liberalisation – for example, Argentina and Thailand – have strong and direct interests in the dismantling of protection; their revenues and income would increase significantly. On the other hand chronic food importers – for example, Bangladesh – would undoubtedly suffer'.[90] The fact that developed country liberalization of trade in agriculture may harm this latter group of countries is taken into account in the Decision on Measures Concerning the Possible Negative Effects of the Reform Programme on Least-Developed and Net Food-Importing Developing Countries.

The Decision commits Trade Ministers of GATT Members to review levels of food aid provided to developing countries to ensure that they are sufficient to meet the legitimate needs of developing countries during the reform programme (Article 3 (i)); to increase the proportion of food aid provided to developing countries as aid or on concessional terms (Article 3 (ii)); and to give 'full consideration' to developing country requests for technical assistance to develop their domestic agricultural sectors (Article 3 (iii)). As well, it is accepted that difficulties in financing imports of food on commercial terms may be a basis for assistance from international financial institutions (Article 5).

Agreement on Textiles and Clothing Of major importance to many developing countries will be the gradual liberalization of protection pursuant to the MFA, as provided for in the Uruguay Round Agreement on Textiles and Clothing. Under the Agreement, all restrictions provided for in bilateral agreements and under the MFA are to be notified to the Textiles Monitoring Body (TMB), and removed according to a graduated schedule. Thus upon entry into force of the Agreement, Members are to remove all MFA-based or bilaterally-agreed restrictions on products accounting for at least 16% of the total volume of their imports in 1990 in the following product groups: tops and yarns, fabrics, made-up textile products, and clothing (a detailed annex listing the individual product classes according to the Harmonized System of Classification is attached to the Agreement on Textiles and Clothing). With respect to restrictions that remain after this initial phase of liberalization, within three years, members must remove restrictions on products accounting for a further 17% of the total volume of imports in 1990 terms. Removal of restrictions on products accounting for at least another 18% of import volume is required after 7 years. All further restrictions are to be eliminated within 10 years of the entry into force of the Agreement. During the transition period, quotas are to be expanded on imports that have not yet been completely derestricted.

It is to be emphasized that the above liberalization commitments apply only to restrictions imposed based upon the MFA or bilateral agreements outside the GATT legal framework. In the case of many of the products in question, the bound MFN tariff rates remain quite high, and are in themselves unaffected by these liberalization commitments. Tariff reductions achieved in the Uruguay Round, while substantial, will nevertheless leave in place tariffs on many textile and apparel items that are much higher than the average for industrial products generally.

It should be noted, as well, that special safeguard provisions apply with respect to the liberalization of MFA-based and bilaterally-negotiated restrictions. A Member may take safeguard action when 'it is demonstrated that a particular product is being imported into its territory in such increased quantities as to cause serious damage, or actual threat thereof, to the domestic industry producing like and/or directly competitive products' (Article 6 (2)). It is specified that 'serious damage or actual threat thereof must demonstrably be caused by such increased quantities in total imports [of the product in question] and not by such other factors as technological changes or changes in consumer preference'. Safeguard protection is to be temporary (a maximum of three years with no right of renewal) and must in any event cease when, pursuant to the liberalization commitments discussed above, all past MFA-based or bilaterally-based restrictions are to have been removed from the product. The level of restraint under the safeguard 'shall be fixed at a level not lower than the actual level of exports or imports from the Member concerned during the twelve-month period terminating two months preceding' the request for safeguard protection (Article 6 (8)). An importing Member seeking to take safeguard action must first attempt a voluntary agreement with the exporting Member before acting unilaterally. However, any such voluntary agreement must be reported to the TMB, which is to determine its consistency with the safeguard provisions of the Agreement on Textiles and Clothing. Finally, safeguards are to be applied on a Member-by-Member basis, rather than to all Members exporting the product in question. Therefore, a determination must be made that serious damage or threat thereof is attributable to *each* Member to whom safeguard action is to be applied (Article 6 (4)).

Finally, Article 8 of the Agreement on Textiles and Clothing sets out the procedures for establishment and operation of the TMB. The TMB is to consist of a Chairman and ten Members. The membership 'shall be balanced and broadly representative of the Members and provide for rotation of its members at appropriate intervals' (Article 8 (1)). The membership of the TMB is to be selected by Members of the WTO designated by the Council for Trade in Goods to serve on the TMB, voting in their personal capacity and not as representatives of their governments. The TMB is charged with a range of monitoring functions, including a major review of the liberalization process, to be conducted after the end of each of the stages (i.e. 3, 6 and 10 years).

Agreement on Technical Barriers to Trade

The Agreement stipulates that developing country Members shall be provided, upon request, with technical assistance and advice from other Members in order to facilitate the process of standardizing technical requirements both through national standardizing bodies, and participation in international standardization exercises (Articles 11(2), 11(4), 11(5)). Such assistance and advice is to occur on 'mutually agreed terms and conditions'. Generally speaking, Article 12, although entitled Special and Differential Treatment of Developing Country Members, does not exempt developing countries from the obligations of the Technical Barriers Agreement with respect to harmonization, standardization, or mutual recognition of technical requirements. Rather, most of the provisions of Article 12 merely require that various special needs of developing countries be taken into account in the interpretation and implementation of the agreement. However, Article 12(4) seems to go further towards an actual modification (or at least, a qualification) of substantive obligations, in stipulating that 'developing country Members should not be expected to use international standards as a basis for their technical regulations or standards, including test methods, which are not appropriate to their development, financial and trade needs'.

Agreement on Implementation of Article VI of the GATT (Dumping)

Article 15 states that 'special regard' is to be given by developed country Members to the 'special situation' of developing countries when considering the imposition of antidumping duties. Members are required to explore the possibility of constructive remedies (i.e. price undertakings) before imposing duties where these would 'affect the essential interests of developing country members'. This provision is essentially identical to Article 13 of the Tokyo Round Dumping Code.

Agreement on Subsidies and Countervailing Measures

The ban on export subsidies in Article 3(1)(a) in Article 3 does not apply to least-developed country Members, and will apply to other developing country Members only after a transition period of 8 years (Article 27(1)). The ban on subsidies 'contingent ... upon the use of domestic over imported goods' shall not apply to developed countries in general for 5 years and to the less-developed countries for 8 years (Article 27(2)). However, once a developing country has achieved 'export competitiveness' in a given product, it is required to phase out export subsidies over a period of two years (Article 27(4)), unless it is one of a listed group of least-developed countries, in which case the phase-out period is extended to 8 years (Article 27(4)). 'Export competitiveness' is deemed to have been achieved where the exports of the developing country in question have reached at least 3.25% of world trade for two consecutive years (Article 27(5)). Finally, the Agreement on Subsidies and Countervailing Measures contains special *de minimis* exemptions from countervailability for developing countries. Thus a countervailing duty investigation is to be terminated when it is determined that a subsidy accounts for less than 2% of value on a per-unit basis or where the *volume* of subsidized imports accounts for less than 4% of the total imports of like products (unless imports of like products from developing countries, taken together, amount to more than 9% of total imports of like products into the importing country) (Article 27 (9)).

Understanding on Rules and Procedures Governing the Settlement of Disputes

The Dispute Settlement Understanding contains several provisions that arguably seek to address long-standing complaints that developing countries have been marginalized or disadvantaged in the GATT dispute settlement process. Article 8(2) includes 'a sufficiently diverse background' as one of the criteria for composition of dispute panels, and – much more specifically – Article 8(10) stipulates that 'when a dispute is between a developing country Member and a developed country Member the panel shall, if the developing country Member so requests, include at least one panellist from a developing country Member'. Within the general time limits established by the Dispute Settlement Understanding, a panel examining a complaint against a developing country Member is to 'accord sufficient time for the developing country Member to prepare and present its argumentation' (Article 12(10)). Furthermore, where a developing country Member is Party to a dispute, the panel must explicitly address in its report the applicability of any special GATT provisions with respect to developing countries, where these provisions have been invoked by the developing country Member that is a Party to the dispute (Article 12(10)).

In the case of least-developed country Members, particular consideration is to be given to the 'special situation' of these Members throughout the dispute settlement process. Members are required to 'exercise due restraint' in making complaints against least-developed country members under the WTO dispute settlement procedures. A special role is contemplated for the Director-General of the WTO or the Chairman of the Dispute Settlement Body (DSB) with respect to facilitating consultations in the event of a dispute involving a least-developed country member (Article 24(1), 24(2)). Finally, the Secretariat of the WTO is charged with the provision of legal advice and assistance to developing country members with respect to dispute settlement (Article 27(2)).

Decision on Measures in Favour of Least-developed Countries

The Decision reflects what remains of the non-reciprocal approach to trade liberalization with developing countries, applied *only* to the least developed countries 'as long as they remain in that category'. With respect to specific commitments and concessions as opposed to compliance with the general rules of the Final Act and its various agreements, least-developed country members will 'only be required to undertake commitments and concessions to the extent consistent with their individual development, financial and trade needs, or their administrative and institutional capabilities' (Article 1). Thus MFN tariff and non-tariff concessions 'on products of export interest to the least-developed countries may be implemented autonomously, in advance and without staging' – i.e. without being tied to reciprocal concessions from these countries.

The above survey of the provisions of the Final Act and related Agreements and Decisions that apply to developing countries clearly suggests that the overall approach is one of full integration of all but the least-developed countries into the GATT/WTO, with some special allowance made for special difficulties that developed countries may experience with respect to full integration, e.g. through longer phase-in periods for compliance with GATT/WTO obligations. Even with respect to the least-developed countries, 'special and differential treatment' falls far short of outright exemption from the main general rules of the GATT/WTO. Overall, the Uruguay Round outcome represents a wager by developing countries in favour of an approach to trade and development premised upon openness and export-led growth. Whether this wager will be won depends significantly on the will of developed countries to offer tariff concession on products of export interest to developing countries. It also depends on the willingness to prevent (sometimes legitimate) concerns about 'fair trade' – e.g. labour and environmental standards – from releasing a new wave of protectionism against developing countries.[91]

CONCLUSION

The empirical evidence to date suggests that developing countries with outward-oriented policies for development and growth, including those that have recently introduced liberalizing reforms, will continue to experience strong growth in exports and more generally in GDP.[92] These are, however, not the only criteria for success in development – in a number of LDCs, political and social structures will be such that the growth in question will not be directly reflected in a better life for the population at large.[93] It is our general view that economic liberalism does help to advance the long-term process of political liberalization and democratization. But although this has been an article of faith for free traders from Montesquieu to Milton Friedman, there is a pressing need for important theoretical work on the interaction between liberal economic and political reforms[94] – especially in light of the fact that some of the most economically successful LDCs, including those that have undertaken liberal economic reform, remain authoritarian regimes and show few signs of intensive movement towards political liberty.

Economic prospects for many of the least developed countries continue to look bleak, especially in Africa, where living standards are generally expected to further decline in the coming years.[95] Widespread social and political instability, including civil and foreign wars, as well as natural disasters such as droughts, continue to plague a large number of these nations. In these circumstances, the kinds of structures required to initiate export-led growth remain distant. But if there is a worldwide economic recovery in the next decade, and the global system of trade and finance remains open, there is at least the hope that we will collectively regain the generosity and the dedication necessary to address the plight of the poorest countries of all.

13

TRADE AND THE ENVIRONMENT

INTRODUCTION

In the last two decades, we have witnessed a remarkable increase in support for environmentalism among citizens of liberal democratic regimes throughout the world. Environmentalism is a very broad concept, extending from concern about traditional forms of pollution, such as emissions of dangerous substances into the air and the water, to the protection of endangered species and the aesthetic purity and integrity of natural landscapes. It has been increasingly recognized that environmental problems cross national boundaries, and that many of the most pressing challenges cannot be addressed adequately without international cooperation and international rules – saving the world's ozone layer from further damage is an obvious and important example.

The relationship between international trade and the environment has only recently attained a prominent place on the trade agenda, although it has been a concern of environmentalists for some time. Much of the debate on this issue is highly emotive and polarized. Often, environmentalists tend to identify liberal trade with environmentally-destructive unrestrained economic growth. Many free traders, on the other hand, are largely dismissive of the environmentalists' concerns as either disguised protectionism or irrational fanaticism.[1]

The links between trade and environment are complex and multi-faceted. In this chapter, we attempt to clearly separate and define the issues, examine existing international trade law that affects environmental concerns, and explore prospects for reform.

In our view there are several crucial distinctions that must be made in order to clarify and better focus the debate. The first is between the use of trade restrictions to protect the domestic environment of the importing state and the use of such restrictions as a response to the environmental policies of *other* states. It is this second category of environmentally-based trade restrictions that is the most controversial and problematic and – as most clearly illustrated by the now notorious *Tuna/Dolphin* GATT decision – that does not fit well

331

within the existing legal framework for international trade. However, within this second category, several further distinctions must be drawn. Among the most important is between environmental and competitiveness aims of environmentally-based trade restrictions.

Some international environmental treaties, such as the Convention on International Traffic in Endangered Species (CITES), use control of trade as a direct means of achieving an environmental purpose. Even where there is no such direct relationship between trade restrictions and environmental regulation, environmentalists may view trade restrictions as appropriate *sanctions* for non-compliance with international environmental standards, as means of imposing such standards where there are none, or a response to the failure of particular nations to engage in negotiations to develop such standards. Whether trade measures are an appropriate or effective means of achieving these ends raises a wide variety of normative and empirical issues.

Environmentalists, in addition to this concern about international standards, are also concerned about the so-called 'race to the bottom' – the possibility that, in response to the competitive advantage that is gained from lower environmental standards in some industries, a greater share of jobs and trade in those industries will shift to countries with lower domestic environmental standards. This, it is feared, will put downward pressure on environmental standards in countries that presently have higher levels of protection. Here, environmentalists are not necessarily seeking adoption by all countries of the same domestic environmental standards but are simply concerned that such standards continue to be sustainable in countries that have already decided to adopt them. Although some free traders are largely dismissive of the problem posed by the 'race to the bottom', our own view is that this problem is real but that there will usually be a better alternative response to increased competitive pressures than the lowering of environmental standards – including better instrument choices in environmental regulation that achieve the same or improved results while imposing lower costs on industrial production, investment in technologies that promise to reduce the cost of complying with higher environmental standards, and adoption of adjustment and exit-oriented measures that shift resources from sectors where comparative advantage continues to depend on lower environmental standards to those where it does not.

By contrast with environmentalists, 'fair traders' are concerned with the impact on trade, not on the environment as such, of other countries' lower environmental standards. They consider it 'unfair' that a country can gain an advantage in trade from lower environmental standards. Unlike the claims of environmentalists, we view these claims of fair traders with great scepticism. First of all, the claims implicitly assume that the importing state's environmental standards are optimal from both a domestic and a global perspective. But absent some defensible international norm or benchmark for environmental standards, this assumption merely reflects the bias of the importing country towards its own regulatory approach. Second, higher environmental standards may actually *confer* a competitive advantage in some sectors, where these standards may create incentives for the development of environmental technologies that can then be exported to other countries as their demand for environmental protection increases. Third, environmental standards and costs must be distinguished. 'Fair traders' are really concerned with differential costs to industry of environmental standards, yet even if standards *were* harmonized, different countries for technological, climatic, other geographical and demographic reasons, could still face vastly different costs of meeting these harmonized standards. Here the arguments of fair traders exhibit the same kind of incoherence that is evident with respect to countervailing duty law, which we have discussed at length in Chapter 6. Briefly, for unfairness to have a normatively defensible meaning it must entail the violation of some neutral, objective baseline for the balance of benefits and burdens that governments create for industries.

In this chapter, we begin by reviewing the existing trade law and jurisprudence that affects environmentally-based trade measures. We pay particular attention to jurisprudence of the GATT and the FTA that has applied a number of key legal norms and principles of international law in environmentally-related contexts. As well, we consider the environmental provisions of the NAFTA, including the environmental side-agreement.[2] Finally, along the lines sketched above, we address the debate over the place of environmentally-related trade measures in the evolving framework of international trade law *and* international environmental law.

THE GATT

Border Measures and National Treatment with respect to Internal Measures

The General Agreement (especially Articles I, II, and XI) prohibits border restrictions on the exportation and importation of goods, subject to a narrow range of exceptions. In addition, the GATT prohibits certain internal measures that discriminate against foreign imports (Article III). Clearly, the vast majority of domestic environmental policies fall into neither of these categories, and hence no potential or real conflict with the GATT is likely to emerge except in a relatively small number of cases.[3] Nevertheless, the number and importance of these cases is growing as many Contracting Parties place increasing priority on protection of the environment. In the case of the FTA, the relevant provisions are closely similar or identical to those of the GATT, including the provisions on National Treatment with respect to trade in goods and the prohibition of quantitative restrictions.

Article XX: A GATT Environmental Charter?

Given that many of the border measures connected with environmental goals are on their face violations of Article XI, much of the jurisprudence has centred on whether such measures can be saved by virtue of any of the exceptions listed in Article XX of the GATT. Article XX exempts certain classes of measures from the strictures of other GATT articles, provided that 'such measures are not applied in a manner which would constitute a means of arbitrary or unjustifiable discrimination between countries where the same conditions prevail, or a disguised restriction on international trade, . .'. Among the classes of measures listed are those 'necessary to protect human, animal or plant life or health' (XX (b)); and 'relating to the conservation of exhaustible natural resources if such measures are made effective in conjunction with restrictions on domestic production or consumption'(XX (g)).

The word 'environment' is not mentioned explicitly in either paragraph. Commentators are divided on whether, nevertheless, these provisions were intended by the drafters to apply to the environment in the broadest sense (including moral and aesthetic concerns) or, alternatively, to a much narrower range of policy concerns. Shrybman, for instance, argues for the latter point of view.[4] It is possible to understand Article XX (b), for example, as intended to cover measures designed either to protect public health against diseases (e.g. from contaminated meat) or to protect animal or health life for commercial reasons (e.g. the economic consequences of crop pestilences). With respect to Article XX (g), its purpose might be to allow a country to protect 'exhaustible natural resources' such as minerals or petroleum that are considered as essential to its economic well-being. In a detailed analysis of the negotiations that produced the General Agreement, Charnovitz has shown, however, that the drafters had at least conservation goals in mind, as well as economic or public health and safety concerns. He argues that the drafters were aware of existing international conventions on conservation, and probably did not include a more explicit environmental exemption precisely because they thought that Articles XX(b) and (g) would suffice for this purpose.[5]

Throughout much of the history of the GATT, the main issues raised by Article XX concerned the potential for protectionism to be disguised as measures taken for health and other goals stated in the Article. For example, phytosanitary measures with respect to livestock were often cited as indirect protectionist measures, as well as other technical barriers such as idiosyncratic product standards or inspection requirements. The explicit language of Article XX presupposes that it is possible to detect instances where measures are in fact 'disguised restrictions on trade'. In practice this has proven far from straightforward in the presence of conflicting scientific evidence as to the non-protectionist justification of particular measures, and also due to the fact that much of the claimed protectionism might be embedded in the manner in which a measure that did have a genuine non-protectionist basis was administered. It is, in significant part, these kinds of difficulties that led to the negotiation of the Tokyo Round Agreement on Technical Barriers to Trade.

The Agreement on Technical Barriers to Trade attempted to address the task of distinguishing genuine non-protectionist measures from disguised trade protection through a multi-faceted approach. First of all, the Parties agreed to use accepted international standards rather than idiosyncratic national ones, where this was possible. Second, Parties deviating from these international standards could be required to demonstrate that the resulting barriers did not constitute 'an unnecessary obstacle to trade'. Significantly, the Agreement on Technical Barriers to Trade permits 'technical regulations and standards' which are 'for the protection of human health or safety, animal or plant life or health or the environment' (Article 2(2)). Here the addition of 'the environment' to language that otherwise duplicates the wording of Article XX(b), may suggest an explicit acknowledgement that the Article XX exemptions are to be interpreted broadly to include measures taken for environmental purposes.[6]

The Jurisprudence of the GATT (including interpretation of GATT provisions by Canada–USA FTA Panels)

In several GATT and FTA Panel decisions during the 1980s, the consistency of environmental measures with Articles III and XI of the GATT was addressed, as well as the application of Article XX to the environment.

The application of Article XX to trade restricting measures to protect the restricting country's own environment was addressed in the *Herring and Salmon* case.[7] Here, the United States was the complainant, arguing that Canadian requirements that salmon and herring caught in Canadian waters be processed in Canada before export violated Article XI of the GATT. Among Canada's arguments in response was that these restrictions were an integral part of its overall scheme for management of West Coast fisheries resources, and therefore 'related to' the 'conservation of exhaustible natural resources' within the meaning of Article XX (g).[8] According to Canada, the export restrictions functioned in the following two ways to support its conservation scheme. First of all, the vulnerability of the species required an extremely accurate catch control system, and the only way of having precise data on the catch was to limit its destination to Canadian fish plants, which were subject to rigorous reporting requirements. Second, because of the cyclical nature of the catch for both species, making the unprocessed fish available exclusively to Canadian plants was the only means of balancing the conservation objective with the goal of sustaining a viable domestic fish processing industry. The implication of this latter claim was that unless

Canadian fish plants were assured of the entire Canadian catch, the Canadian government would be faced with the choice of either accepting the demise of the industry or permitting overfishing when the catch was good.

The United States replied that the Canadian requirements were 'neither necessary nor particularly useful' for the purpose of ensuring an accurate estimate of the Canadian catch, since in the case where unprocessed fish was exported to the United States, 'United States authorities routinely provided to Canada, upon request and for use in the Canadian conservation programme, full data on United States landings of unprocessed fish'.[9] The United States also objected to the broad view of 'conservation' suggested by the notion that conservation measures included measures that balanced conservation goals with socio-economic concerns such as the preservation of a domestic processing industry – in any case, Canada's domestic processing industry would have access to fish imports to make up any shortfall resulting from the combined impact of conservation measures and the cyclical nature of the industry.

Finally, the United States presented evidence that the Canadian government itself had described the export ban as a means of protecting Canadian jobs in its own official literature, and therefore that the measure should be viewed as a disguised restriction on trade.

The GATT Panel interpreted the Article XX (g) requirement that measures be 'related to' conservation of exhaustible natural resources as meaning 'primarily aimed at' such conservation,[10] but it viewed this as weaker than the requirement of 'necessity' imposed by Article XX (b). Among the main factors that led the panel to find that the Canadian export ban was not 'primarily aimed' at conservation was that accurate statistical data could be collected without such a ban, as was done for other species that were subject to conservation measures but whose export in an unprocessed state was not banned. The Panel thus adopted an objective test to determine primary intent, i.e. instead of examining the legislative history of the measure to determine whether its primary aim was protection of the domestic Canadian processing industry, it considered whether other means less restrictive of trade could equally serve the stated conservation purpose.

An important clarification of the meaning of 'necessary' in Article XX (b) occurred in the non-environmental *Thai Cigarette* case.[11] In that case, the United States challenged a ban on imports of cigarettes into Thailand as a violation of Article XI of the GATT. Thailand defended the ban, under Article XX (b), as 'necessary' for the protection of public health. While no comparable ban existed on domestic Thai cigarettes, the Thai Government claimed that American imports were more likely to induce women and young persons to take up smoking, because of sophisticated advertising directed at these groups. Thailand also argued that American cigarettes were somehow more addictive or more likely to be consumed in larger quantities than comparable Thai cigarettes, due to their chemical composition (this claim was largely unsupported, however, by scientific evidence). The Panel ruled that an import ban would only be 'necessary' for public health reasons, within the meaning of Article XX (b) if alternative non-trade restricting measures could not be used to achieve the public health objectives in question. The Panel considered that restrictions or bans on advertising and labelling and content requirements that applied on a non-discriminatory basis to both domestic cigarettes and imports would be satisfactory alternatives to an import ban, and therefore the ban could not be justified under Article XX (b) as 'necessary' for reasons of public health. In coming to this decision, the Panel simply ignored the possibility that the alternative measures might involve high regulatory and compliance costs, or might be impracticable to implement effectively in a developing country.

In the *Salmon and Herring Landing Requirements*[12] case, an FTA Panel considered the scope of the Article XX (g) exception with respect to measures 'primarily aimed at conservation of an exhaustible natural resource'. In that case, the United States challenged provisions of a Canadian law that required that salmon and herring caught on Canada's West Coast be landed and unloaded in Canada before processing. The landing requirement was imposed after Canada's domestic *processing* requirement had been found in violation of Article XI by a GATT Panel, as discussed above.[13] Unlike the measure impugned in the earlier case, the landing requirement did not explicitly prohibit or restrict exports of the unprocessed fish. Nevertheless, its *effect* was to disadvantage American processors, because in the case of fish destined to US processing plants, they would have to be both landed and unloaded in Canada (due to the law) and then repacked, and unloaded again in the United States before processing. The United States claimed that the measure was, in effect, a restriction on 'exportation or sale for export' (i.e. of unprocessed Canadian fish to the United States) and therefore in violation of Article XI of the GATT. Canada argued that even if the landing requirements were in violation of Article XI, the Article XX (g) exception applied, because landing of the fish was necessary for accurate monitoring of the catch pursuant to Canadian conservation programmes. The Panel found that other means less restrictive of trade existed to achieve Canada's objectives of monitoring and compliance with its conservation schemes, including co-operation with US authorities and on-board inspection of catches and cargo, and that (at least implicitly) Canada had adopted more restrictive means for protectionist reasons. The Panel was also prepared to accept that landing of part of the catch might be necessary for sampling in order to achieve Canadian monitoring and compliance objectives, but considered that a requirement that 100% of the catch be landed went farther than was reasonably necessary for these purposes. In consequence, conservation could not be considered the 'primary purpose' of the landing requirements and therefore Article XX (g) did not apply.

Taken together, the *Thai Cigarette* GATT Panel Decision and the *Salmon and Herring Landing Requirements* FTA Panel Decision point to a least-restrictive means test as the appropriate standard of justification for trade-restricting measures under *both* Article XX (b) *and* Article XX (g). This is a very rigorous kind of test that may result in measures taken for genuinely environmental purposes being nevertheless found to violate the GATT (even though on the particular facts of the *Salmon Herring and Landing Requirement* case the Panel had good reason to suspect protectionist motivations given the prior challenged regulation). The strong implication is that avoidance of trade-restricting impacts must be a paramount consideration in domestic choices between alternative instruments of environmental protection.

One justification for such a rigorous test is, of course, that it is needed to deter Contracting Parties from resorting to environmental pretexts for protectionist measures. Arguably, weeding out disguised protection through an objective test such as least-restrictve means is, in a number of respects, preferable to an inquiry into the motivation or subjective intent behind a policy measure for which an environmental exemption is being claimed. Such an inquiry could put a dispute settlement panel in the uncomfortable position of questioning the sincerity or genuineness of a Party's claims, a position at odds with the diplomatic dimension of interstate dispute settlement. Moreover, in many societies, environmental policy measures (like most other policies) are often the result of complex coalitions of legislators and voters, who may support a measure out of widely varying interests or motivations. However strong the intrinsic environmentalist justification for a trade measure, it will undoubtedly *also* attract the support of lobbies demanding trade protection. Demanding purity of intent would thus seem unduly restrictive of measures that have real environmental justifications.

A least-restrictive means test may thus be an attractive alternative to intent- or motivation-based inquiries, and need not necessarily be premised on the privileging of trade liberalization over environmental objectives. Moreover, the alternative of a looser or more flexible balancing or proportionality test, which weighs the environmental gains against the harm to trade, has its own disadvantages, even from an environmentalist perspective. The first is that it invites a cost-benefit analysis whereby the panel is required to weigh injury to trade against the social value or importance of a given environmental objective or result. There are important concerns about institutional and democratic legitimacy surrounding a trade panel second-guessing a country's own judgement about the social value or importance of a particular environmental goal. Moreover, it is far from clear that the kind of cost-benefit analysis a panel would undertake in this regard would do justice to the full range of moral and aesthetic arguments for environmental protection. A least-restrictive means approach, precisely through its rigorous focus on *means*, has the advantage of reconciling the important objective of deterring disguised protectionism with a high level of deference to domestic choices about the ends of environmental policy.

This being said, the *application* of the least-restrictive means test should, arguably reflect sensitivity to the fact that environmental policymakers have limited resources, and often operate under broad background constraints imposed by the political and legal system in their country. The availability of a hypothetically less restrictive means of achieving the same goals should not necessarily mean that the measures under scrutiny fail the least-restrictive means test. The panel should be open to arguments that the hypothetical alternative is not truly available at a reasonable cost to the Contracting Party that has enacted the trade-restricting environmental measure. For instance, in some countries with weakly developed regulatory and legal systems, border controls may be among the few effective ways of addressing some environmental hazards, even if they seem a rather blunt or crude instrument from the perspective of 'state of the art' regulatory theory and practice. To return to the *Thai Cigarette* case, in the abstract, it would have undoubtedly been more rational for the Thai Government to have adopted some of the alternative, less trade-restricting means suggested by the panel, such as consumer warnings, public information campaigns, and so forth. But this simply ignores the issue of whether the kinds of sophisticated techniques of persuasion and psychological manipulation employed by Western cigarette manufacturers could be matched, at reasonable cost (or any cost), by the informational resources available to a developing country government. In the environmental area, a more contextually sensitive application of the least-restrictive means test would arguably require panels to draw upon evidence from the broader environmental policy community as to the available regulatory alternatives and their strengths and limitations in a given set of circumstances. Here again, the *Thai Cigarette* decision sets a bad precedent – the panel simply chose to ignore a report of the World Health Organization suggesting that the Thai Government's approach was a reasonable instrument choice under the circumstances. In the concluding part of this chapter, we shall have more to say about measures that may appropriately broaden the kind of inquiry that panels undertake in applying the least-restrictive means test, and provide access to a wider range of perspectives on environmental regulation.

National treatment and the relationship of Article III to Article XI

A vexing issue, on which the GATT jurisprudence is far from clear, is how to distinguish between border bans that are part of an internal regulatory scheme aimed at both domestic and imported products (permitted by GATT subject only to the Article III National Treatment obligation) and prohibitions or restrictions on imports within the meaning of Article XI (banned by GATT unless strictly justified under Article XX).

In the *Lobster*[14] case, a Canada–US FTA Panel considered whether application of a domestic US minimum size requirement to imports of Canadian lobster should be considered as an Article XI prohibition on imports (i.e. the effect of the measure being the exclusion of all Canadian lobsters beneath a certain size) or as part of an internal regulatory scheme within the meaning of Article III.

The minimum size requirement, as it applied to American lobster, was unquestionably a reasonable conservation measure: the intent was to conserve the stock by ensuring that young lobster would not be taken before they could breed. However, because Canada has colder waters, its mature lobster are in general of smaller size, and accordingly Canada had a lower minimum size requirement, which arguably served in the Canadian context the conservation objective as well as did the higher American size requirement in the US context.

The evidence suggests that imposition of the higher minimum size requirement on imports of Canadian lobster was largely in response to complaints by American fishermen that the domestic US requirement put them at a competitive disadvantage with Canadian fishermen. In its argument to the Panel, however, the US Government attempted to justify the application of its minimum-size requirement to Canadian lobster as necessary to the enforcement of the requirement with respect to American lobster. Since lobsters do not carry passports, it would be costly to determine whether a given lobster was Canadian or American once it had entered the stream of commerce. This difficulty was entirely obviated through application of the size requirement to *all* lobster in the market, whether Canadian or American.

In considering whether to view the extension of the size requirement to Canadian lobster as the application at the border of an internal US regulation, or as a prohibition or restriction on imports within the meaning of Article XI, the majority Panel judgment reviewed a variety of GATT Panel decisions. The majority rejected the view that trade-restricting impacts should be the decisive consideration in classifying a measure as an Article XI measure. This seems in direct contradiction with another FTA Panel's ruling in the *Salmon and Herring Landing Requirement* case, where (as discussed above) the Panel found that the measure in question, while not taking the legal form of a prohibition or restriction on exports or sale for export, had this effect, and should therefore be considered a *prima facie* violation of Article XI.[15] Nor did the *Lobster* Panel consider it of paramount importance whether the measure was to be enforced at the border by customs officials or through internal inspections once the product entered the domestic stream of commerce. Instead, the Panel's majority decision seems to rest upon its acceptance of the United States's position that the import ban was genuinely an integral part of an internal regulatory regime applicable to both foreign and domestic product. As pointed out in the vigorous dissenting judgment by one expert on the Panel, this was precisely how Canada had characterized its landing requirement measure in the *Salmon and Herring Landing Requirement* case, i.e. as connected to the monitoring requirements of its internal conservation regime, and yet in *Salmon and Herring Landing Requirement* the measures were nevertheless categorized as Article XI restrictions or prohibitions on exports.[16]

Of course, even where the measures in question are classified as internal regulations under Article III, complex issues may be implicated in determining whether in fact foreign products are being treated equally. A particularly difficult issue is whether only facially discriminatory measures should be considered in violation of Article III, or whether measures with a 'disparate impact' on foreign producers also, in some circumstances, violate the National Treatment obligation. For instance, a country may impose on both domestic products and imports a requirement of environmentally-safe (e.g. biodegradable) packaging, in circumstances where most domestic producers are already using such packaging. Foreign producers, unlike their domestic equivalents, would be required at considerable cost to change packaging methods and materials in order to sell their goods within one particular foreign market. The more specific and idiosyncratic the requirements, the more likely that any foreign producer who does not possess a large market share in the country concerned will simply find that the costs of adapting the product are prohibitive, and will effectively be excluded from the market. Situations of this kind have led to considerable trade frictions within the European Union, despite the existence of institutional mechanisms for harmonization of national environmental standards.

The issue was addressed somewhat indirectly by a GATT Panel considering the application of Article III to a variety of measures affecting the importation of beer into several Canadian provinces.[17] Among these measures was a tax on beer containers applied to both domestic and imported beer. However, the tax was refundable where a system of collection of the containers for re-bottling and recycling was used. Such a system was readily available to domestic beer producers, as they were permitted to sell their beer through privately owned retail stores that had such a system in place. Imported beer, by contrast, could only be sold at provincial monopoly liquor outlets where no such system for return of containers was in place. As a result, the only way a foreign producer could comply with the conditions for refund of the tax was to set up its own independent system for collection, re-bottling and recycling of beer containers, which would involve considerable if not prohibitive expense. Since the tax applied equally on its face to both domestic and imported beer, the United States argument amounted to a claim that disparate impact of a facially neutral internal measure could constitute a violation of Article III.

The Panel found that the container tax as it applied to imported beer did not violate Article III. In significant part, its reasoning was that the disparate impact in question was really due to another, *explicitly* discriminatory practice that was in itself a violation of Article III, i.e. the effective prohibition of foreign beer producers from sale of their beer through private retail outlets.[18] At a minimum, this finding may be interpreted to mean that a mere disparate impact on imports does not render facially neutral internal environmental measures in contravention of the GATT.

Several GATT Panel decisions have addressed the consistency under the General Agreement of trade measures that address environmental concerns extending beyond the trade restricting country's own territorial boundaries.

The *Superfund* case concerned US taxes on imports of certain petroleum and chemical products, the revenues from which were to go to a fund dedicated to environmental protection purposes.[19] In the case of petroleum products, an excise tax for environmental purposes was applied to both domestic and foreign petroleum. The tax on imports was, however, higher than that on domestic products (11.7 cents as opposed to 8.2 cents per barrel). The United States gave no justification for this discrimination, other than that there was no 'nullification and impairment' of a GATT concession because the difference was so small as not to create a competitive disadvantage for foreign suppliers. The Panel had little difficulty concluding that there was nevertheless a *prima facie* nullification and impairment, and that the discriminatory tax violated the National Treatment obligation of Article III.

The Panel treated quite differently, however, the tax on imported chemicals. The United States argued that this tax was no greater than the tax that would be levied on similar substances when used by American producers to make the same chemicals. Therefore, the USA claimed, the tax met the conditions for an exemption from the National Treatment obligation in Article II:2 (a), being 'equivalent to an internal tax . . . in respect of an article from which the imported product has been manufactured in whole or in part'.

The Panel accepted this claim despite the complainants' objection that the environmental harm from the use of the substances in question in the production of *imported* chemicals occurred not in the United States but in the jurisdiction of manufacture, and thus that the tax represented a United States tax on pollution that was occurring outside its borders. The Panel responded to this objection by stating that the General Agreement provisions on tax adjustment 'do not distinguish between taxes for different policy purposes'.[20] This outcome suggests that one clear means by which Contracting Parties can sanction environmentally harmful conduct outside their borders is through environmental taxes that apply to imported products – provided, of course, that equivalent taxes also apply domestically.

Measures found to be export or import restrictions within the meaning of Article XI have received much stricter scrutiny from GATT Panels than was the case with the environmental tax in the *Superfund* case. The 1979

Canadian Tuna case concerned an American import ban on Canadian tuna, imposed under the US Fishery Conservation and Management Act. The ban followed the seizure by Canadian authorities of 19 US fishing boats within the Canadian 200 mile territorial limit. The United States argued that, although in violation of Article XI of the GATT, the tuna ban represented an essential element of the American approach to the conservation of the species. The interests of conservation required that Canada stop unilaterally enforcing its territorial limit against American fishermen and instead negotiate with the United States jointly-agreed catch limits on this essentially shared fisheries resource: 'it was fruitless [according to the American representative] for one coastal state to limit the catch when a school of tuna was in its waters, if the school would be overfished in another State's waters or the high seas'.[21] The tuna ban was a sanction aimed at inducing Canada to end its unilateral actions against American fishermen and instead to accept a co-operative approach to management of the resource, and therefore could be justified on the basis of Article XX (g) as 'related to the conservation of an exhaustible natural resource'. In reply, Canada claimed that the American action was a direct retaliation for the act of seizure and not a response to more general concerns about Canadian non-acceptance of US approaches to management of tuna stocks. The United States did not deny this, but argued that the wording 'related to' in Article XX (g) did not require conservation objectives to be the sole or even primary cause of the measure in question.[22] A final issue related to the requirement of Article XX (g) that the measures in question be 'made effective in conjunction with domestic restrictions on consumption and production'. Although the United States had domestic production quotas with respect to tuna, these did not apply to at least one of the specific species whose importation from Canada had been banned (i.e. albacore tuna).

In its decision, the Panel began by considering an additional argument, i.e. that the import ban might be justified under Article XI:2, which permits quantitative restrictions where necessary to sustain a system of domestic supply management for primary products (the intent of this provision was arguably to exempt from GATT strictures the border measures required to enforce price and quantity restrictions in domestic agricultural marketing schemes).[23]

The Panel rejected the application of Article XI:2 on two largely technical grounds: (1) domestic restrictions were not consistently in force with respect to species covered by the import ban; (b) the language of Article XI:2(c) was explicitly limited to 'restrictions' on imports and therefore this subparagraph could not be used as a basis for a total ban.

With respect to Article XX (g), the Panel found that this exception did not apply, also for the rather narrow, technical reason that some species of tuna covered by the import ban were not covered by the domestic US restrictions on production. The Panel sidestepped entirely the two extremely fundamental jurisprudential issues raised by the case: first, in what circumstances can unilateral action aimed at inducing another state to accept one's own approach to management of a joint resource be considered a GATT-consistent conservation measure; and second, how closely connected to the purpose of conservation the specific measure adopted must be for Article XX (g) to apply. (The Panel did note that inasmuch as the American action was solely a retaliation for the seizure of American ships, it would not be covered by Article XX, but failed to comment on the application of this observation to the facts at hand.) Moreover, the Panel did find that the import ban on Canadian tuna was not a 'disguised restriction on international trade' within the meaning of Article XX, because it 'had been taken as a trade measure and publicly announced as such'.[24] This interpretation of 'disguised restriction' clearly narrows its significance – a measure that is on its face a trade restriction cannot be considered a 'disguised restriction on international trade' where its conservation purpose is colourable. Instead 'disguised restrictions' would appear to be non-trade measures (perhaps discriminatory internal measures that would otherwise be violations of the Article III National Treatment obligation), whose conservation purpose is colourable. This narrow view of the meaning of 'disguised restriction' can perhaps be justified in the case of XX (g) on the grounds that XX (g) has its own internal test that in effect screens out colourable measures, i.e. whether the measures in question are accompanied by parallel domestic restrictions.

In the *Tuna/Dolphin* case,[25] Mexico complained that an American embargo of its tuna exports violated, *inter alia*, Article XI of the GATT. The embargo was imposed because Mexico had failed to satisfy US authorities that its tuna was caught in a manner that did not risk the destruction of dolphins. The United States argued that because its restrictions on the manner in which tuna was caught applied to American tuna as well, the import ban should be treated as the enforcement of 'laws, regulations and requirements affecting (the) internal sale, offering for sale, purchase, transportation, distribution or use' of imported products within the meaning of Article III, and not as quantitative trade restrictions. Here, the United States relied specifically on an Interpretive Note annexed to Article III, which states that 'any internal law, regulation or requirement of the kind referred to in [Article III:1] which applies to an imported product and the like domestic product and is collected or enforced in the case of the imported product at the time or point of importation' nevertheless is to be treated as an internal measure within the meaning of Article III:1. As discussed earlier in this chapter, the view of Article III suggested by this Interpretative Note has led to considerable disagreement on whether a given measure should be classified as a restriction or prohibition on imports and exports within the meaning of Article XI, or as an internal measure merely enforced through a border ban (in which case the Article III National Treatment obligation alone would apply).

Here, the Panel rejected the view that Article III, rather than Article XI was applicable, on the grounds that what was being regulated was not the actual imported product (tuna) but the manner in which it had been produced, and that Article III concerned measures that applied to and affected the nature of products themselves. The Panel suggested: 'Regulations governing the taking of dolphins incidental to the taking of tuna could not possibly affect tuna as a product'.[26] The Panel thus went on to characterize the import ban as a quantitative restriction within the meaning of Article XI, the issue thus becoming whether either Article XX (b) or Article XX (g) could apply to exempt the ban from Article XI strictures.

With respect to Article XX (b), the Panel simply excluded the possibility that it could apply to the protection of animal life outside the jurisdiction of the Contracting Party taking the measure. Two grounds were provided for this interpretation, neither of which has any textual basis in the General Agreement itself. The first was that the drafting history of Article XX (b) suggested that the essential purpose was to permit sanitary measures to protect human animal and plant health in the importing country. The second ground was that if the broader interpretation of Article XX (b) were accepted,

> each contracting party could unilaterally determine the life or health protection policies from which other contracting parties could not deviate without jeopardizing their legal rights under the General Agreement. The General Agreement would then no longer constitute a multilateral framework for trade among all contracting parties but would provide legal security only in respect of trade between a limited number of contracting parties with identical internal regulations.[27]

Although this finding itself sufficed to make Article XX (b) inapplicable to the US import ban, the Panel went out of its way to further narrow the Article's scope. The Panel claimed that the language of 'necessity' in Article XX (b) meant the United States would have to show that it had exhausted all options less restrictive of trade before resorting to import restrictions. The Panel noted that the possibility of international cooperation with respect to dolphin conservation was an option that the United States had not exhausted.

With respect to Article XX (g), the Panel suggested that, like Article XX (b), it could only be invoked to justify measures aimed at protecting the trade-restricting state's own environment. The Panel based this view, in part, on the notion that Article XX (g) requires that import restrictions be imposed in tandem with internal measures to control production or consumption of the resource. The Panel noted: 'a country can effectively control the production or consumption of an exhaustible natural resource only to the extent that the production or consumption is under its jurisdiction'.

The Panel also suggested that since, at a given moment, Mexico could not know how many dolphins had been killed by American fishermen, it could not know whether it was complying with American law, and therefore whether it could avoid an export ban. In the Panel's view, 'a limitation on trade based on such unpredictable conditions could not be regarded as primarily aimed at conservation'.

The Panel also considered a quite different American measure concerned with the protection of dolphins, the Dolphin Protection Consumer Information Act, which permitted producers to market tuna in the United States with a 'Dolphin-Safe' label, provided US authorities could be satisfied that the tuna were indeed caught in a manner that did not unnecessarily endanger the lives of dolphins. Mexico argued that this law violated Article I:1 of the GATT, the Most Favoured Nation provision, since documentary evidence on the manner in which tuna were harvested was only required where the tuna came from the Eastern Tropical Pacific; thus, less than the full benefit of the label was conferred on tuna producers from countries such as Mexico that fished in the Eastern Tropical Pacific. The Panel rejected this argument, finding that the requirement of documentation would apply equally to any country that wished to fish in the Eastern Tropical Pacific.

The *Tuna/Dolphin* decision has been widely criticized by environmentalists, but vigorously defended by the GATT Secretariat[28] and some trade lawyers.[29] There are many aspects of the decision that are difficult to justify – including the notion that measures that apply to the production process for a product cannot be regarded as internal measures for the purposes of Article III.

The forced reading of the General Agreement that characterizes some aspects of the Panel's decision must be considered, however, in light of its overall interpretation of the normative structure of the GATT, and it is this interpretation that must be the basis of any fundamental critique of the decision. The Panel's view of the GATT is revealed most clearly in the concluding remarks of the Panel:

> The Panel wished to note the fact, made evident during its consideration of this case, that the provisions of the General Agreement impose few constraints on a Contracting Party's implementation of domestic environmental policies. . . . As a corollary to these rights, a contracting party may not restrict imports of a product merely because it originates in a country with environmental policies different from its own. It seemed evident to the Panel that, if the CONTRACTING PARTIES were to permit import restrictions in response to differences in environmental policies under the General Agreement, they would need to impose limits on the range of policy differences justifying such responses and to develop criteria so as to prevent abuse.[30]

346

The fundamental dividing line that the Panel sees is between environ-mental policies for the sake of protecting one's own environment, and policies that somehow dictate to another Contracting Party how it should protect its own environment. This seems a mischaracterization of the problem. First of all, the United States was not aiming paternalistically, as it were, to dictate to Mexico how it should regulate a purely domestic environmental problem. The measure was aimed at the preservation of dolphins as a species surviving in the world's oceans, i.e. of the global environmental commons. There was no domestic Mexican jurisdiction over dolphins that was being encroached upon. Second, the American legislation was not interfering with any specific obligations or rights assigned to Mexican fishermen under Mexican law. Despite the adoption of extra-territoriality language by the Panel, the American dolphin protection measures did not impose any obligations on Mexican fishermen that were in actual conflict with environmental laws or policies of the Mexican government. The Mexican government did not have an environmental policy forcing Mexican consumers to eat dolphin-destructive tuna, for instance, or enjoining Mexican fishermen to kill dolphins when fishing for tuna. Nor was the lifting of the import ban on the tuna necessarily conditional upon the Mexican government adopting identical legislation to the American dolphin protection legislation. Mexico was free to permit access to its own market for dolphin-destructive tuna, whether caught by Mexican or foreign fishermen. As long as Mexican fishermen did not use fishing technology that threatened the lives of dolphins, their tuna was free to enter the United States. It is true that in order for Mexican fishermen to use dolphin-threatening technology *and* for their tuna nevertheless to be admitted to the United States, the Mexican government would be required to adopt similar rules to those in force in the United States. But this is far from the massive intrusion on Mexican legal sovereignty evoked by the Panel's suggestion that the American measures virtually forced the Mexicans either to adopt identical environmental protection laws to those of the United States or give up their legal rights under the GATT.

By making access to the US market depend upon either an American-like regulatory scheme *or* adoption of different technology by Mexican fishermen, the US measures did place a commercial disadvantage or burden on Mexican fishermen, in that if their government failed to act the only way they could get access to the US market was to acquire and use a different fishing technology, presumably less efficient or in any event more costly.

However, the Panel also was prepared to accept that these kinds of commercial disadvantages might be permissible under Article XX (b) if 'necessary' to protect the United States' *own* environment. What is most questionable is the Panel's view that where the preferences of the trade-restricting state are for protection of the global commons rather than for protection of its own domestic environment, Articles XX (b) and XX (g) can *never* be relied on.

This view seems based upon several different arguments, some of which are more explicit than others in the Panel's reasoning. The first is that the drafting history suggests that Article XX (b) was only intended to apply to protection of animal and health life within one's own boundaries. This view of the drafting history is contradicted by evidence that the drafters were likely aware that at the time the GATT was negotiated there were various international conventions and agreements as well as some unilateral legislation that involved import and export restrictions linked to global conservation goals (e.g. for endangered species).[31] In not restricting the wording of XX (b) explicitly to domestic animal and plant life, the drafters may well have intended to make room in the GATT for these pre-existing conservation-related restrictions.

Moreover, other provisions of Article XX suggest that its purpose was not to be limited to exempting measures to protect domestic interests within the trade-restricting state. The clearest example is the exemption for products made with prison labour – clearly what is at issue here is preferences concerning the morality of prison labour in the *exporting* country, not simply in one's own country. Similarly, the general view of Article XX (f) which refers to the 'protection of national treasures of artistic, historic or archaeological value' is that it permits not only restrictions on the export of a Contracting Party's own national treasures, but import and export restrictions on national treasures of *other* Contracting Parties as well.[32]

If there is so little textual basis for the reading that Articles XX (b) and (g) exclude measures adopted due to preferences for global as opposed to domestic environmental welfare, can a basis be found in some broader vision of the GATT as a normative order? The Panel does attempt to elucidate such a basis, however tentatively, in suggesting the legal order of the GATT points towards international cooperation rather than unilateral trade action as a means of resolving differences in domestic policies of Contracting Parties.

This view of the GATT is, indeed, embodied in the Agreement on Technical Barriers, which, as we have seen, obliges Contracting Parties to adopt international standards, wherever possible, as opposed to domestic policies and standards inconsistent with those of other Contracting Parties, in order to vindicate the kinds of purposes listed in Article XX (b). But, clearly, in the case of dolphin protection there were no explicit international standards. The view of the GATT in the Panel's decision thus suggests a very different balance between the desirability of international cooperation and vindication of domestic preferences through unilateral action than that which is struck in the Agreement on Technical Barriers.

The question is whether there is some reason, intrinsic to the GATT, for viewing preferences for protection of one's domestic environment as a superior justification for limits on GATT strictures to preferences for global environmental protection.

Let us first of all consider this problem from the perspective that the GATT's purpose is to maximize the welfare gains from free trade. Is there any reason to believe that the foregone welfare gains due to trade restrictions imposed for domestic environmental reasons will as a rule be any less than in the case of comparable restrictions imposed for global environmental reasons? There seems little basis for such a conclusion. Second, are the benefits of restrictions (in terms of desired environmental protection) likely to outweigh the losses from trade restrictions more often where domestic rather than global environmental welfare is the basis for the restriction? There is no obvious reason why the welfare gains from greater domestic environmental protection would be more likely to outweigh the welfare losses from trade restrictions, than would the welfare gains from greater protection of the global environmental commons. The welfarist view of the GATT thus provides no basis for the Panel's distinction between the permissibility of measures to protect the domestic environment and the impermissibility of measures to protect the global environment, i.e. the environmental commons.

Another view of the GATT is that of a framework for the negotiation on a reciprocal basis of mutually advantageous trade concessions. On this view the GATT's rules in question are aimed in large measure at distinguishing legitimate domestic policy options that the Parties never gave up in their negotiation of trade concessions from the colourable use of domestic policies to claw back some of the protectionism they traded away.[33] This view of the GATT was implicit in the Panel's concern about protectionist abuse of environmental exceptions to GATT strictures. The implication seems to be that if global environmental welfare arguments were possible under Article XX (b) (or (g) for that matter), a whole new and largely uncontrollable set of pretexts for disguised protectionism would be available to Contracting Parties.

However, as explored at length earlier in this chapter, much of Article XX is in fact directed at controlling the use of rationales such as conservation or protection of animal health as a means of disguised protection. Hence the general requirement that Article XX measures not be disguised restrictions on trade. Hence, also, the 'necessity' test in Article XX (b), and the requirement in Article XX (g) that trade measures be taken in conjunction with domestic restrictions on production or consumption. These various aspects of Article XX all provide a means of screening out colourable protectionist measures (i.e. cheating on trade concessions) from measures genuinely enacted for the non-protectionist purposes listed in the Article. However, there is no reason why these aspects of Article XX would not function equally well to screen out global environmental pretexts as well as domestic ones.

A final view, also implicit in the Panel's report, reads into the legal order of the GATT a prohibition on unilateral action to protect the environment beyond one's borders. Undoubtedly, certain kinds of unilateral action that are extraterritorial violate particular rules of international law, both treaty law (e.g. the Law of the Sea Convention) and customary international law.[34] These include direct assertion of control over activity in international waters through the use or threat of military force. Yet apart from the risk described above of increased cheating on trade concessions, it is hard to understand why a *sui generis* rule on non-intervention for environmental purposes should be read into an international regime concerned with preserving and enhancing international commercial exchanges. There is a considerable body of public international law on the issues of non-intervention and the use of economic sanctions against other states. But – at least in its current form – the GATT dispute settlement mechanism has, arguably, neither the institutional competence nor the legitimacy, to interpret and develop these public international law rules. In any event, there is no general public international rule against unilateral action to protect the environment as long as such action does not result in illegal assertion of jurisdiction over international waters or territory or usurpation of the territorial jurisdiction of another state.

Clearly, it would be inappropriate to be simply dismissive of the important sovereignty concerns that underpin the Panel's ruling. In our estimation, however, these concerns were more appropriately addressed in the Panel's observation that the United States had not pursued with sufficient vigour international cooperation as a means of protecting the dolphin population (either bilaterally with Mexico or on a multilateral basis), and therefore that the adoption of unilateral trade restrictions was precipitous and hence not clearly 'necessary' within the meaning of Article XX (b).

THE NORTH AMERICAN FREE TRADE AGREEMENT

The North American Free Trade Agreement (NAFTA) is the first comprehensive trade treaty that deals explicitly with the relationship between trade and environmental protection. Nevertheless, the key NAFTA provisions on environment are unlikely to play any significant role in sustaining or enhancing levels of environmental protection in the member countries, and in the case of the provisions on technical standards, may actually threaten high environmental standards. The NAFTA environmental side-agreement, the North American Agreement on Environmental Co-operation, does not establish any substantive transnational environmental norms or standards. However, it does establish an institutional framework from which such norms or standards may eventually emerge. As well, the side-agreement binds the Parties to effective enforcement of their own domestic environmental laws, and provides for dispute settlement and, ultimately, sanctions where a NAFTA Party persistently fails to enforce these laws.

Article 104:
Environmental and Conservation Agreements

Article 104 states that in the event of an 'inconsistency' between the NAFTA and the trade provisions of several major environmental treaties, including the Convention on International Trade and Endangered Species (CITES), the provisions of the environmental treaty shall prevail 'to the extent of the inconsistency.' The kinds of trade obligations in question are, generally speaking, export and/or import bans, which would normally run afoul of Article 309 of the NAFTA. Article 309 incorporates into the NAFTA the GATT Article XI prohibition on both export and import restrictions and prohibitions.

Since any measure saved by Article 104 is, therefore, likely also to constitute a violation of Article XI of the GATT, will Article 104 have any real significance in enabling the implementation of environmental treaties? This will depend on whether Article 104 applies to the Parties' pre-existing GATT obligations as well as to the provisions of NAFTA. Article 103 (1) of the NAFTA states that 'The Parties affirm their existing rights and obligations with respect to each other under the *General Agreement on Tariffs and Trade* and other agreements to which the Parties are party.' Article 103 (2) then goes on to state: 'In the event of any inconsistency between the provisions of this Agreement and such other agreements, the provisions of this Agreement shall prevail to the extent of the inconsistency, except if otherwise provided in this Agreement.'

Does the expression 'other agreements' in 103 (2) mean any agreement besides the NAFTA to which the Parties are signatories, including GATT, or does it refer to 'other agreements' as defined in Article 103 (1) – i.e. agreements other than the GATT and NAFTA? If the second interpretation is correct (i.e. that NAFTA does not take precedence over GATT although it does over agreements other than GATT), then Article 104 is likely to have very little effect. The one case where Article 104 would still have an impact is if, in the future, an otherwise GATT-inconsistent environmental treaty received a waiver under Article XXV:5 of the General Agreement. In that case, while the treaty would no longer entail violation of the NAFTA Parties' GATT obligations (i.e. due to the waiver), it could still be in violation of their NAFTA obligations. Here, Article 104 *would* apply to resolve the. inconsistency in favour of the environmental treaty. Finally, it is to be noted that any dispute between NAFTA members concerning a treaty listed under Article 104 is to be referred to the NAFTA dispute settlement process rather than to the GATT (Article 2005.3).

351

Chapter Nine: Technical Barriers to Trade

Article 904 (1) states in part that 'Each Party may, in accordance with this Agreement, adopt, maintain and apply standards-related measures, including those relating to safety, the protection of human, animal and plant life and health, the environment, and consumers, and measures to ensure their enforcement or implementation.' This provision goes beyond comparable language in Article XX of the GATT, in that it explicitly mentions environmental measures. However, building on the GATT Agreement on Technical Barriers, Articles 904 to 915 set out a number of quite elaborate constraints on the extent to which Parties may enforce disparate standards, including environmental standards, that have a trade-restricting effect. Here, it is important to realize that it is higher or more rigorous environmental standards that are likely to come under scrutiny according to the provisions of Article 904 – after all, a Party would hardly want to restrict imports where its relevant environmental standards were lower than those of the exporting country. The general thrust of Chapter Nine is to oblige each Party to minimize distinctive national standards that have a trade-restrictive impact, by adopting international standards wherever possible, by recognizing other Parties' standards wherever compatible with its own policy objectives, by actively pursuing harmonization, and by limiting its resort to distinctive standards with trade-restricting impacts to those instances where it is justified by scientific assessment of risk (Article 907).

Of particular concern from an environmentalist perspective is the attempt to subject technical barriers to strict scientific scrutiny. Parties may wish to take environmental protection measures on moral and aesthetic grounds, or where the evidence remains controversial among scientists but is sufficiently strong to create the democratic will to act.[35] This concern is amplified by the fact that the dispute resolution provisions of NAFTA envisage an important role for scientific experts in the resolution of environmental disputes under the NAFTA (Article 2015).

Furthermore, nothing in Chapter Nine suggests that protecting the global environment is a legitimate policy objective that can justify technical standards with trade-restricting impacts. Here, it will be recalled that in the *Tuna/Dolphin* case, a GATT panel interpreted a provision of the GATT similar in wording to Article 904 (i.e. Article XX (b)) to apply only to measures necessary to protect the environment of the trade-restricting country. There is nothing in the wording of the NAFTA that would preclude a similar interpretation of NAFTA Article 904.

Article 1114 – Environmental Measures

Article 1114 (2) states in part that 'The Parties recognize that it is inappropriate to encourage investment by relaxing domestic health, safety, or environmental measures. Accordingly, a Party should not waive or otherwise derogate from, or offer to waive or otherwise derogate from, such measures as an encouragement for the establishment, acquisition, expansion, or retention in its territory of an investor.' This provision is the most innovative of the NAFTA provisions on environment, in that it does recognize explicitly the danger of an environmental 'race to the bottom', where investors are attracted to the NAFTA jurisdiction with the lowest environmental standards – thereby possibly exerting downward pressure on standards elsewhere as the Parties compete for the jobs that come with investment. However, the actual provisions of Article 1114 may be inadequate to its purpose. First of all, and of greatest significance, the language 'a Party should not waive . . .' connotes something less than a full legal obligation – generally, NAFTA obligations are expressed by the more clearly imperative word 'shall'.

One drawback in adopting existing environmental measures as the baseline is that removal or relaxation of some existing environmental measures may actually be justified, from an environmentalist perspective, in light of changes in technology as well as shifts in the choice of environmental instrument, for instance from 'command and control' type regulations to taxes and charges. For example, if Canada implements a new reforestation management system that results in much more rapid reforestation, why should Canada not be able to exploit any competitive advantage that comes from being able to provide producers located in Canada with more liberal quotas for timber than a less effective conservation system in the United States would permit?

Finally, the proposed dispute settlement process with respect to Article 1114 (2) does not appear to lend itself to the kind of in-depth investigation that would be required to determine if a Party was under-enforcing its own laws in order to encourage investment. Thus, Article 1114 (2) states: 'If a Party considers that another Party has offered such an encouragement, it may request consultations with the other Party and the two Parties shall consult with a view to avoiding any such encouragement.' Is this process of 'consultations' intended to exclude further recourse to the normal NAFTA dispute resolution mechanism that allows for in-depth investigation and the assessment of expert opinion? While the normal dispute resolution mechanism applies to all the provisions of NAFTA, it does so '(e)xcept as otherwise provided in this Agreement' (Article 2004). It is unclear whether the provision for consultations in Article 1114 would constitute one of these exceptions to the application of the Chapter Twenty dispute settlement mechanism. It could be argued that the Chapter Twenty mechanism still applies, since elsewhere in the NAFTA when the Parties have wished to exclude recourse to Chapter Twenty procedures, they have done so through an explicit exclusionary clause (see Annex 1137.2 Exclusions from Dispute Settlement).

The NAFTA provisions on environment fall far short of an effective environmental charter, especially if one balances the strict scrutiny of a Party's differentially higher trade-impacting environmental standards provided for in Chapter Nine against the rather weak limits on investment-impacting downward movement in a Party's standards stipulated in Article 1114 (2). It is perhaps not surprising, therefore, that the Clinton Administration would insist on the negotiation of supplemental provisions in a parallel accord. It is to this side-agreement that we shall now turn our attention.

The North American Agreement on Environmental Cooperation

The NAAEC, often referred to as the NAFTA environmental side-agreement, states a set of general objectives that include fostering 'the protection and improvement of the environment in the territories of the Parties', increased 'cooperation . . . to better conserve, protect and enhance the environment, . . .' and the avoidance of 'trade distortions and new trade barriers' (Article I). The NAAEC also contains a set of 'general commitments', which include public reporting and education about environmental matters, assessment of environmental impacts where appropriate, and the promotion of economic instruments of environmental regulation (Article II). In addition, Article III stipulates that 'each Party shall ensure that its laws and regulations provide for high levels of environmental protection and shall strive to continue to improve those laws and regulations'. However, Article III also recognizes 'the right of each Party to establish its own levels of domestic environmental protection, . . .'. It is difficult, but not impossible to reconcile these two aspects of Article III. One approach would be to argue that Article III permits a Party to set its own levels of protection, as long as those levels are 'high' by some objective standard. An alternative interpretation, which would greatly attenuate the significance of Article III, is that each Party must set a level of environmental protection that is 'high', but that the meaning of a 'high' level of environmental protection is to be determined by each Party's domestic values and priorities.

Article 5 requires that 'each Party shall effectively enforce its environmental laws and regulations through appropriate government action, . . .' and gives a list of examples of such actions, ranging from the use of licences and permits to contractual and voluntary arrangements for environmental compliance. Article 6 requires that 'interested persons' be able to request a Party's regulatory authorities to investigate possible violations of domestic environmental laws and regulations. Since the NAAEC does not contain a definition of 'interested persons', whether this includes, for example, environmental NGOs will depend on the standing rules in each Party's domestic legal system.

Of all these obligations, *only* a Party's obligation to enforce effectively its own environmental law can be regarded as 'hard' trade law, for only this obligation carries with it the possibility of binding dispute settlement and, ultimately, sanctions for non-compliance. Thus, where there is a complaint that 'there has been a persistent pattern of failure [of a NAFTA Party] to enforce its environmental law', Part V of the NAAEC provides for a dispute settlement process that closely parallels the general NAFTA dispute settlement process set out in Chapter 20. A rather significant difference is that a request for a panel must be approved by a two-thirds vote of the Parties. This means that where, for instance, Canada requested a panel to investigate an alleged persistent failure of Mexico to enforce its environmental laws, it would have to obtain the agreement of either Mexico or the United States in order for dispute settlement to proceed (Article 24 (1)).

If, in its final report, a panel concludes that in fact, a persistent failure of enforcement has occurred, the Parties to the dispute 'may agree on a mutually satisfactory action plan, which normally shall conform with the determinations and recommendations of the Panel' (Article 33). If no such action plan is agreed upon, then, after 60 days (but within 120 days) of the final report, the complaining Party may request that the panel reconvene and determine an appropriate action plan and/or a monetary assessment against the offending Party. If the panel subsequently determines that an action plan (either mutually agreed upon or stipulated by the panel itself) is not being implemented it may impose monetary assessments against the offending Party (Article 34 (5)(b)). Where the offending Party fails to pay a monetary assessment within 180 days after it is imposed, the complaining Party may suspend concessions under the NAFTA itself 'in an amount no greater than that sufficient to collect the monetary enforcement assessment'. Annex 34 states, *inter alia*, the limits on monetary assessments. 'For the first year after entry into force of the NAAEC, these shall not exceed $20 million US. Thereafter, an assessment may not exceed 0.007 percent of total trade in goods between the Parties during the most recent year for which data are available' (Annex 34, Article 1). Here, 'between the Parties' most logically refers to the total trade between all three NAFTA Parties, not that between the two Parties to the dispute.[36] The latter interpretation would create the arbitrary result that a monetary assessment arising out of exactly the same violation would vary enormously depending, for instance, on whether Canada or the United States was the complainant. Here, it should be stressed that monetary assessments are *not* intended as compensation for injury to the complaining Party's trade from persistent violation of the Agreement, but rather as an enforcement measure or sanction – they are not paid to the complaining Party but rather are paid into a fund to be spent at the direction of the NAFTA Parties for improving or enhancing environmental protection in the territory of the offending Party (Annex 34, Article 3).

In the case of a monetary assessment against Canada, a rather disingenuous procedure replaces withdrawal of trade concessions as the sanction of last resort where the assessment remains unpaid. The panel decision imposing the monetary assessment is to be registered in a domestic Canadian court and to be subject to an enforcement order of that court, just as a foreign civil judgment might be enforced according to principles of conflict of laws (private international law). The ultimate effect is really the same as with the withdrawal of trade concessions, but the insertion of this separate procedure allowed the Canadian government of the day to make the (rather empty if literally true) public claim that it had succeeded in adhering to its position that no trade sanctions should be attached to the violation of environmental obligations.

If only Article 5 obligations are genuinely enforceable through dispute settlement and sanctions, what is the real significance of the various other, more general obligations and commitments in the NAAEC? The answer to this question will lie in the effectiveness of the institutional mechanisms that are aimed at fulfilling the broader promise of the NAAEC through on-going cooperative efforts concerning environmental regulation and standards.

The NAAEC provides for the estabishment of four institutions for environmental cooperation: the Commission, the Council, the Secretariat and the Joint Public Advisory Committee. The Commission is the umbrella organization that encompasses the other three institutions (Article 8). The Council comprises ministerial-level representatives of the Parties who are required to meet at least once a year. The Council may make recommendations with respect to a wide variety of environmental matters, including 'transboundary and border environmental issues, such as the long-range transport of air and marine pollutants' and the 'protection of endangered and threatened species' and 'eco-labelling'. Perhaps most significantly, the Council, 'without reducing levels of environmental protection', may establish a process for developing recommendations on the 'greater compatibility of environmental technical regulations, standards and conformity assessment procedures, . . .'. This, in effect, gives the Council a mandate for the development of harmonized minimum environmental standards. In carrying out these various responsibilities the Council may establish committees, working groups or expert groups, and seek the advice of NGOs (Article 5). It should be noted that recommendations of the Council are to be made by consensus (Article 6), and that a Contracting Party's obligation is merely to 'consider' such recommendations, not to implement them.

The Secretariat consists of a permanent professional staff which provides administrative and technical support to the Council, headed by an Executive Director appointed for a (once renewable) three-year term (Article 11 (1)). In addition to this general support function, the Secretariat is charged with preparing an annual report of the Commission, based upon instructions from the Council (Article 12 (1)). The report is to contain, *inter alia*, data on each Party's compliance with its obligations under the agreement (Article 12 (2) (c)) and 'relevant views and information submitted by non-governmental organizations and persons, . . .' (Article 12 (2) (d)).

Finally, Articles 14 and 15 establish a procedure where a non-governmental organization may bring a submission before the Secretariat asserting that a Party is failing to enforce effectively its own environmental law. Upon approval by a two-thirds vote of the Council (i.e. by two of the three Parties) the Secretariat may prepare a 'factual record' concerning the NGO's claims, based upon the NGO's submissions as well as any 'relevant technical, scientific or other information', including submissions by the Party that is the object of the complaint. The Council may decide, by a two-thirds vote to make the factual record public. It is to be emphasized that no formal dispute settlement or sanctions ensue in consequence of an adverse factual record. However, such a record would provide a strong evidentiary basis for a complaint against the offending Party should either of the other Parties choose to lodge one in accordance with the separate Part V dispute settlement procedures. Once made public, an adverse factual record would also assist environmental NGOs in bringing public pressure to bear upon the other NAFTA Parties to lodge such a complaint.

The Joint Public Advisory Committee consists of 15 members, 5 of which are appointed by each Party (Article 16 (91)). The Committee may participate in the process of developing a factual record in accordance with Article 15. The Secretariat must also provide the Committee, *inter alia*, with the draft annual report, presumably for comment before its final adoption.

In assessing the significance of the NAAEC, at least as much emphasis should be placed on the broader institutional framework it establishes as on the rather limited enforceable legal obligations that it contains. This framework holds the promise of setting in motion a process for the evolution of genuine regional environmental norms, linked (albeit indirectly) to evolution of deeper economic integration among the NAFTA Parties. Although the NAAEC does not, by any means, transcend the state-centric paradigm of traditional international law[37] (i.e. only Parties have direct access to dispute settlement), it does acknowledge in important ways the legitimate stake that NGOs have in the process of monitoring and enforcing NAAEC legal obligations, i.e. that environmental protection is not just a matter between governments, but is of direct concern to individuals throughout the NAFTA region.

THE TRADE/ENVIRONMENT DEBATE AND THE FUTURE OF THE MULTILATERAL TRADING SYSTEM

In this section of the chapter we address the broader debate over trade and environment and suggest some possibilities for reform or clarification of existing multilateral trade rules which we believe have the potential to achieve a principled reconciliation of environmentalist concerns with a liberal global trading order.

The central focus of the debate, as illustrated by the dispute that led to the *Tuna/Dolphin* Panel, is the legitimacy and desirability of using trade restricting measures as a response to the environmental policies of other GATT/WTO Members. Much confusion has been created in this debate by a failure to distinguish between two quite different, although partly interrelated sets of justifications for imposition of trade restrictions in response to concerns about other Members' environmental policies. The first set of justifications may be described as environmentally-based. Here, the concern is with the effect on the environment and on environmental policy of trade measures. Trade measures may be used to enforce international environmental agreements among the signatories, or against 'hold outs' who have refused to sign the agreements; trade measures may be used as sanctions to show moral distaste or outrage at acts that are viewed, either by an individual state or by a broad cross-section of the international community, as harmful to the environment and/or to bring pressure on the state(s) in question to cease these acts; one could also employ trade measures as a 'stick' to bring countries to the negotiating table with a view to solving a 'tragedy of the commons' problem through international co-operation. Finally, trade measures have been proposed as a response to the risk of a 'race to the bottom', i.e. to the possibility that competitive pressures from trading partners will prevent a Member from sustaining high levels of environmental protection which impose relatively higher costs on its domestic producers. All these instances involve the use of trade restricting measures to promote or sustain objectives of environmental protection.

Related to the 'race to the bottom' is a set of arguments in favour of trade restrictions in response to others' environmental policies may be described as 'fair trade'-based, rather than environmentally-based. These claims focus not on harm to the environment and its prevention, but harm to domestic producers due to the supposed competitive disadvantage in having to comply with more stringent environmental standards than one's foreign competitors. Here the logic of the argument points not to the use of trade restrictions as enforcement measures, sanctions, or incentives to global bargaining, but rather to equalize any competitive disadvantage that domestic producers may suffer from the lower environmental standards of others. The closest analogy here is with countervailing duties, and indeed some 'fair-trade'-based claims to environmental trade restrictions entail arguments that countervailing duty laws should be amended so that lax environmental standards may be classified as a countervailable subsidy.[38] These 'fair trade' claims rarely entail the identification of any superior normative interest in a particular level of environmental protection that justifies regarding the domestic standards of the trade-restricting country as a benchmark for 'fair' international competition. Setting one's standards below those of one's trade competitors *is itself* deemed an unfair act or a distortion of international trade – just as in the case of countervailing duty law, there need be no inquiry into whether the subsidy itself is harmful or beneficial to domestic or global welfare, i.e. the 'unfairness' of the subsidy is largely presumed.

Let us first consider how the multilateral trading order should respond to environmental-based claims to trade restrictions that would otherwise constitute violations of GATT/WTO commitments. We should at the outset admit that the normative order of liberal multilateral trade does not have at its disposal any set of principles on which to oppose *as such* some sacrifice of the gains from free trade to the external, non-trade goal of environmental protection. The possibility of such sacrifices does not undermine the internal coherence or integrity of the liberal trading order, nor does it put in question the basic theory of gains from freer trade. Indeed such sacrifices to external goals or norms are already contemplated in the exemptions contained in Articles XX and XXI of the General Agreement. At the same time the liberal multilateral trading order *does* have a significant stake in maintaining a framework in which it is possible to make defensible distinctions between measures that are in fact environmentally-based and those that constitute the use of an environmental pretext to cheat on liberalization commitments. In our view, the ability to identify cheating or defection through legitimate multilateral surveillance and dispute settlement mechanisms is crucial to maintaining the integrity of the system.[39] It follows that the multilateral trading order does have an internal interest in preventing forms of environmental trade action that threaten the capacity to identify and sanction protectionist 'cheating' on trade liberalization commitments. But, as we noted above in our critique of the *Tuna/Dolphin* decision, this interest exists equally with respect to trade measures taken to protect a country's own environment *and* with respect to measures aimed at protecting the global environmental commons. A second, related interest of the multilateral trading order is in avoiding resort to trade restrictions where alternative means are available and perhaps more appropriate to address an environmental problem. This, obviously, involves a judgement of the relationship of means to ends, and such a judgement stands at the intersection of the normative systems of environmentalism and of liberal trade. That is to say, the making of such a judgement appropriately implies that the environmentalist perspective must be brought within the trade dispute settlement process, or more broadly, the GATT/WTO interpretation process. Both normative orders have a legitimate interest in the choice of means – the environmentalist in order to most effectively, in a given context, achieve a given environmental goal, and the free trader, in order to ensure that the means chosen do not gratuitously or unnecessarily restrict trade.

On the basis of these principles we suggest: (1) that environmental trade actions should not be exempted from the requirement of justification under Article XX of the GATT, but that Article XX should be interpreted or, if need be, amended to encompass explicitly not just domestic but also global environmental objectives; (2) that trade measures taken in accordance with multilateral environmental agreements or general principles of international environmental law should normally be viewed as deserving of exemption from GATT strictures, since an external benchmark of environmental justification exists for such measures that allows them to be distinguished from protectionist cheating; and (3) that unilateral trade measures not supported by any existing international environmental norms should generally speaking not be justifiable under GATT, except as a last resort where a country or countries fails to cooperate to evolve a multilateral approach to a global environmental problem or to prevent spillovers that affect the trade-restricting state's own environment.

We shall now examine how this approach can be applied to the various classes of environmentally-based trade measure.

Enforcement of International Environmental Agreements

Earlier in this chapter, we alluded to the existence of international environmental agreements that explicitly provide for trade restrictions as a means of enforcing the agreement or of achieving its environmental objectives. The most obvious example is the CITES Convention,[40] restricting trade in endangered species. Lucrative export markets are often a major incentive for hunters to violate domestic regulations with respect to the protection of endangered species. Domestic monitoring and enforcement of limits or prohibitions on the killing of such species are often of limited effectiveness. Effective border measures may well be an attractive alternative or supplement. Here, the environmental agreement itself embodies an explicit choice for trade restrictions as an instrument of environmental regulation (not merely a sanction). The agreement does not merely permit, but *requires* such restrictions. Such is the case, as well, with the Basel Hazardous Wastes Convention and the Nuclear Non-Proliferation Treaty.

In these kinds of instances, trade measures taken against *signatories* of the international environmental agreement pose no real legal issue for the GATT, as long as the environmental agreement has come into force subsequent to the relevant GATT provisions. This is due to the public international law principle that, in the event of a conflict, the provisions of a later treaty take precedence over those of an earlier one.[41] However, with respect to trade measures taken against non-signatories of the environmental agreement who are Members of GATT/WTO, a legal issue does arise. Even if the Members are non-signatories of the environmental agreement, we see no compelling reason why such measures should not be justified under Article XX, and we would recommend either the amendment of Article XX or the negotiation of an understanding with respect to its interpretation that clearly encompasses trade restrictions taken against non-signatories pursuant to international environmental agreements. There is a lesser risk of countries actually negotiating international environmental agreements for the purpose of cheating on their trade commitments, and so here the concern with protectionist 'cheating' does not justify particularly rigorous scrutiny of the trade measures in question. As well, the trade measures are closely bound up with the structure and purpose of the agreements themselves; the closeness of the interrelationship will, in these instances, often reflect important rationales for choosing trade controls as an environmental instrument, thereby addressing the concern that trade not be unnecessarily or gratuitously restricted for environmental purposes. There is a more general international law issue of whether the use of trade measures against a country based on an agreement that it has not signed represents an unwarranted interference with that state's sovereignty. However, the bounds of state sovereignty (and the very meaning of the concept) are in flux in a number of areas of international law.[42] The range of existing and evolving international norms that affect this issue is very wide, and many of these norms are connected only tangentially to the multilateral liberal trading order. There is no good reason, from the perspective of values internal to the liberal trading order, to freeze within the GATT a rigid, traditionalist concept of sovereign rights in the international environmental context. This is not to say that, under some circumstances, a GATT/WTO Member might have a legitimate complaint that trade measures taken against it for genuine environmental purposes under an agreement it has not signed, violate some sovereignty norm under public international law. Rather, this kind of complaint – again because of the range of international legal issues it raises in an area of rapidly evolving norms – should appropriately be brought before the United Nations or the International Court of Justice.

Even where an international environmental agreement or an international legal norm does not justify or require trade measures for its enforcement, a country may decide to use trade measures as a sanction against another country or countries that it deems in violation of the agreement or norm. Here, serious risks of disguised cheating on trade liberalization commitments do in fact exist. This is especially true where trade measures are imposed based on a unilateral determination that some relatively general or even controversial norm of international environmental law has been violated. As well, there is a genuine concern that trade restrictions do not become the instrument of choice for dealing with disputes about international environmental law, just because they constitute a relatively easy and certainly in many instances a visceral response to such disputes. For both these reasons, such measures should only be exempted from GATT strictures where they pass a rigorous least-restrictive means test of the kind that has emerged in recent GATT jurisprudence on Article XX. Here, it will be important to inquire whether alternative avenues of dispute settlement exist, either under international agreements or within international environmental institutions, whether an attempt has been made to resolve the disagreement through consultations or arbitration aided by international environmental institutions, and whether it is the view of international environmental institutions or authorities[43] that a violation of an international agreement or norm has, indeed, occurred. To facilitate a determination on this last point, we would recommend that an understanding on the interpretation of Article XX in environmental trade disputes include a provision allowing a dispute panel to obtain an advisory opinion from international environmental institutions or authorities.

A final case is that of trade measures that are taken against a country in the absence of any alleged violation of an international agreement or norm, merely on the basis that the citizens of the country in question find the environmental practices or policies of the affected state to be reprehensible and/or they seek to change those policies. Here, trade measures are being used in the first instance as sanctions to support the domestic values of the trade-restricting state. Since there *is* no external benchmark of any kind to assist in distinguishing, on an objective basis, these sanctions from disguised 'cheating' on trade liberalization commitments, the scrutiny of these measures should entail special vigilance in the application of the least-restrictive means test. An understanding on the interpretation of Article XX in environmental trade disputes should list a number of factors that a dispute panel *must* consider in determining whether an environmental exemption from GATT strictures is warranted. Foremost among these is why a multilateral approach has not succeded in the evolution of international agreements or norms. Have attempts at international cooperation been defeated by free-rider problems? Is the state against which the trade restricting measures are directed a hold-out that is frustrating bona fide attempts by other states, including the trade-restricting state, to secure a multilateral solution? Here it is important to consider the extent to which the non-adherence of some states to a multilateral approach will undermine the efforts of others to address a global environmental problem.[44] A second factor that should, arguably, always be taken into account is whether the trade-restricting state has exhausted all avenues of bilateral negotiation and co-operation as a solution to the problem.

Of course, it is fundamental to a determination as to whether all reasonable efforts have been made for an international cooperative solution – either bilateral or multilateral – to know whether the trade restricting state's *terms* for such a settlement are themselves reasonable. This goes to one of the main concerns of developing countries with respect to international environmental law – the costs to these countries of international solutions to global environmental problems. Here, international environmental agreements that contain obligations that are variable according to the circumstances of individual countries[45] may provide a benchmark for determining the reasonableness of the terms on offer for a cooperative solution. This is certainly a matter on which it would be appropriate for a GATT/WTO dispute panel to seek an advisory opinion from international environmental institutions and authorities, as well as international institutions and authorities concerned with the situation of developing countries. In some circumstances, a reasonable offer for a co-operative solution may be deemed to include economic assistance to defray some of the costs of implementing domestically such a solution.[46]

As opposed to the above categories of measures, where we see, at least in some circumstances, a valid justification for exemption of environmentally-based trade measures from GATT strictures, we are considerably more sceptical that measures based upon 'race to the bottom' arguments can be made consistent with the liberal multilateral trading order. Fundamentally, these arguments challenge the notion that regulatory diversity can lead to a legitimate comparative advantage in trade. They suggest that gains from trade can only be considered to be fair when they are not derived from a regulatory approach more favourable to a country's trading interests.

We can identify several levels of incoherence in deployment of 'race to the bottom' arguments in the trade and environment context. At the outset, however, we are prepared to accept, on the basis of the best available empirical evidence, that production and jobs are sometimes shifted from one country to another on account of lower environmental costs. According to a detailed synthesis of the existing evidence Richard Stewart reports that, 'the empirical studies on productivity, trade, and industrial location are broadly consistent with one another. They show that national differences in environmental regulation have had an important impact at the margin in the case of a relatively few "dirty" industries.'[47]

Even in the case of these industries we are far from convinced that trade restrictions are an appropriate response to the pressure on domestic environmental standards due to the competitive advantage of less environmentally-stringent trade competitors. First of all, it may be possible to reduce the gap in environmental costs without lowering standards, by shifting to more efficient instruments of environmental protection, such as incentive-based instruments. Moreover, the pressure from trade competition for domestic industries to find lower-cost means of meeting higher environmental standards may well lead to the development of new technologies which will actually enhance global economic welfare by allowing *all* countries to control environmental risks at lower cost. A related consideration is that higher environmental standards may lead to a comparative advantage in environmental technologies and control methods, which may to some extent compensate for any short run comparative disadvantage from the higher standards themselves. Finally, even if all countries had the same level of environmental consciousness, or even the same general environmental standards, approaches to instrument choice as well as the choice of risks on which to concentrate would still differ widely, due to differing climatic and other geographical or demographic conditions. For these reasons, even in a world where all citizens shared the same environmental preferences, environmental laws and regulations would still be likely to differ substantially between countries, and even where they were the same, the costs to industry of complying with those laws and regulations would still be likely to differ substantially from country to country. There is no coherent reason for not simply considering these differences as akin to other differences in endowments that create a comparative advantage in trade. Moreover, basing trade restrictions on arbitrary judgements as to which endowments do or do not constitute a legitimate source of comparative advantage seems to undermine comparative advantage itself as a foundational normative principle of a multilateral liberal trading order.[48]

Our view of the case for 'fair trade'-based, as opposed to environmentally-based, trade restrictions in the environmental context follows very closely from this assessment of the 'race for the bottom' argument. As with domestic subsidies, we consider it incoherent to single out a particular government policy as providing a country with a comparative advantage with respect to a given product, without comparing the overall burdens and benefits imposed on industry by governments in *both* countries. Given the wide range of government policies that pervasively influence the costs of doing business in most countries such a comparison would be close to impossible to make. Even if these comparisons could be made the consequence for international trade law would be devastating. If trade restrictions could be imposed wherever an identical balance of government-created burdens and benefits did not exist between trading partners, then free trade would only be sustainable within a single world state.

This being said, it may well be the case that certain industries exist that are characterized by intense but imperfect global competition between a few major producers. If, in these industries, environmental costs represent a substantial part of doing business, it is imaginable that governments might selectively and strategically alter environmental regulations or their application in order to help domestic firms prevail in the global competition. Where an industry has particular characteristics that lead to a significant risk of such strategic behaviour, there *may* be a justification for a sectoral accord of some kind, restraining beggar-thy-neighbour government policies. An example, in the subsidies area, would be the GATT Civil Aircraft Code, or the enforcement of constraints on beggar-thy-neighbour subsidies policies in certain industries through competition policy in the European Community.

CONCLUSION

The existing jurisprudence on trade and environment in the GATT displays a lack of coherence and consistency. With respect to measures that a country takes to protect its own environment, measures that are characterized as import or export restrictions within the meaning of Article XI, will only be found to be legal under the GATT if they can be shown to be the least trade restrictive means available to achieve the environmental objectives set out in Articles XX(b) or XX(g) of the General Agreement. On the other hand, measures connected to an internal regulatory scheme, even if enforced through restrictions or prohibitions of imports at the border, can be found consistent with the GATT as long as the National Treatment obligation is met, i.e. without the need for the trade-restricting country to resort to the exemptions under Article XX. At the same time, it is unclear as to when facially neutral internal environmental measures will be found to violate the National Treatment obligation by virtue of a disparate impact on imports.

With respect to trade measures taken with a view to protecting the environmental commons, one GATT Panel decision, the *Superfund* ruling, suggests that where such measures involve the imposition of an environmental tax on imported products that is also imposed on like domestic products, there will be no violation of the GATT. On the other hand, the more recent *Tuna/Dolphin* ruling appears to exclude entirely the possibility of justifying under Articles XX (b) or (g) of the GATT trade measures to protect the environmental commons that are considered to be import or export restrictions within the meaning of Article XI. As we have argued in this chapter, there is a very weak basis in GATT law or trade theory for drawing a hard and fast distinction between measures taken to protect a country's own environment and those taken to protect the global environmental commons. In addition, while much emphasis was placed by the *Tuna/Dolphin* panel on the unilateral nature of the impugned measures, the legal reasoning of the Panel strongly implies that the trade restrictions and sanctions contemplated by international environmental agreements such as CITES and the Montreal Protocol could not be justified under Article XX of the GATT, since these measures are contemplated pursuant to global environmental goals.

Especially given the increasing number of trade conflicts related to environmental matters, the present state of GATT law as just described is far from satisfactory. The case for specific rules (and perhaps even a specific institution) within GATT to address environmental matters is strong, and not only from an environmentalist perspective. The uncertainty and incoherence that characterize the existing jurisprudence only serve to undermine the legitimacy of GATT strictures that affect environmental protection, thereby fuelling increased demands for aggressive unilateralism. In our view, a GATT environmental code or charter should permit trade measures that are legitimately directed at either domestic or global environmental protection goals. This should apply whether the instrument in question is a border restriction on imports and exports, a tax, or an internal measure that discriminates against imports. The most practicable manner for screening out protectionism on environmental pretexts is to require a stringent justification of the measures in terms of their environmental purposes. Clearly, any approach designed to do justice to the twin goals of providing broad scope for legitimate environmental measures and screening out protectionism on environmental pretexts is likely to require value judgements about the costs and benefits of environmental protection. We question whether the GATT Panel process, dominated as it is by trade diplomats and experts, would have the institutional competence and legitimacy to make such judgements. At the same time, the NAFTA approach of involving scientists in dispute settlement also seems too narrow, since the judgements in question implicate not only questions of science but of ethics and fundamental social values. It is important that ways be found to bring these broader perspectives into GATT interpretation and dispute settlement in environmental contexts. We have suggested, for instance, that international environmental institutions such as the United Nations Environmental Program (UNEP) could be called upon to offer advisory opinions in environment-related trade disputes.

There are, surely, broader issues of public international law implicated in whether trade sanctions can be used to enforce an international agreement against a sovereign state that is not a Party to that agreement.[49] Yet concepts of state sovereignty in public international law are shifting, and sovereignty is often no longer viewed as an absolute value, superior to human rights or environmental concerns. Placing a state at some commercial disadvantage if it fails to adhere to international standards for protection of the global environmental commons may well be a defensible balance between sovereignty values and environmental values.[50]

If there are dangers of a protectionist spiral, it is through the importation into the environmental area of 'unfair trade' arguments to justify duties that supposedly neutralize cost advantages to foreign producers in countries with laxer environmental standards. The extension of existing countervailing duty law to encompass this kind of unilateralism should be strongly resisted. Ultimately, however, the more successful the world community becomes in defining genuinely international or at least regional environmental standards and norms, the less likely that the environmental movement will put its full moral force behind the option of unilateral environmental protectionism. For this reason alone, advocates of liberal trade should lend their support to the enterprise of developing international rules and institutions to govern the global environmental commons, which ideally would complement the evolution of GATT norms and interpretation in response to environmental issues.

14

THE INTERNATIONAL MOVEMENT OF PEOPLE

INTRODUCTION

Classical free trade theory assumed that goods could often readily be traded across national borders but that the factors of production employed to produce those goods (land, capital, and labour) were fixed and immobile. In the contemporary world, largely due to technological changes, this has become dramatically untrue of capital, and much less true of labour. However, the frequent political resistance to international mobility of goods is often dramatically intensified in the case of the international mobility of people. Here we move from the domain of international trade policy to the domain of immigration policy. The most critical linkage between the two relates to international trade in services, especially services which require physical proximity between service supplier and service user. As international trade in services of various kinds continues to grow, the line between trade in services and migration of people becomes increasingly blurred.[1] Of the economic integration regimes reviewed in this book, only the EU to date has committed itself to free internal movement of people.

This chapter addresses a question that has confronted all individuals and groups of individuals who, throughout history, have chosen to live in a state of civil society with one another and for whom social, political, and economic relationships are integral to the self-definition of each individual in the community of which they are a part. How does one define and justify the conditions of membership in the community? In the context of the modern nation state, this primarily directs our attention to the substance and procedures of our immigration policies; who may become citizens and who must remain strangers, for nations imply boundaries and boundaries at some point imply closure. Current intense public debates in Canada, the USA, and Western Europe over central features of domestic immigration policies reflect the deep conflicts that immigration issues have always provoked. As of the late 1980s, approximately 100 million people were resident outside their nations of current citizenship. Roughly 35 million are in sub-Sahara Africa, and approximately 13 to 15 million each in the prosperous regions of Western Europe and North America. Another 15 million or so are in the Middle East and Asia.[2] Of the total number of immigrants, about 18 million are refugees.[3]

THE VALUES

Liberty

At the heart of debates in all western democracies over immigration policy now, and in the past, lie two core values which stand in some irreducible degree in opposition to one another: liberty and community. Theories of liberty and community each present themselves with almost endless variations, but for our purposes, the essence of the two values, in the context of immigration policy, can be fairly readily captured. As Carens points out:

> [All liberal] theories begin with some kind of assumption about the equal moral worth of individuals. In one way or another, all treat the individual as prior to the community. Such foundations provide little basis for drawing fundamental distinctions between citizens and aliens who seek to become citizens.[4]

Carens goes on to review three contemporary approaches to liberal theory: libertarianism, social contractarianism and utilitarianism. From the libertarian perspective, exemplified by scholars such as Nozick, individual property rights play a central role.[5] In a state of nature, individuals have rights to acquire and use property and to alienate it voluntarily. The existence of the state is only justified to the extent that it is required to protect property rights and facilitate their voluntary transfer. On this view, if aliens wish to move to Canada or the USA they should be free to do so, provided they do not violate anyone else's rights. To the extent that citizens choose to enter into contracts of employment with them, or sell them land, homes, or businesses, the rights of both citizens and aliens would be violated by externally imposed constraints thereon. From a social contractarian perspective, as exemplified most prominently by the writings of John Rawls,[6] an ideal social constitution would be constructed behind a veil of ignorance, where individuals know nothing about their own personal situations, class, race, sex, natural talents, religious beliefs, individuals goals, values and talents etc. The purpose of the veil of ignorance is 'to nullify the effect of specific contingencies which put men at odds', because natural and social contingencies are 'arbitrary from a moral point of view', and therefore are factors which ought not to influence the choice of principles of justice.

As Carens points out, whether one is a citizen of a rich nation or a poor nation, whether one is already a citizen of a particular state or an alien who wishes to become a citizen, are the kinds of specific contingencies that could set people at odds, and a fair procedure for choosing principles of justice should therefore exclude knowledge of these circumstances, just as it excludes knowledge of one's race, sex or social class. We should therefore take a global, not a national, view of the original position (the 'universal brotherhood of man').[7] Behind this global veil of ignorance, and considering possible restrictions on freedom, we should adopt the perspective of those who would be most disadvantaged by the restrictions, in this case often the perspective of the alien who wants to immigrate. From this perspective, very few restrictions on immigration can be morally justified. Rawls would recognize that liberty may be restricted for the sake of liberty, in the sense that all liberties depend on the existence of public order and security. To cite a metaphor used by Carens, it does no one any good to take so many people into a lifeboat that it is swamped and everyone drowns.[8] But short of a reasonable, as opposed to a hypothetical expectation of this prospect, largely unconstrained immigration would seem implied by Rawls' social contract theory. However, Galloway has recently challenged Carens' implication that a Rawlsian social contract version of liberal theory requires open borders in the sense of a recognition that each person in the world has a right to choose his country of residence. Just as within a given society individuals cannot be viewed as owing duties to facilitate or promote the life plans of others when this would completely undermine the ability of the former to pursue their own life plans, so as between countries members of one society are not under a duty to make every sacrifice required in order to promote the autonomy of individuals in other countries where this would undermine the autonomy of members of the first country.[9]

From a utilitarian perspective, the utilities or disutilities experienced by both aliens and citizens would be entered in the utilitarian calculus.[10] Some citizens would gain from being able to enter into contractual relationships with immigrants, others might lose if wages are depressed through the additional competition they bring to labour markets, while yet other citizens as consumers might benefit from access to cheaper goods or services. Against these costs and benefits accruing to citizens must be set whatever costs and benefits accrue to aliens by being permitted entry – in most cases one assumes that the benefits substantially outweigh the costs otherwise they would presumably not have chosen to resettle in another land. Moreover, to the extent that many aliens will have made the wrenching decision to resettle because of economic privation or religious or political oppression or persecution in their homelands, the gains to them from being permitted to join a new and more congenial community may be very substantial. Thus, from a utilitarian perspective, while perhaps providing more scope for restrictions on immigration than either the libertarian or social contractarian perspective, relatively open borders would in general be dictated.

369

Community

In opposition to these liberal values stand the core values of community. Here, it is asserted, in the context of immigration policy, that control over who may enter is a powerful expression of a nation's identity and autonomy – in other words its sovereignty. Sovereignty entails the unlimited power of a nation, like that of a free individual, to decide whether, under what conditions, and with what effect it will consent to enter into a relationship with a stranger.[11] The most prominent contemporary proponent of this view is Michael Walzer.[12] In justifying this view, he draws analogies between neighbourhoods, clubs, and families. While it is true that in the case of neighbourhoods, people are free, in general, to enter and exit as they please, he argues that to analogize nations to neighbourhoods, permitting unconstrained entry by aliens in any number from anywhere in the world would destroy the concept of neighbourhood. He argues that it is only the nationalization of welfare (or the nationalization of culture and politics) that opens the neighbourhood communities to whoever chooses to come in. Neighbourhoods can be open only if countries are at least potentially closed. Only if the state makes a selection among would-be members and guarantees the loyalty, security, and welfare of the individuals it selects, can local communities take shape as 'different' associations determined solely by personal preference and market capacity. Walzer claims that if states ever become large neighbourhoods, it is likely that neighbourhoods would become little states. Their members would organize to defend the local politics and culture against strangers. Historically, it is claimed, neighbourhoods have turned into closed or parochial communities whenever the state was open. Thus, Walzer rejects the analogy of states to neighbourhoods and rather analogizes states with clubs and families, where members are free to determine the conditions of membership. Walzer concludes:

> The distribution of membership is not pervasively subject to the constraints of justice. Across a considerable range of the decisions that are made, states are simply free to take in strangers (or not) – much as they are free, leaving aside the claims of the needy, to share their wealth with foreign friends, to honor the achievements of foreign artists, scholars, and scientists, to choose their trading partners, and to enter into collective security arrangements with foreign states. But the right to choose an admissions policy is more basic than any of these, for it is not merely a matter of acting in the world, exercising sovereignty, and pursuing national interests. At stake here is the shape of the community that acts in the world, exercises sovereignty, and so on. Admission and exclusion are at the core of communal independence. They suggest the deepest meaning of self-determination. Without them, there could not be *communities of character*, historically stable,

ongoing associations of men and women with some special commitment to one another and some special sense of their common life.[13]

Unlike the liberal theories, which imply no or very few limitations on entry, Walzer's theory, at least without further qualification, appears to permit almost any limitations on entry that a state should choose to impose, including admission policies that are overtly racist. Two controversial features of his theory are the notion that political sovereignty is a near-absolute value – a view increasingly challenged by the evolution of international human rights norms – and that the only communities of character are those that reflect ethnic, religious or cultural commonalities – a view many liberals would challenge on the grounds that common commitments to liberal civic institutions and mutual tolerance of intermediate sub-communities of interest can sustain communities of character. In any event, these two core values of liberty and community clearly frame the major issues that must be confronted in the design of any country's immigration policies.

THE ISSUES

The size of the intake

The issue of the size of the intake of immigrants cannot readily be separated from the composition of the intake, in terms of deducing what kinds of demands the immigrants are likely to make on our community. However, to the extent that the two issues can be separated, regardless of the composition of the intake the notion that any country could accept and absorb millions of immigrants a year without critical features of infrastructure collapsing and congestion externalities being created on all sides is unlikely to be readily accepted. One might, of course, argue that a natural equilibrium is likely to establish itself before this happens – if the intake threatens these conditions, some would-be immigrants will abandon an interest in resettling. However, collective action problems may prevent such an equilibrium emerging at all or at any event quickly or smoothly, and it is not obvious that Rawls' 'public order' qualification on the right of entry tells us anything very helpful about when congestion externalities have reached the point where the lifeboat metaphor can appropriately be invoked. This concern is somewhat reminiscent of the concerns raised by Thomas Malthus in 1798 in his famous essay on the *Principle of Population as it Affects the Future Improvement of Society.* As Heilbroner states the Malthusian thesis:

[The essay on population claimed] that there was a tendency in nature for population to outstrip all possible means of subsistence. Far from ascending to an ever higher level, society was caught in a hopeless trap in which the human reproductive urge would inevitably shove humanity to the sheer brink of the precipice of existence. Instead of being headed for Utopia, the human lot was forever condemned to a losing struggle between ravenous and multiplying mouths and the eternally insufficient stock of Nature's cupboard, however diligently that cupboard might be searched.[14]

In Malthus' view, land, unlike people, cannot be multiplied – land does not breed. While Malthus' fears were subsequently proven to be greatly exaggerated, and most dramatically refuted by the settlement of the New World, where increased population through immigration, in terms of increased labour and capital on the supply-side and increased aggregate demand on the demand-side, made possible the realization of enormous economies of scale and the technological advances that accompanied them. However, as birth rates and destitution levels in many impoverished Third World countries exemplify today, Malthus' concerns were not entirely without foundation, and a totally unrestricted immigration policy may legitimately implicate those concerns. Once some restriction on total intake is recognized as necessary, then the composition of that restricted intake must be addressed.

The composition of the intake

A host of complex and morally sensitive issues arise here. On many of these issues, the core values of liberty and community are likely to yield quite different implications.

A market in entitlements

One method of allocating scarce entitlements to entry that appeals to a number of economists would be for the state to auction off these entitlements on a periodic basis, and allocate them to the highest bidders.[15] It could presumably be claimed on behalf of this allocative mechanism that the successful bidders would be those who valued the right of entry most highly, because the opportunities for them following entry are likely to be greatest, presumably reflecting the greater value that present citizens are likely to place on whatever economic activities these successful bidders intend to engage in. On the other hand, it could be cogently argued that this method of allocation of scarce entitlements offends notions of distributive justice by rewarding ability to pay and disregarding claims that other non-citizens might be able to make for entry, on the grounds of, for example, economic deprivation, religious or ethnic persecution, political oppression in their home countries, family reunification, and where despite their lack of material resources, the opportunity to emigrate may dramatically enhance their individual autonomy and welfare, perhaps to the point of making the difference between life and death.

Lotteries

One could also employ the mechanism of a lottery. That is to say, all aspiring entrants would register their applications, and names of individuals in the applicant pool would be drawn on a periodic basis until the total intake for the period was met. This method of allocation would obviously neutralize the role that wealth would play in the allocation of entitlements to entry, although being entirely insensitive to relative claims of merit or desert that individual members of the applicant pool, and existing citizens, might feel should be vindicated.

Queues (first-come first-served)

Scarce entitlements to entry could be allocated on a queuing – first-come first-served basis, where the order of registration or filing of applications is recorded, and applicants simply selected from the top of the queue until the total, collectively-agreed, intake for the period in question is met. While, like lotteries, this method of allocation is wealth neutral, it is vulnerable to all the same objections in that it is entirely insensitive to relative claims of merit or desert that might be asserted by or on behalf of individual applicants.

Once these three methods of allocation are rejected, either in whole or in part, as the primary allocative mechanisms, administrative (merit) allocation is left as the only major alternative. In formulating the criteria for evaluating relative claims of merit or desert in legislative or administrative policies, the normative considerations surrounding the claims of the following categories of applicants would have to be addressed:

Applicants who pose a national security risk

Obviously, no normative theory of immigration recognizes that an invading country is entitled to unopposed entry on the grounds of free movement of people. Similarly, no theory would recognize an obligation to admit subversives committed to overthrowing the state by force. A more difficult question arises with respect to the admission of significant influxes of people who come from non-liberal societies, even if they do not come with any subversive intent. In other words, how tolerant must we be of the intolerant? Carens argues that there may be a case, even from a liberty perspective, for excluding such people where the cumulative effect of their presence may be to undermine the maintenance of liberal institutions. From a communitarian perspective, given that the state, with certain qualifications, can set any conditions of entry that it pleases, exclusion here would be viewed as unproblematic.

Refugee or asylum claimants

Aliens who have found their way to our country or are displaced in third world countries and seek refugee or asylum status on account of the threat of political, religious, or ethnic persecution in their homelands present a morally compelling claim for admission on most theories of immigration. Liberal theories would readily recognize such claims, given the premise of the recognition of the equal moral worth of all individuals, and given the special concern in Rawlsian social contract theory with the plight of the most disadvantaged. Even on communitarian theories of immigration, at least as articulated by Walzer, a claim arises under the mutual aid or good Samaritan principle which he recognizes as applying where positive assistance is urgently needed by one of the parties and the risks and costs of giving it are relatively low for the other party. Historically, with some exceptions, refugee or asylum claims have tended to involve relatively small numbers of people at any given time so that Walzer's conditions were often readily satisfied. However, in the contemporary world, approximately 18 million individuals have been displaced from their homelands by war, civil unrest or religious or ethnic persecution – up from 8 million in 1980 and 2.5 million in 1970; in addition, another 24 million are displaced within their own countries.[16] With ready means of international mobility now available to many of them, the extent of the principle of mutual aid has become highly contentious. Walzer states: 'I assume that there are limits on our collective liability, but I do not know how to specify them.'[17]

Economically necessitous aliens

This category of claimant embraces aliens who because of simple economic impoverishment in their homelands wish to resettle in our country (sometimes referred to as economic refugees). From a liberal perspective, their claims would be viewed as having different strengths, depending on which strand of liberal theory one espoused. Within a domestic libertarian framework, provided their entry did not interfere with rights of others, they should be admitted. Within a utilitarian framework, much would depend on what they could contribute to our society relative to the costs that they would impose on it, although a global utilitarian framework would also weigh the benefits to them. Within a social contractarian framework they would engage our special concern to the extent that they could properly be characterized as amongst the least advantaged. In contrast, from a communitarian perspective, Walzer claims that we have very limited obligations to such persons, or at least we are free collectively to take that view.[18] Perhaps we have an obligation to provide foreign aid, or as he argues in his criticism of the White Australia policy where a country has large empty land masses it may have an obligation to share these spaces with necessitous aliens. In his view, to recognize a more general claim would be to invite the prospect of a country being overrun by almost unlimited numbers of disadvantaged aliens from around the globe who share very little in common with existing members of the community, and who would thus threaten to undermine its sense of community.

Family members

Both Carens and Walzer recognize that aliens who have family relationships with citizens can make an especially salient normative claim for admission, in Walzer's[19] case because community bonds and affinities are readily embraced by such relatives and, in Carens'[20] case, presumably because to exclude them would be to deny their equal moral worth, although curiously he suggests that more distant relatives would have a weaker claim. A libertarian perspective on family reunification claimants would readily countenance their admission, provided they imposed no costs involuntarily on others. The social contractarian perspective might be ambivalent to the extent that family members do not fall within the category of the least advantaged. A domestic utilitarian perspective might again be somewhat ambivalent, particularly in the case of older or infirm family members who might in some cases be expected to contribute little to our society and conceivably make significant demands on us, although a global utilitarian perspective would also weigh the benefits to them.

Culturally homogeneous aliens

A complex and sensitive issue arises as to whether a state can morally attach conditions of entry for aliens that are designed to maintain the community's cultural homogeneity. On most versions of liberal theory, such discriminatory conditions are likely to be suspect, in the sense that they do not treat all individuals as being of equal moral worth. From a communitarian perspective, the foundational premise is that the community is free to set any terms of entry that it wishes, particularly where the conditions are designed to reinforce shared, common values. Both core values here encounter difficulties. From a liberal perspective, it is necessary to accommodate the aspirations for national self-determination that independence movements around the world, particularly in the post-war years, have strongly evinced. In the contemporary world, the transformation of Eastern Europe and the claims for independence or greater autonomy on the part of many forms of sub-parts of these countries all reflect, to some degree, a claim to an entitlement to recognition and reinforcement of culturally or politically distinct communities. Within Canada, claims advanced on behalf of Quebec's francophone majority to its being a distinct society, and a potential claim to political independence, with a corollary claim in both cases to control the characteristics of its immigrant population, rests in large part on the claim to cultural distinctiveness, which may entail exclusionary implications. Some claims of North American Aboriginal people to self-government, at least on reserves, also rests on a claim to an entitlement to protect and preserve cultural distinctiveness, even where this entails exclusionary elements. Carens, within the liberal egalitarian framework that he adopts, is also prepared to concede that a country or society with a long tradition of close cultural homogeneity might be entitled to maintain a restrictive immigration society, provided that it is applied more or less equally to all aliens.[21]

Better-endowed and less well-endowed aliens

Can a state in setting the terms of admission to the community it represents, morally justify discriminating in favour of more well-endowed and against less well-endowed aliens (in terms of skills or material resources). The different versions of liberal theory might respond to this question differently. Within a libertarian framework, it is more likely that better endowed immigrants, in terms of skills or capital, will be able to establish mutually beneficial contractual relationships with existing members of the admitting community; less well-endowed aliens presumably pose a greater risk of becoming a public burden in terms of health and education costs, unemployment and social welfare costs for example, and all of these programmes involve coercive forms of redistribution to which libertarians traditionally object. Within a domestic utilitarian framework, obviously the more that an alien can contribute to the admitting society in terms of skills or capital, and the fewer demands he makes on that society, the more likely it is that the utilitarian calculus will be met, although from a global utilitarian perspective the calculus may go the other way, with special recognition being accorded to the benefits likely to be derived from immigration by less well-endowed immigrants.

Within a Rawlsian social contract framework, the least well-endowed aliens should engage our special moral concern. Moreover, it might be argued that by adopting a preference towards the better endowed aliens we encourage their exit from their homelands and promote a brain drain or capital drain that reduces the welfare of their communities of origin, which often face severe scarcities of human and financial capital. Carens believes that we cannot justify encroaching on the rights of such individuals on this account. Moreover, the effects of emigration on the welfare of citizens in the sending country are far from clear.[22] Arguably, owners of capital receive a reduced return if wage rates amongst workers who remain increase (and these workers are correspondingly better off). Some negative externalities from population density may be reduced but some advantages from population density and size (e.g. ease of communication and transportation) may also be reduced. While the 'brain drain' has often attracted concern, the concern assumes that highly skilled professionals, business people, or workers are not capturing in their earnings all the value of their skills, but are creating positive externalities that will be lost when they leave (e.g. imparting skills or knowledge to younger individuals). To the extent that their education has been financed by their home governments, their departure may entail a loss of this investment, but on the other hand, taxes paid by parents may, on average, reflect these costs. To the extent that emigrants are younger and more productive than the home population on average, the sending country loses their taxes with which to finance social programmes for older citizens and children. Finally, the substantial remittances sent home by immigrants (about $US66 billion world-wide in 1989) substantially mitigate or even offset many of the above costs to sending countries.[23]

Guest workers

We are familiar with the contemporary phenomenon of 'guest workers' in many countries in Western Europe, where these workers are admitted on a temporary basis for confined categories of tasks and without most of the legal incidents of citizenship[24] and with no formal assurance of ever being able to qualify for citizenship. Programmes for domestic workers and farm workers in North America possess similar features.[25] However, the phenomenon has long historical antecedents – in the past we called such people indentured workers, or more bluntly, coolie labour. In most versions of liberal theory, such arrangements are offensive, simply because they do not treat all individuals as of equal moral worth. This would be particularly so within the libertarian and social contractarian frameworks. A domestic utilitarian framework may be more ambiguous, to the extent that guest worker arrangements are intended to confine aliens to sectors of the economy where indigenous labour is not available, and to prevent competition with, and thus the imposition of costs on, indigenous workers in other sectors. It might also be argued that guest workers introduce desirable degrees of flexibility into domestic labour markets, and reduce the burden on domestic social welfare nets in times of high unemployment by virtue of their transitory status. However, on a global utilitarian calculus, given the typical circumstances of most guest workers, net utility would presumably be maximized by enlarging their rights to encompass full citizenship if they desire it, and indeed it has often proven difficult in fact to expel them once family ties, and economic and social networks have been established. From Walzer's communitarian perspective, he argues that to admit guest workers as residents in one's community and permit them to develop personal, social and occupational ties as members of that community, but to treat them as a community apart, or as 'second class citizens', undermines communal values.[26] While this view might well have force with long-term 'guest-workers', some operational distinction (which may be difficult to draw and maintain) seems required between such workers and those admitted under temporary entry visas (as provided for in the Canada–US Free Trade Agreement) such as are issued to professional, business or technical personnel ancillary to international trade in goods or services.

Illegal immigrants

This category of immigrants embraces those who have taken up residence in a host country without satisfying whatever substantive criteria of permanent admission have been prescribed by law with respect to the various characteristics of claimants described above, or at least without following the procedures that govern those determinations e.g. they are visitors or temporary workers who have outstayed their visas. On the one hand, it can be argued from a liberal perspective that to give priority or preference to immigrants, simply because they are here, over aliens with claims of similar substance who seek admission from outside our boundaries and in accordance with prescribed procedures is to violate the precepts of equal treatment of similarly situated individuals. On the other hand, it might be argued from a communitarian perspective, that where illegal immigrants have been resident in the host country for some significant period of time and have established ties and relationships with existing members of the community, perhaps procreated and reared children in the host community, and contributed positively to the community in productive ways through employment or other activities, we have no right to expel them, and indeed perhaps have an obligation at some point to validate retrospectively their status by according them citizenship (through e.g. amnesty policies), even though at the expense of according recognition to a class of intentional lawbreakers and queue-jumpers.

EMPIRICAL EVIDENCE ON THE WELFARE EFFECTS OF IMMIGRATION

While the welfare effects of immigration policy have not traditionally received anything like the attention that has been devoted to other aspects of international economics, fortunately recent theoretical and empirical work[27] has begun to yield a fairly clear consensus on the effects of immigration, despite the fact that this consensus is sharply at variance, in many respects, with widely held popular perceptions.

First, as with the analysis of international trade, it is crucial to distinguish the national from the cosmopolitan (or global) perspective. From a global economic perspective, it seems largely beyond dispute that open immigration is the optimal global strategy, with some well-defined qualifications. The argument for this is quite straightforward: open immigration encourages human resources to move to their most productive uses, whatever the localized distributional impact in countries of emigration or immigration. Hamilton and Whalley,[28] for example, provide estimates for 1977 that the gain from removing all restrictions on international immigration could exceed world-wide GNP in that year. More qualified estimates would still yield gains constituting a significant proportion of world GNP and exceeding gains from removing all trade restrictions.[29] As Sykes stresses in a recent paper,[30] the most important qualification to this proposition is fiscally-induced migration, driven by a desire to access entitlement systems such as social welfare, social security, and public health care systems in other countries. Obviously, migration induced for these reasons may not entail a redeployment or relocation of human resources to more productive uses. While both the open global immigration base case, and the principal qualification to it, are obvious enough, it is important not to lose sight of either, because from an economic perspective, the base case suggests that domestic debates about immigration policy are almost by definition likely to pertain to distributional issues, about which economics as a discipline has a limited amount to say, beyond clarifying the actual distributional impacts of alternative policies.[31] The qualification to the base case is also important because it suggests economic, as opposed to distributional reasons, for adopting particular selection mechanisms for admitting new immigrants, or alternatively attaching limitations on their access to non-contributory public services or programmes.

The most recent and comprehensive reviews of the empirical evidence on the effects of immigration establish a fairly clear consensus on certain propositions, and some differences on others. First, despite recurrent debates over the course of history of many Western countries as to their 'absorptive capacity', and vacillations between catastrophic Malthusian scenarios and the perception of immigration as the driving force in opening up the New World,[32] recent evidence now appears to establish that immigrants as a whole raise the average income of natives, principally in two ways: a scale effect, and a dependency effect. The scale effect simply means that countries with a larger and more rapidly growing population will be able to sustain some industries and some social infrastructure activities that would not be economically viable at lower population sizes. There is some difference of opinion among analysts on the magnitude of the scale effects. The Economic Council of Canada in its recent study estimates these effects to be quite modest, finding that for every additional one million persons – a figure that could be attained through a net immigration rate of say 100,000 per year over a decade – GDP per capita in Canada would be increased by somewhere between 0.1% and 0.3% (about $71 per present resident). The Council estimates that on the basis of today's production technology and capital investment, a population of approximately 100 million people in Canada (compared to the present 26 million) would maximize income per person as measured by GDP per capita. At that population size, the average income of Canadians would be roughly 7% higher than at today's population.[33] However, long-term projections of this kind, entailing a population increase of this order of magnitude, seem highly unlikely to capture a number of intervening variables that may completely undermine the welfare judgement. Simon, while not assigning specific numeric weights to the gains from scale associated with a larger population, argues that apart from scale effects *per se*, dynamic effects, such as broader diffusion of technological and other ideas and greater possibilities for learning-by-doing, may generate quite significant positive effects on average native incomes from a larger population.[34] Simon's argument is not especially convincing, particularly in a country the size of the USA, and particularly in an international environment where scale effects chiefly in capital rather than labour intensive industries can often be captured by trading into foreign markets and do not require a large local employment or consumer base.

The second reason why immigration is likely to enhance native incomes on average is through the dependency effect. This simply means that because immigrants on average tend to be disproportionately represented in the wage-earning age group, and relatively under-represented in the younger and older age groups, the percentage of immigrants dependent on government transfers will typically be lower than for natives.[35] This implies that on average immigrants will contribute more through taxes and take out less in public expenditures than natives. The Economic Council of Canada recently estimated that the net gain per capita from a doubling of the recently prevailing level of annual immigration to Canada from 0.4 to 0.8% of the present population i.e. going from about 160,000 immigrants a year to 340,000 by the year 2015, would be $78 per capita.[36] Adding the Council's estimated scale gains to the gross savings in tax costs of dependency, and subtracting the expenses associated with processing the extra immigrants yields an estimate that by 2015, a doubling in the immigration rate would raise per capita incomes by $350 – approximately 1% of expected annual income at that time.[37] This increase in average incomes of residents is still quite modest, and because it entails an aggregation function, may obscure quite uneven distributional impacts on different subsets of the resident population. Some of these are mentioned below.

Beyond these general effects of immigration on average native incomes, other propositions are also now reasonably well settled. First, taking immigrants as a group (including refugees), labour force participation rates, unemployment rates, and participation in welfare assistance programmes in both the USA and Canada seem comparable, and in some cases superior, to the performance of the native population on average. Second, the bulk of the evidence, both for the USA and internationally, also suggests that while immigrants, following entry, start off earning less on average than their native counterparts, this gap closes after between 10 and 15 years, and indeed after that point immigrants may earn more on average than their native counterparts. Third, the evidence suggests no or minimal displacement by immigrants of natives in the job market, including less skilled and minority native sub-groups, and no or minimal depression of the natives' incomes.[38] Fourth, the evidence also suggests that immigrants on average are better educated than is the native population on average. Fifth, discriminatory attitudes by residents to immigrants of different racial, ethnic, or cultural backgrounds seem to decline markedly with increased contact (the so-called 'contact hypothesis').[39]

All of this is to suggest that not only do natives gain, perhaps modestly, from immigration, but that immigrants themselves, presumably reflecting a rational calculus favouring moving in the first place, also substantially improve their lot in life, and on most performance measures do at least as well as the native population. Thus, as the Economic Council of Canada concludes:

> Immigration offers a rare chance for a policy change where everyone can gain. Those already here gain a little more real income, a more excitingly diverse society, and the satisfaction of opening up to others the great opportunities that living in Canada gives. Among those who come, some gain safety from persecution, some gain freedom from want, some gain a secure future for their children, and nearly all become economically better off.[40]

CONCLUSION

There is an enormous volume of refugees or otherwise necessitous persons currently seeking resettlement in developed countries of the world who are often from cultural, linguistic, religious, and racial backgrounds that are in many respects quite different from those of refugee claimants in previous periods, and sharply different from the majority of the indigenous population of developed countries. This has placed extreme strains on domestic immigration policies in developed countries, and on the social and political consensus surrounding the appropriate form of these policies. In moderating these strains, it is crucial to identify key linkages between immigration policies and other classes of international and domestic policies and in so doing not to impose on immigration policy more weight than it can reasonably bear.

In this respect, it is clear that the level of demand for resettlement would be substantially diminished if developed countries, through appropriate forms of international cooperation, took stronger and more effective policy stances towards human rights violations and political or religious oppression in many countries of origin. In addition, much more liberal trade policies towards developing country exports, the provision of more generous foreign aid in cases of natural disasters, and more effective developmental aid in forms, or with conditions attached, designed to address (and, if necessary) discipline governmental incompetence and corruption that is often pervasive in many developing and former command economies, are clearly important substitutes for immigration. For foreign aid to be fully effective, developing and former command economies need to be encouraged to adopt domestic policies that promote high levels of economic growth at home. A key element in such policies is outward-looking trade policies that assign substantial weight to export-led growth, and concomitant reduction in reliance on trade and currency restrictions designed to foster often inefficient import-substituting domestic industries. Unfortunately, in this respect, reflecting a massive exercise in hypocrisy on the part of many Western countries, the costs of protectionist policies imposed by developed countries on developing countries currently exceed the entire value of foreign aid provided to these countries.[41]

In short, all other things being equal, it seems clear that most refugees or displaced persons would prefer to return to their homelands, but the policies of most developed countries do not reflect this priority. Instead, the consequences of displacement are seen primarily as an immigration problem, where effective policy responses are highly circumscribed or at any event intensely controversial. It needs to be added that while growth-oriented development policies are likely to reduce migration rates over the long-term, evidence suggests that in the shorter term, the disruptive impacts of rapid development on traditional social and economic structures in developing countries (e.g. rural–urban migration and saturated urban labour markets) may actually increase international migration.[42] This said, however, the insights from recent empirical work on immigration tell us that, perhaps within some broad parameters that we presently seem well inside, we could benefit modestly and potential immigrants very substantially from a much higher level of immigration than most developed countries are presently committed to. Just as with trade policy, the facts (as opposed to the prejudices) suggest that national and cosmopolitan perspectives on immigration policy do not sharply diverge.

15

DISPUTE RESOLUTION IN INTERNATIONAL TRADE

DISPUTE RESOLUTION MECHANISMS IN THE GATT*

Introduction

It is important to remember that the General Agreement on Tariffs and Trade was originally intended as only one element of what was supposed to be a much more ambitious institutional structure. By 1950 it was clear that the US Congress would not accept the International Trade Organization, with the result that the only international organization left for the regulation of world trade was a provisional agreement never intended as a framework for such an organization.[1]

From the beginning, then, the GATT was characterized by temporary measures and *ad hoc* solutions to emerging problems. Administrative services for the GATT were provided by the Interim Commission of the ITO and responsibility for overall direction was taken on by regular meetings of the Contracting Parties, with Geneva as the *de facto* site.[2]

In contradistinction to the ITO draft charter, the GATT in its original terms makes no provision for arbitration, nor does it make any reference to the possibility of appeal to the International Court of Justice in resolving disputes.[3] The emphasis is on consultation and consensus: both of the main provisions dealing with dispute resolution, Articles XXII and XXIII, seek to encourage negotiation; and any action taken to enforce a ruling must be agreed to by all of the Contracting Parties. Indeed, early efforts at formal amendment to the GATT saw the Contracting Parties attempt to enhance the utility of consultation: Article XXII was amended to allow for the Contracting Parties to intervene (and presumably mediate) in consultations if bilateral talks failed to resolve a dispute.[4]

Notwithstanding the genesis of the GATT, the history of GATT dispute resolution has evinced a tendency towards greater reliance on a rule-oriented regime in resolving disputes. The first complaints to come before the GATT were referred to the Chairman of the Contracting Parties at the Second

Session in 1948 (without any warrant for such a procedure in the GATT itself), who gave a ruling on the legality or otherwise of the measures complained of.[5] At that same session, a 'working party' was set up for the first time to report on a dispute between the USA and Cuba regarding the latter's textile regulations. The Working Party, which consisted of GATT representatives from Canada, India, the Netherlands, Cuba, and the USA, was to investigate the matter 'in the light of the factual evidence' and to recommend a 'practical solution' to the Contracting Parties. Three days of meetings led to a compromise satisfactory to both of the disputing parties.[6] In contrast to the 'rulings' given by the Chairman, the working parties were really a forum for encouraging negotiation. This was not a third-party investigation for the purpose of coming to objective conclusions on the merits: such a function was precluded by the participation of the disputants, and the fact that the other representatives were acting on the instructions of their respective countries.

The Third Session, in 1949, saw the advent of something like third-party panel dispute resolution. Chile complained to the Contracting Parties about the practices of Australia with respect to fertilizer subsidies. A Working Party was established, and the report drafted by the neutral countries of the Working Party was accepted by the Contracting Parties notwithstanding the dissent of the Australian representative.[7] But it was not until the Seventh Session, in 1952, that the Contracting Parties resorted to the panel procedures which have now become the standard means of dispute resolution within the GATT.[8] The use of panels marked an important shift for the GATT. They no longer included representatives from the disputing parties; major trading nations like the UK and the USA were not automatically panel members; and the panel and the GATT Secretariat worked together to develop more formal procedures for the functioning of panels.[9] The GATT Secretariat, in a report to the Contracting Parties, identified this move to panel procedures as an attempt to instill greater objectivity in dispute resolution.[10] One GATT insider has called the institution of panels a Secretariat 'conspiracy' to enhance its influence, and lessen that of the larger countries which tended to dominate working parties.[11] Whatever the real reasons for their creation, panels marked a move away from the GATT as an institution for facilitating negotiation towards a greater emphasis on third-party adjudication.

But the move towards third-party adjudication was not written in stone. No sooner had the panel process been instituted than it fell into a degree of disfavour with GATT nations. During the 1960s, very few disputes were brought before panels – there were only six panel complaints in this period – and from 1963 to 1970 no panels were set up at all. Countries resorted to consultation to resolve disputes, and the more contentious issues were dealt with by working groups, which issued reports with recommendations rather than rendered court-like judgments.[12] Several reasons have been suggested for this move away from legalism in procedure.[13]

The 1960s witnessed a growing perception among GATT countries that the rules of the agreement were becoming outdated. This period also saw the emergence of the EU, Japan, and several less-developed countries as important trading powers within the GATT. No one in this group found legalism particularly salutary to their interests: strict interpretations of the Agreement would have interfered with domestic programmes designed to manage international trade in various key sectors.[14] Seen in this light, the legalism of the 1950s was probably more a result of the GATT's domination by the USA than some deeply-felt commitment on the part of GATT members in general. Moreover, the 1960s was a period which saw declining compliance with the GATT through the use of non-tariff barriers (even as tariffs fell dramatically after the Kennedy Round), and sectoral agreements which effectively managed trade.[15] Faced with trade restrictions that challenged the very assumptions of the GATT, its dispute resolution mechanisms appeared increasingly inadequate to the task of ensuring compliance with the Agreement. The 1970s would see a revival of the use of panel procedures, but this was largely the result of a new aggressiveness on the part of the USA.[16] The real challenges facing the GATT had to be dealt with by negotiation.

The Tokyo Round was initiated in part to deal with contentious forms of non-tariff barriers. The USA also hoped to use the Round to strengthen the panels by elaborating their procedures and increasing the predictability of their outcomes. The USA did achieve an important codification of existing practice, and a renewed commitment from GATT countries to use the agreement's dispute resolution mechanisms.[17] As well, some of the subsidiary codes negotiated during the Tokyo Round included their own dispute resolution provisions which set deadlines for dispute resolution, and allowed resort to a panel as of right (rather than at the discretion of other GATT members).[18] But US efforts towards an even greater emphasis on legalism, for example, through the imposition of stricter deadlines, were blocked.[19] Several agreements since the Tokyo Round have further clarified and to some extent enhanced panel dispute resolution, but the results have been less than some want and more than others would like. Dispute resolution reform has been an important item on the agenda during the Uruguay Round and has resulted in a new Understanding on Rules and Procedures Governing the Settlement of Disputes[20] that largely ratifies, on a permanent basis, the Mid-term Review Agreement, adopted on an interim basis in 1988 during the Uruguay Round negotiations.

A description of the Dispute Resolution Mechanism

The principal Dispute Resolution Provisions of the GATT

It is important to emphasize at the outset that there is no single way to resolve disputes under the GATT. In fact, the Agreement supplies a variety of more or less formal means to settle disagreements over international trade: leading American commentators argue that there are really thirty ways of resolving disputes under its auspices.[21] Its text is replete with provisions that provide for consultation over disputes. For example, Article VII:1 provides that a country must review the way it values goods for customs purposes if requested to do so by another Contracting Party. Other clauses are framed to prevent disputes, for example via waivers of obligations under Article XXV:5.[22] Moreover, the GATT operates informally to ensure compliance merely because it is the forum for the discussion of international trade issues. Thus, while panels have been an important means of dispute resolution since 1947, it is probable that informal negotiations have played at least as important a role in settling disagreements.[23] As well, the GATT helps to prevent abuses through its surveillance of international trade and country compliance with GATT rules – in short, by shaming countries into living up to their international commitments.[24]

Nonetheless, when GATT observers refer to formal dispute resolution procedures, they are typically alluding to the body of practice that has grown up around Articles XXII and XXIII of the Agreement. Article XXII requires Contracting Parties to consult with each other in the event of a dispute with respect to any matter affecting the operation of the GATT and to give sympathetic consideration to representations by each other. The Contracting Parties at large (typically through the agency of the GATT Secretariat) may, at the request of a Contracting Party, assist in the consultations. Article XXIII provides that if any Contracting Party considers that any benefit accruing to it directly or indirectly under the GATT is being 'nullified or impaired' or that the attainment of any objective of the Agreement is being impeded as the result of: (1) the failure of another Contracting Party to carry out its obligations under the Agreement; or (2) the application by another Contracting Party of any measure, whether or not it conflicts with the provisions of the Agreement; or (3) the existence of any other situation, and consultations have failed, the aggrieved Contracting Party may request the Contracting Parties to investigate the complaint and if found justified authorize the aggrieved Party to suspend such concessions or other obligations under the Agreement to the Party complained against as they deem appropriate in the event that the latter fails to modify its offending policies or practices.

This chapter reviews past practice under Articles XXII and XXIII, especially as it concerns the formation and activities of panels, and then evaluates various reform proposals, as well as briefly considering dispute resolution processes under the Canada–US FTA and under NAFTA. However, one note of caution must be sounded. The distinction that has been drawn between formal and informal dispute resolution, and the use of words like 'mechanism' or 'procedure' should not mislead the reader into thinking that practice under Articles XXII and XXIII amounts to a well-defined legal process. In fact, the fairly elaborate procedures that have evolved do enjoy a certain legitimacy amongst GATT members. But the precise legal status – the authority – of documents like the 1979 Understanding, which purport to codify panel practice, is still unclear; and difficulties remain concerning the precise status of past practice. However, the *ad hoc* constructions of the last forty years have accumulated enough legitimacy to allow the Contracting Parties to agree on a description of how they have settled disputes in the past. Thus, questions can be asked about the process, and relatively definitive answers given, subject always to the observations above.

Standing

To understand properly the GATT dispute resolution process, it is essential to realize that only Contracting Parties – that is, member states – have standing to put matters before the Contracting Parties. Individuals and firms concerned with the trading practices of another country must approach their governments, and through more or less formal means convince them to take up their cause at the GATT.[25] Both the USA and the EC have adopted legislation which dictates how private parties are to petition for action by their governments.

The US legislation (The Trade Act of 1974, s. 301, as amended) has become increasingly precise with regard to what situations will justify or even require retaliation by the President under domestic law, and those situations do not all depend on foreign violations of international obligations. Nor is s. 301 particularly patient with GATT processes – the legislation is very specific that the USA need not wait for the completion of international adjudication processes to begin retaliatory action.[26] In 1984 the EU adopted similar regulations to allow firms and individuals to petition the EU Commission for an investigation of foreign government practices harmful to EU trade.[27] The protectionist shift is apparent here as well – it is now easier for the Commission to take action against foreign 'unfair practices' over the objections of the EU Council.[28]

Scope of jurisdiction

Insofar as a 'cause of action' is concerned, the Agreement is clear that a violation of its rules is *not* a prerequisite for putting a matter before the Contracting Parties. The complaining country need only show that benefits it reasonably expected[29] under the Agreement have been nullified or impaired by the actions of a trading partner.[30] The Agreement is clear that nullification and impairment must be shown to be the result of: (1) a violation of the terms of the Agreement; (2) the application of a measure whether or not inconsistent with the Agreement; or (3) the existence of any other situation.[31] However, GATT practice has tended to limit complaints to those where a breach of the Agreement is alleged. If a breach is shown, GATT 'law' presumes nullification or impairment of benefits. That is, without proof of adverse trade effects, it finds '*prima facie* nullification', and it is then up to the offending Party to rebut that presumption. On the other hand, if no violation of the Agreement is alleged then the complaining Party will in practice have a difficult time showing nullification or impairment.[32]

Prior consultations

Consultations are the first step in any attempt to resolve a GATT dispute, of whatever kind, and they are available under either Article XXII or XXIII.[33] They are the precondition for the setting up of a panel: Article XXIII:2 seems to require them, and the 1979 Understanding required that Parties to a dispute try to reach an agreement amongst themselves before appealing to the Contracting Parties.[34] Consultations are an extremely important part of the GATT dispute resolution process. No data exist to show what proportion of disputes is settled before recourse is had to a panel, but it is clear that many are settled this way before they ever come to the attention of the Contracting Parties.[35]

Until recently, how Parties chose to go about consulting each other was left largely to their discretion. However, concerns about the timeliness and effectiveness of GATT dispute resolution prompted the Contracting Parties to impose certain procedural constraints on disputants. Thus, according to the Uruguay Round Dispute Settlement Understanding, Contracting Parties must now notify the GATT Council of a request for consultation, and the consultation itself must be in writing and give reasons therefor.[36] The Uruguay Round Understanding also sets some deadlines at this stage. Formerly, Contracting Parties were to respond to requests for consultation 'promptly' and attempt to conclude them 'expeditiously'.[37] Now Contracting Parties are to respond to requests for consultation within ten days, and enter into consultations regarding the matter complained of within thirty days of the initial request by the complaining Party. Failure to comply with these deadlines gives the complainant the right to seek the establishment of a panel without actually holding consultations.[38] Finally, a deadline is set for concluding a satisfactory agreement: if none is reached within sixty days from the date of the initial request for consultation, or if both parties agree that no solution is likely, then the complainant can request a panel.[39] Where the matter is urgent (urgent is defined as 'including those [situations] which concern perishable goods en route'), Parties must enter into consultations within ten days, and a panel can be requested after twenty days from the request if no accord is obtained.[40]

Mediation and arbitration

If consultation does not enable the disputants to reach a satisfactory solution to their problem, several GATT accords since the Agreement provide for the use of the 'good offices' of third Parties. The principle was initially adopted to help LDCs, which often do not have the resources and expertise to negotiate effectively during consultations. The Director General of the GATT might intervene in disputes involving LDC's to help conciliate the dispute.[41] The 1979 Understanding allowed any disputing Parties to seek the intervention of a third-Party conciliator, and the 1982 GATT Ministerial Declaration specified that any country could request the good offices of the Director General in a dispute.[42] However, an insider to the process has pointed out that, in practice, most disputing parties do not resort to third-Party mediation; they seem not to feel the need for third-Party intervention except when all else has failed and what is really needed is an adjudicator.[43]

In the event that consultation fails, the Uruguay Round Understanding provides for the possibility of binding arbitration by agreed-upon third Parties. Its use is subject to the consent of both Parties to a disagreement, and they also set the procedures to be used in the process. Its use must be notified to all GATT Contracting Parties, and the Understanding provides for access by third Parties with an interest in the dispute, subject to the agreement of the original disputants.[44] While in many cases it is difficult to see how arbitration would be more helpful than a GATT panel, in some circumstances it might be a useful way to remove a dispute from the some-times overly-politicized GATT forum. But usually the GATT is overly-politicized precisely because Parties to a dispute make it so. Under such circumstances, Parties are unlikely to wish to submit to binding arbitration in any event.

Request for a Panel or Working Party

If consultation and conciliation fail, the complaining Party can bring the matter before the GATT Council of Representatives, the body which represents the Contracting Parties between Sessions. The complainant must submit the request in writing, indicate whether consultations were held, and outline the factual and legal nature of the dispute. The request for a panel serves to define the issues at the outset: careful drafting is necessary because any subsequent attempt to broaden (or narrow) the scope of a complaint can be difficult.[45] Under Article XXIII:2

> the Contracting Parties shall promptly investigate any matter so referred to them and shall make appropriate recommendations to the contracting parties which they consider to be concerned, or give a ruling on the matter, as appropriate.

As a matter of practice Contracting Parties do not deal with disputes directly; instead they refer them to working Parties or panels. A complainant putting a matter before the Council will usually request a working Party or, more typically, a panel (the choice is understood to be up to the complainant).[46] The Council usually grants the request for a panel as a matter of course, although it might defer a decision in order to give the responding Party time to study the complaint.[47] Under the Uruguay Round Understanding, a panel must be established at the latest at the Council meeting following that at which the request first appears on the agenda (para. 6).

Selection of panellists and determination of terms of reference

Next begins the process of deciding the terms of reference for a panel, and selecting the individuals who will serve on it.[48] Unless the Parties agree otherwise, within twenty days from the establishment of a panel, standard terms of reference are as follows

> To examine, in the light of the relevant provisions in [name of covered agreement] the matter referred to the Dispute Settlement Body by [name of contracting party] in document [. . . .] and to make such findings as will assist the CONTRACTING PARTIES in making the recommendations or in giving the rulings provided for in [that/those agreements].[49]

The terms of reference, if not standard, must be circulated to all Contracting Parties, and any third Party can raise questions regarding the terms at a Council meeting.[50] On occasion, disputants have tried to strengthen their position *ex ante* by altering the terms of reference in order to restrict the investigation of the panel to certain issues.[51] On the other hand, while adoption of the standard terms of reference prevents disputes over the terms of reference from dragging on, it also allows panels to make ill-defined reports which do little to clarify GATT practice or law.[52]

In practice the more difficult task in establishing a panel is finding suitable and willing panellists acceptable to the Parties in a dispute. GATT instruments have tried valiantly to expedite this process by establishing deadlines for the composition of panels, and setting up rosters of qualified individuals, but problems with the process remain.

The 1979 Understanding (para. 12) provided that the Director General should propose nominations of from three to five panel members to the disputing Parties.[53] The panellists, who 'would preferably be governmental', are to serve in their individual capacities, and they are to be selected for their independence of judgement, and diversity of background and experience.[54] The disputants were to respond to such nominations within seven working days. Despite the apparent simplicity of this process, there are many difficulties in appointing panellists, and this has led to significant delays in a few important cases, and several attempts to impose restrictions on the length of time it takes to compose a panel.[55] The composition of a panel must normally be agreed to by the disputing Parties, and they naturally tend to be cautious about whom they allow to serve on a panel.[56] The 1984 Action allows the Director General to complete a panel if the deadline has not been met, but only 'after consulting both parties'. The Uruguay Round Understanding (para. 8.7) allows the Director General, in consultation with the Chair of the Council, to set the composition of the panel if no agreement on its membership has been reached within twenty days of its establishment. Qualified panellists can also be hard to find. About one-fifth of the GATT countries do not maintain permanent delegations in Geneva, with the result that they seldom have personnel qualified to sit on panels. If the EU is involved in a dispute (and it often is), this eliminates people from twelve member countries (interested Parties cannot have nationals on panels). Similarly, Secretariat personnel will know that certain countries have an interest in the outcome of a dispute even though they have not declared it, and this eliminates their delegations from the list of possible candidates as well. The Secretariat must also contend with the political necessity of maintaining a proper geographical and philosophical balance on the panel, and it must deal with the fact that many GATT delegates do not like serving on panels.[57]

To deal with the shortage of panellists the 1979 Understanding (para. 13) provided for the establishment of a roster of qualified individuals who can serve on panels. Contracting Parties were invited to submit lists of such individuals every year. However, this was apparently insufficient to meet the needs of panels. The 1984 Action (at para. 1) asks Contracting Parties to submit the names of qualified *non-governmental* experts who might serve on panels, and the same instrument (at para. 2) expresses again the preference for governmental representatives, but allows for the possibility of non-governmental panellists. The Uruguay Round Understanding goes even further, and dictates the expansion and improvement of the non-governmental roster. The move to secure greater participation by non-governmental experts may be a small step towards the establishment of something like a permanent panel of 'independent' experts.[58] There is a risk, of course, that the process will simply divert conflict to different theatres, as countries vie to ensure that *their* experts get on the right panels, or try to thwart the process in other ways.[59]

Panel procedures

Panels, aided throughout by the Secretariat, basically set their own working procedures, but an outline of the process is simple enough.[60] The panel will begin by establishing a calendar or schedule for the case to encourage the Parties to be prompt in meeting deadlines.[61] It will then commence soliciting information about the dispute. Panels are not wholly dependent on the disputants for the information they receive about the case – any individual or body can be consulted for information or even technical advice.[62] The panel will also request written submissions, first from the complainant, next from the respondent, and from interested third Parties.[63] The complainant is usually required to make the initial submissions first so that the respondent will have a better idea of the case it will have to meet.[64] The burden is on the complainant to show nullification or impairment, unless the complainant can make out a *prima facie* case of such by proving that there has been a violation of the Agreement. In practice, however, panels put questions to both sides and expect both Parties to argue their case forcefully and thoroughly.[65] Finally, oral hearings are held in closed sessions to clarify written submissions. Sometimes defending Parties will not really make a defence until the second such oral hearing – in fact, the prime source of delay in panel deliberations is often the tardiness of Parties in making their arguments.[66]

In recent years, various attempts have been made to address the problem of delay in panel deliberations. One important measure has seen the GATT Secretariat expanded and given greater resources to help speed up the process. The Secretariat is essential to the operations of a panel – it does everything from arranging meeting rooms for oral hearings, to providing advice on procedural and technical matters concerning the GATT, to drafting panel reports – ensuring that it has sufficient wherewithal is a prerequisite for efficient and speedy dispute resolution.[67] Several GATT agreements have also tried to improve the process by imposing more or less strict deadlines on the work of panels. The 1979 Understanding (para. 20) provided that panels should normally submit their reports 'without undue delay'. The Uruguay Round Understanding requires 'as a general rule' that panels take no longer than six months from the time that the composition and terms of reference are agreed on to submit a report and three months in urgent cases. If a panel takes longer than this it must inform the Council in writing of the reasons for the delay, along with an estimate of when its task will be finished. 'In no case' will panel reports take longer than nine months to prepare.[68]

Once a panel has as much information as it thinks necessary it will instruct the Secretariat, in the absence of the disputants, to begin drafting a report, which will be used as the basis for the final panel report to the Contracting Parties.[69] Panels are to make objective assessments of the facts and whether they conform with the Agreement, although sometimes panels are asked to submit technical opinions, or recommendations regarding what remedies would be appropriate.[70] Their reports are to provide reasons for their findings and opinions – the ideal is a clear finding which can provide guidance in future about the particular meaning of a rule.[71] But there is a great deal of pressure on panels to come to a consensus, with the result that panel reports can be difficult to understand, and the virtue of clarity gets lost amidst the wish for agreement.[72] Before a panel sends its report to the

Contracting Parties, a draft of the descriptive sections must be circulated to the disputing Parties for written comment, and then a draft of the entire report including recommendations must be circulated to the disputing Parties for additional comment.[73] The hope here is that the Parties will come to a mutually agreeable solution once the shape of the report that the Contracting Parties will receive is made known to them. If no solution is reached, then the report is circulated to the Contracting Parties, and put on the agenda of the next Council meeting.

Adoption of panel reports by Contracting Parties

A panel report as such has no legal status at all in GATT 'law'. Article XXIII:2 authorizes only the Contracting Parties to investigate and adjudicate complaints. Thus, the next step of the process – the Contracting Parties' consideration of a panel report – is crucial to GATT dispute resolution.

The Chair of a panel will submit its report to the Contracting Parties through the Council, which under the Uruguay Round Understanding will be replaced for this purpose by the integrated Dispute Settlement Body, on which all members of the WTO are entitled to be represented. The Council then begins to consider the report, although it may postpone consideration until the next Council meeting if one Party to the dispute so requests.[74] Reports traditionally have been adopted by consensus, which means that a report becomes a 'decision' only if no Contracting Party voices an objection to it. Of course, this means that Parties to the dispute then have a say in whether or not a report should be adopted: they become 'judges in their own cause'. In practice, reports are almost always adopted promptly by the Council.[75] Sometimes disputes may arise as to what a report means: some reports have been adopted along with an 'interpretation' which may qualify the findings.[76] But until 1986 there were only five cases in which adoption was blocked, and only a few cases saw significant delays in the Council's consideration of a report.[77] Under the Uruguay Round Understanding, the consensus rule has now been modified in a crucial respect: a consensus is now required of Council members in order to block the adoption of a panel report, meaning that the prevailing party can compel its adoption (para. 16.4.).

Implementation

Because a report is adopted does not mean that its recommendations and rulings are automatically followed. Article XXIII:2 provides for the authorization of the suspension of concessions by one Party if another has nullified or impaired benefits accruing to the former under the Agreement. However, such action has only ever been taken once, by the Netherlands, and with little effect.[78] Typically, implementation relies on the moral suasion of a recommendation by the Council (pursuant to a report), which can direct a Contracting Party to withdraw or modify a measure (if the measure was found GATT-'illegal'), or to take some other action to restore the balance of concessions (if a measure was found to be GATT-'legal' but to have nullified benefits reasonably expected under the Agreement). The Council can also seek to ensure compliance by regularly monitoring whether or not a country has complied. Traditionally, the complainant Party had the responsibility of ensuring that such matters were brought to the attention of the Council on a regular basis. The Uruguay Round Understanding now provides that at a Council meeting held within thirty days of the adoption of a report, the Contracting Party whose measures have been successfully challenged must inform the Council of its intentions with respect to implementing the recommendations of the Council. If immediate compliance is impractical, a reasonable period of time can be proposed by the transgressing member subject to approval by the Council, or the disputing Parties can agree on a reasonable time, or a reasonable time can be determined by arbitration, which should not normally exceed fifteen months from adoption of the panel's report. The matter is automatically placed on the agenda of the Council six months following the establishment of a reasonable time for compliance and remains on the Council's agenda until resolved. At least ten days before each Council meeting, the transgressing member must report in writing to the Council on compliance progress.[79]

Perspectives on dispute resolution

In recent years the GATT has been the locus of important disagreements over the rules of international trade, and major members seem increasingly unable to agree on its basic goals and the means for achieving them. For example, three reports by panels established under the Tokyo Code on Subsidies and Countervailing Duties have not been adopted because of fundamental disagreements over the interpretation of the Code's articles.[80] The GATT has been the focus of some criticism for its inability to facilitate the resolution of these problems. There has been a concerted movement over the last decade or so to meet these criticisms by reforming the process.[81] Several aspects of the mechanism have attracted the attention of these critics. They complain that the process is unpredictable and ill-defined, and that some of its substantive concepts (such as 'nullification and impairment') are so vague as to be almost useless for dispute resolution purposes. They claim that the process is too vulnerable to delays at every stage, and that its workings are too often the unfortunate subject of the vagaries of international trade diplomacy. The critics also have attacked the consensus rule governing report adoption, and the problems with implementing and ensuring compliance with panel findings.[82] We will briefly examine the actual record of GATT dispute resolution to assess the strength of these criticisms, and will conclude with a critical analysis of proposals that have been made for further changes to the dispute resolution process.

The potential sources of delay have already been noted: consultations can be protracted, choosing a panel and setting its terms of reference can be a time-consuming and contentious exercise, panel deliberations can sometimes take years, and report adoption and implementation can be blocked at every step by a determined opponent. The Uruguay Round Understanding addresses most of these issues with more or less strict deadlines of admittedly unknown efficacy. It is probably unwise to dwell too much on these criticisms even though they are very important to how observers perceive the GATT. It may be that the Uruguay Round Understanding has dealt with this issue effectively, although it is important to realize the limits of such instruments: the GATT is still an institution based on consensus, and all these instruments can really only amount to suggestions about how quickly disputes should be resolved.

Another concern relates to the expertise brought to panel deliberations. Critics point out in the first place that the technical support given to panels can vary widely because of the way in which GATT cases are assigned within its Secretariat. There are about ten different divisions within the Secretariat dealing with matters such as trade policies and technical cooperation. It was the habit of the Secretariat to assign cases to one or the other of these divisions for technical support, with the result that panels would sometimes receive a particular slant on the problem confronting them.[83] Furthermore, because the EU and the USA were so often involved in disputes, it was often difficult to find panellists. Resort was often had to countries like New Zealand or Norway, but this put a significant burden on their smaller delegations.[84]

Another important criticism of dispute resolution is its ineffectiveness. This supposed vice is seen to stem from two broad sets of factors. In the first place, it is often said that the process does not encourage the development of case law which could help improve the predictability of the process and provide more guidance for Parties engaged in international trade. In this regard, critics have pointed to the paucity of published reports where consultations resolve a dispute. But panel reports themselves are often criticized as of limited efficacy because of their vague language and unwillingness to grapple with the difficult issues at the centre of many trade disputes. It is said that panels often sidestep difficult questions rather than confronting them directly, and as a result their findings are of limited value in ending the immediate conflict, let alone in providing guidance in future disputes.[85] Of course, even if panel reports were always models of clarity and boldness, it needs to be pointed out that their precise status as precedent is unclear even after adoption. Certainly this fact does not aid the development of GATT 'law'.[86]

But an even greater cause of the GATT's ineffectiveness, according to its critics, has been the practice of requiring consensus for the adoption of a report. Aside from the delay that this can occasion, it is felt to be unfair to allow a Party to a dispute to be a judge in its own cause. Moreover, the adoption of a report can be used as another venue for negotiation by a Party adversely affected by a ruling. The Council might be urged to 'interpret' a ruling, in effect to change it, in order to make it more palatable for the country against whom the ruling was made. Many feel that these features of GATT dispute resolution make it a waste of time even when the process manages to work relatively quickly.[87]

Even greater frustration is evident concerning the implementation of reports that have been adopted by the GATT Council. There are a myriad of ways in which a country can impede the effective implementation of a report's recommendations, and of course a country can simply refuse to follow a GATT ruling. The Uruguay Round Understanding has done something to improve surveillance of report implementation, but this does not of itself ensure enhanced compliance. Certainly, the other major GATT weapon for ensuring compliance – retaliation – has attracted little enthusiasm from GATT observers who are quick to point out that it usually accomplishes little in ending trade disputes. It is a clumsy device, which small countries find difficult to wield against larger economies, and which even larger countries often find counter-productive. Retaliation has the effect of protecting domestic industries that may not need it, hurting the consumers of the products targeted by the retaliatory measures, and providing little or no assistance to the industry that was adversely affected by the impugned trade measure in the first place.[88]

Is the GATT's dispute resolution record really as bad as the criticisms would seem to suggest? Or do the criticisms focus too much on how the system might possibly break down, or has broken down in a few cases, without paying much attention to how the system actually works in general? In fact, the GATT dispute resolution process has worked fairly well over its entire history. From 1947–85, it took about two years to resolve a dispute from the moment a complaint was lodged to the implementation of remedial measures.[89] Only ten cases have taken longer than two years, and only one was very protracted indeed.[90] More importantly, a recent detailed review of all GATT disputes between 1948 and 1989 by Hudec, et al.[91] finds a success rate for valid complaints (resulting in full or partial satisfaction of the complaint) of 88%. While the success rate declined somewhat in the 1980s, the compliance record still stood at 81%. Other trends of note that emerge from the Hudec study are: (1) the explosion of complaints in the 1980s – more than half of all GATT complaints were brought in the last of the four decades of GATT history; (2) for the entire 42-year period, 73% of all complaints were filed by the USA, the EU and its present members, Canada, and Australia. The USA, the EU and its members, Canada, and Japan accounted for 83% of all appearances as defendants. Ninety-two per cent of all complaints involved either the USA or the EU (or its members) as a Party; (3) for the entire period, 52% of all complaints related to NTBs, 21% to tariffs, 16% to subsidies, and 10% to antidumping/countervailing duty measures. Over time, NTBs and AD/CVDs have increased as a percentage of complaints while tariffs have sharply declined; (4) in the 1950s only 23% of all complaints involved agriculture while for the period 1960–1984, one-half of the complaints involved agricultural trade measures, many relating to the EU's Common Agricultural Policy. However, compliance rates with rulings in agricultural and non-agricultural complaints are roughly the same; (5) according to the authors, the most important finding of their study is the disproportionate level of non-compliant behaviour by the USA, especially in recent years.

While the effectiveness of the GATT dispute resolution process has clearly declined somewhat over the last decade or so, it is important to ask whether the process, as such, is a significant factor in the genesis of these difficulties? Will reforming its procedures substantially improve the process? There is an ongoing debate amongst legal experts as to the proper balance to be struck by the GATT between a rule-oriented system and a system which is mainly concerned with providing a forum for the diplomatic discussion and resolution of trade issues. Advocates of a rule-based regime – 'the lawyers' – tend to see the institution of rules as an important first step towards restoring the GATT's authority amongst its participants. Adjudication by means of an objective application of previously agreed-upon rules is thought to be the best way of ensuring that right prevails over might, that countries refrain from breaching GATT rules in the first place, and that they comply with GATT rulings even when unfavourable. The lawyers think that those who advocate building the GATT as a forum for discussion – 'the diplomats' – tend to lose sight of the forest for the trees. What is said to matter is not necessarily the satisfactory resolution of a particular dispute, but the overall functioning of the system in terms of its general ability to provide consistent, predictable responses to conflicts generally.[92]

The Uruguay Round Understanding on Dispute Resolution seeks to advance substantially the legal orders conception of the GATT. In addition to rendering permanent most of the provisions of the Mid-Term Review Agreement, the Understanding creates an integrated dispute settlement system, to be administered by a Dispute Settlement Body (DSB), comprising representatives of all members of the WTO, and to be responsible for handling all disputes rising under either the GATT or any collateral codes or agreements. The Understanding also creates an automatic right in a complainant country to the creation of the panel (unless a consensus exists amongst the Contracting Parties to refuse the panel). A report is to be adopted by the Dispute Settlement Body within sixty days unless there is an appeal, or the DSB decides by consensus to reject the report. Thus, it is in the power of the winning side to ensure that a report will be adopted by the DSB. The Uruguay Round Understanding also contemplates a new appeal process. Appeals from panel decisions will be possible on matters of law to panels of three drawn from a rotating pool of seven persons of recognized authority and demonstrated expertise in international trade law, who are to be appointed by the DSB, and who are to be available at all times on short notice. The Appellate Body is to submit its report within sixty days of an appeal being filed.[93] The Uruguay Round Agreement also contemplates the establishment of the World Trade Organization (WTO) which is to provide the common institutional framework for the conduct of trade relations between members of the WTO, and more specifically to administer the integrated dispute settlement system and a trade policy review mechanism.[94] The trade policy review mechanism is of particular interest in the present context, because it would vest in the GATT an independent investigative authority to initiate, on a rotating basis, country-by-country reviews of international and domestic policies that may impact on trading relationships. One virtue often claimed for the trade policy review mechanism is that it would make exposure of non-compliance by Contracting Parties with a GATT obligation less dependent on the dispute resolution process.

These proposals represent a substantial advance in the evolution of the institutional structures of the GATT. However, some proponents of a legal orders conception of the GATT would go even further. It has sometimes been proposed that private parties be given access to the GATT dispute resolution mechanism, rather than being wholly dependent on the willingness of their home government to take up disputes on their behalf, when such willingness may be compromised by diplomatic and foreign policy issues extraneous to the particular dispute in question.[95] While this proposal may have some merit in the abstract, the long history of domestic trade remedy regimes suggests that the privatization of trade remedy law contains substantial potential for protectionist forms of harassment. Moreover, the explosion in the number of complaints that would need to be processed is likely to place an unsustainable burden on the GATT dispute resolution process. This problem could be contained to manageable proportions by creating an appropriate international 'filter' to screen out spurious complaints, although it is not obvious how such a 'filter' would be designed without creating yet another layer of review, in addition to the panel process itself and possible appeals from panel decisions.

A further proposal contemplates that GATT rights and obligations be enforceable in the domestic courts of member countries as an aspect of their domestic law.[96] This would presumably permit judicial review of domestic laws, regulations, and administrative practices for consistency with GATT rights and obligations. While this proposal has some attraction in the abstract, there may be difficulties in putting it into practice in the GATT context. The proposal would entail domestic courts in the hundred-odd members of the GATT interpreting the GATT with respect to the GATT-consistency of various domestic policy measures. Hence, some supranational appellate process would be necessary in order to resolve differences of interpretation by domestic courts. This would then remit us to familiar questions as to how the GATT dispute resolution process might best be designed.

Yet another proposal, drawing on provisions that originally appeared in the Havana Charter, would contemplate that the International Court of Justice might sit as a permanent court of appeal on matters of law pertaining to the interpretation of the GATT. However, many Contracting Parties are unlikely to view the International Court of Justice as possessing the relevant international trade expertise to be entrusted with this role. The new appellate process adopted in the Uruguay Round Understanding, in contrast, would set up an expert appellate process. How well this is likely to work is difficult to predict. One might anticipate that the losing Party, in most panel decisions, will automatically appeal the decision to this appellate body, thus creating in most cases a more protracted, two-stage review process. This will place a formidable burden on the appellate body, and render extremely complicated the politics among the Contracting Parties in appointing members to this body.

Many of these proposals for reform of the GATT process seem to ignore or undervalue an important fact which grounds all the criticisms of the reform proposals: that the GATT has always been mainly a forum for negotiation, and that it is currently the locus of fundamental disagreements over the means and ends of the world-trading system.[97] Such fissures within the GATT – past and present – seem able to explain the vagueness of GATT rules which often complicates substantially the task of panels. This is especially the case with many forms of NTBs, with the traditionally attenuated discipline over agricultural trade, with subsidies, and with the domestic application of AD/CVD laws. The notion that the procedure itself is to blame for cynicism about the GATT is not very credible in light of these more substantive problems.[98] Where the system has well-defined, agreed-upon rules, and disputes are narrowly focused on those rules, it works well to resolve disputes. But where international consensus is lacking to define the rules clearly, and to agree upon how they should be implemented, then the GATT will fail to resolve the disputes coming before it. It seems futile to expect the dispute resolution process to succeed in developing and applying predictable rules of international law where political negotiation has failed to enunciate such rules.

DISPUTE RESOLUTION MECHANISMS IN THE CANADA–US FREE TRADE AGREEMENT

The Canada–US Free Trade Agreement (FTA or 'the Agreement') provides two main avenues for the resolution of disputes between its signatories.

Chapter 18 of the Agreement sets up a Commission to resolve disputes; Chapter 19 details procedures for resolving problems in antidumping and countervailing duty cases. The Chapter 18 and 19 mechanisms involve the use of consultation, negotiation, and panels – all of which resembles dispute resolution mechanisms in the GATT under Article XXIII:2. The Agreement also appears to have benefited from experience under the GATT, and to have adopted some of the improvements which have been introduced into its procedures over the last decade or so.[99] The result is a mechanism which, on its face, has the potential to allow for the efficacious resolution of trade disputes with a minimum of politically unacceptable impairment of sovereignty.[100]

Chapter Eighteen

Article 1801 of the FTA states that Chapter 18 is for the 'avoidance or settlement of all disputes regarding the interpretation or application of this Agreement' except insofar as any dispute relates to the provisions of Chapter 17 (Financial Services) or Chapter 19 (Antidumping and Countervailing Duty Cases).[101] It establishes the Canada–US Trade Commission ('the Commission') to supervise the implementation of the Agreement, to resolve disputes under it, 'to oversee its further elaboration, and to consider any other matter that may affect its operation'.[102] The Commission is composed of representatives of both countries: exactly how many from each side is not clear, but the Agreement provides that the principal representatives 'shall be the cabinet-level officer or Minister primarily responsible for international trade or their designees'.[103] The Commission establishes, by consensus, its own rules and procedures (all the Commission's decisions are made by consensus), and it may delegate responsibility or seek advice as it sees fit. Finally, it is to meet at least once a year to review the operation of the Agreement.[104]

Articles 1803–1804 lay down the procedures for notification and consultation regarding actual or proposed measures that might materially affect the operation of the FTA. The FTA requires the Parties to notify each other of such measures in advance of implementation or as soon thereafter as possible. It also gives each Party the right to ask the other for information regarding these measures.[105] Article 1804 allows each Party the right to consultations regarding any measures or any other matter material to the FTA, and it exhorts the Parties to make every effort to reach mutually agreed upon solutions to problems that arise in these consultations.[106] If consultations do not allow the Parties to resolve their differences within 30 days, then Article 1805 permits either Party to request a meeting of the Commission, which is to convene within 10 days (unless otherwise agreed) to attempt 'to resolve the dispute promptly'.[107]

If a dispute is not resolved within 30 days of being referred to the

Commission, then the Commission *must* in the case of dispute over safe-guard actions or[108] (in the case of other actions) *may* refer the dispute to binding arbitration.[109] If the Commission cannot (because of disagreement) or will not refer a dispute to binding arbitration, then either Party may request the establishment of a panel of experts 'to consider the matter'.[110] The panel is drawn 'wherever possible' from nominated lists of unaffiliated individuals who have been chosen by each country on the basis of their expertise, objectivity, reliability, and sound judgement.[111] A panel will have five members. Two must be from Canada, and two from the USA. Each Party in consultation with the other chooses two panellists, and the fifth panellist, who is also the Chair, is chosen by the Commission. If a Party fails to choose a panellist within 15 days of the request for a panel then the panellist is chosen by lot from the roster.[112] If the Commission cannot agree on a Chair within this time frame then the four panellists will decide amongst themselves. If they cannot agree within 30 days of the request, then the Chair will be chosen by lot as well from the roster.[113]

A panel's procedures are determined by it, unless the Commission decides otherwise. However, the Agreement stipulates that the Parties are to be afforded at least one hearing, as well as the right to present written submissions and rebuttal arguments. It also requires that proceedings be confidential, and that the panel base its decision solely on submissions (unless otherwise agreed by the Parties).[114]

The panel is to present an initial report (or reports – panels need not be unanimous) to the Parties within three months of its Chair being appointed. This report is to contain the findings of fact, whether any measure at issue is inconsistent with the FTA or otherwise nullifies or impairs its benefits, and any recommendations for a resolution of the dispute.[115] Panels are to have made every effort to provide the Parties with an opportunity to comment on the panel's preliminary findings of fact,[116] but in any case a Party which disagrees with an initial report can, within 14 days of its issuance, formally object to it. The panel may then (on its own motion, or that of the Commission or either Party) request the views of both Parties, and reconsider its report. The panel must then issue a final report within 30 days of the issuance of the initial report.[117]

Once the Commission has received the final report, it is to agree on a resolution of the dispute in question 'normally' in conformity with the recommendations of the panel.[118] 'Whenever possible', this resolution is to be the non-implementation or withdrawal of measures not conforming with or causing nullification or impairment of benefits accruing under the FTA.[119] If the Commission cannot reach agreement within 30 days of the receipt of the final report, or if a Party refuses to comply with the findings of a panel under the binding arbitration provisions of Article 1806, then the other Party may suspend the application of equivalent benefits to that Party.[120]

Chapter 18 provides a useful framework for the resolution of disputes, at least in theory. In fact, its provisions have not been resorted to very often. As of the end of 1993, there have been only five disputes remitted to panels under this part of the FTA: one relating to Canadian salmon and herring landing requirements; another relating to the treatment of non-mortgage interest on land or plant and machinery for purposes of rules of origin; another relating to whether exports of durum wheat to the USA by the Canadian Wheat Board were occurring below acquisition cost; and another relating to the adoption of regulations in Puerto Rico that precluded continuing sales of ultra-high temperature (UHT) milk by a Quebec producer to Puerto Rican consumers.

Chapter Nineteen

It should be noted at the outset that Chapter 19 is premised on an agreement that the current means of dealing with AD and CVD disputes are unsatisfactory. Article 1906 calls for an agreement within five years (with the possibility of a two-year extension) on a code between Canada and the USA regarding AD and CVD matters. The Article contemplates the possibility that the Agreement will be terminated (on six months notice by either Party) if no accord is reached on a new regime for resolving disputes in this contentious area.[121] Thus, Chapter 19 is, on its face, a temporary expedient. It begins with two other important limitations on its power and scope. Article 1901:1 states that the Article 1904 provisions outlining the procedures for the review of 'final determinations' in AD and CVD cases apply only to goods which the relevant authority in the *importing* Party has determined come from the other Party. Moreover, Article 1902 reserves the power to apply and amend domestic AD and CVD law to each Party respectively.[122] However, Article 1902 imposes important limits on the capacity to modify existing AD and CVD law: Parties must notify and consult each other about such changes; for changes to apply to the other Party it must be named; and no change can be inconsistent with relevant GATT provisions or 'the object and purpose of this Agreement and this Chapter'.[123] Nonetheless, the limits to Chapter 19 are significant, especially in view of the importance that AD and CVD cases have assumed over the last few years, and the remainder of Chapter 19 might usefully be seen as an attempt to ensure some degree of bilateral accountability in this area.

Articles 1903 and 1904 both are designed to allow bilateral review of the amendment and application of AD and CVD law. Article 1903 allows a Party to request that a panel be set up to examine an amendment to determine whether it is consistent with relevant GATT and FTA provisions, or whether, in addition, it 'has the function and effect of overturning a prior decision' made under Article 1904.[124] If the panel decides that an amendment is in fact objectionable, the Parties are then to enter into consultations to remedy the situation within 90 days, and if remedial legislation is not enacted within 9 months of the end of this consultation period then the other Party is entitled to take comparable action or terminate the Agreement.[125]

Article 1904 provides a set of procedures allowing binational panels to replace judicial review of the 'final determinations' of administrative agencies in AD and CVD cases.[126] At the request of either Party, a panel can review such determinations and issue a *binding decision* as to whether they conform to the AD and CVD law of the importing country subject to a procedure for an extraordinary challenge of a panel's decision to a binational panel of retired judges on various grounds.[127] The standard of primary panel review is that laid down by the relevant statutes (as amended from time to time) of each Party, and by 'the general legal principles that a court of the importing Party would otherwise apply'.[128] Requests for panels must be made within 30 days of the publication of a final determination.[129] Only the Parties have the right to request a panel, but Article 1904: 5 provides that a Party must ask for a panel when petitioned by a person otherwise entitled by domestic law to redress via judicial review.[130] The administrative agency whose determination is being reviewed has the right to be represented by counsel before the panel, as do all other persons entitled by domestic laws to standing before a court reviewing such determinations.[131] The panel reaches its decision by a majority vote of its members, and it issues its reasons (majority, concurring, and dissenting) in a written report.[132] If a panel finds an error in a final determination it may remand the determination to the relevant domestic administrative agency for 'action not inconsistent with the panel's decision'.[133]

Chapter 19 – its committees and panels – is supported and administered by a Secretariat established under Article 1909. It has two branches, each run by a Secretary, one Canadian (located in Ottawa) and the other American (located in Washington, DC). The Secretariat is responsible for servicing the meetings of panels and committees, and if directed to do so it 'may' provide services for the Commission instituted under Article 1802 as well.[134] It is also charged with the task of receiving and filing all official papers connected with the operation of Chapter 19.[135]

The final salient feature of Chapter 19 is its elaborate provisions regarding the composition of panels. Annex 1901.2 sets out the method of choosing these panels, and the pool from which they are to be drawn. The overall method it uses is very similar to that in Chapter 18. A roster is established by consultation between the two Parties of 50 unaffiliated individuals – 25 from each country – who are chosen for their good character, reliability, and objectivity.[136] A panel is composed of five members, a majority of whom must be lawyers. Each Party must choose, in consultation with the other Party, two members; each Party is allowed four peremptory challenges; and if panellists are not chosen within 30 days of the request for a panel, or alternative panellists are not chosen within 45 days then a panellist will be chosen by lot from the Party's candidates on the roster.[137] A fifth member must be chosen within 55 days of the request by the Parties, or, if they cannot agree, within 60 days by the already chosen panellists, or, if they cannot agree, by lot (on the 61st day).[138] The Chair of the panel is picked from among the lawyers by a majority vote of the panellists; if there is no majority vote then the Chair will be chosen by lot.[139]

These are the procedures outlined by Chapters 18 and 19 for the resolution of disputes between the world's two largest trading partners. Early critics of the Agreement argued that the provisions did not go far enough to prevent administrative harassment of exporters by domestic competitors. The critics argued that no effective limits had been placed on the discretion of administrative trade agencies, and that panels would be as ready to defer to these agencies in reviewing their determinations as had been the US Court of International Trade or the Canadian Federal Court of Appeal.[140] But the experience with the mechanisms to date suggests that they do represent a significant improvement over what they replaced. In some instances, they may be able to reduce substantially the time and money involved in challenging ITC or ITA determinations.[141] Moreover, the cases that have been heard by panels to date would suggest that the latter are unwilling to accord agency determination the deference which hitherto had been the norm. Chapter 19 panels have been extensively used. As of October 1993, there had been 44 requests for panel reviews: 29 against US agency determinations, and 15 against Canadian agency determinations. Of the 20 cases that had then resulted in a panel opinion, 15 related to US agency determinations, 5 to Canadian agency determinations. Of the 15 US cases, 10 involved panel remands to the originating agency and of the 5 Canadian cases 4 entailed remands. The panels have shown themselves ready to demand 'sound reasons' and 'substantial evidence' for the findings made by administrative bodies. It is not enough for the ITA or ITC (or their Canadian counterparts) merely to state a conclusion, and then reassure the reader that evidence and reasons exist which support it. The reasoning must be clearly laid out, and it must be sound; the evidence must be relevant and persuasive (if not dispositive). In one case, a panel refused to follow CIT precedent, and sought to bring the applicable law into closer conformity with the GATT.[142] Nevertheless, a defect of the Chapter 19 process is that the panel itself cannot provide relief – it can only refer the matter back to the domestic trade agency or tribunal for redetermination in light of the panel's ruling of law. Here there is a potential for the domestic authorities to skirt around a panel's ruling on a particular aspect of its previous decision by finding other grounds or employing a somewhat different methodological approach that nevertheless results in duties being reimposed or retained. This has been the saga of Canada's pork and soft-wood lumber producers. There have been three extraordinary challenges to panel rulings, all initiated by the US and all unsuccessful.

DISPUTE RESOLUTION MECHANISMS IN NAFTA[143]

Under the proposed North American Free Trade Agreement (NAFTA), the binational panel procedures established under Chapters 18 and 19 of the Canada–US Free Trade Agreement are, in most respects, preserved, and in the case of Chapter 19 binational panel review of antidumping and counter-vailing duty determinations is made permanent. Under NAFTA two potentially important changes to the FTA provisions have been made. First, the roster of panellists 'shall include sitting or retired judges to the fullest extent practicable', as opposed to international trade lawyers, economists, or other experts (Annex 1901.2). Second, the extraordinary challenge procedure pertaining to panel decisions has been extended to permit a challenge in a case where a panel has failed to apply the appropriate standard of review (Article 1904 (13)). These two changes, in combination, carry the potential for reinstating the more traditional and deferential standard of judicial review of agency determinations that applied prior to the creation of the binational panel review process under the FTA. On the other hand, the proposed creation of a permanent trilateral Secretariat (Article 2002) to assist panels may enhance the quality and consistency of panel decisions.

The second round of bilateral negotiations contemplated by the Canada–US Free Trade Agreement on new rules for antidumping, subsidies, and countervailing duties appeared initially to have been abandoned. In their place, NAFTA provides that the trilateral Free Trade Commission shall establish a Working Group on trade and competition to make recommendations to the Commission within five years of the coming into force of the agreement 'on relevant issues concerning the relationship between competition laws and policies and trade in the free trade area'.[144] The Parties further agree to consult on '(a) the potential to develop more effective rules and disciplines concerning the use of governmental subsidies; and (b) the potential for reliance on a substitute system of rules for dealing with unfair transborder pricing practices and government subsidization'.[145] A trilateral side-accord of 2 December 1993 now commits the three governments to establishing a working group on subsidies and anti-dumping duties which is to complete its work by 31 December 1995.

Under the FTA, disputes (other than those relating to antidumping and countervailing duty determinations) arising under that Agreement and the GATT may be settled in either forum at the discretion of the complaining Party, although once an election has been made, this excludes the alternative dispute resolution process (Article 1801). Under NAFTA, there is a similar right of election, except where disputes relate to environmental and conservation matters or sanitary and phytosanitary measures where the responding Party may insist that a complaint be heard by a NAFTA, rather than GATT panel (Article 2005). In such cases, a disputing Party may request, or a panel on its own initiative may solicit, a written report of a scientific review board on any factual issue concerning such matters (Article 2015).

Other innovations proposed in NAFTA with respect to general dispute resolution (Chapter 20) include: (1) instead of separate national rosters of respective panellists, as provided under Chapter 18 of the FTA, the NAFTA contemplates a consensus roster of up to thirty persons acceptable to all member countries; (2) instead of disputing parties selecting nominees from the roster who are their own nationals, NAFTA calls for a process of reverse selection, by which Parties must select from the other country's nationals on the roster; (3) unlike the FTA, NAFTA permits third country and non-member country nationals to serve as a Chair of a panel; (4) unlike the FTA, disputes regarding financial services are fully subject to dispute settlement, through specialized procedures designed to ensure appropriate panel expertise (Chapter 14); and (5) under the investment provisions of NAFTA (Chapter 11) any NAFTA investor who alleges that a host government has breached an obligation of the investment chapter may invoke an arbitral tribunal to hear the matter. Investment obligations include requirements for National Treatment and Most Favoured Nation treatment, as well as certain disciplines on specified performance requirements, rules against restricting transfers, and against expropriation without compensation. Procedures may be based on ICSID or its Additional Facility, or on the UNCITRAL Rules for such arbitrations. Procedures are provided to enable consolidation of cases, to avoid procedural harassment, and for the intervention of governments responsible for the Agreement both individually before the arbitral tribunal or collectively through the issuance of Commission interpretations of the Agreement on questions that may be before the arbitral tribunal. Awards for monetary damages are directly enforceable in the domestic courts of the NAFTA members as if they were domestic court judgments.[146] Thus, in the investment context, private Parties are given direct access to international dispute resolution mechanisms for the first time in an international trade treaty.

CONCLUSION

Measured against a domestic 'legal orders' model, or even against the role of the European Court in interpreting and applying the law of economic integration in the EU, the GATT, FTA and NAFTA dispute settlement mechanisms are likely to appear weak and ineffective. These mechanisms seem to reflect the continuing subordination of law to politics in the realm of international trade. They appear far removed from the direct enforcement of legal rights by the Parties affected, as is the case for much of the EU law on economic integration.[147]

Nevertheless, as we have seen, in many areas the GATT, FTA and NAFTA mechanisms do have potential to work to interpret and clarify basic rules of the game, which govern the largest part of the world's trade. In the case of the GATT, panel decisions have become increasingly characterized by detailed legal reasoning and by a concern for principled justification and for consistency with past rulings.

Where, in practice, the mechanisms do not work as well is in solving disputes that go to the most controversial issues in trade theory and policy today, where the existing rules themselves provide little guidance, or have become problematic, such as agriculture, subsidies, and trade and the environment. In the case of the GATT, where panels have been able to operate within a high degree of general normative consensus among Contracting Parties about what the rules are, they have been effective in both interpreting the rules, and in having the interpretation implemented by the disputants. With respect to the FTA, the Chapter 19 process has provided significant control on abusive or arbitrary application of existing domestic trade remedy laws, but its work is not an effective substitute for substantive rules on countervail and antidump that are agreed on between the Parties.

Thus, it may be that critics who complain about the lack of legalism in the operation of dispute resolution mechanisms have missed the point. It is not procedural or institutional shortcomings in dispute settlement that are the major problem, but the extreme difficulty of evolving legal rules to deal with many of today's most intense trade controversies. Even where new rules are developed, the nature of the issues (such as trade and the environment) may be such that dispute settlement will inevitably involve making many more value judgements about the domestic policy objectives and approaches of the disputants than was the case with traditional rules on trade. This will result in continued pressure on dispute settlement mechanisms, but, again, this should not lead to scepticism about the capacity of these mechanisms to effectively apply the basic rules of the game that remain crucial to sustaining a liberal trading regime.

16

CONCLUSION:
THE FUTURE OF THE GLOBAL TRADING SYSTEM

INTRODUCTION

Over the last several years, we have witnessed momentous changes in global politics and economics: the collapse of the Soviet bloc and the end of the Cold War; the embracing of democracy and markets by a wide range of countries in the Third World; the fundamental deepening of political and economic integration within the European Union. At the broadest philosophical level, all of these developments would appear to enhance the prospects for liberal trade. However, the most momentous of these changes can also be interpreted as raising as many obstacles and fears for the global trading order as they do benefits and hopes. The collapse of the Soviet Empire, for instance, has unleashed a new wave of nationalisms, which pose their own threat to liberal internationalism. With the end of the Cold War, it has been argued, the United States should have less reason to cooperate with former Allies against communism, such as Western Europe and Japan, and therefore should feel free to pursue more aggressively self-interested external economic policies, even at the expense of alienating these powers. Greater integration in the European Union has raised fears of a 'Fortress Europe', an immense trading bloc with the power to conduct increasingly illiberal policies against non-Members.

Coupled with these recent developments have been longer-term trends or tendencies that many have argued fundamentally threaten or challenge liberal trading rules. One example is aggressive unilateralism on the part of the United States, particularly where applied to obtain market access concessions from other countries under threat of GATT-illegal sanctions against those countries' imports into the United States. Has the United States declined as a hegemonic power, or has it instead decided to use that hegemonic power to enforce its own interests at the expense of a liberal international order?

In this concluding chapter, we discuss several of the most pressing challenges facing the world trading system in light of these and other developments and trends. In our judgement, these challenges create a formidable, but not unmanageable, post-Uruguay Round agenda for students and practitioners of the law and policy of international trade. The three major challenges are: (1) disciplining protectionism based on 'fair trade' claims; (2) integrating the Newly Liberalizing Countries of Central and East Europe into the world trading system reconciling the emergence of regional trading blocs with the multilateral system; and (3) managing the interrelationship between regional accords and the multilateral system.

UNFAIR TRADE

The nature of the debate

Many trade scholars – both lawyers and economists – view the increasing preoccupation with 'fair trade' as the most fundamental challenge to liberal rules of trade.[1] This refers to the proliferation of arguments that free trade is only 'fair' where one's trading partners adopt certain kinds of domestic policies and/or refrain from others (whether the policy area be anti-trust law, intellectual property rights, environment, or labour standards). The debate over fair trade implicates both the means and the ends of trade policy, and much of the intellectual confusion that it generates is due to the frequent failure to separate means from ends. 'Fair trade' is frequently identified with aggressive unilateralism, whereby the domestic policies of a trading partner become a basis for imposing new GATT-illegal restrictions on imports. The story becomes complicated by the arguments of some fair trade advocates that the objective of protection is to extract, under threat, further liberalization commitments from trading partners (i.e. greater market access) and that the end result is not only fair trade but *freer* trade.[2] It becomes even more complex when one brings into the picture the arguments of trade scholars and politicians who reject the legitimacy of unilateralism, i.e. who do not espouse protection either to even the odds or to bargain new liberalization, yet consider a range of domestic policies a legitimate subject for further bargaining among trading partners, perhaps with a view to common standards or harmonization. In other words, one can be in favour of fair trade as an *end*, but believe that protectionism is an inefficient, ineffective, and/or unfair means of achieving that end. Alternatively, one may reject the idea of 'fair trade' as an *end*, i.e. one can believe that trade is mutually beneficial and just even between countries with radically different domestic policy choices in areas as sensitive as environment or labour standards, and that what are now domestic policy choices should not even be on the international trade agenda. A further variant is the view that whereas there is nothing intrinsically unfair or inefficient about trade between countries with different domestic policies, the legal order of international trade should be viewed as part of a broader international legal order, and that the benefits of liberal trade should be linked to opting in to the standards or rules of this broader order (e.g. environment or human rights) or that countries should be able to restrict imports whose production is linked to violations of non-trade international rules or standards.

Throughout this book, we have discussed a variety of 'unfair trade' claims. Chapters 5 and 6 have addressed at length the traditional claims about the unfairness of dumping and subsidies, and the justifications for imposing retaliatory duties as a response to these practices. Such duties, as we have emphasized, address only the effects of dumping or subsidies on domestic producers who are competing with the dumped or subsidized imports. We have sought to show that, in fact, there has not been a very close relationship between imposition of such duties and any coherent notion of unfairness. In fact, their use has served, in many if not most cases, as an inferior (from the perspective of the domestic welfare of the country imposing them) substitute for effective safeguards or domestic adjustment assistance policies in sectors threatened by foreign competition. We have thus advanced a number of proposals, admittedly of varying degrees of political realism, for significant constraints or even abolition of the right of GATT Contracting Parties to unilaterally impose such duties. In the alternative, we support a reformed and more effective safeguards or escape clause regime – which would, quite apart from claims about the supposed unfairness of import competition – address what is usually the real issue, that of managing the adjustment costs of increased international competition. We accept that there are very important normative claims surrounding worker displacement and the need for adjustment policies. An enhanced safeguards regime would focus explicitly on these normative claims, permit selective but temporary reneging on trade liberalization commitments where necessary to deal with adjustment pressures from increased imports, but on condition that the reneging country take appropriate domestic policy measures to ensure real adjustment and therefore obviate the necessity in the long-term for resort to renewed protectionism. At the same time, we recognize that in some instances subsidies may raise genuine issues that go beyond the adjustment concern, for instance the beggar-thy-neighbour effects of subsidy wars between trading partners in sectors where international competition for market share is intense.

In addition to the traditional areas of subsidies and dumping, we have also attempted to address the broader range of more recent 'fair trade' claims, including some that have been explicitly addressed in the Uruguay Round (e.g. intellectual property rights) and others, such as labour standards and environment-related claims, for which explicit multilateral trade rules have yet to be developed.

In general, we strongly disagree with the view that for significant gains from trade to be realized, these domestic policies must be harmonized or set on a level playing field. However, as we have discussed in previous chapters, this very reasoning has to some degree already been embedded in the

Uruguay Round Agreement, with respect both to services and to intellectual property. Just as was the case for the Tokyo Round Subsidies Code, bringing into the GATT itself the fair trade approach with respect to intellectual property and services represents a calculated wager that it is worth legitimizing the fair trade approach within a multilateral framework in order to reduce the extent to which it becomes a basis for unilateral protectionist policies.

In our view, having brought into the GATT and to some extent legitimized the fair trade approach with respect to intellectual property and services, it is impossible to sustain principled resistance to consideration of environmental and labour standards-related claims, as well. What is important at the outset is to distinguish the various concepts of fairness at issue in the different kinds of claims and then to consider their consistency with both the liberal theory of trade and most importantly with the basic multilateral framework for liberal trade – both norms and institutions. Are these claims simply indeterminate or open-ended, or can new benchmarks be found, or new institutional avenues established, to develop means of distinguishing legitimate from illegitimate claims, and thereby constraining purely unilateralist approaches?

Environmental or Labour Rights-based Trade Measures

In Chapter 13 (Trade and the Environment) we distinguished between environmentally-based and 'fair trade'-based justifications for trade measures in response to other countries' environmental policies. Environmentally-based claims assert the appropriateness of trade measures as a device for enforcing international environmental agreements, as sanctions to express disapproval of other countries' environmental policies, or as a 'stick' to encourage hold-out countries to enter into global environmental negotiations. Here, the purpose of trade restrictions is to support environmental values and goals. 'Fair trade'-based claims, by contrast, assert the supposed unfairness to one's own producers of having to compete with products from countries with lower environmental standards. They address supposed trade injury rather than harm to the environment as such. A similar distinction can be drawn between human rights-based claims for trade measures related to labour standards and 'fair trade'-based claims. Human rights-based claims do not imply that gains from trade cannot occur where one of the trading partners is using child labour or suppressing independent trade unions, but rather these gains are tainted with conduct that is wrongful according to some standard independent of trade theory.

As is clear from even a cursory reading of Article XX of the GATT, the GATT system has long entertained the legitimacy of placing restrictions on trade for purposes or values external to the liberal multilateral trading order itself. For instance, Article XX (f) provides an exemption from GATT strictures for measures taken with respect to products produced by prison labour.

Although free traders frequently oppose the use of measures that restrict trade for the sake of external values, we are persuaded that the liberal multi-lateral trading order, and indeed the theory of gains from trade itself, do not possess the normative resources to stake a claim that trade liberalization values should always 'trump' environmental or human rights values in the case of a conflict.

Where the multilateral liberal trading order *does* have a legitimate, and indeed crucial, interest is in distinguishing trade measures genuinely aimed at supporting non-trade values such as environmentalism and human rights, from measures that are in fact disguised protectionism on an environmental or human rights pretext. This is necessary in order to be able to identify cheating or defection from commitments to liberal trade and thereby sustain the legitimacy and viability of the liberal multilateral trading order. As well, there is a justified concern that external values and goals do not lead to trade measures that are genuinely motivated by those values but which nevertheless represent a gratuitous or unnecessary restric-tion on trade, given the other means available for supporting and advanc-ing those values and goals. The evolution of international human rights and environmental norms, and of institutional arrangements for the monitoring of these norms, serves to establish objective benchmarks which can assist in distinguishing genuine environmentally- or human rights-based trade actions from 'cheating' under environmental or human rights pretexts. In our view, Article XX of the GATT should be amended, or alternatively, an interpretive understanding negotiated, that clearly permits exemption from GATT strictures for environmental and human rights-based trade actions. But this interpretive understanding should also embody a least-restrictive means test for such measures, with a view to ensuring that they do not constitute protectionist 'cheating' nor entail gratuitous or unnecessarily severe restrictions on trade. The understanding ought, as well, to set out a number of factors to be considered by dispute settlement panels in applying a least-restrictive means test. In particular, considerable weight should be given to whether the trade-restricting state is acting pursuant to international norms or agreements endorsed by a significant part of the world community, and whether the complaining country's view of environmental or human rights policies that supposedly informs its action is consistent with the judgement of international insti-tutions and authorities (for instance, the United Nations Environmental Programme or the International Labour Organization).

Whether a country should be able to impose trade restrictions to protect *its own* environmental or labour standards from downward competitive pressures is a rather different matter. Here, we are concerned with the 'race to the bottom' argument that liberalized trade may lead to a shift of production and jobs from countries with high labour and environmental standards to those with lower standards. As we have noted, at least with respect to environmental standards, there is some empirical evidence of such a shift having occurred at least in a few industries. Clearly, also some industrial production has been relocated to low labour cost jurisdictions. This, it is argued, may lead to irresistible pressure to lower standards in order to retain or regain competitiveness.

A fundamental difficulty with the 'race to the bottom' argument is that downward movement in one's own labour or environmental standards is not an inevitable response to the competitive pressures in question. For instance, where a country finds that with respect to certain products or sectors it can no longer compete with others while continuing to impose the same costs on its producers with respect to labour and environmental standards, then it can if it chooses retain its high standards, and facilitate exit from the sectors or industries in question through worker adjustment programmes and related measures. As well, countries with relatively high environmental standards can respond to competitiveness pressures through shifting to more efficient instruments of environmental protection that permit producers to meet these higher standards at lower cost. Furthermore, the effects of competitiveness pressures from higher environmental and labour standards should be viewed dynamically – while the immediate effect may be a loss of market share, in the longer term these pressures may create salutary incentives for investment in technologies or other measures that allow firms to meet high environmental standards at significantly lower costs, or that permit an increase in worker productivity that offsets relatively high labour costs.

Nevertheless, under circumstances of deep economic integration, where many other factors relevant to comparative advantage have been equalized and most trade barriers eliminated, there may be serious temptations for an individual country to strategically adjust downward environmental or labour policies. This may happen with respect to sectors or industries characterized by thin profit margins and relatively few competitors, where even short-term cost differentials could have the effect of forcing a foreign competitor out of the market altogether. For these reasons it seems appropriate that the kind of deep economic integration contemplated in the Europe 1992 programme of the EU be accompanied by a social agenda and by further harmonization of environmental standards. As well, in particular industries or sectors of the kind just described, where strategic governmental policies can lead to a 'rigging' of the market, it may be appropriate to negotiate specific constraints on such policies among the major main competing nations (an example is the GATT Civil Aircraft Code). Such agreements, however, should be transparent and subject to multilateral scrutiny, to ensure that they do not further restrict trade, through quotas or agreed market shares.

As well, 'race to the bottom' concerns may have salience in regional contexts where, even though other factors have not yet been largely equalized, economic integration may be proceeding to a level where by selectively lowering or not enforcing environmental or labour standards a country may be able to obtain investment or market shares it otherwise might not be capable of attracting. In the case of the North American Free Trade Agreement, for instance, through liberalized foreign investment US and Canadian producers may be able to take with them to Mexico many of the factors in which they have a comparative advantage (technology, processes, methods of production, etc.), while benefiting from low environmental and labour standards in Mexico. In sum, the lower other barriers to trade and investment become, the more likely that labour or environmental standards may be decisive in influencing trade and investment flows. This may argue – from a domestic policy perspective – against very deep integration with countries that have very low standards, unless the domestic policy calculus permits an adjustment-oriented response. But it does not at the same time provide much normative legitimacy for reneging on existing GATT commitments that are situated within a framework of integration that permits a very wide range of domestic policies influencing in various ways comparative advantage. At the same time, a win-win alternative with respect to more closely integrating arrangements may be available through a parallel process of deeper economic integration and standard-raising in the country or countries with far inferior standards – for which the NAFTA side-agreements establish an institutional basis within the North American free trade area.

Unlike the claims discussed above, which take as their normative reference point values external to the liberal multilateral trading order, 'fair trade'-based claims focus on the effects on domestic producers of other countries' environmental and labour policies, and not *per se* the effects of those policies on the environment and on workers. These claims imply that domestic producers are unfairly injured where they lose market share to foreign firms that have lower environmental or labour costs because they are subject to laxer government regulation in these areas. As with countervailable subsidies, the question that must be asked is: why single out a particular policy difference as an unfair source of comparative advantage, in abstraction from the full range of governmentally-created burdens and benefits that affect the costs of domestic and foreign producers? Trade action to neutralize government-created or influenced comparative advantage would only be truly 'fair' if it neutralized *all* differential costs attributable to government. The *real* normative baseline of 'fair traders' is in fact a 'laissez-faire' world in which nothing but supposedly natural endowments determined comparative advantage. From the fair trade perspective, a uniformly low level playing field is as fair as a uniformly high one – in either case, the supposedly 'unfair' impact of regulatory diversity on trade competitiveness is eliminated.

For this very reason, environmentalists and labour rights advocates should be reluctant to form alliances with 'fair traders' – 'fair trade' arguments can as easily be turned against differentially high environmental standards as against differentially low ones.

Reciprocity and the gains from trade

There is a somewhat different set of 'fair trade' arguments premised, directly or indirectly, upon a concept of reciprocity or balanced gains from trade. These arguments deserve serious and separate consideration. Typically, they are advanced by 'fair trade' advocates in the USA, and involve an assertion that, over the last few decades, many other countries have benefited disproportionately from liberal trade rules in comparision with the United States. These other countries have taken advantage of lower tariffs to enter the US market, while adopting domestic policies (whether monopolies in sectors such as telecommunications or idiosyncratic product standards or lax competition policies) that have impeded access to their markets by US exporters of goods and services.

In its broadest sense, the principle of reciprocity has pervaded both multi-lateral and regional efforts at trade liberalization in the post-war period, even though – as we have discussed at various points in this book – it is at odds with the logic of the economic theory of the gains from trade, which suggests the rationality of unilateral liberalization, i.e. the removal of trade barriers even in the absence of reciprocal concessions by trading partners. Nevertheless, reciprocity is in a certain sense rational, for it may be entirely rational to insist on being paid for doing something that it is in one's own interests to do anyhow.

However, the reciprocity demanded by 'fair traders' amounts to requiring concessions that have in fact *never* been negotiated for. There is nothing wrong with the USA demanding negotiations on, say, Japanese competition policies – what is wrong is to require these concessions on the threat of reneging on existing concessions for which the Japanese have already 'paid'.

Once trade agreements are conceptualized as mutually advantageous exchanges, then it is inevitable that issues of fairness or morality of exchange enter the picture. In fact, contract theorists have long struggled with the difficulties presented by situations where, due to changes in circumstances, one of the parties to a long term contract or bargain no longer benefits from it. In such cases, should modifications in the terms in the initial bargain be enforceable, even where the modification has been exacted by one party's implicit or explicit threat to renege on the initial bargain if the revised terms are not accepted? Making such modifications enforceable where no additional advantage or payment accrues to the Party made worse off by the change in terms may well imply acceptance of the legitimacy in some circumstances of exacting more advantageous contractual terms through exercising commercial pressure on the other party or parties to a bargain.[3] The fact is, however, that the United States, by any meaningful measure, *has* benefited enormously from liberalized trade, even if it no longer enjoys the predominance that it did in global markets at the outset of the GATT era.[4]

Diffuse reciprocity

For this reason, the more sophisticated reciprocity-based 'fair trade' claims focus on how the gains from liberalized trade are shared or divided, rather than on the argument that the liberal multilateral trade order has actually become a Pareto-inferior bargain, at least from the perspective of some countries. This variant in the argument is concerned with relative gains from, or equality in, exchange. Proponents of the realist school of international relations theory identify the concern with relative gains as at its core a concern about power – each state is not only concerned with whether a change in its relationship with other states will increase its domestic welfare, but also about the effects of this change on its relative power *vis-à-vis* other states. This leads to a fundamental disagreement between realists and neo-liberals or liberal internationalists. Neo-liberals believe that Pareto-superior bargains or agreements between states can be struck and sustained in the long run provided transaction costs can be managed and appropriate institutions and rules put into place to constrain cheating (the latter exercise may require, at the outset, a hegemon with strong interests in the creation of such institutions and rules).[5] Realists are sceptical of the capacity of states either to create or sustain international agreements or rules for international co-operation, because they believe that states will never voluntarily agree to, or at least continue to adhere to, rules that result in their relative power in the international system being weakened, even if in domestic welfare terms, they benefit from the agreements or rules in question.[6] If the realist interpretation of the concern with relative gains is correct, then the increasing sense that the United States faces a relative loss of power from open rules of trade bodes ill indeed for the sustainability of a liberal trading order in the long run. The realist view, in fact, strikes at the very heart of liberal political economy, for it suggests that enlightened economic self-interest remains secondary in international economic relations to the primordial struggle for relative power among nations.

An alternative interpretation, however, is possible of the concern about relative gains from exchange. This alternative interpretation is based in a normative theory of fairness or equality in exchange, rather than a power-based understanding of state behaviour. On this view, the long-term legitimacy and indeed sustainability of an exchange depends upon the maintenance of a fair distribution of benefits and burdens among the Parties. Pareto-superiority, on this view, is a necessary but not sufficient criterion for the fairness of an exchange or bargain.[7] Unlike pre-liberal 'just price' theorists, contemporary advocates of equality in exchange tend to emphasize the importance of balance and the avoidance of one-sidedness in contractual obligations, rather than the imposition of a requirement of strict equivalence in values exchanged (which would constitute a paternalistic destruction of the freedom of contract ideal). Unlike the power-based perspective of the realists, this perspective suggests that long-term bargains between countries can be sustained much like long-term contracts between individuals, provided that the agreements themselves contain the flexibility required to prevent one-sidedness or imbalance as circumstances change, or alternatively as long as there is a set of general or meta-norms that permit Parties to insist on occasional readjustment of the initial bargain in order to correct emerging imbalances or inequities in rights and responsibilities.

It is important to note that the post-war economic order, of which the GATT is an integral part, contained a mechanism for precisely such rebalancing. The mechanism in question was the Bretton Woods system of exchange rates and payments, characterized by fixed exchange rates backed by gold. If a country's exports substantially exceeded its imports, eventually demand for its currency would exceed its gold reserves. Its currency would then need to be revalued in order to reflect this scarcity. The revaluation would increase imports and reduce exports, thereby correcting the trade imbalance. Similarly, where a country was unable to cover the foreign currency needed to pay for imports with foreign currency it received for its exports, it would have to sell gold to make up the difference. Where its gold reserves began to run out, the country would have to devalue its currency (to increase exports and reduce imports) and maintain its liquidity and convertibility obligations under the IMF Articles. The Bretton Woods system also entailed both explicit and implicit responsibilities of countries to adopt or alter domestic policies so as to avoid payments problems and thereby obviate the need for frequent changes in exchange rates, which would undermine a system of fixed rates by creating constant speculation on markets as to when revaluations and devaluations would occur. In a previous chapter we have described the breakdown of the Bretton Woods system of exchange rates and payments and the largely unsuccessful effort to attempt rebalancing under floating rates through macroeconomic policy coordination among the major economic powers.

Under the rebalancing through the exchange rates and payment systems envisaged by Bretton Woods, a supranational authority, the IMF, was to bear the primary responsibility for determining which countries' domestic policies required what adjustments in order to preserve exchange rate stability and to clear trade and payments imbalances – on the basis, of course, of the Keynesian policy science of macroeconomics. But under contemporary circumstances, there is no supranational authority with the normative legitimacy to decide which, for example, American and/or

Japanese policies should change in order to achieve rebalancing through *trade*. Unlike the realists, we believe that rebalancing can, in theory, be accommodated within long-term bargains and actually serve the goal of sustaining those bargains as circumstances change over time. But there is an important concern that the existing institutions and normative framework of the GATT – built on the assumption that rebalancing would occur through another part of the system – are not adequate to the task of adjudicating or arbitrating claims for rebalancing, and particularly of distinguishing legitimate claims from unjustified cheating, or strategic games of 'up the ante'. A sustained dissensus about what is cheating and what is not could pose a significant long-run threat to the sustainability of the liberal trading system, at least on a neo-liberal or liberal internationalist perspective that views the sustainability of a cooperative equilibrium as dependent on effective means of identifying and sanctioning defection. However, in the short run, the most effective avenue for addressing diffuse reciprocity concerns may be through increasing the range of issues subject to *future* multilateral negotiations. The Uruguay Round itself is an example of this approach, with the addition of services, investment, and intellectual property rights reflecting, in part, a concession to the American concern about rebalancing of benefits and burdens within the liberal multilateral trading order.

Specific reciprocity

The diffuse reciprocity concerns described above usually do not stand on their own but go hand in hand with concerns about reciprocity within specific sectors or with respect to particular products. While the Bretton Woods system as originally conceived seemed to encompass a concept of rebalancing that corresponds to concerns about diffuse reciprocity, it certainly did not contemplate any mechanism for balancing or rebalancing trade within specific sectors or in specific products. Indeed, this would seem tantamount to attempting to suppress comparative advantage itself.

The counterargument from fair traders is that domestic policies in certain highly competitive sectors, like microelectronics, can fundamentally distort comparative advantage or rig the competitive game. Where both global and domestic market share are crucial to survival, if I can arrange my domestic policies (e.g. competition rules, technical standards) such that your producers have little access to my domestic market, while my producers have largely unimpeded access to yours, I may be able to force you out of business. Free trade advocates are likely to reply that most of the domestic policies in question are not intended to rig the game, but are general 'background' policies that should be considered as a normal part of comparative advantage, rather than a distortion of it. Nevertheless, at the limit, some range of domestic policies may be correctly characterized as targeted efforts at capturing market share from foreign competitors – subsidies in the case of civil aircraft are a case in point. As well, while some policies may constitute an integral part of a country's underlying social and economic arrangements, and thus are unlikely to be adaptable to meet fair trade concerns, others may indeed be alterable, at least with respect to their application to specific sectors.

While the demand for sectoral reciprocity, or reciprocal market access in particular sectors, runs the risk of generating a thicket of discriminatory managed trade arrangements in the absence of complete harmonization of domestic policies (a highly unrealistic possibility), in one sense the demand for sectoral reciprocity is more manageable than that for diffuse reciprocity. Because one is dealing with a limited number of domestic policies of a few countries that are major players in specific sectors it is possible to engage in some kind of focused dialogue about the effects of domestic policies on trade reciprocity. Concerns of diffuse reciprocity are more difficult to handle, absent a supranational authority or judge, simply because the value judgements are so open-ended. The Japanese argue that the US budget deficit and debt is the problem, driving up interest rates and the value of the US dollar. Some fair traders will reply that the size of the US debt and deficit are partially attributable to America's global defence responsibilities, from which Japan has actually benefited substantially.

In the case of specific reciprocity, a range of trade-offs concerning domestic policy constraints may be possible by applying certain normative criteria or tests to a limited number of policies. For example, Bhagwati has suggested that principles of proportionality, intentionality, selectivity and proximity can be invoked to evaluate claims that particular domestic policies distort trade unfairly within a specific sector. The proportionality principle would eliminate from scrutiny domestic policies determined to have a minimal impact on trade. The intentionality principle would limit offensive domestic policies to those intended to rig the game. The selectivity principle would limit scrutiny of domestic policies to those targeted to the specific sectors in question. Finally, the proximity principle would limit fair trade claims to those domestic policies that directly affect comparative advantage.[8] Bhagwati himself characterizes these principles as 'pragmatic' in the sense that the distinctions they draw between distortive and non-distortive domestic policies have no real basis in the theory of liberal trade. Applied by domestic trade authorities and tribunals with respect to an indeterminate range of foreigners' policies in the context of unilateral trade actions driven by protectionist demands, these kinds of principles would prove highly manipulable (consider the fate of the injury and specificity tests with respect to countervailing duty actions under domestic US trade law). By contrast, they might function quite well as *lignes directrices* for a structured multilateral negotiation on trade-impacting domestic policies within certain sectors.

These kinds of principles, as well, are not without some normative foundation even within the pre-Uruguay Round GATT. First of all, the jurisprudence of the GATT suggests a willingness to submit to scrutiny domestic policies that may have discriminatory or harmful impacts on trade even where on their face the domestic policies in question do not single out imported products for discriminatory treatment. GATT Panels as well as FTA Panels interpreting the GATT have been prepared to consider the possibility that facially neutral policies mask a discriminatory protectionist intent, or even to take an effects-based approach to key GATT provisions such as Articles III and XI,[9] subjecting to GATT scrutiny some measures that while not in form barriers to trade in products or discriminatory domestic policies, nevertheless appear to have a particularly harmful impact on trade and whose domestic benefits seem disproportionately small relative to the harm they do to the interests of trading partners. Along similar lines, the GATT *Technical Barriers* Code places Contracting Parties under a general obligation to minimize the negative trade effects of distinctive national standards or regulatory requirements with respect to trade in goods, and to adopt internationally recognized standards or norms wherever available and not prejudicial to domestic interests. Finally, supported by some GATT jurisprudence, there is plausibility to the view that, on its terms, Article XXIII of the General Agreement includes a right to relief from 'nullification and impairment' of GATT concessions, even where the actions leading to nullification and impairment do not involve a formal violation of GATT rules.

There thus seems to be some (albeit rather general) normative basis for multilateral sectoral bargaining on trade-impacting domestic policies. This, combined with sound empirical work on the trade impacts of domestic policies, the domestic goals and functions of the policies, and possible alternative policies with fewer negative trade impacts, may allow for sectoral agreements that are widely viewed as legitimate rather than simply as a capitulation to unilateralism. Such agreements are certainly vastly superior to achieving specific reciprocity through discriminatory managed trade arrangements, such as bilateral VERs, the Auto Pact, the Multi-Fibre Arrangement (MFA), and the US–Japan Semi-Conductor Agreement. In this sense, the demand that trade-impacting domestic policies be put on the bargaining table may be inherently less threatening to the normative order of the GATT than traditional managed trade arrangements, which the GATT has been rather ineffective in preventing in the past (witness the tremendous expansion of managed trade in textiles from the 1960s to the 1970s and of VERs in steel and autos during the late 1970s and 1980s[10]), as long as claims of unfairness can be defined, evaluated and constrained within an appropriate normative and institutional framework.

In our view, it would be appropriate to encourage sectoral bargaining with respect to domestic policies in sensitive industries under the auspices of the GATT, along the lines (broadly speaking) of the Civil Aircraft Code, and to establish certain rules for such bargaining. These might involve an obligation to include in negotiations all countries involved in global competition in the sector; a prohibition on explicit agreements with respect to quotas and market shares (i.e. an anti-cartelization rule); a requirement that all market access commitments in the form of adjustment of domestic policies as they apply to foreign producers be offered to all countries party to the agreement (conditional MFN); a general proviso that the agreements not be more restrictive of trade than existing rules; and an obligation to consider interests of non-signatories (both consumer interests and those of *potential* entrants to the market).

INTEGRATING THE NEWLY LIBERALIZING COUNTRIES INTO THE GLOBAL TRADING SYSTEM

Unquestionably one of the greatest challenges confronting the global trading system today is that of integrating into the system the Newly Liberalizing Countries of Central and Eastern Europe, the former Soviet Union and China (the NLCs). Prior to the collapse of communism, these countries' foreign trade was controlled (like most economic activity within the communist bloc) by state fiat or command. Central control over trade was exercised through a combination of state trading enterprises or monopolies, rigid exchange controls, and/or import and export licences and permits. In addition, the cost of producing goods and services, as well as their prices, were determined by a complex system of consumer and production subsidies and cross-subsidies. Moreover, until the collapse of communism most trade (almost 70% of all imports and exports) occurred within the Soviet Bloc under the umbrella of the Council on Mutual Economic Assistance (CMEA, often referred to as Comecon).[11]

In the past, the GATT system was generally viewed as ill-adapted to the participation of command economies. The system was seen as presupposing that Contracting Parties' trade barriers took a transparent and discrete form, such as tariffs or quantitative restrictions, which could be negotiated down and bound, or constrained by rules and principles, such as National Treatment and MFN.[12] Also, given the 'artificial' nature of factor prices in communist economies, traditional rules on subsidies and dumping were considered impossible to apply.

Article XVII of the GATT does address explicitly the phenomenon of state trading enterprises and affirms their consistency with the GATT provided these enterprises operate in a manner consistent with 'commercial considerations' and do not engage in discriminatory practices. However, where demand, supply, prices, and wages are themselves not in any measure determined by 'commercial considerations', ascertaining whether the behaviour of a particular state trading enterprise conforms to commercial considerations is an intractable undertaking. In effect, one would have to ask a formidable counterfactual question: what import or export decisions would this enterprise make if the domestic economy in which it is trading operated according to market forces? Understandably, therefore, Article XVII has not proved a particularly useful vehicle for addressing the place of command economies within the GATT.[13]

Nevertheless, a number of these economies have been able to join the GATT, including Poland, Hungary, Romania and the former Yugoslavia. In each instance, special terms and conditions were imposed as a condition for membership, reflecting concerns about the lack of transparency of trade barriers in command economies, and the absence (in most cases) of significant tariff barriers that could be reduced and bound as a price for entry into the GATT. The terms and conditions varied from country to country, but generally contained a discriminatory safeguard provision which could be interpreted as permitting Contracting Parties to continue to apply discriminatory quantitative restrictions (QRs) against imports from the command economies, even though they were now members of the General Agreement.[14] In the case of Poland, specific commitments to increase imports from other Contracting Parties by 7% per year were the price of admission, and similar (although apparently not as rigid) commitments were also implicated in the Romanian accession.[15] The Hungarian and Yugoslav accessions occurred in the context of these countries' avowed intentions, in the 1970s, of partial reform of their economies, including liberalization and decentralization of foreign trade. Unlike Romania and Poland, the terms of accession focused on surveillance of trade policies and practices in these countries, to ensure that the avowed liberalization was indeed taking place.

In general, as Haus concludes, 'The socialist countries . . . received few tangible benefits upon accession to the GATT. Membership provided them with little in the way of increased access to Western markets, although this had been an important objective for the Eastern countries when they first approached the GATT'.[16] While the countries of the European Union continued to apply discriminatory QRs against the command economy Contracting Parties, the United States invoked Article XXXV of the GATT and dealt with each country on a bilateral basis, refusing MFN treatment, and applying a special system of administered protection that was used only with respect to command economies.[17] Among the justifications for continued high levels of protection were that the command economies themselves engaged in preferential treatment of each other through the CMEA, and that despite the various commitments to liberalization, hidden trade barriers remained pervasive in these countries.

With the collapse of the Soviet Bloc, the CMEA trading system rapidly broke down, and several of the NLCs rapidly reoriented their exports towards the West. Contrary to the widely-held view that the NLCs had little of value that could be sold competitively in the West, with the breakdown of the CMEA exports of several NLCs to OECD countries increased dramatically. Ostry notes: 'Exports from the CSFR (former Czechoslovakia), Hungary and Poland (to the OECD) increased by 41 percent, 22 percent and 15 percent, respectively, in 1991 from a year earlier.'[18] In these three countries, and most strikingly in Poland, reform of the Trade and Payments system was one of the first major liberalizing moves, with a rapid shift towards internal currency convertibility and removal of most export and import controls of an administrative, or 'command' nature.[19]

In the case of Poland and Hungary, it might have seemed that the most obvious response to these encouraging developments would be to hasten the full integration of these economies into the GATT, i.e. to eliminate the special burdens and conditions contained in their accession protocols. With respect to Czechoslovakia, which was a founding member of GATT but became inactive in the GATT following the communist takeover of 1949, a renewed commitment to accept the full obligations of GATT membership might have been sought, in return for the granting of MFN status by the major world trading powers. In the case of other countries, such as Yugoslavia or the Soviet Union, the high level of uncertainty about whether the existing federal arrangements would survive naturally created a difficult predicament for the GATT. And in the case of Romania and Bulgaria (the latter had made a failed attempt to join the GATT during the 1980s) it was far from clear whether market-oriented reform was proceeding at a sufficient pace, and with sufficient depth, to permit full integration into the GATT in the short term.

Even taking into account these dilemmas and uncertainties, the response of the major trading nations to the challenge presented by liberalization in Central and East Europe has been highly disappointing.[20] Providing access to foreign markets and giving the NLCs incentives to open up their own markets is one of the few unambiguously helpful things the West can do for these countries. More export opportunities generate jobs and capital at a time of transition when they are desperately needed. Moreover, since the process of privatizing major state enterprises is proving to be a lengthy one in all these countries,[21] and must be supplemented by a further (or interrelated) process of demonopolization and decartelization, foreign competition is a very attractive short-cut to market discipline. Full membership in GATT would also stimulate foreign investment by providing them the assurance that imports of inputs into and export of finished products out of NLCs will be governed by liberal trade rules.

Unfortunately, the whole process of integrating the NLCs fully into the GATT has been beset by delays and confusion, as Contracting Parties revise constantly their prognosis of how far or deep economic reform has gone in particular countries, and attempt the exercise of determining a 'threshold' beyond which it is safe to admit NLCs as full GATT members without special conditions or safeguards. It is true of course that many large state enterprises remain, and that they still receive subsidies and soft financing, and that some price controls and/or consumer subsidies continue in place or have been reimposed in several of these countries. In this respect, it may be unrealistic to expect full reciprocity of obligations at the outset of GATT membership, and some transitional leeway with regard to NLC compliance may be necessary, i.e. in the short term, something akin to unilateral trade liberalization by the West. What has in fact happened, however, is that several of the NLCs themselves have undertaken a substantial amount of uni-lateral trade liberalization within an unprecedentedly short period of time. For example, these countries have moved in the direction of full currency convertibility and have removed capital controls at a pace far outstripping that of the Western European countries after the Second World War.

While the GATT has remained largely at an impasse with respect to these issues, the EU has been active in negotiating Association Agreements on a bilateral basis with individual NLCs. These agreements have been rather naively viewed by the NLCs, at least to some extent, as an initial step towards full EU membership.[22] The Agreements, while reducing or eliminating discriminatory QRs imposed by EU countries on certain NLCs, are most notable for what amounts to a system of managed trade between the EU and the NLCs that they create with respect to sensitive (and for NLCs, crucial) export sectors such as steel, textiles, and agricultural products.[23] The United States has granted MFN status to most of the NLCs by changing its domestic trade legislation. However, the case-by-case fashion in which this has been done leaves the United States considerable leeway to reverse its decision with respect to any particular NLC whose liberalization is deemed to be in-sufficiently rapid or that becomes a trade irritant to US producer interests.[24]

It would perhaps be an overstatement to suggest that the EU Agreements provide no new meaningful market access to Western Europe for NLCs.[25] However, it is also true that the Agreements create new structures for man-aged trade, and contain a whole range of discriminatory safeguard provisions that will offer an easy route to renewed protectionism against NLC imports if political pressures for such protection become more intense.

In our view, Hungary, Poland, and the Czech Republic should be brought into the GATT as full members on the same terms and conditions as apply to other Contracting Parties. The unilateral liberalization that has occurred to date should constitute a sufficient 'price' for entry into the GATT. Not all the liberalizing domestic policy changes would easily lend themselves to being bound as trade concessions. However, requiring full adherence to the GATT and IMF rules on currency convertibility, balance of payments and exchange control measures is probably sufficient to ensure that these countries do not revert to centrally-managed trade practices. Such practices depend decisively on currency controls – once individual businesses and citizens can exchange domestic currency for foreign currency to buy imports, then the range of instruments available to restrict trade becomes similar to that used by any other GATT member: tariffs, quotas, or prohibitions on imports and/or exports.

In the case of Romania and Bulgaria uncertainty understandably remains concerning the depth and pace of liberalizing reforms. With respect to these countries, it could be argued that special terms and conditions are still needed. However, as suggested above, attempts to define an appropriate 'price' for entry into GATT or a threshold that must be passed by such countries to be entitled to a normal membership are fraught with difficulty. An alternative approach, suggested by Sylvia Ostry,[26] is considerably more attractive: the trade and related domestic policies of the countries concerned would be subject to heightened surveillance under the GATT through an enhanced WTO Trade Policy Review Mechanism, which would operate in consultation with the World Bank, the IMF, and the European Bank for Reconstruction and Development. All these institutions are following closely policy developments in the NLCs, and could be relied upon to provide reporting and advice on the progress of liberalizing reforms. In addition, Ostry recommends that selective safeguard action should be permitted against NLCs (without the compensation requirement now contained in Article XIX) for a limited period of time (5 years) as an *alternative* to anti-dumping and countervailing duty actions.

The case of the former Soviet republics, as well as the former Yugoslavia, presents a rather different and more intractable set of difficulties than that of the Central and East European countries. Political and economic instability is rampant in most of these new states. The Commonwealth of Independent States has proved a fragile and uncertain framework for governing trade and other economic relations between the Republics, and there is a fundamental lack of clarity as to whether these countries should be considered as fully independent in their commercial relations, what the exact nature of their monetary relations will be with Russia and the Russian central bank, and so forth. In addition, between some Republics, a state of civil war exists at present, and trade relations between others have broken down completely. Here, there seems more justification, obviously, for a 'wait and see attitude', and the same could be said for several of the Republics of the former Yugoslavia.

However, we agree with Ostry that providing a framework for eventual integration of these countries must begin now. It should be remembered that the planners of the Bretton Woods institutions were sufficiently farsighted to begin their work *before* the end of the Second World War, and by the time the war had ended a framework had already begun to emerge that permitted the rapid construction of a new world order.

In the case of the former Soviet Republics, Ostry suggests that a framework for integration into the GATT would set out as preconditions for membership stabilization and normalization of trade relations and monetary relations between the Republics, including removal of inter-republican trade barriers, supported by an IMF Stand-By Arrangement.[27] In addition, enhanced trade policy surveillance would be implemented, as with other NLCs. It is clear that at present the Republics individually and collectively are unable to fulfill these preconditions, but setting them out in advance might hasten the pace of stabilization in the CIS, and might also provide a concrete long-term alternative to the proliferation of various bilateral and discriminatory arrangements between NLCs and individual Contracting Parties. Once such a complex system of discriminatory managed trade is in place (and it is already beginning to evolve), it will be difficult to dismantle except through equally complex transitional arrangements (and perhaps not politically possible to completely dismantle), when the Republics have met the preconditions for full GATT membership. Indeed, at the very least, the potential long-term importance of these countries to world trade is such that the GATT should be sufficiently proactive to place some limits on, or develop some guidelines for, bilateral arrangements with these countries. Given the kinds of changes in the former Soviet Bloc that are now occurring, there is an urgent need to rethink the traditional view that Contracting Parties can engage in whatever trade arrangements they wish with non-Parties[28] as long as these do not violate the requirement of MFN treatment for other Contracting Parties.

A different approach to accession by the former Soviet Republics is taken by Leah Haus.[29] She would encourage entry of the Republics into the GATT immediately, but on an 'associate membership' basis. This would involve permission to participate in the GATT as an organization, but not secure access to the full legal rights of GATT membership. The extent to which a Republic would be entitled to such legal rights would be negotiated with each individual Republic. This approach would have the advantage of allowing control through the multilateral forum of the GATT Council over the extent to which Contracting Parties would remain free to engage in discriminatory treatment of the Republics and therefore provide some kind of curb on the proliferation of bilateral arrangements. Nevertheless, it would involve the creation of complex new interim arrangements, which would certainly still permit some discriminatory treatment and bilateral managed trade, and could well be difficult to phase out when full membership becomes appropriate. The Ostry approach, in setting general preconditions, and entailing a temporary safeguard mechanism and policy surveillance mechanism applicable to all the former Republics, would seem inherently easier to wind down or 'phase in' to full membership. Here again, it is to be recalled that with respect to those Soviet Bloc countries that entered the GATT on special terms and conditions, phasing these out or even adjusting them has proven a very difficult and contentious undertaking.

A related issue is the application of China for full GATT membership.[30] With respect to China, we remain unpersuaded that economic reforms to date suggest an unambiguous commitment to an open economy. Instead, the Chinese authorities appear to be engaging in a two-track approach – maintaining an orthodox central planning approach in many economic sectors while permitting limited liberalization in others, especially sectors where liberalization will make China successful in export markets. The threat to reciprocity is evident where much of China's own domestic market remains controlled by central planning and only selectively opened to foreign competition through traditional mechanisms of state trading, but where other sectors operated on market principles provide intense export competition for trading partners.

In addition, increasing attention to linkages between trade and human rights within the global trading order will pose particularly severe problems in the Chinese case, as China would be the one remaining major trading nation that normally takes the dogmatic traditional communist bloc approach that these are strictly 'internal' matters. This being said, it would be inappropriate to wait until some threshold of 'full' liberalization is passed *in practice* before bringing China into the GATT. When China is able to make a credible commitment to gradual abandonment of the totalitarian, command model of social and economic organization, and when it is able to accept the legitimacy of international scrutiny of its human rights record, full membership should be granted.

MULTILATERALISM VERSUS REGIONALISM

As discussed earlier in this book,[31] the rise of regional trading blocs poses a special challenge to the multilateral system. The principle of non-discrimination that lies at the heart of the multilateral system is potentially put at serious risk by regional trading blocs which, by definition, extend more favourable trading rules to members than non-members. The principle of non-discrimination enshrined in the GATT (in the form of the Most Favoured Nation and National Treatment Principles) has important economic and political rationales. From an economic perspective, regional trading blocs always entail some degree of trade diversion as well as trade expansion and thus carry the potential for distorting global trade and reducing global economic welfare. From a political perspective, the principle of non-discrimination is designed to discourage countries from playing favourites with other countries, and inducing the kind of mutually self-destructive forms of factionalism that led to the collapse of the open trading system in the inter-war years.

We believe that both the economic and political rationales for the principle of non-discrimination seen as central to the GATT by its founders remain of paramount importance. In order to preserve these values, consideration should be given to tightening the conditions under which free trade areas or customs unions can be authorized under the GATT. More specifically, several key conditions contained in Article XXIV need to be interpreted and applied more stringently than they often have been in the past. First, the requirement that when a free trade or customs union is formed, substantially all trade between or among member countries must be liberalized should be interpreted to mean exactly what it says, so as to exclude various kinds of bilateral, sectoral, managed trade arrangements. While sectoral agreements with reciprocal market access commitments *may* be liberalizing (e.g. the chapter on financial services in the NAFTA), these agreements also have considerable potential to reinforce restrictive managed trade arrangements, whether directly through measures such as quotas or indirectly, for example, through complex re-adjustment of the rules of origin for particular products or sectors. In sensitive sectors such as textiles, autos and agriculture, the NAFTA seems to take on the character of a managed trade arrangement rather than a free trade arrangement.

Second, the requirement that external duties imposed by member countries of free trade areas or customs unions should not be higher on average than those prevailing before the formation of such an arrangement should be amended to require that such external duties imposed following the formation of regional trading arrangements should not exceed the *lowest* external duties imposed by any member country prior to the formation of the arrangement, thus minimizing the amount of trade diversion likely to be induced. Such a requirement would also reduce the need for complex rules of origin.

To ensure that trade diversion is minimized, it is not sufficient to scrutinize only the external duties imposed following the establishment of regional arrangements. Rules of origin and rules with respect to the extent to which partially or wholly foreign-owned or controlled firms operating within the free trade area can benefit from liberalization commitments on investment or services also have a considerable impact on the extent to which regional arrangements are trade-diverting. In the case of rules of origin, the trade diverting effects may be quite dramatic. The rules determine, with respect to each product grouping, what percentage of value of the finished product must have been added within the free trade area in order to qualify for preferential or duty-free admission into other countries within the area. They can easily be fine-tuned so as to significantly affect the market share of non-members of the free trade area for certain products. To take a hypothetical example, suppose that prior to the existence of a free trade area, producers of widgets in country A have been using an input manufactured in Japan that constitutes 40% of the value of the finished product. If the rule of origin is now set at over 60%, in order to be able to export duty-free the finished product within the free trade area, the producer will have to substitute for the Japanese input one produced within the area. Therefore, assuming that the price advantage of the Japanese input is less than the advantage in terms of lower duties that comes from meeting the rules of origin by selecting an input manufactured within the free trade area, Japanese producers will lose market share. In sum, there is a clear need for scrutiny of the effects of a range of rules in regional arrangements on the trade of non-members.

Third, there is also much to be said for the view that in order for regional trading arrangements to be authorized under the GATT an additional condition should be satisfied - that membership of such an arrangement is open to any country prepared to accept the obligations to which existing members have committed themselves. That is to say, these arrangements should be required to be open to application by new members, through an obligatory accession provision, along the lines of the accession provisions in the GATT (Article XXXIII), and building on the accession provisions contained in NAFTA (Article 2205). Even where (because of particular characteristics of the country concerned or its stage of social and economic development) a country may not be prepared automatically to accept all the obligations of the existing arrangement, there should be a duty at least to enter into negotiations in good faith with a view to admission on terms and conditions that are mutually acceptable. As well, in specific areas such as services, investment and intellectual property rights, members of a regional arrangement should be encouraged to extend the rights provided by the arrangement to non-members who are prepared to accept regional obligations in these areas even if they are not members of the region itself, or if for other reasons it would be inappropriate for them to become full members of the regional arrangement. Here, a precedent exists with respect to the agreements that existed between the EFTA countries and the European Union prior to their decision to join the EU.

While both the GATT and NAFTA accession provisions contemplate a process of negotiation and approval by existing members, where a country seeking membership of a regional trading arrangement is able to demonstrate a willingness to accept all the obligations that existing members are subject to, some right of review by a GATT Working Group or Committee of a negative decision by members would seem to be an important check on arbitrary or discriminatory exclusions. While the findings and recommendations of such a Working Group might not realistically bind existing members, they would improve the transparency and legitimacy of the decision-making process, and provide applicants for membership in regional trading arrangements with additional political leverage.

Quite apart from the potential for increasing the tendency towards managed trade and discrimination, a proliferation of regional arrangements and regional dispute settlement processes for trade disagreements poses a threat to clarity and certainty in trade rules. Overlap between GATT and regional obligations, the latter often stated in similar but not identical terms to those in the GATT, can create confusion with respect to the appropriate interpretation of both sets of rules. Furthermore, free trade areas (as opposed to customs unions, where matters are simplified by a common external policy) increase the regulatory knowledge and burden that trading partners require to engage in effective commercial relations – they must still take account of the trade policies of each individual country and the GATT rules, while also being aware of the meaning and implications of the regional rules as well, and the evolving jurisprudence surrounding those rules. In the pre-Uruguay Round environment, the problem was less pronounced because regional arrangements built on the GATT, and created rules in areas such as intellectual property, services and investment, where the GATT had few or none. However, there are now both GATT and overlapping regional rules in all these areas. Cowhey and Aronson, who are favourably disposed towards regional arrangements, nevertheless see a need eventually to 'multilateralize' these arrangements.[32] In our view, multilateralization would ideally implicate a Working Group of the GATT in the task of harmonizing regional and multilateral rules to the extent possible, as well as addressing on an *ad hoc* basis conflicts that occur with respect to the interaction of regional and multilateral rules, or important divergences in the jurisprudential approaches of different dispute settlement fora.

In sum, in order to minimize the potential threat that regional trading blocs pose to the multilateral system, we consider that some significant rethinking and reworking of the conditions for approval of such arrangements under Article XXIV of the GATT should be an important priority on the future international trade policy agenda.

NOTES

PREFACE

1 E.-U. Petersmann, 'Strengthening GATT Procedures for Settling Trade Disputes', *World Economy*, March 1988, pp. 55–6.

1 THE EVOLUTION OF INTERNATIONAL TRADE THEORY AND POLICY

1 This section draws heavily on three widely accessible accounts of the evolution of international trade theory: Richard G. Harris, *Trade, Industrial Policy and International Competition* (Research Study No. 13, Macdonald Royal Commission and the Economic Union and Development Prospects for Canada, University of Toronto Press, 1985); Jagdish Bhagwati, 'Fair Trade, Reciprocity and Harmonization: The New Challenge to the Theory and Policy of Free Trade', in A. Deardorff and R. Stern (eds) *Analytical and Negotiating Issues in the Global Trading System* (Ann Arbor: University of Michigan Press, forthcoming); and Peter B. Kenen, *The International Economy* (Prentice Hall, 2nd ed., 1989) chs 1–8.

2 See Paul Krugman and Maurice Obstfeld, *International Economics* (New York: Harper Collins, 2nd ed., 1991) p. 521.

3 Adam Smith, *The Wealth of Nations* (1776; New York: Modern Library Edition, 1937) p. 424.

4 Taken from P. Samuelson and A. Scott, *Economics* (Toronto: McGraw-Hill, 1980) p. 807.

5 See Herbert G. Grubel and P.J. Lloyd, *Intra-Industry Trade: The Theory and Measurement of Trade in Differentiated Products* (London: Macmillan, 1975).

6 See e.g. Raymond Vernon, 'International Investment and International Trade in the Product Cycle', (1966) 80 *Quarterly J. of Econs* 190; Vernon, 'The Product Cycle Hypothesis in a New International Economic Environment', (1979) 41 *Oxford Bulletin of Economic Statistics* 255.

7 See Krugman and Obstfeld, *op. cit.*

8 See William R. Cline, '"Reciprocity": A New Approach to World Trade Policy', in Cline, W.R. (ed.) *Trade Policy in the 1980s* (Washington DC: Institute for International Economics, 1983) p. 152.

9 See Cline, *op.cit.*

10 See Beth and Robert Yarborough, 'Reciprocity, Bilateralism and Economic "Hostages": Self-enforcing Agreements in International Trade' (1986) 30 *International Studies Quarterly* 7; Alan O. Sykes, 'Mandatory Retaliation for

Breach of Trade Agreements: Some Thoughts on the Strategic Design of Section 301', (1990) 8 *Boston University International Law Journal* 301.

11 See R. Axelrod and R. Keohane, 'Achieving Co-operation Under Anarchy' in K. Oye (ed.) *Co-operation Under Anarchy* (Princeton NJ: Princeton University Press, 1985).

12 Adam Smith, *op. cit.*, pp. 434–5.

13 See Jagdish Bhagwati and Hugh Patrick (eds) *Aggressive Unilateralism* (Ann Arbor: University of Michigan Press, 1992).

14 See Carolyn Rhodes, 'Reciprocity in Trade: The Utility of a Bargaining Strategy' (1989) 43 *International Organization* 273.

15 See Yarborough and Yarborough, *op. cit.*; Laura Tyson, 'Managed Trade: Making the Best of the Second Best', and Rudiger Dornbusch, 'Policy Options for Free Trade: The Case for Bilateralism', in R. Lawrence and C. Schultz (eds), *An American Trade Strategy: Options for the 1990s* (Washington DC: Brookings Institution, 1990).

16 John Stuart Mill, *Principles of Political Economy* (London: Longman, Greene & Co., 1848) p. 922.

17 See e.g. Paul Krugman (ed.) *Strategic Trade Policy and the New International Economics* (Cambridge MA: MIT Press, 1986); Elhonan Helpman and Paul Krugman, *Trade Policy and Market Structure* (Cambridge MA: MIT Press, 1989); J. David Richardson, 'The Political Economy of Strategic Trade Policy', (1990) 44 *International Organization* 107.

18 See e.g. A. Dixit, 'How Should the United States Respond to Other Countries' Trade Policies?', in R. Stern (ed.) *U.S. Trade Policies in a Changing World Economy* (Cambridge MA: MIT Press, 1987) p. 245.

19 See Chapter 7 below.

20 See Chapter 6.

21 See Chapter 13.

22 Francis Fukuyama, 'The End of History', *The National Interest* (Summer, 1989) p. 3; Fukuyama *The End of History and the Last Man* (New York: Free Press, 1991).

23 George Grant, *Lament for a Nation: The Defeat of Canadian Nationalism* (Toronto: Anansi, 1967).

24 Downs, A., *An Economic Theory of Democracy* (New York: Harper, 1957).

25 Olson, M., *The Logic of Collective Action* (New York: Schoken, 1965).

26 I.M. Destler and J. Odell, *Anti-Protection: Changing Forces in United States Trade Politics* (Washington DC: Institute for International Economics, 1987).

27 H. Milner, 'Trading Places: Industries for Free Trade', *World Politics* XL, 3 (April, 1988) pp. 350–76.

28 H. Milner and D. Yoffie, 'Between Free Trade and Protectionism: Strategic Trade Policy and a Theory of Corporate Demands', (1989) 43(2) *International Organization*.

29 Robert Baldwin, *The Political Economy of Import Policy* (Cambridge MA: MIT Press, 1985) ch. 1.

30 This evidence is reviewed in M. Trebilcock, M. Chandler and R. Howse, *Trade and Transitions* (London: Routledge, 1990) pp. 178–80.

31 Baldwin *op.cit.*, p. 180.

32 See Gilbert Winham, *The Evolution of International Trade Agreements* (University of Toronto Press, 1992) ch. 1.

33 S.B. Clough and C.W. Cole, *Economic History of Europe* (Boston MA: D.C. Heath, 1941) p. 458.

34 Charles P. Kindleberger, 'The Rise of Free Trade in Western Europe, 1820–1874', (1975) 35 *J. of Economic History* 20 at p. 23, and Clough and

Cole, *op. cit.*, pp. 456–8. See also A.G. Kenwood and A.L. Lougheed, *The Growth of the International Economy* (London: Allen & Unwin, 1971) p. 73. In this respect, the situation in the German states around 1815 is especially striking – 8,000km of borders divided the twenty-eight German-speaking states; heavy transit tolls substantially impeded trade.

35 Clough and Cole, *op. cit.*, p. 473. James Foreman-Peck, *A History of the World Economy* (Ottawa: Barnes & Noble, 1983) p. 56 also emphasizes that Britain was fiscally more able to reduce tariffs than most at this time because of the substantial size of her commerce with respect to the economy as a whole, and the relative absence of government debt.

In Prussia, the Junkers, for the most part large exporters of wheat, favoured free trade. Their dominance of national institutions helped solidify support for the policy in Germany until the 1870s. Then a more cohesive manufacturing sector, and stiff competition from overseas wheat helped turn the political tide against free trade. See Kindleberger, *op.cit.*, p. 42.

36 Clough and Cole, *op.cit.*, pp. 469ff. Such trade treaties actually had their genesis in the late-eighteenth century – Britain and France signed a treaty on trade just before the Revolution. The latter saw the renunciation of the treaty almost directly the King was removed from power.

37 Kenwood and Lougheed, *op.cit.*, p. 77; and P. Bairoch, 'European Trade Policy, 1815-1914', in P. Matthias and S. Pollard, (eds) *The Cambridge Economic History of Europe*, vol. 8 (Cambridge MA: Cambridge University Press, 1989) 1 at p. 36.

38 Kenwood and Lougheed, *op.cit.*, p. 78; Clough and Cole, *op. cit.*, pp. 608–9; and P.B. Kenen, *The International Economy op. cit.*

39 Kenwood and Lougheed, *op. cit.*, p. 78.

40 P. Bairoch, 'European Trade Policy, 1815–1914', in Matthias and Pollard, (eds) *op.cit.*, p. 101.

41 Kenen, *op.cit.*, p. 213, and P. Bairoch, 'European Trade Policy, 1815–1914', in Matthias and Pollard, (eds) *op.cit.*, 1 at pp. 51–2.

42 Foreman-Peck, *op.cit.*, p. 57, and Kindleberger, *op.cit.*, p. 45.

43 Foreman-Peck, *op.cit.*, p. 57. Kindleberger, *op.cit.*, p. 33, points out that some English industrialists supported free trade in the 1840s as a means of slowing down European industrialization.

44 Clough and Cole, *op.cit.*, p. 477.

45 P. Bairoch, 'European Trade Policy, 1815–1914', in Matthias and Pollard, (eds) *op.cit.*, 1 at pp. 51–2. For a description of the 'colonial pact' see P. Bairoch, 'European Trade Policy, 1815–1914', in Matthias and Pollard, (eds) *op.cit.*, 1 at p. 103. It should be noted that colonial policy was not a constant. Britain's stance in this respect was largely dictated by protection on the Continent: in mid-century she was dismantling imperial preference (for a description, see Clough and Cole, *op.cit.*, p. 466), and it was only after the return of protection in the 1880s that the idea of imperial preference regained any real legitimacy. See Kenwood and Lougheed, *op.cit.*, p. 79, and Clough and Cole, *op.cit.*, p. 476. Moreover, colonies were not acquired for economic reasons only; nationalism played an important role as well.

46 Kenwood and Lougheed, *op.cit.*, p. 186.

47 Foreman-Peck, *op.cit.*, pp. 215–16.

48 Kenen, *op.cit.*, p. 216.

49 J.H. Jackson and W.J. Davey, *Legal Problems of International Economic Relations* (St. Paul: West, 1986) at c. 5. R.E. Hudec, *The GATT Legal System and World Trade Diplomacy*, 2nd ed. (St. Paul: Butterworth, 1990) Part I, contains a detailed description of the negotiations.

50 Jackson and Davey, *op.cit.*, p. 295. See also Hudec, *op.cit.*, at c. 6.
51 Jackson and Davey, *op.cit.*, pp. 294ff.; J.H. Jackson, *The World Trading System* (Cambridge MA: MIT Press, 1989) at. c. 2; and Hudec, *op.cit.*, c. 7. See also *Review of the Effectiveness of Trade Dispute Settlement Under the GATT and the Tokyo Round Agreements: Report to the Committee on Finance, U.S. Senate* (Washington DC: U.S. International Trade Commission, 1985) pp. 11–12 [hereinafter *ITC Report*]; Hudec, *The Evolution of the Modern GATT Legal System* (Butterworths, USA, 1993).
52 Jackson and Davey, *op.cit.*, at s. 5.4.
53 Jackson and Davey, *op.cit.*, pp. 324ff.; K.W. Dam, *The GATT: Law and International Economic Organization* (Chicago: University of Chicago Press, 1970) at c. 5; and Jackson, *op.cit.*, pp. 52–7.
54 Dam, *op.cit.*, at c. 14. See also R.E. Hudec, *Developing Countries in the GATT Legal System* (London: Gower, 1987); and Jackson, *op.cit.*, at c. 12.
55 For a very useful review of recent developments in international trade policy, see Margaret Kelly and Anne Kenny McGuirk, *Issues and Developments in International Trade Policy* (Washington DC: International Monetary Fund, August 1992).
56 Jackson and Davey, *op.cit.*, at s. 4.2 provide useful citations to sources for EC history.
57 See Chapter 4.

2   THE BASIC ELEMENTS OF THE GATT, THE CANADA–US FREE TRADE AGREEMENT, NAFTA AND THE EUROPEAN UNION

1 For introductory treatments of the GATT, see Olivier Long, *Law and Its Limitations in the GATT Multilateral Trade System* (London: Graham & Trotman, 1987); Frank Stone, *Canada, the GATT and the International Trade System* (Montreal: The Institute for Research on Public Policy, 1984); Michael Hart, *Trade – Why Bother?* (Ottawa: Centre for Trade Policy and Law, Carleton University and University of Ottawa, 1992); Alan Oxley, *The Challenge of Free Trade* (London: Harvester Wheatsheaf, 1990). For more extensive treatments, see Kenneth W. Dam, *The GATT: Law and International Economic Organization* (Chicago: University of Chicago Press, 1970); Robert E. Hudec, *The GATT Legal System and World Trade Diplomacy* (2nd ed. Salem NH: Butterworth Legal Publishers, 1990) and John Jackson *The World Trading System: Law and Policy of International Economic Relations* (Cambridge MA: MIT Press, 1989).
2 For a comprehensive review of international codes and agreements dealing with trade and government procurement, see Arie Reich, *Towards Free Trade in the Public Sector: A Comparative Study of International Agreements on Government Procurement* (S.J.D. thesis, University of Toronto Faculty of Law, 1993).
3 J. Bhagwati, 'Fair Trade, Reciprocity and Harmonization: The New Challenge to the Theory and Policy of Free Trade', in A. Deardorff and R. Stern (eds) *Analytical and Negotiating Issues in the Global Trading System* (Ann Arbor: University of Michigan Press, 1993).
4 See, in general, L. Haus, *Globalizing the GATT: the Soviet Union's Successor States, Eastern Europe, and the International Trading System* (Washington DC: Brookings Institution, 1992).
5 See Chapter 12.
6 The relationship between trade and the environment is discussed in detail in Chapter 13.

CHAPTER 2

7 See Michael J. Hahn, 'Vital Interests and the Law in GATT: An Analysis of GATT's Security Exceptions', (1991) *12 Michigan J. of International Law* 588.

8 *Assessing the Effects of the Uruguay Round*, OECD, Paris, 1993. More generally, see Jeffrey Schott, *The Uruguay Round* (Washington DC: Institute for International Economics, 1994).

9 For treatments of the Canada–USA Free Trade Agreement, see Debra P. Steger *et al.*, *A Concise Guide to the Canada–United States Free Trade Agreement* (Toronto: Carswell, 1988); Jon Johnson and Joel Schacter, *The Free Trade Agreement: A Comprehensive Guide* (Toronto: Canada Law Book, 1988); John D. Richard and Richard G. Dearden, *The Canada–U.S. Free Trade Agreement: Final Text and Analysis* (Toronto: CCH Canadian Ltd., 1988); Peter Morici, *Making Free Trade Work: The Canada–U.S. Agreement* (New York and London: Council of Foreign Relations Press, 1990); *The Free Trade Law Reporter* (Toronto: CCH Canadian Ltd., 1989) (Looseleaf); Duncan Cameron and Ed Finn, (eds) *The Facts on Free Trade* (Toronto: James Lorimer, 1988); John Crispo, (ed) *Free Trade: The Real Story* (Toronto: Gage Educational Publishing Co., 1988); Marc Gold and David Leyton-Brown (eds) *Trade-Offs on Free Trade: The Canada–U.S. Free Trade Agreement* (Toronto: Carswell, 1988); and Bruce Doern and Brian Tomlin, *Faith and Fear: The Free Trade Story* (Toronto: Stoddart Publishing Co. Ltd, 1991).

10 See Donald C. Masters, *The Reciprocity Treaty of 1856* (Toronto: McClelland & Stewart, 1963).

11 For the complete legal text of the NAFTA, see *North American Free Trade Agreement* (Ottawa: Supply and Services, 1992). For discussions of the provisions of NAFTA, see S. Globerman and M. Walker (eds) *Assessing NAFTA: A Trinational Analysis* (Vancouver, B.C.: The Fraser Institute, 1993); G.C. Hufbauer and J.J. Schott, *NAFTA: An Assessment* (Washington DC: Institute for International Economics, 1993); J. Lemco and W.B.P. Robson (eds) *Ties Beyond Trade: Labor and Environmental Issues Under the NAFTA*, (Canadian–American Committee) (Toronto, Ont.: C.D. Howe Institute, 1993); A.R. Riggs and Tom Welk, *Beyond NAFTA: An Economic Political and Sociological Perspective* (Vancouver: The Fraser Institute, 1993); Government of Canada, *NAFTA: What's It All About?* (Ottawa: External Affairs and International Trade Canada, September 1993); R. Lipsey, D. Schwanen and R. Wennacott, *The NAFTA* (Toronto: C.D. Howe Institute, 1994); Jon Johnson, *The North American Free Trade Agreement: A Comprehensive Guide* (Toronto: Canada Law Book Co., 1994).

12 This discussion relies, to a significant extent, on the following sources: F.G. Jacobs and K.L. Karst, 'The "Federal" Legal Order: The U.S.A. and Europe Compared: A Juridical Perspective', in M. Cappelletti, M. Seccombe, and J. Weiler, (eds) *Political Organizations, Integration Techniques, and Judicial Process: Methods, Tools and Institutions*, vol. 1 (Berlin: W. De Gruyter, 1986, (hereinafter, *Integration Through Law*)); T. Heller and J. Pelkmans, 'The Federal Economy: Law and Economic Integration and the Positive State – The U.S.A. and Europe Compared in an Economic Perspective', in *Integration Through Law*; M. Brealey and C. Quigley's 'Introduction', in *Completing the Internal Market of the European Community: 1992 Handbook* (London: Graham and Trotman, 1989); G. Hufbauer, 'An Overview', in G. Hufbauer, (ed.) *Europe 1992: An American Perspective* (Washington DC: Brookings Institution, 1990); D. Swann, *Competition and Industrial Policy in the European Community* (London: Methuen, 1990, chs 1 and 2); P. Leslie, *The European Community: A Political Model for Canada?* (Ottawa: Supply & Services, 1991); and P. Monahan, *Political and Economic Integration: The*

European Experience and Lessons for Canada (Toronto: York University Centre for Public Law and Public Policy, 1992).

13 *Treaty Establishing the European Economic Community,* 25 March 1957, 298 UNTS 11 (hereinafter Treaty of Rome).

14 At the outset, direct enforceability was controversial, as some states adhered to the narrower view of the Treaty as a 'normal' interstate agreement. Early decisions of the Court were of decisive importance in establishing a 'constitutional' status for the Treaty, and in moving the Community towards genuine *integration.* See H. Rasmussen, *Community Law* (Brussels, 1983). Also, see *Van Gend en Loos* v. *Nederlandse Administratie der Belastingen,* Case 26/62 [1963] E.C.R. 1125, and the discussion of this and subsequent cases in D. Wyatt and A. Dashwood, 'The Community Legal Order', in W. Wyatt (ed.) *The Substantive Law of the EEC,* 2nd ed. (London: Sweet and Maxwell, 1990).

15 Brealey and Quigley, *op. cit.,* p. xxii.

16 See Brealey and Quigley, *op.cit.,* p. xxvi.

17 The system is as follows: France, Germany, Italy, and the UK have 10 votes each; Spain, 8; Belgium, Greece, Netherlands, Portugal, 5 each: Denmark and Ireland, 3 each: Luxembourg, 2. The total number of votes is 76, of which 54 are required to pass a directive or regulation by qualified majority. G. Hufbauer, 'Overview', *op.cit.,* p. 53. It will readily be seen that: (a) the minimum number of countries needed to pass a measure is seven; (b) consequently, the big countries cannot pass a measure without some support from the smaller ones; (c) the smaller countries cannot pass a measure without some support from the big ones; (d) to defeat a measure a coalition of at least 3 countries is required since the maximum number of votes that any two countries could muster would be 20 (therefore, solving the hold out problem from unanimity requirements).

18 On the importance of the abandonment of the unanimity requirement to the realization of Europe, 1992, see for example, L. Bergeron, 'L'integration européenne', ch. 2, in Commission sur l'avenir politique et constitutionelle du Québec, *Eléments d'analyse institutionelle, juridique, et demolinguistique pertinent à la révision due status politique et constitutionelle du Québec,* Document du travail, numero 2, Québec City 1991, at 116; see also Tarullo, 'Can the European "social market" survive?', *American Prospect,* Spring 1991; Brealey and Quigley, *op.cit.,* p. xii.

19 The Article reads as follows: 'The provisions of Articles 30 to 34 shall not preclude prohibitions or restrictions on imports, exports or goods in transit justified on grounds of public morality, public policy or public security; the protection of health and life of humans, animals and plants; the protection of national treasures possessing artistic, historic or archaeological value; or the protection of industrial and commercial property. Such prohibitions or restrictions shall not, however, constitute a means of arbitrary discrimination or a disguised restriction on trade between member states.'

20 *Rewe-Zentral AG v Bundesmonopoverwaltung für Branntwein, E.C.J.* 120/78.

21 The notion of mandatory requirements suggests that the measures in question must be pursuant to a mandatory legislative scheme and not a mere exercise of executive or administrative discretion.

22 Case 178/84 (1988) 1 CMLR 780.

23 See Articles 92(1) and 92 of the Treaty.

24 Hufbauer, 'An Overview', *op.cit.,* p. 9.

25 Europe, Documents No. 1759/60, February 1992.

26 For a discussion in greater depth of some of these institutional changes, see P. Ludlow, 'The Maastricht Treaty and the Future of Europe', *Washington*

Quarterly, Autumn 1992, pp. 127–9.

27 Discussed in Chapter 3, on trade, exchange rates, and the balance of payments.
28 See, for a discussion of these issues, R. Portes, 'EMS and EMU After the Fall', 16 *World Economy*, January 1993, pp. 1–15. See also, for a background to some of the tensions among EC Member Countries with respect to macro-economic policy, L. Pauly, 'The politics of European monetary union: national strategies, international implications', 27 *International Journal* 93 (1992).
29 See A. Hartley, 'Europe's New Populism', *National Interest*, Winter 1992/93, pp. 37–40.
30 On the seriousness of the immigration issue, see Hartley, *ibid.*, pp. 39–40.

3   TRADE, EXCHANGE RATES, AND THE BALANCE OF PAYMENTS

1 See R. Gilpin, *The Political Economy of International Relations* (Princeton NJ: Princeton University Press, 1987) p. 121.
2 This is an extremely simplified presentation of the understanding in contem-porary finance theory of equilibrium exchange rates. For a clear elaboration of the complexities, see C. Fred Bergsten and John Williamson, 'Exchange Rates and Trade Policy', in *Trade Policy in the 1980s* (Washington DC: Institute for International Economics, 1983).
3 J.E. Spero, *The Politics of International Economic Relations* (New York: St. Martin's, 1990) pp. 33–4.
4 These arrangements are usefully summarized in S. Fischer, 'International Macroeconomic Policy Coordination', in M. Feldstein, (ed) *International Economic Cooperation* (Chicago: University of Chicago Press, 1988) pp. 25–7. See also, R. Solomon, *The International Monetary System, 1945–1981* (New York: Harper & Row, 1982) and P.B. Kenen, *The International Economy* (3rd ed.) (Cambridge: Cambridge University Press, 1994) ch. 19, 'Evolution of the Monetary System'.
5 P. Volcker, *Changing Fortunes: The World's Money and the Threat to American Leadership* (New York: Times Books 1992) p. 20.
6 For a helpful discussion of the evolution of the international monetary system during this period, see J.C. Pool, *International Economic Policy* (New York: Lexington, 1989) pp. 4–22.
7 S. Fischer, 'International Macroeconomic Policy Coordination', *op. cit.*, p. 15.
8 P.B. Kenen, *The International Economy (3rd ed.)*, *op. cit.*, p. 3.
9 V. Riches, 'Quarante-cinq ans de commerce mondial; régionalisation ou glob-alisation?', in J. Doyère and S. Marti, (eds) *Bilan économique et social 1993* (Paris: Le Monde Dossiers et Documents, 1994) p. 45.
10 See, particularly, S. Strange, *Casino Capitalism* (Oxford: Basil Blackwell Ltd., 1984) ch. 1.
11 J.C. Pool, *International Economic Policy, op. cit.*, pp. 17–18.
12 See W.J. McKibbin and J.D. Sachs, *Global Linkages: Macroeconomic Interdependence and Cooperation in the World Economy* (Washington DC: Brookings Institution, 1991).
13 For instances of their use, see R. Roessler, 'Selective Balance-of-Payments Adjustment Measures Affecting Trade: The Roles of the GATT and the IMF', (1977) *J. of World Trade Law* 238.
14 See, for example, *United Kingdom Temporary Import Charges: Report of the Working Party adopted on 17 November 1966*, L/2675, BISD 15th Supp. (1967) 113.

15 BISD, 26th Supp. (1980), p. 205.

16 E.-U. Petersmann, 'Trade Restrictions for Balance-of-Payments Adjustment Measures', (1986).

17 On the LDC debt crisis and its general impact on trade, see Chapter 12.

18 *Republic of Korea – Restrictions on Imports of Beef – Complaint of the United States*, BISD, 36th Supplement, p. 268.

19 See, for an excellent account of exchange controls and restrictions in OECD countries from the post-war period to the present, OECD (Centre for Co-operation with the European Economies in Transition), *Exchange Control Policy* (Paris: OECD, 1993) Part I, 'Experience of OECD Countries with Exchange Controls'.

20 See J. Gold, 'Convertibility', in *Legal and Institutional Aspects of the International Monetary System: Selected Essays*, vol II (Washington DC: International Monetary Fund, 1984).

21 GATT doc. L/88, 1 May 1953.

22 Roessler, *op. cit.*, p. 39.

23 *Ibid.*

24 See *Liberalization of Capital Movements and Financial Services in the OECD Area* (Paris: OECD, 1990).

25 See Bergsten and Williamson, *op. cit.*, note 2.

26 See Strange, *op. cit.*, note 10; see also Gilpin, *op. cit.*, note 1.

27 Spero, *op. cit.*, note 3, p. 50.

28 This is the position of Deborah Coyne. See D. Coyne, 'Canada in an Interdependent World', unpublished manuscript, 1992, ch. 3.

29 Marston, surveying the empirical evidence available as of 1988, suggests 'despite strong evidence that exchange rate volatility is much greater under flexible than under fixed rates, it has been difficult to establish statistically that this increase in volatility has seriously affected international trade'. R.C. Marston, 'Exchange Rate Policy Reconsidered', in M. Feldstein, (ed.) *International Economic Cooperation* (Chicago: University of Chicago Press, 1988) p. 87.

30 Coyne, *op. cit.*, advocates such a tax, as does J. Tobin, 'A Proposal for International Monetary Reform', in *Essays in Economics* (Cambridge MA: MIT Press, 1982).

31 As is suggested by Cooper, 'What Future for the International Monetary System?', in *International Financial Policy: Essays in Honour of Jacques Polak*, Frankel and Goldstein (eds) (Washington DC: IMF 1991) pp. 140–1.

32 See J. Williamson and M.H. Miller, *Targets and Indicators; A Blueprint for the International Coordination of Economic Policy*, Policy Analysis in International Economics No. 22 (Washington DC: Institute for International Economics, 1983). A succinct discussion and critique of the technical aspects of Williamson's proposal can be found in Kenen, *The International Economy, op. cit.*, pp. 557–8.

33 In Williamson's proposal, the commitment to intervene once a target zone was exceeded would not be absolute or unconditional. Instead, movement of a currency outside the zone would signal the possibility of intervention.

34 Cooper, *op. cit.*, note 31, p. 142.

35 Our discussion of the breakdown of the EMS in September 1992 owes much to R. Portes, 'EMS and EMU After the Fall', 16 *World Economy*, January 1993, pp. 2–15, as well as to coverage of these events throughout the Fall of 1992 and Winter of 1992/3 in the *Economist* magazine.

36 This brief and simplified account owes much to the following more detailed discussions of the EMS crisis: P. Kenen, *The International Economy, op. cit.*,

pp. 546–67; M. Kaelberer, 'Money and Power in Europe: The Political Economy of European Monetary Cooperation', paper presented at the Annual Meeting of the American Political Science Association, 2–5 September 1993, Washington DC; R. Portes, 'EMS and EMU After the Fall', *op. cit.*

37 Here it should be recalled that when capital flows into a country, that country's currency is purchased and the currency in which the capital was originally held is sold, placing downward pressure on the latter. However, when, say, German imports increase and exports decrease, there is the opposite effect on other currencies – since relatively more Deutschmarks are sold for other currencies (i.e. to purchase imports from abroad) than are bought by foreigners to pay for German exports, other currencies rise in value as against the Deutschmark.

38 M. Kaelberer, 'Money and Power in Europe: The Political Economy of European Monetary Cooperation', *op. cit.*, p. 24.

39. P. Kenen, *The International Economy, op. cit.*, p. 553.

40 *Ibid.* p. 553.

4 TARIFFS, THE MFN PRINCIPLE, AND REGIONAL TRADING BLOCS

1 Roy J. Ruffin and Paul R. Gregory, *Principles of Economics* (Glenview ILL: Scott Foresman and Company, 1983) pp. 350–1.

2 See J.M. Finger, 'Trade Liberalization: A Public Choice Perspective', in R. Amacher, G. Haberler and T. Willett (eds) *Challenges to a Liberal International Order* (Washington DC: American Institute Enterprise, 1979); see also Richard Snyder, *The Most Favoured Nation Clause* (New York: Columbia University Press, 1948).

3 J.M. Finger, *op. cit.*

4 We explore these issues more fully in Chapter 12.

5 Samuel Laird and Alexander Yeats, 'Tariff Cutting Formulas – and Complications', in J.M. Finger and Andruzej Olechavski, (eds) *The Uruguay Round: a Handbook on Multilateral Trade Negotiations* (Washington DC: The World Bank, 1987) p. 89.

6 Richard E. Caves and Ronald W. Jones, *World Trade and Payments* (Boston MA: Little Brown & Co., 4th ed., 1985) pp. 233–5.

7 *Ibid.*, p. 235. See also, generally, Jeffrey Schott, *The Uruguay Round* (Washington DC: Institute for International Economics, 1994, pp. 60–5).

8 Quoted by J. Quinn and T. Slayton, 'The GATT and the Deep Structure of Customs Administration', in Quinn and Slayton (eds) *Non-Tariff Barriers After the Tokyo Round* (Montreal: Institute for Research on Public Policy, 1982) p. 237.

9 For a detailed description of current and past valuation systems see M. Irish, *Customs Valuation in Canada* (Montreal: CCH, 1985).

10 J.H. Jackson, *The World Trading System* (Cambridge MA: MIT Press, 1989) pp. 127–8.

11 Canadian Tariff Board, *The GATT Agreement on Customs Valuation* Part One: Proposed Amendments to the Customs Act (1981), p. 6.

12 Jackson, *op. cit.*, p. 124.

13 BISD, 26 Supp. 116 (1980).

14 M. Stark, 'Valuation Principles: Canadian Customs Duties and Sales Tax' (1988) 36 *Canadian Tax J.* 1261 at p. 1262.

15 Agreement on Implementation of Article VII of the GATT, 15 December 1993.

16 Article VII: 2(a).

17 Under the BDV, value was based on a notional concept of valuation, that is, a price at which goods *ought* to be sold under a specified set of circumstances. Because it was not based on any real price it did not achieve a truly uniform valuation standard (G. Winham, *International Trade and the Tokyo Round Negotiations*, Princeton NJ: Princeton University Press, 1986) p. 179.

18 55 UNTS 308 (1947).

19 R.E. Smith, *Customs Valuation in the United States: A Study in Tariff Administration* (Chicago: University of Chicago Press, 1948) p. 141. The ASP provided for the assessment of duty based on the value of 'like or similar goods' produced domestically. This made it possible for domestic producers to inflate their prices and thereby relieve import pressure on a wide range of functionally related products (Winham, *supra*, note 17, pp. 67–8). The ASP was only applied to a few imports but its impact on those exporters was substantial. According to W. M. Snyder 'the ASP . . . led to protection equal to more than a 100% rate of duty' ('Customs Valuation in the European Economic Community' (1981) 11 Georgia. *J. of International Company Law* 79 p. 83).

20 Winham, *op. cit.*, pp. 180–1.

21 Two aspects of the Canadian system were considered inconsistent with these GATT rules: value was based on 'fair market value' in the country of export; and value could be established by ministerial prescription when fair market value could not be determined. These rules directly conflict with the GATT Article VII which states: 'value for customs purposes . . . should not be based on the value of merchandise of national origin or on arbitrary or fictitious values'. See G.E. Salembier, A.R. Moroz and F. Stone, *The Canadian Import File: Trade, Protection and Adjustment* (Montreal: The Institute for Research on Public Policy) c. 5, 103 pp. 111–12 [hereinafter *Canadian Import File*].

22 An attempt was made during the Kennedy Round to abolish the ASP and adopt more uniform standards but the US Congress refused to ratify the agreement.

23 There were many difficulties with the BDV. Even in countries that applied the system in a non-protectionist manner there were large variations in the value assigned to a particular good (Winham, *op. cit.*, p. 179).

24 Twenty-eight countries (including the EC as one) have accepted the code, including five developing countries. Developing countries were of the view that the Code would make unreasonable demands on their administration systems. As a result, a Protocol was added making allowances for special treatment of developing countries (GATT BISD, 26 Supp. 151 (1980)). There are also quite extensive interpretive notes with the Code making it more precise than other GATT codes.

25 The effective date of the EC legislation was 1 July 1980 and the legislation is in the Council Regulation 1224/80 of 28 May 1980, 23 *O.J. Eur. Comm.* (no. L134) 1 (1980); the USA implemented the Code on 1 July 1980, the current legislation is the Trade Agreements Act of 1979, Pub.L. 96–39, 93 U.S. Statutes at Large 144 – 19 USC s. 1401a; in Canada the Code became law on 1 January 1985 and is found in Part III (ss 44-53) of the Customs Act, SC 1986, ch. 1.

26 For detailed descriptions of the provisions of the Tokyo Round Code see: S.L. Sherman and H. Glashoff, *Customs Valuation: Commentary on the GATT Customs Valuation Code* (Deventer: Kluwer, 1988) and D.A. Wyslobicky and J.H. Warnock, 'Customs Valuation: Overview and Problem Areas in Determining Transaction Value', in *Customs and Trade Law Development* (The Canadian Institute, 1989).

27 Article 1,1(a) of the Uruguay Round Customs Valuation Code.

28 Article 1.2. 'Related persons' are defined in Article 15.4.

29 The order of the last two methods may be reversed by the importing country.

30 The last proscription is aimed primarily at the ASP (Snyder, *supra*, note 19, p. 82). The Canadian legislation does not prohibit any methods of valuation.

31 Jackson cites the example of the 1904 Swiss–German Treaty reducing German Tariffs on the imports of ' . . . large dapple mountain cattle or brown cattle reared at a spot at least 300 meters above sea level and having at least one month's grazing each year at a spot at least 800 meters above sea level . . .' (footnote omitted) (*op. cit.*, p. 127).

32 *Canadian Import File, op. cit.*, p. 115.

33 The system became law in Canada on 1 January 1988 and in the USA in September of that year. In addition to Canada and the USA, there are over 50 signatories to the System including the EC and Japan. In addition, nearly 30 other countries use the system but have not signed the convention. See Maureen Irish, *The Harmonized System and Tariff Classification in Canada* (D.C.L. thesis, McGill Law School, 1992).

34 The details of the system are drawn from T. Lindsay, *Outline of Customs in Canada*, 8th ed. (Calgary: Erin, 1991) [unpublished].

35 *Canadian Import File, op. cit.*, p. 114.

36 The seventh and eighth are a tariff classification, and the ninth and tenth are statistical.

37 *FTA*, Chapter 3, Article 301(2). This method of establishing origin is called 'change in tariff classification (or heading)'. The classification system contemplated is the Harmonized System already described.

38 Annex 301.2 of the FTA lists the precise rules.

39 'The U.S. Rules of Origin Proposal to GATT: Monotheism or Polytheism?' (1990) 24 *J. of World Trade* 25 at p. 26.

40 This provision applies to all rules of origin used in non-preferential commercial policy instruments including application of: MFN treatment, antidumping and countervailing duties, safeguard measures, origin marking requirements and any discriminatory quantitative restrictions.

41 A Technical Committee was established to develop a definition of this and other terms.

42 See Jon Johnson, 'The NAFTA Rules of Origin – A New Approach?' Canadian Law Newsletter, American Bar Association, October, 1992.

43 K. Dam, *The GATT: Law and International Economic Organization* (Chicago: University of Chicago Press, 1970) p. 183.

44 Dam, *op.cit.*, p. 181. A recent example of such a fee is discussed by P.G. Justice in 'Customs User Fee: A Survey of Recent Developments' (1987) 17 Georgia. *J. of International and Company Law* 507.

45 See R. Lawrence and R. Litan, 'The World Trading System After the Uruguay Round', (1990) 8 *Boston University International Law Journal* 247.

46 See e.g. Jagdish Bhagwati, *Protectionism* (Cambridge MA.; MIT Press, 1988); Jackson, *op. cit.*

47 See e.g. R.O. Keohane, *After Hegemony* (New York: Princeton Press, 1985); R. Axelrod and R. Keohane, 'Achieving Co-operation Under Anarchy', in K. Oye (ed.) *Co-operation Under Anarchy* (Princeton NJ: Princeton University Press, 1985); I. Ikenbarry, 'The State and Strategies of International Adjustment', (1986) 39 *World Politics* 53; C. Lipson, 'International Co-operation in Economic and Security Affairs', (1984) 37 *World Politics* 1.

48 Axelrod and Keohane, *op. cit.*; Alan O. Sykes, 'Mandating Retaliation for Breach of Trade Agreements: Some Thoughts on Strategic Design of Section 301', (1980) 8 *Boston University International Law Journal* 301; Michael J.

Trebilcock, Marsha A. Chandler, and Robert Howse, *Trade and Transitions* (London: Routledge, 1990) pp. 211–23.

49 Kenichi Ohmae, *The Borderless World: Power and Strategy in the International Economy* (New York: Harper Business, 1990).

50 Peter Drucker, *Frontiers of Management* (New York: Harper & Row, 1987) p. 65.

51 See Peter J. Lloyd, *Regionalization and World Trade* (OECD Economic Studies no. 18, Spring 1992); Jagdish Bhagwati 'Regionalism versus Multilateralism', *World Economy*, September, 1992.

52 See e.g. Kenneth W. Dam, *The GATT* (Chicago: University of Chicago Press, 1970) ch. 16; Anne O. Krueger, 'Free Trade is the Best Policy' in Lawrence and Schultze (eds) *An American Trade Strategy: Options for the 1990s* (Washington DC, Brookings Institution, 1990); Jeffrey J. Schott, *More Free Trade Areas?* (Washington DC: Institute for International Economics, 1989); Michael Aho and Sylvia Ostry, 'Regional Trading Blocks: Pragmatic or Problematic Policy', in William Brock and Robert K. Hormats (eds) *The Global Economy: America's Role in the Decade Ahead* (New York: American Assembly, 1990); Andrew Stoeckel, David Pearce, and Gary Banks, *Western Trade Blocks: Game, Set or Match for Asia Pacific and the World Economy?* (Centre for International Economics, Canberra, Australia, 1990) p. 7.

53 Jacob Viner, *The Customs Union Issue* (New York: Carnegie Endowment for International Peace, 1950).

54 See e.g. Rudiger Dornbusch, 'Policy Options for Free Trade: The Case for Bilateralism', in Robert Lawrence and Charles Schultze (eds) *An American Trade Strategy: Options for the 1990s* (Washington DC: Brookings Institution, 1990).

55 Robert Lawrence and Robert Litan, 'The World Trading System After the Uruguay Round', (1990) 8 *Boston University International Law Journal* 247.

56 See Paul Krugman, 'Regional Blocs: The Good, The Bad and The Ugly', (1991) International Economy (Nov.–Dec.) 54.

57 Stoeckel *et al.*, *op. cit.*, p. 7.

58 At p. xi.

59 *Ibid.*, p. 39.

60 *Ibid.*, p. 18.

61 See Stephen D. Krasner, 'State Power and the Structure of International Trade', in Art and Jervis (eds) *International Politics: Anarchy, Force, Political Economy, and Decision-Making*, (Little, Brown, 1985).

62 Paul Wonnacott and Mark Lutz, 'Is There A Case for More Free Trade Areas?', in Jeffrey J. Schott (ed.) *Free Trade Areas and U.S. Trade Policy* (Washington DC: Institute for International Economics, 1989).

63 Bhagwati, *op. cit.*

64 See Sylvia Ostry, *Governments and Corporations in a Shrinking World* (New York: Council on Foreign Relations, 1990) ch. 2.

65 See e.g. Schott, *op. cit.*, p. 25.

66 See R.J. Wonnacott, 'U.S. Hub-and-Spoke Bilaterals and the Multilateral Trading System' (C.D. Howe Institute Commentary, no. 23, October, 1990, Toronto).

5 ANTIDUMPING LAWS

*   Much of the research and writing for this chapter was undertaken by one of our former students, Presley Warner: see Warner, 'The Canada–US Free Trade Agreement: The Case for Replacing Antidumping with Antitrust', (1992) 23 *Law & Policy in International Business* 791.

CHAPTER 5

1 Sylvia Ostry, 'Antidumping: The Tip of the Iceberg', in M.J. Trebilcock and R.C. York, (eds) *Fair Exchange: Reforming Trade Remedy Laws* (Toronto: C.D. Howe Institute, 1990) 3 at p. 17.

2 GATT, Basic Instruments and Selected Documents, Thirty-sixth through Forty-fourth Session (Geneva: GATT, March 1981 – June 1989) Appendix Tables; Summary of Antidumping Actions and Countervailing Duty Actions; reported in A. Anderson and A. Rugman, 'Country Factor Bias in the Administration of Anti-Dumping and Countervailing Duty Cases', in Trebilcock and York, *op. cit.*, p. 152.

3 In the alternative, according to Article VI, the normal value can be based on either the highest comparable price for the like product for export to any third country in the course of trade, or the cost of production of the product in the country of origin plus a reasonable addition for the selling cost and profit.

4 Both countries used the grandfather clause, contained in the Provincial Protocol of Application governing accessions of countries to membership of the GATT, to retain their own legislation with respect to these duties. For more details on this and other aspects of the development of the GATT antidumping regime, see J.F. Beseler and A.N. Williams, *Antidumping and Antisubsidy Law: The European Communities* (London: Sweet and Maxwell) 1986) p. 3.

5 The actual status of the code, both then and as revised, is more substantive than merely interpretive. See R.M. Bierwagen, *GATT Article VI and the Protectionist Bias in Antidumping Law* (Deventer: Kluwer, 1990) p. 23.

6 Article 8(a).

7 Article 3(a).

8 This Act requires 'a causation link but . . . not . . . that dumped imports must be a principal cause, or a major cause, or a substantial cause of injury caused by all factors contributing to overall injury to an industry' (S.Rep. No. 1298, 93rd Cong., 2nd Sess. 180 (1974), brackets omitted).

9 19 U.S.C. § 160 note (1970).

10 See Beseler and Williams, *op. cit.*, p. 11.

11 Article 3(4). Subsequent references to the GATT Code refer to the 1979 Antidumping Code.

12 Article 3(3).

13 See M. Koulen, 'Some Problems of Interpretation and Implementation of the GATT Antidumping Code', in J.H. Jackson and E.A. Vermulst, (eds) *Antidumping Law and Practice: A Comparative Study* (Ann Arbor: University of Michigan Press, 1989) p. 366.

14 Details of the Canadian regime are drawn from: R.K. Paterson, *Canadian Regulation of International Trade and Investment* (Toronto: Carswell, 1986, p. 106; P.A. Magnus, 'The Canadian Antidumping System', in Jackson and Vermulst *op. cit.*, p. 167; J. Buchanan, 'Antidumping Law and the *Special Import Measures Act*' (1985) 11 *Can.Bus.L.J.* 2; and M. Dutz, 'Enforcement of Canadian Trade Remedy Laws: the Case for Competition Policies as an Antidote for Protection', in J.M. Finger, *Antidumping* (Ann Arbor: University of Michigan Press, 1993). The US regime is described in G. Horlick, 'The United States Antidumping System', in Jackson and Vermulst *op. cit.*; G. Bryan, *Taxing Unfair International Trade Practices* (Lexington MA: Lexington, 1980) chs. 1–7; and J.M. Finger and T. Murray, 'Antidumping and Countervailing Duty Enforcement in the United States', in Finger, *op cit*. For the USA and Canada, see P. Warner, *op cit*. The description of the EC draws primarily on J.F. Bellis 'The EEC Antidumping System', in Jackson and Vermulst *op. cit.*, p. 41. For a more detailed account, see I. Van Bael and J.-F. Bellis, *Antidumping and Other Trade Protection Laws of the EEC* (Bicester: CCH, 1990). For a critical review of the experience under EC

dumping laws, see P. Messerlin, 'The Antidumping Regulations of the European Community: The Privatization of Administered Protection', in M. Trebilcock and R. York *op. cit.*, and A. Eymann and L. Schuknecht, 'Antidumping Enforcement in the European Community', in Finger, *op cit.*

15 An Act to Amend the Customs Tariff, 1897, S.C. 1904 c. 11.

16 R.S.C. 1985, c.S-15.

17 15 U.S.C. ss 71–72 (1988).

18 19 U.S.C. s. 1673 *et seq.* (1988).

19 Council Regulation 2423/88, OJ (1988) L209/1 governs the EC antidumping system. For a detailed description of the development of the EC antidumping regulations, see Beseler and Williams, *op. cit.*, p. 21.

20 SIMA, ss 38–41.

21 Hereinafter, 'Code' refers to the 1993 GATT Antidumping Code.

22 However, the American definition of 'non-negligible' is arguably over-inclusive: the DC regulations provide that a computed dumping margin which exceeds 0.5% will justify a finding of 'dumping': 19 C.F.R. s. 353.6(a) (1991). Cited in N.D. Palmeter, 'Review Essay: The Capture of Antidumping Law' (1989) 14 *Yale J. of International Law* 182.

23 19 U.S.C. paras 1673–1677h (1988).

24 This methodology allows the Community to disregard those export transactions that are above the normal value.

25 Article 2: 1.

26 SIMA, ss 15(a), 16(b); several other conditions for the home market approach are set out in ss 15(a)–(e).

27 The DMNR has some discretion in determining which price is 'preponderant'. See Magnus, *op. cit.*, pp. 195–6.

28 SIMA, s.15(2).

29 *Id.* s.17.

30 19 C.F.R. 353.4 (1980).

31 SIMA, s. 16(2)(a) (Canada); 19 U.S.C. para. 1677a(c) (1988) (U.S.).

32 Article 2(4) allows for the exclusion of sales at prices below the cost of the product if they account for more than 20% of sales and are not in a concentrated period. Since it raises the normal value, the exclusion of below-cost sales increases the chance that dumping will be found. The problems with the treatment of below-cost sales as not 'in the ordinary course of business' are discussed later in the chapter.

33 This aspect of normal-value calculation resulted from the case *Electronic Typewriters*, OJ (1985) L128/39.

34 SIMA, s. 15; Regulations 5(d), 7, 9, and 23 (Canada); 19 C.F.R. 353.15 (1980) (U.S.); Article 2(10) (EC). See Buchanan, *op. cit.*, pp. 17–19; Paterson, *op. cit.*, pp. 111–13.

35 In the EC, the only costs that can affect the home price are those directly related to the sale of the good; any indirect costs such as those related to advertising or marketing are excluded.

36 This ground for departing from the home-market method is only contemplated by the EC Regulations.

37 SIMA, Regulation 9(1)(b)(v).

38 19 U.S.C. para. 1677b(a)(2) (1988).

39 These are known as selling, administration and other general expenses (SGA) and are expenses incurred in selling the product on the domestic, not export, market. These expenses are added even if there are no home sales.

40 The various surrogates for the profit margin are ranked in Article 2(3)(b)(ii) of the regulations.

41 The *Electronic Typewriters* case, *op. cit.* raised the average profit margin used in the calculations.

42 See 'Procedure' below pp. 107–12.

43 Buchanan, *op. cit.* p. 20, finds that past Canadian cases have calculated 'excessive' margins of dumping for goods from socialist countries.

44 The definition of a 'non-market economy' is not specified in the regulation, although there is reference to countries to which certain other regulations apply (Article 2(5)).

45 If no third country provides an adequate basis for comparison the Community may be used in the calculation.

46 Bellis notes that countries at various levels of economic development have been chosen as the analogue country. Which country will be chosen as an analogue is quite unpredictable (Bellis, *op. cit.*, p. 77).

47 According to Tharakan, the Commission is lenient in accepting undertakings from East European exporters because of the unfairness associated with the third country method ('East European State Trading Countries and Antidumping Undertakings', in P.K.M. Tharakan, (ed.) *Policy Implications of Antidumping Measures* (New York: Elsevier, 1991) 269 at p. 271.

48 Jagdish Bhagwati, *Protectionism* (Cambridge MA: MIT Press, 1988) p. 51.

49 SIMA, s. 29.

50 Horlick, *op. cit.*, p. 143.

51 Article 2(8)(a).

52 The biases associated with this construction are discussed by Bellis, *op. cit.*, pp. 79–81.

53 Article 3.4.

54 Article 3.5.

55 Article 4.1.

56 Vermulst suggests that the functional 'uses' approaches adopted by Canadian and American antidumping authorities do not conform to the GATT Code, which focuses solely on physical likeness: 'The Antidumping Systems of Australia, Canada, the EEC and the USA: Have Antidumping Laws Become a Problem in International Trade?', in Jackson and Vermulst *op. cit.*, p. 453.

57 S. 2(1) of the SIMA defines 'like goods'. The Canadian Import Tribunal set out its functional test in *Steam Traps, . . . Produced by or on Behalf of Sarco Co. Inc, Allentown, Pennsylvania, U.S.A.* (ADT–10–76), aff'd by the Federal Court of Appeal in *Sarco Canada* v. *Antidumping Tribunal*, [1979] 1 F.C. 247. See also Magnus, *op. cit.*, pp. 202–5 and L. Herman, 'Injury Findings by the Canadian Import Tribunal: The Decisive Elements' (1987) 1 *Rev. Int'l Bus. Law.* 373 at pp. 388–90.

58 The US legislation defines 'like product' as 'a product which is like, or in the absence of like, most similar in characteristics and uses with [the dumped imports]': 19 U.S.C. para. 1677(10). Horlick, *op. cit.*, pp. 148–9, suggests that to be 'like goods,' domestic goods must have a close degree of physical similarity to the dumped goods.

59 Article 4(5). Some producers may be excluded from the injury investigation on the grounds that they are related to the dumping exporter, have previously imported the dumped product, or sell exclusively in a separate, regional market.

60 The product must be 'identical, i.e. alike in all respects to the product under consideration, or, in the absence of such a product, another product which has characteristics closely resembling those of the product under consideration' (Article 2(12)).

61 Bellis, *op. cit.*, p. 85.

NOTES

62 S. 2(1) of the SIMA defines 'material injury' vaguely but the CITT's Rules adopt the criteria outlined in the GATT Code. See Rule 61, Canadian International Trade Tribunal Rules, SOR/91–499, 125:18, C. Gaz. 1991.II.2912.

63 19 U.S.C. para. 1677(7) (1988).

64 19 U.S.C. para. 1677(7)(A) (1988). The United States did not adopt the *'material'* injury requirement until the Tokyo Round Antidumping Code was adopted, although some commentators suggest that the current ITC injury inquiries ignore this requirement.

65 Bellis, *op. cit.*, p. 89. According to Bellis, the entire volume of exports, not just those dumped, during some period in the past are often considered at this stage of the inquiry. He goes on to point out that this practice is contrary to the regulations.

66 For a discussion of the causation requirements, see A. Rugman and S. Porteous, 'Canadian and U.S. Unfair Trade Laws: A Comparison of Their Legal and Administrative Structures' (1989) *16 Can. Bus. Law Journal* 1 at p. 5.

67 *Certain Wide Flange Shapes Originating in or Exported from Spain,* (CIT-1-85) 7 June 1985.

68 *Drywall Screws Originating in or Exported from Taiwan,* (CIT-1-86) 10 July 1986.

69 Rule 61, CITT Rules, *op. cit.*

70 *Sporting Ammunition (Rimfire, Centrefire and Shotshells) Originating in or Exported from the U.S.A.* (ADT–8–80). Rugman and Porteous, *op. cit.*, provide several other examples.

71 In the case, *Cars Produced By or on behalf of Hyundai Motor Company* (CIT-13-87) the Director argued that the dumping in that case was not responsible for the material injury that was alleged. See M. S. Kronby, 'Kicking the Tires: Assessing the Hyundai Anti-Dumping Decision From a Consumer Welfare Perspective' (1991) 18 *Can. Bus. L.J.* 95.

72 *British Steel Corp.* v. *United States,* 593 F.Supp. 405 (Ct. Int'l Trade 1984).

73 H. Doc. 96–153, Part II, 434–5; cited in I. Feltham *et al.* 'Competition and Antidumping Laws in the Context of the Canada–U.S. Free Trade Agreement', Study for the Committee on Canada–United States Relations of the Canadian Chamber of Commerce and the Chamber of Commerce of the United States, exposure draft 19 December 1990, at para. 72. For a discussion of alternative approaches to causation, see R. Cass, 'Economics in the Administration of US International Trade Law' (Ontario Centre for International Business, International Business and Trade Law Programme Working Paper no. 16 1989).

74 Article 4.

75 Article 5.4.

76 SIMA, s. 42(3).

77 19 U.S.C., para 1671a(b) (1988).

78 Article 5.6.

79 Article 5.7.

80 This is defined in s. 2(1) of the SIMA.

81 SIMA, s. 31(1).

82 Rugman and Porteous, *op. cit.*, p. 9. More than 70% of all preliminary American investigations into Canadian exporters result in positive findings of injury: A. Anderson and A. Rugman, 'The Canada–U.S. Free Trade Agreement: A Legal and Economic Analysis of the Dispute Settlement Mechanisms', 13 *World Competition L. & Econ. Rev.* 43 (1990).

83 Bellis, *op. cit.*, p. 48.

84 Paterson, *op. cit.*, pp. 113–15; Magnus, *op. cit.*, p. 184.

85 On request, the DMNR will disclose the basis on which it determined the provisional margin of dumping and allow parties to make submissions.
86 SIMA, s. 43.
87 Bellis, *op. cit.*, p. 49.
88 Beseler, *op. cit.*, p. 194.
89 Technically, duties are imposed by a 'Dominion customs appraiser', not the DMNR: SIMA s. 56. Customs appraisers may calculate their own dumping margins for goods imported after the CITT's final determination, though Buchanan, *op. cit.*, p. 9 notes that in practice customs appraisers follow the DMNR's calculation of the dumping margin.
90 SIMA, s. 76(5).
91 Palmeter, *op. cit.*, p. 190.
92 19 C.F.R. 353.25 (1991).
93 Article 15. Article 14 also provides for a regular review process a year after the resolution of the case if there is sufficient new evidence to justify reopening the case.
94 Article 13(4)(b).
95 *Ibid.*, Article 16. See Bellis, *op. cit.*, pp. 60–1.
96 According to Bellis, this treatment of new exporters is 'one of the most unfair features of the EEC antidumping system' (*op. cit.*, p. 93).
97 SIMA, s. 45.
98 The Financial Administration Act, R.S.C. 1985, c. F–11, gives the Minister this authority.
99 House of Commons Sub-Committee on Import Policy: *Report on the Special Import Measures Act*, Issue No. 31, 1st Sess., 32nd Parl., 1980–81–82, 9 June 1982; referred to in Paterson, *op. cit.*, pp. 125–6.
100 *Surgical Adhesive Tapes and Plasters, Excluding Plastic Tapes and Plasters, Originating in or Exported from Japan* (CIT–8–85) 4 December 1985; *Grain Corn Originating in or Exported from the United States of America* (CIT–7–86) 6 March 1987; *Fresh Whole Yellow Onions, Originating in or Exported From the United States of America* (CIT–1–87) 30 April 1987. (These cases include countervailing duty cases.)
101 Articles 11(1) and 12(1).
102 Beseler, *op. cit.*, p. 169; Michael Trebilcock, Marsha Chandler and Robert Howse, *Trade and Transitions* (London: Routledge, 1990) pp. 200, 201.
103 SIMA, s. 76(1).
104 *Id.* s. 76(2).
105 *Federal Court Act*, R.S.C. 1985, c. F–7, s. 28.
106 *Id.* s. 31. See Paterson, *op. cit.*, pp. 126–30 for a discussion of the various appeal provisions.
107 28 U.S.C. para. 1581 *et seq.* (1988).
108 See Chapter 15 below.
109 I. Van Bael, 'Lessons for the EC: More Transparency, Less Discretion, and, at Last a Debate' in Jackson and Vermulst *op. cit.*, 405 at p. 407; Messerlin, *op. cit.*
110 J. Viner, *Dumping: A Problem in International Trade* (Chicago: University of Chicago Press, 1933) p. 86.
111 A US Congressional subcommittee remarked: '[Antidumping laws are] designed to free U.S. imports from unfair price discrimination practices [by foreign exporters]'. S. Rep. No. 93–1298, 93rd Cong., 2d Sess. 179, cited in W. Caine, 'A Case For Repealing the Antidumping Provisions of the Tariff Act of 1930' (1981) 13 *Law & Pol'y Int'l Bus.* 681 at p. 682.
112 Competition Act, R.S.C. 1985, c. C–34, ss 50(1)(a), (b).
113 Clayton Act, as amended by the Robinson–Patman Act, ss 2, 3; 15 U.S.C.

para. 13 (1988).

114 B.J. Dunlop, D. McQueen and M.J. Trebilcock, *Canadian Competition Policy: A Legal and Economic Analysis* (Toronto: Canada Law Book, 1987) p. 208.

115 Price discrimination is impossible under perfect competition because sellers who charge a price which is higher or lower than the competitive price will be forced out of the market. For a non-technical discussion of perfect competition and its underlying assumptions see H. Hovenkamp, *Economics and Federal Antitrust Law* (St. Paul, Minn.: West, 1985) pp.1–14. See also R. Posner, *Antitrust Law: An Economic Perspective* (Chicago: University of Chicago Press, 1976) p. 63 [hereinafter *Antitrust Law*].

116 See Dunlop, McQueen and Trebilcock, *op. cit.*, pp. 208–10.

117 Since a monopolist has complete market power any losses from price discrimination will be highest if the discriminator is a monopolist.

118 Richard Posner, 'The Social Costs of Monopoly and Regulation' (1975) 83 *J. Pol. Econ.* 807.

119 The conflicting views are summarized in M.J. Trebilcock, *The Common Law of Restraint of Trade* (Toronto: Carswell, 1986) pp. 364–5.

120 Joan Robinson showed that the output effects of price discrimination depend on the shape of consumer demand curves. See *The Economics of Imperfect Competition* (London: Macmillan, 1933) pp. 188–93. R. Schmalensee, in 'Output and Welfare Implications of Monopolistic Third-degree Price Discrimination' (1981) 71 *Amer. Econ. Rev.* 242, and H. Varian, 'Price Discrimination and Social Welfare' (1985) 75 *Amer. Econ. Rev.* 870, find that welfare effects also depend on the shape of consumer demand curves. Hence, generalizations about the output and welfare effects of price discrimination are impossible.

121 It is not 'dumping' for the seller to charge lower prices in its home market than in its export market and this practice, is not prohibited by current legislation. See Deardorff, 'Economic Perspectives on Antidumping Law', in Jackson and Vermulst, *op. cit.*, p. 26.

122 Trebilcock and Quinn, 'The Canadian Antidumping Act: A Reaction to Professor Slayton' (1979) 2 *Canada–U.S. L.J.* 101 at p. 104.

123 Dunlop, McQueen and Trebilcock, *op. cit.*, p. 208. See generally J. A. Ordover and R. D. Willig, 'An Economic Definition of Predation: Pricing and Product Innovation' (1981) 91 *Yale L.J.* 8.

124 The original US antidumping law, the Antidumping Act of 1916, 19 U.S.C. 1673, made evidence of predatory intent an element of the dumping offence.

125 Competition Act, R.S.C. 1985, c. C-34, ss 50(1)(b), 50(1)(c), and 79.

126 Sherman Act, 15 U.S.C. para. 2 (1988), s. 2. Occasionally predatory pricing is challenged under para. 2 of the Clayton Act, as amended by the Robinson–Patman Act. See Hovenkamp, *op. cit.*, pp. 188–90.

127 Articles 85 and 86 of the Treaty of Rome set out the basis for EC competition law.

128 This is not to say that predatory pricing will never occur. See Dunlop, McQueen and Trebilcock, *op. cit.*, pp. 220–4; Posner, *Antitrust Law, op. cit.*, pp. 183–6; Bork, *The Antitrust Paradox* (New York: Basic Books, 1978) pp. 144–60; and Hovenkamp, *op. cit.*, pp. 172–84.

129 See e.g.: B.S. Yamey, 'Predatory Price Cutting: Notes and Comments' (1972) 15 *J. L. & Econ.* 129; F. Easterbrook, 'The Limits of Antitrust' (1984) 63 *Tex. L. Rev.* 1 at p. 26 and 'Predatory Strategies and Counterstrategies' (1981) 48 *University of Chicago L. Rev.* 263 at p. 268; J. McGee, 'Predatory Pricing Revisited' (1980) 23 *J. L. & Econ.* 289 pp. 295–7.

130 Hovenkamp and Silver-Westrick, 'Predatory Pricing and the Ninth Circuit'

(1983) *Ariz.St.L.J.* 443 at pp. 460–5.

131 McGee, *op. cit.*

132 P. Areeda and D.F. Turner, 'Predatory Pricing and Related Practices Under Section 2 of the Sherman Act' (1975) 88 *Harvard L. Rev.* 697 at p. 698.

133 The marginal cost of one unit of output is the amount by which the seller's total costs (for all units of output) increase when that one additional unit of output is produced. Since accountants typically report average costs, not marginal costs, marginal cost is extremely difficult to calculate.

134 The seller's total costs are the sum of its fixed costs and its variable costs. Variable costs vary with the level of output; fixed costs do not. By definition, average variable costs are lower than average total costs.

135 For the Canadian approach see Dunlop, McQueen and Trebilcock, *op. cit.*, and Roberts, *Anticombines and Antitrust* (1980) pp. 218–29. For the US approach see Bork, *op. cit.*, pp. 144–60, and Hovenkamp, *op. cit.*, pp. 172–84.

136 Deardorff, *op. cit.*, p. 36.

137 For further support for this view, see J. Barceló, 'Antidumping Laws as Barriers to Trade – The United States and the International Antidumping Code' (1972) *Cornell L. Rev.* 491 at pp. 501–3.

138 S. Hutton and M.J. Trebilcock, 'An Empirical Study of the Application of Canadian Antidumping Laws: A Search for Normative Rationales' (1990) 24 *J. of World Trade* 123 at p. 128.

139 For a mathematical proof of this result see S.W. Davies and A.J. McGuiness, 'Dumping at Less Than Marginal Cost' (1982) 12 *J. Int'l Econ.* 169 at pp. 171–6; see also P. Nicolaides, 'The Competition Effects of Dumping,' (1990) 24 *J. of World Trade* 115 at pp. 119, 120.

140 Antidumping duties were imposed in each case. Hutton and Trebilcock, *op. cit.*, p. 128.

141 Deardorff, *op. cit.*

142 This practice is widespread. Bulk mail, for example, often contains free samples. Sellers provide samples hoping customers will be willing to purchase goods after 'experiencing' samples.

143 It may be objected that dumped goods cannot be characterized as 'learning by doing' goods because any technological learning would have the same effect on both the home market and the export market. However, if home market sales were 'insufficient' within the meaning of antidumping legislation, antidumping investigations would examine only the 'fully-allocated costs' of the exporter. If those costs exceeded the export-market price, there would be a positive finding of dumping even if the exporter were merely pricing below-cost (in both markets) to gain technological know-how.

144 In the USA, the legality of aggressive pricing policies to increase market share has been upheld: *Telex Corp.* v. *IBM*, 510 F.2d 894 (10th Cir. 1975), *cert. dismissed*, 423 U.S. 802 (1975); *Berkey Photo* v. *Eastman Kodak Co.*, 603 F.2d 263 (2d Cir. 1979). Canadian courts have also recognized the legitimacy of promotional sales: *R.* v. *Hoffman-La Roche Ltd.* (1981), 28 O.R. (2d) 164 at 196; 109 D.L.R. (3d) 5 at 37 (Ont. C.A.).

145 *op. cit.*, pp. 30–1.

146 For a fuller discussion of intermittent dumping see F. Lazar, 'Antidumping Rules Following the Canada–U.S. Free Trade Agreement' (1989) 23 *J. of World Trade* 45.

147 Four of the thirty cases studied exhibited indications of intermittent dumping (Hutton and Trebilcock, *op. cit.*, p. 61).

148 *Ibid.*

149 See Trebilcock and Quinn, *op. cit.*, pp. 108–11.

150 *Ibid.*

151 Several studies have shown that the cost of capital in markets with strong import competition and demand fluctuation exceeds its cost in markets with constant demand and weak import competition: see W. Wares, *The Theory of Dumping and American Commercial Policy* (Lexington MA: Lexington, 1977, pp. 67–73); Sandomo, 'On the Theory of the Competitive Firm under Price Uncertainty' (1971) 61 *Amer. Econ. Rev.* 65; and Zucker, 'On the Desirability of Price Instability: An Extension of the Discussion' (1965) 22 *Econometrica* 437.

152 Hutton and Trebilcock, *op. cit.*, p. 130.

153 See e.g. Barceló, *op. cit.*

154 S. Rep. No. 249, 96th Cong. 1st Sess. 37 (1980); cited in Palmeter, *op. cit.*, p. 191.

155 *Bingham and Taylor Div. Va. Industries, Inc.* v. *United States*, 815 F.2d 1482, 1485 (Fed. Cir. 1987). See also *Matsushita Electric Industrial Co.* v. *United States*, 823 F.2d 505, 509 (Fed. Cir. 1987).

156 For a useful discussion of both the economic and political elements of unfairness claims see R.E. Hudec, 'Mirror, Mirror, On the Wall: The Concept of Fairness in United States Trade Policy', in *1990 Proceedings*, Canadian Conference on International Law [forthcoming].

157 Bhagwati, *op. cit.*, p. 50.

158 *Ibid.* p. 68.

159 For a brief and incisive discussion of the welfare effects of low-priced imports see J. A. Ordover, A. O. Sykes and R. D. Willig, 'Unfair International Trade Practices' (1983) 15 *Int'l L. & Pol'y* 323 at pp. 330–4.

160 Hutton and Trebilcock, *op. cit.*, p. 124. The issue that is raised is whether antidumping laws are the appropriate tool for vindicating these concerns. Compared to antidumping actions, safeguard actions and domestic adjustment assistance policies are preferable policy instruments to address those impacts. This is discussed further in Chapter 7.

161 See e.g. John Rawls, *A Theory of Justice* (Cambridge MA: Belknap Press, 1971).

162 While shareholders often include pension plans and employee shareholders (and therefore workers) it is likely that pension plans would diversify their assets so that import competition would not significantly erode workers' savings.

163 See e.g. Michael Sandel, *Liberalism and the Limits of Justice* (Cambridgeshire NY: Cambridge University Press, 1982).

164 Hutton and Trebilcock, *op. cit.*, p. 143.

165 *Ibid.*

166 See Nicolaides *op. cit.*; B.M. Hoekman and M.P. Leidy, 'Dumping, Antidumping and Emergency Protection,' (1989) 23 *J. of World Trade* p. 27.

167 See *United Brands* v. *E.C. Commission* [1978] E.C.R. 207; 1 C.M.L.R. 429 C. Ct. of Justice.

168 See e.g. N. Campbell and M.J. Trebilcock, 'International Merger Review: Problems of Multijurisdictional Conflict' in E. Kantzenbach, H.E. Scharrer and L. Waverman (eds) *Competition Policy in an Interdependent World* (Baden-Baden: Nomos Verlagegesellschaft, 1993, p. 129).

169 Warner, *op. cit.*

170 See Hoekman and Leidy, *op. cit.*

171 See more generally, Thomas Boddez and Michael Trebilcock, *Unfinished Business: Reforming Trade Remedy Laws in North America* (Toronto: C.D. Howe Institute, 1993).

172 For an excellent review of the issues, see D.G. McFetridge, 'Globalization and

Competition Policy', in Thomas J. Courchene and Douglas J. Purvis (eds) *Productivity, Growth and Canada's International Competitiveness* (The Bell Canada Papers on Economic and Public Policy, 1993, John Deutsch Institute for the Study of Economic Policy, Queen's University, Canada, p. 133); see also Kantzenbach, Scharrer and Waverman, *op. cit.*

173 See Sylvia Ostry, 'Beyond the Border: The New International Policy Arena', in Kantzenbach *et. al.*, *op. cit.*

174 See Campbell and Trebilcock, *op. cit.*; Campbell and Trebilcock, 'A Comparative Analysis of Merger Law; Canada, The United States and the European Community', (1992) 15 *World Competition* 5.

175 See Leonard Waverman and Shyam Khemani, 'Strategic Alliances: A Threat to Competition?', Centre for International Studies, University of Toronto, 14 January 1993.

176 See Sylvia Ostry, 'Globalization, Domestic Policies and the Need for Harmonization', Centre for the Study of Business and Public Policy, University of California, Santa Barbara, January 1993.

177 See American Bar Association, Section of Antitrust Law, *Report of Special Committee on International Antitrust*, (Chicago, 1 September 1991).

6   SUBSIDIES, COUNTERVAILING DUTIES, AND GOVERNMENT PROCUREMENT

1 This is not the case among member countries of some free trade–common market arrangements, like the EC, where countervailing duties have been abolished.

2 P. Messerlin, 'Antidumping', in J.J. Schott (ed.), *Completing the Uruguay Round: A Results-Oriented Approach to the GATT Trade Negotiations* (Washington DC: Institute for International Economics, 1990), 108 at p. 110.

3 *Ibid.*

4 P. Messerlin, 'Public Subsidies to Industry and Agriculture and Countervailing Duties. Paper prepared for the European Meeting on the Position of the European Community in the New GATT Round' (Spain, 2–4 October 1986) as cited in J.M. Finger, 'Antidumping and Antisubsidy Measures' in J.M. Finger and A. Olechavski (eds) *The Uruguay Round: A Handbook on the Multilateral Trade Negotiations* (Washington DC: The World Bank, 1987) 153 at p. 156.

5 Industrial subsidies as a percentage of GDP at market prices in Canada were 2.6% in 1980–4 and 2.2% in 1985–8. In the United States the same measures show a 0.5% contribution for 1980–4 and 0.7% for 1985–8.

6 E. Fry, *Subsidies and International Trade: The Provincial and State Dimension* (Halifax: Institute for Research and Public Policy, 1990).

7 Fry, *ibid.*; M.G. Smith, 'Overview of Provincial and State Subsidies: Their Implications for Canada–U.S. Trade', in *International Economic Issues* (Halifax: Institute for Research on Public Policy, April 1990).

8 J-F. Bence and M.G. Smith, 'Subsidies and the Trade Laws: The Canada–U.S. Dimension', *International Economic Issues*, May–June 1989.

9 *Ibid.*, pp. 31–2. OECD, *Economic Survey: United States (1991–1992)* (Paris: OECD, 1991) p. 148.

10 Article VI, GATT. Part V of the Uruguay Round Subsidies Code also governs countervailing duties.

11 In the USA, retaliation against certain unfair foreign producers is authorised under s.301 of the *Omnibus Trade and Competition Act*, 1988.

12 Of course, if domestic producers in country C were being harmed then from

the perspective of country C this situation is like the first.

13 There is some evidence that early commentators on trade were concerned about unfair trade and did not sharply distinguish the concepts of dumping and subsidization: J.H. Jackson, *The World Trading System: Law and Policy of International Economic Relations* (Cambridge MA: MIT Press, 1989) p. 255 [hereinafter *World Trading System*]. Even now, because of the overlap between countervailing duty and antidumping complaints, US producers will often initiate both actions against an exporter.

14 This distinction leads some commentators to conclude that countervailing duty actions are more legitimate: these duties offset distortions caused by government interference in a free market, while antidumping duties compound the distortion created by a producer with market power by forcing domestic consumers to pay monopoly prices. See for example, K. Dam, *The GATT: Law and International Economic Organization* (Chicago: University of Chicago Press, 1970) pp. 177–9.

15 Paragraph 4 of Article VI of the GATT.

16 Paragraph 7 of Article VI of the GATT.

17 R.R. Rivers and J.D. Greenwald, 'The Negotiation of a Code on Subsidies and Countervailing Measures: Bridging Fundamental Policy Differences' (1979) 11 *Law & Policy in International Bus.* 1447 at p. 1460.

18 Section B is entitled, 'Additional Provisions on Export Subsidies'. However, there is no definition of export subsidies in the Section or Article.

19 Seventeen developed countries accepted the new section. G. Horlick, R. Quick and E. Vermulst, 'Government Actions Against Domestic Subsidies, An Analysis of the International Rules and an Introduction to United States' Practice' (1986/1) *Legal Issues of European Integration*, pp. 1–51.

20 See Jackson, *World Trading System, op cit.*, p. 256.

21 See J. Jackson, *Legal Problems in International Economic Relations* (1977) p. 756. This list was updated during the Tokyo Round Subsidies Code negotiations.

22 G. Winham, *International Trade and the Tokyo Round Negotiations* (Princeton NJ: Princeton University Press, 1986) p. 116.

23 *Ibid.*, p. 119.

24 The nature of the policy differences and the way in which these differences were resolved is discussed in detail in Rivers and Greenwald, *op cit*. In large part, the conflict on subsidies can be linked to the USA's dissatisfaction with the Common Agricultural Policy of the EC.

25 Article 4, Subsidies Code.

26 J.H. Jackson, *World Trading System, op cit.* p. 258.

27 Rivers and Greenwald, *op cit.* p. 1456.

28 Article 6 of the Code contains the rules for determining the existence of injury.

29 Such factors include the volume and prices of non-subsidized imports of the product in question, contraction of demand or changes in the pattern of consumption.

30 J.J. Barceló III, 'The Two Track Subsidies Code – Countervailing Duties and Trade Retaliation', in Quinn and Slayton, (eds), *Non-Tariff Barriers After the Tokyo Round* (Montreal: Institute for Research on Public Policy, 1982) [hereinafter 'Trade Retaliation'] p. 121.

31 As was the case in the GATT, there is no definition of export subsidies. There is a revised 'Illustrative List of Export Subsidies' in the annex to the Code which is intended as an aid to interpretation. There is some debate about whether the list is relevant to Track I or only Track II of the Code. According to Jackson: 'The U.S. has taken the position that [it] is only useful in inter-

preting a definition of subsidies for purposes of Track 2 of the Code and does not in any way constrain national sovereigns in their definition of "subsidy" for purposes of Track 1' (*World Trading System, op cit.*, pp. 259–60).

32 Article 11(1).

33 Article 11(1) of the Code.

34 Article 11(2).

35 According to Jackson: 'It is not surprising that the Subsidies Code has had a very difficult history subsequent to the completion of the Tokyo Round, since its very language reflects considerable ambivalence about its obligations' (*World Trading System, op cit.*, p. 259).

36 Article 12(3).

37 The Committee is comprised of a representative from each signatory to the agreement.

38 Paragraphs 3, 4 and 5 of Article 18 govern the establishment of panels. Article 18(4) states that in order to facilitate the establishment of panels the Committee shall maintain a list of persons qualified in the fields of trade relations, economic development, and other matters covered by the GATT and the Code who are able to serve on panels. Signatories may nominate individuals who are available for panel assignments.

39 Article 18(2).

40 The application of the assistance must be limited to the following costs: personnel; instruments, equipment, land and buildings used exclusively and permanently for the research activity; consultancy and other similar services used exclusively for the research activity; other overhead costs; and running costs incurred directly as a result of the research activity.

41 For an extensive review of government procurement under international agreements, see: Reich, A., *Toward Free Trade in the Public Sector* (S.J.D. Thesis, Faculty of Law, University of Toronto: 1994).

42 S. Arrowsmith, *Government Procurement and Judicial Review* (Toronto: Carswell, 1988) p. 1.

43 For examples of this 'secondary' use, see Leimkuhler, W.F., 'Enforcing Social and Economic Policy through Government Contracts', in *Annual Survey of American Law* p. 539 (1980).

44 For this topic, see US General Accounting Office, *Government Buy-National Practices of the United States and Other Countries – an Assessment* (1976). On the discriminatory procurement practices of various governments see Baldwin, R., *Nontariff Distortions of International Trade* (1970) pp. 59–70; Krauss, M., *The New Protectionism: The Welfare State and International Trade* (1978) pp. 54–6.

45 For example, the Canadian Content Premium (see Deputy Minister of Supply and Services Directive 637 [10/02/89] Annex A-1) and the Buy American Policy (see the Buy American Act [41 U.S.C., 1976]).

46 See *Selling to Government, A Guide to Government Procurement in Canada* (Ottowa: Minister of Supply and Services Canada, 1989) pp. 48–50.

47 See Long, O., *The Tokyo Round of Multilateral Trade Negotiations*, Report by the Director General of GATT (Geneva, April 1979).

48 The Agreement on Government Procurement (the Code), Published in GATT BISD, 26th Supplement, p.33. The amendments to the Code enacted in 1987 were published as 'Protocol Amending the Agreement on Government Procurement', BISD 34th Supplement, p.12.

49 This threshold was lowered from SDR 150,000 (Article 1:1(b)) by the 1987 amendments. SDR stands for Special Drawing Rights, the IMF's monetary units. The value of the threshold in the currency of each signatory is deter-

mined by the Committee established by the Agreement, in consultation with the signatory in question, and applies throughout a two year period until next determination. SDR 150,000 is approximately $US181,000.

50 See Article 1:1(b), and Article 1:2(3) of the Amendment *supra* note 48.

51 See Article 1:1(a). Note that this has been changed under the Uruguay Round negotiations.

52 See Article 11:4.

53 See Article V.

54 See Articles V:2, V:6, and V:7.

55 Article V:16 limits circumstances for 'single tendering'. On collusion in tendering see: United Nations Conference on Trade and Development, *Collusive Tendering* (1985).

56 See Article V:15(f).

57 See Article VI:6. Usually, no effective remedy is provided. See US International Trade Commission, *Review of the effectiveness of trade dispute settlement under the GATT and the Tokyo Round agreements* (Washington, DC: USITC, 1985).

58 See Article VII:14.

59 Mission of Canada Geneva, '(draft) GATT Agreement on Government Procurement' (15/12/93).

60 *Ibid.*, Article I.

61 *Ibid.*, Article XVI.

62 *Ibid.*, Article XX.

63 Treasury Board of Canada, *Administrative Policy Manual*, Chapter 305, 'Procurement Review', (March 1980).

64 See Minister of Supply and Services, *The Canada–U.S. Free Trade Agreement and Government Procurement: An Assessment*, 1989.

65 'Most Favourable Treatment' obligation under Article 1305:1 of the FTA.

66 Compare Annex 1002.1 of NAFTA with Annex 1304.3 of the FTA.

67 See NAFTA Article 1006.

68 See Council Directive 71/305/EEC, *O.J.* 1971, L 185/5 ('The Works Directive') and Council Directive 77/62/EEC *O.J.* 1977 L 13/1 ('The Supplies Directive'). Also see Council Directive 88/295/EEC *O.J.* 1988 L 127 ('Amending Supplies Directive') and Council Directive 89/440/EEC *O.J.* 1989 L 210 ('Amending Works Directive'). For a recent study on public sector procurement in Europe, see The 'Cost of Non-Europe' *in Public Sector Procurement*, Research on the 'Cost of Non-Europe', Basic Findings, vol.5, by W.S. Atkins Management Consultants (Commission of the European Communities, 1988).

69 For a list of these circumstances, see Article 9 in the Works Directive, and Article 6 in the Supply Directive.

70 Council Directive 89/665/EEC *O.J.* 1989 395/33–35.

71 Council Directive 90/531/EEC *O.J.* 1990 297.

72 Council Directive 92/13/EEC *O.J.* 1992 76, p. 14.

73 For a detailed description of the administration of countervailing duty laws in the USA see: T. Boddez and M. Trebilcock, *Unfinished Business: Reforming Trade Remedy Laws in North America* (Toronto: C.D. Howe, 1993); R. Diamond, 'A Search for Economic and Financial Principles in the Administration of United States Countervailing Duty Law' (1990) 21 *Law and Policy in International Bus.* 507; and T.V. Vakerics, D.I. Wilson and K.G. Weigel, *Antidumping, Countervailing Duty and Other Trade Actions* (New York: Practising Law Institute, 1987) pp. 218–19.

74 The Tariff Act, 19 U.S.C. §§702(a) and 732(a) authorizes the ITA to initiate

investigations. It rarely does so. Most investigations are initiated by complaints from domestic producers.

75 Tariff Act, 19 U.S.C. §1671.
76 Jackson, *World Trading System*, *op cit.*, p. 262.
77 A.O. Sykes, 'Countervailing Duty Law: An Economic Perspective' (1989) *Columbia L. Rev.* 199 at p. 203.
78 See Vakerics, Wilson and Weigel, *op cit.*, pp. 218–19.
79 G.C. Hufbauer and J. Erb, *Subsidies in International Trade* (Washington, DC: Institute for International Economics, 1984).
80 Vakerics, Wilson and Weigel, *op cit.*, p. 221.
81 Tariff Act, §1677(5)(B).
82 See Bello and Homer, 'Subsidies and Natural Resources: Congress Rejects a Lateral Attack on the Specificity Test' (1984) 18 *George Washington J. of Int'l L. and Econ.* 297; Panzarella, 'Is the Specificity Test Generally Applicable?' (1986) 18 *L. and Policy in Int'l Bus.* 417; and Sussman, 'Countervailing Duties and the Specificity Test: An Alternative Approach to the Definition of "Bounty or Grant"' (1986) 18 *L. and Policy in Int'l Bus.* 475.
83 564 F.Supp. 834 (Ct. Int'l Trade 1983).
84 620 F.Supp. 722 (Ct. Int'l Trade 1985).
85 54 *Federal Register* 30774 (1989) at p. 30777.
86 Boddez and Trebilcock, *op cit.*, p. 45 illustrate the problems with the ITA's methodology with a description of the Canadian–US softwood lumber dispute.
87 These aspects are highlighted in Vakerics, Wilson and Weigel, *op cit.*, p. 222.
88 The rationale for this rule is that in a non-market economy there is no valid distinction between government and industry. See, for example, *Carbon Steel Wire Rod from Czechoslovakia*, 49 Fed. Reg. 55014 (1983).
89 Upstream subsidies are defined in 19 U.S.C. §1671–1(a)(1) as subsidies paid or bestowed by a foreign government with respect to an input that is used in the manufacture, in the same country, of merchandise that is the subject of a countervailing duty proceeding.
90 See, for example, *Prestressed Concrete Steel Wire Strands from Spain*, 47 Fed. Reg. 28723, 28726 (1982).
91 Details of the approach of the ITA to these cases can be found in Vakerics, Wilson and Weigel, *op cit.*, p. 230.
92 See, for example, *Certain Iron-Metal Castings from India*, 45 Fed. Reg. 34946 (1980).
93 19 U.S.C. §1671(a)(1)(B). An example of this is found in *Certain Steel Products from the Republic of Korea*, 47 Fed. Reg. 57535 (1982).
94 J. Terry, 'Sovereignty, Subsidies and Countervailing Duties in the Context of the Canada–U.S. Trading Relationship' (1988) 46 *University of Toronto Fac. L. Rev.* 48 at p. 69.
95 G.N. Horlick. 'Subsidies and Suspension Agreements in Countervailing Duty Cases' in, *The Commerce Department Speaks on Dumping and Countervailing Duties* (New York: Practising Law Institute, 1982) p. 31.
96 *Certain Textile Products from Mexico*, 50 Fed. Reg. 10824 (1985).
97 Diamond, *op cit.*, pp. 541–2.
98 See 19 U.S.C. §1677(b).
99 Vakerics, Wilson and Weigel, *op cit.*, p. 221.
100 See Vakerics, Wilson and Weigel, *ibid.*, p. 239 for details on this aspect of US countervailing duty law.
101 Thus, many of the same problems arise that were discussed in Chapter 5.
102 Article 16.1.
103 19 U.S.C. §1677(4)(A).

104 19 U.S.C. §1677(4)(C).

105 19 U.S.C. §1677(10).

106 Inv. No. 701–TA–80, USITC Pub. No. 1191 (1981).

107 In *Certain Carbon Steel Products from Argentina, Australia, Finland, South Africa and Spain*, Inv. No. 701–TA–212, USITC Pub. No. 1510 (1984), there were five separate like products.

108 Article 15.4.

109 Tariff Act, 19 U.S.C. §1677(7)(A).

110 19 U.S.C. §1677(7)(C).

111 *Ibid.*

112 M.S. Knoll, 'An Economic Approach to the Determination of Injury Under United States Antidumping and Countervailing Duty Law' (1989) 22 *New York University J. of Int'l Law & Pol.* 37 at p. 52.

113 For a detailed criticism of ITC methodology see Boddez and Trebilcock, *op. cit.*, 73 at p. 57.

114 Article 15.5.

115 Knoll, *op cit.*, p. 54; and Cass and Schwartz, 'Causality, Coherence, and Transparency in the Implementation of International Trade Law', in Trebilcock and York, (eds) *Fair Exchange: Reforming Trade Remedy Laws* (Toronto: C.D. Howe, 1990) [hereinafter *Fair Exchange*] 24 at p. 43.

116 Cass and Schwartz, *op cit.*, p. 43.

117 *Ibid.*, p. 33.

118 *Ceramica Regiomontana, S.A.* v. *United States*, 810 F.2d 1137 at 1139 (Fed. Cir. 1987).

119 See for example, *Matsushita Electric Industrial Co.* v. United States, 750 F.2d 927 (1984).

120 See Boddez and Trebilcock, *op cit.*, ch. 3 for a detailed analysis of binational panel decisions in antidumping and countervailing duty cases.

121 *Ibid.* p. 75.

122 *Ibid.*, ch. 3. See also Chapter 15 below.

123 J. Terry, *op cit.*, p. 51; and W. Schwartz and E.W. Harper, Jr., 'The Regulation of Subsidies Affecting International Trade' (1972) 70 *Mich. L. Rev.* 831.

124 Schwartz and Harper, *op cit.*, p. 844.

125 See Sykes, *op cit.*

126 Schwartz and Harper, *op cit.*, pp. 834–5. Predatory pricing and international price discrimination are discussed in detail in Chapter 5 above.

127 Robert Hudec, 'Mirror, Mirror on the Wall: The Concept of Fairness in the United States Foreign Trade Policy', (1990) *Proceedings of the Canadian Council on International Law* 88.

128 See Countervailing Duty Law Symposium Issue, (1990) 21 *Law & Policy in International Business*.

129 See Jagdish Bhagwati, 'Fair Trade, Reciprocity, and Harmonization: The New Challenge to the Theory and Policy of Free Trade', in A. Deardorff and R. Stein (eds) *Analytical and Negotiating Issues in the Global Trading System* (Ann Arbor: University of Michigan Press, 1993); Bhagwati, 'Challenges to the Doctrine of Free Trade' (1993) 25 *International Law and Politics* 219.

130 See Hudec, *supra*, note 127.

131 J. Bhagwati, *The World Trading System at Risk* (Princeton NJ: Princeton University Press, 1991) pp. 21–2; see also James Bovard, *The Fair Trade Fraud* (New York: St. Martin's Press, 1991).

132 See Chapter 13 below; and Chapter 7 respectively.

133 See Chapter 5 above.

134 This group would include unskilled, immobile or low-income workers. See, J.

Rawls, *A Theory of Justice* (Cambridge MA: Belknap Press, 1971).

135 For an extensive comparative evaluation of attempts to regulate subsidies in international trade, see R. Behboodi, *The Regulation of Subsidies in International Trade* (London: Routledge, forthcoming).

136 Diamond, *op cit.*; Trebilcock, 'Is the Game Worth the Candle? Comments on Diamond, "A Search for Financial and Economic Principles in the Administration of Countervailing Duty Law" (1990) 21 *Law & Policy in Int'l Bus.* 723 [hereinafter 'Is the Game Worth the Candle?']; Trebilcock, 'Throwing Deep: Trade Remedies in a First-Best World', in Trebilcock and York (eds) *Fair Exchange* (Toronto: C.D. Howe Institute, 1990); and M. Hart, 'Idealism *versus* Pragmatism: Policy and the Academic Analyst', in *Fair Exchange, ibid.*

137 Diamond, *op cit.*, pp. 158–9.

138 Diamond, *op cit.*

139 C. Goetz, L. Granet and W. Schwartz, 'The Meaning of "Subsidy" and "Injury" in the Countervailing Duty Law' (1986) 6 *Int'l. Rev. of Law and Econ.* 17; see also Diamond, 'Economic Foundations of Countervailing Duty Law' (1989) 29 *Virginia J. of Int'l Law* 767.

140 Identifying predatory pricing or setting a reasonable rate of return for a natural monopoly are prominent examples.

141 These would include, for example, cases of inefficiency or mismanagement of domestic firms as well as threats from more efficient third country exporters. At the same time, the subsidy in question may have been conferred principally for home market reasons.

142 See Goetz, Granet and Schwartz, *op cit.*, pp. 26–9; see also Alan Sykes, 'Second-Best Countervailing Duty Policy: A Critique of the Entitlement Approach' (1990) 21 *Law & Policy in International Business* 699.

143 Barceló, 'Subsidies and Countervailing Duties: Analysis and a Proposal' (1977) 9 *Law & Policy in Int'l Bus.* 779.

144 See J.J. Barceló, 'Trade Retaliation' *op cit.*; and A.O. Sykes, *op cit.*

145 See for example, Richard Harris, *Trade, Industrial Policy and International Competition*, Royal Commission on the Economic Union and Development Prospects for Canada Collected Research Studies 13 (Toronto: University of Toronto Press, 1985).

146 See, Jackson, *The Perplexities of Subsidies in International Trade*, Law and Economics Workshop Paper (Toronto: University of Toronto, 1989), and Milner and Yoffie, 'Between Free Trade and Protectionism: Strategic Trade Policy and a Theory of Corporate Trade Demands' (Spring 1989) *International Organization* 238.

147 The Commission has, however, employed some common-sense *de minimis* tests to dispose of cases where the aid in question could have little plausible impact on trade; see, in general, C. Quigley, 'The Notion of a State Aid in the EEC', (1988) 13 *European Law Review* 242; R. Howse, *Economic Union, Social Justice, and Constitutional Reform: Towards a High but Level Playing Field* (Toronto: York Centre for Public Law and Public Policy, 1992) Appendix III.

148 See A. Evans and S. Martin, 'Socially Acceptable Distortion of Competition: Community Policy on State Aid', (1991) 16 *European Law Review* 80.

149 See more generally, Boddez and Trebilcock, *op cit.*

150 These panels hear disputes between Canada and the USA that are unrelated to unfair trade law.

151 T.L. McDorman, 'Using the Dispute Settlement Regime of the Free Trade Agreement: The West Coast Salmon and Herring Problem' (1991) 4 Canada-U.S. *Bus. L. Rev.* 117 at p. 179.

152 See especially, *R. v. Oakes* (1986) 26 D.L.R. (4th) 200 (S.C.C.).

7 TRANSITION COSTS: SAFEGUARD REGIMES, DOMESTIC ADJUSTMENT, AND LABOUR POLICIES

1 Article XIX:1 lays out the grounds for invocation; XIX:2 the notification requirement; and XIX:3 the right to compensation.

2 Compensation usually takes the form of other trade concessions. In the absence of agreement on compensation, the exporting countries can impose import restraints of substantially equivalent value.

3 From G. Sampson, 'Safeguards', in J.M. Finger and A. Olechowski (eds) *The Uruguay Round: A Handbook on the Multilateral Trade Negotiations* (Washington, DC: The World Bank, 1987) 143, table 19.3 p. 147.

4 From P.A. Messerlin, 'Antidumping', in J.J. Schott, (ed.) *Completing the Uruguay Round: A Results Oriented Approach to the GATT Trade Negotiations* (Washington DC: Institute for International Economics, 1990) 108, Table 6.1 p. 110 [hereinafter *Completing the Uruguay Round*] .

5 From M.J. Trebilcock, 'Throwing Deep: Trade Remedies in a First-Best World', in M.J. Trebilcock and R.C. York, (eds) *Fair Exchange: Reforming Trade Remedy Laws* (Toronto: C.D. Howe, 1990) 235, Table A-4 p. 273 [hereinafter *Fair Exchange*]. This figure includes voluntary export restraints, orderly marketing arrangements, export forecasts, basic price systems, industry-to-industry arrangements, and discriminatory import systems.

6 These arrangements are not contemplated by the GATT but are generally believed to be inconsistent with GATT's policy on export restraints. It is difficult for the GATT to control these agreements unless a complaint is lodged; since both Parties usually have an interest in the ERA complaints are infrequent. See J.H. Jackson, *The World Trading System: Law and Policy of International Economic Relations* (Cambridge MA: MIT Press, 1989) p. 179 [hereinafter *The World Trading System*].

7 23 December 1942, Article XI, 57 Stat. 833 (1943); E.A.S. No. 311 (effective 30 January 1943).

8 William L. Clayton, *GATT: An Analysis and Appraisal of the General Agreement on Tariffs and Trade* (U.S. Council of the International Chamber of Commerce, 1955) p. 36, n.8.

9 J.H. Jackson, *World Trade and the Law of GATT* (Ann Arbor: Bobbs-Merrill, 1969) p. 554 [hereinafter *World Trade*].

10 The historical description that follows draws primarily on G. Winham, *International Trade and the Tokyo Round Negotiations* (Princeton: Princeton University Press, 1986).

11 Jackson, *World Trade, op. cit.*, p. 557.

12 According to Sampson: 'Article XIX has rarely, if ever, been interpreted in a way that would appear to be consistent with the text' (*op. cit.*, p. 143).

13 This interpretation of 'increased' was adopted at the Second Session of the GATT Contracting Parties in 1948 (GATT, 2 BISD 39, pp. 44–5 (1952)). The allowance of safeguard actions when imports have not increased absolutely is controversial since it shifts the burden of an economic downturn to foreign producers (Jackson, *World Trade, op. cit.*, p. 558).

14 Jackson, *The World Trading System, op. cit.*, p. 171.

15 *Ibid.*

16 A.O. Sykes, 'Protectionism as "Safeguard": A Positive Analysis of the GATT "Escape Clause" with Normative Speculations' (1991) 58 *University of Chic. L. Rev.* 255 at p. 288 [hereinafter 'Protectionism'].

17 *Ibid.*, p. 287.

18 See *Report on the Withdrawal by the U.S. of a Tariff Concession Under Article XIX of the GATT (the Hatter's Fur Case)* (Geneva, GATT/151–3, 1951).

19 Sampson, *op. cit.*, p. 143.

20 GATT L/76 (1953). The interpretation was developed as part of the negotiations on the International Trade Organisation which was never realized so it has only persuasive value.

21 The legal and practical requirement of nondiscrimination is the subject of some controversy. See Jackson, *The World Trading System, op. cit.*; Bronckers, 'The Nondiscriminatory Application of Article XIX GATT: Tradition or Fiction?' (1981/2) Legal Issues of European Integration (LIEI) 35, 'Reconsidering the Nondiscrimination Principle as Applied to GATT Safeguard Measures' (1983/2) LIEI 113, and *Selective Safeguard Measures in Multilateral Trade Relations* (Deventer: Kluwer, 1985); and Koulen, 'The Nondiscriminatory Interpretation of GATT Article XIX(1): A Reply' (1983/2) *LIEI* 89.

22 See Jackson, *World Trading System, op. cit.*, p. 168.

23 Sykes, 'Protectionism', *op. cit.*

24 *The Canada–U.S. Free Trade Agreement* (Toronto: CCH Canadian, 1988) 364. For a discussion of the FTA provisions, see M.J. Trebilcock, 'Reforming the GATT Safeguards Regime', (1989) 15 *Can. Bus. L.J.* 234.

25 Article 1101. Once the transition period is over bilateral emergency action can only be taken with consent of the other country.

26 These measures contrast with ERAs which typically allow exporters to reap monopoly profits at the expense of domestic consumers.

27 Chapter 8, NAFTA.

28 Kenneth Dam, *The GATT: Law and International Economic Organization* (Chicago: University of Chicago Press, 1970) p. 106.

29 *Ibid.*, p. 99.

30 Sykes, 'Protectionism' *op. cit.*, and A.O. Sykes, 'GATT Safeguards Reform: The Injury Test', in *Fair Exchange, op. cit.*, p. 203 [hereinafter 'The Injury Test'].

31 Sykes, 'Protectionism', *op. cit.*, p. 279.

32 If these two assumptions are false then there is no need for a safeguard clause since countries can either escape their obligations via a substitute for safeguard relief or else simply ignore their trade obligations.

33 Jackson, *The World Trading System, op. cit.*, p. 150.

34 G.C. Hufbauer and H.F. Rosen, *Trade Policy for Troubled Industries* (Washington, DC: Institute for International Economics, 1986).

35 With the remaining four it was too early to make a determination. Successful adjustment cases included cases in which the industry requested further protection following the end of the relief and ITC denied such renewal on the grounds that trade was not causing the injury.

36 See M.J. Trebilcock, M.A. Chandler and R. Howse, *Trade and Transitions: A Comparative Analysis of Adjustment Policies* (London: Routledge, 1990) pp. 42–76.

37 R.W. Crandall, 'Import Quotas and the Automobile Industry: The Costs of Protectionism', 2 *Brookings Review* 4 p. 8.

38 Economic Council of Canada, *Managing Adjustment* (Ottawa: Economic Council of Canada, 1988) pp. 61,70,76.

39 Until midway through 1987 compensation was offered in twenty GATT safeguard clause cases and retaliation occurred in only thirteen. See E.-U. Petersmann, 'Grey Area Trade Policy and the Rule of Law' (1988) 22 *J. of World Trade* 23 p. 36.

40 See Sykes, 'Protectionism', *op. cit.*

41 R.Z. Lawrence, 'GATT Safeguards Reform: A Comment', in *Fair Exchange*, *op. cit.* p. 203.

42 Hamilton and Whalley would include in these alternate measures antidumping and countervailing-duty actions. 'Safeguards', in *Completing the Uruguay Round, op. cit.*, 79 at p. 89.

43 E-U Petersmann, 'Economic, Legal and Political Functions of the Principle of Non-Discrimination', 9 *World Economy*, March, 1986, 113.

44 Marco Bronckers, *Selective Safeguard Measures in Multilateral Trade Relations: Issues of Protectionism in GATT, European Community, and United States Law*, (Deventer: Kluwer Law and Taxation Publishers, 1985) ch. 3.

45 For a fuller elaboration of these arguments, see Bronckers *op. cit.*

46 Winham, *op. cit.*

47 According to Winham, the USA adopted a middle ground. It was sympathetic to the view of developing countries but also saw itself as vulnerable to sudden import increases from low cost suppliers (*op. cit.*, p. 199).

48 Winham, *Ibid.*, pp. 243–4.

49 GATT Secretariat, *The Tokyo Round of Multilateral Trade Negotiations: Supplementary Report* (Geneva: 1980) p. 42.

50 Winham, *op. cit.*, p. 358.

51 A.W. Wolff, 'The Need for New GATT Rules to Govern Safeguard Actions', in W.R. Cline, (ed.) *Trade Policy in the 1980s* (Washington, DC: Institute for International Economics, 1983) 363 at p. 383.

52 *Ibid.*

53 J. Zietz, 'Negotiations on GATT Reform and Political Incentives' (1989) 12 *World Economy* 39.

54 Sykes: 'Protectionism', *op. cit.*; and 'The Injury Test', *op. cit.*

55 Hufbauer and Rosen, *op. cit.*, p. 60.

56 Trebilcock, *op. cit.* (1989) p. 238; J.D. Richardson, 'Safeguards Issues in the Uruguay Round', in R.E. Baldwin and J.D. Richardson, (eds) *Issues in the Uruguay Round* (Cambridge MA: NBER, 1988, 24 at p. 33).

57 *Ibid.*

58 J. Tumlir, 'A Revised Safeguard Clause for GATT?' (1973) 7 *J. of World Trade Law* 404.

59 Wolff, *op. cit.*, p. 380.

60 Trebilcock, *op. cit.*, (1989) p. 238.

61 See M. Trebilcock, M. Chandler and R. Howse, *op. cit.*

62 Report of the Advisory Council on Adjustment (De Grandpré Report), *Adjusting to Win* (Ottawa: Supply and Services Canada, 1989).

63 *Ibid.*, p. xvii.

64 L. Kaplow, 'An Economic Analysis of Legal Transitions', (1986) 99 *Harvard L. Rev.* 509.

65 For a discussion of the difficulties of predicting employment effects with precision, see Economic Council of Canada, *Venturing Forth: An Assessment of the Canada–U.S. Trade Agreement* (Ottawa: Supply and Services, 1988).

66 The evidence is presented in W. Mendling, *The Plant Closure Policy Dilemma: Labor, Law and Bargaining* (1984).

67 See more generally, R. Howse and M. Trebilcock, 'Protecting the Employment Bargain', (1993) 43 *University of Toronto L.J.* 751.

68 See, especially, G. Glenday, G.P. Jenkins, and J. C. Evans, *Worker Adjustment to Liberalized Trade: Costs and Assistance Policies* (Washington DC: World Bank, 1980) pp. 50–5.

69 The seminal study on this phenomenon is J. Elster, *Sour Grapes: Studies in the*

Subversion of Rationality (Cambridge: Cambridge University Press, 1983).

70 See C.R. Leana and D.C. Feldman, *Coping with Job Loss: How Individuals, Organizations, and Communities Respond to Layoffs* (New York: Lexington Books, 1992) ch. 3 'Reactions to Job Loss'.

71 F. Michelman, 'Property, Utility, and Fairness', (1967), *Harvard L. Rev.* 1165.

72 G. Calabresi, *Ideals, Beliefs, Attitudes and the Law* (New York: Syracuse University Press, 1985) p. 109.

73 M. Trebilcock, *The Political Economy of Economic Adjustment* (vol. 8, Research Study prepared for Royal Commission on Economic Union and Development Prospects in Canada, Toronto: University of Toronto Press, 1985).

74 R.Z. Lawrence, and R. Litan, 'Living with the Trade Deficit: Adjustment Strategies to Preserve Free Trade', (1985) 4 *Brookings Review*, 1, pp. 3–13.

75 Hufbauer, and Rosen *op. cit.*

76 P. Morici, 'Transition Mechanisms and Safeguards in a North American Free Trade Agreement', in L. Waverman, (ed.) *Negotiating and Implementing a North American Free Trade Agreement* (Toronto and Vancouver: Fraser Institute and Centre for International Studies, 1992) p. 84.

77 See Daniel Tarullo, 'Beyond Normalcy in the Regulation of International Trade' (1987) 100 *Harvard L. Rev.* 546.

78 R. Howse, 'The Case for Linking a Right to Adjustment with the NAFTA', in J. Lemcoe and W. Robson (eds) *Ties Beyond Trade: Labor and Environmental Issues under the NAFTA* (Toronto and Washington DC: C.D. Howe Institute and National Planning Association, 1993) pp. 79–107. This part of the chapter draws heavily on this article.

79 'Appendix. The Current Enforcement Authority and Procedures: 301, Super 301 and Special 301', in J. Bhagwati and H.T. Patrick (eds) *Aggressive Unilateralism: America's 301 Trade Policy and the World Trading System* (Ann Arbor: University of Michigan Press, 1990) pp. 39–40.

80 See Chapter 12 below for an explanation of the GSP.

81 S. 503, General System of Preferences Renewal Act of 1984.

82 *Ibid.*, and see also, S. Weintraub and J. Gilbreath, 'The Social Side to Free Trade', in Lemco and Robson (eds) *Ties Beyond Trade, op. cit.*, pp. 66–7.

83 Francis Wolf, 'Human Rights and the International Labour Organisation', in Theodor Meron (ed.) *Human Rights in International Law: Legal and Policy Issues*, Vol. II (Oxford: Clarendon Press, 1984) pp. 274–5.

84 See Weintraub and Gilbreath, *op. cit.*, pp. 66–8.

85 *Ibid.*

86 See P. Morici, 'Implications of a Social Charter for the NAFTA', in Lemco and Robson (eds) *op. cit.*, pp. 137–8.

87 See 'Confidential NEC Options Paper on Environment and Labor', in 11 *Inside U.S. Trade* no. 10 (1993) at S-6–S-9.

88 The basic insight behind an emphasis on adjustment as an alternative to renewed or escalating protectionism is that adjustment policies are less costly both in domestic and global welfare terms than policies that purport to resist change itself as opposed to appropriately managing its costs. This is the basic theme developed in M.J. Trebilcock, M.A. Chandler and R. Howse, *Trade and Transitions: A Comparative Analysis of Adjustment Policies* (London: Routledge, 1990, especially ch. 6 'The Reform Agenda').

89 And indeed these disputes are not referable to NAFTA dispute settlement panels, although (at least in the case of the USA and Canada, by virtue of continued application of the FTA provisions on emergency action between these two countries) they may be referred to binding arbitration. See Article 804 of NAFTA.

90 See Tarullo, 'Can the European Social Market Survive 1992?' (1991) 1 *American Prospect* 61.

91 See Howse, 'The Case for Linking a Right to Adjustment with the NAFTA', *op. cit.*, pp. 80–3.

92 United Nations Development Program, *Human Development Report 1991*.

93 See in general, J.D. Sullivan, 'Democracy and Global Economic Growth', *Washington Quarterly* (Spring, 1992), p. 176: Sullivan cites the examples of South Korea, Singapore, Hong Kong and Taiwan.

8   TRADE IN AGRICULTURE

1 See *Issues and Developments in International Trade Policy* (Washington DC: International Monetary Fund, 1992) ch. VI, 'Agricultural Trade Policies Recent Developments and Issues for Reform'.

2 K. Dam, *The GATT: Law and the International Economic Organization* (Chicago: University of Chicago Press, 1970) p. 260.

3 D. Hathaway, *Reforming World Agricultural Trade* (Washington DC: Institute for International Economics, 1988) p. 109.

4 But, note that it does not encompass prohibitions.

5 *Dairy Products from the Netherlands*, BISD, vol II (1952), 116.

6 *Japan: Restrictions on Certain Agricultural Products*, BISD, 35 Supp. (1989) 163.

7 *European Community: Restrictions on Imports of Apples*, BISD 36th Supp. (1990).

8 *France: Assistance to Exports of Wheat and Wheat Flour*, BISD 7th Supp. (1959) 46.

9 *European Community: Subsidies on Export of Wheat Flour*, SCM/42 (21 March 1983). See W.H. Boger III, 'The United States–European Community Agricultural Export Subsidies Dispute', 16 *Law & Policy in International Business* 173 (1984).

10 J. Jackson, *The World Trading System: Law and Policy of International Economic Relations* (Cambridge MA: MIT Press 1988) p. 102.

11 *European Community: Subsidies on Exports of Pasta Products*, SCM/43 (19 May 1983).

12 *European Community: Payments and Subsidies on Oilseeds and Animal-Feed Proteins*, BISD, 37th Supp. (1989) 86.

13 See 'Introduction', in K.A. Ingersent, A.J. Rayner and R.C. Hine, *Agriculture in the Uruguay Round* (London: St. Martin's, 1994) pp. 5–6.

14 J. Hillman, *Technical Barriers to Agricultural Trade* (San Francisco: Westview, 1991) pp. 126–8.

15 See A. Dick, 'The EC Hormone Ban Dispute and the Application of the Dispute Settlement Provisions of the Standards Code', (1989) 10 *Michigan Journal of International Law* 872.

16 The following account of the agricultural provisions of the NAFTA draws extensively on R. Bartichello and T. Josling, 'Agriculture in the NAFTA: A Preliminary Assessment', paper presented at C.D. Howe Institute NAFTA Conference, Toronto, December 1992.

17 T. Grennes and B. Kristoff, 'Agricultural Trade in a North American Free Trade Agreement', (1993) 16 *World Economy* 483.

18 *Ibid.*, pp. 486–7.

19 B. Wilson and P. Finkle, 'Is Agriculture Different? Another Round in the Battle Between Theory and Practice', in G. Skogstad and A.F. Cooper (eds)

CHAPTER 8

Agricultural Trade: Domestic Pressures and International Tensions (Halifax: Institute for Research on Public Policy, 1990) p. 17.

20 L. Martin, 'Global Competition and Canadian Federalism: the Agri-Food Sector' (paper presented at a Conference on Global Competitiveness and Canadian Federalism, Faculty of Law, University of Toronto, 16 September 1990) p. 3.

21 See J.C. Gilson, 'Agriculture and the Uruguay Round of the GATT', in *World Agriculture Changes: Implications for Canada* (Toronto: C.D. Howe Institute, 1988).

22 *Ibid.*

23 See, for example, OECD, *National Policies and Agricultural Trade* (Paris, 1987); World Bank, *World Development Report* (Washington DC, 1986).

24 'Grotesque: A Survey of Agriculture', *Economist*, 12 December 1992, p. 7.

25 See M. Kelly and A.K. McGuirk, *Issues and Developments in International Trade Policy* (Washington DC: IMF, 1992), pp. 59–60. Empirical evidence cited in this study suggests that in the longer term virtually all developing countries would gain from liberalization of agricultural policies in the industrialized countries, as long as the developing countries themselves eliminated domestic distortions in both the agricultural and industrial sectors. See also the economic modelling in R. Tyers and K. Anderson, *Disarray in World Food Markets* (Cambridge and New York: Cambridge University Press, 1992).

26 The members of the Cairns Group are Argentina, Australia, Brazil, Canada, Chile, Colombia, Fiji, Hungary, Indonesia, Malaysia, New Zealand, the Philippines, Thailand and Uruguay. Although Canada was initially very active in the Group, out of concern for its Western grain farmers who have suffered greatly due to export subsidy wars between the USA and the EU, more recently Canada has sought to protect its own system of supply management, particularly with respect to poultry and eggs.

27 *Op. cit.*, p. 7.

28 It is important to note that the United States received strong support for its position that agricultural protection be disciplined in the GATT by the so-called Cairns Group, representing a number of agricultural exporting countries whose agricultural trade was affected by the subsidies wars between the USA and the EC. See A.J. Rayner, K.A. Ingersent and R.C. Hine, 'Agriculture in the Uruguay Round: An Assessment' (1993) 103 *Economic Journal* 1511 at pp. 1516–17.

29 Cited in M. Plain, *Trade Negotiations in the OECD* (London: Kegan Paul, 1993) pp. 120–1.

30 Plain, *Trade Negotiations in the OECD*, *op. cit.*

31 *Ibid.*

32 A.B. Philip, 'The European Community: Balancing Domestic Pressures and International Demands', in G. Skogstad and A.F. Cooper (eds), *op. cit.*, p. 75.

33 Martin, *op. cit.*

34 See, for a discussion of the transitional gains trap problem, M.J. Trebilcock and J. Quinn, 'Compensation, Transition Costs and Regulatory Change', 32 *University of Toronto Law Journal* 117 (1982); see also G. Tullock, 'Achieving Deregulation – A Public Choice Perspective', *Regulation*, Nov.–Dec. 1978. See Gordon Tullock, 'The Transitional Gains Trap', (1975) 6 *Bell Journal of Economics* 671.

35 Significant work was done at the OECD between 1982 and 1987 with respect to developing methodologies for measuring and comparing levels of agricultural protection in various countries. See Plain, *Trade Negotiations in the OECD*, *op. cit.*, pp. 122–3.

36 For an excellent discussion of some of these methodological alternatives, see Gilson, *op. cit.*

37 Some European experts give credence to this US concern. Tarditi for instance suggests the European approach to shifting from price to income support for farmers would involve very significant administrative costs and complexities and be quite vulnerable to widespread fraud by farmers. S. Tarditi, 'Perspectives on EC Agricultural Policy Reform', in Ingersent, Rayner and Hine, (eds) *Agriculture in the Uruguay Round, op. cit.*, pp. 212–14.

38 See K.A. Ingersent, A.J. Rayner and R.C. Hine, 'Agriculture in the Uruguay Round: An Assessment', Ingersent, Rayner and Hine, (eds) *Agriculture in the Uruguay Round* (London: St. Martin's Press, 1994) pp. 268–9.

39 Substitution of income support for price support was a major ingredient in the so-called MacSharry Report on Reform of the CAP, which provided the basis for negotiation *within* the European Community in 1991–93 on liberalization of agricultural policies. Commission of the European Communities, 'The Development and Future of the CAP: Reflections Paper of the European Commission', COM (91) 285 (Final), Brussels, 1991.

40 See J.S. Marsh, 'An EC Approach to Decoupling', in *ibid.*

41 Commission of the European Communities, *op. cit.*

42 'United States Department of Agricultural Statement on US–EC Accord on Oilseeds and the Uruguay Round' (1992) 9 *International Trade Reporter* 2028 (11 November 1992).

43 'Special Report: Progress Made in US–EC Trade Negotiations As of December 7' (1993) 10 *International Trade Reporter* 2042–3(8 December 1993).

44 See the discussion of Annex 2 and Article 13 below at p. 000.

45 An egregious example is a document published simultaneously with the closure of the Uruguay Round by the Canadian Department of Agriculture, which emphasizes that the Canadian system of supply management for dairy and poultry products (which keeps prices far above world prices for these items) will remain in place despite the Uruguay Round Agreement, since the Agreement permits prohibitive tariffs to replace import quotas. The document notes approvingly the 'high level of protection' still allowed under the Agreement; it is completely silent as to any possible benefit to *consumers* from the reductions in protection required by the Agreement. Government of Canada, Department of Agriculture, 'GATT and Agri-food General Information Package', Ottawa, 15 December 1993.

46 Remarks of Peter Sutherland, Director General of the GATT, Centre for International Studies Forum on the Uruguay Round Results, University of Toronto, 21 March 1994.

9 TRADE IN SERVICES

1 K. Sauvant, 'The Tradeability of Services', in P. A. Messerlin and K.P. Sauvant (eds) *The Uruguay Round: Services in the World Economy* (Washington and New York: The World Bank and The United Nations Centre on Transnational Corporations, 1990) 117.

2 See R. Howse and M.J. Trebilcock, 'Protecting the Employment Bargain', (1993) 43 *University of Toronto Law Journal* 751, at pp. 783–4.

3 *Op. cit.*, note 1.

4 B. Hoekman, 'Market Access Through Multilateral Agreement: From Goods to Services' (1992) 15 *The World Economy*, 707 at p. 710.

5 See, in general, R. Howse, J.R.S. Prichard and M.J. Trebilcock, 'Smaller or

CHAPTER 9

Smarter Government?', (1990) 40 *University of Toronto Law Journal* 498.

6 See OECD, *Regulatory Reform, Privatization and Competition Policy* (Paris: OECD, 1992).

7 J.N. Bhagwati, 'Splintering and Disembodiment of Service and Developing Nations' (1984) 7 *World Economy* 133.

8 Sauvant, *op. cit.*, p. 116.

9 An excellent guide to these issues, accessible to the non-specialist, is to be found in J. Bhagwati, 'International Trade in Services and its Relevance for Economic Development', in *Political Economy and International Economics* (Cambridge MA: MIT Press, 1991) ch. 14. See also the review of these issues in P.W. Daniels, *Services in the World Economy* (London: Basil Blackwell, 1993) pp. 1–23.

10 Indeed, one of the main examples we drew upon to illustrate the theory of comparative advantage, that of the lawyer and her secretary is an example of the gains from trade of services.

11 See G. Feketekuty, *International Trade in Services: An Overview and Blueprint for Negotiations* (Cambridge MA: American Enterprise Institute and Ballinger, 1988).

12 P. Nicolaides, 'The Nature of Services' in Messerlin and Sauvant, (eds) *op. cit.*

13 B. Hindley, 'Principles in Factor-related Trade in Services', in Messerlin and Sauvant, (eds) *op. cit.*, note 1, pp. 13–15.

14 See M. Marconini, 'The Uruguay Round Negotiations on Services: An Overview', in Messerlin and Sauvant (eds), *op. cit.*, pp. 20–1.

15 See, for instance, I. Walter, *Liberalization of Trade in Financial Services* (Washington DC: AEI, 1988).

16 See Howse, Prichard and Trebilcock, *op. cit.*

17 See International Monetary Fund (Exchange and Trade Relations Research Departments), *International Capital Markets: Developments and Prospects* (Washington DC: IMF, 1989) particularly pp. 50–60.

18 *Ibid.*

19 See Howse, Prichard and Trebilcock, *op. cit.*

20 Given the conceptual difficulties in defining services discussed earlier in this chapter, it is not surprising that no definition of services appears in the NAFTA. Instead the scope of application of Chapter Twelve is defined in terms of a variety of 'measures relating to border trade in services by service providers'. These include, *inter alia* 'measures respecting . . . the production, distribution, marketing, sale and delivery of a service; . . . the purchase, payment or use of a service' and 'the presence in its territory of a service territory on a service provider of another territory' (Article 1201.1).

21 Organization for Economic Cooperation and Development, Code of Liberalisation of Current Invisible Operations, November 1990.

22 OECD, *Liberalisation of Capital Movements and Financial Services in the OECD Area* (Paris: OECD, 1990) p. 17.

23 The US effort to put services on the international trade agenda began to take shape in the OECD Trade Committee at the end of the 1970s. As early as the Autumn 1982 GATT Ministerial Meeting, the USA was pressing for GATT-based negotiations on services. See W.J. Drake and K. Nicolaidis, 'Ideas, interests, and institutions: "trade in services" and the Uruguay Round', (1992) 46 *International Organization* 45.

24 See M. Marconini, 'The Uruguay Round Negotiations on Services: An Overview', *supra* note 14, pp. 19–20. See also, for a developing country perspective, R. Chakravarthi, *Recolonization: GATT, the Uruguay Round and the Third World* (London: Third World Network, 1990) ch. 5 'Services'.

25 J. Bhagwati, 'Splintering and Disembodiment of Services and Developing Nations', *op. cit.*; 'Trade and Services in the Multilateral Trade Negotiations' in *Political Economy and International Economics*, *op. cit.*, pp. 282–305. See also, B. Balassa, 'Interest of Developing Countries in the Uruguay Round', *World Economy* (March 1988), pp. 39–54.

26 B.M. Hoekman, 'Services-Related Production, Employment, Trade, and Factor Movements', in Messerlin and Sauvant (eds), *op. cit.*, p. 32.

27 *Ibid.* This was the case for Cameroon, Colombia, South Korea, Mexico, Chile, India, Egypt, Kenya, Morocco, the Philippines, Senegal, Singapore, Sudan, Thailand, and Tanzania.

28 For a brief explanation of the purported conceptual basis of this distinction, see 'The nature of services' (this chapter).

29 See Howse, Prichard, and Trebilcock, 'Smaller or Smarter Government', *op. cit.* See also, R. Howse, 'Reform, Retrenchment or Revolution? The Shift to Incentives and the Future of the Regulatory State', (1993) 31 *Alberta Law Review* 455; and R. Daniels and R. Howse, 'Reforming the Reform Process: A Critical Analysis of Privatization Proposals in Central and East Europe', (1992) 25 *New York University Journal of International Law and Politics* 27.

30 See Marconini, *op. cit.*, pp. 20–1.

31 Feketekuty, *op. cit.*

32 It should be noted that some Members have, pursuant to the Understanding on Commitments in Financial Services, already inscribed in their schedules commitments to permit temporary entry of certain specialized personnel in connection with the provision of financial services.

33 I.e. applicable even in the absence of specific multilateral disciplines based on the criteria, as contemplated in Article 6:4.

34 Since the National Treatment obligation applies only to sectors subject to specific commitments in Members' schedules, it appears in Part III of the GATS, to be discussed in the next section.

35 Organization for Economic Co-operation and Development, Code of Liberalisation of Capital Movements, November 1990.

36 See P.A. Messerlin, 'The European Community', in Messerlin and Sauvant (eds) *op. cit.*, pp. 132–49.

37 'Large risk' commercial insurance. Messerlin, *Ibid.*, p. 147.

38 T. Kim, *International Money and Banking* (London: Routledge, 1993) pp. 318–21. The following discussion draws extensively on ch. 14 of this work, 'The EC Framework For Banking Services'.

39 See G. Hufbauer, 'An Overview', in G. Hufbauer, (ed.) *Europe 1992: An American Perspective* (Washington DC: Brookings Institution, 1990).

40 Second Council Directive of 15 December 1989 on the Co-ordination of Laws, Regulations and Administrative Provisions Relating to the Taking Up and Pursuit of the Business of Credit Institutions and Amending Directive 77/80/EEC.

41 T. Kim, *International Money and Banking, op. cit.*, p. 319.

42 The following discussion of banking regulation in Canada and the USA draws on J.F. Chant, 'Free Trade in the Financial Sector: Expectations and Experience', Centre for International Studies/Fraser Institute Conference, 'How is Free Trade Progressing?', University of Toronto, 18–19 November 1991.

43 A clear and comprehensive presentation of Mexico's commitments under the Financial Services Chapter of NAFTA is to be found in B. Gonzalez-Hermosillo and P. Sauvé, 'Financial Services and NAFTA: Implications for Canadian Financial Institutions', paper presented at Conference on NAFTA,

C.D. Howe Institute, Toronto, 5–6 December 1992.

44 'Negotiators Clear Path to GATT Pact by Sweeping Away Remaining Differences', (1993) 10 *International Trade Reporter* 2106 (15 December 1993), at p. 2107.

45 S. Globerman, H.N. Janisch, R.J. Schultz and W.T. Stanbury, 'Canada and the Movement towards Liberalization of the International Telecommunications Regime', in A.C. Cutler and M.W. Zacher, (eds), *Canadian Foreign Policy and International Economic Regimes* (Vancouver: UBC Press, 1992) pp. 262–4.

46 *International Trade Reporter* (15 December 1993), *op. cit.*

47 Howse, Prichard, and Trebilcock, *op. cit.*

10 TRADE-RELATED INTELLECTUAL PROPERTY (TRIPs)

1 See R.A. Epstein, *Takings: Private Property and the Power of Eminent Domain* (Cambridge MA: Harvard University Press, 1985), and R. Nozick, *Anarchy, State, and Utopia* (New York: Basic Books, 1974).

2 For an excellent discussion about the centrality and limits of the idea of private property in liberal democratic theory, in the American context, see J. Nedelsky, *Private Property and the Limits of American Constitutionalism* (Chicago: University of Chicago Press, 1990) pp. 216–64.

3 See the discussion of monopoly power and coercion in M.J. Trebilcock, *The Limits of Freedom of Contract* (Cambridge MA: Harvard University Press, 1993) ch. 4.

4 A good survey is to be found in C.A. Primo Braga, 'Guidance from Economic Theory', in Siebeck, (ed.) *Strengthening Protection of Intellectual Property in Developing Countries: A Survey of the Literature* (Washington DC: The World Bank, 1991).

5 See Primo Braga, *op. cit.*, p. 22.

6 See C. Primo Braga, 'The Developing Country Case For and Against Intellectual Property Protection', Primo Braga, (ed.) *op. cit.*, pp. 77–8.

7 A. Deardorff, 'Should Patent Protection Be Extended To All Developing Countries?' 13 *World Economy* (1990) 13, pp. 497–508.

8 Everson suggests that, with respect to developing countries, 'the literature does not show strong correlations between direct foreign investment and the strength of IPRs'. 'Global Intellectual Property Rights Issues in Perspective', in M.B. Wallerstein, M.E. Mogee and R.A. Schoen, (eds) *Global Dimensions of Intellectual Property Rights* (Washington DC: National Academy Press, 1993) p. 366.

9 Binley challenges the link between strong intellectual property protection and higher levels of foreign investment. She notes: '. . . Korea benefited from technology transfer in numerous industries via licensing arrangements, sub-contracting agreements and the location of foreign subsidiaries during a period in which its intellectual property laws were as weak as any of the other LDCs'. M. Binley, 'Intellectual Property Rights: A Strategic Instrument of Developing Nations', International Business and Trade Law Programme, Working Paper No. 46 (1992), Faculty of Law, University of Toronto, p. 25.

10 See L. Davis, 'Technology Intensity of US, Canadian, and Japanese Manufactures Output and Exports', in J. Niosi, (ed.) *Technology and National Competitiveness* (Kingston and Montreal: McGill-Queens, 1991).

11 See M. Borrus, 'Macroeconomic Perspectives on the Use of Intellectual

Property Rights in Japan's Economic Performance', in F. Rushing and C. Brown, (eds) *Intellectual Property Rights in Science, Technology and Economic Performance: International Comparisons* (Washington DC: U.S. Chamber of Commerce, 1990) pp. 261–7.

12 See J. Niosi, *Canada's Multinationals* (tr. R. Chodos) (Toronto: Between the Lines, 1983).

13 A.V. Deardorff, 'Should Patent Protection be Extended to All Developing Countries?', in 13 *World Economy* 497 (1990).

14 K. Maskus, 'Normative Concerns in the International Protection of Intellectual Property Rights', *World Economy* (1991), at p. 403.

15 G. Grossman and E. Helpman, *Innovation and Growth in the Global Economy* (Cambridge MA: MIT Press, 1991) ch. 11 'Imitation'.

16 For a good discussion of this controversy see J.H. Jackson, 'Remarks of Professor John H. Jackson', (1989) 22 *Vanderbilt Journal of Transnational Law*, pp. 343–4.

17 This case is discussed more extensively below at p. 259–60.

18 Paris Convention for the Protection of Industrial Property, 20 March 1883, 828 UNTS 107.

19 Commission of the European Communities, *Green Paper on Copyright and the Challenge of Technology: Copyright issues requiring immediate attention* (Brussels: European Commission, 1988) p. 233 (hereinafter, EC *Green Paper*).

20 Some commentators, however, read an MFN principle into the national treatment obligation on the basis of the history and general purposes of the Convention. See, for instance, J. Reichman, 'Intellectual Property in International Trade: Opportunities and Risks of a GATT Connection', (1989) 22 *Vanderbilt Journal of Transnational Law* 747 at pp. 843–53.

21 W. Lesser, 'An Overview of Intellectual Property Systems', in C. Primo Braga (ed.) *op. cit.*, p. 11.

22 M. Borrus, 'Macroeconomic Perspectives on the Use of Intellectual Property Rights in Japan's Economic Performance', in F. Rushing and C. Brown, (eds) *Intellectual Property Rights in Science, Technology, and Economic Performance: International Comparisons* (Washington DC: U.S. Chamber of Commerce, 1990) p. 267.

23 C. Primo Braga, 'The Developing Country Case For and Against Intellectual Property Protection', in World Bank Discussion Paper, p. 75.

24 Berne Convention for the Protection of Industrial Property, 20 March 1883, 828 UNTS 107.

25 An exhaustive study of the evolution and contents of the Berne Convention is S. Ricketson, *The Berne Convention for the Protection of Literary and Artistic Works: 1886–1986* (London: Kluwer, 1986). The following section owes much to this work.

26 Hence, 'The expression "literary and artistic works" shall include every production in the literary, scientific and artistic domain, whatever may be the mode or form of its expression, . . .' (Art. 2 (1)).

27 See EC *Green Paper*, see also D. Llewellyn, 'Computers, Software and International Protection', (1986) *VLA Journal of Law and the Arts* 183.

28 'Trade-Related Aspects of Intellectual Property Rights', in T. Stewart, (ed.) *The Uruguay Round: A Negotiating History: vol. III*, pp. 2247–8.

29 Convention Establishing the World Intellectual Property Organization, 14 July 1967, 828 UNTS 3.

30 See E. Wolfhard, 'International Trade in Intellectual Property: The Emerging GATT Regime', (1991) 49 *University of Toronto Faculty L. R.* 106; See also, F.-K. Beier and G. Schricker (eds), *GATT or WIPO? New Ways in the*

Protection of Intellectual Property (VCH: Weinheim, 1989).

31 International Convention for the Protection of Performers, Procurers of Phonograms and Broadcasting Organizations, 26 October 1961, 495–6 UNTS 44.

32 For a discussion of the rationale for the protection of intellectual property rights in the genetic material of plants, see R.L. Marguilies, 'Protecting Biodiversity: Recognizing International Intellectual Property Rights in Plant Genetic Resources', (1993) 14 *Michigan J. Int'l. L.* 322.

33 World Intellectual Property Organization: Treaty on Intellectual Property in Respect of Integrated Circuits, 26 May 1989, 28 *I.L.M.* 1477 (1989).

34 According to Goldberg, 'Chief among the problems that the United States found with the Washington Treaty were the inadequate terms of protection, the lack of specific protection for mask works incorporated in a finished product, broad provisions for compulsory licenses, and excessively permissive treatment of so-called innocent infringers.' M.D. Goldberg, 'Semiconductor Chip Protection as a Case Study', in M.D. Wallerstein, M.E. Mogee and R.A. Schoen, (eds) *Global Dimensions of Intellectual Property Protection* (Washington DC: National Academy Press, 1993) pp. 335–6.

35 But see W. Lesser, 'An Overview of Intellectual Property Systems', in W.E. Siebeck, (ed.) *Strengthening Protection of Intellectual Property in Developing Countries: A Survey of the Literature* (Washington DC: World Bank, 1991).

36 See the discussion of US aggressive unilateralism in Chapter 6.

37 See VanGrasstek Communications, 'Trade-Related Intellectual Property Rights: Developing Countries and the *Uruguay Round*', in United Nations Conference on Trade and Development, *Uruguay Round: Further Papers on Selected Issues* (New York: United Nations, 1990) pp. 79–128.

38 GATT, United States-Section 337 of the Tariff Act of 1930, L 6439 (16 January 1989).

39 See VanGrasstek Communications, *op. cit.*, pp. 103–4.

40 The Instrument does not appear, however, to specify explicitly the nature or level of the retaliation contemplated.

41 See Bourgeois and Laurent, 'Le "nouvel instrument de la politique commerciale": un pas en avant vers l'élimination des obstacles aux échanges internationaux', *Revue trimestrielle de droit européen* (Jan.–Mar. 1985).

42 Commission of the European Communities, *Green Paper on Copyright and the Challenge of Technology: Copyright issues requiring immediate attention, op. cit.*, p. 235.

43 W. Brueckmann, 'Intellectual Property Protection in the European Community', in F. Rushing and C. Brown, (eds) *op. cit.*, pp. 291–310.

44 As Stewart notes, the Conventions and WIPO offer the possibility of accepting the jurisdiction of the International Court of Justice with respect to settlement of disputes, and WIPO itself has attempted to achieve some dispute settlement through the appointment of special informal committees of experts to address particular disagreements about the functioning of the Conventions. T. Stewart, 'Trade-Related Aspects of Intellectual Property Rights', in T. Stewart, (ed.) *The Uruguay Round: A Negotiating History, op. cit.*, pp. 2247–8.

45 C. Primo Braga, 'The Developing Country Case For and Against Intellectual Property Protection', *op. cit.*, pp. 73–5.

46 Indeed, extensive written reasons for a judicial decision are *a*typical of most legal systems in the world, which are based on the civilian approach to the role of courts in decision-making. The court is viewed as applying rules in a code and not as making law from case to case.

47 See G.B. Rathmann, 'Biotechnology Case Study', in M.B. Wallerstein, M.E.

Mogee and R.A. Schoen, (eds) *op. cit.*, pp. 319ff.

48 See W. Lesser, 'Seeds and Plants', in W.E. Siebeck, (ed.) *Strengthening Protection of Intellectual Property in Developing Countries: A Survey of the Literature*, *op. cit.*, pp. 65–8.

49 United Nations Environmental Programme, Framework Convention on Biodiversity, 5 June 1992, Articles 15 (1) and 16 (2). The United States refused to sign the Convention. See Margulies, 'Protecting Biodiversity: Recognizing International Intellectual Property Rights in Plant Genetic Resources', *op. cit.*, pp. 333–4.

50 These are discussed above at p. 257–8.

51 See P. Samuelson, 'A Case Study on Computer Programs', in M.B. Wallerstein, M.E. Mogee and R.A. Schoen, (eds) *Global Dimensions of Intellectual Property Rights in Science and Technology*, *op. cit.*, pp. 309–18.

52 An example would be a mark deemed obscene or associated with racial or religious hatred.

53 For a discussion of the nature of these exemptions, and some concrete examples to which they might apply, see International Bureau of Intellectual Property, *The Paris Convention for the Protection of Intellectual Property from 1883 to 1983* (Geneva: WIPO, 1983) pp. 41–5.

54 See the above discussion of the Canada–USA FTA.

55 For instance the Convention permits member states to make exceptions to protection with regard to private and some journalistic use of recorded material, as well as use for purposes of teaching and scientific research (Article 15).

56 See, on these concerns, Stewart, *The GATT Uruguay Round: A Negotiating History*, *op. cit.*, pp. 2299–30.

57 See C.M. Correa, *Integrated Circuits: Trends in Intellectual Property Protection*, United Nations Industrial Development Organization (UNIDO) Doc. IPCT, 24 October 1989, pp. 21–3.

58 There are certain differences of wording between the Washington Treaty provisions and the applicable TRIPs Agreement provisions, but they are not major. For instance, where the TRIPs Agreement requires that 'adequate' remuneration be paid for a compulsory licence, the Washington Treaty uses the expression 'equitable remuneration' (compare TRIPs Agreement Article 31(h) and Washington Treaty, Article 6.3 (a)).

59 Some adjustment costs may occur in developed countries as well where the Agreement requires extending protection (e.g. in the generic drug industry in Canada). However, no transitional or adjustment provision is available to them.

60 See R.M. Sherwood, 'Intellectual Property and Free Trade in North America', unpublished paper, Centre for International Studies/Fraser Institute Conference, University of Toronto, 18–19 November 1991.

61 See J. Dillon, 'Intellectual Property', in *Analysis of NAFTA Proposals and the Impact on Canada* (Toronto: Ecumenical Coalition for Economic Justice, 1992).

11 TRADE AND INVESTMENT

1 N. Grimwade, *International Trade: New Patterns of Trade, Production and Investment* (London: Routledge, 1989) p. 144.

2 'Trade Related Investment Measures', in T. Stewart, (ed.) *The GATT Uruguay Round: A Negotiating History* (Boston: Kluwer, 1994) p. 2003.

3 M. Kelly and A. McGuirk (eds) *Issues and Developments in International Trade*

Policy (Washington DC: IMF, 1992) p. 8.

4 OECD, *The OECD Declaration and Decisions on International Investment and Multinational Enterprises: 1991 Review* (Paris: OECD, 1991) table 2.

5 See E. Graham and M. Ebert, 'Foreign Direct Investment and U.S. National Security: Fixing Exon-Florio', (1991) 14 *World Economy*; see also, R. Kuttner, *The End of Laissez-Faire: National Purpose and the Global Economy After the Cold War* (New York: Knopf, 1991).

6 See S. Ostry, 'Globalization, Domestic Policies and the Need for Harmonization', Centre for the Study of Business and Public Policy, University of California (Santa Barbara), January 1993, pp. 12–18.

7 S. Strange, *States and Markets* (Cordar: Pinter, 1988).

8 See A. Rugman, *Inside the Multinational: The Economics of Internal Markets* (New York: Columbia University Press, 1981).

9 Recent empirical evidence, surveyed by Jenkins, suggests that a major effect of foreign direct investment in many sectors in developing countries is to make local enterprises more competitive, rather than making them fail for inability to compete with multinationals. In some instances, competition may have resulted in domestic enterprises adopting practices that were arguably regressive or distributively unjust – i.e. with respect to labour and employment practices. Here, foreign investment itself could hardly be considered the root problem as opposed to inadequate labour or other social regulation to which both multinationals and domestic firms operating in the jurisdiction would be subject. See R. Jenkins, 'The Impact of Foreign Investment on Less Developed Countries: Cross-Section Analysis versus Industry Studies', in P. Buckley and J. Clegg, *Multinational Enterprise in Less-Developed Countries* (London: Macmillan, 1991, especially pp. 123–30).

10 See A.J. Easson 'The Design of Tax Incentives for Direct Investment: Some Lessons from the ASEAN Countries', International Business and Trade Law Programme, University of Toronto, 1993.

11 OECD, *Investment Incentives and Disincentives* (Paris: OECD, 1989).

12 See, especially, D. Greenaway, 'Why Are We Negotiating on TRIMs?', in Greenaway *et al.* (eds) *Global Protectionism* (London: Macmillan, 1991).

13 For a discussion of the rationale for singling out export subsidies, and its dubious merits, see Chapter 6.

14 See A. Barnea, R. Haughen and W. Senbet, 'Market Imperfections, Agency Problems, and Capital Structure: A Review', 10 *Financial Management*, Summer 1981. See also, R. Caves, *Multinational Enterprise and Economic Analysis* (New York: Cambridge University Press, 1982). Gilpin notes, the application of the theory of the firm to explain foreign investment is relatively recent; before the 1980s, explanations of foreign investment depended upon assumptions about oligopolistic competition or invoked the 'product cycle' theory of production (according to which countries at different levels of development have a comparative advantage at different stages in the life history of a product, from research and invention downwards to standardized mass-production. R. Gilpin, *The Political Economy of International Relations* (Princeton NJ: Princeton University Press, 1987) p. 237. However, foreign investment has increasingly occurred in sectors not characterized by oligopolistic competition and the 'product cycle' theory cannot explain the existence of increasing foreign investment flows from developed countries to other developed countries.

15 Grimwade, *International Trade: New Patterns of Trade, Production and Investment, supra* note 1, pp. 178–92.

16 On the globalization of production through increasing use of international external contracting mechanisms such as sub-contracting, licensing and inter-

firm agreements, see OECD, *Globalisation of Industrial Activities Four Case Studies: Auto Parts, Chemicals, Construction and Semi-conductors* (Paris: OECD, 1993).

17 P. Nicolaides, 'Investment Policies in an Integrated World Economy', 15 *World Economy* (1992), p. 123.

18 Although, of course, where a firm decided to choose the instrument of Foreign Direct Investment, it may encounter substantial agency costs in enforcing the various internal contracts in the jurisdiction in which it invests. The problem of the security of investors' assets and of expropriation will be discussed briefly later in this chapter.

19 See Grimwade, *International Trade: New Patterns of Trade, Production and Investment, op. cit.*, pp. 170–3.

20 J. Dunning, *Explaining International Production* (London: Unwin Hyman, 1988, especially ch. 2, 'The Eclectic Paradigm of International Production: A Restatement and Some Possible Extensions'). See also, J. Dunning, *Multinationals, Technology, and Competitiveness* (London: Unwin Hyman, 1988).

21 M. Porter, *The Competitive Advantage of Nations* (New York: Free Press, 1990).

22 Transfer prices are the prices at which the firm buys and sells goods and services from and to itself.

23 See, for instance, J. Knubley, W. Krause, and Z. Sadeque, 'Canadian Acquisitions Abroad: Patterns and Motivations', in L. Waverman, *Corporate Globalization through Mergers and Acquisitions* (Calgary: University of Calgary Press, 1991).

24 In general, recent economic literature seems to support the view that the consumer welfare losses from protection in these circumstances are likely to outweigh any gains to domestic welfare from rent-shifting. See A.E. Safarian, *Multinational Enterprise and Public Policy: A Study of the Industrial Countries* (Aldershot: Edward Elgar, 1993) p. 499.

25 See A.E. Safarian, *op. cit.*, pp. 467–70.

26 Indeed, Graham argues that protection-induced investment may actually result in a net loss to domestic economic development, where the foreign firm's access to a protected market reduces the pressure for it to invest in highly competitive production facilities in the host country. E. Graham, 'Strategic Trade Policy and the Multinational Enterprise in Developing Countries', in Buckley and Clegg, *op. cit.*, pp. 89–91. Hence, the economic development case for protection-induced investment depends upon capturing and channelling the rents from protection into directions that are beneficial to economic development.

27 A clear and balanced discussion of these and related concerns about foreign investment and multinationals can be found in R. Gilpin, *The Political Economy of International Relations, op. cit.*, ch. 6, 'Multinational Corporations and International Production'.

28 N. Machiavelli, *The Prince* (trans. M. Musa) (New York: St. Martin's, 1964) chs 6–7.

29 'Trade-related Investment Measures', *op. cit.*, pp. 2036–7. See also, U.N. Centre on Transnational Corporations, *National Legislation and Regulations Relating to Transnational Corporations*, U.N. Doc. ST/CTC/91 (1989).

30 50 U.S.C app. §2170(a) (1990).

31 Stewart, 'Trade-related Investment Measures', *op. cit.*, p. 2038.

32 Nance and Wasserman note, for instance a case where US industry interests complained to the CFIUS about the sale to a West German concern of a US company involved in manufacturing raw material for semiconductors. The

transaction was eventually approved, but not before the German acquirer had sent a letter of intent to the US Government, undertaking, *inter alia*, to continue production in the USA for at least five years, and to make its products available to the US semiconductor industry. D.S. Nance and J. Wasserman, 'Regulation of Imports and Foreign Investment in the United States on National Security Grounds' (1990) 11 *Michigan Journal of Intl. Law* 926, at pp. 973–4. The CFIUS process is particularly suited to the exertion of pressure on foreign investors, and to the striking of such deals or bargains because, as Nance and Wasserman also remark, the process is characterized by a 'complete lack of transparency': there are no hearings, no public submissions, and no administrative record (p. 961).

33 'Foreign Direct Investment and U.S. National Security: Fixing Exon–Florio', *op. cit.*

34 See, in general, A.L.C. de Mestral and T. Gruchalla-Wesierski, *Extraterritorial Application of Export Control Legislation: Canada and the United States* (Boston: Martinus Nijhoff, 1990).

35 See M. Leigh and P. Lichtenbaum, 'Law Without Borders: The Cuban Democracy Act of 1992', (1993) *The Canadian Law Newsletter* 13.

36 See Whitt, 'The Politics of Procedure: An Examination of the GATT Dispute-Settlement Panel and the Article XXI Defense in the Context of the U.S. Embargo of Nicaragua', (1987) 19 *Law & Policy in International Business* 63.

37 See J.G. Castel, A.L.C. de Mestral, and W.C. Graham, *International Business Transactions and Economic Relations* (Toronto: Carswell, 1991) ch.10, 'Extraterritorial Application of Canadian and Foreign Laws Prohibiting Restrictive Business Practices'.

38 OECD, *Decision of the Council: Conflicting Requirements*, Paris, June, 1991.

39 See Chapter 5 on trade and competition policy.

40 For a discussion of these various options, see N. Campbell and M. Trebilcock, 'International Merger Review: Problems of Multi-Jurisdictional Conflict', in E. Kautzenbach, H.-E. Scharrer and L. Waverman, (eds) *Competition Policy in an Interdependent World Economy* (Baden-Baden: Nomos Verlagsgesellschaft, 1993). For a somewhat more sceptical view of the possibility of establishing common rules to govern these inter-jurisdictional disputes, see S. Ostry, 'Globalization, Domestic Policies and the Need for Harmonization', Competition Policy in a Global Economy Project, University of California (Santa Barbara), January 1993 (unpublished).

41 These and related concerns are summarized and discussed in M.J. Trebilcock, *Public Enterprises in Papua New Guinea* (Port Moresby: Institute of National Affairs, 1982).

42 See, generally, for recent work, P.J. Buckley and J. Clegg, *Multinational Enterprise in Less Developed Countries* (London: Macmillan, 1991).

43 See J. Stopford and S. Strange, *Rival states, rival firms: competition for world market shares* (Cambridge: Cambridge University Press, 1991).

44 B. Emmott, 'Multinationals: Back in Fashion', *Economist*, 27 March – 2 April 1993, p. 19.

45 *Canada: Administration of the Foreign Investment Review Act (FIRA)*, BISD 30th Supp. 140 (1984).

46 See D. Greenaway, 'Trade Related Investment Measures: Political Economy Aspects and Issues for GATT", *World Economy* (1992), pp. 375–80.

47 An exhaustive discussion of the various conflicting perspectives that emerged in the Uruguay Round TRIMs negotiations can be found in Stewart, 'Trade-Related Investment Measures', *op. cit.*

48 *Final Act Embodying The Results of the Uruguay Round of Multilateral Trade*

Negotiations (MTN/FA), Geneva, 15 December 1993, II.7 'Agreement on Trade-Related Investment Measures' [hereinafter, 'Agreement on TRIMs'].

49 See M. Bergman, 'Bilateral Investment Protection Treaties: An Examination of the Evolution and Significance of the U.S. Prototype Treaty', 16 *New York University Journal of International Law and Politics*, pp. 19–24.

50 A good discussion of the interrelationship between incentives and disincentives, and the distortive effects of each is to be found in OECD, *Investment Incentives and Disincentives: Effects on International Direct Investment, supra.*

51 More exactly, the language suggests that *overall* treatment with respect to each of the following matters be no less favourable: establishment of new enterprises, acquisition of domestic firms, the conduct and operation of business enterprises, and sale of enterprises (Article 1602 (1) (a–d)).

52 On the US refusal to allow the validity of its Article XXI defence to be included in the terms of reference of the Panel, see R.S. Whitt, 'The Politics of Procedure: An Examination of the GATT Dispute Settlement Panel and the Article XXI Defense in the Context of the U.S. Embargo of Nicaragua', *op. cit.*

53 See M. Gestrin and A.M. Rugman, 'The NAFTA's Impact on the North American Investment Regime', (1993) 42 *C.D. Howe Institute Commentary* 1, at p. 8.

54 There may be some difficult definitional problems as well. For instance, although public health care exists throughout Canada, for purposes of Canadian constitutional law, hospitals, although publicly-funded and regulated, are not viewed as part of government. Therefore, an argument could be made that they are not even covered by Article 1104.1.

55 With the exception of the Treaty of Rome, which is much more than a trade treaty and which may be rightly viewed as establishing the outlines of a supranational *government* that in many matters can act directly on individual citizens.

56 Annexed to OECD, Declaration on International Investment and Multinational Enterprises, Paris, 1976.

57 For a good discussion of the various Codes and guidelines and their perceived impact, see R. Grosse, 'Codes of Conduct for Multinational Enterprises', (1982) 16 *Journal of World Trade Law* 414; see also, M.A. Kwaw, 'Trade Related Investment Measures in the Uruguay Round: Towards a GATT for Investment?' (1991) 16 *North Carolina Journal of International Law and Commercial Regulation* 309, at pp. 315–16.

58 See OECD (Committee on International Investment and Multinational Enterprises), *The OECD Declaration and Decisions on International Investment and Multinational Enterprises: 1991 Review* (Paris: OECD, 1992) pp. 42–54. See also, B. Blanpain, *The OECD Guidelines for Multinational Enterprises and Labour Relations 1982–1984: Experience and Review* (Boston: Kluwer, 1985).

59 The provisions of these Codes are discussed in the context of trade in financial services in Chapter 9 above.

60 OECD (Committee on International Investment and Multinational Enterprises), *National Treatment for Foreign-Controlled Enterprises* (Paris: OECD, 1993) p. 23.

61 OECD Council, National Treatment: Third Revised Decision of the Council (1991), Article 2 (c).

62 *Ibid.*, Article 3.

63 Declaration on International Investment and Multinational Enterprises (1976), *op. cit.*, Article II.1.

64 See P.E. Bondzi-Simpson, *The Legal Relationship Between Transnational*

Corporations and Host States (New York: Quorum, 1990).

65 See, for example, H.W. Baade, 'The Legal Effects of Codes of Conduct for Multinational Enterprises', in N. Horn (ed.) *Legal Problems of Codes of Conduct for Multinational Enterprises* (Deventer: Kluwer, 1980) pp. 32–7.

66 575 UNTS 159.

67 On the various theories concerning ICSID's very limited impact, see O. Unegbu, 'Dispute Settlement in International Investment: A Study of the ICSID Arbitral Regime', LLM thesis, Faculty of Law, University of Toronto, 1991 (unpublished).

12 TRADE AND DEVELOPING COUNTRIES

1 There is no agreed definition for the designation 'developing country.' Sometimes the term is used to refer to countries where per capita income is significantly below that of the major industrialized nations. The United Nations Development Programme (UNDP) has attempted to evolve indices of human development that take into account a broad range of factors, including education and literacy, the condition of women and children, and the level of social infrastructure. The UNDP does not, however, attempt to define a human development threshold below which a country is considered a developing country. Instead, the UNDP classifies all countries other than Europe, Canada, the United States, Australia, New Zealand and Japan as 'developing', including a number of countries that have relatively high per capita incomes, such as Saudi Arabia and Singapore. See UNDP, *Human Development Report* 1991 (New York: Oxford, 1991). For purposes of certain GATT provisions, developing countries are defined as 'contracting parties the economies of which can only support low standards of living and are in the early stages of development' (GATT Article XVIII:1).

2 A. Kruger, 'Global Trading Prospects of Developing Countries', (1992) 15 *World Economy*, p. 9.

3 These were Burma, Ceylon, Chile, Cuba, India, Pakistan, Southern Rhodesia, South Africa and Syria.

4 R. Hudec, *Developing Countries in the GATT Legal System* (London: Gower, 1987).

5 See B. Balassa, 'The Importance of Trade for Developing Countries', in *New Directions in the World Economy* (New York: NYU Press, 1989) p. 17.

6 See Balassa, *ibid.*

7 See R. Gilpin, *The Political Economy of International Relations* (Princeton NJ: Princeton University Press, 1987) pp. 298–302.

8 See, in general, M. Kelly and A.K. McGuirk *et al.*, *Issues and Developments in International Trade Policy* (Washington DC: International Monetary Fund, 1992) pp. 41–3.

9 See, for example, F. Fukuyama, *The End of History and the Last Man* (New York: Free Press, 1992) pp. 98–101.

10 B. Balassa, 'Liberalizing Trade Between Developed and Developing Countries', in B. Balassa, *op. cit.*, p. 360.

11 See Hudec (1987), *op. cit.*, pp. 24–5. See also, OECD (Centre for Cooperation with the European Economies in Transition), *Exchange Control Policy* (Paris: OECD, 1993) pp. 11–15.

12 Developing countries are defined, rather generally or imprecisely, as 'contracting parties the economies of which can only support low standards of living and are in the early stages of development' (XVIII:1).

13 Hudec (1987), *op. cit.*, ch. 2.
14 See, M. Kelly and A.K. McGuirk *et al.*, *op. cit.*, Appendix I ('The GATT System' pp. 74–5).
15 Hudec (1987), *op. cit.*, ch. 4.
16 See B. Balassa, 'The Extent and Cost of Protection in Developed–Developing Country Trade', in B. Balassa (1989) *op. cit.*
17 Hudec (1987), *op. cit.*, p. 83.
18 J.H. Jackson, *The World Trading System: Law and Policy of International Economic Relations* (Cambridge, MA: MIT Press, 1988) p. 99.
19 See Table A15, 'GATT Panels Established Since 1985', in *Issues and Developments in International Trade Policy*, *supra* note 8 pp. 154–63.
20 See Jackson, *op. cit.*, pp. 278–9.
21 See Lomé I (1975), 14 *Intl. Leg. Mat.* 595; Lomé II (1980), 19 *Intl. Leg. Mat.* 327; Lomé III (1985), 24 *Intl. Leg. Mat.* 571.
22 See J.-G.-Castel, A.L.C. DeMestral and W.C. Graham, *International Business Transactions and Economic Relations* (Toronto: Emond Montgomery, 1986) p. 35.
23 Jackson, *op. cit.*, pp. 280–1.
24 Trade and Tariff Act of 1984, Section 505 (b).
25 See R.E. Moore, 'The Level of Development and GSP Treatment', *Journal of World Trade*, December 1992, p. 21.
26 R.I. Meltzer, 'U.S. Renewal of the GSP', 20 *Journal of World Trade Law* 507 (1986).
27 See Jackson, *op. cit.*, pp. 398–9 (footnotes 17–20).
28 With respect to textiles, see the discussion below on the MFA.
29 B. Balassa, 'Liberalizing Trade Between Developed and Developing Countries', in Balassa (1989), *op. cit.*, p. 359.
30 See Table A11 in Statistical Appendix, M. Kelly and A.K. McGuirk *et al.*, *supra*, *Issues and Developments in International Trade Policy*, *op. cit.*
31 Balassa (1989), 'The Extent and Cost of Protection in Developed–Developing Country Trade', *op. cit.*, p. 335.
32 See M. Wolf, 'Managed Trade in Practice: Implications of the Textile Arrangements', in W.R. Cline (ed.) *Trade Policy in the 1980s* (Washington DC: Institute for International Economics, 1983, at pp. 457–9.
33 See Jackson, *op. cit.*, p. 182.
34 See Wolf, *op. cit.*, p. 457.
35 The nature of these competitive pressures, and the costs and benefits to the restricting countries of import controls in the textile and clothing sectors are analysed in M.J. Trebilcock, M.A. Chandler and R. Howse, *Trade and Transitions: A Comparative Analysis of Adjustment Policies* (London: Routledge, 1990) pp. 50–9.
36 Jackson, *op. cit.*, p. 181.
37 G.C. Dao, 'The Developing World and the Multifiber Arrangement', in J. Whalley (ed.) *Developing Countries and the Global Trading System (vol. II)* (London: Macmillan, 1989) p. 85.
38 M. de P. Abreu and W. Fritsch, 'Market Access for Manufactured Exports from Developing Countries: Trends and Prospects', in J. Whalley (ed.) *Developing Countries and the Global Trading System (vol. I)* (London: Macmillan, 1989) p. 117. These estimates are based on UNCTAD, *Protectionism and Structural Adjustment* (Geneva: UNCTAD, 1986).
39 *Ibid.*
40 Dao, *op. cit.*, pp. 87–8.
41 See N.A. Adams, *Worlds Apart: The North South Divide and the International*

System (Atlantic Highlands, NJ: Zed, 1993, especially chs 4–5).

42 Some of these views will be discussed in more detail in the next section of the chapter.

43 Hudec (1987), *op. cit.*, pp. 39–40.

44 See, particularly, *Charter of Economic Rights and Duties of States*, U.N.G.A. Res. 3281, (XXIX), (1974).

45 See M. Agarwal, 'South–South Trade: Building Block or Bargaining Chip?', in J. Whalley, (ed.), *op. cit.*, pp. 196–9.

46 R.E. Hudec, 'The Structure of South–South Trade Preferences in the 1988 GSTP Agreement: Learning to Say MFMFN', in. J. Whalley ed., *op. cit.*, p. 211.

47 *Ibid.*, pp. 213–14.

48 *Ibid.*, pp. 223–9. Space does not permit a discussion of the law of these regional South–South arrangements in this chapter. They include CARICOM (the Caribbean), the Latin American Free Trade Area, the East African Community, West African Economic Community and the Arab Common Market. For a survey of these arrangements and a detailed bibliography, see M. Agarwal, *op. cit.* In general they account only for a small percentage of the total trade of the member countries. This limited potential for South–South economic integration may reflect similarity of endowments among many of the countries concerned.

49 See H.D.B.H. Gunasekera, D. Parsons and M.G. Kirby, 'Liberalizing Agricultural Trade: Some Perspectives for Developing Countries', in J. Whalley, (ed.), *op. cit.*, pp. 253–4.

50 T.A. Oyejide, 'Primary Commodities in the International Trading System', in J. Whalley, (ed.), *op. cit.*, p. 104.

51 *Ibid.*, pp. 105–6.

52 As Ruggie notes, according to Ricardo's presentation of the theory of comparative advantage in the *Principles of Political Economy and Taxation*, 'specialization entailed no important dynamic implications for growth or development, but simply provided static gains from trade that made both parties better off than they would in its absence'. J.G. Ruggie, 'Introduction: International Interdependence and National Welfare', in J.G. Ruggie, (ed.) *The Antinomies of Interdependence: National Welfare and the International Division of Labor* (New York: Columbia University Press, 1983) p. 6. The neo-classical trade theorists launched their analysis from this account of comparative advantage, with little attention to other work of Ricardo and his fellow classical political economists, that emphasized dynamic effects of trade liberalization. See R. Findlay, 'Growth and Development in Trade Models', in P.B. Kenen and R.W. Jones, (eds) *Handbook of International Economics* (Amsterdam: North-Holland, 1984). Milner, as well, emphasizes renewed attention to the work of the classical political economists on the dynamics of growth and development. C. Milner, 'Trade Strategies and Economic Development: Theory and Evidence', in D. Greenaway, (ed.) *Economic Development and International Trade* (London: Macmillan, 1988) pp. 64–5.

53 See, for example, G.M. Grossman and E. Helpman, *Innovation and Growth in the Global Economy* (Cambridge MA: MIT Press, 1991).

54 See R. Gilpin, *The Political Economy of International Relations*, *op. cit.*, pp. 270–90.

55 See, for example, R. Prebisch, *The Economic Development of Latin America and its Principal Problems* (Lake Success NY: United Nations, 1950).

56 See R. Nurkse, *Problems of Capital Formation in Underdeveloped Countries* (New York: Basil Blackwell, 1953).

57 Gilpin, *op. cit.*, p. 275.

58 For a succinct discussion, see J. Bhagwati, 'Export Promoting Trade Strategy: Issues and Evidence' in *Political Economy and International Economics* (Cambridge MA: MIT Press, 1991) pp. 492–3.

59 A useful summary of the characteristics of inward-based growth, import-substitution policies is to be found in A.O. Kruger, *Perspectives on Trade and Development* (Hemel Hempstead: Harvester Wheatsheaf, 1990) pp. 54–7. See also, J. Bhagwati, *Foreign Trade Regimes and Economic Development: Anatomy and Consequences of Exchange Control Regimes* (Cambridge MA: Ballinger, 1978).

60 R. Vernon, 'International Investment and International Trade in the Product Cycle', (1966) 80 *Quarterly Journal of Economics* 190.

61 Grossman and Helpman, *op. cit.*, p. 310.

62 See *Issues and Developments in International Trade Policy*, *op. cit.*, pp. 404.

63 B. Balassa (1989), 'The Cambridge Group and the Developing Countries', *op. cit.*

64 See for a more recent elaboration of the theory, P. Evans, *Dependent Development: The Alliance of Multinational, State, and Local Capital in Brazil* (Princeton: Princeton University Press, 1979).

65 See particularly the 1974 UN Charter of Economic Rights and Duties of States. Article 1 states 'that Every State has the sovereign and inalienable right to choose its economic system as well as its political, social and cultural systems in accordance with the will of its people, without outside interference, coercion or threat in any form whatsoever, . . .'. and Article 2(1) that 'Every State has and shall freely exercise free permanent sovereignty, including possession use and disposal over all its wealth, natural resources and economic activities.'

66 For the empirical evidence, see J. Bhagwati, 'Export-Promoting Trade Strategy: Issues and Evidence', *op. cit.*; B. Balassa, 'The Cambridge Group and the Developing Countries, *op. cit.*; G. Feder, 'On Exports and Economic Growth' (1983) *Journal of Development Economics* 59; V. Thomas, K. Matin and J. Nash, *Lessons in Trade Policy Reform* (Washington DC: World Bank, 1990) p. 5.

67 Kruger, *op. cit.*, p. 51.

68 B. Balassa, 'The Importance of Trade for Developing Countries', *op. cit.* See also, C. Hamilton and J. Whalley, 'Introduction', in J. Whalley, (ed.) *op. cit.*

69 B. Balassa (1989), 'The Importance of Trade for Developing Countries', *op. cit.*

70 J. Bhagwati, 'Export-Promoting Trade Strategy', in J. Bhagwati, *Political Economy and International Economics*, *op. cit.*

71 *Ibid.*

72 See M. Kelly and A.K. McGuirk *et al.*, *op. cit.*, pp. 48–9.

73 Hong Kong is the only one of these countries that actually adopted a thoroughgoing *laissez-faire* approach. See Milner, *op. cit.*, pp. 72–3. The most dramatic contrast with Hong Kong is perhaps Korea, where systematic and pervasive industrial policy measures (including sectoral targeting) went hand-in-hand with liberalization of the external trade regime (i.e. tariffs and exchange rates). On the Korean case, see S. Haggard and C.-I. Moon, 'The South Korean State in the International Economy: Liberal Dependent, or Mercantile?', in J.G. Ruggie, (ed.) *op. cit.*, pp. 147–52.

74 World Bank, *The East Asian Miracle: Economic Growth and Public Policy* (Oxford: Oxford University Press, 1993).

75 See, for the case of one African country, L.K. Mytelka, 'The Limits of Export-Led Development: The Ivory Coast's Experience with Manufactures', in J.G.

Ruggie, (ed.) *op. cit.*, pp. 239–70. See, more generally, 'Africa: A flicker of light', 330 *The Economist* 7853, 5 March 1994, pp. 21–4.

76 See G. Ranis, 'Toward a Model of Development', in L.B. Krause and K. Kihwan, (eds) *Liberalization in the Process of Economic Development* (Berkeley and Los Angeles: University of California Press, 1991) pp. 63–70.

77 But as Przeworski and Limongi note, what must be meant here is an autonomous state that governs in the interests of the whole society, not tyranny or oligarchy where the rulers use their autonomy to engage in self-interested predation of civil society. A. Przeworski and F. Limongi, 'Political Regimes and Economic Growth', (1993) 7 *J. Econ. Perspectives* 51, pp. 64–6.

78 See *Canada, the International Financial Institutions and the Debt Problem of Developing Countries*, Report of the Standing Senate Committee on Foreign Affairs, Parliament of Canada, Ottawa, 1987.

79 Gilpin, *op. cit.*, pp. 318–19.

80 W.R. Rhodes, 'Third-World Debt: The disaster that didn't happen', 324 *The Economist* 7776, 12 September 1992, pp. 21–3.

81 Rhodes, *op. cit.*, p. 22.

82 J.I. Levinson, 'A Perspective on the Debt Crisis', 4 *Amer. University J. Intl. Law and Policy* (1989) 489, at pp. 509–12.

83 Rhodes, *op. cit.*, p. 23.

84 *Issues and Developments in International Trade Policy, op. cit*,. pp. 41–7.

85 *Lessons in Trade Policy Reform, op. cit.*, p. 17.

86 Very recently, however, there are some signs of a change in outlook, although less in the context of assistance to LDCs than of support for the reform process in Central and Eastern Europe. Thus, the World Bank has approved a $100 million loan for labour adjustment in Poland.

87 See D. Papagerogiou, A. Choksi, and M. Michaeli, *Liberalizing Foreign Trade in Developing Countries: Lessons of Experience* (Washington DC: World Bank, 1990).

88 B. Balassa, 'Interests of Developing Countries in the Uruguay Round', *World Economy*, March 1988, pp. 50–1.

89 L.A. Winters, 'The LDC Perspective', in K.A. Ingersent, A.J. Rayner and R.C. Hine, (eds) *Agriculture in the Uruguay Round* (New York: St. Martin's, 1994) p. 159.

90 *Ibid.*

91 See Chapter 13, on trade and the environment, and the Conclusion, on fair trade more generally.

92 See A. Krueger, 'Global Trade and Developing Countries', 15 *World Economy* (1992) at pp. 467–8.

93 See, UNDP, *Human Development Report 1991, op. cit.* ch. 1. The UNDP also notes, however, that rapid economic growth in some of the NICs for example has been followed by greater social expenditures, thereby distributing the gains from growth throughout the population.

94 Some work on this question is now being undertaken within the World Bank, particularly in its efforts to provide countries with advice on regulatory frameworks suitable for private sector development. For example, emphasis has been placed on the importance of stable property rights and transparency, impartiality and consistency in government decision making in stimulating and sustaining private sector activity, i.e. 'the rule of law'. See, for example, *Managing Development: The Governance Dimension*, Discussion Paper (Washington DC: World Bank, 1991).

95 See World Bank, *Adjustment in Africa: Reforms, Results, and the Road Ahead* (Washington DC: World Bank, 1994).

13 TRADE AND THE ENVIRONMENT

1 See generally, Daniel Esty, *Greening the GATT* (Washington DC: Institute for International Economics, 1994).
2 North American Agreement on Environmental Cooperation, 1993.
3 See GATT Secretariat, *Trade and the Environment* (Geneva: GATT Secretariat, 1992, p. 7); see also, E.-U. Petersmann, 'Trade Policy, Environmental Policy and the GATT: Why Trade Rules and Environmental Rules Should be Mutually Consistent', (1991) 46 *Aussenwirtschaft* 197.
4 S. Shrybman, 'International Trade and the Environment: An Environmental Assessment of the General Agreement on Tariffs and Trade', 20 *Ecologist* (1990), at p. 33.
5 S. Charnovitz, 'Exploring the Environmental Exceptions in the GATT', (1991) 25 *Journal of World Trade* 37.
6 The equivalent provision in the Uruguay Round Agreement on Technical Barriers to Trade, Article 2.2, contains identical wording.
7 *Canada – Measures Affecting Exports of Unprocessed Herring and Salmon*, BISD 35S (1988) 98.
8 Canada also argued (unsuccessfully) that the exemption in Article XI (2b) applied, since quality control with respect to the marketing of processed fish required assuring access of the Canadian processing industry to unprocessed fish that were subject to Canadian quality control, implying the need to limit flight of these Canadian quality-controlled unprocessed fish to the United States markets.
9 *Ibid.*, p. 108.
10 *Ibid.*, p. 114.
11 *Thailand: Restrictions On Importation of and Internal Taxes on Cigarettes*, BISD, 37th Supp. (1990) 200–8.
12 *In the Matter of Canada's Landing Requirement for Pacific Coast Salmon and Herring*, Final Report of the Panel, 16 October 1989.
13 *Op. cit.*, and accompanying text.
14 *Lobster From Canada*, Final Report of the Panel (25 May 1990), 3 T.C.T. 8182.
15 Of course, since it was exports and not imports that were affected in the *Salmon and Herring Landing Requirement* case, the Panel could not have dealt with the matter under Article III, which applies only to internal measures affecting *imports*. However, the fact that the Panel had a choice as to whether to apply Article III or Article XI in the *Lobster* case whereas it had no choice in *Salmon and Herring* does not go very far in reconciling the rather different views of Article XI itself that underlie these two decisions.
16 It should be noted, however, that while the Panel found that Article XI did not apply to the ban on undersized Canadian lobster, it did not determine whether in fact the ban violated the National Treatment obligation in Article III. This is because the explicit terms of reference of the Panel did not include the issue of National Treatment.
17 *Canada – Import, Distribution and Sale of Certain Alcoholic Drinks by Provincial Marketing Agencies*, 5 TCT 8003 (1992).
18 *Ibid.*, at 8045.
19 *United States – Taxes on Petroleum and Certain Imported Substances*, BISD, 34th Supp. (1988) 136.
20 *Ibid.*, at 161.
21 *United States – Prohibition of Imports of Tuna and Tuna Products from Canada*, BISD, 29th Supp. (1982) p. 99.
22 *Ibid.*, at 102.
23 See Chapter 8 above.

CHAPTER 13

24 *Ibid.*, at 108.
25 *United States – Restrictions on Imports of Tuna*, 30 I.L.M. 1594 (1991). The panel ruling was not formally adopted by the GATT Council, by mutual agreement of the USA and Mexico.
26 *Ibid.*, at 1618.
27 *Ibid.*, at 1620.
28 See *Trade and Environment, op. cit.*
29 See Ted McDorman, 'The 1991 US–Mexico GATT Panel Report On Tuna and Dolphin: Implications for Trade and Environmental Conflicts', (1991) 17 *North Carolina J. Int'l. L. and Com. Reg* for a defence of the decision.
30 *Op. cit.*, pp. 1622–23.
31 See Charnovitz, *op. cit.*, and accompanying text.
32 See for instance the Canadian Cultural Property Export and Import Act S.C. 1974–75–76, c 50.
33 See Trebilcock, Chandler, and Howse, *Trade and Transitions, op. cit.* (ch. 6).
34 See J.W. Kindt, *Marine Pollution and the Law of the Sea*, vol. IV, (Buffalo NY: Hein & Co., 1986) pp. 2130–44.
35 On this last point, see S.L. Walker, *Environmental Protection versus Trade Liberalization: Finding the Balance – an examination of the legality of environmental regulation under international trade law regimes* (Brussels: 1993, Facultés universitaire Saint Louis, pp. 135–6).
36 This interpretation is also suggested by W.G. Watson, *Environmental and Labor Standards in the NAFTA* (Toronto: C.D. Howe, 1994) p. 14.
37 For a clear presentation of the nature of this paradigm, its limits, and some of the developments in international legal theory and practice that are putting into question traditional notions of sovereignty, see K. Knop, 'Re/Statements: Feminism and State Sovereignty in International Law', (1993) 3 *Transnational Law & Contemporary Problems* 294.
38 Some of these proposals are critically reviewed in J. Barceló, 'Countervailing Against Environmental Subsidies', (1994) 23 *Canadian Business Law Journal* 3.
39 See M.J. Trebilcock, M. Chandler, and R. Howse, *Trade and Transitions: A Comparative Analysis of Adjustment Policies* (London: Routledge, 1990) pp. 21–215.
40 Convention on International Trade in Endangered Species of Wild Fauna and Flora, 3 March 1973, 27 U.S.T. 1087, 993 UNTS 243.
41 This principle of customary international law is now codified in the Vienna Convention on the Law of Treaties, 23 May 1989, 1155 UNTS 331, Article 30, ¶ 3. Since the GATT predates the Vienna Convention, the principle applies to GATT by virtue of customary not treaty law. See K.C. Kennedy, 'Reforming U.S. Trade Policy To Protect the Global Environment: A Multilateral Approach', (1994) 18 *Harvard Environmental Law Review* 185, pp. 207–8.
42 See K. Knop, 'Re/Statements: Feminism and State Sovereignty in International Law', *op. cit.*, pp. 298ff.
43 For example, the United National Environmental Programme (UNEP) or in some instances the World Health Organization (WHO) as well as Secretariats responsible for implementation of specific international agreements.
44 See G. Feketekuty, 'The Link Between Trade and Environmental Policy', (1993) 2 *Minnesota Journal of Global Trade* 171. This article is especially illuminating on the relationship between trade and environment, and is notable for its clear, sophisticated, and sympathetic handling of both the environmental and the trade law values at stake.

45 For instance, the Montreal Protocol on Substances that Deplete the Ozone Layer provides developing countries with a period of time twice as long as that applicable to developed countries to achieve a given level of reductions in per capita consumption of ozone-depleting substances. See D.B. Magraw, 'Legal Treatment of Developing Countries: Differential, Contextual, and Absolute Norms', (1990) 1 *Colorado Journal of International Environmental Law and Policy* 69, pp. 73–81.

46 This linkage is already embodied in the Rio framework for the evolution of international environmental law. See *The Rio Declaration on Environment and Development*, U.N. Conference on Environment and Development, Rio de Janeiro, U.N. Doc. A/CONF.151/5/Rev. 1 (1992).

47 R. Stewart, 'Environmental Regulation and International Competitiveness', (1993) 102 *Yale Law Journal* 2039.

48 See J. Bhagwati, 'Challenges to the Doctrine of Free Trade', (1993) 25 *New York University Journal of International Law and Politics* 219.

49 For a good discussion of these issues, see J.O. Saunders, 'Trade and the environment: the fine line between environmental protection and environmental protectionism', (1991–2) 47 *International Journal* 723, especially pp. 747–50.

50 See, on this issue, G. Palmer, 'New Ways to Make International Environmental Law', (1992), 86 *American Journal of International Law* 259.

14 THE INTERNATIONAL MOVEMENT OF PEOPLE

1 See Sharon Russell and Michael Teitelbaum, *International Migration and International Trade* (Washington DC: World Bank Discussion Paper No. 160, 1992) pp. 36–41.

2 Russell and Teitelbaum, *op. cit.*, pp. 1 and 9.

3 *The Economist*, 23 December 1989, p. 17 *et. seq.*; 3 March 1990, p. 18; 13 November 1993, p. 45.

4 Joseph Carens, 'Aliens and Citizens: The Case for Open Borders', (1987) 47 *The Review of Politics* 251.

5 *Ibid.*, pp. 252–4.

6 *Ibid.*, p. 255.

7 *Ibid.*, p. 256.

8 Joseph Carens, 'Membership and Morality: Admission to Membership in Liberal Democratic States', in *Immigration and the Politics of Citizenship in Europe and North America* (New York : University Press of America, 1989).

9 Donald Galloway, 'Liberalism, Globalism and Immigration', (1993) 18 *Queen's Law Journal* 206

10 Carens, 1987, *op. cit.*, p. 263.

11 Peter H. Schuck, 'The Transformation of Immigration Law' (1984) 84 *Columbia L.R.* 1 at p. 6.

12 Michael Walzer, *Spheres of Justice* (New York: Basic Books, 1983, ch. 2).

13 *Ibid.*, pp. 61–2.

14 Robert L. Heilbroner, *The Worldly Philosophers – The Lives, Times, and Ideas of the Great Economic Thinkers* (New York: Simon and Schuster, 1980, 5th ed., p. 76).

15 See e.g., Julian L. Simon, *The Economic Consequences of Immigration* (Cambridge MA: Basil Blackwell, 1989) pp. 329–35; George J. Borjas, *Friends or Strangers: The Impact of Immigrants on the U.S. Economy* (New York: Basic Books, 1980) pp. 225–7.

16 See 314 *The Economist* 7644, 3 March 1990, p. 18; 329 *The Economist* 7837, 13 November 1993, p. 45.

CHAPTER 14

17 Walzer, *op. cit.*, p. 51.
18 Walzer, *op. cit.*, p. 4.
19 *Ibid.*
20 Carens, 1989, *op. cit.*
21 *Ibid.*
22 For an excellent discussion of the somewhat indeterminate debates on the effects of emigration on developing countries, see Simon, *op. cit.*, ch. 14; see also Jagdish Bhagwati, *Political Economy and Economics* (Cambridge MA: MIT Press, 1991) chs 18–20.
23 See Russell and Teitelbaum, *op. cit.*, pp. 28–32.
24 Carens (1989), *op. cit.*, p. 268.
25 See Audrey Macklin, 'Foreign Domestic Worker: Surrogate Housewife or Mail Order Servant?', (1992) 37 *McGill L.J.* 681.
26 Walzer, *op. cit.*, p. 60.
27 See Julian L. Simon, *op. cit.*; George J. Borjas, *op. cit.*; Economic Council of Canada, *Economic and Social Impacts of Immigration* (Supply and Services, Ottawa, 1991); Lowell Gallaway, Stephen Moore, and Richard Vedder, 'Immigration and Unemployment: New Evidence', (USA: Alexis de Toqueville Institution, 1994).
28 Bob Hamilton and John Whalley, 'Efficiency and Distributional Implications of Global Restrictions on Labour Mobility: Calculations and Policy Implications', (1984) 14 *J. of Development Economics* 61.
29 Hamilton and Whalley *Ibid.*, pp. 73–5.
30 Alan O. Sykes, 'The Welfare Economics of Immigration Law: A Theoretical Survey with an Analysis of U.S. Policy', Law and Economics Working Paper No. 10 (2nd series), University of Chicago Law School, 1992.
31 See W.L. Marr and M.B. Percy, 'Immigration Policy and Canadian Economic Growth', in John Whalley (ed.), *Domestic Policies and the International Economic Environment* (Research Volume No. 12 for the Macdonald Royal Commission on the Economic Union and Development Prospects for Canada, Supply and Services Ottawa, 1985) pp. 71 *et. seq.*
32 See Alan G. Green, *Immigration and the Post-War Canadian Economy* (Toronto: Macmillan, 1976) ch. 1; David Corbett, *Canada's Immigration Policy* (Toronto: University of Toronto Press, 1957) pp. 103 *et. seq.*
33 Economic Council of Canada, *op. cit.*, p. 25.
34 Simon, *op. cit.*, ch. 8.
35 *Ibid.*, ch. 5.
36 Economic Council of Canada, *op. cit.*, p. 50.
37 *Ibid.* p. 51.
38 For a contrary view and related negative empirical assessments, see Donald Huddle, 'The Costs of Immigration', Dept. of Economics, Rice University, Texas, 4 June 1993.
39 Economic Council of Canada, *op. cit.*, ch. 9.
40 *Ibid.* p. 141.
41 See John Whalley, 'The North–South Debate and the Terms of Trade: An Applied Equilibrium Approach' (1984) 66 *Rev. of Economics and Statistics* 224, pp. 231–323.
42 See Russell and Teitelbaum, *op. cit.*, pp. 33, 34.

15 DISPUTE RESOLUTION IN INTERNATIONAL TRADE

* Substantial research and writing for this chapter was undertaken by a former student of ours, John Loukedelis.

1 See J.H. Jackson and W.J. Davey, *Legal Problems of International Economic Relations* (St. Paul: West Publications, 1986, pp. 294–5; see also United States, International Trade Commission, *Review of the Effectiveness of Trade Dispute Settlement under the GATT and the Tokyo Round Agreements* (Washington DC: USITC, 1985) p. 2 [hereinafter *ITC Report*].

2 R.E. Hudec, *The GATT Legal System and World Trade Diplomacy* (Salem NH: Butterworths, 1990, p. 68), and *ITC Report, op. cit.*, p. 11; Hudec, *Enforcing International Trade Law: The Evolution of the Modern GATT Legal System*, (Salem NH: Butterworth, 1993).

3 *ITC Report, op. cit.*, p. 8.

4 *ITC Report, op. cit.*, p. 9.

5 See Hudec, (1980) *op. cit.*, p. 77. See also *ITC Report, op. cit.*, p. 11. The Netherlands complained that Cuba's consular taxes were a violation of Article I (MFN). The matter was referred to the Chairman, who ruled against Cuba which complied with the finding a few months later.

6 *ITC Report, op. cit.*, p. 13.

7 *ITC Report, op. cit.*, p. 14.

8 The *ITC Report, op. cit.*, p. 47 states that between 1975 and 1985 85% of the disputes dealt with by the Contracting Parties went to panels and 15% went to working groups.

9 *ITC Report, op. cit.*, pp. 15–17. The panel procedures adopted during the Seventh Session are basically the same as those used by panels today, although it was not until the Ninth Session that the practice began of appointing panel members in their individual capacity rather than as representatives of their countries. It should be noted that the use of working Parties continued at the Seventh Session. Working Parties continue to be used from time to time.

10 *ITC Report, op. cit.*, p. 17.

11 Rosine Plank, 'An Unofficial Description of How a GATT Panel Works and Does Not' (1987) 4:4 *J. of Int'l. Arbitration* 53 at p. 55.

12 *ITC Report, op. cit.*, p. 20, and J.H. Bello and A.F. Holmer, 'Settling Disputes in the GATT: the Past, Present, and Future' (1990) 24 *The Int'l Lawyer* 519 at p. 521.

13 See the *ITC Report, op. cit.*, p. 20; Robert Hudec, Daniel Kennedy, Mark Sgarbossa, 'A Statistical Profile of GATT Dispute Settlement Cases; 1948–1989, (1993) 2 *Minnesota Journal of Global Trade* 1 at p. 18; Hudec (1993) *op. cit.*

14 Perhaps there are cultural reasons for this aversion to legalism – the Japanese have been conspicuous in their absence from participation in GATT dispute resolution processes, at least as complainants. This reluctance to resort to the GATT is often ascribed to Japanese aversion to confrontation. EC trade officials, as well, are fond of explaining EC–USA clashes over the meaning of dispute resolution as reflecting differences in legal culture. The Europeans are said not to share the American fascination with the vindication of rights through legal processes.

15 The ITC cites the textile agreement of 1962, and the steel export restraints of 1968 as examples. See the *ITC Report, op. cit.*, p. 20.

16 *ITC Report, op. cit.*, p. 23. The *ITC Report* attributes the aggression to American concerns about declining influence within the GATT, and

Congressional concerns about declining exports and growing imports.

17 The 'codification' is the *Understanding Regarding Notification, Consultation, Dispute Settlement, and Surveillance*, GATT BISD, (1979), 26th Supp., p. 210 [hereinafter *1979 Understanding*].

18 *ITC Report, op. cit.*, p. 29. Because of the overall similarity between the Tokyo Codes' dispute resolution mechanisms and the general GATT mechanism, this chapter will make no special attempt to describe ways in which the mechanisms do differ. In any case, few countries have resorted to dispute resolution under the Code mechanisms. Jackson counts only nine disputes between 1979 and 1988 where resort was had to the Code provisions (see J.H. Jackson, *Restructuring the GATT* (London: Pinter, 1990) p. 66; and *ITC Report, op. cit.*, p. 55. Descriptions of the Code provisions on dispute resolution can be found in J.H. Jackson, *The World Trading System* (Cambridge MA: MIT Press, 1991) pp. 97–8; and in the *ITC Report*, pp. 33–4.

19 Jackson, *World Trading System, op. cit.*, p. 96. Jackson blames the EC for blocking US efforts in this direction.

20 Uruguay Round Understanding on Rules and Procedures Governing the Settlement of Disputes, December 1993 (hereinafter Uruguay Round Understanding).

21 Jackson and Davey, *op. cit.*, p. 332. The authors cite several other examples of provisions in the text of the Agreement designed to help resolve disputes.

22 K.W. Dam, *The GATT: Law and International Economic Organization* (Chicago: University of Chicago Press, 1970) p. 354.

23 *ITC Report, op. cit.*, p. 18.

24 Jackson, *The World Trading System, op. cit.*, p. 113.

25 M.C. Bronckers, 'Non-judicial and Judicial Remedies in International Trade Disputes: Some Reflections at the Close of the Uruguay Round' (1990) 24 *J. of World Trade* 121 at p. 121.

26 Jackson, *The World Trading System, op. cit.*, pp. 104–8. For a critique of this legislation see Bronckers, *op. cit.*, p. 122, and R.P. Alford, 'Why a Private Right of Action Against Dumping Would Violate GATT' (1991) 66 *New York University L.R.* 696 at pp. 750–1. For a useful summary and critique of s. 301 and associated legislation (albeit by a critic of the spirit behind its provisions), see J. Bhagwati, *The World Trading System at Risk* (Princeton NJ: Princeton University Press, 1991) p. 126; also J. Bhagwati and Patrick (eds), *Aggressive Unilateralism* (Ann Arbor: University of Michigan Press, 1990). Throughout this chapter it will be assumed that dispute resolution is essentially bilateral. In fact there is nothing to preclude multiple Parties from appearing before a panel, and the Uruguay Round Understanding (para.9) specifies some of the rules necessary for such proceedings. However, there are important practical reasons why panel disputes are usually bilateral, and interested third Parties tend merely to monitor carefully the progress of such disputes, always reserving the right to appear before panels if necessary. See Plank, *op. cit.*, pp. 61–4.

27 Council Regulation (EEC) 2641/84, *OJ* [1984] L.252/1.

28 Jackson, *The World Trading System, op. cit.*, pp. 108–9. It should be noted that the EC regulation *does* require international adjudication procedures to be exhausted before EC counter-measures to the unfair practice can be adopted.

29 'Reasonable expectations' are not mentioned in the Agreement, but this requirement (if such it is) was added in the *Australian Ammonium Sulphate Case* (see *ITC Report, op. cit.*, Appendix I, p. 6 for a brief summary); Jackson, *The World Trading System, op. cit.*, p. 95.

30 Plank, *op. cit.*, p. 58 points out that the language in XXIII:1 regarding

impediments to the objectives of the Agreement is today largely neglected: currently, there is little consensus on what those objectives are.

31 The Agreement, Article XXIII:1.

32 Annex to the *1979 Understanding*, at para. 5. See also Plank, *op. cit.*, p. 58, and Jackson, *World Trading System*, *op. cit.*, p. 95. On the origins of '*prima facie* nullification' see the *ITC Report op. cit.*, p. 21.

33 A Contracting Party may commence consultations under Article XXII:1 'with respect to any matter affecting the operation of this Agreement'. Thus, the absence of nullification or impairment does not preclude consultations altogether.

34 *1979 Understanding*, *op. cit.*, at para. 6 and Annex para. 4. It is generally understood that if consultations begun under Article XXII fail, that will satisfy the requirement that the parties attempt to reconcile their differences under XXIII:1 before resorting to XXIII:2.

35 *ITC Report*, *op. cit.*, p. 56. Hard data are really impossible to compile because their consultations are confidential, and there is no duty to report the results of discussions.

36 Uruguay Round Understanding, para. 4. The *ITC Report*, *op. cit.*, approves of the notification requirement because it enables third Parties who may have a stake in the matter to protect their interests. See *ITC Report*, *op. cit.*, p. 19.

37 *1979 Understanding*; *op. cit.*, para. 4.

38 Uruguay Round Understanding, *op. cit.*, para. 4.3.

39 Uruguay Round Understanding, *op. cit.*, para. 4.7.

40 Uruguay Round Understanding, *op. cit.*, para. 4.8.

41 Dam, *op. cit.*, p. 373. *1979 Understanding*, *op. cit.*, at para. 25 instructs the Secretariat to provide technical aid to LDCs in respect of all matters pertaining to the *1979 Understanding*; (see also Uruguay Round Understanding, para. 24.2).

42 *1979 Understanding*, *op. cit.*, at para. 8 and *1982 GATT Ministerial Declaration*, The GATT: BISD, 29th Supp., 9 at para. (i) [hereinafter *1982 Declaration*].

43 Plank, *op. cit.*, p. 61. The Uruguay Round Understanding outlines the procedures for conciliation: para. 5.

44 Uruguay Round Understanding, para. 25. See also Castel, 'The Uruguay Round and the Improvements to the GATT Dispute Settlement Rules and Procedures' (1989) 38 *Int'l. Comp. L.Q.* 834 at p. 845.

45 Mid-term Review Agreement, *op. cit.*, at para. F(a). See also Plank, *op. cit.*, p. 62.

46 Plank, *op. cit.*, p. 62.

47 *1979 Understanding*, *op. cit.*, at para. 10 and the Annex to the *1979 Understanding*, at para. 6(ii). See also Plank, *op. cit.*, p. 64.

48 Again the focus here is on panels, working Parties are less common. See *1979 Understanding op. cit.*, at para. 6(i) for a description of the panel process.

49 Uruguay Round Understanding, para. 7.1. There were standard terms of reference set out in the *1979 Understanding op. cit.*, at para. 6(ii), but no provision was made for a time limit for agreement on issues other than the terms of reference.

50 Uruguay Round Understanding, para. 7.3.

51 Plank, *op. cit.*, p. 64.

52 *1982 Declaration*, *op. cit.*, at para. (v) expresses a preference for terms of reference which will 'permit a clear finding with respect to any contravention of GATT provisions'.

53 In practice, the Secretariat member assigned the case will have the arduous task

of finding panel members. Three person panels are the rule, but five can be insisted on in difficult or controversial cases. See the Uruguay Round Understanding, para. 8.5 and Plank, *op. cit.*, pp. 64 and 66.

54 *1979 Understanding, op. cit.*, at paras 11 and 14. See also the Annex to the *1979 Understanding*, at para. 6(iii).

55 The *1979 Understanding op. cit.*, at para. 11 states that panel composition should take no longer than thirty days, and the *1982 Declaration op. cit.*, at para. (ii) requires the Director General to inform the Council of any case where a longer period of time is required. See *Action Taken on 30 November 1984 at the Fortieth Session of the Contracting Parties*, [reference] at para. 3 [hereinafter *1984 Action*]. In this context it should be noted that the profile of a case can do much for the image of the GATT. It took three years to establish a panel in the 1973 DISC case, and this has probably done much to shape US perceptions of the GATT. In fact, the *ITC Report op. cit.*, p. 57 points out that most panels seem to be set up within a reasonable time (about two months).

56 The *1979 Understanding op. cit.*, at para. 12 stipulates that Parties are not to oppose a nomination except for 'compelling reasons'. Plank, *op. cit.*, p. 71 states that in fact few countries feel any compunction about rejecting panellists they regard as hostile to their cause.

57 Plank, *op. cit.*, pp. 67–9. Plank points out that many GATT delegates are career diplomats who fear that crossing certain disputants might bar them from serving in important diplomatic posts.

58 *ITC Report op. cit.*, p. 57.

59 The Uruguay Round Understanding is somewhat more explicit about who is qualified to be a panellist – see para. 8.1.

60 Uruguay Round Understanding, para. 12.1 requires panels to follow the detailed procedure laid down in its Annex, unless the panel, after consulting with the Parties decides otherwise.

61 Uruguay Round Understanding para. 12.3.

62 Uruguay Round Understanding. The Understanding requires panels seeking information from individuals or bodies in other jurisdictions to notify the authorities in those jurisdictions beforehand. It should be noted that GATT panels work in circumstances of strict confidentiality. The submissions they receive are distributed to panel members and disputing Parties alone, and not even the Secretariat keeps a record of the panel deliberations over a dispute. See Plank, *op. cit.*, p. 73.

63 Uruguay Round Understanding para. 12.6, para. 10.2. The Annex to the *1979 Understanding op. cit.*, (para. 3) includes constant consultation with disputing Parties as part of a description of the panel process. Paragraph 15 gives any Party having a 'substantial interest in the matter before a panel' the right to be heard as well.

64 Uruguay Round Understanding, para. 12.6.

65 Plank, *op. cit.*, p. 78.

66 Plank, *op. cit.*, p. 80; and *ITC Report op. cit.*, p. 57. Plank notes that panels commonly must require more information from Parties once they turn to consider the submissions. Disputing Parties often use the wrong provision of the Agreement when complaining about a practice, or they do not provide enough information about that practice so that the panel can really understand how it operates.

67 *ITC Report op. cit.*, p. 58; and Plank, *op. cit.*, p. 73.

68 Uruguay Round Understanding para. 12. Paragraph 12.10 makes special provision for extending deadlines where the measures complained about have been taken by an LDC.

69 *1979 Understanding op. cit.*, at Annex para. 6(viii).

70 *1979 Understanding op. cit.*, at para. 16, and at Annex paras 3 and 6(viii).

71 *1979 Understanding op. cit.*, at para. 17.

72 Plank, *op. cit.* p. 83. Panel reports are anonymous (cf. Draft Decision Understanding *op. cit.* at para. 10.7), and not always unanimous. Still, the pressure for consensus is evidently there.

73 Uruguay Round Understanding, para. 15.

74 The Uruguay Round Understanding provides that consideration of a report is not to take place within twenty days of its initial circulation to the Contracting Parties but must be considered by the Council within 60 days (para. 16).

75 *1982 Declaration op. cit.*, at para. (x).

76 Plank, *op. cit.*, p. 88.

77 *ITC Report op. cit.*, pp. 58–9. The *ITC Report* points out that the average time for GATT cases, from the date of the initial complaint to adoption of a report, was about ten months, considerably better than the time it takes many American jurisdictions to deal with civil disputes. On the other hand, it also notes that the average time between 1975 and 1986 was about sixteen months.

78 Cf. *1982 Declaration op. cit.*, at para. (ix). The Netherlands, in September 1951, had filed a complaint against the United States which was upheld by the Contracting Parties. Authorization for the suspension of concessions on US wheat was requested and granted, but the Netherlands itself violated the resulting quota restrictions because US wheat was so cheap.

In the Superfund case, the EC requested authorization to retaliate, and as of 1988 such permission was being held up by the Council. In one case, the USA has retaliated against EC pasta imports because of a dispute over the treatment of US citrus. See Jackson, *The World Trading System, op. cit.*, p. 96.

79 Uruguay Round Understanding, para. 21.

80 The number of reports which have been blocked in this context becomes especially significant given that the Tokyo Codes have not been used very much for establishing panels.

81 An interesting insight into the hesitant course of progress can be culled from the diplomatic language introducing each of the *1979 Understanding, op. cit.*, the *1982 Declaration op. cit.*, the *1984 Action op. cit.*, and the Mid-term Review Agreement *op. cit.*

82 The *ITC Report op. cit.* pp. 71–3 has a fairly exhaustive list of the criticisms commonly made of GATT dispute resolution. See also Bello, *op. cit.*, p. 524.

83 *ITC Report op. cit.*, p. 75.

84 *ITC Report op. cit.*, p. 75.

85 *ITC Report op. cit.*, p. 78.

86 *ITC Report op. cit.*, p. 78, and Jackson, *Restructuring the GATT op. cit.*, p. 68.

87 *ITC Report op. cit.*, pp. 69 and 79.

88 Dam, *op. cit.*, p. 357. The *ITC Report op. cit.*, p. 44 illustrates these problems with an apposite example. US aluminum bat manufacturers at one time enjoyed a commanding lead over their rivals in the Japanese market. In the late 1970s Japan instituted safety standards which had the effect of discriminating against US bats. The US share of the market plummeted, and the US government took the case to the Standards Code committee. Eventually Japan agreed to a settlement favourable to the USA; however, the US manufacturers have since failed to recover anything like their previous share of the Japanese market.

89 The following figures are taken from the *ITC Report op. cit.*, pp. 50–64, supplemented by Jackson, *The World Trading System op. cit.*, pp. 99–100. The ITC study examines 84 cases referred by the Contracting Parties to working

Parties or panels under Article XXIII:2 or the MTN Codes. Cases settled by consultation are not included because of a paucity of data. The ITC estimates that a much larger number of cases never reach the panel stage; consultations are enough to settle the dispute or the case is simply dropped.

90 The 'DISC' case; see *ITC Report op. cit.*, Appendix I.

91 Hudec, Kennedy, and Sgarbossa, *op. cit.*; Hudec (1993) *op. cit.*

92 See Jackson, *The World Trading System op. cit.*, p. 109.

93 Uruguay Round Understanding, para. 17.5.

94 See Agreement Establishing the Multilateral Trade Organization, December 1993; Annex on Trade Policy Review Mechanism, December 1993; see also Victoria Curzon Price, 'New Institutional Developments in GATT', (1992) 1 *Minnesota J. of Global Trade* 87.

95 See E.-U. Petersmann, 'Strengthening GATT Procedures for Settling Disputes', (1988) *World Economy*, 55 at p. 56; Jackson, *World Trading System op. cit.* pp. 111, 112.

96 Petersmann, *ibid.*, pp. 81 *et seq.*

97 Petersmann, *op. cit.*, pp. 73–4. Dam, *op. cit.*, p. 358 claims that there was a decision from the beginning at the GATT to refrain from a rule-based regime, hence the appeal to the Contracting Parties for the resolution of disputes. Plank, *op. cit.*, p. 60 makes a similar argument, citing the emphasis on consultation within the GATT system as evidence for this position.

98 It should be said that advocates of legalism do not necessarily see it as a panacea. See Castel, *op. cit.*, pp. 841–2 and 848.

99 In particular, the FTA is very explicit about setting out detailed schedules for the panel review process.

100 What follows is a summary of the dispute resolution mechanisms in the Agreement itself. Fuller descriptions of the FTA dispute resolution provisions can be found in J.R. Johnson and J.S. Schacter, *The Free Trade Agreement: A Comprehensive Guide* (Toronto: Canada Law Book, 1988) ch. 9; K.B. Ferguson, *Dispute Settlement Under the Canada–US Free Trade Agreement* (Toronto: International Business and Trade Law Programme, 1988); W.C. Graham, *Dispute Resolution in the Canada/U.S. Free Trade Agreement* (Toronto: International Business and Trade Law Programme, 1991, *passim*); and the *Free Trade Law Reporter* (Toronto: CCH International, 1992) [hereinafter *Free Trade Law Reporter*]. The latter contains a regularly updated commentary on the FTA itself and its associated case-law.

101 Canada, Department of External Affairs, *The Canada–US Free Trade Agreement* (Ottawa: Minister of Supply and Services, 1988) at Article 1801:1 [hereinafter *FTA*]. Article 1801:2 provides that trade disputes between the two countries can be resolved *via* either the FTA or the GATT if both Agreements are applicable; but these avenues of redress are mutually exclusive according to Article 1801:3.

102 *FTA*, Article 1802:1.

103 *FTA*, Article 1802:2.

104 *FTA*, Article 1802:3–5.

105 *FTA*, Article 1803.

106 *FTA*, Article 1804.

107 *FTA*, Article 1805:1. Article 1805:2 permits the Commission to consult whatever technical advisers it deems necessary, and it allows for the use of mutually acceptable mediators to assist in resolving disputes.

108 If the matter involves an action taken under Chapter II.

109 *FTA*, Article 1806:1.

110 *FTA*, Article 1807:2.

111 *FTA*, Article 1807:1.

112 *FTA*, Article 1807:3.

113 *FTA*, Article 1807:3.

114 *FTA*, Article 1807:4. GATT panels are not restricted to the Parties' submissions in reaching their 'verdicts'; their procedures can be much more inquisitorial.

115 *FTA*, Article 1807:5.

116 *FTA*, Article 1807:5.

117 *FTA*, Article 1807:6.

118 *FTA*, Article 1807:8.

119 *FTA*, Article 1807:8.

120 *FTA*, Articles 1806:3 and 1807:9. Article 1807:9 requires the Party suspending benefits to consider that its fundamental rights or benefits under the Agreement are or would be impaired by the measure or proposed measure. There is no such stipulation in 1806:3. Article 1807:9 also provides for the termination of such suspension when the offending measure is removed. Again, 1806:3 has no comparable provision.

121 *FTA*, Article 1907 contemplates the creation of a Working Group to propose new legal norms to govern government subsidies and unfair cross-border pricing.

122 *FTA*, Article 1902:2.

123 *FTA*, Article 1902:2.

124 *FTA*, Article 1903:1. Article 1903:2 requires that the panel conduct itself in accordance with the procedures set out in Annex 1903.2, which provides for procedures very similar to those used in Chapter 18. The Annex also allows the panel to make recommendations about how an offending provision can be brought into conformity with Article 1902.

125 *FTA*, Article 1903:3. Article 1908 requires each Party to designate one or more officials who are to be responsible for ensuring that consultations are as expeditious as possible.

126 *FTA*, Article 1904:10 provides that the Agreement is not to affect judicial review of other than 'final determinations'. 'Final determination' is a technical term defined by Article 1911 – it includes determinations made by administrative tribunals under the Special Import Measures Act (Canada) and the Tariff Act of 1930 (USA). See also Article 1904:15(f) regarding amendments to the Special Import Measures Act deeming certain determinations as final for the purposes of the Agreement. For a description of the relevant provisions, as well as the administrative procedures to which they relate see Johnson and Schacter, *op. cit.*, at c. 9.

127 *FTA*, Article 1904:1–2. 'Law' here includes 'statutes, legislative history, regulations, administrative practice, and judicial precedents to the extent that a court of the importing Party would rely on such materials' (Article 1904:2). Article 1904:9 makes a panel decision binding on both Parties; Article 1904:11 precludes judicial review of a final determination if either Party has requested panel review; and Article 1904:11 also forbids either Party from allowing its courts to hear an appeal from a decision of the panel.

Article 1904:13 provides for the 'extraordinary' challenge of panel decisions if a Party alleges that: (a) a panel member was guilty of gross misconduct; (b) the panel flouted procedural rules; or (c) substantive limitations on panel powers were ignored; and any of these transgressions materially affected the panel decision and threatens the integrity of binational panel review. The challenge is heard by a panel of three chosen from a roster of ten judges. They will use the criteria of Article 1904:13 to decide the case (see Annex 1904.13). Article

1910 contemplates an exchange of letters by the two Parties which will establish a code of conduct for panellists and committee members operating under Articles 1903 and 1904.

128 *FTA*, Article 1904:3. The relevant statutes are set out in Article 1911: they are the Federal Court Act (s. 28(1)), and the Tariff Act of 1930 (ss. 516A (b) (1) (A) and 516A (b) (1) (B)).

129 *FTA*, Article 1904:4. 'Publication' means publication in either the *Canada Gazette* or the *Federal Register*. If there is no publication of the determination, then the Party whose tribunal made it must notify the other Party, which then has thirty days to request a panel.

The Agreement is not as detailed as it might be about procedure; details are left to be worked out by the Parties at a later date (see Article 1904:14). However, the Agreement (Article 1904:14) is very clear about the time limits to be allocated to each phase of the panel process, and it sets an overall limit of 315 days, beginning from the date when a request for a panel is made, for the completion of dispute resolution.

130 *FTA*, Article 1904:15 sets out a number of amendments that had to be made to existing legislation to give persons standing so that they could ask a Party to request a panel. Thus, s. 28(4) of the Federal Court Act had to be modified, and rules added such that persons could ask Canada to request a panel if they were entitled to pursue judicial review.

131 *FTA*, Article 1904:7.

132 *FTA*, Annex 1901.2:5.

133 *FTA*, Article 1904:8. This provision also requires the panel to establish as brief a time as possible given the nature of the case for the administrative body to take action 'not inconsistent' with the panel's decision. In no case can the time given be any longer than that provided by the relevant statute for a final determination by the relevant authority.

134 *FTA*, Article 1909:7.

135 *FTA*, Article 1909:9–10.

136 *FTA*, Annex 1901.2:1.

137 *FTA*, Annex 1901.2:2.

138 *FTA*, Annex 1901.2:3.

139 *FTA*, Annex 1901.2:4.

140 For a discussion of this literature, see T.M. Boddez and M.J. Trebilcock, *Unfinished Business: Reforming Trade Remedy Laws in North America* (Toronto: C.D. Howe Institute, 1993).

141 For a favourable assessment of FTA Chapter 19 dispute resolution experience to date, see Boddez and Trebilcock *op. cit.*, ch. 3.

142 *Replacement Parts* [from Canada] *for Self-Propelled Bituminous Paving Equipment* [hereinafter 'Paving Equipment'] (*Free Trade Law Reporter, op. cit.*, at ¶ 75006).

143 See generally, David S. Huntingdon, 'Settling Disputes Under the North American Free Trade Agreement' (1993) 34 *Harvard International L.J.* 407.

144 Article 1504, North American Free Trade Agreement.

145 Article 1907, North American Free Trade Agreement.

146 See Jonathan Fried, 'Dispute Settlement Under the NAFTA', (forthcoming).

147 See D. Wyatt and A. Dashwood, 'The Community Legal Order' in W. Wyatt, (ed.) *The Substantive Law of the EEC* (2nd ed., London: Sweet and Maxwell, 1990).

16 CONCLUSION: THE FUTURE OF THE GLOBAL TRADING SYSTEM

1 See, for example, J. Bhagwati, *The World Trading System at Risk, Aggressive Unilateralism, op. cit.*, and 'Fair Trade, Reciprocity and Harmonization', in A. Deardorff and R. Stern, *Analytical and Negotiating Issues in the Global Trading System* (Ann Arbor: University of Michigan Press, 1993); R. Hudec, 'Mirror, Mirror on the Wall', *op. cit.*

2 L. Tyson, *Who's Bashing Whom? Trade Conflict in High-Technology Industries* (Washington DC: Institute for International Economics, 1993) especially ch. 7.

3 See the discussion of consideration and modification of contracts in M.J. Trebilcock, *The Limits of Freedom of Contract* (Cambridge MA: Harvard University Press, 1993) pp. 136–40, 168–70.

4 See Tyson, *op. cit.*

5 See M.J. Trebilcock, M.A. Chandler, and R. Howse, *Trade and Transitions: A Comparative Analysis of Adjustment Policies* (London: Routledge, 1990) pp. 217–23.

6 See J. Grieco, 'Anarchy and the Limits of cooperation: a realist critique of the newest liberal internationalism' (1990) 42 *International Organization* 485.

7 See J. Gordley, 'Equality in Exchange' (1981) 69 *California Law Review* 1587.

8 Bhagwati, 'Fair Trade, Reciprocity and Harmonization: The New Challenge to the Theory and Policy of Free Trade', *op. cit.*, p. 28.

9 As did an FTA panel in the *Salmon and Herring Landing Requirement* case.

10 For the evidence, see Trebilcock, Chandler and Howse, *Trade and Transitions: A Comparative Analysis of Adjustment Policies, op. cit.*, ch. 2.

11 See S. Ostry, *The Threat of Managed Trade to Transforming Economies* (Washington DC, Group of Thirty, 1993) pp. 3–4.

12 See P. Mackenzie, 'China's Application to the GATT: State Trading and the Problem of Market Access', (1990) 24 *Journal of World Trade* 133, at pp. 135–6.

13 See K.W. Dam, *The GATT: Law and the International Economic Organization* (Chicago: University of Chicago Press, 1970) ch. 18.

14 See L. Haus, *Globalizing the GATT: the Soviet Union's Successor States, Eastern Europe, and the International Trading System* (Washington DC: Brookings Institution, 1992), for a clear and comprehensive discussion of the accession of each of these countries to the GATT. Our discussion of NLCs and the global trading order owes much to this superb work.

15 L. Haus, *ibid.*, pp. 60–1.

16 *Ibid.*, at p. 62.

17 Article XXXV allows a Contracting Party to stipulate that the obligations of the GATT do not apply as between it and another Contracting Party.

18 Ostry, *op. cit.* p. 3.

19 For a summary of these policy reforms, see IMF, *Developments in World Trade Policy* (Washington DC: IMF, 1992).

20 See *Economist*, 1–7 May 1993, pp. 54–6.

21 See R. Daniels and R. Howse, 'Reforming the Reform Process: A Critique of Proposals for Privatization in Central and Eastern Europe', (1992) 25 *New York University Journal of International Law and Politics* 27. For a useful discussion of the difficulties of large-scale privatization in the Polish context, see 'Poland: Against the Grain', *The Economist* 16–22 April 1994.

22 See D. Kennedy and D. Webb, 'Integration: Eastern Europe and the European Economic Communities', (1990) 28 *Columbia Journal of Transnational Law* 633 at pp. 652–3.

23 Ostry, *op. cit.*, pp.10–16. See also, *Economist*, 1–7 May 1993 *op. cit.*
24 Haus, *op. cit.*, p. 67.
25 Kennedy and Webb, *op. cit.*, take a more sanguine view of their content than Ostry, emphasizing that in some areas quotas and other QRs have genuinely been removed without new offsetting restrictions.
26 Ostry, *op. cit.*, pp. 20–3.
27 Ostry, *op. cit.*, pp. 28–9.
28 The provisions on customs unions and free trade areas in Article XXIV of the GATT apply only to such arrangements 'as between the territories of contracting parties'. (Article XXIV: 5)
29 *Op. cit.*
30 See P. Mackenzie, *op. cit.*
31 See Chapter 4.
32 P. Cowhey and J.D. Aronson, 'A New Trade Order', (1993/4) 72 *Foreign Affairs*, at p. 192.

INDEX

absolute advantage, theory of 1–2
Africa 94, 226, 318, 321, 329, 367
agricultural protectionism: costs and benefits of 203–5; domestic price control and management systems 201–3; instruments of 201–5; price instability and 199–200; rationales for 199–201 and rural ways of life 200–1; and self-sufficiency 199
agriculture: in FTA 41, 197–8; multilateral trade liberalization with LDCs 324–5; in NAFTA 45–6, 198–9; protectionism in see agriculture protectionism; SPS measures in Uruguay Round Agreement 212–13; trade in see trade in agriculture; Uruguay Round Agreement on 205–12
alcoholic beverages, in FTA 41
aliens, movement of: culturally homogeneous 375–6; economically necessitous 374–5; as refugees or asylum seekers 375
American Selling Price see ASP
AMS (Aggregate Measure of Support), in Uruguay Round 208, 210–11
Anderson, K. 204
Anti-Dumping Codes 33–4, 98–100; complaints under see anti-dumping complaints; Kennedy Round 32, 98–9; and LDCs, trade with 307; Tokyo Round 32, 99; Uruguay Round 38, 99–100
anti-dumping complaints: disputes, in FTA 403–6; disputes, in GATT 398; duties, assessment of 110–11; formal investigations 108–9; preliminary investigations 108;

standing of complainants 107–8
anti-dumping laws 97–125; Canada 101–12; and competition and trade 122–4; EU 101–12; economic rationales for 112–19; GATT provisions 97–101; institutional arrangements 101–2; non-efficiency rationales for 119–20; procedure in 107–12; reform of 121–2; revision of 32; substantive law on 102–7; theoretical rationale for 112–20; USA 101–12
ANZCERTA (Australia-New Zealand Closer Economic Relations Trade Agreement) 121
arbitration in dispute resolution mechanisms in GATT 389
Areeda, P. 115
Argentina 96, 317, 324
Aronson, J.D. 430
Asia 35, 151, 187, 226, 285, 385; future of global trading 428–9; non-tariff barriers 93; trade-related intellectual property 248, 260; and development 318–19, 321, 324. See also Japan; NICs
ASP (American Selling Price) valuation system 86
asylum seeking, in movement of people 375
Australia: agriculture 195, 204; antidumping laws 97, 121; dispute resolution 384, 396; GATT and regional trading blocs 29, 32; LDCs 308; movement of people 374; tariffs 83–4; transition costs 162, 181
Australia-New Zealand Closer

494